D0334642

MANAGEMENT
An Introduction

Visit the *Management, third edition* Companion Website at **www.pearsoned.co.uk/boddy** to find valuable **student** learning material including:

- Multiple choice questions to help test your learning
- Weblinks to key companies mentioned in the text
- An online glossary to explain key terms
- Flashcards to test your understanding of key topics

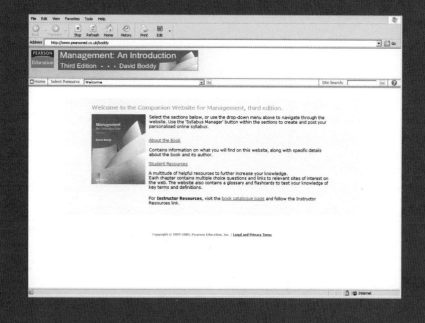

MANAGEMENT
An Introduction

THIRD EDITION

DAVID BODDY

University of Glasgow

FT Prentice Hall
FINANCIAL TIMES

An imprint of **Pearson Education**
Harlow, England • London • New York • Boston • San Francisco • Toronto
Sydney • Tokyo • Singapore • Hong Kong • Seoul • Taipei • New Delhi
Cape Town • Madrid • Mexico City • Amsterdam • Munich • Paris • Milan

Pearson Education Limited

Edinburgh Gate
Harlow
Essex CM20 2JE
England

and Associated Companies around the world

Visit us on the World Wide Web at:
www.pearsoned.co.uk

First published 1998 under the Prentice Hall Europe imprint
Second edition published 2002
Third edition published 2005

ISBN-10: 0-273-69586-X
ISBN-13: 978-0-273-69586-8

British Library Cataloguing-in-Publication Data
A catalogue record for this book can be obtained from the British Library.

Library of Congress Cataloging-in-Publication Data
A catalog record for this book is available from the Library of Congress.

10 9 8 7 6 5 4 3
09 08 07 06

Typeset in 10.5/12.5pt Minion by 30
Printed and bound by Mateu Cromo, Spain

The publisher's policy is to use paper manufactured from sustainable forests.

Brief contents

Contents

Part 1
AN INTRODUCTION TO MANAGEMENT

Chapter 1
Managing in organisations

Chapter 2
Models of management

Part 2
THE ENVIRONMENT OF MANAGEMENT

Chapter 3
The business environment

Chapter 4
The international context of management

Chapter 5
Corporate responsibility   132

Part 3
PLANNING

Chapter 6
Planning   166

Chapter 7
Decision making   194

Chapter 8
Strategy   222

Part 4
ORGANISING

CONTENTS

Part 5
LEADING

Chapter 14
Influence and power   **448**

Chapter 15
Motivation   **478**

Chapter 16
Communication   **518**

Chapter 17
Teams   **550**

Supporting resources

Visit **www.pearsoned.co.uk/boddy** to find valuable online resources

Companion Website for students

● Multiple choice questions to help test your learning

● Weblinks to key companies mentioned in the text

● An online glossary to explain key terms

● Flashcards to test your understanding of key topics

For instructors

● Complete, downloadable Instructor's Manual

● PowerPoint slides that can be downloaded and used as OHTs

● Testbank of question material

Also: The Companion Website provides the following features:

● Search tool to help locate specific items of content

● E-mail results and profile tools to send results of quizzes to instructors

● Online help and support to assist with website usage and troubleshooting

For more information please contact your local Pearson Education sales representative or visit **www.pearsoned.co.uk/boddy**

Preface to the first edition

This book is intended for readers who are undertaking their first systematic exposure to the study of management. Most will be first-year undergraduates following courses leading to a qualification in management or business. Some will also be taking an introductory course in management as part of other qualifications (these may be in engineering, accountancy, law, information technology, science, nursing or social work) and others will be following a course in management as an element in their respective examination schemes. The book should also be useful to readers with a first degree or equivalent qualification in a non-management subject who are taking further studies leading to Certificate, Diploma or MBA qualifications.

The book has the following three main objectives:

- to provide newcomers to the formal study of management with an introduction to the topic;
- to show that ideas on management apply to most areas of human activity, not just to commercial enterprises; and
- to make the topic attractive to students from many backgrounds and with diverse career intentions.

Most research and reflection on management has focused on commercial organisations. However, there are now many people working in the public sector and in not-for-profit organisations (charities, pressure groups, voluntary organisations and so on) who have begun to adapt management ideas to their own areas of work. The text reflects this wider interest in the topic. It should be as useful to those who plan to enter public or not-for-profit work as to those entering the commercial sector.

European perspective

The book presents the ideas from a European perspective. While many management concepts have developed in the United States, the text encourages readers to consider how their particular context shapes management practice. There are significant cultural differences that influence this practice, and the text alerts the reader to these – not only as part of

an increasingly integrated Europe but as part of a wider international management community. So the text recognises European experience and research in management. The case studies and other material build an awareness of cultural diversity and the implications of this for working in organisations with different managerial styles and backgrounds.

Integrated perspective

To help the reader see management as a coherent whole, the material is presented within an integrative model of management and demonstrates the relationships between the many academic perspectives. The intention is to help the reader to see management as an integrating activity relating to the organisation as a whole, rather than as something confined to any one disciplinary or functional perspective.

While the text aims to introduce readers to the traditional mainstream perspectives on management which form the basis of each chapter, it also recognises that there is a newer body of ideas which looks at developments such as the weakening of national boundaries and the spread of information technology. Since they will affect the organisations in which readers will spend their working lives, these newer perspectives are introduced where appropriate. The text also recognises the more critical perspectives that some writers now take towards management and organisational activities. These are part of the intellectual world in which management takes place and have important practical implications for the way people interpret their role within organisations. The text introduces these perspectives at several points.

Relating to personal experience

The text assumes that many readers will have little if any experience of managing in conventional organisations, and equally little prior knowledge of relevant evidence and theory. However, all will have experience of being managed and all will have managed activities in their domestic and social lives. Wherever possible the book encourages readers to use and share such experiences from everyday life in order to explore the ideas presented. In this way the book tries to show that management is not a remote activity performed by others, but a process in which all are engaged in some way.

Most readers' careers are likely to be more fragmented and uncertain than was once the case and many will be working for medium-sized and smaller enterprises. They will probably be working close to customers and in organisations that incorporate diverse cultures, values and interests. The text therefore provides many opportunities for readers to develop skills of gathering data, comparing evidence, reflecting and generally enhancing self-awareness. It not only transmits knowledge but also aims to support the development of transferable skills through individual activities in the text and through linked tutorial work. The many cases and data collection activities are designed to develop generic skills such as communication, teamwork, problem solving and organising – while at the same time acquiring relevant knowledge.

Preface to the third edition

This third edition takes account of helpful comments from staff and students who used the first edition, and the suggestions of reviewers (please see below). The book retains the structure of six parts which found favour with the reviewers. The most obvious change is the inclusion, at the suggestion of the reviewers, of new chapters on Planning and Decision Making respectively, which are included in the enlarged Part 3 – Planning.

There are 12 completely new chapter cases – Ryanair, Starbucks, DSM (a Dutch chemical business), Wipro (an Indian IT business), Manchester United, Oxfam, Vodafone/ Ericsson, Semco, Nissan, Cisco Systems, BASF and The Student Loan Company. There are more specific examples of current Management in Practice features in each chapter, and there are over 180 new references.

Again in response to reviewers' suggestions, at least two of the Activity features in each chapter now invite the reader to engage in some critical reflection – making some connections between the idea or case being discussed and their organisation. This should appeal to readers with management experience, such as those on Executive MBA courses. Many of the Case Questions and Activities have been rewritten to make a closer connection with the theories being presented. The Summary section is presented more clearly and

there are additional suggestions for Further Reading.

A major innovation is that each chapter concludes with a Critical Reflection and a web-based activity. The former is expected to appeal most to experienced managers on MBA programmes. It uses the format for critical reflection suggested by Thomas (2003) – introduced in Chapter 1 – to invite readers to seek some critical connection between several themes in the chapter and their respective organisations.

The web-based activities may appeal most to undergraduates, as they invite them to visit the websites of companies mentioned in the chapter (or others in which they have an interest) and seek new or additional information on some of the themes in the chapter. This should add interest and help retain the topicality of the cases.

There is a new Part Case in Part 6 – Airbus Industries. The Part Cases are now at the end of each Part, which seems a more logical arrangement: the questions should allow students to reinforce the ideas they have worked on earlier in the Part by applying them to the Part Case. Each Part now concludes with several skills development activities, drawing on and in some cases integrating ideas from several of the chapters in that Part.

List of reviewers

We would like to express thanks to the original reviewers and review panel members who have been involved in the development of this book. We are extremely grateful for their insight and helpful recommendations.

Reviewers of the second edition

John Clark (London Metropolitan University)
James Edgar (Queens University, Belfast)
Olaf Sigurjonsson (Reykjavik University, Iceland)
Eddie Pargeter (Birmingham College of Food, Tourism and Creative Study)
Bart Bossink (Vrije University, Amsterdam)
Ian Parkinson (Hull College)
Nicky Metcalf (St Martin's College, Lancaster)
Jackie Shaw (Macclesfield College)

Jos Weel (Hogeschool van Amsterdam)
Peter Williams (Leeds Metropolitan University)
Iraj Tavakolo (Brighton University)
Ray Rogers (Coventry)
John Chamberlain (Derby)
Siobhan Tiernan (University of Limerick)
Andrew Godley (University of Reading)

Reviewers of the third edition

Peter Falconer (Glasgow Caledonian University)
Ad van Iterson (Maastricht University)
Gail Shepherd (Coventry University)
Abby Cathcart (University of Sunderland)
Paschal McNeill (University College, Dublin)

Guided tour of the book

Case studies engage student interest and encourage critical analysis.

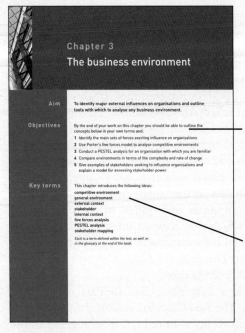

Chapter openers provide a brief introduction to chapter **aims** and **objectives**.

A list of **Key terms** introduces the main ideas covered in the chapter.

Case questions encourage students to test their understanding of, often complex, managerial issues.

Activities enable students to personally engage and investigate managerial theory and practice.

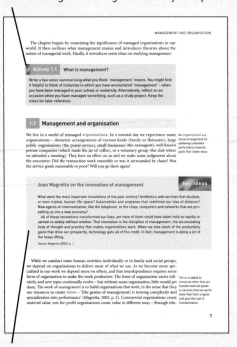

Key ideas are short vignettes which bring management to life by illustrating how past developments in management influence practice today.

Key terms are defined alongside the text for easy reference and to aid understanding.

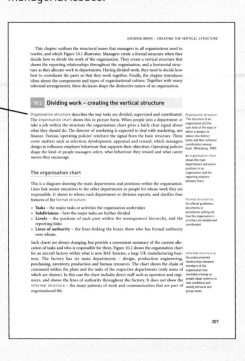

Skills development sections include tasks which allow students to relate key managerial themes to personal experience.

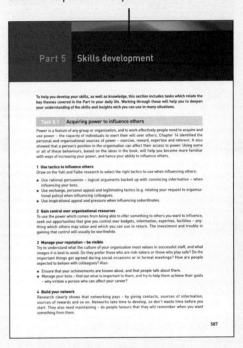

Management in practice boxes provide real world examples and encourage students to identify and engage with managerial issues and challenges.

Review questions enable students to check their understanding of the main themes and concepts.

Concluding critical reflections are a series of questions intended to develop critical thinking skills and analysis of key debates.

Chapter **Summaries** aid revision by supplying a concise synopsis of the main chapter topics.

Guided tour of the website

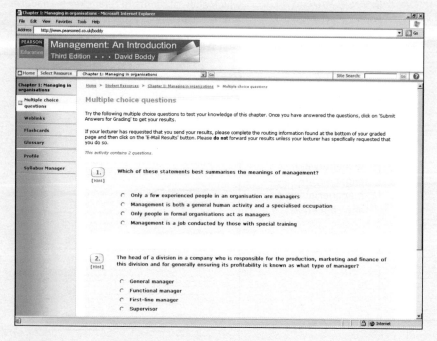

Multiple choice questions

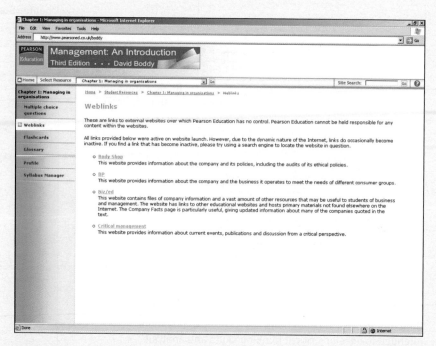

Weblinks

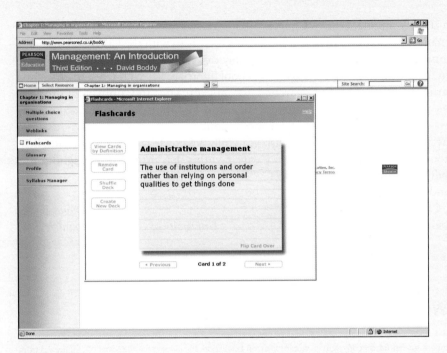

Flashcards

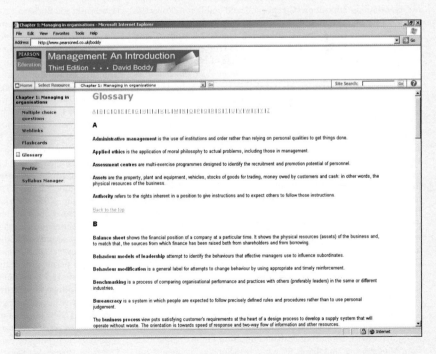

Glossary

Acknowledgements

This book has benefited from the comments, criticisms and suggestions of many colleagues and reviewers of the second edition. It also reflects the reactions and comments of students who have used sections of the material and earlier versions of some of the case material. Their advice and feedback have been of immense help.

Most of the chapters were written by the author, who has also edited the text throughout. I am grateful to these colleagues who contributed specific chapters: Bob Marshall, Chapters 8 and 9; Professor Phil Beaumont and Dr Judy Pate, Chapter 11; Douglas Briggs, Chapter 18; and Professor Douglas Macbeth,

Chapter 19. I am also grateful to Stuart Cotterell and Ian McKay for their help with the Cisco and Students Loan Company cases respectively. Janie Ferguson, the Business School librarian, has willingly and efficiently searched for appropriate and unusual European sources. The errors and omissions in the text are my responsibility alone.

I also gratefully acknowledge the support and help that my wife, Cynthia, has provided throughout this project.

David Boddy
University of Glasgow, December 2004

Publisher's acknowledgements

We are grateful to the following for permission to reproduce copyright material: Figure 2.2 from *Becoming a Master Manager*, 3rd edition (Quinn et.al. 2003), © 2003 John Wiley & Sons, Inc. This material is used by permission of John Wiley & Sons, Inc; Figure 2.3 from *Behavior in Organizations*, 5th edition (Greenberg, Jerald and Baron, Robert A. 1997) © Pearson Education 1997. Reprinted by permission of Pearson Education, Inc., Upper Saddle River, NJ; Figure 2.6 from *Chaos, Management and Economics*, Hobart Paper 125 (Parker, D. and Stacey, R. 1994) reprinted by permission of the Institute of Economic Affairs; Figure 3.2 from *Competitive Strategy: Techniques for Analyzing Industries and Competitors*, p. 5 (Porter, M. E. 1980) © 1980, 1998 by The Free Press. Reprinted with the permission of The Free Press, a division of Simon & Schuster Adult Publishing Group. All rights reserved; Figures 3.3 and 3.6 from *Exploring Corporate Strategy*, 6th edition (Johnson and Scholes 2002), with permission from Pearson Education Limited; Table 4.1 from *The Management of a Multicultural Workforce* (Tayeb, M.H. 1996) © 1996 John Wiley & Sons Limited. Reproduced with permission; Figure 5.1 from *Management*, 5th edition, p.135 (Daft 2000) © 2000. Reprinted with permission of South-Western, a division of Thomson Learning: www.thomsonrights.com. Fax 800 730-2215; Figure 5.3 from *Business and Society*, 38(3) (Carroll 1999) © 1999 Reprinted with permission of South-Western, a division of Thomson Learning: www.thomsonrights.com. Fax 800 730-2215; Chapter 6 Table in Key Ideas Box, p.187, from 'Strategic Planning, Autonomous Actions and Corporate Performance' in *Long Range Planning*, 30(3), pp. 442-5 (Anderson, 2000).With permission from Elsevier; Figure 6.4 and Table 13.3 from *Managing Projects: Building and Leading the Team* (Boddy 2002), with permission from Pearson Education Limited; Figures 6.7, 16.2, 20.1, 20.2 and 20.3 from *Managing Information Systems: An Organisational Perspective*, 2nd edition (Boddy, Boonstra and Kennedy 2005), with permission from Pearson Education Limited; Figure 7.2 from *Management*, 7th Edition, fig. 6.8, p.161 (Robbins, Stephen P. and Coulter, Mary 2003) © Pearson Education 2003. Reprinted by permis-

sion of Pearson Education, Inc., Upper Saddle River, NJ; Figure 7.3 from *Making Management Decisions*, 2nd edition (Cooke and Slack 1991), with permission from Pearson Education Limited; Figure 7.7 and Table 13.5 from *Organizational Behaviour: An Introductory Text*, 5th edition (Huczynski and Buchanan 2003) © A.A. Huczynski and D.A. Buchanan, 2001, with permission from Pearson Education Limited; Figure 7.8 from *Leadership and Decision-making*, p.188 (Vroom, Victor H. and Yetton, Philip W. 1973) by permission of the University of Pittsburgh Press. © 1973 by University of Pittsburgh Press; Table 8.1 © 2004 Commission for Healthcare Audit and Inspection from www.health-carecommission.org.uk; Figures 8.2, 8.4 and 20.8 from *Competitive Advantage: Creating and Sustaining Superior Performance* (Porter, M. E. 1985) © 1985, 1998 by Michael E, Porter. Reprinted by permission of The Free Press, a division of Simon & Schuster Adult Publishing Group. All rights reserved; Table 8.3 from *The Rise and Fall of Strategic Management*, p.24 (Mintzberg 1994), with permission from Pearson Education Limited; Table 9.1 from *Cases in Marketing Management*, 2nd edition (Moutinho 1995), with permission from Pearson Education Limited; Figures 9.2 and 9.3 from *Marketing Management*, 11th Edition (Kotler, Philip 2003) © Pearson Education 2003. Reprinted by permission of Pearson Education, Inc., Upper Saddle River, NJ; Table 11.1 from *The Occupational Psychologist*, February 1998 (Guest, D. 1988), reprinted by permission of the British Psychological Society; Figure 12.5 from *Management and Technology*, (Woodward, J. 1958), HMSO, reproduced with permission of the Controller of Her Majesty's Stationery Office; Figure 12.7 from *Management* 4th edition, (Daft 1997) © 1997. Reprinted with permission from South-Western, a division of Thomson Learning: www.thomsonrights.com. Fax 800 730-2215; Figure 12.8 from fig. 1.1 'New forms of organizing: the multiple indicators', p.12 in *Innovative Forms of Organizing* (Pettigrew, Andrew 2003), © Pettigrew *et al.* 2003. Reprinted by permission of Sage Publications Ltd; Figure 12.9 from *Partnership Sourcing: An Integrated Supply Chain Approach* (Macbeth and Ferguson 1994), with permission from Pearson

Education Limited; Figure 13.4 from *Project Management*, 8th Edition (Lock, D. 2003), © 2003. By permission of Gower Publishing Ltd; Figure 14.4 from an exhibit in 'How to Choose a Leadership Pattern' in *Harvard Business Review*, 37 (Tannenbaum and Schmidt 1973). Original article translated and reprinted by permission of *Harvard Business Review*. This article was originally published under the English title, 'How to Choose a Leadership Pattern', 37, March-April 1958, reprinted in May-June 1973. Copyright © 1973 by the Harvard Business School Publishing Corporation. All rights reserved. This translation, Copyright © 1973 by the Harvard Business School Publishing Corporation; Figure 14.6 taken from *Leadership Skills* (Adair, J. 1997) © 1997 with the permission of the publisher, the Chartered Institute of Personnel and Development, London; Figure 15.3 from *Psychological Contracts*, p.2 (Rousseau and Schalk 2000), © 2000 Sage Publications; Figure 15.5 from 'One More Time: How do you Motivate Employees?' in *Harvard Business Review*, 65 (Herzberg, F. 1987). Original article was translated and reprinted by permission of *Harvard Business Review*. This article was originally published under the English title 'One More Time' by Hertzberg (vol.65) Sept-Oct 1987. Copyright © 1987 by the Harvard Business School Publishing Corporation. All rights reserved. This translation, Copyright © 1987 by the Harvard Business School Publishing Corporation; Table 15.3 from 'The Changing Psychological Contract: The Human Resources Challenge of the 1990s', in *European Management Journal* 13(2), pp.288-94 (Hiltrop, J.M. 1995), Copyright © 1995, with permission from Elsevier Science; Figure 15.7 Copyright © 1975 by The Regents of the University of California. Reprinted from the *California Management Review*, 17(4). By permission of The Regents; Table 17.1 and Figure 17.3 from *The Wisdom of Teams* (Katzenbach and Smith 1993). Original material translated and reprinted by permission of *Harvard Business Review*. The article was originally published under the English title 'The Wisdom of Teams' by Katzenbach and Smith. Copyright © 1993 by the Harvard Business School Publishing Corporation. All rights reserved. This translation, Copyright © 1993 by the Harvard Business School Publishing Corporation; Figure 17.2 from *The Human* Organisation, p.50 (Likert, R. 1967) Copyright © 1967 McGraw-Hill, reproduced by permission of The McGraw-Hill Companies; Table 17.2 reprinted from *Groups that Work (And Those That Don't)*, p.489 (Hackman, J.R. 1990) © 1990 Jossey-Bass, San Francisco. This material is used by permission of John Wiley & Sons, Inc.; Figure 17.4 from *Business Structures* (video) (2004) by permission of TV Choice Productions; Table 17.6 from *Team Roles at Work*, p.36 (Belbin, 1993) © 1993. With permission from Elsevier; Figure 19.3 from 'Operations Management: Productivity and Quality Performance' (Sprague) in *The Portable MBA*, p.290 (Collins, E.G.C. and Devana, M.A. 1990) © 1990. This material is used by permission of John Wiley & Sons, Inc; We are also grateful to the following for permission to reproduce textual material: The Random House Group Ltd for extracts from *Body and Soul* by Anita Roddick published by Ebury and *The Seven Day Weekend* by Richardo Semler published by Century; The Body Shop International Plc for extracts from *The Body Shop Annual Report and Accounts 2003, Cash Flow Statement* year ending 28th February 2004 and *Annual Report 2004*; INSEAD for *Strategy and Performance at DSM Case* written by Marjolein Bloemhof, Research Associate at INSEAD, 2004, under the supervision of Philippe Haspeslagh, Professor of Strategy and Management, and Regine Slagmulder, Associate Professor of Accounting and Control, both at INSEAD. It is intended to be used as a basis for class discussion rather than to illustrate either effective or ineffective handling of an administrative situation. Support from DSM in assembling the information presented in the case is gratefully acknowledged. Some case facts have been disguised for confidentiality reasons; Penguin Books Ltd for an extract from *Understanding*

Organizations by Charles Handy © Handy, 1976, 1981,1985, 1993, 1999; McGraw Hill Companies for an extract from 'Microsoft's mid-life crisis?' published in *Business Week* 19th April 2004; Elsevier Ltd for an extract from 'Transforming the Vodafone/Ericsson relationship' by Ibbott and O'Keefe published in *Long Range Planning* vol 37 no 3, 2004; The Economist for an extract from 'The flowering of feudalism' published in *The Economist* 27th February 1993; Pearson Education Inc for a table adapted from *Developing Management Skills* 6th edition by David A. Whetton and Kim S. Cameron © 2005; BASF Plc for extracts from *Operating Report* year ending 31st December 2003; VNU Business Publications for an extract from 'IFRS2 to hit company profits' by Kevin Reed published in *Accountancy Age* 11th August 2004; Marks & Spencer for an extract from the *Marks and Spencer Annual Reports 2001–2004*. Business and Diversity: Towards a more civil service from *The Financial Times Limited*, 10 May 2004, © Sarah Murray; Marketing brand Me from *The Financial Times Limited*, 22 December 2000, © John Hunt.

We are grateful to the Financial Times Limited for permission to reprint the following material: Keeping the brewery solid as a rock, © *Financial Times*, 25 July 2003; Companies UK: At last someone is getting to grips with the transport system that Londoners love to hate, © *Financial Times*, 20 February 2004; Inside Track: Balancing act between jobs and profits, © *Financial Times*, 22 January 2003; Companies UK: Lamb chops and changes to engineer a recovery at IMI, © *Financial Times*, 4 February 2004; Features: In the 1st of a 2-part series, Jonathan Guthrie finds that there is plenty of room for improvement in a British workforce, © *Financial Times*, 12 February 2004; Features: Intel insider looks to Asia, © *Financial Times*, 22 September 2003; Inside Track: Italy's firm family ties, © *Financial Times*, 24 March 2003; Inside Track: when the word on the street is danger, © *Financial Times*, 5 March 2003; Coca-cola finds formula for India, © *Financial Times*, 18 June 2003; Companies and Finance the Americas: Telecoms groups 'booked fictitious revenues', © *Financial Times*, 25 September 2002; Companies and Finance International: Brewer's head promises to pull no punches, © *Financial Times*, 22 November 2002; Outsider who now has inside view, © *Financial Times*, 28 April 2004; Sport: Out of the dogfight and into the final, © *Financial Times*, 15 May 2003; Back page: 1st section: Hunter gathers all the plaudits, © *Financial Times*, 18 November 2002; Features: Siemens clocks up top results, © *Financial Times*, 19 August 2003; Inside Track: Chameleon at the centre of expansion: under the skin of Lesley Macdonagh, quote from Lesley Macdonagh, © *Financial Times*, 15 February 2001; Table 14.2 World's most respected companies 5: Displaying the ability to make a measurable difference, © *Financial Times*, 15 December 2000; Inside Track: If at first you do succeed…Profile Jorma Ollila, Nokia, © *Financial Times*, 8 December 2000; Companies UK: Chief puts his money where his mouth is, © *Financial Times*, 6 June 2003; News Corps wooing of Beijing pays off, © *Financial Times*, 9 January 2003; Chairman knows the value of a little help from his friends, © *Financial Times*, 21 February 2003; Table 15.1 FT best workplaces, © *Financial Times*, 28 April 2004; Quote from Kevin Smith in 'Smith takes over with a Lancashire lesson', © *Financial Times*, 20 December 2002; W R Grace: Building on the team structure, © *Financial Times*, 21 January 2004; Figure 18.1 Pre-tax profits compares: Halifax/Bank of Scotland, Lex column, © *Financial Times*, 5/6 May 2001; Bringing Business Technology out into the open, © *Financial Times*, 17 September 2003; Better prognosis after slow start, FT.com, © *Financial Times*, 21 May 2003.

In some instances we have been unable to trace the owners of copyright material and we would appreciate any information that would enable us to do so.

AN INTRODUCTION
TO MANAGEMENT

Part 1

Introduction

This part considers why management exists and what it contributes to human wealth and well-being. Management is both a universal human activity and a distinct occupation. We all manage in the first sense, as we organise our lives and deal with family and other relationships. As employees and customers we experience the activities of those who manage in the second sense, as members of an organisation with which we deal. This part offers some ways of making sense of the complex and contradictory activity of managing.

Chapter 1 clarifies the nature and emergence of management and the different ways in which people describe the role. It argues that management is not a neutral, technical activity: it inevitably involves some degree of controversy as the manager balances the expectations of stakeholders and interest groups. They have different views about what counts as success. The chapter concludes with some discussion and ideas about managing your study of the topic. You are likely to benefit most by actively linking your work on this book to events in real organisations, and the chapter includes some ideas on that.

Chapter 2 sets out the main theoretical perspectives on management and shows how these can complement each other despite the apparently competing values about the nature of the management task. Be active in relating these theoretical perspectives to real events as this will help you to understand and test the theory.

The Part Case concerns The Body Shop, a leading retailer with extensive international operations. It is an organisation with two missions: to produce personal care products for a profit, and to create a vehicle for environmental education and practical social activism. It developed a controversial approach to management which contrasted sharply with that of conventional businesses, though this may now be a less prominent aspect of the company than it was in the early days.

Chapter 1

Managing in organisations

Aim

To introduce the tasks, processes and context of managerial work in organisations.

Objectives

By the end of your work on this chapter you should be able to outline the concepts below in your own terms and:

1 Summarise the functions of organisations and how management affects their performance

2 Describe how management is both a universal activity and a distinct occupational role

3 Distinguish between the roles of general, functional, line, staff and project managers

4 Summarise the activities that make up the tasks (or content) of managerial work

5 Outline the conclusions of research by Stewart, Mintzberg and Luthans on the process of managerial work

6 Identify the elements of the organisational context in which managers work

7 Explain the meaning of a critical perspective on management.

Key terms

This chapter introduces the following ideas:

organisation
value
management as a general human activity
manager
management as a specialist occupation
role
general manager
functional manager
line manager
staff manager
project manager
management
management task
management role
critical perspective

Each is a term defined within the text, as well as in the glossary at the end of the book.

In 2004 Ryanair, based in Dublin, was Europe's fastest growing 'no-frills' airline. It was created in 1985 to offer services between Dublin and London, in competition with the established national carrier, Aer Lingus. In the early years the airline changed its business several times – initially a conventional, though slightly cheaper competitor for Aer Lingus, then a charter company, at times offering a cargo service. A crisis in 1990 resulting from the Gulf War caused a general fall in air traffic, with the result that the company continued to lose money – even though it was carrying more passengers. Managers decided to focus the airline as a 'no-frills' operator, in which many of the traditional features of air travel (free food, drink and newspapers, allocated seats at check-in) were no longer available. It aimed to serve a group of flyers who wanted a functional and efficient service, rather than luxury.

In 1997 changes in European Union regulations on air travel enabled new carriers to enter markets previously dominated by the established national carriers such as Air France and British Airways. Ryanair quickly took advantage of this, opening new routes between Dublin and continental Europe. Managers were also quick to spot the potential of the Internet, and in 2000 opened Ryanair.com, a booking site: within a year it sold 75 per cent of seats online, and now sells almost all seats this way. It also entered a long-term deal with Boeing to purchase 150 new aircraft over the next eight years.

Several factors enable Ryanair to offer fares to its customers that are significantly below those of traditional carriers:

- Simple fleet – using a single aircraft type (Boeing 737) simplifies maintenance, training and crew scheduling.
- Secondary airports – using airports away from major cities keeps landing charges low, sometimes as little as £1 per passenger against £10 at a major airport.
- Fast turnrounds – staff typically turn an aircraft round between flights in 25 minutes, compared to an hour

Thierry Tronnel/Corbis

for older airlines. This enables aircraft to spend more time in the air, earning revenue (11 hours compared to 7 at BA).
- Simplified operations – not assigning seats at check-in simplifies ticketing and administrative processes, and also ensures that passengers arrive early to get their preferred seat. Flying directly between cities avoids the problems of transferring passengers and baggage between flights, which is where costly mistakes and delays frequently occur.
- Cabin staff collect rubbish before and after landing, saving the cost of expensive standby cleaning crews which the established carriers choose to use.

Source: *The Economist*, 10 July 2004, and other published information.

Case questions

- What functions is Ryanair performing?
- What did 'management' contribute to the growth of the airline?
- Identify three points at which managers changed what the organisation does and how it works.

1.1 Introduction

The Ryanair case illustrates several aspects of management. A group of entrepreneurs created an organisation to offer a new service which they believed customers would want to buy. The company does this by bringing resources together and transforming them into something with greater value – which they sell to the customers. They differ from their competitors in that they use a different set of resources (e.g. secondary airports) and have different ways of transforming these into outputs (e.g. short turnrounds). They have been innovative in the way they run the business, such as in identifying what some customers valued in a flight – cost rather than luxury. However, the business environment is turbulent, and after a period of rapid growth profits fell sharply in 2004.

Managers like Michael O'Leary of Ryanair are always looking for ways to innovate and make the most of new opportunities. Other managers face a different challenge – to meet growing demand with fewer resources. In almost every public healthcare organisation managers face a growing demand for treatment, but find it difficult to secure the resources they require to meet that demand. A new management team at Shell is working to restore confidence in the group after previous senior managers seriously overstated the value of the company's oil reserves. This is leading to major changes in the structure of the company, and in the way many staff work.

Organisations of all kinds – from small but growing operations like Ryanair to large established businesses like Shell or H&M (the Swedish fashion retailer) – depend on people at all levels who can run the current business efficiently, and also initiate change. This book is about the knowledge and skills that enable people to meet these expectations, and so build a satisfying and rewarding management career.

Figure 1.1 illustrates the themes of this chapter. It represents the fact that people draw resources from the external environment and manage their transformation into an output that they hope is of greater value than the inputs. They pass the outputs back to the environment and the value they obtain in return (money, reputation, goodwill, etc.) enables them to continue attracting resources to continue in business (shown by the feedback arrow from output to input). If the outputs fail to generate sufficient new resources the enterprise will fail – it has not performed well enough to generate the support it needs.

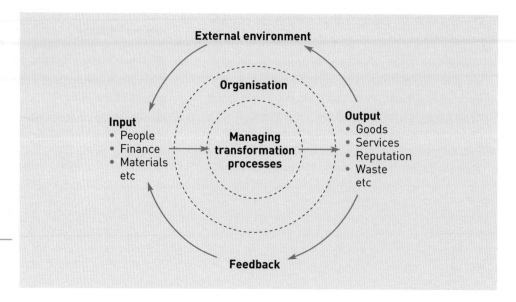

Figure 1.1

Managing
organisation and
environment

The chapter begins by examining the significance of managed organisations in our world. It then outlines what management means and introduces theories about the nature of managerial work. Finally, it introduces some ideas on studying management.

1.2   Management and organisation

We live in a world of managed **organisations**. In a normal day we experience many organisations – domestic arrangements of various kinds (family or flatmates), large public organisations (the postal service), small businesses (the newsagent), well-known private companies (which made the jar of coffee), or a voluntary group (the club where we attended a meeting). They have an effect on us and we make some judgement about the encounter. Did the transaction work smoothly or was it surrounded by chaos? Was the service good, reasonable or poor? Will you go there again?

> An **organisation** is a social arrangement for achieving controlled performance towards goals that create value.

Joan Magretta on the innovation of management

What were the most important innovations of the past century? Antibiotics and vaccines that doubled, or even tripled, human life spans? Automobiles and airplanes that redefined our idea of distance? New agents of communication, like the telephone, or the chips, computers and networks that are propelling us into a new economy?

All of these innovations transformed our lives, yet none of them could have taken hold so rapidly or spread so widely without another. That innovation is the discipline of management, the accumulating body of thought and practice that makes organizations work. When we take stock of the productivity gains that drive our prosperity, technology gets all of the credit. In fact, management is doing a lot of the heavy lifting.

Source: Magretta (2002), p. 1.

While we conduct some human activities individually or in family and social groups, we depend on organisations to deliver most of what we use. As we become more specialised in our work we depend more on others, and that interdependence requires some form of organisation to make the work productive. The form of organisation varies infinitely, and new types continually evolve – but without some organisation, little would get done. The work of management is to build organisations that work, in the sense that they use resources to create **value** – '[the genius of management] is turning complexity and specialization into performance' (Magretta, 2002, p. 2). Commercial organisations create material value, not-for-profit organisations create value in different ways – through edu-

> **Value** is added to resources when they are transformed into goods or services that are worth more than their original cost plus the cost of transformation.

cating people, counselling the troubled, caring for the sick. Theatres, opera companies and orchestras create value by offering people inspiration, new perspectives or unexpected insights.

Well-managed organisations create value in many different ways. If you buy a ticket from easyJet or Ryanair, you can easily see the direct money value which the company has created for you. In other purchases the value will be intangible. In fashion goods or services customers value the look of a product, what it feels or smells like, how trendy it is, or whether it fits their personal self-image. Others value good service, or a clear set of instructions on how to assemble and use their purchase. Good managers understand what customers value, and build an organisation to deliver it – whether in commercial or non-profit enterprises.

 ## Creating value in a pub and brewery company

Ralph Findlay (a former geology student) has been Chief Executive of Wolverhampton and Dudley Breweries since 2001. In 2004 the company owned about 1600 pubs and brewed Banks's and Pedigree ales. Findlay knows that he works in an industry where success often comes down to paying attention to detail – such as a lick of paint, flower-boxes or a non-smoking patio. He says:

> We are in a business that is not actually that complicated. You can overcomplicate it ... A lot of the time it is about somebody in a place like this who has got a smile on his face and wants to welcome his customers. Provided he makes them feel good about coming in, they will keep coming back and that is what it is really about.

FT

Source: From an article by Adam Jones, *Financial Times*, 25 July 2003.

Some organisations work inefficiently, use resources to do things that people do not value, or create pollution and waste. Management is then reducing value and destroying wealth. They sometimes destroy assets that other people in a society value. If the managers of a motorway construction site do a good job they will be creating value for road-users, residents of bypassed villages and their shareholders. Those who opposed the motorway (perhaps because it destroys an ancient woodland) will see it differently. From their perspective the company has used resources to destroy some natural wealth and has reduced, not created, value. The idea of creating value is subjective and relative.

Organisations perform functions other than economic ones. They enable people to share common causes and interests. Charities such as Oxfam or Greenpeace were created by a few like-minded individuals. They have become worldwide organisations with significant resources and operations for raising funds and managing their charitable activities. Other organisations serve particular interests – such as Unison, a trade union that represents workers in the UK public sector, or the Law Society, which defends the interests of lawyers. Firms in most industries create trade organisations to protect their interests by lobbying or public relations work. Organisations of all kinds can provide psychological support for members and non-members. Corporate scandals at prominent companies like Enron and Parmalat have indicated the greed and self-interest of some directors and senior managers, who clearly saw these businesses as vehicles for their personal enrichment. Table 1.1 summarises these organisational functions.

Whatever its function, how well an organisation performs depends on those who work within it. Luck plays a part, but most of the time it is the quality of management which makes the difference between an organisation that fails and one that succeeds.

Table 1.1

Some functions of organisations

Function	Description	Examples
Create value, wealth or human well-being	By providing goods and services that people value	Commercial and public organisations
Articulate and implement ideals	Individuals with an interest in a topic, or a passion to change something, usually need the tangible or moral support of others	Charities, protest groups, political parties
Gain power to protect sectional interests	Large organisations have access to political and economic resources beyond those of individuals	Trade unions, professional associations, industry groups
Give people work, status and social contact	A source of careers and training as well as immediate jobs, of contact with others, of a wider outlook, a source of structure in life	Any long-lasting and respected organisation
Enrich directors or senior managers	When those in charge operate to maximise their personal wealth, by providing misleading information to shareholders or regulators	Scandals at Enron (US) or Parmalat (Italy)

Activity 1.2   Managing in a voluntary organisation

Voluntary bodies are organisations too. Charities and other kinds of voluntary group are big business. A recent estimate is that the 160,000 charities in England and Wales have an annual income of £30 billion and assets of £70 billion. Ninety per cent of this income is received by the 10,000 largest charities such as Age Concern and the Royal Society for the Protection of Birds (Charities Commission Annual Report for 2002–03, available at **www.charitycommission.gov.uk**). All that needs managing. If you are connected with a voluntary group of any kind, reflect on how it is managed. How is it different from a business?

1.3   Meanings of management

Management as a general human activity

People called managers are not alone in requiring the skills of management. As individuals we run our own lives and careers: in this respect we are managing. Parents manage children, elderly dependants and households. Management is both a **general human activity** and a distinct occupation. In the first sense, people manage an infinite range of activities as well as economic ones:

> When human beings 'manage' their work, they take responsibility for its purpose, progress and outcome by exercising the quintessentially human capacity to stand back from experience and to regard it prospectively, in terms of what will happen; reflectively, in terms of what is happening; and retrospectively, in terms of what has happened. Thus management is an expression of human agency, the capacity actively to shape and direct the world, rather than simply react to it. (Hales, 2001, p. 2)

Management as a general human activity occurs whenever people take responsibility for an activity and consciously try to shape its progress and outcome.

9

*A **manager** is someone who gets things done with the aid of other people.*

Rosemary Stewart (1967) expressed this idea of the universality of management when she described a **manager** as someone who gets things done with the aid of other people. So described, the activity takes place in a great variety of human circumstances – domestic, social and political, as well as in formally established organisations.

In pre-industrial societies people typically work on their own or in family units. They retain control of their time and other resources used in producing goods or delivering services. They decide what to make, how to make it and where to sell it. They combine management and work to create value. Self-employed craftworkers, professionals in small practices, and individuals running a one-person business do this every day. We all do it in household tasks or voluntary activities in which we do the work (planting trees or selling raffle tickets) and the management activities (planning the winter programme).

Activity 1.3   Critical reflection on the definition

● Does Rosemary Stewart's definition accurately describe 'management'? Test it by choosing some domestic, community or business activity you have undertaken.

● Does it capture, very broadly, what you did?

● What more specific things did you do to 'get things done with the aid of other people'?

Management as a specialist occupation

Human action can also separate these activities so that the 'management' element becomes distinct from the 'work' element. This separation creates 'managers' who are in some degree separated from those doing the work.

Management as a specialist occupation develops when activities previously embedded in the work itself become the responsibility not of the employee, but of owners or their agents.

Management as a specialist occupation emerges when external agents, such as a private owner of capital, or the state, gain some control of a work process that a person used to complete in its entirety. They then decide what to make, how to make it and where to sell it. They take responsibility for some elements of management previously integrated with the work – even if their job titles do not include the term 'management'. Previously independent workers become employees, selling their labour rather than the results of their labour. During the process of industrialisation in western economies, factory owners took control of the physical and financial means of production. They also tried to take control of the time, behaviour and skills of those who were now employees rather than autonomous workers.

The same evolution takes place when an individual or a partnership starts an enterprise. A one- or two-person operation combines the management and ownership functions. The owner or the partners perform all the management functions as well as the work itself. If the business grows and engages employees, the owners or partners probably take over certain management activities, leaving employees with more limited responsibilities. This creates the distinct occupational role of management – a **role** being the sum of the expectations that others have of a person occupying a position.

*A **role** is the sum of the expectations that other people have of a person occupying a position.*

This separation of management and non-management work is not inevitable or permanent. People have deliberately separated the roles, and on other occasions have brought them together. As Henri Fayol (1949) (an early French writer on management, of whom you will read more in Chapter 2) observed:

Tony Watson on separating roles

All humans are managers in some way. But some of them also take on the formal occupational work of being managers. They take on a role of shaping ... work organisations. But these managers are not super-men and women. They have all the human anxieties, inadequacies and needs for meaning to be found in those whom they are meant to 'manage'. Managers' work thus involves a double ... task: managing others at the same time as managing themselves. But the very notion of 'managers' being separate people from the 'managed', a notion at the heart of traditional management thinking, undermines a capacity to handle this. Managers are pressured to be technical experts, devising rational and emotionally neutral systems and corporate structures to 'solve problems', 'make decisions', 'run the business'. These 'scientific' and rational–analytic practices give reassurance but can leave managers so distanced from the 'managed' that their capacity to control events is undermined. And they also tend to leave managers isolated from the essentially human community which the organisation might be. This can mean that their own emotional and security needs are not handled, with the effect that they retreat into all kinds of defensive, backbiting and ritualistic behaviour which further undermines their effectiveness.

Source: Watson (1994), pp. 12–13.

Management ... is neither an exclusive privilege nor a particular responsibility of the head or senior members of a business; it is an activity spread, like all other activities, between head and members of the body corporate. (p. 6)

Someone in charge of part of an organisation, say a production department, will usually be treated as a manager, and referred to as one. The people who operate the machines will be called something else. In a rapidly growing business like Ryanair the boundary between 'managers' and 'non-managers' is likely to be very fluid, with all being ready to perform a range of tasks, irrespective of their title.

1.4 Specialisation between areas of management

As organisations become larger, senior managers create separate functions and a hierarchy, so that management itself becomes divided.

Functional specialisation

General managers typically head a complete unit of the organisation, such as a division or a subsidiary, within which there will be several functions. The general manager is responsible for the overall performance of the unit, and therefore relies on the managers in charge of particular functions. A small organisation will have just one or two general managers, who will also manage specific functions. At Shell UK the most senior general manager in 2004 was Clive Mather, the Chairman.

Functional managers are those responsible for a single common activity within the organisation, such as research, marketing or production. At Shell, as in most organisations, there are managers in charge of both line and staff functions.

Line managers are in charge of a function that is directly involved in creating value (supplying products or services) to customers. Depending on their level, they will be in charge of a retail store, a group of nurses, a social work department or a manufacturing area. Their performance significantly affects business performance and image, as they

General managers are responsible for the performance of a distinct unit of the organisation.

Functional managers are responsible for the performance of a common area of technical or professional work.

Line managers are responsible for the performance of activities that directly meet customers' needs.

and their staff are in direct contact with the customers or clients. At Shell, Emma Fitzgerald was (in 2004) the Managing Director responsible for the Liquid Petroleum Gas business in the UK, while Ken Rivers was manager of the Stanlow Refinery.

Staff managers are in charge of support functions such as finance, personnel, purchasing or legal affairs. These functions do not earn income directly for the organisation, and their staff are not usually in direct contact with external customers. Their customers are the line departments of their own organisation, so their impact on outside customers is indirect. In managing their departments they operate as line managers. At Shell, Engelhardt Robbe was Finance Director, and Nic Turner was in charge of providing professional advice to other Shell managers on employment policy and employee relations.

Project managers are responsible for a temporary team that has been created to plan and implement a change – a new product or system, for example. Mike Buckingham, an engineer, was responsible for managing a project to invest millions of pounds in new manufacturing systems at a van plant now owned by LDV. He still had line responsibilities for some aspects of manufacturing, but worked for most of the time on the project. To help him, he had a team of technical specialists from around the organisation. When the project was complete he went back to his line job for a few months and then took on another change project.

Staff managers are responsible for the performance of functions that provide support to line managers.

A project manager is someone who is responsible for managing a project, usually intended to change some aspect of an organisation.

Management hierarchies

As organisations grow, senior managers usually create a hierarchy of positions. The amount of 'management' and 'non-management' work within these positions varies.

Performing direct operations

People who perform direct operations do the manual and mental work to produce and deliver products or services. These range from low-skilled ancillary activities, through skilled or technical work, to highly paid professionals such as lawyers and doctors. The activity is likely to contain some aspects of management work, though in lower-level jobs this will be limited. People running a small business combine significant management work with direct work to deliver the products or services.

Managing staff on direct operations

Sometimes called supervisors or first-line managers, these managers ensure that staff perform the daily operations of the organisation. They also help to overcome any difficulties that arise. Examples would include the supervisor of a production team, the head chef in a hotel, a nurse in charge of other nurses in a hospital ward or the manager of a bank branch. They probably spend less time on direct operations than their subordinates, except in small companies.

Managing managers

Usually referred to as middle managers (a very numerous group), these managers – such as an engineering manager at Ryanair – are expected to ensure that supervisors work in line with broader company policies. They check whether they are meeting performance targets, monitor what they are doing and provide support or pressure. They also provide a communication link, ensuring that information flows up and down the organisation. They tell first-line managers what they expect, and brief senior management about events deep down in the business. They spend time influencing other managers at the same level, and those above them in the hierarchy. Some have close and frequent links with managers in other organisations (suppliers or customers) on whom they depend. The performance of middle managers depends largely on how well they manage other managers.

Managing the business

Managing the business is the work of a relatively small group of people, usually called the Board of Directors, who are responsible for the overall direction and performance of the organisation. They establish policy and have a particular responsibility for managing relations with people and institutions in the world outside, such as shareholders, media or elected representatives. They need to understand the internal detail, but spend most of their time looking to the future or dealing with external affairs. The Board includes several non-executive directors – senior managers from other companies who are intended to bring a wider, more independent view to the discussions, supplementing the internal view of the executive directors. The Board will not usually spend time on current management issues – except in small firms.

The Board of The Body Shop www.the-body-shop.com

management in practice

The Board of Directors, which currently consists of three Executive and five Non-executive Directors, determines the strategic direction of the Group, and is responsible for the Group's system of corporate governance. The Board meets regularly throughout the year to review the operating and financial position of the group ... The Non-executive Directors are independent with wide business experience ... Responsibility for management of the group's operations is delegated to the Executive Committee which consists of the Chief Executive Officer, the Finance Director and a number of other senior managers.

Source: The Body Shop PLC, 2003 *Annual Report and Accounts*, p. 24. Reproduced with kind permission of The Body Shop International PLC.

1.5 The tasks of management

This section presents a model of what people do as they manage the transformation of resources into more valuable outputs. **Management** is the activity of getting things done with the aid of people and other resources. Building on Figure 1.1, this involves the **management tasks** of planning, organising, leading and controlling the use of resources to 'get things done'. Whatever their level, people who perform these tasks are managing. The amount of each varies with the job and the person, and they do not perform them in any particular sequence. They do so more or less simultaneously, switching rapidly between them as the situation requires – but these tasks make up the content of management work.

Figure 1.2 illustrates the elements of this definition. It expands the central 'transforming' circle of Figure 1.1 to show the tasks that together make up the transformation process. People draw inputs (resources) from the environment and transform them through the tasks of planning, organising, leading and controlling. This results in goods and services that they pass as output into the environment. The feedback loop indicates that this output is the source of future resources.

Management is the activity of getting things done with the aid of people and other resources.

Management tasks are those of planning, organising, leading and controlling the use of resources to add value to them.

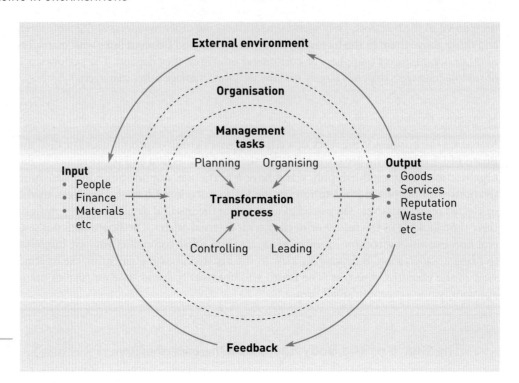

Figure 1.2

The tasks of management

Environment

Organisations depend on the external environment for the resources to sustain them. These are most clearly those of finance, people, ideas, materials and information. They could also include more intangible resources such as goodwill, licences, permissions and authorisations to undertake certain activities. Equally an organisation depends on players in the external environment being willing to buy or recognise what it produces. It depends on this cash, recognition or reputation to secure the resources to survive. Commercial firms sell goods and services and use the receipts to buy future resources. Public organisations depend on relevant authorities being sufficiently satisfied with what they do to provide future budgets. Charities depend on convincing donors that they have used their contributions well. Part 2 of the book deals with the external environment.

Planning

Planning deals with the overall direction of the work to be done. It includes forecasting future trends, assessing actual and potential resources, and developing objectives and targets for future performance. Any work activity raises choices about where to concentrate effort and resources.

As more people and interests become involved and the cost of resources increases, setting objectives, targets and plans becomes more essential than ever. Managers therefore invest time and effort in developing a sense of direction for the organisation, or their part of it, and express this in a set of objectives for the activity. Part 3 of the book deals with planning.

David Simon – planning targets at BP www.bp.com

David Simon was chairman and chief executive of BP from 1992 to 1995. He believes that setting simple goals is an important part of developing a culture of continual performance improvement. He made it clear to BP employees that they should be cost and profit conscious. He has a golden rule for attaining goals: 'Targeting is fundamental to achieving. If you do not target, you do not measure and you do not achieve.' He believes that:

> **Picking the right targets is a skill in itself. The difficulty of leadership is picking the targets and having a dialogue as you progress towards that goal so that, when it is achieved, it seems the easiest thing in the world. Then you can pick another target.**

One top executive described Simon's accomplishment: 'What he has done so well is pull the company together in a very calming way, setting clear targets and telling people how they can achieve them.'

Source: See BP Case Study at end of Part 2.

Organising

Organising is the activity of moving abstract plans closer to realisation, by deciding how to allocate time and effort. It includes defining the primary business processes required to meet the objectives, and deciding on the technologies and other facilities that people will need. The whole needs to be organised into a structure to allocate and coordinate work. This establishes who is responsible for which activities, and how their work links to that of others. At more detailed levels it includes matters like selecting staff, revising payment systems, or choosing suppliers. Part 4 deals with organising.

Reorganising Diageo's distribution in the US www.diageo.com

Diageo, based in the UK, is the world's leading premium drinks business, whose brands include Smirnoff, Guinness, J&B and Baileys. To make the most of its already strong position in the United States, it announced in 2004 that it had completed a major reorganisation of its distribution in that country. It had reduced the number of distributors handling the brands in each state, and in return had required the remaining distributors to do more. For example, they have to employ staff who only sell Diageo brands. The benefits included better retail displays for its products – a key influence on a consumer's choice of drink. The company believed that this change in organisation had contributed to a 10 per cent growth in sales and a small increase in market share.

Source: Company announcement of half-yearly results, February 2004, available at **www.diageo.com**.

Leading

Leading is the activity of generating effort and commitment towards meeting objectives. It includes influencing and motivating other people to work in support of the plans. The more complex an organisation becomes, divided into horizontal and vertical specialisms, the more the task of securing the required commitment and action from others becomes problematic. People exercise choice over what they do at work, and managers cannot assume that others will act as they would like them to. For David Simon at BP, setting targets was itself a vital part of his leadership. Part 5 deals with this topic.

Controlling and learning

Control is the task of monitoring progress, comparing it with the plan, and if necessary taking some corrective action. Managers set a budget for a housing department, an out-patients' clinic, or business travel. They then ensure that a system is in place to collect information regularly on expenditure or performance so that they can check that they are keeping to budget. If not, they can decide how they bring actual costs back into line with budgeted costs. Are the outcomes consistent with the objectives? If so, they can leave things alone. But if by Wednesday it is clear that the week's production target will not be met, or if the level of customer complaints in March is well above the monthly average, then managers need to act. They may be able to deal with the deviation by a very short-term response – such as to authorise some overtime to catch up. Other deviations are so severe that the board decides to leave a business altogether – such as when senior management at Philips stopped making mobile phones in 2001, as the company was losing so much money from the activity.

 **The dangers of less control at Shell** www.shell.com

In early 2004 Shell received some damaging publicity when the (then) Chairman admitted that the company had overstated its oil reserves – a key part of an oil company's value. Many observers believed that the source of the trouble lay in the company's history – including the dismantling of well-established systems of internal controls during a period of growth in the 1990s. As senior managers encouraged growth and a more entrepreneurial spirit ('people were wearing T-shirts saying "grow at 15 per cent a year"') controls were gradually removed as they were seen as a hindrance. Where previously systems were in place to track projects, it became almost impossible to find out how much money had been committed. Executive committees for main business units were given more responsibility, and were expected to make speedier decisions with fewer restrictions and checks. That this decreased internal control, and opened the way for top management to manipulate data, was not seen as dangerous at the time.

Source: Based on an article by Ian Bickerton, *Financial Times*, 18 June 2004.

Control also provides an opportunity to learn from past events. The ability of managers to learn from their experience is critical to their performance. This does not mean sending people on external courses, but creating and using opportunities to learn from what they are doing. The box gives an example of this; Part 6 deals with control.

The tasks in practice

Managers typically switch between tasks many times a day. They deal with them in an intermittent and often parallel fashion, touching on many different parts of the job. However, they can usually identify these elements in their job, as this manager in a housing association explains:

> My role involves each of these functions to some extent. Planning is an important element in that I am part of a team which is allocated a budget of £8 million to spend in pursuit of specific objectives, and to promote particular forms of housing. So planning or profiling where we will spend the money is very important. Organising and leading are important too, as staff have to

Encouraging learning

The organisation is a national charity that runs residential homes for people with severe learning disabilities. It has a high reputation not only for the quality of the care it gives to users, but also for the attention it gives to developing the carers it employs. Managers throughout the organisation take whatever opportunities they can to help staff gain confidence in the difficult and often stressful work. Research into how they do this indicates examples such as:

> Staff in one area described how their manager supported their studies by creating a file for them containing information on relevant policies and legislation. The same manager recognised that a night shift worker doing a qualification was not getting the full range of experience necessary to complete college assessments: 'So she took me to a review last week and also took me to a referral for a service user. That was new for me because I'd never seen that side before – but now I can relate to the stuff that will come up at college. It's about giving you the fuller picture, because sometimes the night shift can be quite isolating.'

Source: Unpublished research.

be clear on which projects to take forward, clear on objectives and clear on deadlines. Controlling also forms part of my role, as I have to compare the actual money spent with the planned budget and take corrective action as necessary.

And a manager in a legal firm:

As a manager in a professional firm, I find that each assignment involves all the elements in the list, to ensure that we carry it out properly. For example, I have to set clear objectives for the assignment, organise the necessary staff and information to perform the work, supervise staff and counsel them if necessary, and evaluate the results. However, all the roles interrelate with each other and there are no clear stages for each one.

Case question 1.1

- In what ways has the business environment affected the development of Ryanair?
- What specific tasks do you expect managers at Ryanair would be performing under each of the headings (planning, leading, organising and controlling)?

1.6 The process of management

Management tasks make up the content of management work – *what* managers do. It is also useful to be aware of the process perspective – *how* managers work. Research by Rosemary Stewart, Henry Mintzberg and Fred Luthans gives some insights.

Rosemary Stewart – how managers spend their time

What are managers' jobs like? Do they resemble an orderly, methodical process – or a constant rush from one problem to the next? One of the best-known studies was that conducted in the 1960s by Rosemary Stewart (1967), an academic at Oxford University. She persuaded 160 senior and middle managers to keep a diary for four weeks, and it remains the largest study of its kind. The managers (from different functions and from large and small organisations) completed the diary in a way that allowed the researchers to establish how the managers spent their time.

The results showed that managers worked in a fragmented, interrupted fashion. This was measured by the number of times the manager was alone long enough to concentrate on a problem. The study also measured the number of brief contacts the manager had, and the number of separate diary entries, each signifying the start of a new activity or a continuation after an interruption. Over the four weeks, the managers had, on average, only nine periods of 30 minutes or more alone, 12 brief contacts each day, and 13 diary entries each day. They spent 36 per cent of their time on paperwork (writing, dictating, reading, calculating) and 43 per cent in informal discussion. They spent the remainder on formal meetings, telephoning and social activities.

Stewart also found great variety between managers. For example, the proportion of time they spent on paperwork ranged from 7 to 84 per cent. The research team analysed the data to show different profiles of management work, based not on level or function but on how they spent their time (see box).

---

key ideas   Rosemary Stewart's management profiles

- **The Emissaries** spent much of their time out of the organisation, meeting customers, suppliers or contractors.
- **The Writers** spent most of their time alone reading and writing, and had the fewest contacts with other managers. If they had meetings they were usually with just one other person.
- **The Discussers** spent most of their time with other people and with their colleagues.
- **The Troubleshooters** had the most fragmented work pattern of all, with many diary entries and many fleeting contacts, especially with their subordinates.
- **The Committee Members** had a wide range of internal contacts, and spent much time in formal meetings. They spent half their time in discussions with more than one other person.

Source: Stewart (1967).

Fragmentation and diversity are the key messages of Rosemary Stewart's research. While some find the fragmented pattern of work stressful, others accept it as the only way to keep in touch with events. Her conclusions about fragmentation and variety have been broadly supported in later work by Mintzberg and Luthans.

Henry Mintzberg – ten management roles

Mintzberg (1973) developed the most widely quoted challenge to the traditional perceptions of management functions. His research built on earlier empirical studies by Carlson (1951) and Stewart (1967) and used structured observation to gather the data – albeit from only five chief executives. Despite this limitation, other studies, such as that by Martinko and Gardner (1990) of 41 school managers, have supported his conclusions. Mintzberg concluded, like Stewart, that managers' work was varied, brief and fragmented and that they spent much time on interpersonal activities. He identified ten **management roles** in the three categories shown in Table 1.2: informational, interpersonal and decisional.

Management role is the sum of the expectations which others have of a manager.

Table 1.2

Mintzberg's ten
management roles

Category	Role	Activity
Informational	**Monitor**	Seek and receive information, scan papers and reports, maintain interpersonal contacts
	Disseminator	Forward information to others, send memos, make phone calls
	Spokesperson	Represent the unit to outsiders in speeches and reports
Interpersonal	**Figurehead**	Perform ceremonial and symbolic duties, receive visitors
	Leader	Direct and motivate subordinates, train, advise and influence
	Liaison	Maintain information links in and beyond the organisation
Decisional	**Entrepreneur**	Initiate new projects, spot opportunities, identify areas of business development
	Disturbance handler	Take corrective action during crises, resolve conflicts amongst staff, adapt to external changes
	Resource allocator	Decide who gets resources, schedule, budget, set priorities
	Negotiator	Represent department during negotiations with unions, suppliers, and generally defend interests

Source: Based on Mintzberg (1973).

Informational roles

Managing depends on obtaining information about external and internal events, and passing information to others. The *monitor role* involves seeking out, receiving and screening information to understand the organisation and its environment. It comes from papers and reports, but equally usefully from chance conversations with customers or new contacts at conferences and exhibitions. Much of the information received is oral (from hearsay as well as formal meetings), building on personal contacts. In the *disseminator role* the manager shares information with subordinates and other members of the team or organisation. By forwarding reports and papers, telephoning to pass on gossip or briefing staff about impending changes, the manager ensures others are aware of relevant events. As a *spokesperson* the manager transmits information to people outside the organisation. This happens when the manager gives information at a conference on behalf of the organisation, speaks to the media or gives his or her department's view at a company meeting. Michael O'Leary at Ryanair is renowned for this role, frequently making flamboyant statements to the media about competitors or officials in the European Commission.

Interpersonal roles

Interpersonal roles arise directly from a manager's formal authority and status, and involve relationships with other people both in and out of the organisation. In the *figurehead role* the manager is a symbol, representing the unit in legal and ceremonial duties such as greeting a visitor, signing legal documents, presenting retirement gifts or receiving a quality award. The *leader role* defines the manager's relationship with other people (not just subordinates), including motivating, communicating and developing their skills and confidence:

> I am conscious that due to conflicting priorities I am unable to spend as much time interacting with staff members as I would like. I try to overcome this by leaving my door open whenever I am alone as an invitation to staff to come in and interrupt me, and encourage the staff to come to me to discuss any problems which may arise.

The *liaison role* focuses on a manager's contacts with people outside the immediate organisational unit. Managers maintain a network in which they trade information and favours for mutual benefit with clients, government officials, customers and suppliers. For some managers, particularly chief executives and sales managers, the liaison role is paramount, taking a high proportion of their time and energy.

Strengthening interpersonal roles

A company restructured its regional operations, closed a sales office in Bordeaux and transferred the work to Paris. The sales manager responsible for south-west France was now geographically distant from her immediate boss and the rest of the team. This caused severe problems of communication and loss of teamwork. She concluded that the interpersonal aspects of the role were vital as a basis for the informational and decisional roles. The decision to close the office had broken these links.

She and her boss agreed to try the following solutions:

- A 'one-to-one' session of quality time to discuss key issues during monthly visits to head office
- Daily telephone contact to ensure speed of response and that respective communication needs were met
- Use of fax and e-mail at home to speed up communications.

These overcame the break in interpersonal roles caused by the location change.

Source: Private communication.

Decisional roles

In the *entrepreneurial role* managers initiate change. They see opportunities or problems and create projects to deal with them. Managers play this role when they introduce a new product or create a major change programme – as Bob Horton did at BP when he became chief executive, determined to change what he saw as a very established and inflexible culture, unsuited to the newly competitive oil business. Managers play the *disturbance-handler role* when they deal with problems and changes that are unexpected.

Two examples of handling disturbance

In early 2004 Doreen Tobin, chief financial officer of Vivendi Universal, the French media and communications group that has owned Universal Music Group since 2000, announced that it planned to cut 400m euros from its cost base by 2005. The company had just reported a loss of 1.1bn euros, which she blamed on the recent contraction in the music industry. The saving will come from cuts in back-office staff, lower royalties to artists, and a reduction in the number of artists whose work it promotes.

In the same year the chief executive of Lego, the Danish toy maker, unveiled a wide-ranging restructuring programme, under which it will cut jobs, reduce costs and sell non-core businesses. He said that it had recently misjudged part of the market and lost substantial sales, but that it now wanted to deal with its serious earnings crisis by improving its competitive edge and returning the focus to basic play materials.

Source: Various published information.

The *resource-allocator role* involves choosing among competing demands for money, equipment, personnel and other demands on a manager's time. How much of her budget should the housing manager quoted on page 16 spend on different types of project? What proportion of the budget should a company spend on advertising and what on improving an existing product line? The manager of an ambulance service regularly has to decide whether to pay overtime to other staff to replace an absent team member, or let the speed of the service decline until a new shift starts. Closely linked to the resource-allocator role is the *negotiator role*, in which managers seek to reach agreement with other parties on whom they depend. When managers at Sun Microsystems want to change the prices at which they buy a component, they negotiate the new deal with their suppliers.

Activity 1.4   Critical reflection on Mintzberg's model

Reflect on a time when you have been responsible for managing an activity. Consider how closely the results of Mintzberg's research compare with your job.

- Do the ten roles cover all of the roles you performed, or did you do things that are not covered by his list? What are they?
- Give examples of activities under (say) five of the roles.
- Were there any of these roles to which you would prefer to give more time? Or less?

Mintzberg proposed that every manager's job combines these roles, with their relative importance varying between the manager's level and their type of business. Managers can usually identify with many of the roles, and see them as complementing rather than contradicting the traditional framework. They view the roles as describing how they perform the tasks of management.

Ryanair – the case continues   www.ryanair.com   CASE STUDY

The company carried 45 per cent more passengers in 2003 than in the previous year. However, some observers noted that its growth may be hampered by a dispute with the European Commission over subsidies. The company was persuaded to fly to Charleroi Airport in Belgium by subsidies offered by the regional government and the company operating the airport. The European Commission has ruled that such subsidies are illegal, and the company feared that this would lead to the subsidies it receives at other state-owned airports being withdrawn: 'Bureaucrats in Brussels wish to prevent privately owned airlines from developing low-cost arrangements for the benefit of consumers', said Michael O'Leary, the chief executive.

Ryanair's rivals were meanwhile lobbying in support of the Commission, urging them to stand firm against state aid. Rod Eddington, head of British Airways, argued that 'No-one should receive special treatment'.

The company also announced that despite the growing passenger numbers, it needed to cut costs further to remain profitable. It had therefore decided that its new aircraft would not have window blinds, headrests or reclining seats in order to save money. Managers believed these 'frills' would not be missed as most journeys were of less than an hour.

Source: *Business Week*, 15 December 2003, p. 21; *Economist*, 31 January 2004; and other sources.

Case questions 1.2

- Which of Mintzberg's management roles can you identify being exercised in the latest stage of the Ryanair case?
- Which two of these roles are likely to be most critical in the next stage of the company's development, and why?

Managers often highlight two roles that are missing from Mintzberg's list – manager as subordinate and manager as worker. Most managers have subordinates but, except for those at the very top, they are subordinates themselves. Part of their role is to advise, assist and influence their boss. This is the role of 'managing up'. Much management work involves such attempts to influence people over whom the manager has no formal authority. In today's fluid and fast-moving organisation managers often cannot wait to go through the 'right' channels: in order to get things done they need to persuade people higher up the organisation that their ideas will work, or that they need a larger budget. A project manager recalled:

> This is the second time we have been back to the management team, to propose how we wish to move forward, and to try and get the resources that are required. It is, however, worth taking the time up front to get all members fully supportive of what we are trying to do. Although it takes a bit longer we should, by pressure and by other individuals demonstrating the benefits of the system we are proposing, eventually move the [top team] forward.

Many managers, especially those in small organisations or those in junior positions in large ones, spend some of their time doing the work of the organisation. A director of a small property company helps with sales visits, or an engineering director helps with difficult technical problems. A lawyer running a small practice performs both professional and managerial roles. A final point is that changes in the environment will affect managers' ability to perform their role, as the Management in Practice feature at the end of Section 1.9 shows.

Fred Luthans – managers as networkers and politicians

Does the way in which managers interpret their role affect their performance? Mintzberg's study gave no evidence on this point, but work by Luthans (1988) showed a link between the time managers spent on specific roles and their performance. The team studied 292 managers at different levels in four organisations. Trained staff observed each manager over a two-week period, and recorded their behaviours in agreed categories. The research team also developed measures to distinguish between levels of 'success' (relatively rapid promotion) and 'effectiveness' (work-unit performance and subordinates' satisfaction). The behavioural categories were:

Communicating	Exchanging information and paperwork
Traditional management	Planning, decision making, controlling
Networking	Interacting with outsiders, socialising/politicking
Human resource management	Motivating, managing conflict, staffing, training

The conclusion was that *successful* managers spent considerably more time networking (socialising, politicking, interacting with outsiders) than the less successful managers. Human resource management took least time. In contrast, *effective* managers spent most time on communication and human resource management activities. They spent little time networking. These results implied that managers who want to rise to more senior positions should spend relatively large amounts of time and effort on networking and on the political skills of management. A later study by Aslani and Luthans (2003) with another group of managers broadly confirmed these conclusions.

1.7   Managers and their context (or environment)

Internal context

Figures 1.1 and 1.2 showed the links between managers, their organisation and the external environment. Figure 1.3 enlarges the 'organisation' circle of the earlier figures to show more fully the elements that make up the internal environment within which managers work. Any organisation contains these elements – they represent the immediate context of the manager's work. For example, as Jorma Ollilia has built Nokia into a major business, he and his management team have made significant changes to technology, business processes – and indeed to all the organisational elements shown in the figure (Steinbock, 2001).

The following list describes these elements briefly – later chapters give more detail.

- **Objectives** – sometimes called purposes or goals, these represent some future desired state of the organisation, or a unit within it.
- **Business processes** – the activities that people and technologies perform on materials and information to meet the objectives. They include processes for designing products, receiving orders, making the product, delivery, receiving payment and many more.
- **Technology** – the type and location of physical facilities, machinery, and information systems that people use to transform inputs into useful outputs.
- **Finance** – the financial resources available to the organisation.
- **Structure** – the way tasks are divided and coordinated; this includes formal and informal structures, which can have equally important effects on meeting objectives.
- **People** – their knowledge, skills, attitudes and goals; it is sometimes useful to include here people from outside the organisation as well as regular employees, if they influence performance.

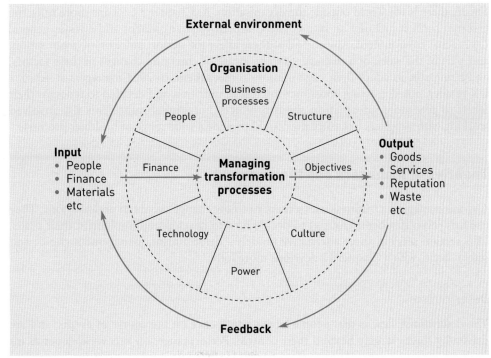

Figure 1.3

The internal and external context of management

- **Culture** – norms, beliefs and underlying values that characterise the unit.
- **Power** – the amount and distribution of power with which to influence others.

Models like this bring out the fact that managers work within constraints – they are to some degree helped or hindered by the elements in Figure 1.3. They do not necessarily accept their context passively – they try to change one or more of the elements to meet personal and organisational objectives (see Chapter 13). There is continuing debate in most large organisations about the kind of structure, information technology and culture that will best help people to meet their unit's objectives.

Historical context

Management also takes place within a flow of historical events. What people do now reflects the influence of past events and future uncertainties. Managers naturally focus on dealing with the tangible details of current operations – the urgency of present issues. They work to bring resources together to achieve some performance target. They try to ensure that things run properly, sense trouble, make the organisation work. At the same time, history exerts an influence through the structure and culture of the organisation. People remember successes and failures, and this affects how they respond to current proposals.

Management also means looking to the future. However good the present situation, or the present operation, effective managers look outwards, and to the future. This means questioning present systems and seeking improvements, observing how the environment changes and what that means for them. Does work need to be redirected towards another purpose? Are resources being used too wastefully, requiring some changes in method? What are others doing? All of these pose issues for most kinds of human activity, and they are resolved through the tasks and processes of management.

External context

Finally there is the world outside the organisation. As Chapter 3 explains more fully, the external context includes an immediate competitive environment and a wider general (or macro) environment. Any and all of these affect the performance of an organisation, and part of the work of a manager is to be aware of emerging changes in these factors, and being able to adapt their organisation to meet them. In 2004 managers at Tesco, a UK retailer, noted growing consumer interest in nutrition and decided to redesign their labels to give more information about products' nutritional value. This also involved working with suppliers to ensure they could provide a wide range of healthier products.

Theories of managers and their context

Anyone managing a business uses a theory of how change occurs in organisations. They use this (even if subconsciously) to decide how to develop and implement their plans. This section sets out three alternative models – determinism, management choice and interaction – which Chapter 12 develops more fully.

Determinism

The determinist view is that people have no influence on the course of events, and are driven by forces largely beyond their control. Performance, on this view, depends on broad economic and environmental factors, such as the industry one is in, government policy or the rate of economic growth. Managers have little choice but to adapt their policies to suit external changes and have little influence over the direction of the business. Organisations have to use the latest technologies to survive. People expect banks to have cash machines and to offer Internet banking, so banks have little choice but to use these technologies if they wish to remain in business. On this view, the context is an independent variable: Figure 1.4(a) represents this position.

Management choice

An alternative view is that people have free will and can influence the course of events. People in powerful positions can shape aspects of their environment, have minds of their own and choose which businesses to enter or leave, and which countries to operate in. They use lobbying organisations to influence government policy on taxation, regulations and most other things. Many observers believe that major companies influence trade policy generally in their interests. On this view, the context is a dependent variable, reflecting human activities. Figure 1.4(b) shows this position.

Interaction

The interaction approach expresses the idea that people are influenced by, and can themselves influence, the context in which they and others work. It implies that people interpret the existing context and act to change it to promote personal, local or organisational objectives. A manager may see a change in the company's external environment, and respond by, say, advocating the purchase of a computer system (technology) or a change in reporting relationships (structure). Others interpret this proposal in the light of *their* perspective on the situation. All the players try to influence decisions in a way that suits their interests. The evolving outcomes from these interactions affect the context in some way – which now provides the historical background to future action. The essential idea is that the relation between the manager and the context works both ways – as shown in Figure 1.4(c). People shape the context, and the context shapes people.

Throughout the book there are many examples of management actions which record the way managers have interacted with their context.

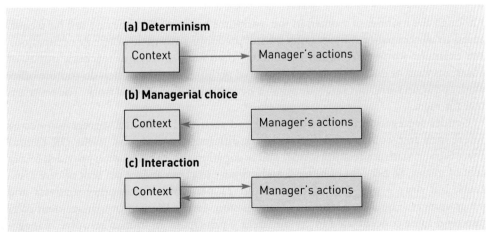

(a) Determinism

Context → Manager's actions

(b) Managerial choice

Context ← Manager's actions

(c) Interaction

Context ⇄ Manager's actions

Figure 1.4

Alternative models of managers and their context

1.8 Managing diversity

Managers in many countries work in a context in which the workforce is becoming increasingly diverse. In the UK 58 per cent of women were in employment in 1984, while by 2003 that figure that had risen to 70 per cent; the proportion of workplaces with employees from ethnic minority groups rose from 36 per cent in 1980 to 48 per cent in 1998. Managing this increasingly diverse workforce is needed both to comply with the law and to gain the benefits of workforce diversity.

Gender and ethnic origin are but two dimensions of diversity. Anti-discrimination legislation has largely concentrated on demographic or visible diversity, now including disability, age and sexual orientation. Some researchers argue that managing a diverse workforce proactively is likely to bring business benefits, in that it may lead to:

- Greater access to a wider range of individual strengths, experiences and perspectives
- A greater understanding of the diverse groups of potential and existing customers represented within a workforce
- Better communication with these diverse groups of potential and existing customers (Anderson and Metcalf, 2003, p. 1x).

key ideas   An argument for diversity

Diversity is a reality in labour markets and customer markets today. To be successful in working with and gaining value from this diversity requires a sustained, systematic approach and long-term commitment. Success is facilitated by a perspective that considers diversity to be an opportunity for everyone in an organisation to learn from each other how better to accomplish their work and an occasion that requires a supportive and co-operative organisational culture as well as group leadership and process skills that can facilitate effective group functioning. Organisations that invest their resource are taking advantage of the opportunities that diversity offers and should outperform those that fail to make such investments.

Source: Kochan *et al.* (2003), p. 18.

Gendered segregation

Although the number of women in the workforce has increased, they do not have equal access to all occupations. Many tasks are still predominantly male or female occupations. For example, women are much more likely than men to work as teachers, nurses or librarians than as doctors, judges or chartered accountants. They often do routine office work and shop work, but rarely do what is defined as skilled manual work. The reverse is true for men.

Gender segregation is both horizontal and vertical. Horizontal segregation occurs where men and women are associated with different types of jobs. In the UK Labour Force Survey, statistics relating gender and occupation show that women provided 89 per cent of nurses, 86 per cent of nursery and primary teachers and 92 per cent of care assistants, but only 3 per cent of drivers and 21 per cent of computer analysts and programmers (Equal Opportunities Commission, 1999). Women in management roles also tend to be concentrated in certain areas – principally in human resource management and other staff functions, rather than in line functions.

If women are confined to lower occupational positions and to less responsible work they will have fewer opportunities for professional growth and promotion. This in turn distances them from positions of power and the exercise of formal authority. This results in vertical segregation – men in the higher ranks of an organisation and women in the lower. A study of the proportion of women in senior management positions in large UK companies showed that of the 1048 directors of the 100 largest UK companies by market value, only 58, less than 7 per cent, were women (Linstead *et al.* 2004, p. 59). Alvesson and Billing (2000) concluded that in Sweden gender division of labour was as pronounced as in most Western countries – 'in most high-level jobs male over-representation is very strong. Only about 10–15 per cent of higher middle and senior managers and seven per cent of all professors are women' (p. 4).

Gender in management

Another question is whether men and women differ in the way they interpret and perform the management role. Researchers have focused on identifying distinctive characteristics of 'masculine' and 'feminine' management styles. Rosener (1997) found that male managers tended to adopt what she termed a transactional style. This uses the principle of exchange as the dominant way of managing – giving rewards for things done well, and punishing failure. Male respondents tended to rely mainly on their positional authority – the status conferred on them by their formal role to influence others. Women, in contrast, tended to use a relational style, motivating staff by persuasion, encouragement and using personal qualities rather than position: they generally try to make staff feel good about themselves. She believes that this female model of leadership is more suited to modern, turbulent conditions than the command and control styles typical of the male managers in her research.

Other studies have found similar differences in the styles of women – Helgesen (1995), for example, suggesting that women are better at developing cooperation, creativity and intuition than men. She also found that women prefer to manage through relationships rather than by their place in the hierarchy, and claims that they listen and empathise more than men. However, those in a position to make promotion decisions may see it differently, and use the supposedly masculine nature of organisational work to prevent women reaching senior positions (Knights and Murray, 1994). Managers who emphasise the value of hard analytical skills above soft interpersonal skills support, perhaps unwittingly, the progression of men and discourage that of women. Stressing competitiveness, tension and long unsocial working hours has a similar effect. It drives some women away from senior positions owing to domestic responsibilities that continue to be primarily theirs.

1.9 Current challenges

Most considerations of the nature of management stress two particularly difficult challenges that managers face. The first is the need to build the internal capability to meet increasingly demanding customers, and the second is to balance long-term and short-term requirements.

External demands and internal capabilities

Many companies are in markets where customers are becoming more demanding, expecting more individual products or services. They also work in an increasingly international environment in which they face both local and global competitors, many of whom are able to work from locations with low costs. To meet these demands they need to be able not only to identify trends in the external context, but also to build an organisation that can meet these demands profitably – by changing some or all of the elements in Figure 1.3.

Balancing external and internal at H&M

H&M, the trading name of Swedish fashion retailer Hennes & Mauritz, is one of Europe's top performing companies. Its net income rose by 49 per cent in 2002 and by a further 35 per cent in 2003. In 2004 it had over 900 stores in 17 countries, selling clothes cheaply to young, style-conscious customers. The company's secret weapon is its quick turnround time: H&M's in-house design team of 95 designers can move a garment from the design board to shop floor in as little as three weeks. Quick reflexes enable H&M to stay on the cutting edge of trends and minimise the impact of fashion disasters. Costs are kept low by outsourcing manufacturing to a network of more than 900 apparel contractors in low-wage countries such as Bangladesh, China and Turkey.

Source: *Business Week*, 28 July 2003, 24 June 2004, and other sources.

This account suggests that the company's managers have chosen to work in a particularly volatile section of the market (they could clearly have chosen a less demanding sector). They have been successful by managing aspects of both the external and internal contexts. Rapidly improving information and transport systems have enabled them to draw supplies from low-wage countries, while internally they have created processes and structures which allow them to manage a very rapid design-to-delivery system. This highlights how one company has met the challenges that many face in building an organisation that can respond well to external demands.

More generally, managers need to seek ways of building the resilience of their organisations – their ability to adapt and change themselves to be able to cope with ever-changing external conditions.

Balancing the long-term and short-term

Managers also experience endless conflict between short-term and long-term expectations. Senior managers, shareholders and the financial press tend to emphasise quick, visible improvements in performance, and there is always the threat of a hostile takeover by another company if managers are unable or unwilling to deliver. It is comparatively easy for a manager under pressure to find ways to cut costs, by postponing training, investment or advertising. When Richard Baker took over as Chief Executive of Boots (a UK health and beauty retailer) in 2003 he commented that the company had recently fallen down on basic retail principles, including keeping products in stock, serving customers well and adapting opening hours. Stores had not had enough investment and looked shabby, while the group had become introspective: 'The current performance is a function of under-investment and insufficient focus on the core for the last decade' (*Financial Times*, 7 November 2003).

In the pharmaceutical industry managers at companies like GlaxoSmithKline are continually having to decide how much to spend on competing scientific research teams, in a field where it is notoriously difficult to predict the results of research. They could easily cut costs and boost short-term profits by reducing this area, and any business can save money by cutting the time it spends training customer service staff.

When company profit margins are under pressure, boards of directors typically urge managers to make short-term savings to make the organisation appear more efficient. They tend to cut back on expenditure on advertising, marketing or training, which can quickly boost short-term profits. But cutting research teams reduces the flow of new drugs which are essential for the future of the company; if they stop investing in training, customer service starts to slip. What is much harder to predict is the effect on future returns. The research team that was closed down might have produced the breakthrough drug; poor service may lead to a loss of customers who are hard to regain. Earnings won at the cost of long-term competitive advantage only briefly add value.

Balancing present and future at Global Instruments

Lisa Scott, European account manager at Global Instruments, on the dilemma she faced in working for the plant's survival:

> There had never been a marketing function as such in the UK, so I was brought in to try to look at that. I set up the marketing function, and especially to look after our three major accounts. There was a marketing function at headquarters, but it didn't pay much attention to Europe.
>
> We need to be able to anticipate what the customers require, and come up with innovative ideas, be proactive. But I also have to spend a lot of time at the moment dealing with existing customers. We are renegotiating a contract with one of them, so a lot of time is taken on that, and not enough on marketing.
>
> I am still having to deal with current issues, with current customers, rather than being able to concentrate on the strategy bit. That's a big tension, because it's two different people: analysing inventory and costings, negotiating pricing; and then turning the mind to what we need to be producing next year. That's my biggest problem, because the short term always takes priority. Yet people are asking a lot of questions of me, about what we are going to do.

1.10 Conventional and critical perspectives

Management takes place in a social setting in which people and institutions hold and express many different values, priorities and interests. These reflect deeper divisions in wealth, power and opportunity. Alvesson and Wilmott (1996) argue that, in capitalist societies, the development of management as an occupational group limits the risks of ownership and protects established positions. Managers act as agents of the owners and represent their interests. They are accountable to the owners of the business, not to employees, consumers or wider communities.

> The rise of management has institutionalised the lack of democratic control over the allocation of resources within, and by, work organisations. This lack of accountability increases the social and ecological risks for employees, customers and citizens. Once management becomes a separate social group the idea of a community of interest becomes problematical, especially when there is little or no accountability of managers to the managed. (p. 12)

A **critical perspective** is one which evaluates an institution or practice in terms of its contribution to human autonomy, responsibility, democracy and ecologically sustainable activity.

In consequence, management is not a neutral, professional process. It reflects existing unequal divisions within societies and within organisations. Writers such as Alvesson and Wilmott use a **critical perspective** to challenge institutions and practices that obstruct the search for alternative ways to manage cooperative activity. They do not see 'best practice' in terms of how best to achieve current ends (such as profitable growth or market share). Instead they ask what a practice contributes to objectives such as autonomy, responsibility, democracy and ecologically sustainable development.

They argue that a critical perspective is not 'anti-management'. Rather, their aim is to raise a broader set of questions not only about ways of accomplishing existing ends, but about whether the '*existing ends routinely generate needless waste and divisiveness*' (p. 3, emphasis in original). The technical and other skills of management remain highly relevant – solving technical problems is an essential activity in complex organisations. Their argument is that society will benefit more from such technical skills within a less socially divisive practice of management.

Managing in the hope of adding value and creating wealth is not a logical or rational process – it cannot be so when it takes place within a human institution. Organisations have a history that shapes how people respond to events, and the choices they make. People manage within a social and political context, where the values of other interest groups influence what happens. It is therefore about managing both internally and externally in order to create wealth or well-being in a way that is acceptable to a wide range of stakeholders.

1.11 Studying management

Courses in management have been a rapidly growing area of European higher education in recent years as students seek courses with greater perceived relevance to their future. Do not confuse relevance in such a complex topic as management with easy examples or simple prescriptions. Managers often disagree about ends and means, especially over the strategic issues that determine the future direction and shape of the business. Simple prescriptions and ready solutions rarely work in the complex and ambiguous reality of a particular organisation.

Taking a critical perspective will deepen your understanding of management. Thomas (2003) cites these components of critical thinking:

- Identifying and challenging assumptions
- Creating contextual awareness
- Identifying alternatives
- Developing reflective scepticism.

This does not imply a 'do-nothing' cynicism, 'treating everything and everyone with suspicion and doubt' (p. 7). A critical perspective lays the foundation for a successful management career, as it helps to ensure well-founded proposals and arguments.

Studying management is itself a task to be managed – and so an opportunity to gain some practice in the subject. You can go through the processes of planning what you want to achieve and of organising the resources you will need. You will also experience various controls as you go through the course – such as your examinations. Studying management will also develop mental and personal skills, and as you work on this book you will have opportunities to improve your skills of literacy, understanding arguments, numeracy, communicating, problem solving and teamwork.

The most accessible sources of ideas and theory about management that you will have are this book, and your lectures and tutorials. There are many other ways in which you can supplement this material that should add to your interest and enrich your understanding. Such resources include media, the World Wide Web, and films or novels, such as *The Goal* (Goldratt and Cox, 1989) or *Nice Work* (Lodge, 1989), which give unusual insights into the work of managing. You can also draw on the experience of friends and

Ways of thinking critically

1 Identifying and challenging assumptions about:
- the nature of management, its tasks, skills and purposes
- the nature of people and why they behave as they do
- the nature of organisations
- learning, knowing and acting
- values, goals and ends.

2 Creating contextual awareness by understanding:
- how management practices have developed historically
- how people in other societies see management
- the implications of different contexts for management
- the interrelationship between organisations and society.

3 Identifying alternatives by:
- becoming aware of the variety of ways in which managing and organising can be undertaken
- inventing and imagining new ways of managing
- specifying new goals and priorities.

4 Developing reflective scepticism by:
- adopting a questioning, quizzical attitude
- recognising the limitations of much that passes for knowledge in the management field
- knowing how to evaluate knowledge claims
- developing a resistance to dogma and propaganda
- being able to distinguish systematic argument and reasoned judgement from sloppy thinking and simplistic formulae.

Source: Based on Thomas (2003), p. 7.

relatives to help with some of the activities and discussion points in the book. These help you to gather information about current practices, which you can compare with that of other members of your tutorial group and with the theories in the book. Remember too that as you go about your educational and social lives you are experiencing organisations, and in some cases helping to manage them. Actively reflecting on these experiences will support your study of management.

Summary

1 Summarise the functions of organisations and how management affects their performance:
- Organisations enable people to create value by transforming inputs into outputs of greater value – though the concept of creating value is subjective and open to different interpretations. Management is the process of building organisations in which inputs are transformed into outputs.

2 Describe how management is both a universal activity and a distinct occupational role:
- Management is an activity that everyone undertakes to some extent as they manage their daily lives. In another sense management is an activity within organisations, conducted in varying degrees by a wide variety of people. It is not exclusive to people called 'managers'. People create the distinct occupational role when they separate the

management of work from the work itself and allocate the tasks to different people. The distinction between management and non-management work is fluid and the result of human action.

3 **Distinguish between the roles of general, functional, line, staff and project managers:**

- General managers are responsible for a complete business or a unit within it. They depend on functional managers who can be either in charge of line departments meeting customer needs, such as manufacturing and sales, or in staff departments such as finance which provide advice or services to line managers. Project managers are in charge of temporary activities usually directed at implementing change.

4 **Summarise the activities that make up the tasks of managerial work:**

- Planning is the activity of developing the broad direction of an organisation's work, to meet customer expectations, taking into account internal capabilities. Organising is the activity of deciding how to deploy resources to meet plans, while leading is to ensure that people work with commitment to achieve plans. Control monitors activity against plans, so that people can adjust either if required.

5 **Outline the conclusions of research by Stewart, Mintzberg and Luthans on the process of managerial work:**

- Rosemary Stewart drew attention to the fragmented and interrupted nature of management work, while Mintzberg identified ten management roles in three groups which he labelled informational, interpersonal and decisional. Luthans observed that successful managers were likely to be those who spent most time networking and politicking.

6 **Identify the elements of the organisational context in which managers work:**

- The organisational context consists of eight elements which help or hinder the manager's work – objectives, technology, business processes, finance, structure, culture, power, and people. The historical context also influences events, as does the external context made up of the competitive and general environments.

7 **Explain the meaning of a critical perspective on management:**

- A critical perspective emphasises the benefits to a management career of being willing to identify and challenge assumptions, to be aware of the unique context in which management takes place, to identify alternatives and to develop reflective scepticism.

Review questions

1 Apart from delivering goods and services, what other functions do organisations perform?

2 What is the difference between management as a general human activity and management as a specialised occupation? How has this division happened, and what are some of its effects?

3 What examples are there in the chapter of this boundary being changed, and what were the effects?

4 Describe, with examples, the differences between general, functional, line, staff and project managers.

5 Give examples from your experience or observation of each of the four tasks of management.

6 How does Mintzberg's theory of management roles complement that which identifies the tasks of management?

7 What is the significance to someone starting a career in management of Luthans' theory about roles and performance?

8 In what ways could the way managers deal with diversity affect organisational performance?

9 How can a critical perspective help managers do their job more effectively?

10 Review and revise the definition of management that you gave in Activity 1.1.

Concluding critical reflection

Think about the way managers in your company, or one with which you are familiar, go about their work. Review the material in the chapter, and make notes on these questions:

- Which of the issues discussed in this chapter are most relevant to the way you and your colleagues manage?

- What assumptions about the role of management appear to guide the way you manage? Which aspects of the content and process of managing are you expected to focus on – or are you unsure? Does your observation support, or contradict, Luthans' theory?

- What aspects of the historical or current context of the company appear to influence how you, and others, interpret your management role? Do people have different interpretations?

- Can you compare your role with that of colleagues on your course? Does this suggest any plausible alternative ways of constructing your management role, in terms of where you devote your time and energy? How much scope do you have to change it?

Further reading

Magretta, J. (2002), *What Management Is (and why it is everyone's business)*, Profile Books, London.

This small book by a former editor at the *Harvard Business Review* offers a brief, readable and jargon-free account of the work of general management. Highly recommended.

Thompson, P. and McHugh, D. (2002), *Work Organisations: A critical introduction*, (3rd edn.) Macmillan, Basingstoke.

Alvesson, M. and Wilmott, H. (1996), *Making Sense of Management*, Sage, London.

Both provide very detailed discussion of management from a critical perspective, with numerous further references.

Handy, C. (1988), *Understanding Voluntary Organisations*, Penguin, Harmondsworth.

This chapter has stressed that management is not confined to commercial organisations, and Handy's book offers a valuable perspective for anyone wanting to consider management in the voluntary sector more fully.

Roddick, A. (2000), *Business as Unusual*, Thorsons, London.

More background from the founder of The Body Shop.

Drucker, P. (1999), *Management Challenges for the 21st Century*, Butterworth/Heinemann, London.

> Worth reading as a collection of insightful observations from the enquiring mind of this great management theorist.

Mezias, J.M. and Starbuck, W.H. (2003), 'Studying the accuracy of managers' perceptions: a research odyssey', *British Journal of Management*, vol. 14, no. 1, pp. 3–17.

> Since this chapter has stressed the significance of managers interpreting and interacting with their context, this paper is a timely reminder of how fallible those perceptions can be. The other articles in this symposium are also valuable in providing further perspectives on how managers see their world.

Hales, C. (2002), '"Bureaucracy-lite" and continuities in managerial work', *British Journal of Management*, vol. 13, no. 1, pp. 51–66.

> Valuable conclusions from case study research about the changing role of management, contrasting these observations with some less empirically-based predictions.

Weblinks

These websites have appeared in the chapter:

www.ryanair.com
www.bp.com
www.shell.com
www.the-body-shop.com
www.diageo.com

Visit two of the business sites in the list, or those of other organisations in which you are interested, and navigate to the pages dealing with recent news, press or investor relations.

- What are the main issues which the organisation appears to be facing?
- Compare and contrast the issues you identify on the two sites.
- What challenges may they imply for those working in, and managing, these organisations?

Annotated weblinks, multiple choice questions and other
useful resources can be found on
www.pearsoned.co.uk/boddy

Chapter 2

Models of management

Aim

To present the major theoretical perspectives on management and to show how they relate to each other.

Objectives

By the end of your work on this chapter you should be able to outline the concepts below in your own terms and:

1 Understand the value of models, and compare unitary, pluralist and critical perspectives

2 Outline Morgan's 'images of organisation' and show your understanding by giving original examples

3 Outline the structure of the competing values framework

4 Outline the main elements of rational goal, internal process, human relations and open systems models, and their contribution to the management agenda

5 Compare the approaches in terms of their contribution to specific management situations

6 Explain the influence on management of uncertain conditions and the assumptions of non-linear models of management.

Key terms

This chapter introduces the following ideas:

model
metaphor
scientific management
operational research
bureaucracy
administrative management
human relations approach
system
open system
system boundary
feedback
subsystem
sociotechnical system
contingency approach
'non-linear' system

*Each is a term defined within the text, as well as
in the glossary at the end of the book.*

Robert Owen – an early management innovator   CASE STUDY

Robert Owen (1771–1856) was a successful manufacturer of textiles, who ran mills in England and at New Lanark in Scotland, which he bought in 1801. New Lanark was an unusually large business unit for the time, requiring a range of management and production control techniques beyond the needs of the owner of a smaller enterprise. The mills were in poor shape when Owen took them over, and he quickly tried to improve the quality of the labour force. Most employees, at this stage of the Industrial Revolution, had little or no experience of factory work. He found 'the great majority of them were idle, intemperate, dishonest [and] devoid of truth' (quoted in Butt, 1971). He also had 'to deal with slack managers who had tolerated widespread theft and embezzlement, immorality and drunkenness' (Butt, 1971).

Owen quickly introduced new management practices. These included daily and weekly measurements of stocks, output and productivity; a system of labour costing and measures of work-in-progress. He used a novel technique to control employees. A small, four-sided piece of wood, with a different colour on each side, hung beside every worker. The colour set to the front indicated the previous day's standard of work – black indicating bad. Everyone could see this measure of the worker's performance. Overseers recorded this to check any trends in a person's work. Owen was keen on discipline, and introduced community singing 'to counteract incipient lawlessness'. The workers are reported to have been less than enthusiastic.

Owen actively managed the links between his business and the wider world. On buying the mills he quickly became part of the Glasgow business establishment, and was closely involved in the activities of the Chamber of Commerce. He took a prominent role in the social and political life of the city. He used these links in particular to argue the case for reforms in the educational and economic systems, and was critical of the effect that industrialisation was having upon working-class life. Owen believed that education in useful skills would help to release working-class children from poverty. He pro-

vided a nursery for workers' children over one year old, allowing both parents to continue working, and promoted the case for wider educational provision. He also developed several experiments in cooperation and community building, though with only limited success. More broadly, he sought new ways of organising the economic system in a way that would raise wages and increase security of employment, at a time of severe business fluctuations. For example, in 1815 he persuaded allies in Parliament to propose a bill on child labour. This would have made it illegal for children under 10 to work in mills. It would also have limited their working hours to 10 a day. The measure met strong opposition from mill owners and a much weaker measure became law in 1819, to Owen's disappointment.

Case questions

- What management issues was Owen dealing with at New Lanark?
- How did the wider context affect Owen's management activities, and how did Owen try to change that context?

2.1 Introduction

The brief historical sketch of Robert Owen illustrates three themes that run through this book. First, he was active in devising management systems of all kinds to improve the performance of his mills, and paid particular attention to ways of controlling the workforce to ensure productive activity. Second, Owen engaged with the wider social environment in which he lived – especially with a workforce unused to the factory system and with different values from his own. He criticised the effects of industrialisation on that social system and tried to influence local and national policy – advocating the end of child labour, for example. His practice of providing nurseries for employees' children from the age of one year would be rare even today. Third, he was managing at a time of transition from an agricultural to an industrial economy, and many of the practices he invented were attempts to resolve the conflicts between these two systems.

Managers today cope with similar issues. They too need to recruit willing and capable staff, and ensure that their work creates value. Many also share Owen's concerns with the social context of work. They see that family circumstances affect staff performance, and take steps to balance the two. Littlewoods, the UK retail chain, offers 'family-friendly' policies such as subsidised child care and flexible working hours to make it easier for people with family responsibilities to continue working if they wish.

Managers operate in a world that is going through changes equal to those facing Owen. In the newer industrial countries of Eastern Europe and Asia the transition is again from agriculture to industry. All are coping with the transition from a world in which people conducted most business within their nation to one in which ever more business is done on a global scale. The Internet is enabling great changes in the way people organise economic activity, equivalent to the Industrial Revolution of which Owen was part. It has encouraged the growth of 'pure' Internet companies such as lastminute.com, and transformed the way established companies use information. Sustained climate change will affect many businesses in unknown, yet substantial, ways.

In coping with such changes managers, like Owen before them, have searched for ways to manage their enterprises and to overcome the pressing issues of their time. Through trial and error they developed practices that are now part of business and management history. Understanding this history helps present and future managers shape their practice to suit current circumstances.

This chapter traces the evolution of ideas about management. The next section introduces the idea of management models, and how they can illuminate the activity of managing. Later sections present four such models. The final section indicates some of the issues facing managers today – and the new models that may represent these conditions.

2.2 Why study models of management?

A **model** represents a complex phenomenon by identifying the major elements and relationships.

A **model** (or theory) represents a more complex reality. Focusing on the essential elements and their relationship helps to understand that complexity, and how change may affect it. Most management problems can only be understood by examining them from several perspectives, so no model offers a complete solution. Those managing a globally competitive business such as motor vehicle production require flexibility, quality *and* low-cost production. Managers at Ford or DaimlerChrysler want models of the production process that help them organise it efficiently from a technical perspective. They also want models of human behaviour that will help them to organise production in a way that encourages staff to work in an enthusiastic and committed way. The management task is to reconcile both approaches into an acceptable solution.

Managers act in accordance with their theory or perspective about the task in hand. To understand management action we need to know the range of perspectives available and how people use them to guide practice.

Models help to understand complexity

Models and theories aim to identify the key variables, suggest possible relationships and predict the outcomes of change. In the messy, uncertain management task of 'getting things done with the aid of people and other resources' in which every situation is unique, many experienced managers question the need for, and benefit of, abstract theory. But 'without a theory of some sort it's hard to make sense of what's happening in the world around you. If you want to know whether you work for a well-managed organization – as opposed to whether you like your boss – you need a working theory of management' (Magretta, 2002, p. 10). The more accurately theories represent reality, the more useful they are to people as they try to cope with the complexity of managing. Good theories form a person's mental toolkit, helping them to reflect consciously on the situation and to anticipate the possible results of their actions.

Many people find models and theories of management vague and imprecise, especially if they have previously studied in the physical or natural sciences. The fixed laws governing those scientific phenomena allow people to predict relationships accurately. Management has few such certainties. One reason is the number of variables that affect the situation. Figure 2.1 develops Figure 1.3 to show some more specific variables within each of the elements of the internal context within which managers work. Moreover, these elements interact: the ability and motivation of *people* will affect output. These depend, amongst other things, on the budgets for training, pay and other benefits

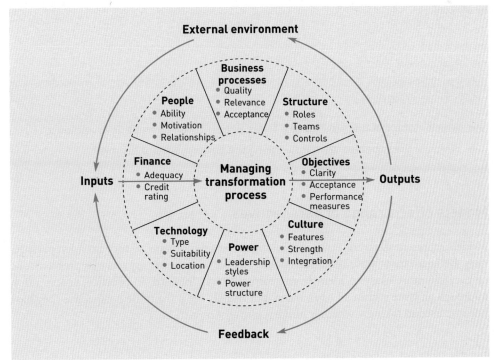

Figure 2.1

Some variables within the internal context of management

(*finance*) – which reflect the relative *power* of those involved in setting the budgets. External events (see Chapter 3) shape all of these.

Scientific phenomena also embody numerous variables. The difference in developing theories of management is that the variables in Figure 2.1 are hard to measure, and people will interpret them in different ways. People have unique experiences, interests and objectives which affect what information they attend to, the significance they attach to it and how they act. There is an example in Chapter 10 of a study of the organisational culture within a retail business, in which senior managers, store managers and shop-floor staff attached different meanings to the culture in which they worked. People act on the basis of subjective interpretations of information, which means that predicting their reaction is hazardous, though essential.

Practice reflects managers' theories

The following examples illustrate contrasting theories which these managers hold about motivation.

Motivating managers: Tim O'Toole, who became chief executive of London Underground in 2003, put in a new management structure, appointing a general manager for each line, to improve accountability.

> Now there's a human being who is judged on how that line is performing and I want them to feel that kind of intense anxiety in the stomach that comes when there's a stalled train and they realise that it's their stalled train. (From an article by Simon London, *Financial Times*, 20 February 2004)

Motivating staff: Joe Roelandts is CEO of Xilinx (a company that makes advanced products in the electronics industry) and which (exceptionally) did not make staff redundant during a period of low industry demand.

> The decision to avoid lay-offs was a better business decision. It protected the minds of the people who work on the future; it keeps their minds free to continue to innovate. No-one can innovate when they are worried about their jobs. (From an article by Simon London, *Financial Times*, 22 January 2003).

Find out more at **www.xilinx.com**.

FT

Case question 2.1

- Which of the variables in Figure 2.1 was Robert Owen attempting to influence?
- Which of the variables were influencing the performance of his mill?

Models offer a range of perspectives

Models represent different ways of thinking about phenomena, so they broaden perspectives. Being aware of several models enables people to see more aspects of a problem, and so they are more likely to identify an acceptable way forward. In practice, people rarely approach an issue within an open mind, but usually see it from the perspective they have become used to taking – whether unitary, pluralist or critical.

Unitary

Someone who takes a unitary perspective tends to emphasise the common purpose of the organisation, and to believe that members share and accept this purpose. They expect members to subordinate individual interests to the good of the whole. They see disagreement or dissent as a sign of disloyalty or failure, and expect all the parts to work together for the common good. They often use analogies of sporting teams ('let's play to win') or ships ('we're all in the same boat'), and stress the importance of loyalty.

Pluralist

People who take a pluralist view see the organisation as a coalition of interest groups. Each has its own objectives that will sometimes coincide and at other times conflict with those of other groups. They see that members have personal goals and competing loyalties – to colleagues, their profession, business unit, family or local community – as well as to the organisation. Pluralists expect that people will reflect these loyalties in debate within the organisation about both ends and means. They see disagreement as a sign of strength, not of weakness. Pluralists compare organisations to nation states in which political systems and processes resolve divergent, but equally legitimate, views.

Critical

Those who take a critical perspective believe organisations reflect the divisions and inequalities of society. They believe that organisations are not just vehicles for the efficient delivery of services but are also tools for achieving personal or group interests. Some stakeholders are more powerful than others, so that apparently democratic debate will always favour those in more powerful positions. Those with a critical perspective stress the underlying differences of power in organisations and society, and believe that 'rational' methods attempt to disguise underlying sectional interests.

Models reflect their context

People develop models and theories in response to circumstances, in this case to the most pressing issues facing managers at the time. In the late nineteenth century skilled labour was scarce, unskilled labour plentiful, and management was keen to increase its control of both. The pressing problem was how to control vast numbers of people with limited experience whom factory owners had recruited to work for them. Managers trying to increase production to meet growing demand wanted theories about making production as efficient as possible. They looked for ways to simplify tasks so that they could use less-skilled employees, and early management theories gave priority to these issues. People often refer to this focus on efficiency as a manufacturing mindset.

In an influential book Peter Drucker (1954) observed that customers do not buy products, but the satisfaction of particular needs. This implied that what a customer values may be different from what producers think they are selling. Efficiency is still necessary, but is not sufficient. People, Drucker argued, should develop a marketing mindset, focusing on what customers want, and how much they are prepared to pay. Both the manufacturing and the marketing mindset remain relevant, as managers seek ways of meeting rapidly changing customer needs quickly and at low cost. They are interested in models about organising work for maximum flexibility. As business conditions change, new theories will evolve to help people navigate a route for their organisations.

key ideas   Gareth Morgan's images of organisation

Since organisations are complex and contradictory creations, no single perspective or theory can explain them adequately. We need to see them from several viewpoints, each of which will illuminate one aspect or feature – while at the same time obscuring others. Gareth Morgan (1997) shows how alternative mental images and **metaphors** can represent organisations. Metaphors are a way of thinking about a phenomenon, attaching labels to it, which vividly indicate the image being used. We express alternative images in different theoretical constructions, focusing on different ways of looking at the problem. Images help understanding – but also obscure or distort understanding if we use the wrong image. Morgan explores eight images, which represent organisations as:

- **Machines** – mechanical thinking and the rise of the bureaucratic organisation
- **Organisms** – recognising organisational needs, and how the health of organisations is affected by the environment
- **Brains** – an information-processing, learning and self-organising perspective
- **Cultures** – a perspective focusing on the underlying assumptions, beliefs and values
- **Political systems** – the role of interests, conflicts and power in shaping organisations
- **Psychic prisons** – how people can become imprisoned or confined by modes of thinking and acting that become habitual
- **Flux and transformation** – a focus on change and renewal, and the logic behind them
- **Instruments of domination** – the exploitation of members, nations and environments.

A **metaphor** is an image used to signify the essential characteristics of a phenomenon.

2.3   The competing values framework

The range of models of management appears confusing and contradictory. Researchers study different variables, in different contexts and with different aims. It is not immediately obvious how the different approaches relate to each other. The Quinn *et al.* (2003) 'competing values' framework relates models to each other by highlighting the values that lie behind them. Figure 2.2 shows the framework.

Quinn and his colleagues (Quinn *et al.*, 2003) argue that while each model adds to our knowledge of management, none is sufficient – they are complementary elements in a larger whole. The vertical axis represents control and flexibility. Control is a pervasive concern of management as they try to ensure that activities are in line with expectations. Others emphasise ways of enhancing flexibility – apparently the opposite of control. The horizontal axis distinguishes an internal focus from an external one. Some theories are primarily inward looking, while others focus on the links between an organisation and its external environment.

The labels within the circle indicate the primary concerns of theories in that segment. The four broad models that have sought to address those concerns appear around the outside. The human relations model, upper left in the figure, stresses the human-centred criteria of commitment, participation and openness. The open systems model, upper right in the figure, stresses criteria of innovation, adaptation and growth. The rational goal model in the lower right focuses on productivity, direction and goal clarity. Lastly, the internal process model stresses stability, documentation and control.

Finally, the outer ring indicates general values associated with each of the models. For example, it shows that the value associated with the rational goal model is that of maximising output, while the human relations model emphasises developing people.

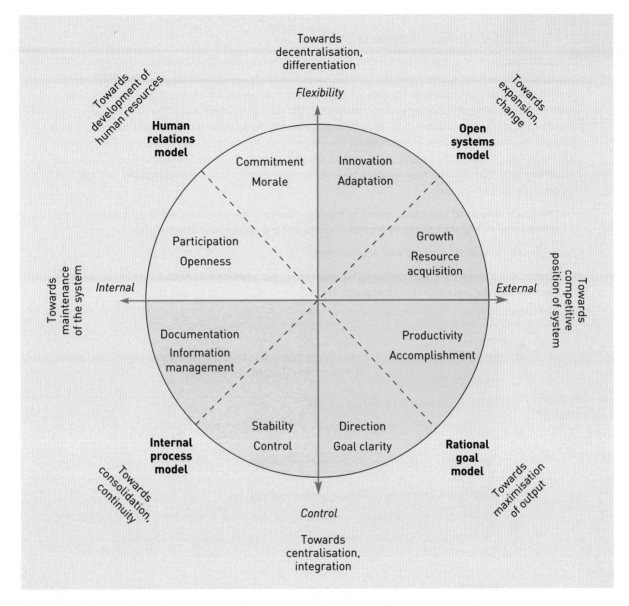

Figure 2.2   Competing values framework
Source: Quinn *et al.* (2003), p. 13.

Quinn uses the overall framework to relate the main models of management to each other. He uses the term 'competing' values, as each of the models seems to carry a competing message. They may, however, be complementary, in that each illuminates a different aspect of managing. Each model has a perceptual opposite: human relations, defined by flexibility and internal focus, is in sharp contrast to the rational goal model, defined by control and external focus. The first values people for themselves while the second values them as contributors to goals. Quinn stresses that the parallels among the models are also important. Both the human relations and the open systems models emphasise flexibility; internal process and rational goal models emphasise control.

Competing values at IMI?

management in practice

Since Martin Lamb took control of IMI (the UK's seventh largest engineering group) in 2001 he has introduced significant changes. He has tried to rebuild the group, which had suffered a decline in business like many other engineering businesses, by switching more manufacturing to low-cost countries and set in train a switch in management culture to forge close links with key customers and to boost innovation. He is also concentrating the business on five sectors of engineering, each associated with high-value products and a strong chance of growth in the next few years. About 40 skilled engineers at 'vision centres' have to identify technologies from other industries that IMI can adapt to its own use. Mr Lamb says:

> This is a fundamental transition, aimed at moving IMI away from an old-established manufacturing enterprise to a company focused on product development and applications of knowledge.

Someone who knew the company well commented:

> I always had the feeling ... that IMI was a bit introverted and anything that (makes) the company more aggressive on the sales side is to be applauded.

FT

Source: Extracts from an article in *Financial Times*, 4 February 2004.

Activity 2.1   Critical reflection on the model

Using the model to reflect on IMI

- Which of the competing values were most dominant in 2000, and which is most dominant now?
- What examples can you find in the case that correspond to the Open Systems model?

Using the model to reflect on your organisation

- Which of the competing values are most dominant in, say, three separate departments?
- How does that affect the way people in them manage the operation?

2.4   Rational goal models

A rarely quoted example of early entrepreneurs developing ways to manage large numbers of people is found in the slave plantations in the United States, where several 'modern management practices were to be found in the operation of the ante-bellum plantations' (Cooke, 2003). Cooke quotes a contemporary account of work on a cotton plantation which records how owners divided slaves into gangs according to their abilities, and then allocated predetermined tasks to each:

> 1st the best hands, embracing those of good judgement and quick motion. 2nd those of the weakest and most inefficient class. 3rd the second class of hoe hands. Thus classified, the first class run ahead and open a small hole about seven to ten inches apart, into which the second class drop from four to five cotton seed, and the third class follow and cover with a rake. (Fogel, 1989: quoted in Cooke, 2003, p. 1908)

More widely, the availability of powered machinery during the Industrial Revolution enabled the transformation of manufacturing and mining processes. These technological innovations encouraged, but were not the only reason for, the growth of the factory system. The earlier 'putting-out' system of manufacture, in which people worked at home on materials supplied and collected by entrepreneurs, allowed great freedom over hours, pace and methods of work. It was difficult to control the quantity and quality of output. Emerging capitalist entrepreneurs found that they could secure more control if they brought workers together in a factory. Having all workers on a single site meant that:

> coercive authority could be more easily applied, including systems of fines, supervision … the paraphernalia of bells and clocks, and incentive payments. The employer could dictate the general conditions of work, time and space; including the division of labour, overall organisational layout and design, rules governing movement, shouting, singing and other forms of disobedience. (Thompson and McHugh 2002, p. 22)

This still left entrepreneurs across Europe and later the United States (and now China – see Management in Practice) with the problem of how to manage these new factories profitably. Although domestic and export demand for manufactured goods was high, so was the risk of business failure.

Incentives at TCL, China

TCL Corporation is one of the top producers of electronics products in China, and its chairman and chief executive Tomson Li boasts of the long hours his employees put in. Signs posted next to production lines encourage workers to push themselves to do even more. 'If you don't diligently work today', one warns ominously, 'you'll diligently look for work tomorrow.'

Source: Based on 'Bursting out of China', *Business Week*, 17 November 2003, pp. 24–5.

Adam Smith and Charles Babbage

Adam Smith, the Scottish economist, had written enthusiastically in 1776 of the way in which pin manufacturers in Glasgow had broken a job previously done by one man into several small steps. A single worker now performed each of these steps repetitively. This greatly reduced the discretion that workers had over their work but, because each was able to specialise, output increased dramatically. Smith believed that this was one of the key ways in which the new industrial system was increasing the wealth of the country.

Charles Babbage supported and developed Smith's observations. He was an English mathematician better known as the inventor of the first calculating engine. During his work on that project he visited many workshops and factories in England and on the Continent. He then published his reflections on 'the many curious processes and interesting facts' that had come to his attention (Babbage, 1835). He believed that 'perhaps the most important principle on which the economy of a manufacture depends is the division of labour amongst the persons who perform the work' (p. 169). There were several reasons why this method – in which 'each process by which any article is produced is the sole occupation of one individual' – had become so widespread. It reduced training costs, saved the time of moving between jobs and increased the skill that people working at one task would acquire. This in turn meant that workers were able to suggest improvements to the process (pp. 169–76).

Babbage also observed that employers in the mining industry had applied the idea to what he called 'mental labour'. 'Great improvements have resulted … from the judicious distribution of duties … amongst those responsible for the whole system of the mine and its government' (p. 202). He also recommended that managers should know the precise expense of every stage in production. Factories should also be large enough to secure the economies made possible by the division of labour and the new machinery.

Frederick Taylor

Scientific management The school of management called 'scientific' attempted to create a science of factory production.

The fullest answer to the problems of factory organisation came in the work of Frederick W. Taylor (1856–1915), who is always associated with the ideas of '**scientific management**'. An American mechanical engineer, Taylor focused on the relationship between the worker and the machine-based production systems that by then were in widespread use. He wrote that 'the principal object of management should be to secure the maximum prosperity for the employer, coupled with the maximum prosperity for each employee. The words 'maximum prosperity are used ... to mean the development of every branch of the business to its highest state of excellence, so that the prosperity may be permanent' (Taylor, 1917, p. 9). He believed the way to achieve this was to ensure that each worker reached their state of maximum efficiency, so that each was doing 'the highest grade of work for which his natural abilities fit him' (p. 9). This would follow from detailed control of the process, which would become the primary responsibility of management, not of the worker. Management should concentrate on understanding the production systems, and use this knowledge to specify every aspect of the operation. In terms of Morgan's images, the appropriate metaphor would be the machine. Taylor advocated five principles to help managers achieve control and predictability:

- Use scientific methods to determine the one best way of doing a task, rather than rely on the older 'rule of thumb' methods.
- Select the best person to do the job so defined, ensuring that their physical and mental qualities were appropriate for the task.
- Train, teach and develop the worker to follow the defined procedures precisely.
- Provide financial incentives to ensure people work to the prescribed method.
- Move responsibility for planning and organising from the worker to the manager.

Taylor's underlying philosophy was that scientific analysis and fact, not guesswork, should inform management. Like Smith and Babbage before him, he believed that efficiency rose if tasks were as routine and predictable as possible. He advocated techniques such as time and motion studies, standardised tools and individual incentives. Breaking work into small, specific tasks would increase control. Specialist managerial staff would design these tasks, and organise the workers:

> The work of every workman is fully planned out by the management at least one day in advance, and each man receives in most cases complete written instructions, describing in detail the task which he is to accomplish, as well as the means to be used in doing the work ... This task specifies not only what is to be done but how it is to be done and the exact time allowed for doing it. (Taylor, 1917, p. 39)

Managers in the industrialised economies adopted Taylor's ideas widely, if selectively, during the 1920s and 1930s (Thompson and McHugh, 2002). His methods allowed productivity to rise many times, and semi-skilled workers following set routines of work replaced skilled workers. Taylor also influenced the development of administrative systems such as record keeping and stock control to support manufacturing. Henry Ford was an enthusiastic advocate of Taylor's ideas. When he introduced the assembly line in 1914 he reduced the time taken to assemble a car from over 700 hours to 93 minutes. Ford also developed his systems of materials flow and plant layout, a significant contribution to scientific management (Biggs, 1996; Williams *et al.*, 1992).

However, the gains in worker productivity were often achieved at great human cost. The trade unions in the United States believed Taylor's methods increased unemployment, and vigorously opposed them. For many people, work on an assembly line or similarly routine operation is boring and alienating, devoid of much human meaning. In

Ford's Highland Park plant

Ford's plant at Highland Park, completed in 1914, introduced predictability and order 'that eliminates all questions of how work is to be done, who will do it, and when it will be done. The rational factory, then, is a factory that runs like a machine' (Biggs, 1996, p. 6). Biggs provides abundant evidence of the effects of applying rational production methods:

> The advances made in Ford's New Shop allowed the engineers to control work better. The most obvious and startling change in the entire factory was, of course, the constant movement, and the speed of that movement, not only the speed of the assembly line, but the speed of every moving person or object in the plant. When workers moved from one place to another, they were instructed to move fast. Laborers who moved parts were ordered to go faster. And everyone on a moving line worked as fast as the line dictated. Not only were workers expected to produce at a certain rate in order to earn a day's wages but they also had no choice but to work at the pace dictated by the machine. By 1914 the company employed supervisors called pushers (not the materials handlers) to 'push' the men to work faster.

> The 1914 jobs of most Ford workers bore little resemblance to what they had been just four years earlier, and few liked the transformation. ... As early as 1912, job restructuring sought an 'exceptionally specialized division of labor [to bring] the human element into [the] condition of performing automatically with machine-like regularity and speed' (Biggs, 1996, p. 132).

extreme cases the time taken to complete an operation before starting to repeat it – the cycle-time – is less than a minute, and uses few human abilities.

Frank and Lillian Gilbreth

Frank and Lillian Gilbreth (1868–1924 and 1878–1972) worked as a husband and wife team, and enthusiastically promoted the development of scientific management. Frank Gilbreth had been a bricklayer, observing practices that made the work slow and output unpredictable. He used film to study the movements in laying bricks and used this to find the most economical motions for each task. He also specified exactly what the employer should provide, such as trestles at the right height and materials at the right time. Supplies of mortar and bricks (arranged the right way up) should arrive at a time which did not interrupt work. In an influential book (Gilbreth, 1911) he gave precise guidance on how to reduce unnecessary actions, and hence fatigue, while laying bricks. He claimed his methods reduced the number of actions from 18 to five. He gave equally precise guidance on how to train apprentices so that they followed the correct systems: 'These rules and charts will enable the apprentice to earn large wages immediately, because he has here a series of instructions that show each and every motion in the proper sequence. They eliminate the "wrong" way [and] all experimenting' (quoted in Spriegel and Myers, 1953, p. 57).

Lillian Gilbreth focused on the psychological aspects of management, and on promoting the welfare of the individual worker. She too promoted the ideas of scientific management, believing that, properly applied, they would enable individuals to reach their full human potential. Through careful development of systems, careful selection, clearly planned training and proper equipment, workers would build their self-respect and pride. In *The Psychology of Management* (1914) she argued that if workers did something well, and that was made public, they would develop pride in their work and in themselves. She recognised that workers had enquiring minds, and that management should take time to explain the reasons for work processes: 'Unless the man knows why he is doing the thing, his judgment will never reinforce his work ... His work will not enlist his zeal unless he knows exactly why he is made to work in the particular manner prescribed' (quoted in Spriegel and Myers, 1953, p. 431).

> ### Activity 2.2   What assumptions did they make?
>
> What assumptions did Frederick Taylor and Lillian Gilbreth make about the interests and abilities of industrial workers?

Operational research

Operational research attempts to solve complex problems by developing mathematical models to analyse the many variables.

Another perspective that is included within the rational goal model is operational research (OR). This originated during the early 1940s, when the UK War Department faced severe management problems. To solve these it formed what were called operational research teams, which pooled the expertise of various scientific disciplines such as mathematics and physics. The teams produced significant results, especially when early computers supported their intellectual expertise.

After the war, managers in industry and government saw that operational research techniques could also help to run complex civil organisations. The scale and complexity of business was increasing, and required new techniques to analyse the many interrelated variables. Mathematical models could help, and computing developments supported the increasing sophistication of the models the scientists produced. This led to the continuing growth of the 'management science approach'.

This approach usually begins by putting together a team from relevant disciplines to analyse the issue and propose a solution. The team constructs a mathematical model showing the links between all the relevant factors. By changing the values of variables in the model (such as increasing transport costs) and comparing different forms of the equations, the team can establish the quantitative effects of each change. They can present management with apparently objective analyses of alternatives to guide their decisions.

Large organisations in both the public and private sectors use the techniques of management science. The model supports the planning function in areas such as production scheduling, cash flow management and estimating the inventory required for different levels of production. It also contributes to the control function by helping to specify and measure appropriate performance levels.

One difficulty with management science is that some managers find the mathematical basis forbidding and inaccessible. A second difficulty is that it cannot take into account the human and social uncertainties of modern organisations. The assumptions built into the models may in practice be invalid, especially if they involve political interests. The technique can clearly contribute to the analysis of management problems, and probably does so best when recognised as only one, relatively technical, part of the total solution.

Current status

Table 2.1 summarises principles common to the rational goal models of management and indicates their modern application.

Principles of the rational model	Current applications
Systematic work methods	Work study and process engineering departments develop precise specifications for processes and job descriptions for staff
Detailed division of labour	Where staff focus on one type of work or customer in manufacturing or service operations
Centralised planning and control	Modern information systems increase the scope for central control of worldwide operations – for example in the electronics industry
'Low-involvement' employment relationship	Using temporary staff as required, rather than permanent employees

Table 2.1

Modern applications of the rational goal model

Examples of rational goal approaches are common in manufacturing and service organisations. Watch the staff in a bank or a travel agency dealing with a routine transaction with a customer. The chances are that they will follow a set of prompts on their computer screen, key in the answer, and the system then prompts the next question. This limits the scope for error and deviation from the prescribed route (Gabrial, 1988; Ritzer, 1993).

Using technology to control staff

management in practice

A successful travel company introduced a networked computer system linking all of its branches to head office. Many benefits were expected and achieved. One of these was that, having sold a holiday, staff should work in a more disciplined routine to complete the administrative details. The information technology director commented:

> We are finding that paper is never a standard system – there are always different ways you can handle paper. You can always choose to fill in a form or not fill it in, choose to complete a box or not. We expect that automation will finally provide the disciplined system that people must adhere to.

Source: Boddy and Gunson (1996).

Case question 2.2

● Which of the ideas in the rational model of management was Owen experimenting with at New Lanark?

● Would you describe Owen's approach to management as low involvement?

● What assumptions did he make about the motivation of workers?

Activity 2.3 Finding current examples

Try to find an original example of work that has been designed on rational goal principles. There are examples in office and service areas as well as in factories. Compare your examples with those of colleagues.

2.5 Internal process models

Max Weber

A major contribution to the search for ways of managing organisations efficiently came from Max Weber (1947). Weber (1864–1920) was a German social historian who drew attention to the growing significance of large organisations. As societies became more complex, responsibility for core activities became concentrated in specialised units. They could only operate with systems that institutionalised the management process by creating organisations that relied on rules and regulations, hierarchy, precise division of labour and detailed procedures. Weber was one of the first to write extensively about the problems of organisations and to observe that the process of **bureaucracy** was bringing routine to office operations just as machines had to production.

Bureaucratic management is usually associated with the six characteristics shown in the Key Ideas box.

Bureaucracy is a system in which people are expected to follow precisely defined rules and procedures rather than to use personal judgement.

key ideas The characteristics of bureaucratic management

Rules and regulations The formal guidelines that define and control the behaviour of all employees while they are working. This formal system helps to provide the discipline that an organisation needs to exercise control and reach its goals. Adherence to rules and regulations ensures uniformity of procedures and operations, regardless of an individual manager's or employee's personal desires. Rules and regulations also enable top management to direct and coordinate the efforts of middle managers and, through them, the efforts of first-line managers and employees. Managers leave, so rules help to stabilise the organisation.

Impersonality Reliance on rules and regulations leads to impersonality, which protects employees from the personal whims of managers. Although the term often has negative connotations, Weber believed that impersonality ensured fairness for employees. An impersonal superior evaluates subordinates objectively on performance and expertise rather than subjectively on personal or emotional considerations. In other words, impersonality heightens a manager's objectivity and minimises discretion and the scope for favouritism.

Division of labour Managers and employees perform officially prescribed and assigned duties based on specialisation and expertise, with the benefits originally noted by Adam Smith. This enables management to set people to work on jobs that are relatively easy to learn and control.

Hierarchical structure Weber advocated the use of a clear hierarchical structure in which jobs were ranked vertically by the amount of authority the holder had to make decisions. Typically, power and authority increase through each level up to the top of the hierarchy. Each lower position is under the control and direction of a higher position.

Authority structure A system based on rules, regulations, impersonality, division of labour and hierarchical structure is tied together by an authority structure – the right to make decisions of varying importance at different levels within the organisation.

Rationality The last characteristic of bureaucratic management, rationality, refers to using the most efficient means to achieve the organisation's objectives. Managers should run their organisations logically and 'scientifically' so that all decisions help to achieve the objectives.

Activity 2.4 Bureaucratic management in education?

Reflect on your role as a student and how rules have affected the experience. Try to identify one example of your own to add to those below or that illustrates the point specifically within your institution:

- Rules and regulations – the number of courses you need to pass for a degree
- Impersonality – admission criteria, emphasising previous exam performance, not friendship
- Division of labour – chemists not teaching management, and vice versa
- Hierarchical structure – to whom your lecturer reports, and to whom they report
- Authority structure – who decides whether to recruit an additional lecturer
- Rationality – appointing new staff to departments that have the highest ratio of students to staff.

Compare your examples with those of other students and consider the effects of these features of bureaucracy on the institution and its students.

Weber was aware that, as well as creating bureaucratic structures, managers were using scientific management techniques to control production systems. He welcomed this as the ideal vehicle for imposing discipline on factory work. The two systems complemented each other. Formal structures of management centralise power, and hierarchical organisation aids functional specialisation. Fragmenting tasks, imposing close discipline on employees and minimising their discretion ensures controlled, predictable performance (Thompson and McHugh, 2002). Job descriptions that define the work expected and performance measures that assess the output have the same effect.

While Weber's recommendations on organising work were consistent with those of scientific management, his ideas on the employment relationship were new. He stressed the importance of a career structure clearly linked to the position a person held in the hierarchy. This would allow them to move up the hierarchy in a predictable, defined and open way, which would increase their commitment to the organisation.

He also believed that officials should work within a framework of rules. The right to give instructions was based on a person's authority derived from impersonal rules set by those higher in the organisation. This in turn reflected a rational analysis of how staff should do the work. This approach worked well in large public and private organisations, such as government departments and banks.

Activity 2.5 Critical reflection on bureaucracy

Rules and regulations often get a bad press, and we have all been frustrated at times by rules that got in the way of what we wanted to do. Are they always bad news? Think back to a job that you or a friend has held, or of the organisation in which you work.

- Do the supervisors appear to operate within a framework of rules, or do they do as they wish? What are the effects?
- Do clear rules guide selection and promotion procedures? What are the effects?
- As a customer of an organisation, how have rules and regulations affected your experience?

The systems had both positive and negative aspects for staff. They may have objected to rules that overspecified how they should do their job, but they probably welcomed those on selection and promotion. Rules brought some fairness to these processes at a time when nepotism and favouritism were common.

Henri Fayol

Administrative management is the use of institutions and order rather than relying on personal qualities to get things done.

Managers were also able to draw on the ideas of **administrative management** developed by Henri Fayol (1841–1925), whose work echoes that of Taylor and Weber. While Taylor's scientific management focused on the production systems, Fayol devised management principles that would apply to the whole organisation. Fayol was a French mining engineer who from 1860 to 1918 worked for a major coal mining company. From 1888 until his retirement he was managing director of the Commentry–Fourchambault–Decazeville combine, turning it from an almost bankrupt business into one of the success stories of French industry. Throughout his career he maintained close contacts with French business and government. From 1918 until his death in 1925 he worked to publicise his ideas on business administration. His book *Administration, industrielle et générale* only became widely available in English in 1949 (Fayol, 1949).

Fayol credited his success as a manager to the methods he used, not to his personal qualities. He believed that managers should use certain principles in performing their functions, and these are listed in the Key Ideas box. The term 'principles' did not imply they were rigid or absolute:

> It is all a question of proportion … allowance must be made for different changing circumstances … the principles are flexible and capable of adaptation to every need; it is a matter of knowing how to make use of them, which is a difficult art requiring intelligence, experience, decision and proportion. (Fayol, 1949, p. 14)

---

key ideas **Fayol's principles of management**

1 **Division of work** If people specialise, the more can they concentrate on the same matters and so acquire an ability and accuracy, which increases their output. However, 'it has its limits which experience teaches us may not be exceeded.'

2 **Authority and responsibility** The right to give orders and to exact obedience, derived from either a manager's official authority or his or her personal authority. 'Wherever authority is exercised, responsibility arises.'

3 **Discipline** 'Essential for the smooth running of business … without discipline no enterprise could prosper.'

4 **Unity of command** 'For any action whatsoever, an employee should receive orders from one superior only' – to avoid conflicting instructions and resulting confusion.

5 **Unity of direction** 'One head and one plan for a group of activities having the same objective … essential to unity of action, co-ordination of strength and focusing of effort.'

6 **Subordination of individual interest to general interest** 'The interests of one employee or group of employees should not prevail over that of the concern.'

7 **Remuneration of personnel** 'Should be fair and, as far as possible, afford satisfaction both to personnel and firm.'

8 **Centralisation** 'The question of centralisation or decentralisation is a simple question of proportion … of finding the optimum degree for the particular concern … [the] share of initiative to be left to [subordinates] depends on the character of the manager, the reliability of the subordinates and the condition of the business. The degree of centralisation must vary according to different cases.'

9 **Scalar chain** 'The chain of superiors from the ultimate authority to the lowest ranks – the route followed by all communications which start from or go to the ultimate authority ... is at times disastrously lengthy in large concerns, especially governmental ones.' Fayol pointed out that many activities depend on speedy action. Then it was appropriate for people at the same level of the chain to communicate directly, as long as their immediate superiors approved of the contact. 'It provides for the usual exercise of some measure of initiative at all levels of authority.'

10 **Order** Materials should be in the right place to avoid loss, and the posts essential for the smooth running of the business filled by capable people.

11 **Equity** Managers should be both friendly and fair to their subordinates – 'equity requires much good sense, experience and good nature'.

12 **Stability of tenure of personnel** A high employee turnover is not efficient – 'Instability of tenure is at one and the same time cause and effect of bad running.'

13 **Initiative** 'The initiative of all represents a great source of strength for businesses. This is particularly apparent at difficult times; hence it is essential to encourage and develop this capacity to the full. The manager must be able to sacrifice some personal vanity in order to grant this satisfaction to subordinates ... a manager able to do so is infinitely superior to one who cannot.'

14 **Esprit de corps** 'Harmony, union among the personnel of a concern is a great strength in that concern. Effort, then, should be made to establish it.' Fayol went on to suggest two ways of doing so: avoid sowing dissension amongst subordinates, and use verbal rather than written communication when it is simpler and quicker.

Source: Fayol (1949).

Current status

Table 2.2 summarises some principles common to the internal process models of management and indicates their modern application.

Some principles of the internal process model	Current applications
Rules and regulations	All organisations have these, covering areas such as expenditure, safety, recruitment and confidentiality
Impersonality	Appraisal processes based on objective criteria or team assessments, not personal preference
Division of labour	Setting narrow limits to employees' areas of responsibility – found in many organisations
Hierarchical structure	Most company organisation charts show managers in a hierarchy – with subordinates below them
Authority structure	Holders of a particular post in the hierarchy have authority over matters relating to that post, and not to matters which are the responsibility of others
Centralisation	Organisations balance central control of (say) finance or online services with local control of (say) pricing or recruitment
Initiative	Current practice in some firms to increase the power and responsibility of operating staff
Rationality	Managers expected to focus on things that support the organisation's objectives, and assess issues on the basis of fact, not preference

Table 2.2

Modern applications of the internal process model

Some organisations have been spectacularly successful with these methods, especially when they have many geographically dispersed outlets. Hotel groups, estate agents, retail chains and banks are usually like this – customers expect them to deliver a common and predictable service in each location. So they centralise design and development activities to ensure a standard product. Manuals set out precisely how to deliver the service. They also set out standards and procedures that managers should follow in running the operation. These include how to recruit and train staff and what the premises must look like. The manuals explain how to treat customers, how to conduct the transaction and how to handle the finance. As Fayol advised, these procedures must be applied 'in proportion', allowing for unusual circumstances. Applied clumsily, they dehumanise work and annoy customers.

The main danger stems from the fact that the principles were designed to support management in predictable, routine situations. Parts of business life are still like that, and in those circumstances the internal process models are valuable. They are unlikely to work in situations that require change and innovation.

2.6 Human relations models

In the early twentieth century several writers such as Follett and Mayo recognised the limitations of the scientific management perspective as a complete answer.

Mary Parker Follett

Mary Parker Follett (1868–1933) graduated with distinction from Radcliffe College (now part of Harvard University) in 1898, having studied economics, law and philosophy. She took up social work and quickly acquired a reputation as an imaginative and effective professional, both in creating innovative policies and in putting them into practice. Local and national government sought her advice. As well as being a practical manager she was a keen observer of events. She was learning at first hand about the dynamics of group process – how people work together to develop and implement plans and tasks. She became impressed by the creativity of the group process and realised the potential it offered for truly democratic government – which people themselves would have to create.

Follett advocated replacing bureaucratic institutions by group networks in which people themselves analysed their problems and then produced and implemented their solutions. True democracy depended on tapping the potential of all members of society

key ideas Mary Parker Follett on groups

Follett saw the group as an intermediate institution between the solitary individual and the abstract society, and argued that it was through the institution of the group that people organised cooperative action. In 1926 she wrote:

> Early psychology was based on the study of the individual; early sociology was based on the study of society. But there is no such thing as the 'individual', there is no such thing as 'society'; there is only the group and the group-unit – the social individual. Social psychology must begin with an intensive study of the group, of the selective processes which go on within it, the differentiated reactions, the likenesses and the unlikenesses, and the spiritual energy which unites them.

Source: Graham (1995), p. 230.

by enabling individuals to take part in groups organised to solve particular problems and accepting personal responsibility for the result. If the essence of democracy is creating, the technique of democracy is group life. Such ideas are finding renewed relevance today in the work of institutions such as community action and tenants' groups.

In the 1920s Follett became involved in the business world, when managers invited her to investigate business problems. She again advocated the application of the self-governing principle that would facilitate the growth both of individuals and of the group to which they belonged. Conflict was essential if people brought valuable differences of view to bear on a problem. The group then had to solve the conflict in a way that helped to create what she called an integrative unity among the people concerned. The essential point about a common belief or policy was not that people shared it, but that they had *produced* it in common, through processes aimed at integrating the differences.

She agreed that organisations had to optimise production, but did not accept that the strict division of labour advocated by scientific management was the right way to achieve this (Follett, 1920). The notion of individual workers performing repetitive tasks under close supervision devalued human creativity. The human side should not be separated from the mechanical side, as the two are bound up together. She believed that people, whether managers or workers, behave as they do because of the reciprocal response that occurs in any relationship. If managers tell people to behave as if they are extensions of the assembly line they will do so. This implied that, to achieve effective results, managers should not manipulate their subordinates but train them in the use of responsible power – 'managers should give workers a chance to grow capacity or power for themselves'.

Follett also wrote about leadership, pointing out that leadership shifts from one person to another as a situation evolves. The situation determines what needs to be done, but not who should do it. The person who discovers how best to deal with the situation should take over the leadership. Graham (1995) provides an excellent review of Follett's work.

Mayo's perspective

Elton Mayo was a professor at the Harvard Business School who drew attention to aspects of human behaviour that practitioners of scientific management had neglected. In terms of Morgan's images, the appropriate metaphor would be the living organism which has needs that it can satisfy in interaction with the environment. Mayo's insight grew out of attempts to discover the social and psychological factors that affected performance. His team conducted a series of studies at the Hawthorne plant, owned by the Western Electric Company. The work began in 1924 as a series of experiments to discover the effect on output of changing defined environmental factors. With the emphasis on the physical working conditions, and how they might affect productivity, the questions were similar to ones Taylor might have asked.

The first group of experiments was into the effect of lighting. The researchers established a control and an experimental group, then gradually varied the level of illumination and measured the output. As light rose, so did output. More surprisingly, as lighting fell, making it harder to see the components being assembled, output continued to rise. Even stranger was the fact that output in the control group also rose, even though there had been no change in their lighting. Clearly the physical conditions had only a small effect on the results. The team set up a more comprehensive set of experiments to identify the other factors.

They assembled a small group of workers in a separate room and altered several variables in turn. These included the working hours, the length of breaks and the provision of refreshments. The experienced workers were assembling small components into telephone equipment. A supervisor was in charge of them. There was also an observer to record the experiments and how the workers reacted. Great care was taken to prevent external factors disrupting the effects of the variables under investigation. The researchers were careful to explain what was happening and to ensure that the workers understood what they were expected to do. They also took into account the workers' views on aspects of the working situation.

The experiment began, with conditions being varied every two or three weeks and output measured regularly by the supervisor. The trend in output showed a gradual, if erratic, increase – even when the researchers returned conditions to those prevailing at an earlier stage. Figure 2.3 shows the trend.

Activity 2.6	**Explaining the trend**

Describe the pattern shown in Figure 2.3. Compare in particular the output in periods 7, 10 and 13. Before reading on, what explanations would you put forward for this?

During the experiments, Mayo and some associates from Harvard tried to interpret the results (Roethlisberger and Dickson, 1939; Mayo, 1949). They concluded that the increase in productivity was not related to the physical changes, but to a change in the social situation in which the group was working:

> the major experimental change was introduced when those in charge sought to hold the situation humanly steady (in the interests of critical changes to be introduced) by getting the co-operation of the workers. What actually happened was that 6 individuals became a team and the team gave itself wholeheartedly and spontaneously to co-operation in the environment. (Mayo, 1949, p. 64)

The group felt they were special: managers asked for their views, were involved with them, paid attention to them and they had the chance to influence some aspects of the work.

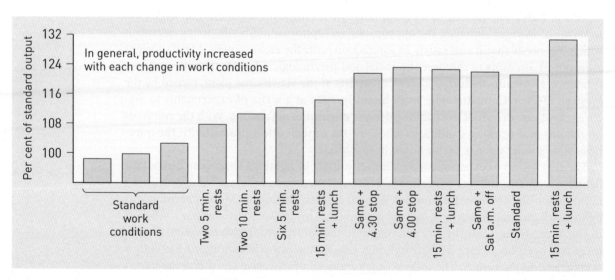

Figure 2.3 The relay assembly test room – average hourly output per week (as percentage of standard) in successive experimental periods

Source: Based on data from Roethlisberger and Dickson (1939). From *Behavior in Organizations,* 6th edition, Greenberg and Baron, © 1997. Reprinted by permission of Pearson Education, Inc. Upper Saddle River, NJ.

The research team also observed another part of the factory, the bank wiring room. This revealed a different aspect of group working. Workers in this area received their wages according to a piece-rate system. This is a system in which management pays workers a set amount for each item, or piece, that they produce. Such schemes reflect the theory that financial incentives will encourage staff to work.

Mayo's researchers were surprised to observe that employees regularly produced much less than they could have done. The reason was that the group had developed their own sense of what a normal rate of output should be, and ensured that all members of the team adhered to this rate. The workers believed that if they produced, and earned, too much, management would reduce the piece-rate, so that employees would have to work harder for the same pay. Group members therefore exercised informal sanctions against colleagues who worked too hard (or too slowly), until they came into line. Members who did too much were known as 'rate-busters' while those who did too little were 'chisellers'. Anyone who told the supervisor about the norms was a 'squealer'. Sanctions included being 'binged' – tapped on the shoulder to let them know that what they were doing was wrong. Managers had little or no control over these groups, who appointed an informal leader.

Finally, the research team conducted an extensive interviewing programme of employees. The team began by asking fairly direct questions about the working environment, how employees felt about their job, and then moved on to questions about the employees' life in general. The responses showed that there were often close links between work and domestic life. Work experiences went much more deeply into people's wider life than had been expected. Conversely, events in their domestic life affected their feelings about work. The implication was that supervisors needed to pay attention to emotional needs of subordinates.

Activity 2.7 A comparison with Taylor

How does this evidence compare with Frederick Taylor's belief that piece-rates would be an incentive to individuals to raise their performance?

Overall, these and similar observations led Mayo to introduce the idea of 'social man', in contrast to the 'economic man' who was at the centre of the earlier theories. While financial rewards would influence the latter, work group relationships and loyalties would influence the former. These would outweigh management pressure.

On financial incentives, Mayo wrote:

> Man's desire to be continuously associated in work with his fellows is a strong, if not the strongest, human characteristic. Any disregard of it by management or any ill-advised attempt to defeat this human impulse leads instantly to some form of defeat for management itself. In [a study] the efficiency experts had assumed the primacy of financial incentive; in this they were wrong; not until the conditions of working group formation were satisfied did the financial incentives come into operation. (Mayo, 1949, p. 99)

People had social needs that they sought to satisfy – and how they did so may be either in line with management interests or in opposition to them. Mayo's study also drew attention to the informal groups existing alongside the formal organisation designed by management.

Later analysis of the experimental data by Greenwood *et al.* (1983) suggested that the research team had underestimated the influence of financial incentives on performance. For example, becoming a member of the experimental group in itself increased the worker's income. Despite the possibly inaccurate interpretation of the data, the findings

key ideas Women and research

The Hawthorne studies are often quoted as an example of theorists' failure to pay attention to the significance of gender (Acker and Van Houton, 1992; Wilson, 1996). Despite the striking differences between the findings of the relay assembly test female group and the male group in the bank wiring observation room, generalisations made were equally applicable to workers of both genders. The female group increased their output and showed increasingly cooperative attitudes towards management. The male group restricted their output, contrary to management's efforts. These observations rightly led the researchers to acknowledge the significance of group dynamics.

However, when Acker and Van Houton (1992) re-examined the Hawthorne studies they found that the researchers failed to pay attention to the possible effect of the different sex of the subjects in the two rooms. They 'also seem to have taken no notice of the possible effects of variation in research procedures and the interaction of those variations with the sex of the subjects' (p. 21). The analysis of the experiments ignored the fact that the women in the relay assembly test room were individually and informally selected by the plant manager to make sure that they really wanted to participate. Further to this, when two of these women were uncooperative to managers' strenuous efforts to control, they were replaced. In contrast to the female group, in the male-based experiment the pressure to participate in the research was on the group rather than on the individuals. During this experiment no one was replaced, even though 'there was slowing down, laughing and talking'.

stimulated interest in the influence of social factors in the workplace. The research therefore added another dimension to knowledge of the management process. Scientific management stressed the technical aspects of work, and the importance of designing that correctly. The Hawthorne studies implied that management should give at least as much attention to human factors, leading to the **human relations approach**. This advocates that employees will work more effectively if management shows some interest in their well-being through more humane supervisory practices.

Human relations approach is a school of management which emphasises the importance of social processes at work.

Case question 2.3

- In what ways did Robert Owen anticipate the conclusions of the Hawthorne experiments?
- Which of the practices that he used took account of workers' social needs?

Current status

The Hawthorne studies themselves have been controversial, and the interpretations questioned. Also, the idea of social man is itself now seen as an incomplete picture of people at work. Providing good supervision and decent working environments may increase satisfaction, but not necessarily productivity. The influences on performance are certainly more complex than Taylor assumed – but are also more complex than Mayo assumed.

Other writers have followed and developed Mayo's emphasis on the human side of organisations. McGregor (1960), Maslow (1970) and Alderfer (1972) have suggested ways of integrating human needs with those of the organisation as expressed by management. Some of this reflected a human relations concern for employees' own well-being. A much stronger influence was the changing external environments of organisations,

Ricardo Semler and Semco

Semco is a successful Brazilian company which in 2004 employed 3000 people in three countries. It was founded by Ricardo Semler's father in the early 1950s and is now a federation of about ten companies engaged in highly engineered, high quality products which they offer in carefully chosen market niches. These include industrial machinery, cooling systems for commercial properties, managing buildings and properties, and environmental consulting.

The most distinctive feature of the company, and what makes it of great interest to managers at other companies, is the philosophy which underlies the way people work in the business. Semler is committed to the view that:

> the repetition, boredom and aggravation that too many accept as an inherent part of working can be replaced with joy, inspiration and freedom. (p. x)

The company lacks formal structure, so that workers can follow their interests and their instincts when choosing jobs or projects. Semler insists on workers seeking personal challenges and satisfaction before trying to meet the company's goals – and above all that they continually ask 'why?':

> At Semco we spur people to question everything they hear – to undo, dismantle and restart every concept or instruction. We don't do it to sow contention, but because more than once it has led to new opportunities for us. (p. 6)

Unusual features of the company include flexible working times (to enable people to balance work and life), no fixed office spaces for any staff, and the gradual decentralising of the headquarters to satellite office buildings. Semler does not plan the future of the company: he believes that the employees shape it with their effort, interests and initiatives.

Source: Semler (2003).

which have become much less predictable since the time of Frederick Taylor and Elton Mayo. The theoretical roots of these ideas are contained in open systems models.

2.7 Open systems models

The open systems approach builds on earlier work in general systems theory, and has been widely used to help understand management and organisational issues. The basic idea is to think of the organisation not as a **system**, but as an **open system**.

The open systems approach draws attention to the links between the internal parts of a system, and to the links between the whole system and the outside world. The system is separated from its environment by the **system boundary**. It is sustained by flows of energy and materials, which enter it from the environment across this boundary, undergo some transformation process within the system, and leave the system as goods and services. The central theme of the open systems view of management is that organisations depend on the wider environment for inputs if they are to survive and prosper. Figure 2.4 (based on Figure 1.1) is a simple model of the organisation as an open system.

The figure shows input and output processes, conversion processes and feedback loops. The organisation must satisfy those in the wider environment well enough to ensure that they continue to provide resources. The management task is to sustain those links if the organisation is to thrive. **Feedback** refers to information about the performance of the system. It may be deliberate, through customer surveys, or unplanned, such as the loss of business to a competitor. Feedback enables those managing the system to take remedial action.

> A **system** is a set of interrelated parts designed to achieve a purpose.

> An **open system** is one that interacts with its environment.

> A **system boundary** separates the system from its environment.

> **Feedback** occurs as the receiver expresses his or her reaction to the sender's message.

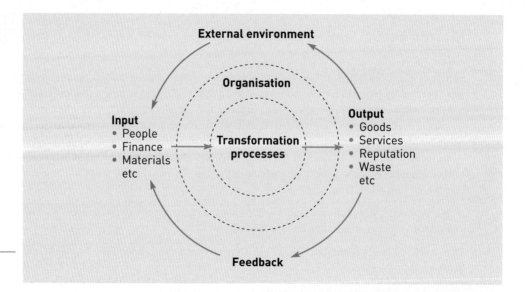

Figure 2.4

The systems model

Case question 2.4

A systems diagram of Owen's mill

- Draw a systems diagram detailing the main inputs, transformation and outputs of Robert Owen's mill.

- Which aspects of the environment probably had most influence on his management practices?

Subsystems are the separate but related parts that make up the total system.

Another key idea is that of **subsystems**. A course is a subsystem within a department or faculty, the faculty is a subsystem of a university, the university is a subsystem of the higher education system. This in turn is part of the whole education system. A course itself will consist of several systems – one for quality assurance, one for enrolling students, one for teaching, another for assessment, and so on. In terms of Figure 2.1, each of the organisational elements is itself a subsystem – there is a technical subsystem, a people subsystem, a finance subsytem and so on, as Figure 2.5 shows.

These subsystems interact with each other, and how well people manage these links affects the functioning of the whole system: when universities move their teaching from three terms to two semesters this has implications across the system – such as accommodation (*technology*), costs (*finance*), arrangements for admission and examinations (*business processes*).

A systems approach emphasises the links between systems, and reminds managers that a change in one will have consequences for others. What counts as the environment depends on the level at which the analysis is being conducted. If a team at British Airways is discussing a new strategy to concentrate on business passengers, the relevant environmental factors will be mainly outside the organisation – the strategies of competing airlines, the level of demand for the more expensive service, whether better-timed landing slots can be negotiated. If the discussion is about the reservations procedures then the relevant environment would mainly include related systems within the airline (such as their call centres and information systems) and the links to travel agents. In either case the principle is the same: take account of the systems that surround the immediate one. That implies being ready and able to scan those environments, to sense changes in them, and to act accordingly.

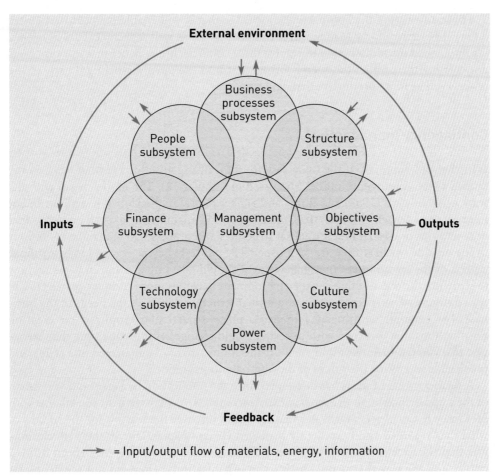

Figure 2.5

Interacting subsystems in organisations

= Input/output flow of materials, energy, information

Sociotechnical systems

An important variant of systems theory is the idea of the **sociotechnical system**. The approach developed from the work of Eric Trist and Ken Bamforth at the Tavistock Institute in London during the 1950s. Their most prominent study was of an attempt by the coal industry to mechanise the mining system. Introducing what were in essence assembly line technologies and methods at the coalface had severe consequences for the social system that the older pattern of working had encouraged. The technological system destroyed the fabric of the social system, and the solution lay in reconciling the needs of both systems.

This and similar studies in many different countries showed the benefits of seeing a work system as a combination of a material technology (tools, machinery, techniques) and a social organisation (people, relationships, constitutional arrangements). In other words, an organisation has technical and social subsystems. Each affects the other, so people need to manage them together for them to work in harmony.

The general message of systems theory is that in designing any kind of system it is necessary to take account of the interdependencies between the various elements of the system. The sociotechnical view, in particular, argues that organisations are best understood as interdependent systems. Analysis should deal with both the social and technical components. The aim is to integrate them rather than to optimise one without regard to the other. The experience of applying the approach in many practical management situations is reflected in a set of principles to be used in designing organisations (Cherns, 1987), a topic discussed in Chapter 12.

A sociotechnical system is one in which outcomes depend on the interaction of both the technical and social subsystems.

61

Those advocating the approach acknowledge that it will enable people to articulate different objectives for a system, if it is to satisfy social as well as technical criteria. They recommended open discussion to resolve these conflicts, in the belief that this process is not creating the conflict but merely bringing it into the open. Resolving it early in the process will be more productive than ignoring it.

Contingency management

A further development of the open systems view of organisations is what has become known as the contingency model (discussed in Chapter 12). The model began with the work of Woodward (1958) and Burns and Stalker (1961) in the United Kingdom, and of Lawrence and Lorsch (1967) in the United States. The main theme of such models is that organisations must adapt their internal structures and processes to match the conditions in the outside world if they are to prosper. The **contingency approach** looks for those aspects of the environment that management should take into account in deciding how to structure the organisation. As the environment becomes more complex managers can use contingency perspectives to examine what structure will meet the needs of the business. For example, contingency theorists place a particular emphasis on creating organisations that can cope with uncertainty and change. At the same time they recognise that some functions within such organisations need to be managed in a stable and predictable way, using the values of the internal process model.

> **Contingency approaches** to organisational structure are those based on the idea that the performance of an organisation depends on having a structure that is appropriate to its environment.

A further group of ideas has developed since the publication by Peters and Waterman of their best-selling book *In Search of Excellence* (1982). As management consultants with McKinsey & Co., Peters and Waterman set out to discover the reasons for the success of what they regarded as 43 excellently managed US companies. One of their conclusions was that the excellent companies had a distinctive set of philosophies about human nature and the way that people interact in organisations. They did not see people as rational beings, motivated by fear and willing to accept a low-involvement employment relationship. Instead, the excellent companies regarded people as emotional, intuitive and creative social beings who like to celebrate victories, however small, who value self-control, but who also need and want the security and meaning of achieving goals through organisations. From this, Peters and Waterman deduced some general rules for treating workers with dignity and respect. This was not out of a sense of philanthropy, but to ensure that people did quality work in an increasingly uncertain environment. In his later work, Peters (1987) continued to stress that people were not components in a rational machine but were the main source of ideas and creativity. Only by tapping the full ingenuity of its staff could management succeed in the current business world.

In Search of Excellence had a significant influence on management thinking and practice. It reflected a move away from rational goal approaches that emphasised complex and usually quantitative analytical techniques as the route to effective management. Peters and Waterman criticised management for having become too reliant on analytical techniques at the expense of the more intuitive and human aspects of business. This, they believed, led to inflexibility and an inability to innovate through experimentation, especially through encouraging attention to the culture and values of organisations. In this they developed the ideas associated with the human relations school, such as those of Douglas McGregor.

The excellent companies appeared to have succeeded by developing strong cultures. As Watson (1994) suggested:

> people do not wander away from serving the key purposes of the organisation's founders or leaders. The tightness of control comes from people choosing to do what is required of them

because they wish to serve the values which they share with those in charge. These values, typically focusing on quality of service to customers, are transmitted and manifested in the organisations' culture. This culture uses stories, myths and legends to keep these values alive and people tend to be happy to share these values and subscribe to the corporate legends because to do so is to find meaning in their lives. (p. 16)

Despite some criticism of the empirical basis of their work, Watson went on to observe that these shortcomings in themselves should not obscure the importance of Peters and Waterman's underlying message. Thompson and McHugh (2002), while critical of much writing on the topic, observe that:

Creating a culture resonant with the overall goals is relevant to any organisation, whether it be a trade union, voluntary group or producer co-operative. Indeed, it is more important in such consensual groupings. Co-operatives, for example, can degenerate organisationally because they fail to develop adequate mechanisms for transmitting the original ideals from founders to new members and sustaining them through shared experiences. (pp. 208–9)

Current status

Those writing about management in the late nineteenth and early twentieth centuries were well aware of the external world. They could observe the massive shift from an agricultural to an industrial economy and the often severe economic fluctuations and political changes that periodically affected organisations. Yet there were also significant sources of stability. Communication systems were such that most organisations were able to operate in a local market with relatively little risk of new competition. Scientific discoveries opened up new possibilities and threatened old businesses, but more slowly than today. There was widespread conflict between management and labour, but the fundamental power of capitalist enterprises remained intact.

These may explain why the emphasis in the early theorists' work was on ways of perfecting the internal arrangements of business so that it could cope with, to modern eyes, a relatively stable business environment. Hence they appear to have viewed organisations as if they were closed systems, and paid relatively little attention to the external world.

An open systems perspective is different, emphasising that people need to plan with the environment of the system in mind. This not only affects the need to adjust objectives and plans more rapidly to external change but also raises the need to find new ways of motivating people to act appropriately in these new conditions.

Yet identifying successful management practice in such conditions is hazardous. The subsequent history of the 'excellent' companies identified by Peters and Waterman demonstrates this. Richard Pascale (1990) found that within five years of publication of their book only 14 of the original 43 companies were still regarded as excellent, and some were in serious trouble. He argued that the pursuit of excellence should not be seen as an end in itself but as a never-ending task. What produced excellence at one time may not do so later.

It is important to recall that organisations in themselves achieve nothing: any change in policy depends on the initiative and action of individuals. Open systems models draw attention to the wide, theoretically infinite, range of issues that affect an organisation. They affect internal affairs only when a person notes an issue and chooses to do something that places it on the management agenda. Whether issues are noticed, how they are interpreted, and what action is taken on them depends on the goals, interests and power of individuals. Factors such as these shape an organisation's response to uncertain conditions.

2.8 Management theories for uncertain conditions

Although theories of management develop at particular times in response to current problems, this does not mean that newer is better. While new concerns bring out new theories, old concerns usually remain. Hence, while current theories are heavily weighted towards ways of encouraging flexibility and change, management still seeks control. Rather than thinking of theoretical development as a linear process, see it as a circular or iterative process in which certain themes recur as new concerns arise.

The competing values approach is useful in that way, in that it captures the main theoretical developments in one framework and shows the relationships between them. Table 2.3 summarises the model and the earlier discussion in a comparative way.

The emerging management challenges come from many sources. One is the increasingly global nature of the economic system (electronics, branded consumer products). Another is the deregulation of many areas of activity, allowing new competitors to enter previously protected markets (airlines, financial services). Still another is the closer integration between many previously separate areas of business (telecommunications, consumer electronics and entertainment). Consumer expectations are increasing and computer-based information systems are developing rapidly. Some radical solutions are being sought by management thinkers – just as was done at the start of the Industrial Revolution.

Some argue that traditional notions of efficiency and asset management may not be adequate to meet the new tasks. They talk instead of *resource leverage*, signifying a search for ways to exploit more fully the physical and especially the invisible intellectual resources of the company. This leads to an emphasis not on size to achieve economies of scale, but on speed and flexibility; on integration, not specialisation; and on management that encourages innovation, not control.

Another new theme in management thinking in such volatile conditions is to consider the implications of feedback. People in organisations, both as individuals and as members of a web of working relationships, can choose how they react to an event or to an attempt to influence their behaviour. That reaction in turn leads to a further response – setting off a complex feedback process. Figure 2.6 illustrates this for three individuals, X, Y and Z.

Table 2.3

Summary of the models within the competing values framework

Features/model	Rational goal	Internal process	Human relations	Open systems
Main exponents	Taylor Gilbreths	Fayol Weber	Mayo Follett Barnard	Trist and Bamforth Woodward Burns and Stalker Lawrence and Lorsch Peters and Waterman
Criteria of effectiveness	Productivity, profit	Stability, continuity	Commitment, morale, cohesion	Adaptability, external support
Means/ends theory	Clear direction leads to productive outcomes	Routinisation leads to stability	Involvement leads to commitment	Continual innovation secures external support
Emphasis	Rational analysis, measurement	Defining responsibility, documentation	Participation, consensus building	Creative problem solving, innovation
Role of manager	Director and planner	Monitor and coordinator	Mentor and facilitator	Innovator and broker

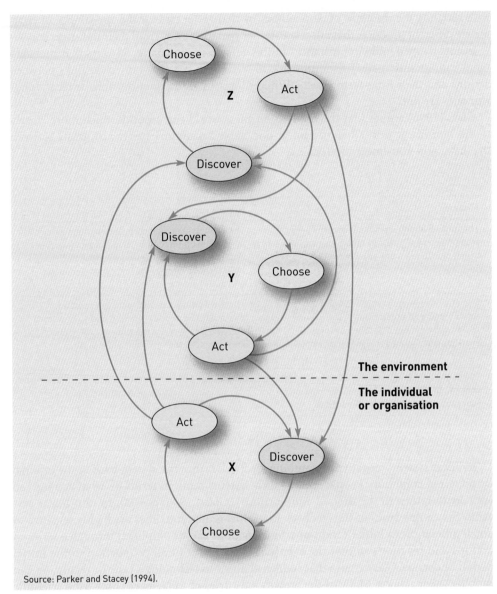

Source: Parker and Stacey (1994).

Figure 2.6

Feedback in non-linear systems

If we look at the situation in Figure 2.6 from the perspective of X, then X is in an environment made up of Y and Z. X discovers what Y and Z are doing, chooses how to respond and then acts. That action has consequences for Y and Z, which they discover. This leads them to choose a response, which has consequences that X then discovers, and acts on. This continues indefinitely. Every act X takes feeds back to have an impact on Y and Z's next action – and the same is true of Y and Z. Hence, as they interact, they make up a feedback system – and what is true of individuals as depicted in the diagram can also be used to indicate the interactions of three groups or three organisations. It can then extend to large numbers of organisations operating in their economic and social environment.

A key element in this way of thinking about organisations is to understand the difference between what are called 'linear' and 'non-linear' systems. 'Linear' describes systems in which an action leads to a predictable reaction. If you light a fire in a room, the thermostat will turn the central heating down. 'Non-linear' systems are those in which outcomes are less predictable. If a company reduces the price of a product it will be surprised if sales in the following period accord exactly with expectations – the company cannot predict

Non-linear systems are those in which small changes are amplified through many interactions with other variables so that the eventual effect is unpredictable.

with certainty the reactions of competitors, of changes in taste or the appearance of completely different products that attract customer spending away from their industry.

Events happen and circumstances in the outside world change in ways that management cannot anticipate. It is impossible to trace with certainty any clear links between actions and their long-term effects. While short-run consequences may be clear, long-run ones are not.

Glass (1996) argues that the modern business world corresponds much more closely to this non-linear world than to a linear one. Table 2.4 summarises the contrasts between the linear and non-linear models.

Table 2.4

Contrasting assumptions in linear and non-linear systems

Linear	Non-linear
The organisation is a closed system. Generally, what it decides to do will take place without too much disruption from outside events.	The organisation is a complex open system, constantly influenced by, and influencing, other systems. Intended actions will often be diverted by external events or by the internal political and cultural processes.
The environment is stable enough for management to understand it sufficiently well to develop a relevant detailed strategy. That strategy will still be relevant when implemented.	The environment is changing too rapidly for management to understand it and to develop a detailed strategy. By the time a strategy is implemented the environment will have changed.
There are defined levers within an organisation that cause a known response when applied (cut staff numbers, increase profits).	Actions lead to unexpected consequences, which can be either positive or negative.

In linear systems, negative or damping feedback brings the system back to the original or preferred condition. People used to such systems think in terms of 'what actions can we take to return to the desired equilibrium?' (Glass, 1996, p. 102). In non-linear systems, the complexities of the feedback loops mean that outcomes are highly sensitive to small differences in initial conditions. Small actions can be amplified through a series of actions and reactions so that the eventual effect is out of all proportion to the initial action or change. Glass argues that sudden changes in technology, taste or regulation can amplify small actions. Many of the growth industries of today have come from scientific breakthroughs that have been aggressively exploited. He goes on:

A manager's way of thinking and acting are quite different if they see the world as being in something near stable equilibrium, than if they believe they are operating in chaos ... In stable equilibrium the manager is constantly trying to bring a situation back to a pre-planned state. In chaos, managers have goals but are also looking for the kind of positive amplification that can give extraordinary, rather than just ordinary, results. (p. 102)

Summary

1 Understand the value of models, and compare unitary, pluralist and critical perspectives:
- Models represent more complex realities, help to understand complexity and offer a range of perspectives on the topic. Their predictive effect is limited by the fact that people interpret information subjectively in deciding how to act.

- A unitary perspective emphasises the common purpose of organisational members, while the pluralist draws attention to competing interest groups. Those who take a critical perspective believe that organisations reflect deep divisions in society, and that attempts to integrate different interests through negotiation ignore persistent differences in the distribution of power.

2 **Outline Morgan's 'images of organisation' and show your understanding by giving original examples:**
   - Morgan suggests that organisations can be viewed from eight alternative perspectives as machines, organisms, brains, cultures, political systems, psychic prisons, in flux and transformation, and as instruments of domination.

3 **Outline the structure of the competing values framework:**
   - A way of integrating the otherwise confusing range of theories of management. Organisations experience tensions between control and flexibility and between an external and an internal focus. Placing these on two axes allows theories to be allocated to one of four types – rational goal, internal process, human relations and open systems.

4 **Outline the main elements of the rational goal, internal process, human relations and open systems models, and their contribution to the management agenda:**
   - Rational goal (Taylor, the Gilbreths and operational research):
     - clear direction leads to productive outcomes, with an emphasis on rational analysis and measurement.
   - Internal process (Weber, Fayol):
     - routinisation leads to stability, so an emphasis on defining responsibility and on comprehensive documentation and administrative processes.
   - Human relations (Follett, Mayo):
     - people are motivated by social needs, and managers who recognise these will secure commitment. Practices include considerate supervision, participation and seeking consensus.
   - Open systems (sociotechnical, contingency and chaos):
     - Continual innovation secures external support, achieved by creative problem solving.

   These theories have contributed to the management agendas in these ways:
   - Rational goal – through techniques like time and motion study, work measurement and a variety of techniques for planning operations; also the narrow specification of duties, and the separation of management and non-management work.
   - Internal process – clear targets and measurement systems, and the creation of clear management and reporting structures. Making decisions objectively on the basis of rules and procedures, rather than on favouritism or family connections.
   - Human relations – considerate supervision, consultation and participation in decisions affecting people.
   - Open systems – understanding external factors and being able and willing to respond to them through individual and organizational flexibility.

5 **Compare the approaches in terms of their contribution to specific management situations:**
   - Rational goal – most likely to be useful when the system depends on minimising costs, and where people are willing to accept the tight controls on their autonomy

that it advises. Low-cost manufacturing countries and mass-production service operations use these techniques.

- Internal process – routine departments running established IT systems, or in public authorities.
- Human relations – professional and personal service organisations such as architects and counselling services.
- Open systems – business development units, marketing or research departments.

6 **Explain the influence of uncertain conditions on management and the assumptions of non-linear models of management:**

- Uncertain conditions mean that it is hard to predict the outcome of an action. Complex feedback loops between the many elements in a situation mean that outcomes are affected by small differences in conditions. The eventual effect is out of all proportion to the initial action or event.
- Linear – closed system, relatively stable environment in which planning is feasible, and identifiable actions with predictable effects are available.
- Non-linear – open system, influenced by other systems; rapidly changing environment, and actions lead to unexpected consequences.

Review questions

1 Name three ways in which theoretical models help the study of management.

2 What are the different assumptions of the unitary, pluralist and critical perspectives on organisations?

3 Name at least four of Morgan's organisational images and give an original example of each.

4 Draw the two axes of the competing values framework, and then place the theories outlined in this chapter in the most appropriate sector.

5 List Taylor's five principles of scientific management and evaluate their use in examples of your choice.

6 What was the particular contribution that Lillian Gilbreth made concerning how workers' mental capacities should be treated?

7 What did Follett consider to be the value of groups in community as well as business?

8 Compare Taylor's assumptions about people with those of Mayo. Evaluate the accuracy of these views by reference to an organisation of your choice.

9 Compare the conclusions reached by the Hawthorne experimenters in the relay assembly test room with those in the bank wiring room.

10 Is an open system harder to manage than a closed system, and if so, why?

11 How does uncertainty affect organisations and how do non-linear perspectives help to understand this?

Concluding critical reflection

Think about the way your company, or one with which you are familiar, approaches the task of management, and the theories that seem to lie behind the way people manage themselves and others. Review the material in the chapter, and perhaps visit some of the websites identified. Then make notes on these questions:

- What examples of the issues discussed in this chapter are currently relevant to your company?

- In responding to these issues, what assumptions about the nature of management appear to guide what people do? Do they reflect rational goal, internal process, human relations or open systems perspectives? Or a combination of several? Do these assumptions reflect a unitary or pluralist perspective, and if so, why?

- What factors such as the history or current context of the company appear to have influenced the prevailing view? Does the approach appear to be right for the company, its employees, and other stakeholders? Do people question those assumptions, in the way that Semler does within Semco?

- Have people put forward alternative ways of managing the business, or even a small part of it, based on evidence about other companies? Does the competing values model suggest other approaches to managing, in addition to the current pattern? How might others react to such alternatives?

Further reading

Drucker, P. (1954), *The Practice of Management*, Harper, New York.

   Still the classic introduction to general management.

Taylor, F.W. (1917), *The Principles of Scientific Management*, Harper, New York.

Fayol, H. (1949), *General and Industrial Management*, Pitman, London.

   The original works of these writers are short and lucid. Taylor (1917) contains illuminating detail that brings the ideas to life, and Fayol's (1949) surviving ideas came from only two short chapters, which again are worth reading in the original.

Biggs, L. (1996), *The Rational Factory*, The Johns Hopkins University Press, Baltimore, MD.

   A short and clear overview of the development of production systems from the eighteenth to the early twentieth centuries in a range of industries, including much detail on Ford's Highland Park plant.

Graham, P. (1995), *Mary Parker Follett: Prophet of management*, Harvard Business School Press, Boston, MA.

   The contribution of Mary Parker Follett has been rather ignored, perhaps overshadowed by Mayo's Hawthorne studies – or perhaps it was because she was a woman. This book gives a full appreciation of her work.

Gillespie, R. (1991), *Manufacturing Knowledge: A history of the Hawthorne experiments*, Cambridge University Press, Cambridge.

Alvesson, M. and Wilmott, H. (1996), *Making Sense of Management*, Sage, London.

Thompson, P. and McHugh, D. (2002), *Work Organisations: A critical introduction*, Macmillan, Basingstoke.

Morgan, G. (1997), *Images of Organization*, Sage, London.

These last four books discuss the ideas in this chapter from a critical perspective.

Semler, R. (2003), *The Seven Day Weekend: Finding the work/life balance*, Century, London.

Well worth reading for an absorbing insight into a radically different approach to managing.

Annotated weblinks, multiple choice questions and other
useful resources can be found on
www.pearsoned.co.uk/boddy

The Body Shop International

www.the-body-shop.com

Anita Roddick opened the first Body Shop in 1976:

My main motivation for going into the cosmetics business was irritation: I was annoyed that you couldn't buy small sizes of everyday cosmetics ... I also recognised that a lot of the money I was paying for a product was being spent on fancy packaging which I didn't want. So I opened a small shop to sell a small range of cosmetics made from natural ingredients in ... the cheapest possible plastic containers. (Roddick, 1991, p. 19)

The company grew rapidly and in June 2004 had over 2000 outlets around the world.

What is wonderful about The Body Shop is that we still don't know the rules. Instead we have a basic understanding that to run this business you don't have to know anything. Skill is not the answer, neither is money. What you need is optimism, humanism, enthusiasm, intuition, curiosity, love, humour, magic and fun and that secret

© The Body Shop International

ingredient – euphoria. The status quo says that the business of business is to make profits. We have always challenged that. For us the business of business is to keep the company alive and breathlessly excited, to protect the workforce, to be a force for good in society and then, after all that, to think of the speculators. I have never kow-towed to the speculators or considered them to be my first responsibility. They play the market without much concern for the company or its values.

Social and environmental issues are woven into the fabric of the company itself. They are neither first or last among our objectives, but an ongoing part of what we do. Not a single decision is ever taken in The Body Shop without considering environmental and social issues. We have an Environmental Projects Department which monitors the company's practices and products to ensure they are environmentally sound and up to date. We have a simple credo. You can run a business differently from the way most businesses are run: you can share your prosperity with your employees and empower them without being in fear of them: you can rewrite the book of how a company interacts with the community: you can rewrite the book on third world trade and on global responsibility and on the role of educating the company, customers and shareholders. You

can do all this and still play the game according to the City, still raise money, delight the institutions and give shareholders a wondrous return on their money. (p. 24)

The Body Shop's mission – *'Our reason for being'* – is 'To dedicate our business to the pursuit of social and environmental change'. The mission statement is followed by five objectives intended to support it:

● To creatively balance the financial and human needs of our stakeholders: employees, customers, franchisees, suppliers and shareholders.

● To courageously ensure that our business is ecologically sustainable, meeting the needs of the present without compromising the future.

● To meaningfully contribute to local, national and international communities in which we trade, by adopting a code of conduct which ensures care, honesty, fairness and respect.

- To passionately campaign for the protection of the environment and human and civil rights, and against animal testing within the cosmetics and toiletries industry.
- To tirelessly work to narrow the gap between principle and practice, while making fun, passion and care part of our daily lives.

These values clearly stem from Anita Roddick's personal principles that guided her in building The Body Shop. She and her husband Gordon believe fervently that business must be a force for social and environmental change. Business organisations are not just for profit – their resources can be used to promote wider purposes. This inspiration and the associated set of values guide the trading principles of The Body Shop management, which are:

- Against Animal Testing: We consider testing products or ingredients on animals to be morally and scientifically indefensible.
- Support Community Trade: We support small producer communities around the world who supply us with accessories and natural ingredients.
- Activate Self-Esteem: We know that you're unique, and we'll always treat you like an individual. We like you just the way you are.
- Defend Human Rights: We believe that it is the responsibility of every individual to actively support those who have human rights denied to them.
- Protect Our Planet: We believe that a global business has the responsibility to protect the environment in which it operates, locally and globally.

For many years the products were sold in refillable containers as part of the company's commitment to reducing packaging and waste. The company discontinued this in 2003 as fewer than 1 per cent of customers used the scheme. Instead, they introduced a new policy of including recycled plastic in the majority of their product bottles. Other environmental policies include using renewable energy in as many shops as possible, and at their main contract manufacturer.

In the past, the cosmetics industry routinely tested new products on animals. The Body Shop campaigned vigorously against this. It raised public awareness of the issue through its campaigns, and it monitors the ingredients used to ensure that the suppliers have not tested them on animals.

Many of its ingredients come from suppliers in poor countries. The company uses its resources not just to buy the products but also to help the communities from whom it buys to achieve sustainable economic independence. It buys directly from the small producers (rather than through intermediate trading companies). It also supplies technical assistance to them to ensure sustainable and good quality supplies, as well as supporting the wider aspects of a community's development. Dismayed by the economic conditions in a deprived part of Glasgow, the company set up a plant in the area to make most of its soap.

The structure of the company is shown in Figure 1. About three-quarters of the shops are owned by franchisees. These are business people who provide the

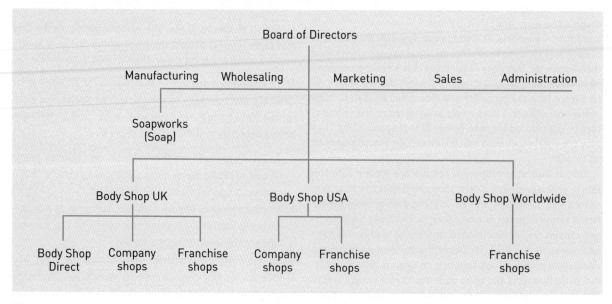

Figure 1 Partial organisation chart of The Body Shop International

capital for a shop and the stock, and then run the shop. They do this under strict The Body Shop guidelines which ensure that the brand image is projected consistently. The Body Shop provides advice and support in setting up and running the outlet but the franchisee is responsible for recruiting and managing staff and for making the shop a success.

This charisma helped to hold the company together in the early days. As it grew and prepared to issue shares to the public in 1984 (to finance further expansion), more systematic ways of managing the business were needed and more professional managers were recruited. There is a constant need to balance the values and the commercial needs of the business. The table summarises the company's turnover and profit for the financial years 2003 and 2002.

	2003 £m	2002 £m
Retail sales	699.5	697.1
Profit attributable to shareholders	30.3	24.3
Earnings per share (p)	10.7	6.8

Anita Roddick is no longer involved actively in managing the company. The company experienced difficult trading conditions for several years, as the market for natural cosmetics matured, and many competitors, including supermarkets, have entered the cosmetics market. The pioneering approach to environmental and corporate responsibility has also been widely copied, so that The Body Shop gained less attention from this aspect of the work. In 2002 commentators were saying that the company appeared to have lost its way.

A new management team was appointed, and in 2004 the group appeared to be recovering. The Chief Executive in 2004 was Peter Saunders, and in his report on the results for 2003 he referred to the difficult trading conditions – though the group had been able to increase pre-tax profits by about 40 per cent. Adrian Bellamy, the executive chairman, said there were opportunities in areas where they had no presence, such as South America and Eastern Europe. The company plans to revitalise the retail outlets, including opening 300 stores over the next three years – its most significant expansion plan for over a decade. It also plans to improve products, improve supply chain performance through investments in technology and strengthen links with the franchisees. In doing so it 'will remained committed to our social and environmental principles and demonstrate integrity and transparency in our relationships with stakeholders'.

Sources: Extracts from Roddick (1991); 'The Body Shop: a case study', Kellogg School, North Western University, Case No. 495-019-8; Company Annual Report 2003; website: www.the-body-shop.com. Extracts from company and website reproduced with kind permission of The Body Shop International PLC.

Part case questions

- How did the management approach of Anita Roddick in the early days of the company compare with that of Robert Owen?
- If you have not done so, visit a branch of The Body Shop so that you are familiar with the physical aspects of the case. What campaigns is it running at the moment? You could also build up a file of press cuttings on the company's performance to update this account.
- What organisational functions does The Body Shop perform?
- In what ways are managers in The Body Shop adding value to the resources they use?
- How does The Body Shop compare with other companies selling similar products? Is it distinctive?
- What clues are there in the case about ways in which the individual founder tried to institutionalise her ideas in the growing company?
- What dilemmas are there likely to be for management in an organisation with two missions?
- In what ways, if at all, are the models in the competing values framework supported by the evidence of The Body Shop case?

To help you develop your skills as well as knowledge, this section includes tasks which relate the key themes covered in the Part to your daily life. Working through these will help you to deepen your understanding of the topic, and develop skills and insights which you can use in many situations.

Task 1.1   Managing your time

Managers often say that they do not have enough time to do their job as well as they would like. People often find that reflecting carefully on how they, and others, spend time helps to improve the way they use it: 'when one is very busy and under pressure, it is difficult to find the time to take stock of the way one works. Yet the effort is worthwhile. Those who do usually find they can organise more effectively both what they do and how they do it' (Stewart, 1967).

To help you begin this reflective process, think back over your recent work as a student or in an organisation, and then:

● list examples of time being badly used, and identify what led to that
● list examples of time being well used, and identify what led to that.

Form a group of three or four colleagues, and exchange information about what you have found. Identify any common themes, and agree at least one practice that you will try to use to improve the way you use your time, either as a student or in an organisation.

Task 1.2   Understanding your roles

The term 'role' refers to the set of expectations which others have of someone occupying a position. The task below should help relate these ideas to your situation.

Part A – creating a role map

The aim of this exercise is to help you identify those people or groups (stakeholders) who have expectations of you in your role as a student *or* in an organisation. What do they expect of you, and what does that mean for where you spend time and energy?

1 Draw a circle in the middle of a page – this represents you in your studying or managing role.

2 Around the sheet draw other circles, each with the name of a person or group (stakeholder) that has expectations of you. Your map should include, amongst others:

   ● the organisation or the boss – respresenting what people formally expect
   ● colleagues – the people who work for you or with you
   ● families and others beyond the immediate role.

Place those where the links are particularly strong nearer the centre, and those that are less critical nearer the edge.

Part B – analysing expectations

Lay out a sheet of paper with the headings below across the top, and a deep row for each main stakeholder. Select three of the stakeholders you identified in Part A, list them in the left-hand column, and make notes on each of the questions in the other columns.

Other person or institution (stakeholder)	[1] What are they expecting of you, and you of them?	[2] In view of (1), what are the three or four study or management tasks you must do well?	[3] Are there situations where the expectations in (1) cause difficulty?	[4] How did you resolve this, or how might you do so?

Part C – comparing with others

Using the role analysis you have carried out, work in pairs or trios with other colleagues on your course. In turn, outline your maps and your analysis in Part B. Your objective is to clarify your awareness of your role, by explaining to your partner(s) what you have written, and then revising it if necessary. Also seek their ideas on the column headed (4).

Part D – connecting theory and practice

Refer to Mintzberg's theory of management roles in Chapter 1. Which (several) of the roles he identified may be most important in helping you to meet the main expectations that others have of you?

Task 1.3 Managing your career

If you have not yet begun your management career, this activity may help you to think about the options and opportunities. Visit major online career websites, such as:

- www.monster.co.uk
- www.fish4jobs.co.uk
- www.prospects.ac.uk

You will be asked to enter a search word for jobs that interest you such as 'marketing' or 'information technology', or to choose a term from a list. This will probably return many possible opportunities – select three, and print the job description. Compile a list of the educational and experience requirements, and of aspects of the job that appeal to you, or which you find unattractive.

Another exercise is to select three of the companies featured on the site, or that are mentioned in this Part, or that interest you. Go to their website and then to the section on 'careers' or 'jobs with us' – again identify some possible jobs, and do as in the previous exercise.

What clues can you find in the information about how the job requirements relate to the tasks of managing (planning, organising, leading and controlling)?

Task 1.4 Identifying what makes a manager effective

You will all have worked with or for people who were managing an activity, either in an organisation or in some other human activity. What makes some better managers than others? Form a group with three or four others on your course and share your experience of managers – good and bad. List what those who were good managers did, which led you to regard them favourably.

Then answer these questions:

- To which of the management tasks or roles identified in Chapter 1 do these seem to relate?
- Are there any which do not fit the theories?
- How would you judge your skills in dealing with the tasks and roles you identified? Be ready to share your conclusions in class.

THE ENVIRONMENT
OF MANAGEMENT

Part 2

Introduction

Management takes place within a context, and this part examines several aspects of the external context of organisations. A key management task is to be familiar with that external environment. People do not need to accept it passively – they can try to influence it by lobbying powerful players, by reaching agreement with competitors or by trying to shape public opinion. Nevertheless, since the organisation draws its resources from the external world, it needs to deliver goods or services well enough to persuade decision makers in that environment to continue their support. This is most obvious in commercial organisations. It is equally relevant in the public service: if a department set up to deliver care is managed badly it will not deliver. Taxpayers or clients will press their elected representatives to improve performance, and they in turn will demand improved performance from management and staff. All those involved with the organisation have some expectations of it. How satisfied they are will affect whether or not they are willing to continue their support. If they do not, the enterprise will fail.

Chapter 3 offers some tools for analysing systematically the relevant forces in the competitive and general environment, and what the most influential players expect of the organisation. Chapter 4 reflects the growing internationalisation of business, by examining some international features of the general environment – political developments such as the European Union, international economic factors and differences in national cultures.

Organisations can no longer act as if their shareholders were the only legitimate external interests. Pressure from interest groups and many consumers has ecouraged some companies to take a positive approach to issues of corporate responsibilities and ethical behaviour. There are conflicting interests here and difficult dilemmas: Chapter 5 presents some concepts and tools that help to consider these issues in a coherent and well-informed way.

The Part Case is BP – a leading player in the world oil business. The business itself is inherently international, being affected by political and economic developments around the world. The case also raises issues of social responsibility in environmental as well as political terms.

Chapter 3

The business environment

Aim

To identify major external influences on organisations and outline tools with which to analyse any business environment.

Objectives

By the end of your work on this chapter you should be able to outline the concepts below in your own terms and:

1 Identify the main sets of forces exerting influence on organisations

2 Use Porter's five forces model to analyse competitive environments

3 Conduct a PESTEL analysis for an organisation with which you are familiar

4 Compare environments in terms of the complexity and rate of change

5 Give examples of stakeholders seeking to influence organisations and explain a model for assessing stakeholder power.

Key terms

This chapter introduces the following ideas:

competitive environment
general environment
external context
stakeholder
internal context
five forces analysis
PESTEL analysis
stakeholder mapping

Each is a term defined within the text, as well as in the glossary at the end of the book.

Nokia is the world's leading manufacturer of mobile phones. With a market share of 35 per cent, it sold twice as many handsets in 2003 as second-placed Motorola and was far ahead of other rivals such as Samsung, Ericsson and Siemens. A Finnish company, founded in 1895 as a paper manufacturer, Nokia grew into a conglomerate with interests including electronics, cable manufacture, rubber, chemicals, electricity generation and, by the 1960s, telephone equipment. In the early 1990s the company decided to focus on the mobile phone industry, then still in its infancy.

A number of factors favoured this move. First, the Finnish government had taken an early lead in telecoms deregulation and Nokia was already competing vigorously with other manufacturers supplying equipment to the national phone company. Second, the European Union (EU) adopted a single standard – the Global System for Mobile Telephony (GSM) – for Europe's second generation (digital) phones. Not only did this create an opportunity to build economy of scale, but it also coincided with Finland's entry into the EU. The GSM standard is now used by two-thirds of the world's mobile phone subscribers. Finland's links with its Nordic neighbours also helped, as people in these sparsely populated countries adopted mobile phones enthusiastically.

Nokia has strong design skills, but above all managers were quick to recognise that mobile phones are not just a commodity but a fashion accessory. Offering smart designs, different ring tones and coloured covers allowed Nokia to establish itself as the 'cool' mobile brand for fashion-conscious individuals. Nokia has also mastered the logistics of getting millions of phones to customers around the world.

While many competitors subcontract the manufacture of their handsets, Nokia assembles most of its own, with factories in countries including Brazil, Finland and China. Managers believe this gives them an understanding of the market and the manufacturing process that it would not otherwise have. Nokia buys about 80 billion components

© Nokia

a year, and has developed close working relationships with the most important of its 150 suppliers.

While all of these factors lie behind Nokia's success, Matti Alahuhta, Director of Strategy, believes there was a further reason. Although competitors such as Motorola and Ericsson already had advantages of scale, experience and distribution networks, the arrival of the new digital technology changed the rules of the game, forcing all players to start from scratch. Mr Alahuhta acknowledges that some external factors have helped Nokia but also comments that 'good luck favours the prepared mind'.

Source: Based on *Financial Times*, 29 June 2001, 16 December 2003; *The Economist*, 16 June 2001.

Case questions

- How has the environment favoured the development of Nokia?
- How could the same factors turn to the disadvantage of the company?
- Visit Nokia's website, and read their most recent trading statement (under investor relations). What have been the main developments in the business?

<table>
</table>

3.1 | Introduction

Nokia's success depends on the ability of its managers to interpret and respond to signals from the outside world – the business environment in which it operates. The early success of the company in mobile phones was helped, for example, by policies of the European Union, and especially the Finnish government, in establishing common standards and promoting mobile use. Nokia was also skilful in recognising that to many users a mobile is as much a fashion item as a phone – and used its design skills to meet that need. More recently it suffered some loss of market when it was slower to anticipate market change than some of its rivals.

All organisations operate in a wider environment, and how people understand, interpret and interact with that outside world affects their performance. Each business is unique, so the external forces that affect them (and which they try to influence) will differ between them. Forces differ by industry and within the same industry: Mercedes and Renault both produce cars, but a government regulation that bans the import of luxury goods would affect only one of them. Managers analyse these forces in the environment as they try to plan the future of the business.

Figure 3.1 shows four environmental forces. The inner circle represents the organisation's immediate **competitive environment** – the industry-specific environment

A **competitive environment** is the industry-specific environment comprising the organisation's customers, suppliers and competitors.

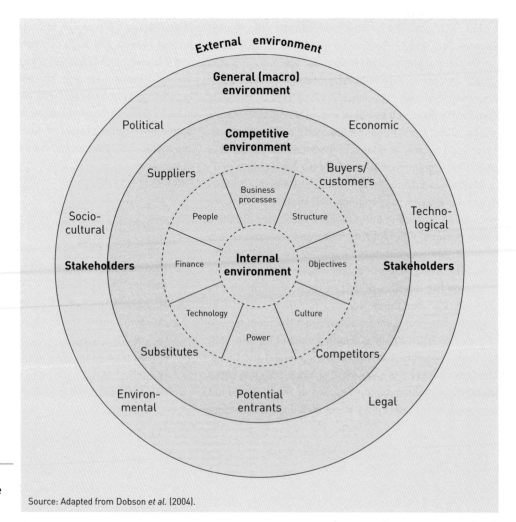

Figure 3.1

Environmental influences on the organisation

Source: Adapted from Dobson *et al.* (2004).

comprising customers, suppliers, competitors and potential substitute products. The outer circle shows the **general environment**, sometimes known as the macro-environment. This is a range of political, economic, social and technological factors that affect all organisations. Forces in the competitive environment usually have more impact on, and are more open to influence by, the organisation than those in the wider environment.

For most organisations the **external environment** (or **context**) is a constantly changing source of threats and opportunities. Performance depends on how well people cope with these uncertainties. Part of the management role is to sense external forces and then to initiate suitable internal changes – adapting factors in areas at the centre of Figure 3.1 such as structure, financial resources and culture. So while looking outwards, managers also need to look inwards to assess how able the organisation is to deal with external change.

While it is easy to list the forces in the external environment, two variables affect their significance for managers. Environmental forces do not affect practice of their own accord. They become part of the agenda only when one or more **stakeholders** pay attention to them and act to place them on the management agenda. Stakeholders are individuals, groups or organisations with an interest in, or who are affected by, what the organisation does. They may be internal (employees, managers, owners, shareholders) or external (customers, bankers, pressure groups and government). In terms of Figure 3.1, they are a third set of forces acting on the organisation.

A related point is that stakeholders interpret environmental forces subjectively. BP and Shell publicly acknowledge climate change, and have specific policies to address it. In contrast, managers at Exxon-Mobil do not yet (in 2004) publicly acknowledge a proven scientific link between burning hydrocarbons and climate. Environmental forces are not objective phenomena, but something which people observe selectively and interpret uniquely.

Managers (who are themselves stakeholders) balance conflicting interpretations of environmental developments. They try to assess actual and potential changes in the environment, and what they mean for the organisation – such as an opportunity to develop a new market or a threat from an unexpected competitor. They then consider what, if any, they would imply for the **internal environment** (or **context**) – which Figure 1.3 illustrated more fully. As Figure 3.1 shows, assessing the environment entails analysing:

- the competitive environment
- the general environment
- stakeholders' expectations
- the ability of the organisation (the internal context) to change.

This chapter concentrates on the first three, Chapter 13 deals with the fourth. The chapter begins by showing how management can analyse the competitive environment facing their unique business. It then presents a model for analysing the general environment. It contrasts different forms of external environment and the practical issues that management must deal with in assessing the external environment. It concludes by introducing the idea of stakeholder analysis.

The **general environment** (sometimes known as the macro-environment) includes economic, political, social and technological factors that generally affect all organisations.

The **external context** consists of elements beyond the oranisation such as competitors, or the wider PESTEL factors.

Stakeholders are individuals, groups or other organisations with an interest in, or who are affected by, what the organisation does.

The **internal context** consists of elements within the organisation such as its technology, structure or business processes.

3.2 The competitive environment – Porter's five forces

Managers are most concerned with the forces in their immediate competitive environment. According to Porter (1980a, 1985) the ability of a firm to earn an acceptable return depends on five forces – the ability of new competitors to enter the industry, the threat of substitute products, the bargaining power of buyers, the bargaining power of suppliers and the rivalry amongst existing competitors. Figure 3.2 shows Porter's **five forces analysis**.

Five forces analysis is a technique for identifying and listing those aspects of the five forces most relevant to the profitability of an organisation at that time.

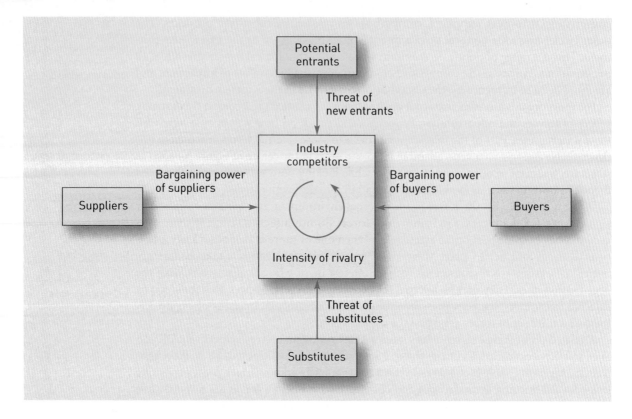

Figure 3.2 The five forces of industry competition

Porter argues that it is the *collective* strength of the five forces that determines industry profitability. The stronger the forces, collectively, the less likely an industry is to be profitable in the long term; conversely, the weaker the forces the greater the opportunity for high profits. These forces influence profitability because they influence prices, costs and investment requirements – which are the fundamentals of return on investment. Buyer power, for example, influences the prices a firm can charge, as does the threat of substitutes. The bargaining power of suppliers determines the cost of raw materials and other inputs. It is in a company's interest to examine these forces in detail to establish the industry strengths and weaknesses. Knowing these forces, and how they are likely to affect their industry, enables managers to decide on future direction.

Potential new entrants

The threat of new competitors to an industry depends on the ease with which they can enter a market. Major barriers to entry are:

- the need for economies of scale (to compete on the basis of cost), which are difficult to achieve in the short run
- high entry costs, where significant capital investment is required (for example in plant and machinery)
- lack of distribution channels
- legislation or other government policy such as selective subsidies, which benefit existing firms at the expense of potential new entrants

- cost advantages of existing firms, such as access to raw materials or know-how
- strong product or service differentiation – customers are loyal to the brand.

As examples, GlaxoSmithKline (a leading Anglo-American drugs group) is, like all similar companies, facing a growing threat from generic (unbranded) versions of its top-selling drugs, while growing low-cost airlines in Asia threaten Cathay Pacific.

Intensity of rivalry amongst competitors

Strong competitive rivalry is likely to result in low margins and profitability; it is likely to occur when:

- there are many firms in an industry, but none is dominant
- there is slow market growth, which means companies fight for market share
- fixed costs are high, as this encourages firms to use capacity and overproduce
- there are high exit costs; specialised assets (which may be hard to sell) or management loyalty (for example in long-established family firms) can create exit barriers which prolong excess capacity and low profitability
- products are similar, so customers can easily switch to other suppliers.

A highly competitive market will also be one in which the threat of new entrants is high. While Nokia still dominated the mobile phone industry in 2004, it was facing growing pressure from established competitors Motorola, Siemens and Ericsson, and from new entrants from Asia.

management
in practice

Competition amongst Chinese brewers

SABMiller and Anheuser-Busch both sought to enter the Chinese market by buying an existing major player, Harbin (with Anheuser-Busch quickly winning the contest). They were attracted by the fact that China is the world's largest market for beer, growing at 6–8 per cent a year. However, it is also fiercely competitive as there are over 400 brewers competing for sales: this keeps prices down, and profits are on average less than 0.5 per cent of sales.

Source: *The Economist*, 15 May 2004.

Buyers (customers)

Buyers (customers) tend to seek lower prices or higher quality at constant prices, thus forcing down prices and industry profitability. Buyer power is likely to be high when:

- the buyer purchases a large part of a supplier's output
- there are plenty of substitute products, allowing easy switching
- the product represents a major proportion of the buyer's total costs, creating the incentive to seek lower prices
- buyers can plausibly threaten to supply their needs from within their own business.

 **management in practice** **Wal-Mart's power as a buyer** www.walmart.com

Wal-Mart (which owns Asda in the UK) is the world's largest company, and is three times the size of the second largest retailer, the French company Carrefour. Its rapid growth has enabled it to become by far the largest purchaser in America, controlling a large and rapidly increasing share of the business done by almost every major US consumer-products company. It accounts for 30 per cent of hair care products sold, 26 per cent of toothpaste, 20 per cent of pet food and 20 per cent of all sales of CDs, videos and DVDs. This gives it great power over companies in these industries, since their dependency on the Wal-Mart business reduces their bargaining power.

Source: *Business Week*, 6 October 2003, pp. 48–53, and other sources.

Suppliers

Conditions that increase the bargaining power of suppliers are the opposite of those applying to buyers. Their power of suppliers relative to customers is high when:

- there are few suppliers, giving them more power over prices or terms
- their product is easy to distinguish, so that loyal customers are reluctant to switch
- the cost to the customer of switching to another supplier is high (e.g. if a company has invested heavily in one supplier's software, it is costly to switch)
- the supplier can plausibly threaten to extend their business to compete with the customer
- the customer is not important (a small or irregular purchaser).

Substitutes

In Porter's model, substitute products refer to products in other industries that can perform the same *function* as the product of the industry, for example using aluminium cans instead of plastic bottles for soft drinks. Close substitutes constrain the ability of firms in an industry to raise prices and this can undermine industry attractiveness. The threat of substitutes typically affects an industry through price competition, and is high when buyers are able and willing to change their buying habits. Technological change and the risk of obsolescence pose a further threat of substitution. Newspapers depend on recruitment advertising for much of their revenue – as companies recruit more staff through their company website, this will reduce the revenue of traditional newspapers.

 **Activity 3.1** **Critical reflection on the five forces**

Conduct a five forces analysis for an organisation with which you are familiar. Discuss with a manager of the organisation how useful he or she finds the technique. Does it capture the main competitive variables in his or her industry? Are any variables missing? You could also compare the analysis with that which you did for Nokia – what similarities and differences do you notice in the forces affecting both companies?

Nokia – the case continues www.nokia.com

In early 2004 the company announced a new internal structure. In addition to the main handsets business and the mobile infrastructure unit (which builds networks for operators such as Vodafone), it created two new divisions. One would focus on offering multimedia services and the other on enterprise solutions. Analysts saw this as an attempt to diversify into new growth areas, and to reduce dependence on handsets.

In May 2004 the company surprised the market by announcing that its share of the handset market in the first quarter of 2004 had slipped to 29 per cent, against 35 per cent the previous year. However, it also pointed out that demand was growing rapidly in China, India and Russia, and many consumers in established markets were upgrading to colour screens and camera phones. Sales of 3G infrastructure equipment were growing as operators became more confident in the success of that technology.

One explanation for the fall in market share was that the company had been slow to offer folding models, which had quickly become very popular with customers, especially in Asia. Some observers believed that the company faced deeper problems:

- It was no longer perceived to be the leader in design – competitors were producing more stylish handsets. For example, Ericsson had teamed up with Sony to created a new design team, and now had a more attractive product range.
- Its market share in Europe was falling, as it faced sharper competition at the low end of the market from Siemens, and at the high end from Samsung and a revitalised Sony-Ericsson.

- The network operators were keen to reduce their dependence on Nokia, and were turning to new, smaller vendors in Asia to supply them with handsets, often as 'own-brand' models.
- The reorganisation had distracted managers: while they created a structure to deliver new devices for games and music, they forgot that most people just wanted a phone.

The power balance in the industry seemed to be shifting from Nokia to the network operators and Asian handset makers. Nokia's management remained positive about the company's future but its outlook is more uncertain than it has been for years. It cut the prices of most of its handsets in 2004, and issued a profits warning. It was not clear whether 2004 was just a short-term upset, or a sign that Nokia's dominance of the industry was ending. Mr Alahuhta observed: 'Difficult times make companies stronger'.

Source: *Financial Times*, 16 December 2003, 23 February 2004, 8 April 2004; *The Economist*, 19 June 2004.

Case questions 3.1

Gather some information about current developments in the mobile phone industry. Also collect information on Nokia.

- What are the main factors in the competitive environment affecting the industry?
- Which of these factors may have contributed to Nokia's difficulties?

Analysing the key forces in the competitive environment enables managers to seize opportunities, counter threats and generally improve their position relative to competitors. They can consider how to alter the strength of the forces to improve their position by, for example, building barriers to entry or increasing their power over suppliers or buyers. Analysing the industry in this way enables managers to judge the likely profitability of different industries, and how they might be able to influence the forces, and hence their profitability. Chapter 8 (Strategy) examines the steps organisations can take to improve their position within the competitive environment.

Analysing the general environment – PESTEL

PESTEL analysis is a technique for identifying and listing the political, economic, social, technological, environmental and legal factors in the general environment most relevant to an organisation.

As well as the immediate environment, forces in the wider world also shape management policies. They can use a **PESTEL analysis** (short for political, economic, socio-cultural and technological, environmental and legal) to identify likely factors – which Figure 3.3 summarises.

Political factors

Political systems vary between countries and often shape what managers can and cannot do. Governments often regulate industries such as power supply, telecommunications, postal services and transport by specifying, amongst other things, who can offer services, the conditions they must meet, and what they can charge. Regulations differ between countries and are a major factor in managers' decisions.

When the UK and most European governments altered the law on financial services, non-financial companies like Virgin and Sainsbury's quickly began to offer banking services. Deregulating air transport stimulated the growth of low-cost airlines, especially in the US (e.g. Southwest Airlines), Europe (easyJet), Australia (Virgin Blue) and parts of Asia (Air Asia), though as the Ryanair case on p. 21 shows, these companies still work in

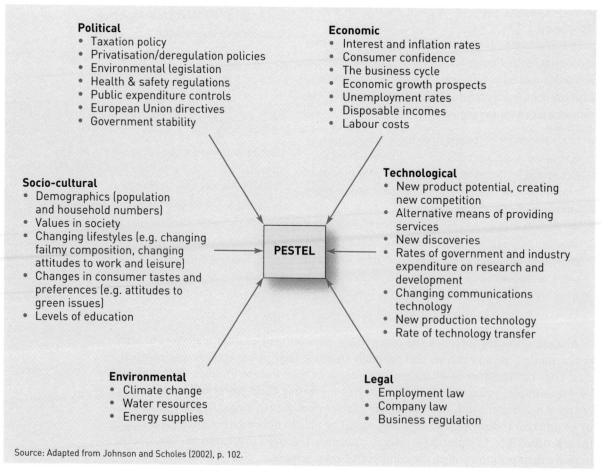

Political
- Taxation policy
- Privatisation/deregulation policies
- Environmental legislation
- Health & safety regulations
- Public expenditure controls
- European Union directives
- Government stability

Economic
- Interest and inflation rates
- Consumer confidence
- The business cycle
- Economic growth prospects
- Unemployment rates
- Disposable incomes
- Labour costs

Socio-cultural
- Demographics (population and household numbers)
- Values in society
- Changing lifestyles (e.g. changing failmy composition, changing attitudes to work and leisure)
- Changes in consumer tastes and preferences (e.g. attitudes to green issues)
- Levels of education

Technological
- New product potential, creating new competition
- Alternative means of providing services
- New discoveries
- Rates of government and industry expenditure on research and development
- Changing communications technology
- New production technology
- Rate of technology transfer

PESTEL

Environmental
- Climate change
- Water resources
- Energy supplies

Legal
- Employment law
- Company law
- Business regulation

Source: Adapted from Johnson and Scholes (2002), p. 102.

Figure 3.3 Identifying environmental influences – PESTEL analysis

The French government blocks a takeover

Novartis is the largest French pharmaceutical company. In early 2004 it received a hostile takeover bid from its smaller French rival, Sanofi. This bid was then topped by the Swiss company Aventis which offered a higher price for the company. Although the European Commission did not object to the merger the French government did, citing the need to have a domestically controlled supply of vaccines in the event of a terrorist threat. It eventually forced Novartis to merge with Sanofi.

Source: *The Economist*, 15 December 2003, and other sources.

a political environment. The European Union is developing regulations to try to manage the environmentally friendly disposal of the millions of personal computers and mobile phones that consumers scrap each year.

Legislation governing employment rights and environmental practices influences company policy. When Motorola responded to the global downturn in sales of mobile phones in 2001 it decided to close a manufacturing plant in the United Kingdom rather than in Germany as redundancy terms are less costly in the former. Intergovernmental agreements to control toxic emissions are forcing oil companies to produce cleaner fuels and car manufacturers to fit catalytic converters and improve fuel efficiency.

Economic factors

Economic factors such as wage levels, inflation and interest rates are critical in an organisation's costs. Globalisation is being driven by increasing competition and the search for cost advantages. Electronics companies such as National Semiconductor or Seagate have switched many production facilities to low-wage economies in Asia to cut costs. Similarly, Marks & Spencer chose to sever long-standing relationships with British clothing manufacturers in order to source supplies from lower-cost countries such as Turkey and India.

Build in Slovakia or Poland?

Slovakia is increasingly popular with car makers building new plants, helped by the decision of the government that was re-elected in 2002 to cut personal and corporate tax to 19 per cent. Poland, which was Slovakia's main rival for the new Kia plant (which will produce 200,000 cars a year by 2007), lost the South Korean company's investment because of poor infrastructure and the complicated and unpredictable tax system.

Source: *The Economist*, 6 March 2004.

The general state of the economy is a major influence on organisational well-being and change in one of the major economies has far-reaching effects. Rising US interest rates would affect businesses throughout the world. Growing incomes lead to increased demand for luxury goods and services, larger homes and foreign travel. It is worth noting that government policy often shapes economic factors, illustrating the interrelationships that exist between factors.

Socio-cultural factors

A key force for most organisations is demographic change, since changes in the size and age of the population affect the demand for particular products and services. An ageing population increases the demand for healthcare, pharmaceuticals and financial services. Fidelity Investments announced in 2004 that it was changing its strategy to take advantage of demographic change in the US and elsewhere. It would offer a broader range of financial advice than previously, to capitalise on the fact that by 2010, 75 per cent of the financial assets in the US would be held by people aged 55 and over. A growing proportion of single people affects the design of housing, holidays and life assurance. Demographics also shape an organisation's publicity – to ensure, for example, that advertising acknowledges the racial diversity of a community. In the late 1990s Motorola lost market share to Nokia when it failed to see that mobile phone demand was driven by fashion, not just engineering – which led to a fall in market share from about 26 per cent in 1997 to less than 15 per cent in 2003.

key ideas   The vanishing mass market

Many consumer businesses such as Coca-Cola, Procter & Gamble and Unilever have prospered by selling standard products to large numbers of consumers – the so-called mass marketing approach. They relied on TV commercials and print advertisements to reach millions of consumers who were all willing to buy the same products. They are now changing direction, and developing many smaller brands directed at small, distinctive groups of consumers. This reflects the growing diversity of the population, with many personal and individual preferences. This in turn has severe implications for media that relied on income from the advertisements that the mass marketers placed.

Source: More information in *Business Week*, 12 July 2004.

management in practice   Inadequate skills affects performance

A survey by the Learning and Skills Council published in 2004 showed that the UK's skills deficit was a drag on the economy. About 2.4m workers were 'incompetent', employers said, and more than two-fifths of employers suffering from skills shortages said they were losing business because of it. According to Iain Murray, a senior policy adviser at the Trades Union Congress:

> Around 20 per cent of the productivity gap which separates the UK from France and Germany is due to lower skills here.

FT

Source: From a report by Jonathan Guthrie, *Financial Times*, 12 February 2004.

Consumer tastes and preferences change. Commenting on a decision to increase the number of healthier products, Peter Brabeck, chief executive of Nestlé said in 2004:

> I think this shows you where the future direction of the company is. This emphasis on (healthier products) is a strategic decision, reflecting changing economic and demographic conditions.

Sales of Miller Lite surged dramatically as many consumers turned to low carbohydrate diets such as the Atkins and South Beach plans.

Technological factors

The physical infrastructure has major implications for management – such as the power and transport systems. Above all, advances in information technology have dramatically changed the business environment for many companies. This is affecting all aspects, from the way companies plan their overall strategy to the way they manage marketing, design, production and distribution. The growing use of the Internet makes it possible to use new distribution channels for many services, enabling new competitors to enter an industry (such as Virgin Financial Services and Kwik-Fit Insurance Services), often with lower costs than the established players. Technology is also changing the nature of work, for instance by enabling employees to work at remote locations. Chapters 12 and 20 have more on the influence of developments in information technology for organisations.

Advances in technology do not only affect data systems. Computers traditionally handled data, while other systems handled voice (telephones) and pictures (film and video). These three devices at the front of the information revolution – the telephone, the computer and the television – have been around for more than half a century. They are in widespread daily use throughout the developed world, and have developed independently of each other. They are familiar to us as separate devices.

Recent developments are eroding the boundaries between them. The primary development here is the new ability to process and transmit information in a common digital format. Computers have always handled information this way, while telephones and television used an analogue method. Now that all use digital methods there is a common platform between the three communication devices which greatly increases their ability to exchange information. Personal computers can download television broadcasts over the Internet, while telephones can display information held on a company database, download music or send an email or a picture. Televisions allow users to interact with retailers to order goods and pay for them over a system linked to their bank or credit card company. Cumulatively these changes revolutionise the availability of information, and have major implications for organisations.

Environmental factors

The natural environment is a further aspect of the business context. One aspect of this is the natural resources available in an economy – including minerals, agricultural land and the prevailing climate. These have fundamental impacts on the kind of businesses that managers create. Currently attention focuses on climate change, and what that means for countries and businesses within them – insurance companies, house builders and water companies are only the most visible examples of companies that are being affected by local and wider environmental changes.

Legal factors

Governments create the legal framework within which companies operate, most obviously in areas like health and safety, employment and monopolies legislation. More fundamentally, they create the legal basis for creating businesses – such as when the UK parliament passed the Joint Stock Companies Act in 1862. Previously people were discouraged from putting their money into a business as they were personally liable for the whole of a company's debts if it failed. The Act of 1862 limited their liability to the value of the shares they held in the company – they could lose their investment, but not the rest of their wealth. This stimulated company formation and other countries soon passed similar legislation, paving the way for the countless 'limited liability' companies that exist today (Micklethwait and Wooldridge, 2003).

The PESTEL analysis is just as relevant to public and voluntary sector organisations. Many public service organisations are in business to do things that the market does not, so a PESTEL analysis can identify emerging issues that need attention. A clear example is the changing age structure of the population, with growing numbers of elderly people that will impact upon community care services, the benefits system and hospitals. Public sector organisations are often unable to expand their operations where new problems or needs are identified, but the results can be used to lobby for increased funding or to better target their existing budgets.

Case questions 3.2

Use the PESTEL framework to identify the general environmental factors that:
- were important in Nokia's development in the 1990s
- are posing threats for Nokia and the mobile telecoms industry in 2005.

By providing a checklist of possible environmental influences, the PESTEL framework is a useful starting point for analysis. However, the aim is not just to produce a list of factors that might affect organisational performance. Its aim is to help managers identify those forces that seem to be the most relevant and critical to the organisation's business both now and in the future, and provide the stimulus for considering the possible effects of change in these key forces on the organisation.

Activity 3.2 Critical reflection on a PESTEL analysis

Conduct a PESTEL analysis for your organisation, or one with which you are familiar. Which of the external forces you have identified has most implications for the business? Reflect on the extent to which the organisation's policy has taken account of these forces. You could also compare this analysis with that which you did for Nokia – what similarities and differences do you notice in the forces affecting both companies?

3.4 The nature of the external environment

The five forces vary between industries and organisations and over time. Managers need both to identify the forces in their environment and to anticipate future trends. How they do this depends on the nature of their environment. The two axes in Figure 3.4 show two variables which shape how people see their environment – the degree of change and the degree of complexity.

In a relatively *stable* environment competitors offer the same products and services at much the same prices, there are rarely new entrants to the market and no technological breakthroughs by current competitors. Few forces affect business and they are predictable. Some aspects of health and education, where demand is driven largely by

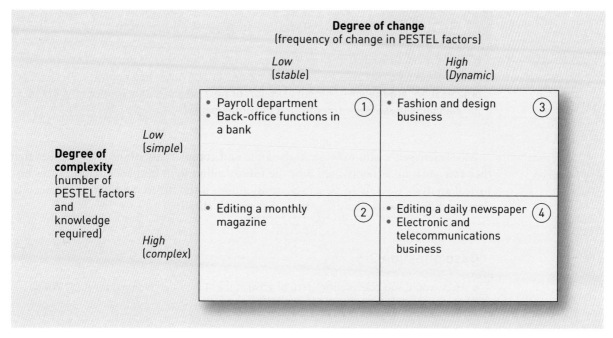

Figure 3.4 Types of environment

demographic change, may fit this pattern: the capacity needed in primary and secondary schools is easy to predict several years ahead.

In contrast, EMI, Universal and other music publishers face a highly *dynamic* environment, as new technologies for downloading music change the industry. The mobile phone industry is also highly uncertain with Nokia, Motorola, Siemens, Ericsson and several others battling to launch new products which appeal to a fashion-conscious market.

Simple environments are relatively straightforward in terms of their business processes and technology. Examples include some routine types of legal work such as house sales and wills, and traditional trades such as joinery. People can use past trends to predict the future with a reasonable degree of confidence. But there are very few static environments nowadays, and changing technology in particular is affecting previously stable businesses.

Complex environments are those in which many factors influence an organisation, and especially where there are connections between them. This makes it hard to isolate cause and effect and to predict future events. Multinationals like Shell and BP experience great complexity, operating across diverse political, legal and cultural systems. Local government, as a multifunctional service provider, also faces complexity, although some services operate in less dynamic environments than others.

Each cell in Figure 3.4 represents a different combination of complexity and change. Managers running a business (or a unit) whose environment corresponds to Cell 1 (stable and simple) face much less environmental uncertainty than those whose unit is in Cell 4 (dynamic and complex). Those in Cell 1 have greater control over events than those in Cell 4, where environmental forces are much more difficult to deal with. In current business conditions, more managers feel that they are operating in the unstable, complex conditions of Cell 4. Eric Schmidt (Chief Executive of Google) has said that in many high tech and other industries today:

> the environment is changing so fast that it requires improvisation in terms of strategy, products and even day-to-day operations. Just when you think you understand the technology landscape, you see a major disruption.

Activity 3.3   Critical reflection on type of environment

Use Figure 3.4 to analyse the environment in which your unit of the organisation works. Then try to do the same analysis for one or two other units of the organisation. Are the environments similar, or not? What are the implications of that for managing these departments, and the organisation?

Most managers claim to work in dynamic and complex situations. This implies that they face great uncertainty over how the future will unfold. In these circumstances historical analysis is likely to be a less useful guide to the future and managers need to develop different ways of anticipating what may lie ahead.

Case question 3.3

● How would you classify the form of environment in which Nokia operates? Which factors contributed to your answer?

3.5 Stakeholder analysis

All organisations have a wide range of internal and external stakeholders. Often their interests will conflict because, as groups or as individuals, stakeholders are themselves subject to a wide range of influences that condition or shape their views and what they expect of organisations. External stakeholders include suppliers, financiers, central and local government, shareholders and customers. They have expectations of organisations and will seek to influence them in various ways. They may be able to influence staff or board members directly through personal contact, or they may seek to exert influence indirectly, for instance by the use of the press and other media to raise issues of concern.

Influential shareholders have long been critical of companies for paying senior (and often failed) managers excessive sums, but are now turning their attention to corporate

The interests of managers and shareholders

While senior managers often claim to be trying to align their interests with those of shareholders, the two often conflict. Mergers often appear to benefit senior managers and their professional advisers rather than shareholders. Acquiring companies often pay too much for the target, but executives inside the enlarged company receive higher pay. Professional advisers (investment bankers) make money on both the merger and the break-up.

Using company money to buy the company's shares in the market uses money that can't be spent on dividends. From the vantage point of many CEOs, paying dividends is about the last thing they would want to do with corporate earnings. In theory, a CEO is carrying out shareholder wishes. In practice, as the spate of recent scandals has shown, the interests of chief executives and their shareholders can widely diverge.

Source: Based on extracts from an article by Robert Kuttner, *Business Week*, 9 September 2002.

Shareholders
- Growth in dividend payments
- Growth in share price
- Consistent dividend payments
- Growth in net asset value

Customers
- Competitive price
- Emphasis on product/service quality
- Return and replacement policies
- Warranty/guarantee provisions
- Product reliability

Suppliers
- Timely payment of debt by company
- Adequate liquidity
- Integrity and public standing of directors
- Negotiating ability of the purchasing manager

Employees
- Good compensation and benefits
- Job security
- Sense of meaning or purpose in the job
- Opportunities for personal development
- Amount of interesting work

Government
- Efficient user of energy and natural resources
- Adhering to the country's laws
- Paying taxes
- Providing employment
- Value for money in the use of public funds

Lenders
- Financial strength of the company
- Quality of company management
- Quality of assets available for security
- Ability to repay interest and capital on due date

Figure 3.5

Examples of possible stakeholder expectations

responsibility. Controversies over climate change, obesity, and the child labour employed by some overseas suppliers are causing investors to fear that negative publicity or litigation could damage the value of their shares.

Figure 3.5 indicates the different expectations that stakeholders may have.

Much of the literature on this subject conveys the impression that organisations should aim to *balance* the interests of stakeholders, but there are different opinions on what this means. Campbell (1997) argues that survival ultimately depends on companies' ability to win 'the loyalty of all the "active" stakeholders – shareholders, customers, employees and suppliers' because companies compete in each of the relevant markets for capital, labour and customers.

Argenti (1997), on the other hand, assumes 'balance' to mean 'equality' and argues that 'some stakeholders are vastly more equal than others'. He considers, for example, that a retailer contemplating longer opening hours will '*not* attempt to balance the convenience of employees with that of customers', but will instead 'ask what effect each decision might have on profits. That is how all legitimate decisions are made in companies – they are, by definition, profit-making organisations.' Since profit is the objective criterion by which the capitalist company will act, shareholders are, in Argenti's view, the stakeholders whose interests should come first. While he recognises that performance would suffer if companies fail to engage everyone affected by their operations, he maintains that 'an organisation designed to serve more than one set of people will fail to satisfy any'.

Both Campbell and Argenti make valid points. The overall message is that it is important to the long-run success of organisations to embrace stakeholder expectations, but that the degree of priority they give to each is unequal and changing.

Stakeholder power

The inequality to which Argenti refers is a reflection of the extent to which different stakeholder groups exert power over organisations. Chapter 14 outlines a model of the sources of power, which external stakeholders can use:

- **Formal power** This may be exercised by stakeholders who are members of influential outside bodies or committees such as those concerned with legislative or regulatory matters.
- **Resource power** Many small companies depend on large customers, such as those in the car and electronics industries. These large buyers often dictate product quality and prices. Some suppliers may exercise control over strategic assets: an example is the collective power of oil-producing countries to control world oil prices. Resource dependence is also a key feature of public services: those that control access to resources (usually government or its agents) are in a strong position to shape the objectives and strategies of organisations that depend on them for funding.
- **Expert power** Superior knowledge of customers held, for example, by retailers may enable them to dictate terms (say on design, quality or price) to manufacturers.

Stakeholder mapping is a means of identifying the expectations and power of different stakeholders.

An analysis of stakeholders must therefore assess how much their expectations matter to the business. A structured approach to this task is **stakeholder mapping**. According to Johnson and Scholes (2002), this aims to assess:

- how interested each stakeholder group is in influencing the organisation, and therefore how likely it is that it will seek to do so
- whether each group has the means, or the power, to do so, as this will determine its ability to influence the organisation.

Stakeholders can be categorised in a power–interest matrix, according to the degree of interest and power they are perceived to hold, as shown in Figure 3.6. Those who have both a high interest and high power may be regarded as the 'key players' and those whom the organisation must seek, in particular, to satisfy. Conversely those groups with low levels of both interest and power may require only minimal attention from the organisation. As a tool, stakeholder mapping helps to determine which stakeholders are the most important to keep on board when major decisions are being taken. It also suggests that communication strategies, ranging from simple provision of information to direct involvement, are likely to differ for each group.

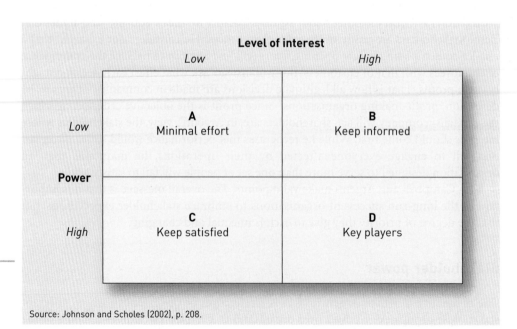

Figure 3.6

Stakeholder mapping – the power–interest matrix

Source: Johnson and Scholes (2002), p. 208.

Case questions 3.4

● Who are the main stakeholders in Nokia?

● What are their interests in the success of the company?

● How could management ensure it maintained the support of the most important stakeholders?

A final point is that the exercise of power works in both directions. Just as external stakeholders seek to influence the people inside the organisation, managers influence the perceptions and expectations of its external stakeholders – through professional lobbying, public relations campaigns and direct personal links to senior politicians.

Siemens and the German Government www.siemens.com

Siemens is the world's sixth biggest manufacturer, with interests in automation, medical equipment, power generation, transportation and many other information technology applications. The head of the group, Heinrich von Pierer, was appointed in 1992, and has transformed the company into a profitable, international business. Forty per cent of its staff still work in Germany, whose government introduced policies on taxation and pensions that were unfavourable to business. Some German business leaders issued strongly worded criticism of Gerhard Schroder, the Chancellor, but Mr Pierer regards such confrontation as counter-productive. He has made a point of keeping open close lines of communication with the Chancellor, with whom he sometimes shares a game of tennis.

Source: Based on an article in *Financial Times*, 4 December 2002.

In some organisations this extends to the active involvement of major external players. In the competitive environment companies can seek to gain advantage over competitors by building relationships with suppliers or customers or by making it harder for other firms to enter their territory. The growth in alliances and partnerships (see Chapter 12) demonstrates this type of collaboration between stakeholders.

Summary

1 **Identify the main sets of forces exerting influence on organisations:**
   ● They include the immediate competitive environment, the wider general (or macro) environment and the organisation's stakeholders.

2 **Use Porter's five forces model to analyse competitive environments:**
   ● This identifies the degree of competitive rivalry, customers, competitors, suppliers and potential substitute goods and services.

3 **Conduct a PESTEL analysis for an organisation with which you are familiar:**
   ● The PESTEL model of the wider external environment identifies political, economic, social, technological, environmental and legal forces.

4 **Compare environments in terms of the complexity and rate of change:**
   ● Environments can be evaluated in terms of their rate of change (stable/dynamic) and complexity (low/high).

5 Give examples of stakeholders seeking to influence organisations and explain a model for assessing stakeholder power:

● Managers can assess the relative power of stakeholders in terms of their interest in and power to affect an issue.

Review questions

1 Identify the relative influence of Porter's five forces on an organisation of your choice and compare your results with a colleague's. What can you learn from that comparison?

2 How should managers decide which of the many factors easily identified in a PESTEL analysis they should attend to? If they have to be selective, what is the value of the PESTEL method?

3 Since people interpret the nature of environmental forces from unique perspectives, what meaning can people attach to statements about external pressures?

4 Illustrate the stakeholder idea with an example of your own, focusing on what affects the relative power of the stakeholders to influence an organisation's policy.

5 Evaluate Argenti's comment on stakeholder power in view of your answer to question 2.

Concluding critical reflection

Think about the way managers in your company, or one with which you are familiar, go about monitoring and assessing the external environment. Review the material in the chapter, and make notes on these questions:

● Which of the issues discussed in this chapter are most relevant to the way you and your colleagues manage? What are the main factors in the external environment affecting your business? Do you all attach the same significance to them, or do views vary? Why is that?

● What assumptions do people make in your business about the environment in which you work? How do they see that affecting the nature of your tasks as managers, and indeed the nature of your organisation?

● What is the dominant view about which changes in the environment will most affect the business? Why do they think that? Do people have different interpretations?

● Can you compare your business environment with that of colleagues on your course, especially those in similar industries? Do you have similar or different views of the future?

Further reading

Johnson, G. and **Scholes, K.** (2002), *Exploring Corporate Strategy* (6th edn), Financial Times/Prentice Hall, Harlow.

Dobson, P., **Starkey, K.** and **Richards, J.** (2004), *Strategic Management: Issues and cases*, Blackwell, Oxford.

Both texts cover Porter's five forces, PESTEL analysis and stakeholder analysis at greater length.

Smith, R.J. (1994), *Strategic Management and Planning in the Public Sector*, Longman/Civil Service College, Harlow.

> Approaches the topics from a public sector perspective and includes a summary of forecasting and market research techniques.

Steinbock, D. (2001), *The Nokia Revolution*, American Management Association, New York.

> This is an authoritative account of the development of the company, and its interaction with the external environment.

The weekly publication *The Economist* often contains useful articles in its leader pages or business section that highlight the impact of environmental factors on particular industries or companies.

Weblinks

These websites have appeared in the chapter:

www.nokia.com
www.walmart.com

Visit both of the business sites in the list, or any other companies which interest you, and navigate to the pages dealing with recent news, press or investor relations.

- What are the main forces in the external environment which the organisation appears to be facing?
- What assessment would you make of the nature of that environment?
- Compare and contrast the issues you identify on the two sites.
- What challenges may they imply for those working in, and managing, these organisations?

Annotated weblinks, multiple choice questions and other useful resources can be found on
www.pearsoned.co.uk/boddy

Chapter 4

The international context of management

Starbucks sells coffee, pastries, confectionery and coffee-related accessories through over 6000 retail stores. Three entrepreneurs created the company in 1971 to sell coffee in Seattle, and by 1981 they had five stores. The owners decided to sell the business in 1987 and Howard Schultz (a former employee) bought the company which he then expanded rapidly, so that by 1991 there were 114 Starbucks stores. The company was also innovative with new products to attract customers – such as introducing low-fat iced coffee for the diet conscious. It grew by about 20 per cent a year during the 1990s, but by the end of the decade the market in the US was becoming saturated.

To maintain this rate of growth, the company began to expand overseas, through Starbucks Coffee International, a wholly owned subsidiary. In 1996 Starbucks entered Japan through a joint venture with Sazaby's Inc. (a leading Japanese teashop company) and it then expanded into South-east Asia, Europe and the Middle East. By March 2003 it had 1500 stores (23 per cent of the total) outside the US.

It entered the Asia Pacific rim first, as the growing eagerness of young people in those countries to imitate western lifestyles made them attractive markets for Starbucks. The company used joint ventures, licensing or wholly owned subsidiaries to enter new markets. Initially it opened a few stores in trendy parts of the country, with the company's managers from Seattle handling the operation. Local *baristas* (brew masters) were trained in Seattle for 13 weeks, to ensure consistent standards across the world. Similar products were stocked, and all stores were 'No Smoking'.

However, the company's managers also took the advice of their local partners and adapted the business to local tastes – such as offering curry puffs and meat buns in Asian markets, as Asians generally prefer to eat something while having coffee. In the Middle East the coffee shops had segregated sections for ladies. In 1998 the company opened in Europe, with stores in the UK, Switzerland, Germany and Greece. The company believed that it was successful not because it was selling coffee, but because it was selling an experience. In many markets it faces local competition and is subject to the same economic conditions as other businesses of its type.

Alamy

It has attracted criticism in some overseas markets – in common with many United States businesses. In Starbucks' case this has also focused on the sources of its coffee. Growers in poor countries complain that they receive very low prices for their crops, and that many workers in the coffee plantations are exploited. Advocates of fair trade argue that big coffee buyers like Starbucks should do more to ensure that they buy coffee at fair prices from growers who do not exploit workers.

Source: Based on published sources.

Case questions

- What encouraged managers at Starbucks to expand overseas, and what influenced their choice of countries in which to operate?
- What are the main risks that Starbucks faces in expanding rapidly in overseas markets?
- What does the story so far suggest about the management issues it will face in operating internationally?

<table>
<tr><td>4.1</td><td>## Introduction</td></tr>
</table>

Managers at Starbucks, like those in many other companies, have decided to expand their business overseas, and in doing so are likely to face common problems in moving to a global operation. The company will face new management questions about staffing, management development, product quality and the balance between maintaining a global brand and adapting it to local tastes.

Most managers sense that they work in an international rather than a national or local setting. New communication technologies are reducing the cost of transmitting information and physical products, while at the same time political changes (such as the enlargement of the European Union) further encourage trade across national boundaries. Rapid economic development in China and other Asian countries is transforming them into major players in world trade, competing strongly with Western manufacturers. For some products (especially those that are high in value and low in weight) the whole world is a potential market – increasing the possibility of both growth and competition. Even managers in a company which does not trade overseas add an international dimension to their work if they acquire an overseas business, or are themselves acquired.

Major retailers like Tesco and Carrefour are extending their international operations, despite the problems of understanding different customer tastes and shopping habits. Managers in companies like McDonald's and The Body Shop with large overseas sales balance the consistency of the brand with growing expectations of local customisation. Software companies have to decide how far to 'localise' software: this provided a business opportunity for companies in Ireland, which offers leading software companies (including Microsoft) facilities to adapt products to suit different markets. Manufacturers like Ford and service providers like Lloyds TSB Bank have transferred many types of work to people in low-wage countries such as China and India. Doing so, of course, then raises new management problems – such as, for Ford, how best to manage a joint venture with the Chong Qing Group in China to manufacture a compact family car. Managers investing overseas consider not only the economic or market aspects, but also, for example, whether the legal system will protect their investments and whether the country is politically stable.

The value-adding processes of design, manufacture and distribution remain much the same across the world. So also are the management tasks of planning, organising, leading and controlling. Yet performing these on an international or global scale brings additional complexities: the environment of management outlined in Chapter 3 now includes some international dimensions.

International management is the practice of managing business operations in more than one country.

From a career point of view, **international management** (managing business operations in more than one country) can mean:

- working as an *expatriate manager* in another country
- joining or managing an *international team* with members from several countries
- managing in a *global organisation* whose employees, systems and structures are truly international in that they no longer reflect its original, national base.

ABB is an example. Formed by the merger of a Swiss and a Swedish business, it retains only a small head office in Zürich, and the board deliberately contains people of different nationalities.

This chapter introduces some models and perspectives that help understand the issues people face in managing internationally. It begins by outlining the driving forces behind the growth of international business, and the different ways in which companies take part in it. Later sections outline the major contextual influences on international business – the political, economic, socio-cultural, technical, environmental and legal dimensions. It then introduces the idea of national (or regional) management systems, and compares those of the United States, Europe and Asia. It outlines the arguments surrounding globalisation, and considers the winners and losers from that process. It concludes by relating the themes presented to the generic functions of management, and the potential implications for the roles of managers. Figure 4.1 indicates the main issues that managers operating on a global scale look for as they work across national boundaries.

4.2 The growth of international business

Driving forces

There has been international trade since the earliest times. The founding of the East India Company in London in 1599, to develop trade with the spice islands in South-east Asia (in close and violent competition with the Dutch East India Company, founded in 1602), signified the practice being put on a more formal basis. By the nineteenth century many great trading businesses were operating across the world. What is new today is the much greater proportion of production that crosses national boundaries. Much of this trade is organised by businesses operating not on a national but on a regional or global scale.

In some areas of business global operations are inevitable. Logistics companies such as Federal Express and Maas operate services on a global scale and develop practices and structures accordingly. Oil companies such as BP and Esso and mining companies such

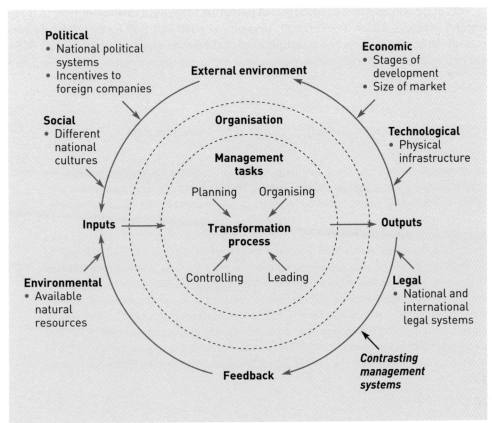

Figure 4.1

Themes in managing in an international context

as Lonrho necessarily secure resources in some parts of the world and sell them in others. A newer development is the way many financial businesses such as ABN AMRO (a Dutch bank), telecommunications businesses such as Nortel and BT, and retailers such as Tesco and Carrefour have ambitions to operate on a global scale.

Two forces have an especially strong influence on this growth – capital and information technology (IT). The availability of capital makes it possible for companies to finance direct investment in a foreign country – as when Ford decided to build an engine plant in Spain. Instead of investing capital in a US plant and exporting the product, Ford invested in Spain and made vehicles there. Capital is mobile and most countries compete for investment. This is most visible in the publicity surrounding attempts to attract major manufacturing investments to less prosperous regions, whether of Europe, Asia or South America. Investment in services – financial, legal, design and other forms of intellectual capital – also increases world trade. One estimate is that one-third of all trade takes place within transnational companies, quite apart from external sales of foreign subsidiaries.

Developments in IT also stimulate trade, both as a product and as a way of supporting dispersed production systems. Electronic products are assembled from many small components. These have a high value-to-weight ratio, so they are cheap to transport long distances. Much of the growth in international trade is due to the emergence of countries in Asia as suppliers of electronic components. These flow in vast numbers every day to US, European and Japanese assembly plants.

Information technology also helps to manage the efficient flow of data on which international operations depend. The complex supply and manufacturing networks depend on computer systems to track and monitor the flow of orders, components and payments. Without information systems of the kind now common, world trade could not have grown to the present scale.

Within those broad trends, managers in particular firms have various motives to try to expand overseas, which Tayeb (2000) presents as push and pull factors. Push factors include saturation and excessive competition in the home market. Starbucks and IKEA are examples of companies whose managers want to continue to grow the business, but

IBM becomes more globally integrated www.ibm.com

IBM has long been a major, and at one time a dominant, player in the world electronics industry. Yet until quite recently the separate business units and manufacturing operations operated with a high degree of independence from each other. Each manufacturing unit made their supply arrangements independently.

In 1996 management centralised the function into 17 Global Commodity Councils. Each manages the supply of a group of parts (such as drives or monitors) for the whole company. Global Commodity Managers handle strategic relations with suppliers, regularly agreeing prices and forecast volumes for the following quarter, based on the requirements of all the company's divisions. The suppliers, most of whom are themselves global players, then deliver as required to any of the company's manufacturing facilities around the world. Each facility has some staff who are part of the Global Procurement Organisation, helping to manage the strategic aspects of the supply chain. Each site also has buyers who work within the manufacturing function to deal with the day-to-day execution of requirements to meet current needs from the overall schedule agreed between the Global team and a particular supplier.

Source: Information provided by the company.

can do so only by expanding outside of their traditional markets. Pull factors include lower wages and less rigorous environmental regulations (major factors attracting Western companies to move production to China or Eastern Europe). Other firms find they can gain competitive advantage by extending their brand on to a global scale. The larger consulting companies, for example, have found that they are better able to meet the needs of global clients by themselves organising as global businesses.

4.3   Ways of conducting business internationally

Managers who decide to extend the international operations of their company have several ways of doing so, each with advantages and disadvantages.

Exporting and importing

The longest established way of dealing with overseas customers and suppliers is by transporting physical products (raw materials or finished goods) or delivering services (a retail shop, consultancy or legal advice) across national boundaries. If the final distribution of exports is arranged through an agent in the receiving country, then the implications for those in the exporting company are quite limited, apart from those directly involved in managing the transactions.

Licensing

Here a business grants the right to a firm in another country to produce and sell its products or services for a specified period of time. The licensing firm receives a royalty payment for each unit that is sold, while the licensee takes the risks of investing in the manufacturing and distribution arrangements. An example is the deal which Imperial Tobacco signed in 2003 with a Chinese group to produce and distribute Imperial brands in the world's largest cigarette market. For the licensing firm, the risks of this method are low and so, usually, are the profits. Franchising is a similar arrangement, commonly used by firms in the service industry that wish to expand their brand rapidly beyond their country of origin.

Joint ventures and strategic alliances

These enable firms in two or more countries to share the risks and resources required for international business. Most joint ventures involve a foreign firm and one in the host country which has access to distribution arrangements and knows the local customs, politics and ways of working. They usually involve both firms investing in the venture to develop or sell a new product or process. Starbucks typically uses joint ventures in overseas markets: in Germany this is with KarstadtQuelle, a department store group. The hazards of this approach lie in cultural differences between the partners, or in misunderstandings about what each expects.

Wholly owned subsidiary

Managers who want to retain close control over a company's international activities are likely to create a subsidiary in another country. This is a costly method, but if the venture works all profits stay within the company. It retains control over its expertise, technology

A Chinese company aims to become a global player www.tcl.com

TCL Corporation is one of the top producers of electronics products in China, and having become one of the most prominent brands in China, the company's entrepreneurial management wants to make the company a global player. In November 2003 they formed a joint venture with French electronics maker Thomson to create the world's largest producer of televisions. For TCL Thomson's brand names – which include RCA and Thomson – were the keys to the deal. Through its sales operations in Europe and the US, Thomson sold 7.4 million TVs in 2002 – TCL wants to use that network to extend its own reach.

Source: Based on 'Bursting out of China', *Business Week*, 17 November 2003.

and marketing, and can secure local knowledge by employing local staff to run the subsidiary. The company may establish the subsidiary as a new entity, or, if time is scarce, it may acquire an existing company. This will be costly, and still brings the problem of managing across different cultures.

Managers will often use each of the above forms at the same time to take account of, say, trade regulations or the availability of suitable partners in particular countries. They also develop different forms of organisation through which to conduct their international business, for which convenient labels are multinational, transnational and global.

Multinational companies are based in one country, but have significant production and marketing operations in many others.

Transnational companies operate in many countries and delegate many decisions to local managers.

Global companies work in many countries, securing resources and finding markets in whichever country is most suitable.

Multinational companies are from one country, but have significant production and marketing operations in many other countries – with these perhaps accounting for more than a third of total sales. Despite their wide geographical spread, major decisions affecting the business are made in the home country.

Transnational companies also operate in many countries, but differ in that they decentralise many decisions to local managers. They develop the business using their local knowledge, developing market and product strategies they consider best suited to the area, while still projecting the consistent company image. Coca-Cola has distribution arrangements with many local companies that promote and distribute the product.

Global companies work in a wide range of countries, securing resources and finding markets in whichever countries are most suitable – ownership, control and top managers are likely to be spread among many countries and nationalities. Most aspects of the production or service process are performed, and integrated, across many global locations. Trend Micro, an anti-virus software company, has organised in a way that allows its staff to respond rapidly to new viruses that appear anywhere and spread very quickly. Trend's

Intel ww.intel.com

More than a third of the employees of Intel (the US-based silicon chip maker) now work offshore, and the company does most of its core product development work in Taiwan. Says Craig Barrett, the Chief Executive:

> Essentially all PC and handheld design work is done in Taipei: so I put my engineers where the action is. We are going to go after the best international resources wherever they are. There are great engineers in China and they also happen to cost less than in the US. China happens to be our fastest growing marketplace and having your presence there is important.

FT

Source: *Financial Times*, 22 September 2003.

financial headquarters is in Tokyo; product development is in Taiwan (many staff with PhD's); and sales is in California – inside the huge US market. Nestlé is another example since, although its headquarters are in Switzerland, 98 per cent of sales and 96 per cent of employees are not. Such global businesses are often organised on product lines, with those in charge of each line being free to resource their operations from whichever country is most profitable. Many possess economic resources greater than some of the countries in which they operate, and typify the (controversial) globalisation of business to which we return in Section 4.12.

An Indian supplier to Wal-Mart www.walmart.com

Deep in the Punjab heartland, in the town of Barnala, Rajinder Gupta is a star supplier to the world's biggest company – Wal-Mart. Gupta's Abhishek Industries exports Rs 200 crore (2 billion) worth of towels annually and he's twice been judged the Wal-Mart International Supplier of the year. Now he's expanding his product range to rugs and bed-sheets and says:

We've grown with Wal-Mart since we first began supplying to them five years ago. Now we've created a dedicated capacity for them, with systems geared to their needs.

From tanneries in Kanpur and rug weavers in Mumbai to shirt manufacturers in Tirupur, Wal-Mart has zeroed in on 142 low-cost quality manufacturing units across India, which will supply to its stores in the US and twelve other countries ... It recently set up Wal-Mart Global Procurement Company in Bangalore where a staff of 54 are working towards further expanding business with India. A company official said:

Indian suppliers are capable, qualified and quality-focused and we intend to grow India as a source of supply, especially in categories like textiles, shoes, jewellery and gift items.

Source: Based on 'Wal-Mart Effect', *Times of India Corporate Dossier*, 28 May 2004.

Activity 4.1 Choosing between approaches

Consider the different ways of expanding a business internationally. For each of the methods outlined above note the advantages and disadvantages, and find one new example to illustrate each method.

Case question 4.1

Consider how Starbucks conducts its business. Is it closest to a multinational, transnational or global firm?

Whichever of these methods companies use, the cumulative result has been a steady growth in the volume of business transactions across national borders relative to those within them. National boundaries become less significant barriers to the movement of goods and services – most clearly seen in the growing trade in electronically transmitted information products. These trends imply an equally steady growth in the proportion of

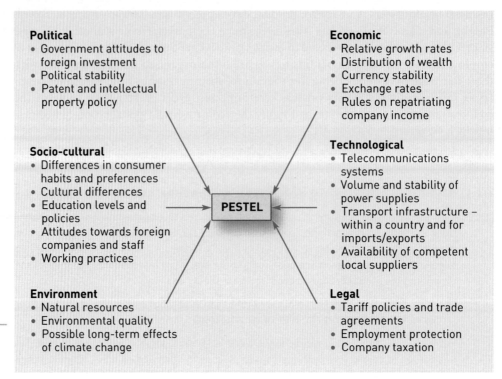

Political
- Government attitudes to foreign investment
- Political stability
- Patent and intellectual property policy

Economic
- Relative growth rates
- Distribution of wealth
- Currency stability
- Exchange rates
- Rules on repatriating company income

Socio-cultural
- Differences in consumer habits and preferences
- Cultural differences
- Education levels and policies
- Attitudes towards foreign companies and staff
- Working practices

Technological
- Telecommunications systems
- Volume and stability of power supplies
- Transport infrastructure – within a country and for imports/exports
- Availability of competent local suppliers

Environment
- Natural resources
- Environmental quality
- Possible long-term effects of climate change

Legal
- Tariff policies and trade agreements
- Employment protection
- Company taxation

Figure 4.2

An international view of a PESTEL analysis

people who work with colleagues from countries, organisations, institutions and cultures widely different from their own. To handle this well means more than learning foreign languages, though that clearly helps. It means being aware of the main international aspects of the general business environment outlined in Chapter 3: the PESTEL framework takes on an international flavour. Figure 4.2 summarises these.

4.4 Political context

Whitley (1996) shows how differences in national institutional features lead to different forms of organisation. These include things such as the extent of state involvement in business, and the features of the financial systems that shape a country's practices for overseeing the management of enterprises. In some countries such as Japan, Germany and France firms are typically part of a network of mutual relations with banks, state agencies, suppliers and unions. In others these links are much weaker or do not exist at all, so that organisations work in relative isolation. Management is then able to act much more autonomously.

At one extreme are the Japanese networks of interdependent relations. Here the tradition is of mutual ownership between different but friendly business units. Companies have close financial and obligational links with companies in other sectors. The Ministry of Industry actively supports and guides the strategic direction of major areas of business. The firms create a network of mutually dependent organisations with interlocking obligations. They decide strategy by negotiation with stakeholders, which are mainly other companies and financial institutions.

In contrast, firms in the United Kingdom and the United States work in a more isolated way. They receive less direct support from banks, which have traditionally avoided long-term investments. Their boards rarely contain representatives of companies with common interests.

key ideas

Whitley's elements of national institutional features

Cultural conventions
- Strength of institutions governing trust relations and collective loyalties

State structure and policies
- Extent to which state dominates economic system
- Level of risk sharing with private economic actors
- State support for cooperation between firms
- Formal regulation of entry to and exit from markets

Financial system
- Credit-based financial system

Labour system
- Significance of labour in strategic decision making
- Centralisation of bargaining
- Collaboration in training

Source: Whitley (1996), p. 51.

The level of dependence affects companies' attitudes towards growth and profitability. Whitley suggests that a high level of dependence on the state encourages growth but discourages concern over profit, and he cites France as an example of this. In Japan firms seek market share and growth within their sector, but not beyond it. The network of relations between Japanese firms and their customers and suppliers restricts unrelated diversification, but there is a strong collective interest in expansion. In contrast the more isolated UK and US firms, where owners operate as portfolio holders, find growth goals limited by the need to meet profit targets and expectations of the capital market. Dividends and share price are more significant measures of corporate performance than growth. Family-owned businesses may also grow slowly if the family is reluctant to share control and prefer to increase family wealth rather than the size of the firm.

Ownership and control have traditionally been closely connected in Continental Europe. For example, in France at the end of the 1980s 44 per cent of top industrial and commercial organisations were under family control and 13 per cent were state owned (Mayer and Whittington, 1996). In Germany and France the banks are much more closely involved in providing long-term finance for business through extended credit-based systems, and they are represented on company boards of directors.

Doing business internationally inevitably involves unfamiliar political and legal risks. Foreign companies are often seen as intruders in a country, threatening the political or economic sovereignty of the host nation. Political activists sometimes attack or damage the property of foreign companies. Unstable governments increase the risk that the terms on which a company is permitted to enter a country may be revoked if there is a change in power.

The Italian private/public model

Managerial capitalism is taking root in Italy – but the country's tradition of public companies controlled by powerful founding families is not yet ready to bow out.

It is almost impossible to exaggerate the importance of family business for the Italian economy. It is probably even more difficult to overstate the role played by the late Gianni Agnelli, the patriarch of the century-old Fiat car empire, as the father figure of postwar Italian family capitalism.

His death in January, and the deepening crisis at Fiat, have inevitably raised questions not only on the future of the country's largest industrial group but on the broader consequences for a corporate model ... widely known as the 'Italian private/public company' – a group of large, publicly quoted companies managed and controlled by founding families.

Italian corporate dynasties have traditionally controlled their industrial and financial groups via a complex structure involving a cascade of holding companies, often quoted, with minimum capital outlay. They further strengthened their hold on their groups through friendly shareholder syndicates and cross-shareholdings based on the principle of 'don't hurt me and I won't hurt you.' ....

But for all the problems at Fiat and other large family companies, the 'private/public company' model is still alive and kicking, although perhaps its public component is getting bigger. But the tenacity of the family business culture in Italy is such that even Silvio Berlusconi, the prime minister, has failed to resolve a conflict of interest between his extensive business empire ... and his political office. **FT**

Source: Extracts from an article by Paul Betts, *Financial Times*, 24 March 2003.

4.5 Economic context

The economic context of a country includes such factors as its state of economic development, the quality of its communications and other infrastructure, and its systems of markets. It also includes aspects of the current economic situation such as inflation, exchange rates and levels of debt.

Stage of economic development

The wide difference between countries in their stage of economic development is a major factor in international management. The measure usually used is income per head of population – a measure of a country's total production, adjusted for size of population. Lower-income countries are concentrated in the southern hemisphere, and include many in Asia, Africa and South America. The richer, developed countries tend to be in the northern hemisphere, which is where most international business firms are located.

Companies from the wealthier countries are attracted to those in less developed areas by their large potential markets. Consumer products companies (especially those in the tobacco business such as British American Tobacco or Phillip Morris) are reaching the limits of their markets in the developed countries. They are attracted by countries in the developing world, whose high birth rates mean a growing number of young and adult consumers. Companies with strong brand names are attracted to the more prosperous of these countries, such as China, Malaysia and South Africa, by the prospect of large and growing markets. Others see them as sources of cheap labour from which to obtain supplies of products and components.

Starbucks – the case continues www.starbucks.com **CASE STUDY**

By late 2002 reports were appearing that Starbucks' Japanese venture was in trouble, and the company announced that it was expecting to trade at a loss in 2003. The company chairman, Howard Schultz, blamed the poor state of the Japanese economy, but others wondered if consumers were already tiring of the brand. Several rival companies had also entered the Japanese market – which was still the company's largest overseas business, and where it had planned to have 1000 shops by 2007.

While coffee drinking is an ingrained part of US culture, in Japan the company is fighting centuries of green-tea sipping. It has tried to overcome the sales problem by broadening the menu by adding local food items – but these did not catch on. It was trying to cut costs by importing more of its supplies from low-cost firms in South-east Asia, rather than importing them from the US. It also decided to slow the rate of expan-

sion, opening only 80 stores in 2003 against 115 the previous year. It would also close some that were making heavy losses.

It was experiencing similar problems in other countries – where rivals often charge less for similar products. Some also queried the method it used for its overseas expansion, mainly joint ventures. While the company gets a revenue from sales and profits, and also gets a licence income from the sale of its coffee, it is harder to control costs in a joint venture. Moreover, the costs for premises and labour are higher overseas than in the US. Others questioned the rate of expansion – 'By opening more stores, name recognition will increase but scarcity value, which is crucial in maintaining brand image, will decline'.

Source: Based on 'Losing the taste for latte already?', *Business Week*, 9 June 2003; and other sources.

Markets

Managers contemplating international expansion are likely to focus on countries and regions where the market for their service appears to be strong. Thus a Hong Kong Disneyland opening in 2005–06 reflects the company's belief that Asia is a market with high growth potential in the media and entertainment areas. The Chinese government has a 57 per cent stake in the project, which Disney hopes will help it win favourable terms for other business ventures in China – such as TV, motion pictures, advertising and consumer products (from an article by Tim Burt, *Financial Times*, 30 October 2003).

Egg (the UK Internet bank) discovered the risks of entering an unfamiliar market when it opened an operation in France. The bank had hoped to replicate its UK success when it bought a French online business in 2002. However, as one banking analyst observed:

> the market is not yet ready to embrace the concept of a pure online bank. There is a clear attachment to the branch network in France, which is not such a factor in the UK, and means people are not ready to commit their entire banking relationship to a company without a network of branches they can go and visit.

Its credit cards were not a success either, as that market is not as fully developed in France as in the UK, and French consumers are more likely to use store cards (from an article by Martin Arnold and Jane Croft, *Financial Times*, 25 April 2003, p. 23). Egg withdrew from the French market in 2004.

4.6 Technological context

Infrastructure includes all of the physical facilities that support economic activities – ports, airports, surface transport and, increasingly, telecommunications facilities. Companies operating abroad, especially in less developed countries, are closely interested in the quality of this aspect of a country as it has a huge effect on the cost and convenience of conducting business in the area. Security of staff in politically troubled countries is a growing problem.

The hazards of interviewing

Market research is not normally classed a dangerous profession, unless you count occasional abuse from people unwilling to take part in a street survey. But in the world's trouble spots, researchers have to take extraordinary measures to protect field workers and ensure they interview a representative sample of the population.

In Argentina, where the long economic crisis has led to a rise in crime, police or fire officers sometimes accompany field workers into the most dangerous neighbourhoods. Face-to-face interviews are necessary because only about 60 per cent of households have a telephone, says Anibal Cantarian, managing director of Taylor Nelson Sofres (TNS) Gallup Argentina.

We try not to interview after the sun goes down, and in neighbourhoods where crime has grown it becomes difficult to enter houses because people are afraid to open the door.

Face-to-face questioning remains the norm in Argentina. In Israel, however, the security crisis has caused a big shift to telephone interviewing, so that only about 20 per cent is face to face. **FT**

Source: *Financial Times*, 5 March 2003.

Conversely a poor infrastructure is an opportunity for those supplying such facilities. European water companies have contracts to apply their expertise to providing water and sanitation services to many less developed countries.

4.7 Environmental context

The natural environment is a further aspect of the business context. One aspect of this is the natural resources available in an economy – including oil, coal and other minerals, agricultural land and the prevailing climate. A key distinction in considering natural resources is between those that are renewable and those that are not: land can be used for several purposes in succession, timber is renewable – but oil is not.

These considerations have fundamental impacts on the kind of businesses which people create in different countries, and on the pattern of world trade. Technological developments enable the discovery of previously unknown resources (new oil reserves are being discovered in Central Asia, for example), and permit the fuller use of some that were previously uneconomic. This brings great potential benefits to the countries concerned, and to the foreign companies who are frequently involved in exploiting them.

Power shortages in China

During 2004 many parts of China experienced severe shortages of power, and many factories had to close for two days a week as electricity was interrupted. Retailers in the rest of the world who now depend on imports from China found that their supplies were being delayed: one said that 'the cost advantage in China is still so great that we'll continue doing business here, but ultimately if they can't deliver in a timely fashion we'll start looking.'

Demand for power had increased by almost 70 per cent in four years, and other infrastructure problems had contributed to the power shortages – such as an overloaded railway system that could not deliver enough coal to power stations. While plans were in place to increase supplies by 2007, in the meantime the power crisis was damaging company performance.

Source: *Business Week*, 5 July 2004.

The process is also controversial, as when foreign mining or oil companies come into conflict with local populations whose land they occupy, or over the commercial terms of the concessions. Many also express concern at the environmental degradation that timber or mineral exploitation causes, whose negative effects may be felt over much wider areas (such as when rivers are polluted in one country before they flow into another). Economic development itself causes pollution, which is both a problem for people in the area, and a business opportunity for foreign businesses that specialise in environmental control and remediation.

4.8 Legal context – trade agreements and trading blocs

Each jurisdiction has its own regulations affecting business practice, which they expect companies operating in the country to meet. Ensuring that the company complies with this often implies working with a local partner, able to negotiate in the local context.

Companies also query the legal system of a country in which they plan to work, and whether it will give sufficient protection in the event of legal disputes arising. The most significant developments in the political–legal environment are those associated with international trade agreements and regional economic alliances.

GATT and the World Trade Organisation

The General Agreement on Tariffs and Trade (GATT) reduces the propensity of national governments to put tariffs on physical goods to protect domestic companies. Its main tool is tariff concessions, whereby member countries agree to limit the level of tariffs they impose on imports from other GATT members (now more than 100 countries). GATT has also sponsored a series of international trade negotiations aimed at reducing restrictions on trade. The most recent of these was the Uruguay Round which involved 125 countries and led to the establishment of the World Trade Organisation (WTO).

The World Trade Organisation is a permanent global institution which monitors international trade, and arbitrates in disputes between countries over the interpretation of tariffs and other barriers to trade. It is also seeking a world agreement on rules governing foreign investment – both to encourage it and, where thought necessary, to control it.

European Union

The EU is credited with being the model for many other regional trade groupings (Dent, 1997; Mercado *et al.*, 2001). Since the Treaty of Rome was signed in 1959 the aim has been to gradually eliminate tariffs and other restrictions that national governments use to protect domestic industries. This was broadly achieved by 1968, and led to further efforts to bring about closer economic integration between the member states. This culminated in the Single European Act of 1986 that aimed to create a single internal market – by 2004 this covered 25 member states. Introducing the euro as a common currency for many of the member states encouraged further changes in the European economy by unifying capital markets and making price comparisons more transparent.

The European Commission (responsible for proposing and implementing policy) is encouraging this liberalisation by proposing changes in national laws to make cross-border trade easier. For example, one project will make it easier for investment businesses to sell investment products across Europe – most at present operate only in their home country. This and similar deals have encouraged a rapid growth in trade within the region. Car companies such as Ford and DaimlerChrysler have plants in several countries, specialising in particular components or models. They then simultaneously import and export their products between the countries as part of a region-wide production system, leading to growth in intra-industry trade.

In 2004 the EU widened its membership when ten new members (many from Eastern Europe) joined the existing 15. It is also deepening integration in the sense of continuously widening the scope of EU prerogatives beyond the customs union with which it started. The intention is gradually to establish common European policy on a range of matters affecting business and competitiveness. These include policies on industry (such as subsidies for local businesses and/or foreign investment), mergers, employment rights, transport and environmental protection.

Activity 4.2   Access the European Union website

Access the European Union website at **http://europa.eu.int/comm**. Go to the page for the internal market and then to the scorecard that the Commission regularly publishes on progress towards the single market.

● What is the latest score, and what is the recent trend?

● Check further and try to establish how the scorecard is compiled, and what it means.

4.9   Socio-cultural context

While people have a great deal in common in the biological sense, people in a country or region develop a distinct culture. As a business becomes more international, its managers balance a common approach to business throughout the world with the unique cultures of the countries in which they operate.

Perspectives on culture

Edgar Schein (1985) defined culture as follows:

> Culture is the pattern of basic assumptions that a given group has invented, discovered or developed and [that is] therefore taught to new members as the correct way to perceive, think and feel in relation to [the organisation's] problems.

Social groupings of all kinds develop a distinct culture, which to some degree sets them apart from other groupings. Teams, clubs, long-term work groups, organisations and nations develop values and beliefs that guide members – how they react to events, what they regard as important. There is growing evidence of identifiable differences in the degree to which national cultures hold certain values and attitudes. For example, a study by Cranfield School of Management concluded that 'the French, although more sensitive to people, are slightly more into power/political styles of management, but less disciplined than the Germans who freely admit less sensitivity to people but a greater adherence to organisational disciplines and systems' (Kakabadse, 1993, quoted in Adams, 1996).

Cultural variety in the European Commission

Marcello Burattini was head of protocol for the European Commission. On the 40th anniversary of the Treaty of Rome he recalled the early days of the Commission:

> At the beginning of the 1960s the rules, based on the principles of Franco-Prussian administration, were strict, formal modes of address, and ties were *de rigueur* … Then certain political leaders decided to enlarge [the Community]. Thus the British and the Irish arrived, bringing with them the English language, humour, simplicity in human relations, many original ideas – for example, pragmatism – somewhat softening the rigorous orthodoxy. The Danes taught us to be less formal, and were astonished by our way of doing things – and by the fact that secretaries made coffee for their bosses.

Source: *The European*, 27 March 1997.

Social beliefs affect what managers expect from their job, how work relates to family life and what reward they expect. Tayeb (1996) contrasts US and Japanese managers. She suggests the former typically give priority to things that are of personal importance to them. These include their long-term professional career, their individual personal development and the quality of family relationships. They come from:

> an individualistic culture in which 'self' takes precedence over group. For the Japanese manager the company's performance and victory … comes first. And if this means sacrificing private leisure time so be it. [They] come from a collectivist culture, where group takes precedence over self. (p. 37)

Tayeb goes on to argue that people learn their culture in the family, from religious influences and through the history of the nation, illustrating this last point with Australia:

> Australia is another example of the influence of history on people's values and attitudes. The origins of modern Australia go back to the eighteenth century, when Britain used to send her convicted political and social offenders there. The convicts carried with them their lack of respect for authority. On the ships that took them there everyone was on an equal footing with their fellow passengers. This combination of low respect for authority and a belief in equality has over time evolved into a democratic political system which (with New Zealand) is more or less unique within their immediate neighbouring region.

Today, Australians are as law abiding as the citizens of any other nation, but they are sceptical about people in positions of power, such as politicians, police and judges. Their federal system of government reflects their belief in decentralisation and delegation of authority. (p. 41)

> **Activity 4.3** **Comparing cultures**
>
> Form a group amongst your student colleagues made up of people from different countries and cultures. Identify some of the main characteristics of the respective cultures that affect management. Note them down and compare your evidence with that from Hofstede's research (see below).

Organisations and their management operate within this cultural context. Employees, including managers, bring their prevailing values, attitudes and beliefs into the work-place as part of their cultural heritage. Tayeb identifies further aspects of culture relevant to the work situation, namely high- and low-context cultures and attitudes to conflict.

High-context and low-context cultures

Low-context cultures are those where people are more psychologically distant so that information needs to be explicit if members are to understand it.

High-context cultures are those in which information is implicit and can only be fully understood by those with shared experiences in the culture.

In a **low-context culture** information is explicit and clear. A **high-context culture** is one in which information is implicit, and can only be fully understood in conjunction with shared experience, assumptions and various forms of verbal codes. High-context cultures occur when people live closely with each other, where deep mutual understandings develop, that then provide a rich context within which specific communication takes place. Low-context cultures occur where people are typically distant from each other so that information needs to be very explicit:

> Japanese, Arabs and Mediterranean people, who have extensive information networks among family, friends, colleagues and clients and who are involved in close personal relationships, are examples of high context cultures. Low context peoples include Americans, Germans, Swiss, Scandinavians and other northern Europeans; they compartmentalise their personal relationships, their work and many aspects of day-to-day life. (Tayeb, 1996, pp. 55–6)

Attitude to conflict and harmony

Disagreements and conflict arise in all societies. The management interest is in how different societies have developed different ways of handling conflict. Individualistic cultures such as those of the United States or the Netherlands see conflict as healthy, on the basis that everyone has a right to express their views. People are encouraged to bring contentious issues into the open and to discuss conflicts rather than suppress them. Other cultures place greater value on social harmony and on not disturbing the way things are:

> The notion of harmony is central in almost all East Asian cultures, such as Korea, Taiwan, Singapore and Hong Kong, through their common Confucian heritage. In the context of Korea, for instance, Meek and Song argue that the traditional implicit rules of proper behaviour provide appropriate role behaviour for individuals in the junior and subordinate roles of an interpersonal relationship. (Tayeb, 1996, p. 60)

Other clear differences between nations include their view of change and their time orientation.

View of change

This varies greatly between cultures. In the West, many take a proactive view of change. People believe that they can shape what happens, things do not have to be as they are, and change is part of the nature of the world. Other cultures see change as something that is slow, inevitable and not greatly influenced by human beings. The notion that events will take their natural course and that human intervention will probably be fruitless is difficult for a Western manager in a non-Western culture to accept.

Time orientation

Managers in Western organisations typically view time as a scarce commodity. They take courses on how to manage it better. They expect others to meet deadlines and to arrive for meetings at the appointed time. Not all cultures see time this way. Some view it as a limitless resource, unbounded by death. Time is inexhaustible, so that the widespread Western concern about saving time is seen as curious.

Tayeb (1996) suggested that the significance of cultural issues for managers depends on the nature of the firm's involvement in intenational business – Table 4.1 sums up the options.

Table 4.1

Company strategies and relevance of national culture

Character of the firm	Relevance of national culture to foreign culture
Domestic, single-nation firm with no foreign interests	nil
Single-nation firm with import/export activities	low to moderate
Multinational firm with franchising and licensing activities	moderate to high
Multinational firm with manufacturing and/or service units abroad	high
Global firm with business activities in most parts of the world	high

Source: Tayeb (2000), p. 87.

Overemphasising diversity?
key ideas

The chapter has illustrated the diversity of national cultures. There is another view that the underlying fundamentals of management may outweigh cultural variations in detailed processes. One powerful constraint on diversity is the economic context of an essentially capitalist economic system. This places similar requirements on managers wherever they are. They have to provide acceptable returns, create a coherent organisational structure, maintain relations with stakeholders and try to keep control.

Further, if managers work in a multinational organisation that has developed a distinctive corporate culture, will that influence their behaviour more than the local national culture?

Another constraint is the dramatic spread of integrated information systems across companies (and their suppliers) operating internationally. Some companies use such systems to place new and common reporting requirements on managers irrespective of their location. Such integration is often of competitive significance, and serves to tie units more closely together. This is also likely to bring convergence in the work of management.

These are unresolved questions to remember throughout this chapter. Look for evidence as you read that supports or contradicts either point of view.

> **Activity 4.4** **Critical reflection on PESTEL factors**
>
> ● If you have worked in a company operating internationally, reflect on which of the forces outlined above had most helped or hindered the venture, or otherwise affected management actions. Within each PESTEL heading, which of the factors listed had most impact?
> ● Which forces NOT listed had a significant impact?
> ● How did people deal with any adverse factors?

4.10 Hofstede's comparison of national cultures

Geert Hofstede (1980), a Dutch academic, provided a widely quoted insight into national cultural differences. He had the opportunity to survey the attitudes of employees of IBM, one of the earliest global companies. He defined culture as a collective programming of people's minds, which influences how they react to events in the workplace. He defined four dimensions of culture (described below), and was able to establish how this varied amongst people in the different countries in which IBM operated.

Power distance

Power distance is the extent to which the less powerful members of organisations within a country expect and accept that power is distributed unevenly.

Hofstede defined **power distance** (PD) as 'the extent to which the less powerful members of ... organisations within a country expect and accept that power is distributed unevenly' (Hofstede, 1991, p. 28). One of the ways in which countries differ is in how power and authority are distributed. A related difference is the way they view any resultant inequality. In some the existence of inequality in boss/subordinate relationships is seen as problematic. Others see it as part of the natural order of things. The questionnaire allowed the researchers to calculate scores for PD, countries with a high PD being those where people accepted inequality. Those with high scores included Belgium, France, Argentina, Brazil and Spain. Those with low PD scores included Sweden, Britain and Germany.

Uncertainty avoidance

Uncertainty avoidance is the extent to which members of a culture feel threatened by uncertain or unknown situations.

Uncertainty avoidance is 'the extent to which the members of a culture feel threatened by uncertain or unknown situations' (Hofstede, 1991, p. 113). People in some cultures tolerate ambiguity and uncertainty quite readily – if things are not clear they will improvise or use their initiative. Others are reluctant to move without clear rules or instructions. High scores, indicating low tolerance of uncertainty, were obtained in the Latin American, Latin European and Mediterranean countries, and for Japan and Korea. Low scores were recorded in the Asian countries other than Japan and Korea, and in most of the Anglo and Nordic countries. The United Kingdom was 47th in the list – similar to the United States, Canada and Australia. Germany ranked 29th, indicating a lower tolerance of uncertainty than Anglo-American countries.

Individualism/collectivism

Hofstede distinguishes between **individualism** and **collectivism** as follows:

> Individualism pertains to societies in which the ties between individuals are loose: everyone is expected to look after himself or herself and his or her immediate family. Collectivism as its opposite pertains to societies in which people, from birth onwards, are integrated into strong, cohesive in-groups which throughout people's lifetime continue to protect them in exchange for unquestioning loyalty. (1991, p. 51)

Some people live in societies in which the power of the group prevails: there is an emphasis on collective action and mutual responsibility, and on helping each other through difficulties. Other societies emphasise the individual, and his or her responsibility for their position in life. High scores on the individualism dimension occurred in wealthy countries such as the United States, Australia, the United Kingdom and Canada. Low scores occurred in poor countries such as the less developed South American and Asian countries. Germany, the Netherlands, the Nordic countries and Japan showed medium individualism.

Individualism pertains to societies in which the ties between individuals are loose.

Collectivism 'describes societies in which people, from birth onwards, are integrated into strong, cohesive in-groups which... protect them in exchange for unquestioning loyalty.' (Hofstede, 1991, p. 51)

Activity 4.5　Implications of cultural differences

- Consider the implications of differences on Hofstede's first two dimensions of culture for management in the countries concerned. For example, what would Hofstede's conclusions lead you to predict about the method that a French or Argentinian manager would use if he or she wanted a subordinate to perform a task, and what method would the subordinate expect his or her manager to use?
- How would your answers differ if the manager and subordinates were Swedish?

Masculinity/femininity

Hofstede defines the two characteristics, as they pertain to society, as follows:

> **masculinity** pertains to societies in which social gender roles are clearly distinct (i.e. men are supposed to be assertive, tough and focused on material success, whereas women are supposed to be more modest, tender and concerned with the quality of life); **femininity** pertains to societies in which social gender roles overlap (i.e. both men and women are supposed to be modest, tender and concerned with the quality of life). (1991, pp. 82–3)

Hofstede argues that societies differ in the desirability of assertive behaviour (which he labels as masculinity) and of modest behaviour (femininity). He sees a common trend in many societies that expect men to seek achievements outside the home while women care for things within the home. Masculinity scores were not related to economic wealth: 'we find both rich and poor masculine countries, and rich and poor feminine countries' (p. 84). The most feminine countries were Sweden, Norway, the Netherlands and Denmark. Masculine countries included Japan, Austria, Germany, Italy and the United States.

Masculinity pertains to societies in which social gender roles are clearly distinct.

Femininity pertains to societies in which social gender roles overlap.

Limitations of Hofstede's work

Other scholars have questioned the significance of Hofstede's work on several grounds. The number of respondents in some countries was very small, fewer than 100 in some cases, and so not necessarily representative of a nation. Moreover, even when the sample was large, employees of a technologically advanced computer company may not be very representative of a whole nation. A more fundamental issue of method is the assumption that since all respondents worked for IBM, they would shared a common organisational culture: this implied that any differences in responses must reflect national differences. However, as McSweeney (2002) has pointed out, there are likely to have been several cultures within IBM, rather than a single one (see Chapter 10 for a discussion of subcultures within organisations). Therefore during the study period there were cultural differences both within and between each IBM unit, not the cultural uniformity that Hofstede originally claimed.

Hofstede sought to indicate the attitudes typically held by people in different national cultures to four dimensions, and Hoppe (1993) found support for the theory in a study of R&D engineers in 17 Western European countries. Trompennaars (1993) also developed a rather more complex typology, using a different method. Even if the precision of the results is questionable, they can be useful as a starting point for managers working internationally to think about the culture in which they operate, and to reflect on their own cultural biases. People operating internationally need to develop an ability to deal with the cultural contexts in which they will work.

Adams (1996) examined several models attempting to identify the competences required to manage internationally. For example, Barham and Wills (1992) found that one of several competences that successful international managers possessed was the ability to act as 'intercultural mediator and change agent'. They defined this as:

> switching one's frame of reference rapidly between different cultures; being aware of one's own cultural underpinnings and of the need to be sensitive to cultural differences; managing change in different contexts and pushing the boundaries of different cultures; and balancing the need for speed and the need for sensitivity. (p. 49)

It is also worth distinguishing between the details and minutiae of interpersonal behaviour across cultures and those behaviours with significant effects on business performance. Again we can only infer that there is a link. There are visible and illuminating examples but it is always dangerous to draw general conclusions from good anecdotes.

Case question 4.2

Below are some of the countries in which Starbucks operates. If Hofstede's analysis is accurate, what may be the implications for managing the business in each of those countries, and for a manager who needs to work with colleagues in each? Check the text for the cultural features which Hofstede identified for each country, and then compare them.

- United States
- Japan
- France
- United Kingdom

Activity 4.6   Critical reflection on cultural differences

- If you have worked in an organisation with international operations, reflect on whether your experience leads you to agree or disagree with the ideas in this section. For example, can you recognise the differences in national cultures identified by Hofstede?
- If so, in what ways did they affect the way people at all levels managed the business?
- How did company culture relate to national culture?

4.11 Contrasting management systems

Management takes place in a social context that influences its character, and this chapter has indicated many aspects of the context. As outlined earlier, Whitley (1996) offered one framework for analysing and comparing national management systems. Table 4.2 draws on material throughout the chapter to present a list of themes with which to compare different systems. The relative importance of each theme will vary with the purpose, and judgements will be subjective.

Context factor	Examples for analysis
Political/legal	Extent to which state dominates economic system State support for cooperation between firms Extent of regulations for entry to and exit from markets State support for trade union activities
Economic	Degree of reliance on capital markets for finance Relative roles of family and private shareholding in economy Level, growth and distribution of income
Socio-cultural	Profit-maximising or corporate responsibility view of business (see Chapter 5) Low-context or high-context culture Dominant Hofstede cultural type Role of social formalities, clear boundaries in relationships Emphasis on role of friends and family in business decisions
Technological	Infrastructure – communications, security etc.

Table 4.2

Summary of factors distinguishing national management systems

Thurley and Wirdenius (1989) summarised the distinctive features of the US and Japanese styles. They believed that the US was characterised by an emphasis on individualism with people pursuing their self-interest and business being conducted in a relatively rational way. This was in contrast to the Japanese management style which emphasised equality as the basis of competition and cooperation. This rejects the implicit technocratic approach of US scientific management, and includes a greater sense of collective responsibility for the success of the organisation. Other cultures are now challenging the Western and Japanese models, for example Islamic beliefs influence management in the Arab world. Arab executives are more person oriented than work oriented, and more susceptible to pressures from families, friends and the wider community.

Such models are highly generalised summaries of diverse populations. Their value is to give some clues about broad differences in approach to management. Above all, they show the variety of ways in which management is practised and encourage people to be ready to adapt the way they work to local circumstances (see also Chen, 2004). Others take a more robust view of cultural differences and try to eliminate their influence within the organisation. Steve Chang is the Taiwanese founder and chairman of Trend Micro (see pages 106–7), an anti-virus software company operating in many countries:

> The curse is that national cultures are very different. We have to figure out how to convert everybody to one business culture – no matter where they're from. (*Business Week*, 22 September 2003)

---

key ideas **National culture or corporate culture?**

A study by Laurent (1983) surveying successive groups of managers participating in executive development programmes at INSEAD (a leading European centre for management education and development) provides support for the view that differences in national cultures override the influence of corporate cultures.

The managers came from many different companies and many different organisations. When their responses were analysed, it appeared that the most powerful determinant of their assumptions about the role of management was their nationality. Across 56 different items of enquiry, it was found that nationality had three times more influence on the shaping of managerial assumptions than any of the respondents' other characteristics such as age, education, function or type of company.

One of the most illustrative examples of national differences in management assumptions was reflected in the respondents' reaction to the following statement: 'It is important for a manager to have at hand precise answers to most of the questions that his subordinates may raise about their work' (p. 86).

While only a minority of Northern American and Northern European managers agreed with this statement, a majority of Southern Europeans and South East Asians did. The research results indicated that managers from different national cultures vary widely as to their basic conception of what management is all about.

Laurent found that conceptions of organisations varied widely across national cultures, as managers from Latin cultures (French and Italian) consistently perceived organisations as social systems of relationships monitored by power, authority and hierarchy to a much greater extent than their northern counterparts did. US managers held an 'instrumental' view of the organisation as a set of tasks to be achieved through a problem-solving hierarchy where positions are defined in terms of tasks and functions and where authority is functionally based. French managers held a 'social' view of the organisation as a collective of people to be managed through a formal hierarchy, where positions are defined in terms of levels of authority and status and where authority is more attached to individuals than it is to their offices or functions.

The research led to the conclusion that deep-seated managerial assumptions are strongly shaped by national cultures and appear quite insensitive to the more transient culture of organisations.

Source: Laurent (1983).

4.12 Views on globalisation

The globalisation of markets?

Globalisation refers to the increasing integration of internationally dispersed economic activities.

If you travel to another country, you immediately see many familiar consumer products or services – things that epitomise the idea that global brands are steadily displacing local products. In several industries identical products (Canon cameras, Sony Walkman, Famous Grouse whisky) are sold across the globe without modification. This trend towards **globalisation** was observed by Theodore Levitt – see Key Ideas below.

Levitt's argument soon influenced practice in many global businesses. In the mid-1980s British Airways developed an advertisement ('The world's favourite airline') and (after dubbing it into 20 languages) showed it in identical form in all 35 countries with a developed TV network. Consumer companies like Coca-Cola and McDonald's began promoting themselves as identical global brands, with standard practices and a centralised management structure.

By the end of the 1990s, managers began to change their approach. Customers were finding that new local brands offered better value and, as producers adopted Western

The globalisation of markets

key ideas

Theodore Levitt, a Professor at Harvard Business School, argued that advances in communications technology were increasingly inspiring consumers around the world to want the same things. 'The world's needs and desires have been irrevocably homogenized. This makes the multinational corporation obsolete and the global corporation absolute' (p. 93). He believed therefore that international companies should cease to act as 'multinationals' that customised their products to fit local markets and tastes. Instead they should become 'global' by standardising the production, distribution and marketing of their products across all countries. Sameness meant efficiency and would be more profitable than difference. From economies of scale would flow competitive advantage.

Source: Based on Levitt (1983).

methods, good quality. Global brands, offering standard products regardless of local tastes, lost market share. So rather than 'going global' they began to 'go local' – Coca-Cola, for instance, owns not one brand but 200, many of them in only one or two markets; McDonald's varies its menu to suit local tastes; Nestlé has about 200 varieties of its instant coffee; and MTV varies programming to suit different countries and regions.

Coca-Cola finds formula for India www.cocacola.com

management in practice

Coca-Cola India totally misjudged rural India, home to two-thirds of the country's 1bn population, when it re-entered the country in 1993. It paid a high price for the then market leader, Thumbs Up, and then tried to kill it off in the mistaken belief that this would pave the way for Coca-Cola's rise. The approach failed – best illustrated by the fact that India is one of the few markets where Pepsi-Cola leads Coca-Cola. 'We were just not addressing the masses', admitted Sanjeev Gupta, Coca-Cola's operations chief. In 2000 management decided to change their approach – by focusing on the distinctive needs of the Indian rural consumer. This meant using smaller bottles, lower prices, more outlets and an advertising campaign (featuring Bollywood stars) that makes sense to villagers as well as city-dwellers. **FT**

Source: Extracts from an article by Khozem Merchant, *Financial Times*, 18 June 2003.

Rugman (2000) offers another view on globalisation, arguing that the world has become divided into three regions – North America, the European Union and Japan/East Asia. He notes that almost three-quarters of exports from EU members went to other EU countries – and exports to North America accounted for less than 10 per cent of the total. He concluded that we are seeing not so much globalisation as regionalisation – with the three groupings having very different traditions and ways of doing business. 'Only in a few sectors is globalization a successful firm strategy … For most manufacturers and all services, regionalization is much more relevant than globalization' (p. 18).

The globalisation of production

Since the 1960s a growing number of firms in the developed world have noted that labour-intensive manufacturing and service operations in their home country is a costly way of working. This was especially the case in electrical and electronic goods, clothing, footwear and toys, which faced growing competition from cheaper imports. Managers looked for new sources of supply, and received a very positive response from a small group of Asian countries – Taiwan, Hong Kong, South Korea and especially Singapore. These countries took the opportunity over the next 30 years to become major 'outsourcing' centres, supplying finished goods and components to companies around the world. They have also developed their education systems so that they can do work of higher value, so that the range of products has also widened greatly – including a growing trade in services such as software development and the back-office functions of airlines and banks. Table 4.3 gives some examples.

Table 4.3

Examples of the globalisation of production

Company	Years	Work transferred	Reasons given
HSBC	2004–06	Relocate 4000 jobs in administrative work and telephone enquiries to India, Malaysia and China	'Need to remain efficient and competitive'
Gillette	2005–07	Close three factories (two UK and one German) and transfer work to new factory in Eastern Europe'	'Significantly reduce costs and improve operating efficiency'
Dyson	2003–04	Moved production of vacuum cleaners and washing machines from UK to Malaysia	'Reduce manufacturing costs and help protect UK jobs in design and development'

Concerns about globalisation

Supporters of more liberal world trade argue that it brings benefits of wider access to markets and cheaper goods and services. The growth in trade that follows benefits both consumers and workers by encouraging innovation and investment. It has given many consumers a much wider choice of goods, by being able to attract supplies from around the world, often much more cheaply than those produced locally. Others take a much more critical view, pointing out that moves towards liberalisation through bodies such as the WTO are driven by the rich countries. They believe the agreements reached serve the interests of multinational businesses and richer economies rather than indigenous producers in local economies.

Activity 4.7 **Debating globalisation**

Arrange a debate or discussion on these questions:

- Has globalisation increased people's power as consumers, or diminished their power as employees?
- Has it lifted millions out of poverty, or has it widened the gap between rich and poor?
- Has it widened consumer choice, or has it encouraged levels of industrialisation and consumption which make unsustainable demands on the earth's natural resources?
- Does globalisation heighten aesthetic awareness of different cultures, or does it expose people to a stream of superficial images?
- Does it enable more people to experience diversity, or does it lead to a bland homogenisation of local cultures into a global view?

Globalisation: what it means to small nations

management in practice

In July 1996 the then prime minister of Malaysia, Dr Mahathir, gave a lecture in which he questioned whether globalisation would bring benefits to poorer countries. Some extracts from his speech were reported as follows.

A globalised world is not going to be a very democratic world but will belong to powerful, dominant countries. Those countries would impose their will on the rest who will be no better off than when they were colonies of the rich. Fifty years ago, the process of decolonisation began and in about 20 years it was virtually completed. But before any had become truly and fully independent, recolonisation has begun. This is what globalisation may be about. It does not contain much hope for the weak and poor. But unfortunately it is entirely possible.

Dr Mahathir said that globalisation might bring about a utopia but nothing that had happened so far seemed to justify this dream. As interpreted by developed countries, it meant breaking down boundaries so that every country had access to others.

The poor countries will have access to the markets of the rich, unrestricted. In return, or rather by right, the rich will have access to the markets of the poor. This sounds absolutely fair. The playing field will be level, not tilted to favour anyone. It will be a borderless world. But if there is only one global entity there cannot be nations. Everyone would be equal citizens of the globe. But will they be truly equal?

Dr Mahathir said that, after 30 years or more of 'independence', the former colonies of the West have found out the emptiness of the independence they had won. They have found that their politics, their economy, their social and behavioural systems are all under the control, directly or indirectly, of the old colonial masters and the great powers. He added that it was clear that the developed countries wished to use the World Trade Organisation to impose conditions on the developing countries. This will result not in improving human rights or labour practices or greater care for the environment but in stunting their growth and, consequently, in suffering for their people. If the developing countries were competing with the West in any way then their records were scrutinised and threats issued. The net effect is to prevent the development of these newly industrialising economies.

Dr Mahathir said globalisation would leave these countries totally exposed and unable to protect themselves, adding that true globalisation might result in increasing foreign investment in these countries. The effect would be the demise of the small companies based in the developing countries: 'Large international corporations, originating in the developed countries will take over everything.'

Source: *New Straits Times*, July 1996.

Activity 4.8 Understanding a critic of globalisation

- Malaysia has attracted much foreign direct investment, especially from IT companies. It is a leading player in South-east Asia with little unemployment. Yet the architect of its economic success clearly has serious doubts about the emergence of the global economy. What are his main concerns?
- Can you find examples of global companies using their economic bargaining power to take advantage of the weaker countries in which they operate?

All of these developments imply much greater patterns of contact between managers in different countries. Legislative changes and treaties remove some barriers to trade, but they do not solve the management problems of making those economic activities work efficiently. Above all, they bring many managers face to face with the need to manage cultural differences.

Managing in an international context

Managing internationally brings managers into direct contact with diverse cultures and institutions, requiring a new level of awareness of and sensitivity to these differences. These are likely to affect each of the management functions. People perform management functions in ways that are compatible with the prevailing economic, institutional and cultural context of their country. As business spreads, management makes contact with ever more diverse cultures, and meets different ways of interpreting the roles of management (van Houten, 1989). While recognising the dangers of overgeneralisation, the following points are offered for discussion – Tayeb (2000) includes a fuller discussion of strategic, organisational and HRM issues raised by managing internationally.

Planning

Increased opportunities for regional and global trade mean that the environment is bringing in new forms of competition to businesses – others can now compete in their home market. By the same token, businesses can develop their objectives towards extending their market into a wider area. Planning to achieve those objectives on a global scale raises new workflow and logistical challenges. People in countries with high power distance scores will expect managers to make plans and subordinates to implement them without complaint or disagreement. Attempts to involve subordinates in discussing the alternatives would be greeted with puzzlement.

Organising

Major challenges arise in developing the appropriate structural forms for international business. New organisational structures are created to manage internationally, which are usually supported by developments in information technology. In shaping these changes management and staff need to take account of the diversity of national cultures. People in high power distance countries will tend to expect structures to be centralised, formal and with strict job descriptions. People in low power distance countries will prefer more fluid structures that allow them to use their initiative.

As companies choose to respond to apparent international opportunities they need to deal with structural issues such as:

- managing matrix structures where products are made and sold in several countries
- improving the links between research, marketing and production to speed the introduction of new products
- facilitating knowledge transfer between the national components of the business
- encouraging tactical and local flexibility while maintaining strategic coherence.

Leading

Internationalisation clearly means more stakeholders, especially when companies develop complex trading networks across national boundaries. Managers need to influence these stakeholders, which include the governments and communities in which they work as well as other commercial organisations. The interests and ways of working of these players will have been shaped by local cultures and institutions. These cultural differences also affect how management can influence the behaviour of those whose support it needs – methods acceptable in one culture may not work in another.

This is particularly necessary in generating willing action and commitment from people who may have different perspectives on work. As with planning, people in high power distance countries may expect to be told what to do. In low power distance countries people expect to be asked for their opinions.

Leadership and national culture

People in different cultures have different beliefs about appropriate leadership behaviour. Suutari (1996) surveyed 149 managers in a company in the metal industry, which operated in Denmark, Finland, Germany, the United Kingdom and Sweden. The questionnaire sought their beliefs about the way a manager ought to behave on 14 dimensions of leadership. Six factors showed statistically significant differences between managers in the five countries. These were:

- **Decision participation** Danish and Finnish managers were more likely than German and British managers to accept the participation of subordinates in decision making.
- **Autonomy and delegation** Same as for decision participation.
- **Rewarding** Danish managers most frequently believed that companies should reward subordinates for good performance.
- **Role clarification** British and German managers tended more frequently than managers from the Nordic countries to see a need for role clarification.
- **Conflict management** British and German managers tended more than Finnish and Danish managers to emphasise conflict management behaviours.
- **Individualism** British and Danish managers were more likely than the others to see a need for managers to pay personal attention to the hopes and needs of individuals.

Overall, the study supported the view that 'management methods developed in one country are applicable in other countries to only a limited extent'.

Source: Suutari (1996), p. 405.

Controlling and learning

The more widespread an organisation's business, the more it must rely on formal systems of control. Nations differ in their views on exercising control. Some systems favour tight, centralised and supervisory controls; the current pattern in many Western organisations is to emphasise the benefits of self-control in semi-autonomous teams. Different attitudes to collective action and learning also illuminate the diversity of management practice across the globe. In individualist societies people acknowledge individual responsibility for results, whereas in collectivist ones they will be more inclined to stress collective action and mutual responsibility. There will be more resistance to attempts to reward or punish individuals.

The primary lesson is that managing internationally will involve significant learning and reflection. How the ideas and models outlined in this chapter affect management practice in a particular location is essentially unpredictable, being a combination of so many individual, corporate, cultural and national influences. Entering a situation with at least an awareness of the differences outlined in this chapter is a start; reflecting on the experience of working in different cultures will add greatly to their value.

Summary

1 **Outline how the internationalisation of business affects the management role:**

- More stakeholders (including governments and communities) to deal with, whose interests and ways of working of these players will be shaped by local cultures and institutions. These affect how managers influence behaviour, as methods acceptable in one culture may not work in another.

2 **Contrast the ways in which organisations take part in international business:**

- Exporting, licensing, joint ventures, wholly owned subsidiaries
- Multinational (independent operations in many countries, run from centre); transnational (independent operations in many countries, decentralised); global (linked and interdependent operations in many countries, closely coordinated).

3 **Explain the significance of national cultures, and evaluate Hofstede's research:**

- Low-context – information explicit and clear; high-context – information is implicit and can only be understood through shared experience, values and assumptions.
- Hofstede distinguished between cultures in terms of power distance (acceptance of variations in power); uncertainty avoidance (willingness to tolerate ambiguity); individualism/collectivism (emphasis on individual or collective action); and masculinity/femininity (preferences for assertive or modest behaviour).

4 **Compare the main features of different national management systems:**

- These shape the way people interpret generic activities of management:
  - US – individualistic, rational approach, contingent design of organisations
  - Europe – collective, rational approach, pragmatic
  - Japan – collective responsibility, trust of subordinates, consensus building.

5 **Outline the forces driving and restraining the internationalisation of business:**

- Drivers include capital, information technology and pressure for growth.
- Restraints include support for local institutions and the costs of managing international businesses.

6 **Set out the benefits and costs of globalisation to different players and the dilemmas these create for management:**

- Benefits include growth, economic development, wider choice for consumers.
- Costs include loss of income by local producers.
- Management issues include balancing local needs with company styles and methods.

Review questions

1 What factors are stimulating the growth in world trade?

2 Compare internationalisation and globalisation. Give a specific example of a company of each type about which you have obtained some information.

3 Outline the difference between a high- and a low-context culture and give an example of each from direct observation or discussion.

4 Explain accurately to another person Hofstede's four dimensions of national cultures. Evaluate his conclusions on the basis of discussions with your colleagues from any of the countries in his study. Evaluate the limitations and criticisms of his study.

5 Give some illustrations of your own about the way in which the history of a country has affected its culture, and how that in turn affects the management of organisations there.

6 What are the distinctive features of Japanese, European and US management systems?

7 Compare the implications of globalisation for (a) national governments, (b) their citizens, (c) the management of global companies, (d) the environment.

8 How is the growth of international business likely to affect management functions?

Concluding critical reflection

Think about the way managers in your company, or one with which you are familiar, deal with the international aspects of business. Review the material in the chapter, and make notes on these questions:

- Which of the issues discussed in this chapter are most relevant to the way you and your colleagues manage? For example, what structure(s) do you use to manage the international aspects of the business? Which of the PESTEL factors have most effect in your situation?

- What assumptions appear to guide the way people manage internationally? Do they assume that cultural factors are significant or insignificant? Do they see globalisation as a benefit or a threat? Do they acknowledge any responsibilities to those who may be damaged by it?

- What aspects of the historical or current context of the company appear to influence your company's approach to internationalisation and globalisation? Do people see it as a threat or an opportunity, and why? Are there different views on how you should deal with this aspect of the business?

- Can you compare your approach with that of other companies in which colleagues on your course work? Does this suggest any plausible alternative ways of managing internationally? How much scope do you have to change this?

Further reading

Mercado, S., Welford, R. and Prescott, K. (2001), *European Business*, Financial Times/Prentice Hall, Harlow.

A thorough discussion of the development of the European Union as it affects business, including many case studies of current management practice.

Daniels, J.D., Radebaugh, L.H. and Sullivan, D.P. (2004), *International Business: Environments and operations* (10th edn), Pearson/Prentice Hall, Upper Saddle River, NJ.

Provides a comprehensive exposure to many aspects of international business, combining a strong theoretical base with many current examples.

Trompennaars, F. (1993), *Riding the Waves of Culture: Understanding cultural diversity in business*, The Economist Books, London.

Uses a different research method to that used by Hofstede, and develops another set of dimensions on national culture.

Chen, M. (2004), *Asian Management Systems*, Thomson, London.

Comparative review of the management systems in Japan, mainland China, overseas Chinese and Korean. These are compared with Western approaches to management.

Harris, N. (1999), *European Business* (2nd edn), Macmillan Business, Basingstoke.

Dent, C.M. (1997), *The European Economy: The global context*, Routledge, London.

Both trace the development of a more integrated European economy and its place within wider global trends.

Monbiot, G. (2000), *The Captive State*, Macmillan, Basingstoke.

A critique of multinational corporations and the way they seek to subvert democratic institutions.

Tayeb, M.H. (2000), *The Management of International Enterprises: A socio-political view*, Macmillan, Basingstoke.

A short, lucid account of the factors stimulating the growth of international businesses, and a discussion of the strategic, organisational and HRM issues which those managing such enterprises need to deal with.

European Management Journal regularly publishes case studies and accessible research with an international perspective.

Weblinks

These websites have appeared in the chapter:

www.starbucks.com
www.ibm.com
www.tcl.com
www.intel.com
www.walmart.com
www.cocacola.com

Visit two of the business sites in the list, or others which interest you, and navigate to the pages dealing with recent news, press or investor relations.

● What signs are there of the international nature of the business, and what are the main issues in this area that the business appears to be facing?

● Compare and contrast the issues you identify on the two sites.

● What challenges may they imply for those working in, and managing, these organisations?

Annotated weblinks, multiple choice questions and other
useful resources can be found on
www.pearsoned.co.uk/boddy

Chapter 5
Corporate responsibility

Aim

To introduce the dilemmas of ethical and responsible behaviour that managers face, and offer some tools that help to consider them coherently.

Objectives

By the end of your work on this chapter you should be able to outline the concepts below in your own terms and:

1 Identify some of the major ethical issues within business practice
2 Compare contrasting views on the role of business within society
3 Outline four ways of justifying a decision as ethical
4 Explain how consumers can influence corporate practice
5 Illustrate the potential competitive advantage from responsible corporate practice
6 Outline the structures and frameworks for corporate governance which managers can use to encourage responsible behaviour.

Key terms

This chapter introduces the following ideas:

philanthropy
enlightened self-interest
applied ethics
social contract
ethical relativism
ethical decision-making models
corporate responsibility
ethical investors
ethical consumer
ethical audit

Each is a term defined within the text, as well as in the glossary at the end of the book.

In the late 1960s the US automobile industry's home market was under threat from overseas competitors. Lee Iacocca, then president of Ford, was determined to face the competition head-on, by having a new car, the Ford Pinto, on the market by the 1971 model year. This meant reducing the standard 'concept to production' time of a year and a half, and making changes on the production line rather than the drawing board.

In testing its new design Ford used current and proposed legislation. Crash tests indicated that the petrol tank tended to rupture when it was struck from behind at 20 mph, posing a significant risk to those inside. This contravened proposed national legislation which required that cars be able to withstand an impact at 30 mph without fuel loss. No one informed Iacocca of these findings, for fear of being fired. He was fond of saying 'safety doesn't sell'.

Management had to decide between production deadlines to meet competitive requirements and passenger safety. The engineers costed the design improvements at $11 per car, and turned to cost–benefit analysis to help quantify the dilemma. Using government figures that estimated the loss to society for every traffic accident at $200,000, Ford's calculations were:

Bettmann/Corbis

Benefits of altering design

Savings:	180 deaths; 180 serious injuries; 2100 vehicles
Unit cost:	$200,000 per death; $67,000 per serious injury; $700 per vehicle
Total benefit:	$49.5 million

Costs of altering the design

Sales:	11 million cars; 1.5 million light trucks
Unit cost:	$11 per car; $11 per truck
Total cost:	$137.5 million

From this calculation Ford determined that the costs of altering the design outweighed the benefits, so they would produce the Pinto in its original form. They reasoned that the current design met all the applicable federal regulatory safety standards. While it did not meet proposed future legislation, it was as safe as current competing models.

Ford therefore launched the Pinto in 1971. Observers estimate that from 1971 to 1978 between 1700 and 2500 people died in fires involving Pintos. In 1977 the proposed fuel tank legislation was adopted. Ford recalled all 1971–76 Pintos to modify their fuel tanks. Civil action was brought against Ford and resulted in a payout of $250 million in damage awards. Many courts concluded that the Pinto's design was legally defective. However, when charged with criminal homicide, Ford was found not guilty in 1980.

Source: Based on Shaw (1991) and Birsh and Fielder (1994).

Case questions

- As a marketing or production manager at Ford at the time, what dilemmas would you face?
- How would you express these dilemmas within the company?

5.1 Introduction

Ford managers dealing with the Pinto problem chose to put short-term profit before safety. As things turned out, they also failed to achieve their profit targets when they had to meet the cost of the legal claims against the company. So perhaps they made a poor business decision as well as an ethically questionable one. Yet they did not act illegally, and customers were not as interested in safety features then as they are today. A manager who tried to delay the model launch would have damaged their career, and their family's economic well-being. A delay may have harmed the company – and the livelihood of other Ford workers. But about 2000 people died because of those managers' decisions.

Most people only become conscious of business ethics when there is a problem. Events such as the collapse of Enron (Swartz and Watkins, 2002), Arthur Andersen (Toffler and Reingold, 2003) and Parmalat (an Italian dairy company with wide international operations), and the high severance payments and pensions paid to senior managers who lose their jobs, increase public distrust of corporate bodies (Clarke, 2003). Controversies about food safety raise questions about producers, retailers and government, as do stories about the use of child labour in the Far East to produce some of the garments sold in Western stores. They also raise questions about the ethics of such companies and their sense of corporate responsibility.

While such situations seem clear-cut, most ethical issues are ambiguous and complex. There are usually several ways of seeing the ethical dimensions in a business issue, and managers have to balance different interests and claims. Each party believes that their position is the most ethical or responsible in the circumstances. There are few rules to guide the manager, yet the issues arise in many areas of business such as promotion, discrimination and environmental degradation. Managers look for some tools that help them approach the issues in a structured way.

The chapter begins with some examples of contrasting behaviour by people in organisations – from the early days of modern business to the present. It then compares two views of the role of business in society and introduces the topic of business ethics, including four ways of evaluating whether a decision is ethical. Finally the chapter shows how some managers try to encourage more responsible behaviour within their companies by creating formal structures, including a framework of corporate governance.

 **Fixing the numbers**

Congressional investigators yesterday accused senior executives at Global Crossing and Qwest of engaging in deals with each other that had no purpose other than to illicitly boost revenues and meet (stock market) expectations. Citing emails and memos uncovered as part of the inquiry ... the chairman of the panel said the telecoms companies booked 'fictitious revenues' by swapping unneeded fibre-optic capacity with each other so that both companies could count the transactions as sales. ...

Former employees at Global Crossing testified that they were under intense pressure to meet quarterly targets at almost any cost.

FT

Source: *Financial Times*, 25 September 2002.

5.2 Contrasts in business practice

The Pinto case shows that (whether they realised it or not) managers have faced ethical dilemmas for years. Indeed the history of economic development shows the scope for unethical business behaviour – not least in the employment of children as young as eight in the mines and mills of nineteenth-century Britain (a practice still common in some parts of the world). Table 5.1 gives some recent examples.

Paradoxically, there is an equally long tradition of ethical behaviour in business. From the start of the Industrial Revolution some entrepreneurs (as well as Robert Owen, the subject of the Chapter 2 case) acted with philanthropy:

1803–76	Titus Salt	Textiles	Employee welfare; Saltaire Village
1830–98	Jeremiah Coleman	Mustard	Charities; Salvation Army; YMCA
1839–1922	George Cadbury	Chocolate	Employee welfare; Bournville Village
1836–1925	Joseph Rowntree	Chocolate	Employee welfare; New Earswick Village
1851–1925	William Lever	Soap	Employee welfare; Port Sunlight Village

Philanthropy is the practice of contributing personal wealth to charitable or similar causes.

They recognised the social impact of industry and its potential to improve social conditions. By fostering an ethos of care, these industrialists developed the traditional notion of individual charity and redefined the responsibilities of business. They offered a different business model and showed society what was possible. Their **philanthropy** helped define **enlightened self-interest** as a viable approach to business. Some were committed Quakers who believed it was morally unacceptable to exploit their workers to make money. They were also owner-managers and so free to give their money to charity if they

Enlightened self-interest is the practice of acting in a way that is costly or inconvenient at present, but which is believed to be in one's best interest in the long term.

Table 5.1 Recent examples of questionable business practices

Company	Incident	Outcome
Boeing Co., 2003	Chief Financial Officer hired a member of the US Air Force while she was in a position to influence the award of contracts.	Chief Executive removes CFO for unethical behaviour, and Board then sacks CEO. Pentagon launches investigation into other Boeing practices it thought could be unethical.
Statoil, 2003, a Norwegian oil company	Accused of giving bribes to help its business in Iran.	Chief Executive resigns.
Enron, 2001, a US trading company	Company collapsed in 2001, amid allegations of accounting practices that artificially inflated earnings and share prices, to benefit top managers.	Thousands of employees lost jobs and pensions, senior managers received huge financial benefits. Court proceedings began iin 2004.
Arthur Andersen, 2002, accounting and consulting firm	Found guilt of obstructing justice by shredding thousands of documents to hide malpractice at Enron, one of its clients.	CEO resigns, firm collapses, and 85,000 staff around the world lose their job.
Parmalat, 2004, an Italian dairy company	Managers found to have claimed assets in bank accounts that did not exist, to cover growing liabilities. CEO accused of diverting £600m to his own use.	Italian investigators developing charges against senior managers, and possibly the company's auditors who failed to uncover the fraudulent transactions.
Shell, 2003, oil company	Admits overstating its oil reserves.	Chairman resigns, accused of creating a culture which encouraged misreporting, and for delay in admitting the error.

Sources: *Business Week*, 8 December 2003, 12 January 2004; *Financial Times*, 19 June 2003, 24 September 2003, 20 February 2004.

wished. Managers of today's public companies are responsible to the shareholders and the communities in which they exist.

Business Week publishes an annual report on philanthropic donations in the United States, the most recent analysing donations between 1999 and 2003. Bill Gates (founder of Microsoft) was at the top, having given $22 billion to health and educational causes. Michael Dell (Dell Computers, and number 6 in the list) gave $1.2 billion to children's healthcare, while the Walton family (founders of Wal-Mart, the world's largest retail chain) gave $750 million to education. A newcomer to the list was Catherine Reynolds who had made her money in the student-loan business – and donated $135 million to the arts and education. In 2003 Jeff Skoll (the ex-president of eBay, the online auction business) announced a gift of £5m to the Said Business School at Oxford University.

While the early philanthropists owned their business, most businesses today are owned by many individual or institutional shareholders, who are unlikely to have a coherent view of philanthropy. Moreover, the institutions have responsibilities to those holding insurance or pension policies. Donations to another group of people may damage their interests, so directors are likely to be cautious about philanthropy. However, public interest in corporate behaviour has encouraged most companies to set up corporate responsibility departments, and to report publicly on how they manage this aspect of their business. Some, like The Body Shop and the Co-operative Bank, make a point of testing decisions against criteria of responsible corporate behaviour.

Applied ethics is the application of moral philosophy to actual problems, including those in management.

A problem managers face is that problems in this area of **applied ethics** are complex, variable and constantly evolving. It is usually impossible to determine the definitively correct response to ethical issues in the workplace. It is often easier to ignore the problem by invoking the economic imperative rather than grapple with ethical concerns.

Activity 5.1   Looking for responsible business activity

- Collect at least two examples of organisations that seem to be taking the matter seriously by introducing explicit policies on environmental, social or ethical matters. You could check company websites to find what they say about responsible corporate behaviour – see Section 5.7 for some award-winning sites.
- What aspects of the company's operations does the policy cover?
- How did management develop the policy (which people or groups took part in forming it)?
- How do they ensure that people follow the policy and that it has the expected effects?

5.3   The role of business in society

There are two major schools of thought on the role of business in society. One follows Milton Friedman, a US economist who argued that the role of business is to create wealth by providing goods, services and employment. The other is based on the idea of corporate responsibility, where the emphasis is on public good rather than private gain.

The Friedmanite position

Milton Friedman was clear:

> [In a free economy] there is one and only one social responsibility of business – to use its resources and engage in activities designed to increase its profits so long as it stays within the rules of the game, which is to say, engages in open and free competition, without deception or fraud. (Friedman, 1962, p. 133)

As an economist, Friedman believed that operating business 'without deception or fraud' provided sufficient social benefit through the creation of wealth or employment. For a business to give money away to charitable purposes was equivalent to self-imposed taxation. He argued that those who had been put in charge of a business (the managers/board of directors) had no right to give away the owners' (the shareholders) money. They were employed to generate wealth for shareholders, not to give it away.

This stance sees the role of business in society as being solely concerned with operating in a competitive market economy. For an individual business to undertake any additional roles is to operate beyond the remit of business. Henderson (2001) develops this view, arguing that for business to take on responsibilities that are properly the domain of government would harm, rather than enhance, human welfare.

The corporate responsibility position

Others disagree with Friedman. They argue that business does not have an unquestioned right to operate in society and to do as it wishes. They see business as one of many subsystems in the wider social system. Just as society depends on business organisations for goods and services, those managing them should recognise that they depend on society. They rely on inputs from society in the form of employees, capital and physical resources. They also depend on socially created institutions to operate – such as laws, enforcement agencies and educational systems. People have (changing) expectations of business behaviour, and these are wider than generating economic wealth.

Writers on business ethics seek to encourage managers to give parity of esteem to ethical considerations, alongside the other factors that shape their decisions. For example, they argue that a manager using Porter's 'five forces' model should also consider the ethical dimension as a further force affecting competitive rivalry. Similarly, in conducting a PESTEL analysis, they advocate adding an ethical element to identify how issues under that heading may affect the business. This would position ethical issues on the same status as those to which managers conventionally pay attention when they decide what to do.

Activity 5.2 Critical reflection on the role of business

Try to gather information from acquaintances or relatives in business about which of these views (Friedman and corporate responsibility):
- they personally favour
- they believe has most influence on practice in their company.

- If you work in an organisation which view guides policy?
- Do you agree with that balance?
- How would practice change if the other view was dominant?

The **social contract** consists of the mutual obligations that society and business recognise they have to each other.

The idea of corporate responsibility reflects this interdependency: society and business depend on each other and have mutual obligations within a **social contract**. However, what people expect of companies changes. The Pinto case shows that producers had little interest in safety in the late 1960s – and most motorists were equally unconcerned; today companies see safety as a major selling point. Society has become more demanding, obliging governments to legislate to protect consumers from undesirable selling practices or faulty goods and services. Public demand for recycled or more environmentally friendly goods has prompted changes in corporate behaviour and products. Many now recognise the poor working conditions in countries that produce clothing and footwear and support the 'fair trade' movement by being awarded the Fair Trade Mark:

- Typhoo Tea changing its practices and being awarded the Fair Trade Mark
- Café Direct successfully competing with the coffee giants
- Smaller fair trade brands such as Green and Black, Divine and Dubble being able to enter the chocolate market.

Case question 5.1

- Did Ford act unethically at that time? Should the law be the only influence on a corporation's actions? What responsibilities do you think a major company has?
- Ford used cost–benefit analysis to decide what to do – could this have been improved? Was it a useful decision tool in this case?
- Imagine you were a Ford manager at this time. What would you have done, and why? List the social costs and benefits to the company and society of the alternatives to help you determine your answer.
- Imagine you worked for Ford as an engineer and were aware of this potential design fault. What would you do? What, if any, are your responsibilities to the customer and/or your employer?

Taking a Friedmanite position implies a relatively simple prescription for managers – do what is best for the business and the shareholders. However, if large numbers of consumers expect companies to behave in a socially responsible way, managers may be damaging shareholder interests by ignoring their wider responsibilities. The difficulty in trying to act in a socially responsible way is that people have different views about what is best for society. The next section introduces four views of an ethical action.

5.4 What is business ethics?

Before looking at some tools for exploring the ethical dilemmas facing management, use Activity 5.3 to locate your ethical position.

'Ethics' refers to a code of moral principles and values that guide the actions of people and groups. They set standards as to what is acceptable behaviour, especially when an action or decision may harm others. We can understand ethics more clearly if we compare the term with behaviours that are governed by law and by free choice. Figure 5.1 illustrates three categories of human behaviour. The first is that which falls within the legal framework – some types of action are the subject of legislation and can be enforced in the courts. It is illegal in most European countries for managers to allow effluent from

Activity 5.3   Reflecting on your ethics

You are walking down the street. There is no one nearby and you see: (a) a 50 pence piece, (b) a £5 note, (c) a £50 note, (d) a £100 note, (e) £1000.

- Do you keep it? Yes or no?
- The money you find was actually in a wallet with the owner's name and address in it. Does this make a difference?
- That name indicates to you that it belongs to: (a) a wealthy person, (b) a pensioner of modest means, (c) a single parent. Does this make a difference?
- Suppose there were some people nearby. Does this make a difference?

Explore your reasons for each of your decisions.

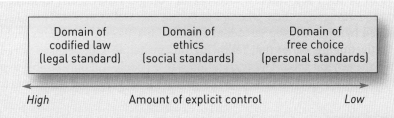

Source: From *Management*; 5th edition by Daft (2000). © Copyright 2000. Reprinted with permission of South-Western, a division of Thomson Learning. **www.thomsonrights.com**. Fax 800 730-2215

Figure 5.1

Three domains of human action

their factories to pollute rivers. At the other extreme are decisions which lie in the area of free choice – managers are free to choose how much to produce next week.

In between are decisions which have an ethical dimension. Laws do not prescribe behaviour, but managers are not completely free to choose: they are subject to some shared principles and values about acceptable behaviour in those circumstances. An ethically acceptable decision is one that both is legal and meets the shared ethical standards of the community – which of course can raise questions about how those standards are formed and expressed. Ethical dilemmas arise when all the choices may cause some harm, as well as bringing some benefit.

Most ethical dilemmas involve a conflict between the needs of the part and the whole – the individual and the organisation, or the organisation and society. For example, should a company monitor the websites that staff visit to check they are not downloading pornography or paedophilia? Should airlines routinely test pilots for alcohol before they go on duty? Should food companies design and advertise products in a way that adds to the obesity of children? Should a company extend a quarry in (and bring employment to) an area of outstanding natural beauty which has high unemployment? Philosophers have identified principles that people use to justify a decision – four of which are moral principles, utilitarianism, human rights and individualism.

- **Moral principles** This approach evaluates whether a decision is consistent with an accepted moral principle. Societies have developed certain rules that members generally accept (e.g. that people do not rob or deliberately injure each other) which are valid in many situations, including organisational ones (Honderich, 1995, pp. 887–8). If the decision fits such an accepted principle, it is ethically justified. This implies that a senior manager who accepts a high salary and bonus even if the company has performed badly would be acting unethically, as most people would feel it violated accepted ideas of fairness and equity.

● **Utilitarianism** This looks at a decision from the perspective of who gains from it, and suggests that what is good for the greatest number is right (Honderich, 1995, pp. 890–2). On this view, making 20 per cent of a company's workforce redundant during a business downturn can be justified if it enables the company to survive and save the jobs of the others.

● **Human rights** This is the idea that people have fundamental rights and liberties, and an ethically correct decision is one that best maintains the human rights of those affected. These rights could include those of consent, privacy, conscience, free speech, fair treatment, and to life and safety. Decisions that violate these rights may be unethical – so monitoring employee emails could be seen as violating the right to privacy; penalising an employee after an incident without hearing their side of the story would violate the right to fair treatment.

● **Individualism** This is the 'ethics of self-interest', which claims that an act is moral if it protects the individual's best long-term interests. Individuals should act in what they believe to be their self-interest, because in doing do they learn to make practical accommodations for others who are pursuing *their* self-interest. This idea was first developed by the philosopher Adam Smith in his *Wealth of Nations*, published in 1776, reflecting his belief that following this principle will, perhaps paradoxically, result in the general good. The assumption is that people will only be able to maximise their personal self-interest if they do things that others value and are willing to pay for.

Activity 5.4 Justifying decisions

Think about times when you have justified a decision you have made on the grounds that (a) it was fair to those affected, (b) it was the right thing to do, (c) it was the best option for yourself, and (d) more people gained than lost. Which of the ethical philosophies outlined above matches each reason?

These tools from moral philosophy enable a more informed and analytical insight into management dilemmas. They may, however, lead to more questions than answers. Table 5.2 identifies some questions under each philosophical approach.

In this chapter, as in much of management, there are no right or wrong answers. These philosophical tools enable people to recognise the arguments that others use to support an action. They can then evaluate them critically, and suggest an alternative philosophy that leads to a different decision. This makes the debate more transparent, and shows the complexities of business ethics and of major management decisions.

Table 5.2

Dilemmas within each philosophy

Philosophy	Dilemma
Moral principles	Who determines that a moral principle is 'generally accepted'? What if others claim that a principle leading to a different decision is equally 'accepted'?
Utilitarianism	Who determines the majority, and the population of which it is the greatest number? Is the benefit to them assessed over the short term or the long term?
Human rights	Actions usually involve several people – what if the decision would protect the rights of some, but breach the rights of others? How do you compare them?
Individualism	Whose self-interest is central to the debate? What if the action of one damages the self-interest of another?

Activity 5.5 Visualising a management dilemma

Consider the situation facing the European car manufacturers. The industry has built too much capacity in Europe so that there is a gap of 7 million units between production capacity and forecast demand. Many manufacturers are considering the closure of one entire manufacturing plant.

Imagine you are the chair of a global motor company. While as a global company you are profitable, in Europe you are losing money. Your shareholders expect profits. You need to reduce costs across the group, and you are aware that this high level of overcapacity in Europe suggests closing a plant. You know that other car manufacturers are also considering this, and that union and government opposition to that approach is growing.

- Your company has several plants in Europe. What criteria should you use to select the one to close? Do you have enough information to make this decision? What other options are available? Do you ask for further information on the social impact that any closure might have?
- Might it be better to reduce the size of several plants rather than close one? Should you take social concerns into account in your decision?
- Can you determine the solution provided by each of the ethical philosophies?

Activity 5.6 introduces another level of complexity.

Activity 5.6 Working on a bigger dilemma

What if the problem is not that of reducing capacity but of relocating it? Demand in the developing world is potentially immense, especially for more basic models. So the major companies are tempted to reallocate capacity to these areas.

- Should a plant be relocated from an economically dependent and deprived European region to a country in South-east Asia whose government is offering favourable incentives? The plant itself is currently not losing money but in the long term the financial returns will be higher in Indonesia or China. It could operate with a cheaper workforce, less demanding health and safety regulations, weak trade unions and few environmental conditions. It would also be contributing to the economic development and modernisation of the area.
- What are the ethics of moving production from one country to another – and to whose standards should you operate when abroad?
- Look for companies that have created policies stating how they will operate across the world – which international standards do they adhere to?

The fact that there are no easy answers leads some to argue that business ethics has not come to terms with practice. They criticise it for being too general, theoretical and impractical for a manager to apply (Stark, 1993), especially when compared with the apparent clarity of data on financial performance (though see Chapter 18). There is an additional philosophy called **ethical relativism** that managers, especially those in corporations operating in many countries, use to justify what they do.

Ethical relativism is the principle that ethical judgements cannot be made independently of the culture in which they are made.

Ethical relativism

Ethical relativism argues that morality depends on a particular society. There is no absolute ethical standard independent of cultural context. What is right is determined by what members of a culture or society says is right, so that what is right in one place may be wrong in another.

This view allows managers to use different standards depending on the culture or country in which they are conducting business. In some countries bribes are an expected part of business. For companies that operate internationally ethical relativism is a convenient philosophy, especially when their competitors are from countries with different moral codes. This causes difficulties for individual managers who may have personal ethical views, which may be more absolute than relative. The issue arises in dramatic ways when major deals for armaments or construction projects are offered to competitive tender from international companies.

Think again about some of the ethical decisions you have already considered in this chapter. Does ethical relativism help? Would it depend on what country you were in? It has been suggested that 'a bribe is only a bribe when it is taken as such'. Does ethical relativism help us think about the validity of corporate gift giving? Some managers consider that it is standard industry practice to exchange gifts and therefore this creates a level playing field – so it cannot be an incentive. Others have a policy that no gift to employees from any other company is acceptable as it may affect employees' judgement.

Activity 5.7   Accepting a gift

In your job as a buyer for a multinational company you receive a gift from one of your minor suppliers at Christmas. It is: (a) a calendar with their brand name on it, (b) a pen set with their brand name on it, (c) chocolates, (d) a bottle of wine, (e) a bottle of whisky, (f) a case of whisky.

- Which offer can you accept, if any? What should you do with it? What would stop you accepting these gifts?

- Should your employer have a policy that outlines solutions to such ethical problems so as to avoid the variety of approaches which may otherwise develop?

- Research a chosen company to find out whether they have an ethics policy. What areas of concern are highlighted? Do you think all companies should state their ethical expectations? Can they be the same across the world, in all countries?

Ethical decision-making models

A problem with using ethical criteria such as those set out above is that this directs attention towards the ethical beliefs of the individual, which are the product of the unique features of the person's life history. It therefore tends to ignore the social context in which they work and in which they confront ethical decisions. Conversely, those who see ethics as derived from the culture of the organisation emphasise the socialisation process by which people are accepted into it, and come to accept the prevailing ways of working. This approach ignores the scope for individual choice and action.

A widely used way of reconciling these two apparently contradictory perspectives is to adopt an **ethical decision-making** framework. Models of this kind examine the influence of both individual characteristics (such as personal value systems) and organisational contexts (such as its structure and distribution of power) on ethical decision making. One example of this approach is that put forward by Trevino (1986), which, as Figure 5.2 shows, sees ethical (or unethical) behaviour as the result of the interaction between individual and situational components. Faced with an ethical dilemma (such as those in Activities 5.5 and 5.6), an individual's way of thinking about ethical problems is then moderated by individual and situational moderators. Bartlett (2003) contains an extensive review of this and similar models.

Ethical decision-making models examine the influence of individual characteristics and organisational policies on ethical decisions.

Case question 5.2

- Did Ford make the right decision *for that time*?
- Would it be the right decision *now*?
- If you have given different answers, why is that?

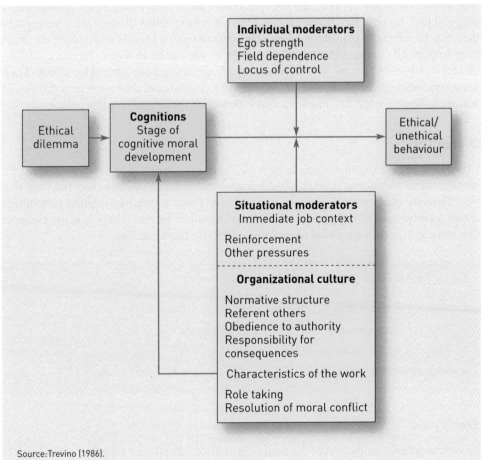

Source: Trevino (1986).

Figure 5.2

Trevino's model of ethical decision making

5.5 | Corporate responsibility

Corporate responsibility is the awareness, acceptance and management of the implications and effects of all corporate decision making.

Like ethics, people interpret the term **corporate responsibility** in different ways. The core idea is that corporate actions have social implications, and that managers have a responsibility to act in ways that benefit society as well as the organisation. That said, people have different views of what actions most benefit society, or which members will benefit. Stakeholder theory enables managers to take account of these different interests.

Stakeholder theory

Chapter 3 introduced stakeholder theory – the idea that people in organisations have responsibilities to internal and external stakeholder groups with an interest in, or who are affected by, what the organisation does. As well as shareholders these will typically include customers, employees, suppliers and the communities in which the organisation works. Many now add the natural environment to the list of wider responsibilities.

Shareholders

Ethical investors are people who only invest in businesses that meet specified criteria of ethical behaviour.

Traditionally management has assumed that the main concern of shareholders lies in maximising their wealth. This assumption is largely accurate, though with two qualifications. Shareholders will vary in their time horizon. If they judge performance over the short term they will have no time for considerations of social responsibility. If they take a longer view they may be willing to consider evidence that managing in a socially responsible way helps long-term profits. Several unit trusts only invest in companies that meet certain guidelines on social responsibility, and have attracted significant funds from '**ethical investors**'. These are people who place social priorities higher than maximising their own personal wealth and are willing to invest in companies that follow clear socially responsible policies.

Customers

Customers expect organisations to provide them with goods and services. Within the specific relationship that is established between individual customers and the organisation there are many implicit, unstated conditions. There is often an implied assumption about quality, durability, performance, safety and other factors. There is some evidence that more consumers are aware of issues of corporate responsibility.

Case questions 5.3

- What did customers of Ford expect of the Pinto at that time?
- Would customers today have different expectations?
- Does that affect your view of the company's actions?
- What other stakeholders would have been affected by Ford's decisions?

Employees

As well as gaining employment from an organisation, employees expect organisations to meet a range of needs such as security, safe working conditions, rewarding work and fairness, as well as esteem and personal development. The area of human resource management has developed to explore the legal as well as ethical implications of a range of issues in the workplace: equal opportunities, promotion practices, employment continuity, remuneration and substance abuse.

Suppliers/business associates

Suppliers have expectations of organisations with whom they trade. They expect to be paid in full by the agreed date. Many are now developing much closer long-term relationships with customers (see Chapter 19) and so the range of mutual expectations between the parties is wider and more complex.

The community

The immediate area plays a central part in the creation of the corporation, its reputation and its continued operation. It was recognised earlier that with the creation of large multinational companies the direct link between manufacturers and their local community is not so distinct. However, the communities in which corporations operate are where their customers and workers live and so remain important.

The natural environment

The natural environment features more prominently in business discussion, prompted by public interest in the environmental impact of corporate actions. However, the level at which recognition and respect for the environment is demonstrated by a corporation varies considerably. The Body Shop International has led the way for many consumers in allowing them to indicate their preference for environmentally friendly goods. Such companies recognise the wisdom of considering not only the environment of the organisation but also the impact of the organisation on its environment.

Ecover – environmentally friendly cleaning www.ecover.com

Ecover (a Belgian company) makes washing-up liquid, dishwasher tablets and a range of clothes cleaning products. The company uses ingredients based on renewable raw materials that degrade more quickly than those of its competitors. The problem for Ecover is that its philosophy has not translated into sales. The company, which began in the late 1980s, has an annual turnover of only £12m – microsopic by detergent industry standards. At first its products did not work as well as conventional ones, but technical developments enable the company to claim that they now have a product that is still environmentally friendly, but works almost as well as conventional ones. The UK is their largest market, with 44 per cent of sales, mainly through supermarkets. It also has alliances with charities and pressure groups such as Greenpeace and the World Wide Fund for Nature.

Source: Company website (www.ecover.com) and various published sources.

Management comes to pay more attention to environmental and other issues as it recognises the links between corporate action and wider implications. This stakeholder approach to business is providing a competitive advantage for companies, as it can enhance corporate reputation, customer loyalty and goodwill, as well as media coverage.

The problem in such decision making is not just determining who is affected, but whose interests should have priority. Considering the community as one group quickly

> ## Activity 5.8 Revising Activity 5.5
>
> ● Using the stakeholders listed above, try again to solve the dilemma of closing the factory in Activity 5.5. Whose 'stake' within the company should be given priority above the others? What did you decide?
>
> ● Do you think that, as a global company, you have specific local responsibilities or a major responsibility to maintain a profitable company for the good of shareholders, customers and workers worldwide?

> ## key ideas Planet Earth
>
> Planet Earth is 4600 million years old. If we condense this to an understandable concept, the Earth is a 46-year-old person.
>
> ● Not until the age of 42 did the Earth begin to flower.
>
> ● Dinosaurs appeared when the planet was 45.
>
> ● Mammals arrived only 8 months ago.
>
> ● Modern man has been around for *four hours*.
>
> ● The Industrial Revolution began *one minute ago*
>
> ● ... and during those 60 seconds of biological time, man has made a rubbish tip of paradise.
>
> Source: Adapted from *Paradise Lost – Countdown to Destruction*, Greenpeace (**www.greenpeace.com**).

shows that this contains many interests – employees' families, neighbours, government agencies and so on. There may be divisions within these groups, and Figure 3.5 shows how to assess their respective power and interest. This approach can focus corporate thinking upon the impact of decisions and help managers recognise the social fallout from corporate activities. It alerts them to potential problems and helps them formulate suitable strategies to address current responsibility issues.

The issues on which people expect companies to act responsibly are constantly changing in response to events, public opinion and media campaigns. This contributes to the evolving nature of corporate responsibility. For example, while the area of equal opportunities was until recently an ethical concern it has gained a critical mass, which has resulted in an improved legal reality for many groups that had previously suffered discrimination in the workplace.

Evaluating corporate responsibility

Figure 5.3 presents a way of evaluating how managers in an organisation have responded to ideas and opportunities of socially responsible behaviour. Four possibilities (Carroll, 1999) are placed in a continuum, from economic responsibilities on the left-hand side through to discretionary responsibilities on the other.

This builds on the ideas in Figure 5.1, and locates ethical issues between the areas of legal and freely discretionary actions.

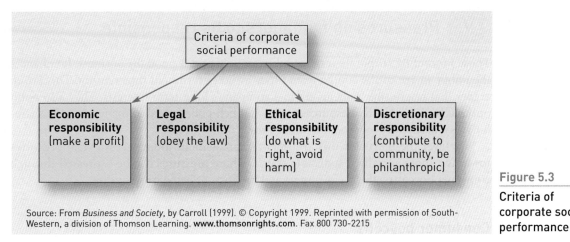

Source: From *Business and Society*, by Carroll (1999). © Copyright 1999. Reprinted with permission of South-Western, a division of Thomson Learning. **www.thomsonrights.com**. Fax 800 730-2215

Figure 5.3

Criteria of corporate social performance

Economic responsibilities

Here managers focus only on meeting the best economic interests of the company and its shareholders. They act in ways that they believe will support that aim, regardless of the effects on communities, environmental pollution or any other consideration. Taken to its extreme this can mean evading legal requirements by, for example, falsifying records used to calculate tax, or exporting weapons in breach of a United Nations arms embargo.

Legal responsibilities

All organisations are subject to a wide and increasing range of laws setting out what they can and cannot do. A company that intentionally fails to meet these requirements would be failing this criterion of responsible behaviour – polluting air or rivers, selling faulty goods or providing potential investors with misleading information. These issues reflect areas that society has at various times decided were sufficiently important to pass laws regulating company behaviour in the wider interest. Some companies will take these responsibilities seriously – but will go no further. If what they do is legal, then that is the only criterion they will use – even if the decision has damaging consequences for others.

Ethical responsibilities

This area includes actions that are not specified by law, and may not serve a company's narrow economic interests. Managers take these actions because they believe they meet some wider social interest, such as discouraging tobacco consumption, protecting the natural environment or supporting a socially disadvantaged group.

Discretionary responsibilities

This covers actions which are entirely voluntary, not being shaped by economic legal or ethical considerations. They include anonymous donations with no expectation or possibility of a pay-back, sponsorship of local events and contributions to charities.

These criteria can be used to evaluate corporate performance in this area. Many will be able to point to activities that are ethical and/or discretionary: the issue then is the scale and magnitude of the decisions under these areas.

5.6   Pressures on managers to be responsible

Those promoting corporate responsibility argue that it is good for business. It enhances the public image of the company and may avoid government intervention. This group argues that responsible policies are in a company's long-term interests. They also point out that business has the resources to pursue such policies and in many cases the shareholders will support some action in this area.

Whatever the merits of this argument, management today faces several pressures towards a more socially responsible stance. These pressures can be expressed through consumer boycotts, ethical consumers and the costs of being irresponsible.

Consumer boycotts

Boycotts reflect the active disapproval of society and can generate media interest that then spreads the news of corporate misdemeanour across the globe. They register the displeasure of consumers with the corporation. There are examples of boycotts achieving their objectives (such as when Barclays Bank was persuaded during the 1980s that its involvement in South Africa supported apartheid), but sustained boycotts are rare. However, they remain a way in which groups of consumers who disapprove of a company's actions can express their views publicly.

Ethical consumers

Ethical consumers are those who take ethical issues into account in deciding what to purchase.

Ethical consumers take ethical issues into account when making a purchase: they will try to avoid buying products from companies that damage the environment, deal with oppressive regimes, have a poor record on animal rights or pay low wages. Such consumer action is not solely a negative response to corporate activities. Many shoppers use their 'ethical purchase votes' (Smith, 1990) to support the actions of companies that conduct business responsibly. Café Direct and Green and Black Chocolate have been the biggest successes of 'fairly traded' products. Many other companies are seeing the advantage in being responsible in areas of social concern and are responding to society's demands. For example, Reebok and Nike have introduced codes of practice to eliminate child labour in the production of their products, in the face of increasing concerns about the exploitation of children in the clothing industry in the developing world. The major supermarkets hold an increasing stock of organic and fair trade products. The Co-operative Bank (**www.cfs.co.uk**) produces an annual survey on the shopping habits of a sample of consumers who join their ethical panel: the latest 'ethical consumerism research report' is available on the ethical policy pages of the website.

Negative publicity

Campaigning organisations monitor corporate actions and report adverse information widely to their members and through the media. Conversely, several also work closely with companies to advise and encourage best practice and to help them audit their corporate responsibility policies. Leading international groups include:

- Business in the Community
- Flora and Fauna International

- Friends of the Earth
- Greenpeace
- FairTrade Alliance.

Competitive advantage

Some companies have positioned corporate responsibility at the heart of their business, as the issues reflect the underlying beliefs and values of founders and senior managers. Their activities gain media attention and increase customer loyalty with little advertising. Familiar examples are The Body Shop (see Part 1 Case) and the Co-operative Bank. This approach worked well for The Body Shop, and helped it become a major retailing group. However, its unique position was eroded – partly by its own success. Animal testing of cosmetics (one of the firm's early campaigns) was stopped, and more people are aware of environmental issues. So what was a strategically valuable position, bringing great benefits to those it aimed to help, came under competitive threat. The financial performance of The Body Shop was poor for several years, though it improved in 2003.

Another example of a company taking a strategic approach to responsible business practice is the Co-operative Bank (now known as Co-operative Financial Services) which was founded upon cooperative principles in the 1870s. It launched its present ethical policy in May 1992 and is now one of the leading examples of this approach.

Co-operative Financial Services www.cfs.co.uk

management in practice

The Bank calculated that in 2002 it lost £4.4m worth of business from companies it turned down on ethical and environmental grounds. It gave the information in its annual Partnership Report for 2003, including turning down business worth £275,000 from a container board manufacturer because of evidence that it was buying raw materials from tropical rainforests in an unsustainable fashion. It also lost more than £240,000 by declining to work with weapons companies supplying oppressive regimes.

While the ethical stance clearly led to the loss of some business, the bank's customer value analysis showed that the policy had a positive impact on bank profits overall. The Annual Report for 2003 (now under the CFS name) shows that the ethical policy was responsible for 30 per cent of pre-tax profits (up from 24 per cent the previous year). The bank calculates this figure from an analysis of the reasons customers give for opening accounts and buying other products from the bank – 47 per cent cited the ethical policies as important or most important reasons for opening an account (37 per cent the previous year).

Source: *Financial Times*, 6 May 2003; CFS *Annual Report 2003* at **www.cfs.co.uk**.

Activity 5.9 Critical reflection on ethical policies

Visit the CFS website (**www.cfs.co.uk**).

- Which partners does it identify?
- Take any one of those partners, and find out from the site what the company believes to be their main concerns, and how it tries to meet them.
- How does CFS monitor its ethical performance?

If you work in an organisation:

- Which, if any, of these sources of pressure have influenced management practice?

Others have begun to follow sustainable policies not out of philanthropy but because it fits their business strategy. Using energy efficiently, avoiding or recycling waste and treating staff with respect are established daily practices in many companies – some of whom now present such practices as part of a responsible image.

Many companies differentiate themselves from others less by the products they sell, and more by ideas, emotions and images that their brand conveys. Managers who allow their brand to become associated with being hostile to people, communities or the natural environment are taking a grave risk. Adopting a range of responsible practices gives them the opportunity to imbue the brand with the positive themes that coincide with the beliefs of many customers. It can pay to cultivate an image of corporate responsibility – as Paul Sternberg, communications director of Business in the Community, said:

> A growing number of companies are beginning to understand that the way they respond to wider community issues does have an impact on their profitability and their long-term reputation.

Sustainable coffee www.kraft.com

Kraft Foods, which buys about 10 per cent of the world's coffee, has agreed to blend sustainably produced beans into its main European brands, which include Kenco, Jacobs and Carte Noire. The deal with the non-profit Rainforest Alliance is the most serious attempt by a big coffee purchaser to tackle the crisis that has pushed down the commodity price, which is often below the cost of production. This threatens the livelihood of 25m coffee farmers, and the long-term supply of beans. Said a senior Kraft commodity manager:

> **We need to make sure we can get the coffees we need 20 years from now. This is not philanthropy. This is about incorporating sustainable coffee into our mainstream brands as a way to have a more efficient and competitive way of doing business.**

Kraft will buy £5m of Rainforest Alliance-certified coffee in the first year, paying farmers a premium of 20 per cent. The company also plans to introduce a brand of coffee aimed at the away-from-home market, which includes universities and other institutions seen as sensitive to issues of global equity.

Brokers said the deal would send a signal to the entire supply chain, particularly producers, that roasters are concerned about more than just the purity of the coffee and may pay more to know that the beans have been produced using good environmental practices by workers who are adequately paid.

Source: *Financial Times*, 7 October 2003; Company website at **www.kraft.com**.

Clearly, as Egan and Wilson (2002) point out, some companies have been able to balance 'responsibility and corporate success, and that the enlightened shareholder understands that it is in his or her best long-term interests that the company performs' (in a way that satisfies all stakeholders), (p. 174).

5.7 Managing company ethics

Managers who wish to improve the level of socially responsible behaviour in their company use several methods to do so, including leading by example, codes of ethics, ethical structures and supporting whistle-blowers.

Leading by example

Researchers in this area believe that the example of those at the top of the company is crucial to a company's stance on responsible behaviour. Leaders set the tone for an organisation by their actions. If others can see that they are acting in line with stated ethical principles, their credibility will rise and others are likely to follow suit. Conversely, leaders who are known to be engaging in malpractice are likely to encourage that to spread throughout the business.

Code of ethics

A code of ethics is a formal statement of the company's values on ethics and social issues. Some set out general principles about the company's beliefs on matters such as quality, employees or the environment. Others set out the procedures to be used in specific ethical situations – such as conflicts of interest or the acceptance of gifts. The effectiveness or otherwise of such codes of ethics depends on the extent to which top management supports them with sanctions and rewards.

Ethical structures

These are the formal systems and roles that a company may create to support the practical implementation of ethical behaviour. An ethics committee is a group of executives appointed to oversee the working of the company's ethics policy. It may provide rulings on difficult ethical issues, and take disciplinary action against those who break the rules. It may also be responsible for clarifying, developing and communicating the policy to employees and other relevant stakeholders – through training programmes, for example.

Large companies (including Vodafone) are appointing directors of corporate responsibility. The box gives an indication of their role in that company.

Director of corporate responsibility at Vodafone www.vodafone.com

Charlotte Grezo was appointed as director of corporate responsibility at Vodafone in 2001. Her brief was to create a group-wide strategy for corporate responsibility. Her team works closely with staff in the operating companies to decide the issues to put to the group operational review committee which sits just below the board.

She refers to corporate responsibility simply as being responsible in the way we run our business and interact with society and the environment, saying:

> We don't define what corporate responsibility is. It's the outside world that decides what it expects of business. That changes the whole time.

Amongst the concerns raised by investors was 'adult content'. The company is working to address these concerns, but as a multinational must be careful not to impose moral standards or limit customer choice. The company issues an annual responsibility report, which lists the areas of current activity. These are supply chain standards (such as ensuring that raw materials for handsets are mined sustainably); responsible marketing (preventing children accessing pornography via a handset); electro-magnetic fields and health; energy efficiency; handset recycling; waste management; and wireless applications with social benefits.

Source: Company website at **www.vodafone.com**.

Ethical reporting and websites

Ethical audits are the practice of systematically reviewing the extent to which an organisation's actions are consistent with its stated ethical intentions.

Most companies now include a statement on their social responsibility policies in their Annual Reports, and post them on their websites. This can include an **ethical audit** which profiles current practice in various areas of the business, and identifies topics for possible attention. A survey in 2003 ranked reports in terms of their reporting on the 'triple bottom line' – a company's economic, social and environmental impact. European companies took the top seven places:

- Co-operative Financial Services (**www.cfs.co.uk**)
- Novo Nordisk (**www.novonordisk.com**)
- BAA (**www.baa.com**)
- BT (**www.bt.com**)
- Rio Tinto (**www.riotinto.com**)
- Royal Dutch Shell (**www.shell.com**)
- BP (**www.bp.com**)

5.8 Corporate governance

How managers deal with issues of ethics and corporate responsibility will be strongly influenced by the framework of corporate governance within which they work. This establishes who the organisation is there to serve, how this should be decided, and by whom. The issue arises because in capitalist economies ownership almost inevitably becomes separated from operational control – managers gradually become detached from ownership. Initially the founder provides the capital and runs the business. If it grows, it will require further capital which is supplied (depending on the local economic system) by external parties.

In Anglo-American economies this usually means issuing shares in the business, with the result that ownership becomes increasingly diffuse – the shares are held by many separate individuals and financial institutions such as pension funds, which cannot practically supervise management decisions closely, and in any case lack the knowledge to do so – so it becomes possible for managers to run a corporation to serve their own ends. Scandals such as those at Enron and Parmalat have only served to give new urgency to long-running debates about what mechanisms would best ensure that managers act in the interests of shareholders.

While some see corporate governance as being essentially a matter between managers and shareholders (Sternberg, 2004), others broaden the debate to include a wide range of stakeholders and considerations (Egan and Wilson, 2002). On this view, the framework of governance should be designed to ensure that managers act in the interests not only of shareholders, but of a wider range of stakeholders – such as communities, customers and environmental campaigners.

Whichever view people take, the key concept in corporate governance is accountability – 'that individuals and institutions are answerable for what they do: they must account to others for their conduct and for their use of resources' (Sternberg, 2004, p. 41). In Anglo-American systems the main mechanisms for corporate governance are:

- the powers and responsibilities of directors
- the requirement that directors report periodically to shareholders
- the requirement that certain appointments and types of action require explicit shareholder approval.

Directors and senior executives

There is a fundamental difference between the responsibilities of directors and those of senior executives. The main responsibility of the board of directors is to set policy, authorise key decisions, appoint senior executives and auditors, monitor executive performance and decide executive pay. The responsibility of senior executives is to implement decisions of the board – though of course they will usually have been active in proposing and designing those decisions. A key issue is the extent to which directors are able and willing to challenge executive actions: several scandals appear to have arisen when directors, for whatever reason, failed to probe sufficiently closely the information that executives provided to them.

As well as the main board, large companies will usually have several board committees, overseeing different aspects of the business – see Management in Practice.

Corporate governance at BP

BP has five senior committees, each of which includes several non-executive directors – people with relevant experience from outside the organisation.

Chairman's committee	Comprises all the non-executive directors and deals with broad issues of governance, including matters referred to it for an opinion from any other board committee.
Audit committee	Monitors all reporting, accounting, financial and control aspects of the executive management's activities.
Ethics and environment	Monitors all non-financial aspects of the executive management's activities.
Remuneration committee	Determines performance contracts, targets and the structure of rewards for the group chief executive and the executive directors.
Nominations committee	Identifies and evaluates candidates for appointment or reappointment as directors.

Source: *BP Annual Report and Accounts 2003*.

Periodic reports

A second mechanism for ensuring accountability is through providing information about performance to shareholders or a wider group of stakeholders. The annual report and accounts are intended to give shareholders the information they need to judge the performance of the directors and senior executives. These accounts are based on financial data from within the company, but are scrutinised by specialist firms of external auditors (appointed by the shareholders at the annual meeting). The audit ensures that the accounts have been compiled in a way that conforms to current accounting standards (see Chapter 18), and give a true and fair view of the financial state of the company.

Responding to external pressures, many companies now produce Corporate Responsibility Reports, setting out how well they have met their targets in these areas.

Annual meeting

The Annual General Meeting (AGM) is another mechanism for ensuring directors are accountable to shareholders, as they are an opportunity for the shareholders to review company performance. As well as approving (or not) the annual report and accounts, the shareholders can hear statements from the Chairman and other directors (usually including the Chief Executive and the Finance Director), and question them about their work and plans. They also appoint directors and auditors, and vote on any specific decisions as required by the company's rules – such as donations to political parties.

These meetings can be attended by anyone holding shares in the company. Many pressure groups buy a token share in companies of which they disapprove and attend the AGM to challenge certain company actions, notably on environmental issues.

Other systems

The accountability systems sketched above reflect the methods typically used in countries modelled on UK and American practice. Other countries have different systems. German companies are structurally different from Anglo-American ones, most notably in having what is called a 'two-tier' board structure. German law has required (since the nineteenth century) that companies have both a management board and a supervisory board. The management board consists of senior executives and is responsible for managing the company. The supervisory board, which may not include executives, is responsible for appointing and supervising the management board. It consists of external representatives (including employees) of those with an interest in the company, such as suppliers and bankers.

Japanese companies typically have a single board, made up of executives of the company, and of the many other companies with shares in the business. The distinctive feature of Japanese companies is that they are closely linked to other companies in related lines of business, often with mutual shareholdings.

There is a continuing debate about the respective merits of alternative governance systems. For example, some argue that the Anglo-American system encourages a short-term view of the business, since shareholders can press managements to pursue short-term gains at the expense of long-term investment, and thus discourage them from giving due weight to environmental or other issues. Conversely, critics of the German and Japanese systems claim that they protect managers from the force of market pressure, producing lower returns on capital invested. Continuing concern about corporate performance, whether from a shareholder or broader stakeholder perspective, ensures that governments will continue to look closely at ways of strengthening corporate governance frameworks.

Summary

1 Identify some of the major ethical issues within business practice:
   ● These potentially arise at all stages of the transformation process, from the way in which the company deals with suppliers (fair terms of payment) and potential employees (discrimination or equal treatment), how it conducts its internal processes (fair treatment of staff) and its relationship with customers (misleading labels). It also includes the way it interacts with the competitive and wider environment (pollution).

2 Compare contrasting views on the role of business within society:

- Milton Friedman's view that the only function of business is to act legally in the interests of shareholders.
- The social responsibility view that business has wider responsibilities, since it depends on aspects of the society in which it operates. It recognises the legitimate claims of a range of stakeholders and seeks an acceptable balance between them.

3 Outline four ways of justifying a decision as ethical:

- Moral principles – the decision is consistent with generally accepted principles.
- Utilitarianism – the decision that benefits the greatest number of people is the right one to take.
- Human rights – decisions that support one of several human rights (such as privacy) are right.
- Individualism – decisions that serve the individual's self-interest are right – in the long run they will benefit society as well.

4 Explain how consumers can influence corporate practice:

- Boycotts, ethical consumers, negative publicity, and awareness of the costs of being irresponsible.

5 Illustrate the potential competitive advantage from responsible corporate practice:

- Several cases were presented.

6 Outline the structures and frameworks for corporate governance that managers can use to encourage responsible behaviour:

- Structures for encouraging ethical behaviour include leading by example, codes of ethics, ethics committees, ethical audits and ethical reporting.
- Corporate governance frameworks depend on systems for providing adequate information, and this implies clarifying the roles of directors in relation to executives, annual reporting and annual meetings of shareholders.

Review questions

1 Identify two recent examples of corporate philanthropy. What are the benefits to the donor and the recipient?

2 List the reasons why you think 'business ethics' is important to the success of firms.

3 Summarise the Friedman and social contract positions on social responsibility with an example of each being applied.

4 List three major ethical issues facing management at the present time, and give reasons for your choices.

5 Describe in your own terms each of the four schools of ethical thought and illustrate each with an example of how it has been used to justify a decision.

6 Outline the ways in which the consumer can affect business practice, and decide whether this is effective or not.

7 List the stakeholders in the Pinto case and prioritise them in order to justify the decision to manufacture.

8 What could Ford staff have done to promote the communication of these difficult issues to higher management?

9 Who should determine a company's level of acceptance of social responsibilities?

10 Are The Body Shop International and the Co-operative Bank responsible companies or are they operating a form of enlightened self-interest?

Concluding critical reflection

Think about the way your company, or one with which you are familiar, approaches issues of corporate responsibility. Review the material in the chapter, and perhaps visit some of the websites identified. Then make notes on these questions:

● What examples of the issues discussed in this chapter are currently relevant to your company?

● In responding to these issues, what assumptions about the role of business in society appear to have guided what people have done? Are they closer to the Friedmanite or the social responsibility view?

● What factors such as the history or current context of the company appear to have influenced the prevailing view? Does the approach appear to be right for the company, its employees, and other stakeholders? Have any stakeholders tried to challenge company policy?

● Have people put forward alternative ways of dealing with these issues, based on evidence about other companies? If you could find such evidence, how may it affect company practice?

Further reading

Megone, C. and Robinson, S.J. (2002), *Case Histories in Business Ethics*, Routledge, London.

Clarke, F.L. (2003), *Corporate Collapse: Accounting, regulatory and ethical failure*, Cambridge University Press, Cambridge.

Egan, J. and Wilson, D. (2002), *Private Business – Public Battleground*, Palgrave, Basingstoke.

Develops the case for companies that are structured in a way that takes account of a range of stakeholder interests.

Jackall, R. (1998), *Moral Mazes: The world of corporate managers*, Oxford University Press, Oxford.

Focuses on the managerial role in tackling the complexity of ethical issues.

Ackroyd, S. and Thompson, P. (1999), *Organizational Misbehaviour*, Sage, London.

Looks at the larger corporate view of 'organisational misbehaviour'.

Bartlett, D. (2003), 'Management and business ethics: a critique and integration of ethical decision-making models', *British Journal of Management*, vol. 14, no. 3, pp. 223–235.

Useful as an overview of recent attempts to resolve the dilemmas between organisational and individual approaches to ethical questions.

Weblinks

These websites have appeared in the chapter:

www.ecover.com
www.cfs.co.uk
www.kraft.com
www.baa.com
www.bp.com
www.shell.com
www.bt.com
www.riotinto.com
www.novonordisk.com
www.greenpeace.com

Visit two of the business sites in the list, and navigate to the pages dealing with corporate responsibility, sustainability or corporate governance.

● What are the main concerns that they seem to be addressing?

● What information can you find about their policies?

● Compare and contrast the concerns and policies expressed on the sites.

● Gather information from the media or pressure group websites which relate to these companies. What differences are there between these perspectives? What dilemmas does that imply that managers in these companies are dealing with?

> Annotated weblinks, multiple choice questions and other
> useful resources can be found on
> www.pearsoned.co.uk/boddy

In 2004 BP was the world's second largest oil and natural gas producer, having recently grown through mergers and joint ventures – such as its deal with major Russian producer TNK in 2003. By its nature it is engaged in international business, with a strong interest in managing the political, economic and technological aspects of the environment. Some criticise the oil industry for contributing to climate change – though companies differ in how they respond to these and other issues of corporate responsibility.

BP is a British registered company, but 40 per cent of its assets are in the United States, and it is that country's largest gas producer. It does 80 per cent of its business outside the UK, and is inevitably involved with political considerations. CEO John Browne suggests that Britain must encourage companies such as his to remain there, by introducing acceptable taxation and related policies. With so much business in the United States, the company is also sensitive to policy there – such as US policy on the Middle East. In 2001 he observed that while BP would be perfectly entitled to follow Royal Dutch Shell and make production agreements with Iran, it would be 'inappropriate' for the company to ignore US sanctions on Iran.

Though Browne has been in charge since 1995, the strong position of the company (recognised in a *Financial Times* survey as one of the world's best-managed companies) is the culmination of a period of radical change in line with the changing environment. This began when Robert Horton was chairman and CEO between 1990 and 1992 and continued under both David Simon and John Browne.

When David Simon took over in 1992 it was clear the organisation needed to revise its strategy to reverse losses, and to repay billions of dollars of debt. Simon moved fast to implement a three-year plan with a simple name: '1-2-5' – cut debt by $1 billion per year, build profits to $2 billion per year and keep capital spending below $5 billion per year. Over the following two years he sold many marginal businesses and reduced staff by almost 50 per cent, with a large reduction in middle management. He narrowed BP's core

BP plc. 2005

interest to petroleum only – 'finding it, extracting it, shipping it, refining it, converting it and selling it', as he put it – through three main divisions: exploration, oil and chemicals.

He is described as 'wily, subtle, diplomatic, and knowledgeable about the undercurrents of the British establishment'. Despite his mild demeanour, he has a mind like a steel trap. 'He knows the figures like the night sky', says a colleague, 'and that allows [him] to navigate [his] way through a group as complex as BP.' He is good at anticipating issues that no one else has focused on.

David Simon has said that setting simple goals is an important part of developing a culture of continual performance improvement. He tells the symbolic story of his visit to a multi-million dollar oil-drilling platform:

I asked the workers, 'What are you doing?' 'Drilling oil', they replied. 'How much money are you making?' I asked them. The workers had no idea. I wanted to know how much money they were making there, and they said they could tell me how much oil they produced. I told them I wasn't interested in how much oil they produced. The platform is a factory, for me. Where's the money? That oil is relevant only in terms of money for the shareholders, not in terms of barrels.

Since then, Simon has made it clear to BP employees that they should be cost and profit conscious. He has a golden rule for attaining goals:

Targeting is fundamental to achieving. If you do not target, you do not measure and you do not achieve.

One top executive described Simon's accomplishment:

What he has done so well is pull the company together in a very calming way, setting clear targets and telling people how they can achieve them.

An outside analyst commented:

I think you have to put an awful lot of BP's recovery down to him. A complete cultural change has been put into place.

John Browne took over from Simon in 1995, and continued to persuade the board and managers that BP must keep changing. He has stated that:

To achieve distinctive performance from a portfolio of first-class assets requires continuous development of our organisation and management processes. We are further decentralising the organisation in order to encourage personal initiative and creativity. Simultaneously, we are strengthening the sharing of experience and best practice so that BP's total competitive strength is greater than the sum of its parts.

Yet the firm prides itself on its collegiate management style, with large amounts of power passed to senior managers below CEO level. So bosses have to rule with a bit of medieval cunning, using strength of personality to chivvy along this potentially fractious group of mini-potentates.

Browne is said to lead by power of intellect. Everything pivots around his ability to absorb vast amounts of information, keeping on top of what is happening anywhere in the company. He carries a heavy workload, even by the standards of multinational bosses.

He is extremely bright, extremely well-organised and is a very good lateral thinker. Very strong on the numbers side, financially extremely astute, but the same also goes for the technological side. He understands geopolitics and has got the nose for a deal.

He has greatly increased BP's oil reserves not only by exploration but also by acquisitions and joint ventures. In 2003 he reached a deal with the Russian oil producer TNK, for £32 billion. This was a strategically important deal as apart from its intrinsic merits it opened the way for further deals related to Russian oil and gas reserves – which are the largest in the world. It also fitted a wider political strategy of developing Russian fields to reduce the West's dependence on Middle Eastern supplies. Rather than own the new company, the deal is for BP to own 50 per cent, and take management control. This was to help ensure that Russian investors felt equally treated, and to secure their help in lobbying the Russian government.

Dealing head-on with the industry's impact on the environment has become one of the keynote principles of his leadership.

These are issues of tremendous complexity. Do you want a clean environment or do you want hydrocarbons? False trade-off. You have to ask if you want both, and in the service of gaining both usually comes technology and better ways of doing things. The industry hasn't handled it well. Consumers want to consume more, they recognise the consequences of consumption, they don't want to shoulder the burden of that themselves, so they transfer it on to the shoulders of the oil and gas companies ... The reality is it's a shared responsibility. We can do a lot but so must consumers.

Browne has impressed green campaigners, who see him as the first oil leader to take the issues seriously. This stance on green issues is dictated by BP staff. Browne asked how they felt about it and the answer was that they worry about global warming, their children talk to them about it, they think the company ought to get on the front foot about it. When Browne asked for suggestions internally on how the company might hit new, greener targets he was deluged with email: 'People believe that this is a principal value of this company: green.'

One potentially controversial aspect of the deal with TNK is that some of the facilities they will now be managing in Russia are old, and could raise serious environmental concerns. While no longer a member of the group lobbying to open the Alaskan National Wildlife Refuge for drilling, Browne believes they should be opened. Although he reckons that new technology would allow this to be done with minuscule damage, he recognises that this would bring BP into conflict with some environmental lobby groups: 'While this would dent Sir John's carefully cultivated "green" image, he claims to have always been in the business of pragmatic trade-offs between nature and the world's insatiable thirst for oil.'

Sources: European Case Clearing House Case No. 497-013-1, 'British Petroleum: transformational leadership in a transnational organisation', by Elizabeth Florent-Treacy and Manfred Kets de Vries, 1997; *Financial Times*, 21 January 2003; *Business Week*, 27 October 2003; and other sources.

Part case questions

- Analyse the five forces acting on BP. Which of them appear to bring the greatest threat to the company?
- Construct a PESTEL analysis to establish the main aspects of the external environment that affect BP.
- Make a list of stakeholders for BP. Assess their sources of power, and rank them according to the likely degree of influence they hold.
- In what ways will managing in BP, with such an international exposure, be different from managing in a national company with no international business? List the three most significant.
- What has BP done to indicate that it is acting in a socially responsible manner?
- A major issue for the company is to balance different stakeholder groups. What argument, from an ethical standpoint, could BP use to support the case for opening new oil fields in the Alaskan National Wildlife Refuge?

Part 2 Skills development

To help you develop your skills as well as knowledge, this section includes tasks which relate the key themes covered in the Part to your daily life. Working through these will help you to deepen your understanding of the topics, and develop skills and insights which you can use in many situations.

Task 2.1 Dimensions of the competitive environment

Select an industry in which you have an interest (perhaps for a potential career), and write a one- to two-page paper describing the main competing players in that industry, and the major issues the industry is facing. Identify the companies in which you are interested by checking articles about the industry in sources such as **www.hoovers.com**, **www.ft.com** or **www.economist.com** (these sites are mainly subscription only once you get beyond the headlines) and then go to the companies' websites for more detailed information.

Task 2.2 Dimensions of the general environment

Changes in a country's demography have significant implications for managers, as they affect the resources available as inputs to organisations, the outputs that are likely to be in demand, and aspects of the transformation process (such as the growing desire for flexible working times). Information about these trends is available from official websites – such as (in the UK) **www.statistics.gov.uk**.

Go to that site, or the equivalent in your country, and find out: (1) the total number of people in the country now, and the predictions for 5 and 10 years on; (2) the changing age distribution; (3) the number of people with Internet access; (4) other data which interest you as a student of management.

What implications may your results have for business in five years' time?

Task 2.3 Comparing industry environments

While all organisations face opportunities and threats from their competitive and general environments, these differ. Summarise the work you have done in the earlier activities so that you can set out the main threats and opportunities facing one industry. Then compare your conclusions with another student who has studied a different industry. List those factors that are the same, and those that are different.

Task 2.4 Tracking multinationals

Since an increasing amount of business is done through multinational businesses, it pays to become familiar with some of them. Select three businesses that have a major international presence (preferably not limited to the most obvious ones) and go to their websites. Find out about their main products and services, the countries in which they operate, the broad structure of the organisation, and their statements about social responsibility. You could also check their careers page.

Compare what you have found with a colleague, identifying what is similar about the companies, and what is different.

Task 2.5   Country studies for a multinational

Suppose that one of the companies you have worked with in Task 2.4 is considering launching a valuable new product in one of the following countries: Malaysia, Singapore, Brazil or Australia. One issue in their decision will be the status of regional trading alliances affecting these countries. Use the Internet to establish whether these countries are part of any such alliances. If so, compile a one-page report on that alliance for presentation to the company. The managers of the company would also like information on the main PESTEL factors in each country. Prepare a one-page report outlining the main PESTEL factors for one of the countries identified. They are also interested in what environmental constraints they may face in that country – try to include a commentary on this aspect, as in some industries it will be critical part of an investment decision, if you can find adequate information.

PLANNING

Part 3

Introduction

This part examines the generic management activities of planning and decision making, and then looks at two substantive applications of these ideas – to strategy and marketing respectively. Both areas depend on understanding the environment of the business and the stakeholders within it. They also both depend on building an internal capability to deliver whatever direction management decides upon.

Chapter 6 provides an overview of planning in organisations, setting out the types and purposes of plans, and the tasks which help people to prepare a comprehensive and useful plan. While all these tasks are likely to be part of the process, their shape will always depend on the circumstances for which a plan is being made.

Decision making is closely linked to planning, made necessary by finite resources and infinite demands. People in organisations must continually decide on inputs, transformation processes and outputs – and the quality of those decisions affects organisational performance. Chapter 7 therefore introduces the main decision-making processes, and contrasts several theories of decision making in organisations.

Chapter 8 outlines the strategy process, and introduces techniques that managers use to analyse the options facing businesses of all kinds. This analysis can then lead to clearer choices about future direction.

A critical aspect of that is the markets which the organisation chooses to serve. Chapter 9 argues that marketing is not just a functional area within the organisation, but is closely allied to the core strategy process. Like strategy, it uses external and internal analysis to establish a way forward, and like strategy it depends on other functions if the organisation is to meet the customer expectations profitably.

The Part Case is The Virgin Group, illustrating the interaction of the external environment with the developing corporate and marketing strategies.

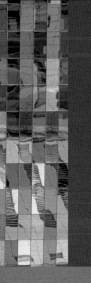

Chapter 6

Planning

Aim

To describe the purposes of planning in organisations, and illustrate the iterative tasks that people can perform when they plan.

Objectives

By the end of your work on this chapter you should be able to outline the concepts below in your own terms and:

1 Describe different types of plan and the potential benefits of planning

2 Outline the seven iterative steps in making a plan

3 Understand and use models to gather information relevant for planning

4 Explain the problem of multiple goals and evaluate a statement of goals

5 Use a model to identify the action and resources a plan should specify

6 Explain the procedural and wider factors that affect whether a plan is implemented successfully

7 Consider the value of planning in rapidly changing conditions.

Key terms

This chapter introduces the following ideas:

planning
goal
business plan
strategic plan
strategic business unit
operational plans
corporate strategy
SWOT analysis
critical success factor
sensitivity analysis
scenario planning
mission statement
stated goal
real goal

*Each is a term defined within the text, as well as
in the glossary at the end of the book.*

© DSM

In 1902 the Dutch government created Dutch State Mines (DSM) as a state-owned coal mining company. Although it stopped mining coal years ago, its headquarters are at Heerlen in the south of the Netherlands, close to the original mines. It has been through many changes since then, and is now mainly in the speciality chemicals business. The Dutch government sold the business in 1989 and it now operates entirely in the private sector.

By 2004 the company had more than 24,000 employees working in over 200 offices and production sites in 40 countries. It has a decentralised structure, with 15 business groups that are empowered to perform all business functions. They form three strategic clusters – Life Science Products, Performance Materials and Industrial Chemicals. Each of the 15 companies is headed by a Business Group Director, who reports directly to the Managing Board of Directors. This has five members, responsible for strategy, the portfolio (the range of businesses in the company) and resource allocation.

Until the mid-1990s the company operated a traditional strategic planning process, with a Corporate Planning Department setting out 3–5 year plans, supplemented by an annual budget cycle. Senior managers became dissatisfied with this as it was 'owned' by the Corporate Planning Department, and had become a routine 'numbers' exercise.

The company therefore introduced a new arrangement. There is a Corporate Strategic Dialogue every three years, in which about 50 executives take part. It develops a long-term strategy for the business, deciding on the portfolio, investment priorities and geographical spread. The results of the last such exercise – 'Vision 2005: Focus and Value' – are now being implemented through the activities of the business groups.

Within Industrial Chemicals is DSM Melamine, which supplies about one-third of the world demand for melamine, a chemical used to make highly resistant surfaces. It is run by Hans Dijkman who realises that, as a commodity business within a company whose strategy is now focused on speciality chemicals, it will be hard to persuade the Board to provide the resources he needs to develop this business.

Source: Based on extracts from Bloemhof, Haspeslagh and Slagmulder (2004). Copyright 2004 INSEAD, Fontainebleau, France.

Case questions

Visit the DSM website (see above).

- What are the main elements of 'Vision 2005: Focus and Value'?
- What effects may the plan have had on what managers in the business do?
- What kind of environment do you think the company is operating in (Chapter 3, Section 3.4)?

6.1 Introduction

The DSM story outlines how managers in that company have developed an approach to planning that seeks to balance the need for overall strategic direction with a high degree of autonomy for the main business units. DSM operates around the world in several technologically advanced businesses – like many other prominent businesses. They too face the issue of how to identify relevant trends in the business environment.

Changes in these external forces create both opportunities and threats to an organisation's position – but above all they create uncertainty. Planning offers a systematic way to cope with uncertainty and adapt to new conditions. It enables people to set objectives for an activity, to specify and coordinate actions to achieve them, and to monitor progress. It is concerned with both ends (what to do) and means (how to do it).

Some plans are very informal – they are not written down, nor are they widely or consistently shared. This can work perfectly well in managing domestic and social life, or in small businesses where the owner-manager and a few staff can see what everyone is doing and adapt to changing circumstances. Some larger organisations also manage with little formal planning – though they run the risk of duplication or of ignoring important information.

The focus here is on more formal plans, which express the goals of a business or unit for some future period, and the actions to achieve them, in written form. When senior management at the electronics company Motorola decided in 2002 that they needed to act quickly to bring the company back to profit, they developed a five-point turnaround plan which included replacing many senior managers, developing new products, reassessing whether to continue in all of the current businesses, cutting costs and reducing debt. When two entrepreneurs decided to create the City Inn hotel chain they planned in detail the kind of hotels they would be – which included contemporary, city centre, newly built, 'active and open' atmosphere, and a consistent room design across the group. Plans like this can then be communicated to relevant players, to ensure that actions in different places and at different times are coherent.

Figure 6.1 provides an overview of the themes in the chapter. At the centre are seven generic tasks in making a plan – but people vary in the order in which they do them, and in how much attention they give to each. This depends on the type of plan, and the person's perspective on planning. How they manage these issues will affect whether planning helps or hinders performance.

The chapter begins by outlining different types of plan, and the potential benefits of planning. The following sections outline in turn the seven generic steps in making a plan

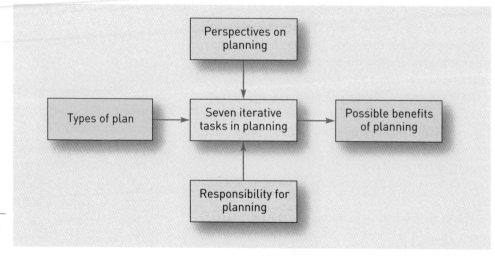

Figure 6.1

An overview of the chapter

– while stressing throughout that their form depends on circumstances. A final section examines different ways of locating responsibility for planning within an organisation.

6.2 Types of plan

While people use different terms, the activity of **planning** essentially involves establishing the objectives (or **goals**) for the task being planned, specifying how to achieve them, implementing the plan and evaluating the results. Goals are a desired future state of an organisation or part of it, and planning to meet them typically includes allocating the resources and specifying what people need to do. It also includes setting interim goals and schedules that enable people to assess progress towards completing the plan. The activity produces a plan which people can use to guide their actions.

People seeking funds to start a new business or expand an existing one invariably need to prepare a **business plan** – a document which sets out the markets the business intends to serve, how it will do so and what finance they require (Blackwell, 2004). They do so to convince potential investors to lend money. Managers in divisions of a business seeking capital investment or other corporate resources also need to convince senior managers to allocate a share of the capital budget to them – which they do by presenting a convincing plan setting out their divisional goals and plans.

Plans vary in the level and breadth of the business they cover and in how far ahead they look. **Strategic plans** apply to the whole organisation or business unit. They set out the overall direction for the business, are broad in scope and cover all the major activities. Chandler (1962) defined strategic plans as determining 'the basic long-term goals and objectives of an enterprise and the adoption of courses of action and the allocation of resources necessary for carrying out these goals'. Strategy is concerned with deciding what business an organisation should be in, where it wants to be and how it is going to get there. These decisions have long-term effects, involve major resource commitments and usually require a series of consequential operational decisions.

In a large business there will then be tactical or divisional plans for each major unit of the business. If subsidiaries operate as autonomous **strategic business units** (SBUs) they probably develop their plans with limited inputs from the rest of the company. This is because an SBU consists of a distinct set of products aimed at a limited market, with little connection to other parts of the company.

Planning is the task of setting objectives, specifying how to achieve them, implementing the plan and evaluating the results.

A **goal** is a desired future state for an activity or organisational unit.

A **business plan** is a document which sets out the markets the business intends to serve, how it will do so and what finance they require.

A **strategic plan** sets out the overall direction for the business, is broad in scope and covers all the major activities.

A **strategic business unit** consists of a number of closely related products for which it is meaningful to formulate a separate strategy.

Fiat's restructuring plan www.fiat.co.uk

In 2003 Fiat Group, owner of the Italian car maker, decided to retain the struggling Fiat Auto, and to invest in returning the company to profit. The plan included:

● cutting manufacturing costs by £700m

● increasing Research and Development expenditure by £750m

● reducing European capacity to 1.6m vehicles a year

● boosting sales in Europe by 9 per cent with the launch of new models

● investing £100m a year for three years to expand the dealer network.

Within that broad plan, the sports car division which makes the Alfa Romeo was making its own plans to restore excitement to the range before re-entering the US market in 2007.

Source: *Business Week*, 21 April 2003.

Operational plans detail how the overall objectives are to be achieved, by specifying what senior management expects from specific departments or functions.

Corporate strategy 'is concerned with the firm's choice of business, markets and activities' (Kay, 1996), and thus it defines the overall scope and direction of the business.

Operational plans detail how the overall objectives are to be achieved. They are narrower in scope, indicating what senior management expects individual departments or functions to do, so that they support the overall plan. So there may be a 'family' of related plans forming a hierarchy – a strategic plan for the organisation, tactical plans for each division and several operational plans for departments or teams. Each will contain linked objectives and plans that become more specific as they move down the organisation. Management hopes that those at lower levels, or for separate divisions, are consistent with the overall **corporate strategy**. Table 6.1 shows this hierarchical arrangement, and how the character of plans changes at each level.

Strategic plans are usually long term in form, looking up to three years ahead – though in businesses with long lead times (such as oil or aircraft manufacture) they include some longer-term analyses, however tentative. Most businesses also develop short-term or annual plans which deal mainly with the financial aspects of the business and set out budgets for the coming year, but necessarily include sales, marketing, production or technology plans as well. EasyJet announced in 2003 that it planned to grow capacity by 20 per cent in the following year, and set out a plan showing the financial and other implications of enlarging the fleet, recruiting staff and opening new routes. These short-term plans are expected to be consistent with the longer-term strategy, but take account of immediate developments and changes since the strategic plan was prepared.

Table 6.1

The planning hierarchy

Type of plan	Organisational	Tactical – divisional or strategic business unit	Operational
Level	Organisation-wide	Particular division, function or market	Functions/Departments
Focus	Direction and strategy for whole organisation	Direction and strategies for particular markets	Resources and actions needed to deliver corporate objectives
Nature	Broad, general direction	More detail on required goals and tasks	Specific detail on goals and tasks
Timescale	Long term (2–3 years?)	Medium (1–2 years?)	Short term (up to 1 year?)

Figure 6.2 contrasts specific and directional plans. Specific plans are clearly defined and leave no room for interpretation. They have specific, unambiguous, mainly quantified objectives and leave little room for misunderstandings. For example, a manager who seeks to increase his or her unit's work output by 8 per cent over the next 12 months could establish specific procedures, budget allocations and schedules of activities to reach that goal. In some situations that could work well – but not in conditions where the future is unpredictable.

In conditions that are highly uncertain, management must be flexible so that they can respond to unexpected changes. In these circumstances directional plans are preferable. They give a looser guidance – providing focus but not locking managers into over-specific goals or courses of action. Instead of detailing a specific plan to cut costs by 4 per cent and increase revenue by 6 per cent in the next six months, managers might formulate a directional plan for improving profits by 5 to 10 per cent over the next six months. The flexibility inherent in directional plans must be weighed against the loss of clarity provided by specific plans.

Managers also prepare many special-purpose plans for projects or aspects of the business. For example, they may have plans for disaster recovery (after, say, a major computer failure or terrorist action), and develop project plans to organise and implement specific

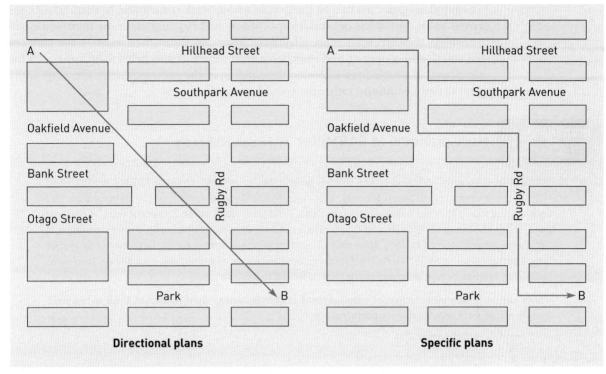

Figure 6.2 Specific and directional plans

changes, such as introducing a new computer system or launching a new product. When The Royal Bank of Scotland took over NatWest Bank in 2002 managers quickly developed a collection of over 160 interlocking plans to incorporate NatWest operations into those of RBS to secure the cost-savings they had promised investors. On a much smaller scale, a manager in a department who needs to recruit a new member of staff will make a simple plan to organise the process. Standing plans specify how to deal with routine, regularly recurring issues like recruitment or dealing with customer complaints. People plan throughout an organisation, at all levels and in all degrees of formality.

6.3 Purposes of planning

Planning, if done well, brings four main benefits – it can clarify direction, motivate people, help use resources efficiently and provide a way to measure progress. The act of planning may in itself add value, by ensuring that people make decisions on the basis of a wider range of evidence than if there was no planning system (Sinha, 1990). If done badly, planning has the opposite effect, leading to confusion, frustration and waste.

Good plans give direction to the people whose work contributes to them. If all concerned know where the organisation or work unit is going and how their work will contribute, they can work more effectively. They can adjust their work to the plan (or vice versa), and cooperate and coordinate with others. It also helps them cope with the unexpected. If people have a good understanding of the end-result, they can more easily adapt to new conditions, rather than wait for new directions.

management in practice · More planning at SABMiller www.sabmiller.com

South African Brewers (SAB) purchased the US brewer Miller in 2002, to form SABMiller. The chief executive of the company, Graham Mackay, was reported to be very critical of the company he had bought, saying that it was not a finely tuned, focused, effective organisation. In recent years it had lost market share to Anheuser-Busch and Coors. He would be exporting the South African company's direct management style to Miller's Milwaukee home, bringing a tighter focus on planning, objective setting and appraisal to Miller staff. The typical middle manager at Miller will be working to clearer objectives as well as having their pay more closely linked to performance:

> **There will be a very much stronger management of consequences than there has been in the past. People will be held accountable for performance.**

Source: *Financial Times*, 22 November 2002.

FT

Planning can reduce overlapping activities, and conversely ensure that someone is made responsible for each significant activity. A plan helps people coordinate their separate tasks, so saving time and resources; without a plan they may work at cross-purposes. If people are clear on the end-result they can spot inefficiencies or unnecessary delays in the activity, and correct or eliminate them.

key ideas · Does planning help new ventures?

Delmar and Shane (2003) developed a theoretical model of why planning would be useful in new ventures, and then tested their hypotheses in 223 Swedish new businesses. They started from the idea that planning facilitates goal attainment in many domains of human action, and in the area of new venture creation helps by:

- enabling founders to make decisions more quickly, by identifying missing information, than with trial and error learning
- providing a tool for managing supply and demand of resources to minimise bottlenecks
- identifying actions to achieve broader goals in a timely manner.

Their hypotheses were that business planning:

- reduces the hazards of new venture disbanding
- facilitates product development in new ventures
- facilitates venture-organising activities in new ventures.

Their study gathered extensive data from the 223 firms at their start-up in 1998, and then at regular intervals over the next three years. Statistical analysis of the results provided support for each of their hypotheses, leading them to conclude that planning did indeed support the creation of successful new ventures.

Source: Delmar and Shane (2003).

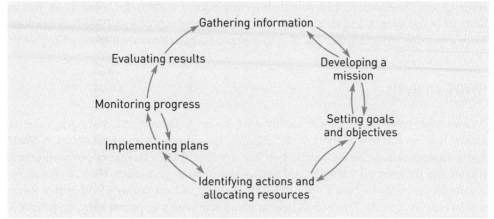

Figure 6.3

Seven iterative
tasks in making
a plan

Finally, planning establishes goals and standards that help people to monitor progress. Until goals and targets are clear, no one can be sure whether or not they have completed the task. Plans also include time-scales, setting out the tasks and their time of completion. This enables people to compare actual progress against the goals, identify significant deviations, and either adjust the goal or change the way resources are being used. A plan, however directional in form, enables people to monitor and control how they are using resources and whether they are adding value to them. These purposes of planning apply to all types of plan – strategic or operational, long-term or short, and special purpose.

Figure 6.3 shows the seven generic tasks which people can perform when they make a plan. They use them iteratively, often going back to an earlier stage when they find new information that implies, say, that they need to reshape the original goals. And of course they may miss a stage, or spend too little or too much time on them: the figure only indicates a way of analysing the stages of planning.

6.4 Gathering information

Any plan depends on information that people can use to guide their choices in building the plan. This includes both informal, soft information gained from casual encounters with colleagues, competitors and customers and formal analyses of economic and market trends. This will reflect the form of plan, but an indication of the range available can begin with the strategic level – people use simpler version for plans which are more limited in level or scope.

Chapter 3 outlined the general and competitive environments, and those involved in planning will usually begin by drawing on what information they can about these contexts. To do so they collect, analyse and interpret information from many internal and external sources. Companies, especially with the aid of computer-based information systems, hold a great deal of valuable information about their customers. The main benefit of loyalty cards for retailers is that they can track each customer's purchasing patterns and map them against the personal information they hold about them, from the form they filled in to obtain the card. Tesco has been particularly skilled at analysing customer data, and this is one of the reasons for its success in the UK market, as it enables their planners to predict likely future demand, especially for new products.

External sources include government economic and demographic statistics, industry surveys and general business intelligence services. Managers also commission market research on, for example, individual shopping patterns, attitudes towards particular firms or brand names, and satisfaction with existing products or services. Many firms use focus groups to test consumer reaction to new products (for more on this see Chapter 9).

SWOT analysis

A **SWOT analysis** is a way of summarising the organisation's main strengths and weaknesses relative to external opportunities and threats.

At a strategic level, planning will usually combine an analysis of external environmental factors with an internal analysis of the organisation's strengths and weaknesses. A **SWOT analysis** does this, bringing together in one document the external opportunities and threats and the internal strengths and weaknesses of an organisation. The external analysis would probably be based on a PESTEL analysis and on Porter's (1980) five forces model (see Chapter 3). These tools help to identify the main opportunities and threats in the external world that people believe could affect the business. Internally, they would seek to analyse the strengths and weaknesses of the resources within, or available to, the organisation (Grant, 1991) – such as a firm's distinctive research capability, or its skill in integrating acquired companies.

A SWOT analysis at Cable & Wireless www.cw.com

Cable & Wireless is a global telecommunications business. One of its most successful areas has been its Caribbean operation, but in 2002 it experienced growing competition from new rivals, especially a company called Digicel. C&W took the threat sufficiently seriously to commission a report that compared the company with Digicel, using the SWOT technique. This provides a useful public example of the technique.

Strengths	Opportunities
• Established customer base • Diversified revenue structure that can absorb losses • Strong knowledge of local culture • Strong technical support	• Take advantage of regionalisation and economies of scale • Offer more coverage before Digicel arrives • Market growth potential • Ability to remain the market leader
Weaknesses	**Threats**
• C&W network not as good as Digicel's • Capital spending restrictions • Poor image across the Caribbean • Low motivation of sales team	• Global entrants to market • Loss of key staff to competitors • Rapid technological innovation • Poor market image

Source: Based on *Financial Times*, 10 December 2002.

Given the diversity and complexity of organisational environments it is easy to have too much information. Management needs to focus on the few trends and events that are likely to be of greatest significance. De Wit and Meyer (2004) report that in relation to the general environment Royal Dutch/Shell focus on critical factors such as oil demand (economic), refining capacity (political and economic), the likelihood of government intervention (political) and alternative sources of fuel (technological).

Critical success factors analysis

In considering whether to enter a new market, a widely used planning technique is to assess the **critical success factors** (Hardaker and Ward, 1987) in that market. These are the things which customers in that particular market most value about a product or service – and they therefore play a key role as people plan whether to move into a line of business. Some value price, others quality, others some curious aspect of the product's features – but in all cases they are things that a company must be able to do well to succeed in that market.

> **Critical success factors** are those aspects of a strategy that *must* be achieved to secure competitive advantage.

Forecasting

Forecasts or predictions of the future are often based on an analysis of past trends in factors such as input prices (wages, components, etc.), sales patterns or demographic characteristics. All forecasts are based on assumptions. In relatively simple environments people can reasonably assume that past trends will continue, but in uncertain conditions they need alternative assumptions. A new market might support rapid sales growth, whereas in a saturated market (e.g. basic foods, paid-for newspapers) it might be more realistic to assume a lower or nil growth rate.

Forecasting is big business, with several organisations specialising in the sale of general or industry analyses to business and government, using techniques such as time-series analysis, econometric modelling and simulation. However, because forecasts rely heavily on extrapolations of past trends, users need to question their inherent assumptions as they interpret the results.

Sensitivity analysis

One way of testing the assumptions is by including a **sensitivity analysis** of key variables in a plan to increase confidence in the choice made. A plan may assume that the company will attain a 10 per cent share of a market within a year: what will be the effect on the calculations if they secure 5 per cent, or 15 per cent? What if interest rates rise, increasing the cost of financing the projects? This enables those making the decision to compare the robustness of the options they are examining and so be better able to assess the relative risks. It gives people greater confidence in the decision, or alternatively may show that it is too risky to be worthwhile. Johnson and Scholes (2002) give a worked example that illustrates the method (pp. 396–7). This task can now be done very easily using computer packages.

> **A sensitivity analysis** tests the effect on a plan of several alternative values of the key variables.

Scenario planning

Forecasting is still relevant in dynamic and complex situations but cannot be relied on as uncertainty increases and where the rate of environmental change shows signs of discontinuity (marked and often rapid changes from trend). In these situations some companies build scenarios of what the future may look like. Johnson and Scholes (2002, p. 107) note that:

> **Scenario planning** is an attempt to build plausible views of a small number of different possible futures for an organisation.

> **scenario planning** does not attempt to predict the unpredictable (but) considers multiple, equally plausible, futures. These scenarios are not just based on a hunch; they are logically consistent but different from each other.

Scenarios typically begin by considering how some major forces in the external environment such as the Internet, an ageing population or climate change might affect a company's business over the next 5–10 years. Doing so can bring new ideas about their environment into the heads of managers, thus enabling them to recognise new and previously unthinkable possibilities. No one can predict the future, but advocates (Van der Heijden, 1996; Schwartz, 2003) claim two main benefits of scenario planning. The first is that it discourages reliance on what is sometimes referred to as 'single-point forecasting', that is a single view of the future; and the second is that it encourages organisations to develop contingency plans or strategies to cope with outcomes that depart from the most likely case scenario.

However, few companies use the technique as it is time consuming and costly. Moreover, while systematic thinking about possible futures may yield new information, that only becomes useful if senior managers make noticeable adjustments to strategy as a result.

 **Scenario planning at Shell** www.shell.com

In today's global and fast-changing environment, extrapolating from historical performance using medium- and long-term forecasting techniques has not proved very reliable, and managers in some companies use scenarios to test their plans. Royal Dutch/Shell was one of the earliest to adopt this approach. Traditionally, Shell planners would forecast refining plant requirements for several years ahead by extrapolating from current demand. However, the volatility in the oil market makes accurate prediction difficult. Shell underestimated oil demand in the 1950s and 1960s and overestimated it in the 1970s. Rather than rely on a single projection, Shell develops a range of possible scenarios for, say, future crude oil supply. One scenario could be that it continues as now, another that many new fields become available and a third that Saudi Arabia experiences major political turmoil and ceases to export oil. Major capital investment projects are evaluated against each scenario, with the aim of ensuring that they have a positive return under each. Scenario planning helps generate projects that are more robust under a variety of alternative futures. It also encourages people to ask deeper questions – for example about whether the oil companies, or the political leaders in the oil-rich countries where the wells are drilled, would be deciding the supply of oil.

'Scenario thinking now underpins the established way of thinking at Shell. It has become a part of the culture, such that people throughout the company, dealing with significant decisions, normally will think in terms of multiple, but equally plausible futures to provide a context for decision making' (Van der Heijden, 1996, p. 21).

Source: Van der Heijden (1996).

A combination of PESTEL and five forces analysis should ensure that managers recognise all the major influences in the external environment. Forecasting and scenario planning then enable them to consider the possible implications for the business at the start of the planning process.

DSM – the case continues   www.dsm.com

The planning process introduced at DSM in the 1990s requires that each Business Group conducts a Business Strategy Dialogue (BSD) about every three years. The purpose of a BSD was to provide a consistent method and terminology to structure the development process and improve its quality. Usually the whole management team of the business group conducts the dialogue, supported by specialists from within the organisation. The reviews have five phases:

- **Characterising the business situation** Collecting information on questions such as what business are you in, who are the competitors, how attractive is the industry in terms of growth and profitability, how do you compare with competitors, what are the main trends?
- **Analysing the business system (macro)** Analysing the industry in which the business unit competes, using Porter's Five Forces model. It also analyses the strategies that competitors are using, to identify the different ways in which a business could compete in an industry.
- **Analysing the business system (micro)** This looks at the internal processes of the business, including its internal value chain, benchmarking of functions, and the strengths and weaknesses of the unit.
- **Options and strategic choice** This phase compares the results of earlier phases – the competitive environment and the Key Success Factors required, and its internal capabilities to deliver those. This allows the unit to choose which strategic option it should pursue and what is required for successful implementation.
- **Action planning and performance measurement** The chosen strategy is then turned into an action plan and linked to performance measurement. The team sets performance indicators such as market share, new product development, customer satisfaction and cost per unit of output. These enable managers to monitor the implementation of the strategy.

Each unit reviews progress on the implementation of its BSD quarterly in its management reporting, and annually in the ASR. With these building blocks from the businesses, the ASR monitors progress on DSM's overall execution of its CSD, like 'Vision 2005: Focus and Value'.

Source: Based on extracts from Bloemhof, Haspeslagh and Slagmulder (2004). Copyright 2004 INSEAD, Fontainebleau, France.

Activity 6.2   Developing a mission

- What benefits can you envisage that managers at DSM Melamine obtain from this company's process?
- How does it compare with the planning process at your organisation?

6.5   Developing a mission

A clear plan depends on being clear about the ultimate purpose of a task – whether this is a small local project or a major organisational change. This seems obvious, but many managers are instinctively drawn towards action rather than planning – especially the more abstract ideas of agreeing on purposes. Yet until people involved in planning have spent time thinking and debating the wider purpose, and can set out why the job is worth doing, they will find it difficult to agree on details.

A fashionable medium for expressing purpose at the level of the whole organisation is the **mission statement**, which is a way of expressing a realistic vision of what the future could be if the plan were to succeed. The same idea can be expressed at departmental or business unit level – setting out what participants see as distinctive about their activities.

A **mission statement** is a broad definition of an organisation's operations and scope, aiming to distinguish it from similar organisations.

key ideas — A method for clarifying purposes

Start by writing the name of the project at the bottom of a large sheet of paper, and then ask 'why?'. Answer by one or more sentences beginning with the phrase 'in order to ...', and write these answers above the project task. For each of these answers, repeat the process of asking 'why?', and answering with 'in order to ...', writing your answers on the sheet. Repeat this several times, until it makes sense to stop – by which time you will probably have some broad, long-term purposes which the project can serve.

Figure 6.4 illustrates the method, and the chart will need to be worked over several times to ensure agreement and understanding among those working on it.

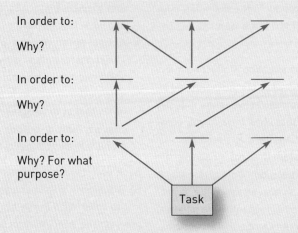

Figure 6.4 Method for clarifying long-term purposes

Source: Boddy (2002), p. 142.

Many projects begin life as a very ill-defined set of ideas and possibilities, and here again spending time clarifying the overall purpose can help to focus the subsequent work on specific objectives. Boddy (2002) points out that many project managers are faced with a very vaguely defined problem as they start to plan their project. For example:

> The size and specification of the project – the tonnages of oil to be made, and the specifications of the products – was not handled well by the commercial functions within the company. (p. 194)

In this example, the project is still vague and poorly defined, a messy problem with an unclear scope. One way to reconcile apparently conflicting objectives is to try to relate them to a wider set of purposes by developing a 'why/how network'. This can make it easier to relate immediate, tangible and possibly conflicting objectives to a wider, and perhaps less conflicting, set of purposes for the activity. The Key Ideas box sets out the method.

While being clear about purposes can be valuable, there is a danger that people become too enthusiastic about them and set them at unrealistic levels, ignoring the project's limited resources. The same danger accompanies organisation-wide visions and strategic mission statements, discussed in Chapter 8.

6.6 Setting goals and objectives

Goals (or objectives – the terms mean the same thing) are desired outcomes for individuals, groups, and entire organisations. They turn the generalities of mission statements

Table 6.2

Examples of
published goals

Company	Published goals
Unilever – 'Path to Growth' 2000–2005	Annual sales growth of 5–6% Operating margins of over 16% Earnings per share growth of 12%
British Airways – Future Shape and Size (2001–2005)	Deliver operating margins of at least 10% Reduce capacity and destinations served Reduce aircraft fleet by 10%
Toyota – European expansion plan to 2006	Sell 800,000 cars in Europe in 2006 (reached in 2004) Invest to improve product range Increase profit per car sold
Nestlé – long-term growth target	In 2003 set new targets of 5–6 % organic growth over 3–5 years, to focus managers' efforts on profit margins rather than sales

Source: Company announcements.

into specific commitments – what is to be done by when. They provide the focus or reference point for other decisions and the criteria against which to measure performance. Most plans include quantified objectives in the areas of financial objectives – such as earnings per share, return on shareholders' funds and cash flow. They are also likely to quantify sales targets, cost reductions, and R&D expenditure. Table 6.2 lists some stated goals of high-profile projects.

However convincingly set out, statements of goals only have value if they guide human action. Effective goal setting involves balancing multiple goals, considering whether they meet the SMART criteria, and evaluating their likely motivational effects.

Single or multiple goals?

Company statements of goals – whether long-term or short – are usually expressed in the plural, for the fundamental reason that a single measure cannot indicate the success or failure of an organisation or a project. Emphasis on one goal, such as growth, ignores others such as dividends for shareholders. Growth takes time and investment – which takes away from profits available for distribution to shareholders now. Managers have to balance multiple, possibly conflicting objectives, of even one group of stakeholders. As Gerry Murphy, who became chief executive of Kingfisher (a UK DIY retailer) in 2004, recalled:

> Alan Sheppard, my boss at Grand Metropolitan and one of my mentors, used to say that senior management shouldn't have the luxury of single point objectives. Delivering growth without returns or returns without growth is not something I find attractive or acceptable. Over time we are going to do both. (*Financial Times*, 28 April 2004, p. 23)

As senior managers try to take account of stakeholders other than those with shares in the company, they anticipate their various expectations. This means (merely as examples) balancing profits (or growth) to satisfy shareholders, quality to satisfy customer interests, and sustainability to satisfy environmental interests. All are legitimate, but mean that managers are juggling conflicting goals. This can lead to conflict between stated goals, as reflected in public announcements, and real goals, which are those to which people work. **Stated goals** are those that appear and are given prominence in

Stated goals are those which are prominent in company publications and websites.

Real goals are those to which people give most attention.

company publications and websites. Establishing the **real goals** – those to which people give most attention – depends on observing what they do. Actions reflect the priorities that senior managers express through what they say and do within the company, and how they reward and discipline managers.

Motivating effect of goals

Setting goals can have a strong motivational effect on people. Goal theory (Locke and Latham, 1990) has established four empirically supported propositions:

- **Challenging goals** lead to higher levels of performance than simple goals that are easy to attain. Difficult goals are sometimes called 'stretch' goals because they encourage people to try harder (though if people believe the goal is impossible to attain the effect is the opposite).
- **Specific goals** lead to higher levels of performance than vague goals such as 'do better' or 'make the customers happier'. People find it easier to adjust their behaviour when they have something precise to aim for, and they are less likely to become involved in distracting discussion about what a vague goal really means.
- **Participation in setting goals**, especially when people have experience in the process, increases their commitment – though goals set by management can also be motivating *provided* that managers adequately explain and justify them.
- **Knowledge of the results** of past performance helps to create a positive motivational climate.

The Key Ideas box indicates how those making a plan can use these ideas to help ensure that people support the plan and try to make it work.

key ideas Practical uses of goal-setting theory

Goal theory offers some practical implications for those making plans – whether for a small local project or a strategic change:

- **Goal difficulty**: set goals for work performance at levels that will stretch employees but are just within their ability.
- **Goal specificity**: express goals in clear, precise and if possible quantifiable terms, and avoid setting ambiguous or confusing goals.
- **Participation**: where practicable, encourage staff to take part in setting goals to increase their commitment to achieving them.
- **Feedback**: provide information on the results of performance to allow people to adjust their behaviour and perhaps improve their achievement of future plans.

Source: Locke and Latham (1990).

Criteria for assessing goals

The SMART acronym summarises some criteria for assessing a set of goals. What form of each is effective depends on circumstances (specific goals are not necessarily better than directional ones). The list simply offers some measures against which to evaluate a statement of goals in a plan – whether strategic, operational or special purpose.

- **Specific** Does the goal set out the specific targets for the activity? People are often reluctant to commit to specific goals, fearing that they make it too easy for others to see whether they have succeeded or not. People who are planning a meeting can set specific goals for what they hope to achieve, such as:

  > By the end of the meeting we will have convinced them to withdraw their current proposal, and to have set a date (within the next two weeks) at which we will start to develop an alternative plan.

  Having a clear statement of what the meeting (or any other activity in a plan) is intended to achieve helps people to focus what they do and say on achieving that goal: it will work better than if they are vague and unclear about the result they want.
- **Measurable** Some goals may be quantified ('increase sales of product X by 5 per cent a year over the next three years') but others, equally important, are more qualitative ('to offer a congenial working environment'). Quantitative goals are not more useful than qualitative ones – what can be measured is not necessarily important. The important point is whether goals have been defined precisely enough so that people can measure progress towards them, whatever the form of those measures.
- **Attainable** Goals should be challenging, but not unreasonably difficult. If people perceive a goal they have been set as unrealistic, they see that they are destined to fail – which decreases commitment. Equally goals should not be too easy, as they too undermine motivation. Some now advocate 'stretch goals' in which people are set ever more demanding standards. However, a manager contemplating this should ensure they are consistent with time, equipment and other resources.
- **Rewarded** Can people who are expected to work to meet the goals see a reward at the end? Rewards give meaning and help ensure commitment – though if the failure to meet a goal is due to circumstances beyond the employees' control this needs to be attended to.
- **Timed** Does the goal specify the time over which it will be achieved, and is that also a reasonable and acceptable standard? It may also be possible to build in intermediate times at which interim assessments can be made of whether the plan is on track, or if some adjustment is needed – especially valuable if the plan is a longer-term strategic one.

Activity 6.3   Critical reflection on goals

Choose a significant plan that someone has produced in your organisation within the last year. Assess the goals that it expresses – are they mutually consistent? Do they meet the criteria of being motivational? Are they SMART? Then try to set out how you would amend the goals to meet these criteria more fully. Alternatively, comment on how the criteria set out in the text could be modified, in the light of your experience with these goals.

6.7   Identifying actions and allocating resources

This part of the planning process involves deciding what actions need to be taken to achieve the objectives, and who will do them. In a small activity like planning a project in a club this would just mean listing the tasks and dividing them clearly amongst a few able and willing members. At the other extreme, the plan to build Ford's new car plant in

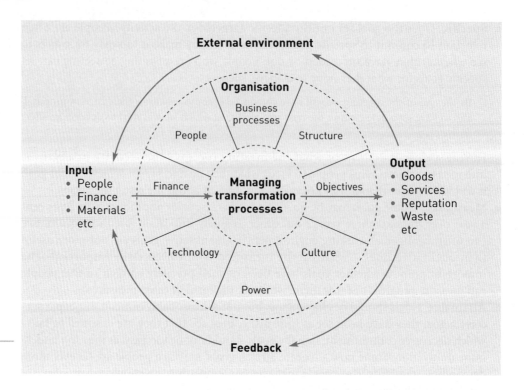

External environment

Organisation

Business processes

People   Structure

Input
• People   **Managing**   **Output**
• Finance Finance **transformation** Objectives • Goods
• Materials   **processes**   • Services
  etc   • Reputation
                                       • Waste
                                         etc

Technology   Culture

Power

Feedback

Figure 6.5

Possible action areas in a plan

China would probably run to several volumes. Figure 1.3 (reproduced as Figure 6.5) provides a model to help envisage the implications of a goal – what, if any, changes need to be made to each of the organisational elements shown?

Deciding the actions

If the objective is to launch a new product, which parts of the organisation will be affected (structure), what investment is needed (finance), how will we take orders, send out invoices (business processes) and so on? New technology projects, for example, often fail because those planning them pay too much attention to the technological aspects, and too little to the human aspects of structure, culture and people (Boddy *et al.*, 2005). Each main heading will then require many further actions that people can identify and assign.

Lynch (2003) points out that, depending on circumstances, managers handle this aspect of planning comprehensively, incrementally or selectively.

- **Comprehensive (specific) plan** This happens if managers decide to make a clear-cut change in direction, in response to a reassessment of the market, a financial crisis or a technological development. Implementing the strategy successfully depends on driving the new changes rapidly and in a coordinated way across the organisation – which implies a comprehensive plan.
- **Incremental (directional) plan** People use this approach when conditions are uncertain – such as rapidly changing markets or when direction depends on the outcomes of research and development. This means that tasks, times and even the objective are likely to change depending on the outcomes of current and planned activities – 'Important strategic areas may be left deliberately unclear until the outcomes of current events have been established' (Lynch, 2003, p. 633).
- **Selective plan** This approach may work when neither of the other methods is the best way forward – such as when managers wish to make a comprehensive change, but are

unable to do so because of deep opposition in some area affected by the plan. They may then try implement the major change in only some areas of the business which, while not their preferred choice, may enable them to make some progress towards the objectives.

A hierarchy of objectives

Those advocating a **traditional goal setting** approach to planning recommend building a hierarchy of objectives, in which the overall objectives are transformed into more specific objectives for different parts of the organisation – such as marketing, finance, operations and human resources. Managers in each of those areas will develop plans setting out the actions, times and resource requirements which they must undertake to meet the overall objective.

Figure 6.6 illustrates the relationship between the issues planned at each level, using IKEA's planned expansion in Japan. To continue to meet its plan of growing sales, managers plan to open many stores across Asia, of which the first group will be in Japan. That has evolved into a plan for their probable location, and then into a precise plan for two near Tokyo, for which land has been bought. That in turn is leading managers to develop progressively more detailed plans for the thousands of details that will need to be in good order if the venture is to succeed.

When the environment is changing rapidly it is very difficult to specify durable objectives and tasks – by the time they have been agreed and communicated the environment will have changed. As this happens the objectives can become impossible to meet, or not sufficiently ambitious. Managers can then try to:

● Be flexible about the objectives within an agreed broad vision

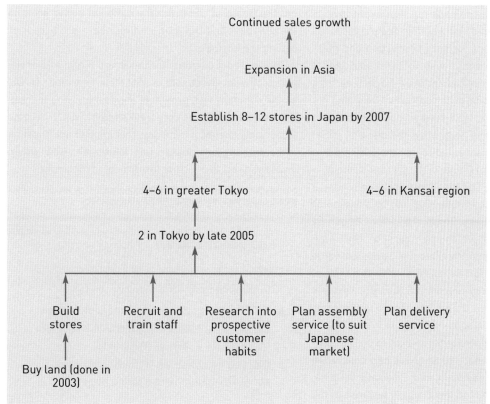

Figure 6.6

Developing a plan for IKEA (Japan)

- Empower those closest to particular changes (such as particular markets or technologies) to be able to respond quickly
- Monitor events closely to ensure that empowerment does not lead people to act in ways that inadvertently endanger the company.

Communicating the actions

In a small organisation or where the plan deals with only one area, communication in any formal or extensive way is probably unnecessary. Equally, those who have been involved in developing the objectives and plans will be well aware of it. However, in larger enterprises managers will probably invest time and effort in communicating both the objectives and the actions required throughout the areas affected. They do this to:

- Ensure that everyone understands the plan
- Allow them to resolve any confusion and ambiguity
- Communicate the judgements and assumptions that underlie the plan
- Ensure that the various activities around the organisation are coordinted in practice as well as on paper.

DSM – the case continues www.dsm.com   CASE STUDY

Managers at DSM Melamine had conducted four BSDs by 2003 and believed that this formal planning process had helped the unit to improve its performance dramatically. It had helped to make the case for significant investments in a new plant, and also a shift in geographic focus towards South-east Asia for both production and markets. The company's image was of a reliable global supplier in Europe, Americas and Asia-Pacific, earning half of its sales from long-term contracts. China had not featured largely in the 1999 review, but the dramatic growth in the Chinese economy meant that DSM Melamine management wanted to use the 2003 BSD to investigate the impact of China on the current strategy.

All members of the DSM Melamine team attended a kick-off meeting in September 2002, led by a facilitator from within the Business Group. The event began by identifying 35 issues which members of the team thought should feature in the Dialogue. So-called 'value teams' were created for each issue, with the task of gathering and analysing information over the next few months. These ensured that many people in the company took part in the dialogue.

The main issue for decision turned out to be the company's position on China. The analysis had concluded that demand in South-east Asia, and especially in China, was expected to continue to grow rapidly because of the

increasing production of laminates for domestic use and exports. Yet the company had no production facility in China. The outcome was that management would present the Board of DSM with the option of either growing the business (as Dijkman and his team preferred) or selling the business.

This posed a dilemma for the Board. From a financial perspective an investment in DSM Melamine made sense, as the company was profitable and in a growing market. On the other hand, the corporate strategy was to become a speciality chemical company: that implied not investing in commodity businesses like Melamine. How would investors react to a further investment in melamine?

Source: Based on extracts from Bloemhof, Haspeslagh and Slagmulder (2004). Copyright 2004 INSEAD, Fontainebleau, France.

Case questions 6.1

- Comment on the range of people taking part in the Dialogue – too many or too few?
- Visit the company website and look for evidence about Melamine's position within the business: is it core or marginal?
- Can you establish what the Board decided about DSM Melamine's China project?

6.8 Implementing plans

However good the plan, nothing worthwhile happens until people implement it, acting to make visible, physical changes to the organisation and the way people work within it. Many managers find this the most challenging part of the process – when plans, however well developed, are brought into contact with the processes people expect them to change. Those implementing the plan then come up against a variety of organisational and environmental obstacles – and possibly find that some of the assumptions in the plan are incorrect. When a new chief executive took over at Woolworths he commented that he had joined the group because of the great opportunities it offered to recover after a difficult trading period:

> but I did not know how much of the work to be done was executional and how much about strategic positioning. Now I know that it is 80 per cent executional.

Organisations are slower to change than plans are to prepare, yet the slower they change the greater the danger of people acting in ways that are no longer appropriate. Miller *et al.* (2004) conducted a long-term study of decisions to examine how managers tried to put strategic plans into action and how those actions related to performance. 'The … strategic decisions (for example) to reorganise corporate structures … or to enter an alliance are managers' attempts to put an overall strategy (say increase market share by 15 per cent a year) into action.'

The team revisited 150 decisions which they had studied in the 1980s, to establish what had been the outcome of the decision. They defined implementation as 'all the processes and outcomes which accrue to a strategic decision once authorisation has been given to … put the decision into practice' (Miller *et al.*, 2004, p. 203). Their intention was to identify the conditions in which implementation occurs, the managerial activities involved in putting decisions into practice, and the extent to which the objectives of the plans were achieved.

Their main conclusion was that success is heavily influenced by:

- managers' experience of the issue, and
- the readiness of the organisation for the change being implemented.

'Having relevant experience of what has to be done … enables managers to assess the objectives, specify the tasks and resource implementation appropriately, leading [those affected to accept the process]' (p. 206). Readiness means a receptive organisational climate that enables managers to implement the change within a positive environment.

The statistical results were illustrated by cases which showed, for example, how managers in a successful company were able to implement a plan to upgrade their computer systems because they had *experience* of many similar changes. They were 'able to set targets, detail what needed doing and allocate the resources … That is, they could plan and control the implementation effectively'. In another illustration, a regional brewer extending into the London area had no directly relevant experience, and so was not able to plan and control the move very tightly. But it had an organisation in which people were very *receptive* to new challenges, and were therefore able to implement the move successfully, even with little formal planning.

The authors concluded that the activities of planning do not in themselves lead to success, but are a means for gaining acceptance of what has to be done when it is implemented. Planning helps by inducing confidence in the process, leading to high levels of acceptability from those involved. 'Planning is a necessary part of this approach to success, but it is not sufficient in itself' (p. 210).

6.9 Monitoring progress and evaluating results

The final stage in developing a plan is to set up a system that will allow people to monitor progress towards the goals. This happens at all levels of planning – from a project manager monitoring and controlling the detail of individual activities and tasks to a Board committee monitoring the plan for a broad strategic change – such as the launch of a new product or entry to a new line of business. The programme manager focuses on the interdependencies between and around the individual projects.

Project plans define and display every task and activity, but someone managing a programme of several linked projects would soon become swamped with such detail. Thus the standard project management tools, such as bar charts, are of little use when managing several projects at once. Each has its interdependencies, resource requirements, deadlines, milestones, issues and delivery phases. The office wall is simply not big enough, so programme management needs a new toolkit. It needs to be able to deal with a large amount of rapidly changing information, and to track progress in the projects. The toolkit takes data from project managers and distils it to show the overall situation. Tools include the overview chart, reporting systems and an issues management system.

The programme overview chart

The programme manager needs to maintain a quick-to-understand snapshot of the programme. This should show progress to date, the main events being planned, interdependencies, issues, and expected completion dates. This also helps the programme manager to communicate with senior executives and project managers.

One way to do this is to create a single chart with a simplified view of each project on an indicative timeline. Figure 6.7 illustrates this. Details vary but the main features are usually:

- An indicative timeline, along which the individual projects are plotted
- A simplified representation of the major milestones in each project, or change area

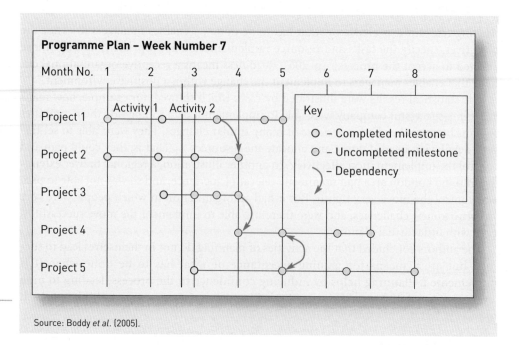

Figure 6.7

A programme overview chart

Source: Boddy *et al.* (2005).

- Descriptions of progress made against that expected for each project
- Indications of interdependencies between projects.

Weekly project reports and the composite plan report

Senior managers will also expect the programme manager to provide a written report on progress. This will be at a high level, but draws information from the projects. A common method is to establish a weekly reporting mechanism whereby project managers feed details on their progress into the overall report. This used to be a paper exercise, but is now likely to use shared files on a computer network, or an intranet site.

Figure 6.8 shows an example Weekly Project Report which would feed into the broader Composite Plan Report. This can then provide the programme owners (the budget holders and executive decision-makers) with a quick and accurate update on the overall programme situation.

6.10 Planning in uncertain conditions

The benefits of planning, especially at the strategic level, have long been advocated by writers such as Ansoff (1965, 1991) and Armstrong (1982). They believe that central planning is essential to coordinate responsive actions across the organisation, and to help spur adaptive strategic thinking. While most managers regularly engage in some form of strategic planning (Glaister and Falshaw, 1999), an influential group of writers (notably Mintzberg, 1994) have questioned its value. They play down the role of centralised strategic planning, instead focusing on the autonomous actions of managers throughout the organisation. They argue that these actions by those familiar with local circumstances are the sources of significant strategic change, which planning tends to inhibit.

Andersen (2000) sought to reconcile these views by studying the use of strategic planning and autonomous action in three industries with different external conditions. He concluded that strategic planning was associated with superior organisational performance in all industrial settings. Whether industries were complex and dynamic or stable and simple, companies that planned performed better than those that did not. In addition, he found that in complex dynamic industries a formal planning process was accompanied by autonomous actions by managers, and this served to further enhance their performance (see Key Ideas).

Does planning affect performance?

key ideas

Many empirical studies have examined industries in different types of environment to see whether the use of strategic planning tools (such as PESTEL and five forces analysis) affect company performance. Andersen (2000) investigated the position in three industry groups for which he calculated indices of environmental complexity and dynamism as shown below. He also concluded that there was a positive association between planning and performance, particularly in dynamic and complex environmental settings.

Industry group	Dynamism index	Complexity index
Food and household products	1.5	8.3
Computer products	7.6	24.5
Banking	4.4	12.1

Source: Andersen (2000).

PROGRAMME OFFICE
Weekly Progress Report

Project: System Development Phase 2 – Funtionality Enhancements
Project Manager: Allana Carruthers
Week Ending: – 7 April 2004
Project Status (Red/Amber/Green): AMBER

> Reasons for Amber/Red: Difficulties with retaining key staff are impacting on deadlines. Recruitment programme commenced with HR and new team members expected to be available by mid-May. Meantime, overtime being offered to minimise slippage.

Activities This Week:
- On-going discussions with respective parties (auditors, SE, bankers, management) to firm up on the exact forms of reporting
- Meeting to analyse accounting policy differencs and consider approach to address them
- External/internal recruitment under way
- Commenced detailed analysis of acquisition implications

Activities Planned for Next Week:
- Progress completion coding and test scripting
- Conclude external reporting formats
- Legal meeting and identification of issues and approaches
- Analysis of detailed accounting implications

Forthcoming Milestones	Completion date Baseline	Estimated	Actual
Preliminary coding modules completed	4 April	7 April	7 April
Summary report formats completed	15 April latest		
Legal issues, including decision on deal making processes defined	15 April		7 April
Decide on processes for maintenance of account figures	20 April	25 April	
Completion reports defined	30 April		
Completion reports coded	5 May		
Test scripts agreed	15 May		

Issues/Action Required
1. Fast-track internal recruitment processes to allow earliest possible start dates.
   Project Director to discuss with HR Director.
2. The uncertainty of external reporting requirements impacts a number of areas.
   Conclude discussions as fast as possible.

Figure 6.8 Example of a weekly progress record
Source: Boddy *et al.* (2005).

A study by Brews and Hunt (1999) also sought to reconcile the planning and learning schools through a study of the planning process in 656 firms. The authors concluded that formal, specific strategic planning had a positive effect on performance, irrespective of environmental conditions. However, planning was even more effective if it was flexible, especially in unstable environments. That is, managers must be prepared to amend and rework plans as they implement them. They also noted that introducing formal planning did not bring immediate benefits – it was likely to be at least four years before the effort devoted to planning was visible in improved performance.

Activity 6.4   How does uncertainty affect planning?

Reflect on the plans you have used in earlier Activities. Were they in a certain or an uncertain environment? If uncertain, how did that affect the planning process? How did people develop plans that were still useful, even if subject to change?

In practice, the different styles are not mutually exclusive. Empirical studies have found that most organisations adopt an explicit and deliberate approach to strategy formulation and most agree that 'strategic planning' is important (Glaister and Falshaw, 1999). But resource constraints, political processes and an ever-changing environment mean that strategy develops through a mix of the planned and emergent styles.

Changes in planning style at PowerGen   www.powergen.co.uk

management in practice

PowerGen (now owned by the German company E.on) was formed in 1991 from the assets of a state-owned electricity company. By 2001 it was a leading multi-utility supplying electricity, gas and telephone services in domestic and overseas markets. As a private and diversifying company, PowerGen moved into a more complex and uncertain environment with new competition and changing regulations, and the company's corporate planning process had to evolve. The company has retained a formal process with a five-year planning horizon, but there have been some significant changes.

Planning is a more devolved process: a much smaller central team focuses on overall corporate strategy while business units have a greater role in developing business strategy and more freedom to consider a wider range of options to cope with their particular competitive situations.

The previous emphasis on long-range demand forecasting, often found to be unreliable and inappropriate for anticipating changes in regulatory requirements, has given way to a greater use of scenario planning with participation by both planning and operational staff across the business. To stimulate strategic thinking, staff are encouraged to use a variety of techniques in the analysis of competitive forces, core competences and resources and in the development and appraisal of strategic options. Business unit plans have become shorter and are no longer required to follow a prescribed format. The overall planning cycle is completed in a shorter period of time. All of these developments have created a more adaptive style of planning that is consistent with the increased uncertainty of the company's business environment.

Source: Jennings (2000).

The same is likely to be true of other forms of plans. Major projects involving extensive allocation of resources to work on interdependent parts of a major change need to be carefully planned to ensure an adequate degree of coordination. But equally those doing the work are bound to confront changing conditions as they implement the plans, and will be expected to adapt to changing circumstances as they go.

Summary

1 **Describe different types of plan and the potential benefits of planning:**
   - Plans can be at strategic, tactical and operational levels, and in new businesses people prepare business plans to secure capital. Strategic business units also prepare plans relatively independently of the parent. There are also special-purpose or project plans, and standing plans. All can be either specific or directional in nature.
   - Effective plans can clarify direction, motivate people, use resources efficiently and allow people to measure progress towards objectives.

2 **Outline the seven iterative tasks in making a plan:**
   - Recycling through the tasks of gathering information, developing a mission, setting goals, identifying actions and allocating resources, implementing plans, monitoring progress and evaluating results.

3 **Understand and use models to gather information relevant for planning:**
   - Planners draw information from the general and competitive environments using tools such as Porter's Five Forces Analysis. They can do this within the framework of a SWOT analysis which relates external opportunities and threats to internal strengths and weaknesses. Other tools include forecasting, sensitivity analysis, critical success factors and scenario planning.

4 **Explain the problem of multiple goals, and evaluate a statement of goals:**
   - People in organisations inevitably pursue several goals at the same time, and some of these will conflict – such as long-term growth and short-term profitability. If they also set goals that will satisfy groups other than shareholders, those too are likely to be a source of conflict. Goals can be evaluated in terms of whether they are specific, measurable, attainable, rewarded and timed.

5 **Use a model to identify the areas of action which a plan should specify:**
   - The 'wheel' provides a model for recalling the likely areas in an organisation which a plan should cover, indicating the likely ripple effects of change in one area on others. Some organisations set out a hierarchy of objectives and plan to guide those at different levels and functions on the actions expected of them to meet the goals of the plan.

6 **Explain the procedural and wider factors that affect whether a plan is implemented successfully:**
   - The value of a plan depends on people implementing it, but whether that happens depends not only on the plan, but on the experience of those implementing it, and the receptivity of the organisation to change.

7 **Consider the value of planning in rapidly changing conditions:**
   - There is clear evidence that companies that plan in uncertain conditions perform better than those that don't – but success depends on encouraging people to be willing to adapt plans as conditions change.

1 What types of planning do you do in your personal life? Describe them in terms of whether they are (a) strategic or operational, (b) short or long term, (c) specific or directional.

2 What are four benefits that people in organisations may gain from planning?

3 What are the main sources of information that managers can use in planning? What models can they use to structure this information?

4 In what ways can a goal be motivational? What practical things can people do in forming plans that take account of goal-setting theory?

5 What is meant by the term 'hierarchy of objectives', and how can that idea help people to build a consistent plan? What else would managers need to do once they have agreed a hierarchy of objectives?

6 Explain the term 'organisational receptivity', and how people can use the idea in developing a plan that is more likely to work.

7 What are the main ways of monitoring progress on a plan, and why is this so vital a task in planning?

8 As environments become more uncertain, will planning become more or less useful? How can managers plan effectively in a rapidly changing environment?

Concluding critical reflection

Think about the way your company, or one with which you are familiar, makes plans. Review the material in the chapter, and perhaps visit some of the websites identified. Then make notes on these questions:

- What examples of the themes discussed in this chapter are currently relevant to your company? What types of plans are you most closely involved with? Which of the techniques suggested do you and your colleagues typically use, and why? What techniques do you use that are not mentioned here?

- In responding to these issues, what assumptions about the nature of planning in business appear to guide your approach? Are the prevailing assumptions closer to the planning or emergent perspectives, and why do you think that is?

- What factors in the context of the company appear to shape your approach to planning – what kind of environment are you working in, for example? To what extent does your planning process involve people from other organisations – and why is that?

- Have you considered whether you plan too much, or too little? Have you compared your planning processes with those in other companies? How do they plan?

Further reading

Johnson, G. and Scholes, K. (2002), *Exploring Corporate Strategy* (6th edn), Financial Times Prentice Hall, Harlow.

> The best-selling European text on corporate strategy. Although more detailed than required at introductory level, a number of sections usefully build on this chapter.

Dobson, P., Starkey, K. and Richards, J. (2004), *Strategic Management: Issues and cases*, Blackwell, Oxford.

Smith, R.J. (1994), *Strategic Management and Planning in the Public Sector*, Longman/Civil Service College, Harlow.

> Both cover the main elements in the strategic planning process and explain, with the use of examples, some planning tools in addition to those covered in this chapter. Smith's book also contains useful chapters on definitions and terminology and options analysis.

Long Range Planning and *Strategic Management Journal* often contain useful articles.

Weblinks

These websites have appeared in the chapter:

www.dsm.com
www.fiat.co.uk
www.sabmiller.com
www.cw.com
www.shell.com
www.powergen.co.uk

Visit two of the business sites in the list, and navigate to the pages dealing with corporate news, or investor relations.

● What planning issues can you identify that managers in the company are likely to be dealing with?

● What kind of environment are they likely to be working in, and how will that affect their planning methods and processes?

> Annotated weblinks, multiple choice questions and other
> useful resources can be found on
> **www.pearsoned.co.uk/boddy**

Chapter 7

Decision making

Aim

To identify major aspects of decision making in organisations and to outline alternative ways of making decisions.

Objectives

By the end of your work on this chapter you should be able to outline the concepts below in your own terms and:

1 Explain with examples why decisions affect performance and how the process of making a decision affects the outcome

2 Explain, and give examples of, programmed and non-programmed decisions

3 Distinguish between certainty, risk, uncertainty and ambiguity

4 Explain the tasks involved in making a decision

5 Contrast rational, administrative, political and garbage can decision models

6 Describe the Vroom and Yetton model of decision-making styles

7 Discuss the benefits and costs of wider participation in decision making.

Key terms

This chapter introduces the following ideas:

decision
decision making
programmed decision
procedure
rule
policy
non-programmed decision
certainty
risk
uncertainty
ambiguity
problem
opportunity
decision criteria
rational model of decision making
administrative model of decision making
bounded rationality
satisficing
incremental model
escalation of commitment
political model

Each is a term defined within the text, as well as in the glossary at the end of the book.

Wipro www.wipro.com

Wipro is a leading IT services company which provides a growing range of IT services to companies such as Microsoft, Nokia, Norwich Union (a UK insurer) and TeliaSonera (a Scandinavian telecoms business). Based in India, it employed 23,000 staff in 2004, and sales had recently been growing by about 25 per cent each year. Azim Premji is chairman of the company and still follows an exhausting work routine even though he is India's richest person:

[His day begins at 7 with] meetings with visiting customers or government officials. That's followed by meetings where he focuses on the minutiae of business – the cost of airline tickets or whether frequent-travelling Wipro salespeople should have permanent (office space). Before the sun is overhead Premji has already worked seven hours, with another seven to go. Frequently Premji ends his day on a commercial flight – there is no corporate jet – to Bombay, San Francisco or London – anywhere his sales team needs a boost.

The company has grown from being a small producer of cooking oil (Western India Vegetable Products) founded by his father. He took charge in 1966 when he was 21 and immediately began to professionalise the company, hiring MBAs and letting them run things as they saw fit. Gradually the company diversified into toilet soaps, competing profitably with major brands.

In 1977 the Indian government told IBM to leave India, creating an opportunity for Indian companies to enter the market for computer hardware. Premji took the opportunity, and by 1981 the company was selling the computer it had designed – these became India's top-selling machines for many years. In 1984 it moved into software with a spreadsheet and word-processing package – which failed. Premji commented:

I don't agonize over failures. One must learn from them.

Software services now provide 85 per cent of Wipro's profits but there is also a computer-hardware unit, a light bulb company, a hi-tech joint venture with GE Medical Systems – and the soap and cooking oil businesses.

The goal is to turn Wipro into one of the world's top ten IT service companies, providing services of greater

Wipro

complexity and value. A few years ago most of the work was in low-value software coding and maintenance, but it is now in more advanced areas of designing software and complete IT systems. The company has recently expanded into call centre work and has invested in software expertise in healthcare, retailing and energy. Premji has also expanded his reach into areas such as the Middle East where US companies are unwelcome.

Recent decisions have involved moving the Technology Division's HQ to California to be closer to the customers, and buying a leading Indian call centre company and several IT consultancies in the US. Wipro acquired these companies just as global competition was rising and IT spending was falling.

Source: Based on *The Economist*, 6 February 2003; *Business Week*, 13 October 2003; and *Financial Times*, 20 January 2004.

Case questions

- Make a note of the decisions which Mr Premji has made in the story so far.
- How have they affected the development of the business?
- Visit Wipro's website, and note examples of recent decisions which have shaped Wipro.

7.1 Introduction

The case recounts the recent history of one of India's biggest and most successful companies, which is now becoming a global player in the market for IT services. To develop the business from a local cooking oil firm to its present position managers needed to decide where to allocate their time, effort and other resources. They made some poor decisions (such as the early word-processing systems) but over the years their decisions have paid off. Further decisions now arise, such as how to continue to attract customers and well-qualified staff in the face of growing competition from established global companies. The company also faces the possibility of political reactions from foreign governments about the loss of local jobs when work is outsourced to companies like Wipro. How managers decide these matters will affect Wipro's future.

The performance of every organisation reflects (as well as luck and good fortune) the decisions which people make. People continually make choices (including that of ignoring an issue and so not making a decision), as they see problems which may need attention, and ideas or proposals which they may be able to use. Resources are limited, there are many demands on them, and people have different goals. Their choices relate to all aspects of the management task – decisions about inputs (how to raise capital, who to employ), outputs (what products to make, how to distribute them) and transformations (how to organise the delivery of a new service, how to manage the finances). The choices they make affect how well the organisation uses resources, and whether it transforms them in a way that creates sufficient value (as seen by customers) to ensure it survives – 'Like management itself, decision-making is a generic process that is applicable to all forms of organised activity' (Harrison, 1999, p. 8).

While some choices are clear and straightforward, many are profoundly difficult and complex – and these are usually the ones of greatest significance to the business. Managers cannot wait passively for someone to place an issue before them – they will typically be looking for problems (inside or outside the organisation) that need to be resolved, as well as noting ideas or information that may be useful. Some conjunction of events sets off a decision-making process, which takes place in an environment of confusing and contradictory evidence, different opinions, and other matters requiring urgent attention. Choice is a source of tension as it implies anxiety about 'what if' the other choice had been made (Schwartz, 2004).

J.K. Rowling offered the manuscript of the original Harry Potter story to several leading publishers, whose editors decided to reject it: an editor at Bloomsbury chose to accept it. Hewlett-Packard and Dell are battling to dominate the personal computer market – H-P managers decided to base their strategy on being more innovative than Dell, in the belief that customers will pay a higher price for advanced features. The managers of the European Airbus 380 project announced in July 2004 that they would increase production from 20 to 30 a year. They believed that demand would rise so that the extra aircraft will be sold profitably, and worth the risk of a wrong decision.

Business decisions like these are complex because people make them in a context – which has both historical and contemporary dimensions. For most organisations the external environment is a source of constantly changing threats and opportunities. Performance depends on the decisions people make about these uncertainties. Part of the management role is to sense external forces and then to initiate decisions about suitable internal changes – adapting factors in the centre of Figure 1.3 such as structure, financial resources or culture. A decision about any of the elements in the internal context may have implications for other elements, which adds to the complexity. These may be of a technical nature, but may also involve issues of culture or power. And history will

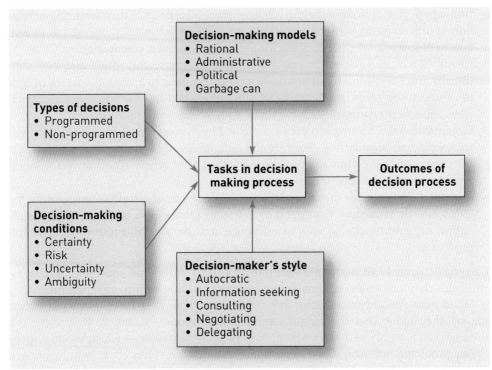

Figure 7.1

Overview of decision making in organisations

play a part – past decisions frequently influence the range of choices available, and the positions that different players involved take towards the issue.

Making decisions involves dealing with stakeholders who, as described in Chapter 3, are individuals, groups or organisations with an interest in, or who are affected by, the decisions that people make. They are likely to have different objectives, different interpretations of events – and therefore a different view of the decision. Figure 7.1 summarises the issues discussed so far, as a model for the chapter.

Figure 7.1 implies that decision making involves:

- identifying the type of decision
- identifying the conditions surrounding the decision
- using one or more models of the process to guide the approach
- selecting a decision-making style
- working through the process and implementing the decision.

Since decisions are so central to organisational performance, there are many competing explanations of the process, which this chapter examines. It begins by identifying different types of decision, outlines the different conditions in which people take decisions and then presents the generic tasks involved in making a decision. It then compares four models of the decision-making process, and finally examines a method for deciding how much to involve others in making decisions.

7.2 Types of decisions

A **decision** is a specific commitment to action (usually a commitment of resources). People make such choices at several levels – individual, group, organisational and societal (Harrison, 1999).

A **decision** is a specific commitment to action (usually a commitment of resources).

- **Individual** People make individual choices about all aspects of their lives, and in relation to organisations they make choices about careers, whether to change job or not, how hard to work, whether to apply for promotion or make a complaint.
- **Group** Much organisational work is done in groups or teams, whose members continually make decisions about how to work together, how to accomplish a task or how to choose a new member. Members are still individuals, but the way they reach decisions will reflect relationships and mutual expectations within the group.
- **Organisational** This refers to decision making by managers and others acting in their roles within an organisation. They are still individuals and will often be part of a team resolving a problem – but will be working within what others expect of them, and in relation to organisational policies and practices.
- **Societal** People outside the organisation make decisions which affect those within it – either directly (awarding a contract) or indirectly (changing a tax regulation). People within organisations also seek to influence, and be part of, these wider decision processes.

Chapters 15 and 17 in particular examine aspects of individual and group decisions, while this chapter focuses on decisions and decision making within organisations.

When managers at Nokia wanted to increase the company's share of the mobile phone market, they had to choose which of several possible models to launch. That choice is a decision, but it is only part of a wider process of **decision making** – which includes identifying problems, opportunities and possible solutions. It involves effort both before and after the actual choice. In deciding whether to select Jean, Bob or Rasul for a job the manager would probably, amongst other things, have to

> **Decision making** is the process of identifying problems and opportunities and then resolving them.

- identify the need for a new member of staff
- perhaps persuade his or her boss to authorise the budget
- decide where to advertise the post
- interview candidates
- select the preferred candidate
- decide whether or not to agree to their request for a better deal, and
- arrange their induction into the job so that they work effectively.

At each of these stages (and others could be added) the manager may have to go back in the process to reconsider what to do, or to deal with another set of decisions – such as the sensitive area of who to include on the selection committee. In Nokia's case the choice of model would have been preceded by choices between aiming to increase market share and aiming to increase profit, which part of the market to aim for – and would be followed by many other choices regarding production volumes, features and price.

While attention often focuses on the decision, the effect on performance depends on the actions that follow from the decision – when someone implements the decision. It is also the case that the visible, public actions that tell us about a decision are preceded by many invisible choices. A manager is making small but potentially significant decisions all the time – which of several urgent jobs to deal with next, whose advice to seek about them, which report to read and which to ignore, which customer to call and which to pass to someone else to deal with. These shape the way people use their time, and the issues they decide are sufficiently important to earn a place on the agenda.

Strategic and operational decisions

Strategic decisions have greater implications for the organisation than operational ones. As Chapter 8 shows, strategy is the business of developing the future direction of the

---

Activity 7.1 | **Critical reflection on types of decisions**

Reflect on your experience and identify new examples of these types of decision:

- **Clear choice** – choosing between two candidates
- **Competing choice** – whether to appoint new staff, outsource the work or close the service
- **Choice avoidance** – not acknowledging that current staff cannot provide adequate service
- **Choice suppression** – not introducing feedback forms that would make complaints visible.

Compare your examples with those of other students. Are these categories the only ones – do some of your examples not fit any of them? How did those involved make each decision?

---

organisation, by committing major resources to one area rather than another. Strategic decisions relate to the world outside the organisation – to develop a new product, to agree a merger with a former competitor, to establish an operation in an overseas market, or to introduce a major change in price. Strategic decisions affect the future of large parts of the organisation – such as when managers at BT decided to make radical changes to telephone charges in response to rivals such as Carphone Warehouse and Tesco.

McDonald's decides a new menu

In 2004 McDonald's, the world's largest fast food chain and a popular target for those concerned about obesity, announced that it would introduce a new range of salads in its European restaurants. Dennis Hennequin, executive vice-president for Europe, promised that space for the new products would be created by eliminating two traditional burgers from the menu. The company is also phasing out several super-size portions of fries and drinks. Mr Hennequin had taken on his present job earlier in the year, in recognition of his success in turning France into McDonald's fastest-growing European market. His decisions there to upgrade restaurants and modernise menus will be the template for what will be done elsewhere in Europe. The menu will include many new ingredients, and reflect Hennequin's belief that the company must start catering to a new customer awareness of the need for a well-balanced diet.

Source: Based on *Financial Times*, 9 March 2004.

Operational decisions are more day to day, and within the boundaries of established policy – whether to recruit another member of staff, to replace a machine that has been causing trouble, to offer a small discount to a customer whose order is late.

Programmed and non-programmed decisions

Programmed decisions (Simon, 1960) deal with problems that are familiar, and where the information required is easy to define and obtain – the situation is well structured. If a store manager notices that a product is selling more than expected there will be a

A **programmed decision** is a repetitive decision that can be handled by a routine approach.

simple, routine procedure for deciding how much extra to order from the supplier. Decisions are structured to the extent that they arise frequently and can be dealt with routinely by following an established **procedure** – a series of related steps, often set out in a manual, to deal with a structured problem. They may also reach a decision by using an established **rule**, which sets out what someone can or cannot do in a given situation. They may also refer to a **policy** – a guideline that establishes some general principles for making a decision.

A **procedure** is a series of related steps to deal with a structured problem.

A **rule** sets out what someone can or cannot do in a given situation.

A **policy** is a guideline that establishes some general principles for making a decision.

A **non-programmed decision** is a unique decision that requires a custom-made solution when information is lacking or unclear.

People make programmed decisions to resolve recurring organisational problems – to reorder supplies when stocks drop below a defined level, to set the qualifications required for a specified job, to decide whether to lend money to a bank customer. Once managers formulate procedures, rules or policies, others can usually make the decisions. Computers handle many decisions of this type – the checkout system in supermarkets automatically calculates how many items they have sold, and orders replenishments from suppliers.

Simon (1960) also observed that people make **non-programmed decisions** to deal with situations that are unstructured, and so require a unique solution. The issue has not previously arisen in quite that form, and the information required is unclear, vague or open to many interpretations. Most major management decisions are of this type – such as the choice which managers at Virgin faced over whether to delay their order for Airbus 380 planes for 18 months until the weight of the new airliner was reduced to that originally promised. Several solutions were being studied and tested, but it was not clear when they would be ready, nor how passengers would react to lighter fittings. Most issues of strategy are of this type, because they involve great uncertainty and involve many parties and interests.

Programmed and non-programmed decisions require that people deal with them in different ways. The former are amenable to procedures, routines, rules and quantitative analytical techniques such as those associated with operational research (see Chapter 2). They are also suitable for resolution by modern information systems. Non-programmed decisions depend more on judgement and intuition and a variety of creative approaches to making decisions such as brainstorming.

Figure 7.2 relates the type of decision to the levels of the organisation. Those lower in the organisation typically deal with routine, structured problems which they can resolve by applying established procedures. As people advance up the hierarchy, they face correspondingly more unstructured decisions. It is easy to see why this happens – lower-level staff hand decisions that do not fit the rules to someone above them to deal with; those higher up pass routine matters to subordinates.

A non-programmed decision – a merger for Deutsche Bank?

On 5 May 2004 the German Chancellor Gerhard Schröder told an audience of bankers that they should start merging. His audience knew that this was aimed particularly at Deutsche Bank, Germany's largest bank, as a strong hint that it should find a way of becoming bigger. While Germany is Europe's largest economy, it has none of the Continent's top banks – which rankles German policy makers. Schroder's speech reopened a long-standing dispute that has divided senior management at the bank. Some favour a merger with another German bank to create a solid customer base in Europe's biggest market. Others advocate a merger with a foreign bank to create a strong international bank. Each carries a great many uncertainties and ambiguities, such as how the European Commission may react, or which of several local or foreign banks would best fit with Deutsche Bank.

Source: *Business Week*, 24 May 2004.

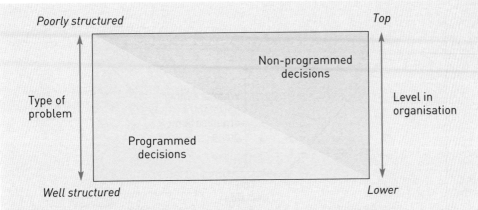

Source: Robbins, Stephen P., Coulter, Mary, *Management*, 7th edition, © 2002. Reprinted by permission of Pearson Education, Inc. Upper Saddle River, NJ.

Figure 7.2

Types of decision, types of problem and level in the organisation

Many decisions cannot easily be described as either programmed or non-programmed – they have elements of each. In considering a decision, it is advisable to consider the extent to which it is programmed or non-programmed, and which elements of the problem correspond to either type. Even non-programmed decisions will probably contain elements that can be handled in a programmed way.

Activity 7.2   Programmed and non-programmed decisions

Identify examples of the types of decision set out above. Try to identify one example of your own to add to those below or that illustrates the point specifically within your institution:

● **Programmed decision** – whether to reorder stock

● **Non-programmed decision** – whether to launch a new service in a new market.

Compare your examples with those of other students and consider how those responsible made each decision. What examples of programmed and non-programmed decisions can you see in the Wipro case? How easy is it to divide decisions between these two categories – how useful are they as distinguishing characteristics?

Dependent or independent

Another way to categorise decisions is in terms of their links to other decisions. People make decisions in a historical and social context and so are influenced by past and possible future decisions and the influence of other parts of the organisation.

Many decisions are influenced by previous decisions – which constrain, or enable, what can be done now. When Hutcheson began to offer third-generation (3G) mobile services in 2004 it was able to offer more competitive prices than established companies. The latter were concerned that if they cut charges on their third-generation services this would affect revenues from existing customers. Hutcheson, as the new entrant, did not depend on revenues from earlier decisions. Legacy computer systems (the result of earlier decisions) frequently constrain how quickly a company can adopt new systems.

Decisions are also influenced by their anticipated consequences for the participants or relevant stakeholders. People will be anticipating the effects on them and their unit, and

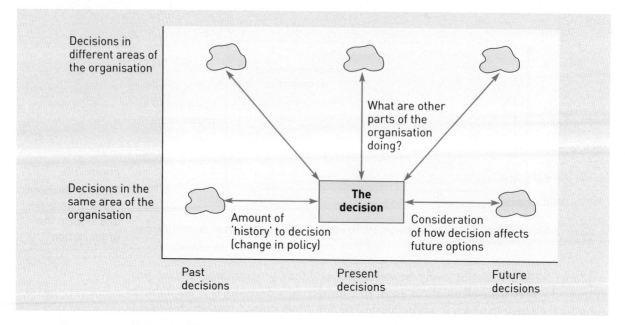

Figure 7.3 Possible relationships between decisions
Source: Cooke and Slack (1991), p. 24.

on other players with whom they interact. Their evaluation of these effects will influence how they act to influence the nature and timing of the decision.

Some decisions have few implications beyond their immediate area, but others have significant ripples around the organisation. Changes in technology, for example, usually require consistent, supportive changes in structures and processes if they are to be effective – but decisions on these areas are harder to make than those affecting the technology. More generally, local units may be limited in their decisions by wider company policies. Figure 7.3 illustrates this.

7.3 Decision-making conditions

Decisions arise within a wider context, and the conditions in this context materially affect the decision process.

Certainty, risk, uncertainty and ambiguity

A major factor distinguishing structured from unstructured decisions relates to the degree of certainty managers deal with in making the decision. Some aspects of a decision are unknowable – what Nokia's competitors will be charging next year, whether GSK's pharmaceutical research programme will deliver the new drugs on the scale the company needs to keep revenue growing. Decisions based on assumptions about these future conditions may not turn out as people hope. Managers try to obtain information about the options facing them to reduce this uncertainty.

Figure 7.4 relates the nature of the problem to the type of decision. Whereas people can deal with conditions of certainty by making programmed decisions, many situations are both uncertain and ambiguous. Here people need to be able to use a non-programmed approach.

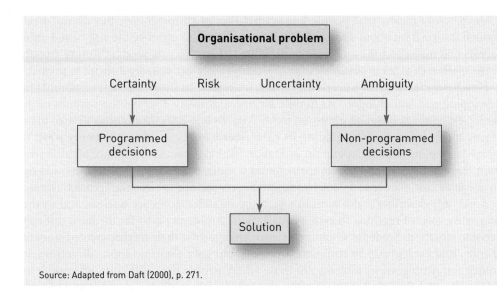

Source: Adapted from Daft (2000), p. 271.

Figure 7.4
Degree of uncertainty and decision-making type

Certainty describes the situation when all the information the decision maker needs is fully available. The decision maker is fully informed about resource costs or constraints, and about the costs and benefits of each alternative action. A company treasurer wanting to place reserve funds can readily compare comparative rates of interest from a range of secure and reliable banks, and calculate exactly the return from each one. However, few decisions are that certain, and most contain risk and/or uncertainty.

Certainty describes the situation when all the information the decision maker needs is available.

Risk refers to situations in which the decision maker can estimate the likelihood of the alternative outcomes. Outcomes are still subject to chance, but people have enough information to allow them to estimate the probable outcome of each alternative, possibly using statistical tools. Banks have developed complex tools for assessing the credit risk of those to whom they lend money – to reduce the risk that the borrower will not repay the loan. The questions on an application form for a loan (home ownership, time at this address, employer's name, etc.) gather information which enables the bank to assess the risk of lending money to that person.

Risk refers to situations in which the decision maker is able to estimate the likelihood of the alternative outcomes.

Risk and uncertainty for a football club chairman

Rupert Lowe was Chairman of Southampton Football Club in 2003, and reflected on the big financial decisions the club faced. He believed that its relative success had been achieved through careful planning and decisions about investment, as well as willingness to assume a certain amount of risk.

> You can't be in football if you don't like risk. We built a new stadium and saddled the club with a debt of £25m, which we will pay off over the next 25 years. The stadium had to be built. Yes, it's a risk, and it puts financial pressure on us, but it's not like spending £25m on players. This is an asset that will allow the club to grow.

Pitching the level of investment in the playing staff is the key decision for any football chairman and his manager. Lowe finds the right balance is agonisingly difficult when the cost of failure and relegation is so great, and the rewards of a place in the Champions' League so rich and tempting.

> If you don't invest enough, then you don't win football matches and move forwards. If you invest too much, you slip off the tightrope the other way, and when you hit the bottom there's no safety net. **FT**

Source: *Financial Times*, 15 May 2003.

Uncertainty is when people are clear about their goals, but have little information about which course of action is most likely to succeed.

Uncertainty means that people know what they wish to achieve, but do not have enough information about alternatives and future events to estimate the risk confidently. Factors that may affect the outcomes of deciding to launch a new product (future growth in the market, changes in customer interests, competitors' actions) are difficult to predict.

Hutcheson faced great uncertainty when it decided to invest million of pounds in developing and launching its 3G mobile service, and many doubted the wisdom of its choice, especially as it was an unproven technology. By late 2004 the decision seemed to be paying off, as it was rapidly building its subscriber base. Egg faced uncertainty when it opened an online banking operation in France. Banking practices in France are different from those in the UK, and the company found it much harder than expected to build up an adequate customer base. In 2004 senior managers decided to close the French business.

Ambiguity is when people are uncertain about their goals and how best to achieve them.

Ambiguity describes a situation in which the intended goals are unclear, and so the alternative ways of reaching them are equally fluid. Ambiguity is by far the most difficult decision situation. Students would experience ambiguity if their teacher created student groups, told each group to complete a project, but gave them no topic, direction, or guidelines. Ambiguous problems are those where people have difficulty in coming to grips with the issues, and they are often associated with conflicts over ends and means, rapidly changing circumstances, fuzzy information, and unclear links between decision elements. Sometimes we come up with a 'solution' only to realise that it may not address what now seems to be the main problem.

Case questions 7.1

- Reflect on the decisions at Wipro which you identified earlier. What risks, uncertainties or ambiguities were probably associated with them?
- When the company moved its technology division to California, what dependencies would that have involved (use Figure 7.3 to structure your answer)?
- If the company expands its business in the Middle East, what dependencies might that raise?

7.4 Tasks in making decisions

As people make decisions (whether in business or about family and domestic matters) they attend in varying degrees to several tasks. Figure 7.5 shows these tasks in a sequence, but also note that the arrows show the iterative nature of the process – people rarely follow these steps in a single sequence. They move between the tasks iteratively, repeatedly going back to an earlier stage. This represents what we see every day – as we move through an activity we find new information, reconsider what we are doing, go back a stage or two and perhaps decide on a different route. People may also miss a step, or pay too much attention to some and too little to others. Putting just enough time and effort into each step is a decision-making skill.

Recognising a problem and setting objectives

A **problem** is a gap between an existing and a desired state of affairs.

People make decisions (such as to commit time and other resources to something) to try to meet an objective. They do so when they become aware of a **problem** – a gap between an

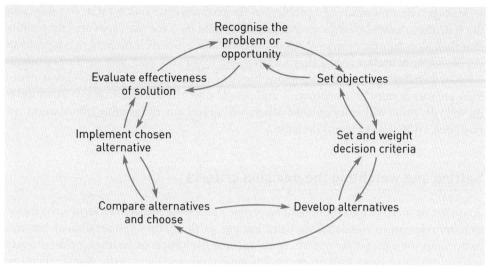

Figure 7.5

Tasks in making decisions

existing and a desired state of affairs, or an **opportunity** – the chance to do something not previously expected. An example to illustrate the steps would be a manager who needs to decide whether to buy new laptops for members of their sales team. The team have been complaining that their present machines are too slow and do not have enough capacity for the volume of work. The sales manager now has a problem, but in real life few problems are that obvious. Is a 5 per cent drop in sales a problem? It may be quite good in terms of what is happening in the rest of the industry, and perhaps the lost customers were unprofitable anyway. So identifying a problem, seeing it as something significant to be placed on the management agenda, is a subjective matter, upon which people may disagree. Before a problem (or opportunity) gets onto the agenda, enough people have to be aware of it and feel sufficient pressure to act. Managers at Microsoft were slow to realise that Linux software was a serious threat to their growth, and this delay in admitting the extent of the threat lost them valuable time in planning a response.

An **opportunity** is the chance to do something not previously expected.

Denial at P&G www.pg.com

management in practice

Procter and Gamble (P&G), the world's largest consumer products company (brands include Tide, Pampers and Crest), is undergoing radical change to increase profitability. This drive is being led by A.G. Laffley, a long-term manager at the company, who became CEO in 2000.

For most of its history P&G was one of America's leading companies, with brands that have become household names in many parts of the world. Many of its management techniques have also been widely adopted – such as the idea of having competing brands within the same company, to encourage performance. But by the 1990s, P&G was in danger of becoming another Eastman Kodak or Xerox, a once-great company that had lost its way. Sales of most of its top 18 brands were slowing; the company was losing ground to more focused rivals such as Kimberly-Clark and Colgate-Palmolive. At the same time, the dynamics of the industry were changing as power shifted from manufacturers to massive retailers.

Through all of this, much of senior management was in denial. Laffley says:

'Nobody wanted to talk about it. Without a doubt (I and a few others) were in the camp of 'We need a much bigger change'.

Source: *Business Week*, 7 July 2003.

Managers become aware of a problem as they compare the existing state of things with the state they desire. If things are not as they should be – the sales reps are complaining that their slow laptops prevent them doing their jobs properly – then there is a problem. People are only likely to act if they feel pressure to do so – such as a rep threatening to leave or a customer complaining about the time it takes to download the latest prices. Pressure comes from many sources – and people differ in whether they pay attention to the signals: some will react quickly, others will ignore uncomfortable information and postpone a difficult (to them) decision.

Setting and weighting the decision criteria

Decision criteria define the factors that are relevant in making a decision.

To decide between two or more options people need some **decision criteria** – the factors that are relevant to the decision. Until people set these, they cannot choose between options: in the laptop case criteria could include usefulness of features, price, delivery, warranty, compatibility with other systems, ease of use and many more. Some criteria are more important than others and the decision process needs to represent this in some way – perhaps by assigning 100 points between the factors depending on their relative importance. Also note that people can measure some of these criteria (price or delivery) quite objectively, while others (features, ease of use) are more subjective.

Like problem recognition, setting criteria is subjective: people vary in the factors they wish to include, and the weights they assign to them. They may also have private and unexpressed criteria – such as 'will cause least trouble', 'will do what the boss expects', 'will help my career'. Changing the criteria or their relative weights will change the decision – so the manager in the laptop case also has to decide whether to set and weight the criteria herself, or to invite the views of the reps.

Developing alternatives

Another task is to identify several alternative solutions to the problem. In the laptop case this is a matter of identifying currently available brands and is not difficult. In more complex problems the alternatives themselves may need to be developed. A practical issue is how many alternatives to develop – and how much time and effort to put into the process. Developing too many alternatives will be costly and time consuming, but developing too few may lead to a less imaginative response. This a key message in Barry Schwartz's (2004) examination of individual decision making – that the widening range of choices which consumers face in all aspects of their lives means that they are having to spend more time and effort making choices.

Comparing alternatives and making a choice

As in daily life, management decisions depend on some system for comparing the alternatives and making a choice. Which bar to go to, where to go on holiday, whether to make an offer for that house – people can use the criteria they set to compare the alternatives and decide which comes out best. In a simple case, that begins to show the relative strengths and weaknesses of each alternative – and that might give a clear signal as to which option best meets the criteria. Since the criteria and their weights are subjective, the choice of one may lead to further argument and disagreement – those who do not like the choice may reopen the debate by invoking different criteria.

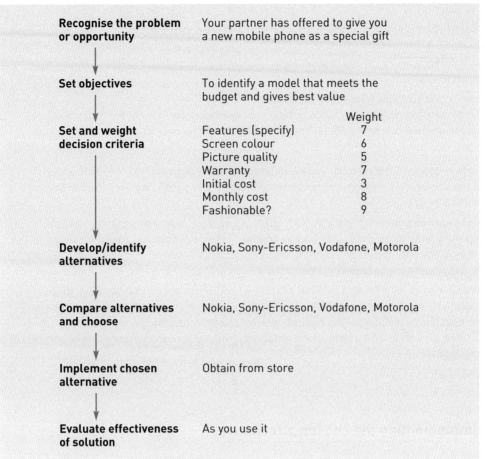

Recognise the problem or opportunity	Your partner has offered to give you a new mobile phone as a special gift	
Set objectives	To identify a model that meets the budget and gives best value	
		Weight
Set and weight decision criteria	Features (specify)	7
	Screen colour	6
	Picture quality	5
	Warranty	7
	Initial cost	3
	Monthly cost	8
	Fashionable?	9
Develop/identify alternatives	Nokia, Sony-Ericsson, Vodafone, Motorola	
Compare alternatives and choose	Nokia, Sony-Ericsson, Vodafone, Motorola	
Implement chosen alternative	Obtain from store	
Evaluate effectiveness of solution	As you use it	

Figure 7.6

Illustrating the decision-making tasks – a new mobile phone

Figure 7.6 illustrates the tasks in making a decision through a simple personal example. Although superficially simple, people find these choices difficult – mainly in the area of setting criteria. Some are easy to state and compare (price, warranty) but others are inherently subjective (in fashion?) and so open to wide differences of interpretation. The more people involved, the more difficult it may be to resolve these issues.

Activity 7.3   Critical reflection on making a decision

Work through the steps in Figure 7.6 for a decision you currently face – such as where to go on holiday, which courses to choose next year, or which job to apply for. Then do the same for a decision that involves several other people, such as which assignment to do in your study group or where to go for a night out together.

If you work in an organisation, select two business decisions as the focus of your work.

- How did working through the steps affect the way you reached a decision?
- Did it help you think more widely about the alternatives?
- How did the second decision, involving more people, affect the usefulness of the method?
- Then reflect on the technique itself – did it give insight into the decision process? What other tasks should it include?

key ideas **Mintzberg's study of major unstructured decisions**

Henry Mintzberg and his colleagues studied 25 major, unstructured decisions in 25 organisations. This showed that the techniques of rational decision making could not cope with the complexity of decision processes at the strategic level of organisations.

Only two of the 25 decisions involved a choice between ready-made alternatives; the great majority involved decisions to develop custom-made (or modified) solutions. The research led to observations that:

- Whether people recognised the need for a decision depended on the strength of the stimuli, the reputation of the source, and the availability of a potential solution: people did not typically devote energy to insoluble problems.

- Most decisions depended on designing a custom-made solution (a new organisation structure, a new product, a new technology, etc.). This was a complex, iterative procedure, typically leading to the 'design of *only one* fully-developed custom-made solution' (Mintzberg *et al.*, 1976, p. 256). It incorporated many selections between options as the design gradually narrowed to a single model.

- The choice phase, rather than being a rational process of setting criteria and evaluating alternatives (see Figure 7.5), was a far less significant part of the process than design – it was essentially ratifying a solution that was determined implicitly during design. Most choices were made on the judgement of one individual or by bargaining among a group of decision makers; they rarely involved formal analysis.

Source: Mintzberg *et al.*, (1976).

Implementing the chosen alternative

In the laptop case this is a simple matter – provided the manager has conducted the process satisfactorily. In bigger decisions this will be a much more problematic stage as it is here that the decision is translated, or not, into visible action. Even then it depends what is meant by 'implementation'. If the decision concerns a new computer system then one measure of implementation could be that the equipment is bought and installed. Another (and more useful) view would be that implementation refers to the wide acceptance and use of the system so that people are using it effectively to improve the service they offer.

This will be a much more protracted process, and will depend on people making many other decisions elsewhere in the organisation. This is also where the way in which a person conducts the decision-making process will become evident. If implementation depends on the cooperation of other people (for example, a major change in the way they work) then their willingness to do so will be affected by the extent to which they were involved in the decision process.

Evaluating the effectiveness of the decision

The final stage is that of evaluation – looking back at the decision to see whether it has resolved the problem in the way expected, and what can be learned from that. It is another way of expressing the activity of control. The evidence is that people are reluctant to do this formally, and typically turn their attention to future tasks, rather than reflect on the past. That choice inhibits their ability to learn from the experience.

Having given this simple and rather abstract overview of the process, the following sections outline models that seek to explain how people make decisions in practice.

7.5 Decision-making models

Scholars have developed several models of organisational decision making. Although sometimes presented as competing, people engaged in complex decisions may act in ways consistent with each of the models at different stages in the process. Managers may have personal preferences for one of the styles, and the choice of model may also reflect the type of decision they are making.

James Thompson (1967) distinguished decisions on two dimensions – agreement or disagreement over goals, and the beliefs that decision makers hold about the relationship between cause and effect. A decision can be mapped on these two dimensions – whether or not there is agreement on goals, and how certain people are about the consequences of their decisions. Figure 7.7 shows these, and an approach to making decisions that seems best suited to each cell.

Computational strategy – rational model

The **rational model of decision making** is based on economic assumptions. Traditional economic models suggested that the role of a manager was to maximise the economic return to the firm, and that they did this by making decisions on economically rational criteria. The assumptions underlying this model are that the decision maker:

- aims for goals that are known and agreed by all concerned, and that the problem is well structured
- strives for conditions of certainty, gathering complete information and calculating the likely results of each alternative
- selects the alternative that will maximise economic returns
- is rational and logical in assigning values, setting preferences and evaluating alternatives to reach a decision that will maximise returns.

> The **rational model of decision making** assumes that people make consistent choices to maximise economic value within specified constraints.

Consensus on goals or problem definition?		
	Agree	*Disagree*
Certainty	I Computational strategy Rational model	III Compromise strategy Political model
Uncertainty	II Judgemental strategy Incremental model	IV Inspirational strategy Garbage can model

Beliefs about cause-and-effect relationships

Figure 7.7

Conditions favouring different decision-making processes

Source: Buchanan and Huczynski (2003, p. 781).

The rational model is normative, in that it defines how a decision maker should act. It does not describe how managers actually make decisions – rather it provides guidelines on how managers would reach an ideal outcome for the organisation. It aims to help decision makers act more rationally, rather than rely solely on intuition and personal preferences. It is most valuable when applied to programmed decisions where there is little significant conflict over ends or means. Where the information required is available and people can agree the criteria for choice, the approach can work well. The approach can be applied by using computer-based quantitative decision techniques such as payoff matrices, break-even analysis, linear programming, forecasting, and operational research. The use of advanced database technologies also supports the use of rational approaches. However, when decisions are more complex and controversial, the rational approach in itself will not be able to resolve a decision – it can still play a part, but only as one input to a wider set of methods.

---

key ideas   **A behavioural theory of decision making**

Richard Cyert, James March and Herbert Simon (Simon, 1960; Cyert and March, 1963; March, 1988) developed an influential model of decision making. It is sometimes referred to as the behavioural theory of decision making since it treats decision making as an aspect of human behaviour. Also referred to as the administrative model, it recognises that in the real world people are restricted in their decision processes, and therefore have to accept what is probably a less than perfect solution. It introduced the concepts of bounded rationality and satisficing to the study of decision making.

Judgemental strategy – administrative and incremental models

The **administrative model of decision making** describes how people make decisions in uncertain, ambiguous situations.

Simon's (1960) **administrative model of decision making** aims to describe how managers actually make decisions in difficult situations, such as those characterised by uncertainty and ambiguity. Many management problems are unstructured and not suitable for the precise quantitative analysis implied by the rational model. People rely heavily on their judgement to resolve such issues.

Simon based the model on two central concepts – bounded rationality and satisficing. **Bounded rationality** expresses the fact that people have mental limits, or boundaries, on how rational they can be. While organisations and their environments become increasingly complex and uncertain, people are only able to process a limited amount of the available information. This places boundaries on their ability to operate in the way envisaged by the rational model, which they deal with by satisficing. **Satisficing** means that decision makers choose the first solution that is 'good enough'. While continuing to search for other options may eventually produce a better return, identifying and evaluating them costs more than the likely benefits. Suppose we are in a strange city and need coffee before a meeting. We will look for the first acceptable coffee shop that looks as if it will provide what we need. We have neither the time nor the knowledge to explore several alternatives for variety and price – we satisfice by choosing one that looks good enough for the immediate problem. In a similar fashion, managers generate alternatives for complex problems only until they find one they believe will work.

Bounded rationality is behaviour that is rational within a decision process which is limited (bounded) by an individual's ability to process information.

Satisficing is the acceptance by decision makers of the first solution that is 'good enough'.

The administrative model focuses on the human and organisational factors that influence decisions. It is more realistic than the rational model for non-programmed, ambiguous decisions. According to the administrative model, managers:

Satisficing in an IT project

Symon and Clegg (1991) studied a project to introduce a Computer-aided Design and Computer-aided Manufacturing (CAD-CAM) system into a manufacturing plant. The system itself was technically complex, but to secure the fullest benefits managers would also need to make significant changes throughout the organisation. The processes for managing orders would need to change, as would the work of staff and the responsibilities of managers. After several years of operation, the system was producing some modest benefits, but nothing like the benefits that the investment could have produced. The research team concluded that managers had unconsciously decided to satisfice – it was working, producing some benefits which they could demonstrate: to secure the full potential would require more effort than they were willing to give.

Source: Symon and Clegg (1991).

- have goals that are typically vague and conflicting, and are unable to reach a consensus on what to do – as indicated by the Deutsche Bank example on page 200
- have different levels of interest in the problems or opportunities facing the business, and interpret information subjectively
- rarely use rational procedures, or use them in a way that does not reflect the full complexity of the issue
- limit their search for alternatives
- usually settle for a satisficing rather than a maximising solution – having both limited information and only vague criteria of what would be 'maximising'.

The administrative model is descriptive, aiming to show how managers make decisions in complex situations rather than stating how they should make them.

Charles Lindblom (1959) developed what he termed an **incremental model** of decision making, which he observed people used when they were uncertain about the consequences of their choice. In the rational model these are known, but people face many decisions in which they cannot know with any certainty what the effects will be. Lindblom therefore built upon Simon's idea of bounded rationality to show that if people made only a limited search for options their chosen solution would differ only slightly from what already existed. Current choices would be heavily influenced by past choices – and would not move far from them.

> People use an **incremental model** of decision making when they are uncertain about the consequences. They search for a limited range of options, and policy unfolds from a series of cumulative small decisions.

On this view, policy unfolds not as a single event, but as the result of a series of cumulative small decisions. By making small decisions people avoid the risk of making a mistake in situations where cause–effect relationships are unclear – and if the effects are undesirable it is easier to reverse the decision. He referred to this as incrementalism, or as the 'science of muddling through'. Instead of looking rationally at the whole problem and a range of possible ways forward, the decision maker simplifies the problem by contemplating only the margins at which things might be changed. This means that the choice is easy to understand, and even then people consider only a restricted number of alternatives: to do more may prevent them from reaching any decision at all.

The incremental model (like the administrative model) recognises human limitations, and that people will be influenced by cultural, political and historical features of the organisation. They may also be influenced by the phenomenon known as the **escalation of commitment**, which is an increased commitment to a previous decision despite evidence that it may have been wrong (Drummond, 1996). People are reluctant to admit mistakes, and may persist in committing further resources to a project despite its evident failure. Rather than search for a new solution, they increase their commitment to the original decision.

> **Escalation of commitment** is an increased commitment to a previous decision despite evidence that it may have been wrong.

A study of escalation – Taurus at the Stock Exchange

Helga Drummond studied the attempt by management at the London Stock Exchange to implement a computerised system to deal with the settlement of shares traded on the Exchange. The project was announced in May 1986 and was due to be completed by 1989 at a cost of £6m. After many crises and difficulties, the Stock Exchange finally abandoned the project in March 1993. By that time the Exchange had spent £80m on developing a non-existent system. Drummond interviewed many key participants to explore the reasons for this disaster – which occurred despite the commitment of the system designers.

She concluded that the project suffered from fundamental structural problems, in that it challenged several powerful vested interests in the financial community, each of whom had their own idea about what should be done. Each new demand, reflecting this continuing power struggle, made the system more complicated. However, while many interests needed to work together, structural barriers throughout the organisation prevented this. There was little upward communication, so that senior managers were largely unaware of staff concerns about the timetable commitments being made.

Senior managers continued to claim the project was on track until a few days before it was finally, and very publicly, terminated. The lack of proper mechanisms to identify pressing issues lulled those making decisions into a false sense of security about the state of the project.

Source: Drummond (1996).

George Klein (1997) studied how effective decision makers work, including those working under extreme time pressure like surgeons, fire fighters and nurses. He found that they rarely used classical decision theory to weigh up the options: instead they used pattern recognition to relate the situation before them to their experience. They act on their intuition – a subconscious process of making decisions on the basis of experience and accumulated judgement – sometimes called 'tacit knowledge'. Effective decision makers use their intuition as much as formal processes – perhaps using both formal analysis and intuition as the situation demands. Experienced managers can act quickly on what seems like very little information. Rather than do a formal analysis, they draw quickly on experience and judgement to decide what to do. It may be that intuition is better described as 'recognition'.

When people build a depth of experience and knowledge in an area the right decision often comes quickly and effortlessly, as the subconscious mind recognises information that the conscious mind has forgotten. Jurgen Schrempp, CEO of DaimlerChrysler, is said to be like that – a risk-taker who always trusts his instincts, and to whom the need for bold moves is so evident that he becomes annoyed when investors question his strategy. In similar vein, Damasio (2000) argues that emotion and reason have to work together to achieve competent decisions, as rational models may leave out key aspects of the problem. They may not reveal the tacit knowledge and experience which are critical aspects of a problem.

Compromise strategy – political model

The **political model** is a model of decision making that reflects the view that an organisation consists of groups with different interests, goals and values.

The **political model** examines how people make decisions when managers disagree over goals and how to pursue them (Pfeffer, 1992; Buchanan and Badham, 1999). It recognises that an organisation is not only a working system, but also a political system, which establishes the relative power of people and functions. A significant decision will enhance the power of some people or units and limit that of others. People will pursue goals relating to personal and sub-unit interests, as well as those of the organisation as a whole. They will evaluate a decision in terms of its likely effects on those possible conflicting objectives.

They will often try to support their position by building a coalition – an informal alliance among managers who support a specific goal – with others who share their interest in the problem. A manager who develops a proposal to, say, increase the company's growth by acquiring another company will talk informally to other executives to seek their support. Coalition building gives others the opportunity to contribute their ideas and enhances their commitment to the decision if it is adopted.

The political model recognises that decisions are complex, information is often ambiguous, and disagreement and conflict amongst the many people involved are normal. The basic assumptions are:

- Organisations are made up of groups with diverse interests, goals and values. Managers disagree about problem priorities and may not understand or share the goals and interests of other managers.
- Information is ambiguous and incomplete. Rationality is limited by the complexity of many problems as well as personal interests.
- Managers engage in the push and pull of debate to decide goals and discuss alternatives. Decisions are the result of bargaining and discussion among coalition members.

Politics at Pensco

Pensco was a medium-sized life insurance business which went through major change, as did the rest of the industry. A new General Manager (GM) introduced a market-led strategy. He introduced a new pensions product which placed major demands on the Information Systems Division (IS). He also recruited a Director of IS from his previous company who had a reputation as an autocratic and aggressive manager. The research highlighted significant conflicts between departments, especially Sales and Marketing (S&M), Customer Services (CS) and IS.

Staff in S&M were dismissive of new products proposed by the Actuarial Division (AD), as they interpreted the market in a different way. S&M actively lobbied for their view, which the Board accepted. However, while the field staff in S&M were enthusiastic about the new products, Customer Services (CS) (who administer the sales and deal with customer queries) were less so. The new products meant retraining and reorganising, and managers doubted if the computer systems that IS was developing would provide enough support.

There were deep differences of view about the success of the project. Management mounted a triumphant presentation to all staff, lauding the success of the pensions product and the great market prospects facing the company. IS staff were bemused by the presentation, 'finding it difficult to link the presentation, which stressed the careful implementation of a carefully conceived and controlled project, with the organisation reality they had [experienced]' (Knights and Murray, 1994, p. 161).

Knights and Murray observed that conflicts over product and systems development policy led the company to incur large (but unpublicised) increases in costs. The management structure was unable to make the decisions necessary to resolve differences in departmental priorities.

Source: Knights and Murray (1994).

Inspirational strategy – garbage can model

This approach is likely when those concerned are not only unclear about cause-and-effect relationships, but are also uncertain about the outcome they seek. James March observed that in this situation the processes of reaching a decision become separated from the decisions reached. In the other models there is an assumption that the processes which the decision makers pass through lead to a decision. In this situation of extreme uncertainty the elements that constitute the decision problem are independent of each other, coming together in random ways.

March argued that decisions arise when four independent streams of activities meet – and when this happens will depend largely on accident or chance. The four streams are:

Choice opportunities	Organisations have occasions at which there is an expectation that a decision will be made – budgets must be set, there are regular management meetings, etc.
Participants	A stream of people who have the opportunity to shape decisions
Problems	A stream of problems which represent matters of concern to people – a lost sale, a new opportunity, a vacancy
Solutions	A stream of potential solutions seeking problems – ideas, proposals, information – that people continually generate

In this view, the choice opportunities (scheduled or unscheduled meetings) act as the container (garbage can) for the mixture of participants, problems and solutions. One combination of the three may be such that enough participants are interested in a solution, which they can match to a problem – and take a decision accordingly. Another group of participants may not have made those connections, or made them in a different way, so creating a different outcome.

This may at first sight seem an unlikely way to run a business, yet in highly uncertain, volatile environments this approach can work. Creative businesses depend on a rapid interchange of ideas, not only about specified problems but on information about new discoveries, research at other companies, what someone heard at a conference. They

 **Oticon builds a better garbage can** www.oticon.com

Oticon, a leading maker of sophisticated hearing aids, underwent a massive transformation in the early 1990s, in which the Chief Executive, Lars Kolind, broke down all barriers to communication. He realised that the key to success in the face of severe competition was to ensure that the talents of staff in the company were applied to any problems that arose. In March's terms, problems were expressed as a project, for which a member of staff (a participant) took responsibility, depending on other staff to suggest or help develop a solution.

> Any and all measures were taken to encourage contact and informal communication between employees. Elevators were made inoperable so that employees would meet each other on the stairs, where they were more likely to engage in conversation. Bars were installed on all three floors where coffee was served and meetings could be organised – standing up. Rooms with circular sofas were provided, complete with small coffee tables, to encourage discussion. (Rivard *et al.*, 2004, p. 170)

These discussions centred on reaching fast and creative decisions about problems and new product ideas – and the arrangement is credited with helping the continuing success of the company.

Source: Rivard *et al.* (2004); see also Chapter 12 Case.

depend on people bringing these solutions and problems together – and deliberately foster structures that maximise opportunities for face-to-face contact and rapid decisions.

Table 7.1 summarises these four models.

Table 7.1 Four models of decision making

Rational	Administrative/incremental	Political	Garbage can
Clear problem and goals	Vague problems and goals	Conflict over goals	Goals and solutions independent
Condition of certainty	Condition of uncertainty	Uncertainty/conflict	Ambiguity
Full information about costs and benefits of alternatives	Little information about costs and benefits of alternatives	Inconsistent views about costs and benefits of alternatives	Costs and benefits unconnected
Rational choice to maximise benefit	Satisficing choice – good enough	Choice by bargaining amongst players	Choice by accidental merging of streams

7.6 Participation in decision making

Vroom and Yetton's decision model

The idea behind Vroom and Yetton's (1973) contingency model of decision making is to influence the quality and acceptability of decisions. This depends on the manager choosing how best to involve subordinates in making a decision – and being willing to change their style to match the situation. The model defines five leadership styles and seven characteristics of problems. Managers can use these characteristics to diagnose the situation. They can find the recommended way of reaching a decision on that problem by using the decision tree shown in Figure 7.8. The five leadership styles defined are:

- *AI (Autocratic)* You solve the problem or make the decision yourself using information available to you at that time.
- *AII (Information-seeking)* You obtain the necessary information from your subordinate(s), then decide on the solution to the problem yourself. You may or may not tell your subordinates what the problem is in getting the information from them. The role played by your subordinates in making the decision is clearly one of providing the necessary information to you rather than generating or evaluating alternative solutions.
- *CI (Consulting)* You share the problem with relevant subordinates individually, getting their ideas and suggestions without bringing them together as a group. Then *you* make the decision that may or may not reflect your subordinates' influence.
- *CII (Negotiating)* You share the problem with your subordinates as a group, obtaining their collective ideas and suggestions. Then you make the decision that may or may not reflect your subordinates' influence.
- *G (Group)* You share the problem with your subordinates as a group. Together you generate and evaluate alternatives and attempt to reach agreement (consensus) on a solution. Your role is much like that of a chairperson. You do not try to influence the group to adopt 'your' solution, and you are willing to accept and implement any solution that has the support of the entire group.

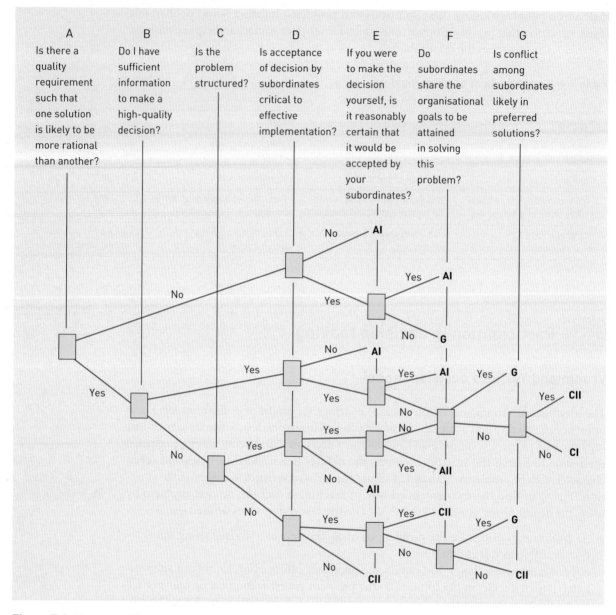

Figure 7.8 Vroom and Yetton's decision tree

Source: Reprinted from Vroom and Yetton (1973), p. 188 by permission of the University of Pittsburgh Press, copyright © 1973 by University of Pittsburgh Press.

The idea behind the model is that no style is in itself better than another. Some believe that consultative or delegating styles are inherently preferable to autocratic approaches, as being more in keeping with democratic principles. Vroom and Yetton argue otherwise. In some situations (such as when time is short or the manager has all the information needed for a minor decision) going through the process of consultation will waste time and add little value. In other situations, such as where the subordinates have the relevant information, it is essential to consult them. The point of the model is to make managers more aware of the range of factors to take into account in using a particular decision-making style.

The problem criteria are expressed in seven diagnostic questions:

- Is one solution likely to be better than another?
- Does the manager have enough information to make a high-quality decision?
- Is the problem structured?
- Is acceptance of the decision by subordinates critical to effective implementation?
- If the manager makes the decision alone, is it likely to be accepted by subordinates?
- Do subordinates share organisational goals?
- Is conflict likely amongst subordinates over preferred solutions?

The Vroom–Yetton decision model implies that managers need to be flexible in the style they adopt. The style should be appropriate to the situation rather than consistent amongst all situations. The problem with this is that managers may find it difficult to switch between styles, perhaps several times a day. Although the approach appears objective, it still depends on the manager answering the questions. Requiring a simple yes or no answer to complex questions is too simple, and managers often want to say 'it all depends' – on other historical or contextual factors.

Decision-making style at Rexam www.rexam.com

Rexam is a UK-based packaging business (and the world's leading beverage can maker), run by Chief Executive Swede Rolf Borjesson from 1996 until 2004 (when he became Chairman). He made many changes to the business, selling more than 100 companies and integrating many newly acquired ones. His management style is described by colleagues as collegial, combined with ruthlessness in delivering results. When it comes to key decisions about the business he says:

I always use the analogy that when you have an idea it is like when you empty your bath-tub.

He waves a hand in the air describing the circles his idea is bobbing on.

You talk to people, not necessarily saying 'I have an idea'. You have a discussion and you get a feeling for how they look at it. And then the whole process starts to accelerate.

His circles speed up as the imaginary idea whirls towards the plug-hole.

And suddenly you are all through the hole and we reach a consensus.
It doesn't mean I am after consensus all the time. I want to test where the organisation is, or where my closest colleagues are, when it comes to important decisions, and then I have to make up my mind what to do. It is very, very critical to the success of the company that the team is very much involved. If you try to run it yourself and you take all the decisions, you turn around to look back and there is no one behind you.

FT

Source: *Financial Times*, 18 November 2002.

Nevertheless the model is used in management training to alert managers to the style they prefer to use and to the range of options available. It also prompts managers to consider systematically whether that preferred style is always appropriate. They may then handle situations more deliberately than if they relied only on their preferred style or intuition.

Delegation

The model also relates to the issue of *delegation* which managers frequently face – whether or not to delegate more of their tasks to others, including how far to enable them to participate in decisions. As managers cope with increasingly demanding and uncertain conditions and as staff become more educated and confident, it will often make sense to widen the range of people taking part in decisions. This enables a wider range of experience and perspectives to be brought into consideration, as well as the motivational and development benefits.

However, the model indicates that this may not always be the best approach – such as if time is too short for wide consultation, or if conflicting views would delay, but not necessarily affect, the implementation of a decision. Equally if the decision is in effect already made for circumstances beyond the manager's control, staff would see a show of participation as an empty gesture. The model brings in the notion of management style being contingent on the specific situation, a topic to which later parts of the book will return.

Summary

1 **Explain with examples why decisions affect performance and how the process of making a decision affects the outcome:**
   - Decisions are choices about how to act in relation to organisational inputs, outputs and transformation processes. While some decisions can be made in a relatively mechanical way, most affect other interests, whose response to the decision will be affected by the way others conducted the wider process of making the decision.

2 **Explain, and give examples of, programmed and non-programmed decisions:**
   - Programmed decisions deal with familiar issues within existing policy – recruitment, minor capital expenditure, small price changes.
   - Non-programmed decisions move the business in a new direction – new markets, mergers, a major investment decision.

3 **Distinguish between certainty, risk, uncertainty and ambiguity:**
   - Certainty – decision makers have all the information they need, especially the costs and benefits of each alternative action.
   - Risk – where the decision maker can estimate the likelihood of the alternative outcomes. These are still subject to chance, but decision makers have enough information to estimate probabilities.
   - Uncertainty – when people know what they wish to achieve, but information about alternatives and future events is incomplete. They cannot be clear about alternatives or estimate their risk.
   - Ambiguity – when people are unsure about their objectives and about the relation between cause and effect.

4 **Explain the tasks involved in making a decision:**
   - Recognise the problem – which may depend on seeing and attending to ambiguous signals.
   - Set and weight criteria – the features of the result most likely to meet problem requirements, and that can guide the choice between alternatives.
   - Develop alternatives – identify existing or develop custom-built ways of dealing with the problem.
   - Compare and choose – using the criteria to select the preferred alternative.
   - Implement – the task that turns a decision into an action.
   - Evaluate – check whether the decision resolved the problem.

People work through these iteratively, frequently cycling back to earlier stages and changing direction.

5 **Contrast rational, administrative, political and garbage can decision models:**
   - Rational models are based on economic assumptions which suggest that the role of a manager is to maximise the economic return to the firm, and that they do this by making decisions on economically rational criteria.
   - The administrative model aims to describe how managers actually make decisions in situations of uncertainty and ambiguity. Many management problems are unstructured and not suitable for the precise quantitative analysis implied by the rational model.
   - The political model examines how people make decisions when conditions are uncertain, information is limited, and there is disagreement among managers over goals and how to pursue them. It recognises that an organisation is not only a working system, but also a political system, which establishes the relative power of people and functions.
   - The garbage can model identifies four independent streams of activities which enable a decision when they meet. When participants, problems and solutions come together in a relevant forum (a 'garbage can'), then a decision will be made.

6 **Describe the Vroom and Yetton model of decision-making styles:**
   - Outlines five ways of involving subordinates in reaching a decision (Autocratic, Information-seeking, Consulting, Negotiating and Delegating), and argues that the choice between them depends on characteristics of the situation – such as whether the manager has the information to reach a decision.

7 **Discuss the benefits and costs of wider participation in decision making:**
   - Participation may encourage commitment to implementing the decision, and by increasing the amount of relevant information available may raise the quality of the decision. The disadvantages are that it may take more time than is available, and lead to unduly high expectations about the real degree of influence participants have over events.

Review questions

1 Why does the quality of decisions that people make in an organisation affect its performance?

2 Explain the difference between risk and ambiguity. How may people make decisions in different ways for each situation?

3 List three decisions you have recently observed or taken part in. Which of them were programmed, and which unprogrammed?

4 The Vroom–Yetton model describes five styles. How should the manager decide which style to use?

5 What are the major differences between the rational and administrative models of decision making?

6 What is meant by satisficing in decision making? Can you illustrate the concept with an example from your experience? Why did those involved not try to achieve an economically superior decision?

7 What did Henry Mintzberg's research on decision making contribute to our understanding of the process?

Concluding critical reflection

Think about the ways in which your company, or one with which you are familiar, makes decisions. Review the material in the chapter, and perhaps visit some of the websites identified. Then make notes on these questions:

- What examples of the issues discussed in this chapter struck you as being relevant to practice in your company?
- Are people you work with typically dealing mainly with programmed or non-programmed decisions? What assumptions about the nature of decision making appear to guide their approach – rational, administrative, political or garbage can? On balance, do their assumptions accurately reflect the reality you see?
- What factors such as the history or current context of the company appear to influence the way people are expected to reach decisions? Does the current approach appear to be right for the company in its context – or would a different view of the context lead to a different approach? (Perhaps refer to some of the Management in Practice features for how different contexts encourage different approaches.)
- Have people put forward alternative approaches to decision making, based on evidence about other companies? If you could find such evidence, how may it affect company practice?

Further reading

Bazerman, M.H. (1998), *Judgment in Managerial Decision Making* (4th edn), John Wiley, New York.

> Comprehensive and interactive account, aimed at developing the skill of judgement among students, and so enabling them to improve how they make decisions.

Harrison, E.F. (1999), *The Managerial Decision-Making Process* (5th edn), Houghton Mifflin, Boston, MA.

> Comprehensive interdisciplinary approach to the generic process of decision making, with a focus on the strategic level. The author draws on a wide range of scholarly perspectives and presents them in a lucid and well-organised way.

Buchanan, D.A. and Badham, R. (1999), *Power, Politics and Organizational Change: Winning the turf game*, Sage, London.

> Theories and research dealing with politics in organisations, increasingly seen as a key part of making decisions.

Schwartz, B. (2004), *The Paradox of Choice*, Ecco, New York.

> An excellent study of decision making at the individual level. It shows how people in modern society face an ever-widening and increasingly bewildering range of choices, which is a source of increasing tension and stress. Many of the issues the author raises apply equally well to decision making in organisations.

Weblinks

These websites have appeared in the chapter:

www.wipro.com
www.pg.com
www.oticon.com
www.rexam.com

Visit two of the business sites in the list, or any other company that interests you, and navigate to the pages dealing with recent news or investor relations.

- What examples of decisions which the company has recently had to take can you find?
- How would you classify those decisions in terms of the models in this chapter?
- Gather information from the media websites (such as **www.FT.com**) which relate to the companies you have chosen. What stories can you find that indicate something about the decisions the companies have faced, and what the outcomes have been?

> Annotated weblinks, multiple choice questions and other
> useful resources can be found on
> **www.pearsoned.co.uk/boddy**

Chapter 8
Strategy

Aim

To describe and illustrate the main elements of strategy and to show the flexible nature of the process.

Objectives

By the end of your work on this chapter you should be able to outline the concepts below in your own terms and:

1 Explain how the strategy process contributes to the management of organisations

2 Describe the main stages and elements in the strategy process

3 Explain the concept of competitive advantage, and show how value chain analysis can identify its sources

4 Use the product/market matrix to identify alternative strategic directions

5 Explain and distinguish the main generic strategies an organisation may follow

6 Illustrate alternative methods of delivering a strategy

7 Compare planning, learning and political perspectives on strategy.

Key terms

This chapter introduces the following ideas:

strategy
competitive advantage
competitive strategy
benchmarking
value for money
institutional advantage
organisational capability
core competence
value chain
Balanced Scorecard
cost leadership strategy
differentiation strategy
focus strategy
strategic management
emergent strategy

Each is a term defined within the text, as well as in the glossary at the end of the book.

Marks & Spencer   www.marksandspencer.com

Originating in 1884 as a market stall, Marks & Spencer (M&S) is today one of the UK's leading retailers of clothes, food, home products and financial services, with a turnover of £7.3bn. There are 375 UK stores, employing 65,000 employees. Each week, 10 million people shop with M&S and three-quarters of UK adults have shopped there in the last 12 months. There are 155 franchised stores in Europe, the Middle East, Asia and the Far East. M&S also owns the US supermarket group, Kings Super Markets. Following an unprecedented programme of expansion at home and abroad in the late 1990s, profits started to slide.

Clothing is the biggest business, accounting for 50 per cent of its UK retail sales. There is a wide range of clothing for all ages and, although sales fell in 2003, M&S still holds an 11 per cent share of the UK market. Food sales account for 43 per cent of turnover and grew by 5 per cent in 2003. New 'metro' store concepts are being tested in city centre and high street stores.

The main strategic decision facing M&S is how to position its weakening clothing business. At the 2004 AGM, the new CEO (Stuart Rose) conceded that the brand is in decline and that customer relationships are weakening due to confusion and disappointment. Although it has a high share of the market, there is intense rivalry with competitors who can establish strong brands in well-defined segments. Some think that M&S targets too many segments and loses understanding of customer needs.

The traditional bases for competition (quality, trust) for which customers paid a premium appear to be changing: differentiating competitors (Next, Gap) offer attractive ranges with similar terms of trade; cost competitors (Matalan, TK Maxx, Tesco) offer acceptable

Marks & Spencer

quality basic clothing at lower prices. As well as adopting a more focused strategy, Rose has also pointed to the need for better internal operations, including improved store layout and streamlined logistics.

Case questions

Visit an M&S store, and also visit their website (**www.marksandspencer.com**).

- What have been the main additions or deletions to the M&S business?
- Comment on these statements from the M&S Chairman Paul Myners (July 2004):
  - '... the business has not performed as well as it should have. Our sales growth faltered during the second half and we lost market share in several core segments ...'
  - '... our product proposition in a number of important areas failed to meet the high standards expected by our customers.'

8.1 Introduction

All businesses in the competitive environment are affected by strategy and strategic issues – if not their own, then those of the competition or the external environment. At a time when the business environment is changing rapidly, all managements (not just those in trouble) are paying more attention to strategy. Established organisations such as BT are in a growing and diversifying telecommunications market – but face new competition that threatens their core business. Should the company try to compete in all areas, or concentrate on one sector, as Vodafone has done? Should Virgin continue to extend the brand into ever more diverse areas of activity, or would it gain more by building profits in the existing areas, and achieving more synergies across the group? Some charities face declining income – should their managers just continue as they are now, or will they serve their cause better by initiating a radical review of their strategy? These are just a few examples of the strategic part of the management task.

Strategy links the organisation to the external world, and Chapter 3 showed how the external environment influences management practice within any organisation. The PESTEL framework summarises factors common to all organisations, while Porter's model identifies five forces specific to a particular industry's competitive environment. Changes in these external forces create both opportunities and threats to an organisation's position – but above all they create uncertainty. You read in Chapter 6 that planning offers a systematic means of coping with uncertainty and adapting to change. It enables managers to consider how to grasp opportunities and avoid problems, to establish and coordinate appropriate courses of action, and to set targets for achievement.

The chapter begins by outlining different types of strategy. It then describes the elements and stages of the strategy process, before examining the main stages in more detail. These include developing objectives, analysing the value chain, conducting a SWOT analysis, deciding on strategic direction, and finally a process of implementing and review. The chapter concludes with a review of different perspectives on the strategy process.

8.2 Types of strategy

Strategy is concerned with deciding what business an organisation should be in, where it wants to be, and how it is going to get there.

Competitive advantage 'arises from discovering and implementing ways of competing that are unique and distinctive from those of rivals, and that can be sustained over time' (Porter, 1994).

Competitive or business strategy 'is concerned with the firm's position relative to its competitors in the markets which it has chosen' (Kay, 1996).

While people use different terms, the activity of **strategy** essentially involves dealing with *what* is to be achieved, *for whom* and *how*. In traditional strategic planning, people establish a vision and/or mission (e.g. M&S's vision: *to be the standard against which all others are measured*; mission: *to make aspirational quality available to all*), set some more tangible goals, and then design the strategy – how to achieve the goals. As you will see, strategic planning is rarely as neat as this – strategies can emerge, alter and disappear, sometimes very quickly.

For most organisations the underlying purpose in developing strategy is to perform well against competitors over a sustained time period. Ultimate measures of competitive performance are financial, such as profitability, return on capital employed or market share. This raises a concept of central importance in discussing strategy, that of **competitive advantage**. Introduced by Porter (1980b, 1985), the concept is concerned with the factors that give an organisation an edge over its competitors and enable it to achieve higher levels of profitability or other financial measure. Section 8.5 discusses these factors.

Strategy defined in this competitive sense – which seeks to identify and sustain sources of competitive advantage – is called **competitive strategy**. It is concerned with how managers respond to the five forces in the competitive environment. In summary, strategy is the direction and scope of an organisation over the long term, which achieves advantage for the organisation through its configuration of resources within a changing environment and to fulfil stakeholder expectations (Johnson and Scholes, 2002).

Not-for-profit strategy

The concept of competitive advantage does not apply directly to not-for-profit (NFP) organisations (Goold, 1997). While in many respects NFPs display similar characteristics to the profit-seeking firm, there are fundamental differences in (a) their goals, (b) their funding and external influence, and (c) their internal power relationships (Bowman and Asch, 1996). Some NFPs have direct competitors: Oxfam, for example, competes for donations and for customers through shop and mail order networks. Others compete for resources, media attention and volunteers.

In the public and education sectors, there is a clear trend to **benchmarking** for resource allocation, a system of comparing an organisation's practices and performance with others. Large NHS Healthcare Trusts in England compete for star status on a scale from one to three stars and with the possibility of becoming a Foundation Trust. Higher scores in this benchmarking exercise lead to greater resource allocation and independence. This incentive can be the most powerful force in driving Trust strategy. UK Higher Education institutions compete for resources via the Research Assessment Exercise.

The analogue to profit in the public sector is frequently **value for money**, i.e. provision of a project or service as economically, efficiently and effectively as possible. Not-for-profits try to maximise value for money, rather than profit. Goold (1997) suggests a better term is **institutional advantage**, which 'is held when a not-for-profit body performs its tasks more effectively than other comparable organisations'.

Benchmarking is a process of comparing organisational performance and practices with others (preferably leaders).

A **value for money service** is one that is provided economically, efficiently and effectively.

Institutional advantage 'is when a not-for-profit body performs its tasks more effectively than other comparable organisations' (Goold, 1997).

Competition between nations or cities

Porter (1990) has also written about competition between nations. Nation states and, within them, individual cities compete with each other, vying to secure inward investment by multinational companies, the right to host events such as the Olympic Games, or to hold titles such as 'European City of Culture'. Such events can bring major employment and income benefits. Competing in this way, countries and cities seek to identify sources of competitive advantage, which might include the levels of education and skill amongst the workforce and the attractiveness of the physical environment.

8.3 Elements and purpose of strategy

Figure 8.1 illustrates that developing an organisational strategy involves three main elements – strategic analysis, strategic choice and strategy implementation. Each of these contains further steps, corresponding to a series of questions that form the basis of strategic decision taking.

Marks & Spencer – the case continues
www.marksandspencer.com

The M&S brand is strongly associated with the company's values of quality, value, service and trust. These have been severely tested during the difficulties in 2001–2004, but Marks & Spencer believes it has a number of 'unique fundamental strengths' that will help its recovery. It has a good record of new product development. In food it has a leading share in fast-growing markets, such as ready meals; it has strong food development capabilities, changing a quarter of its food range every year, and has introduced bakeries, butcher's shops and hot food counters. Of the company's lines, 40 per cent are suitable for vegetarians and it was the first retailer in the world to respond to customers' health and nutrition concerns by appointing teams of food technologists and animal welfare specialists. All of this is reflected in the growth of the food business (turnover up 6 per cent in the year to April 2004).

In clothing, product ranges are constantly upgraded and the company is proud of its innovative 'magic fabrics' such as non-iron cotton, machine-washable wool and non-polish shoes. The company's scale facilitates innovation and also gives it buying power, although the close supplier relationships for which M&S is renowned were damaged by its decision to increase overseas sourcing in search of cost advantage.

Across the business the company stresses its high ethical trading standards and strong sense of environmental and social responsibility.

Sources: M&S *Annual Reports* 2001–2004; M&S website; *Financial Times* (various, 2004).

Case questions 8.1

- What are the main factors that M&S believes give it an edge over its competitors?
- Do you agree with them?
- What does the company do in respect of its commitment to society? (See the website.)
- Do you think these commitments give M&S competitive advantage? Are they likely to encourage people to shop in M&S stores?

Strategic analysis

The foundation of strategy is a definition of organisational purpose. This defines the business of an organisation and what type of organisation it wants to be. Many organisations develop broad statements of purpose, aims or mission; these form the springboard for the development of more specific objectives and the choice of strategies to achieve them.

Environmental analysis – assessing both the external and internal environments – is the next element in the strategy process. Chapter 3 explained how the external environment presents both opportunities and threats. Managers need to assess these in the light of the organisation's strengths and weaknesses (compared with the competition), and of what stakeholders expect.

Strategic choice

The analysis stage provides the basis for strategic choice. It allows managers to consider what the organisation could do, given its mission, environment and capabilities – a choice which also reflects the values of managers and other stakeholders (Dobson *et al.*, 2004). These choices are about the overall scope and direction of the business – what

Elements in strategy process	Questions	Description
STRATEGY FORMULATION		
Strategic analysis		
Defining organisational purpose	What is our purpose? What kind of organisation do we want to be?	A clarification of the purpose of the business, sometime expressed in a mission statement. Some organisations also determine the values to which they wish to subscribe
Environmental analysis	Where are we now?	Environmental analysis involves the gathering and analysis of 'intelligence' on the business environment. This encompasses the external environment (general and competitive forces), the internal environment (resources, competences, performance relative to competitors), and stakeholder expectations
Strategic choice		
Objectives	Where do we want to be?	Objectives provide a more detailed articulation of purpose and a basis for monitoring performance
Strategies	How are we going to get there?	Strategies describe how the objectives are to be achieved
Options analysis	Are there alternative routes?	Alternative strategic options may be identified; options require to be appraised in order that the best can be selected
STRATEGY IMPLEMENTATION		
Actions	How do we turn plans into reality?	A specification of the operational activities and tasks required to enable strategies to be implemented
Monitoring and control	How will we know if we are getting there?	Monitoring performance and progress in meeting objectives, taking corrective action as necessary and reviewing strategy

Figure 8.1 Elements in the strategy process
Source: Adapted from Catterick (1995, p. 14) and Johnson and Scholes (2002).

 **Examples of objectives**

The Kingfisher Group's mission is to be the world's best international home improvement retailer. It has three core objectives for its home improvement division: (a) major growth at B&Q, Costorama, Brico and Screwfix; (b) driving best practice and scale benefits throughout the sector; and (c) building an international store network beyond the United Kingdom and France.

The Higher Education Council for England states as its mission: working in partnership, to promote and fund high-quality, cost-effective teaching and research, meeting the diverse needs of students, the economy and society. It has four core strategic aims:

1 Widening participation and fair access
2 Enhancing excellence in learning and teaching
3 Enhancing excellence in research
4 Enhancing the contribution of HE to the economy and society.

products to offer, and in what markets. These decisions allow it to set more specific goals or objectives which might specify where people are expected to focus their efforts.

With a more specific set of objectives to hand, managers can then plan how to achieve them. Given its stated mission to be the best in the world, Kingfisher, for example, could expand internationally by building new stores, by buying existing overseas companies, or both. Firms also need to decide the *basis* on which they are going to compete with rivals – by offering standard products and competing through price, or by differentiating their products in some other way.

Since managers usually face several strategic options, they often need to analyse these in terms of their feasibility, suitability and acceptability before finally deciding on their direction.

Strategy implementation

Implementation depends on ensuring that the organisation has a suitable structure, the right resources and competences (skills, finance, technology, etc.) and culture. Strategy depends on operational factors being put into place. Finally, organisations set up some monitoring and control systems, developing standards and targets to judge performance.

 **Linn Products, suppliers of hi-fi equipment** www.linn.co.uk

Linn Products was founded in 1972 with a clear purpose: 'to reproduce, through superior sound, the thrills and emotion of a live performance'. The commitment is to quality and accurate performance. The company is an independent precision-engineering company specialising in top-performance sound reproduction. It makes a portfolio of products, including CD players, tuners, amplifiers and speakers, which it exports to more than 50 countries. Linn entertainment systems can be found throughout the world in royal residences, luxury homes, performance motorcars and yachts.

A market leader in specialised sound systems, Linn exhibits a clear, consistent philosophy, being true to the music and being directly coupled to its sources. As the sound technology leader, Linn has earned a unique reputation in the world of specialist hi-fi and multi-channel sound recording and reproduction, providing pitch-accurate sound reproduction. Linn has its own record label: artists include Claire Martin, Barb Jungr and the internationally acclaimed Carole Kidd. This helps Linn to control, monitor and compare every stage in the sound reproduction process, from artist performance to listener.

Market channels are strictly controlled: agents and distributors are intensively trained in the Linn philosophy. The jeans-clad, single-minded founder and CEO, Ivor Tiefenbrun, notes: '.. the traditional kind of (dealer) approach is inadequate to sustain growth in our industry. And retailers who want to build a business, or who want to grow with their customers, have got to meet their changing requirements ...'.

Today, the Linn mission is 'To thrill customers who want the most out of life from music, information and entertainment systems that benefit from quality sound'.

Competition is growing more active. Tiefenbrun says: 'I don't think there's much wrong with the way hi-fi's sold now in the sense that the people who sell it and the people who buy it are quite happy with that programme. But hi-fi is falling down people's lists of priorities. Our customers are changing, and we recognize that the world has changed from the time of the classic enthusiast hobbyist like myself 20 years ago. There are more products and more issues competing for those individuals' attention'.

Source: Interviews with managers, published information and company website.

Activity 8.1   Comparing practice with the model

- How would Linn's planning framework compare with conventional planning models? How would it work when Linn is predominantly marketing through dealers?
- Which strategy processes can you identify?
- What do you think are the bases for competition in this market?

Strategy in practice

Figure 8.1 shows that the seven steps in the strategy process fall into two broad phases – formulation and implementation – though in practice the two interact closely. Good strategists know that implementation rarely proceeds according to plan, partly because the constantly changing external environment brings new opportunities or threats; there may also be inadequate internal competences. Since these may lead management to change the plan, there will be frequent interaction between the activities of formulating and implementing strategy, and management may need to return and reformulate the plan. The important process is not producing a plan – it is the *process* of planning that allows the internal stakeholders to understand and exploit the organisation's competences.

Despite the propensity to change, a structured approach to strategy planning brings several benefits (Smith, 1995; Robbins, 2000):

- It reduces uncertainty: planning forces managers to look ahead, anticipate change and develop appropriate responses. It also encourages managers to consider the risks associated with alternative responses or options.
- It provides a link between long and short terms: planning establishes a means of co-ordination between strategic objectives and the operational activities that support the objectives.
- It provides clarity and unity of purpose: by setting out the organisation's overall strategic objectives and ensuring that these are reflected at operational level. Planning helps departments to move in the same direction towards the same set of goals.
- It facilitates control: by setting out objectives or standards, planning provides a basis for measuring actual performance.

However, the changing environment means that the strategy process is continuous if it is to maintain its 'fit'. Although physical planning documents might be produced periodically, the strategy will require regular review and adjustment to changing circumstances and to sustain advantage in a range of environments. In an economy of constantly changing competitors, alliances and customer requirements, strategic process needs to be flexible and continuous (Obeng, 2001).

8.4 Defining organisational purpose

A clear plan depends on defining organisational purpose. This may seem obvious, but many managers find it useful to debate periodically what their organisation is about, what they want it to become, and what differentiates it from others. Such clarity can provide focus and direction for all the members. Even in public sector organisations, whose basic business is generally prescribed by government, the exercise can be valuable.

A fashionable medium for expressing purpose is the mission statement. Some use the term 'vision' to express what management would like the future to be like. According to Dobson *et al.* (2004) good mission statements should clarify:

- the principal business or activities of an organisation
- its key aims or objectives
- the beliefs or values of the company – defining what the organisation represents, such as the balance between profit and other values such as reputation and community involvement
- the organisation's main stakeholders.

Statements should also be short, clear and easy to understand. Some examples of mission statements are set out below.

 **Examples of mission and vision statements**

IKEA (www.ikea.com)
A better everyday life. The IKEA business idea is to offer a wide range of home furnishings with good design and function at prices so low that as many people as possible will be able to afford them. And still have money left!

Unilever (www.unilever.com)
Unilever's mission is to add vitality to life. We meet the everyday needs for nutrition, hygiene and personal care with brands that help people feel good, look good and get more out of life.

Royal Society for the Protection of Birds (www.rspb.org.uk)
The RSPB is the UK charity working to secure a healthy environment for birds and wildlife, helping to create a better world for us all.

Higher Education Funding Council for England (www.hefce.ac.uk)
Working in partnership, we promote and fund high-quality, cost-effective teaching and research, meeting the diverse needs of students, the economy and society.

Nokia (www.nokia.com)
By connecting people, we help fulfil a fundamental human need for social connections and contact. Nokia builds bridges between people – both when they are far apart and face-to-face – and also bridges the gap between people and the information they need.

Activity 8.2	Critical reflection on mission statements

- Do you think that the examples above satisfy all of the requirements of a good mission statement (as defined by Dobson et al.)?
- Does the M&S statement of vision, mission and values meet those requirements?
- Give examples of the ways in which the company's values are reflected in its business activities.
- Does your organisation have a mission statement, and does it meet the Dobson et al. criteria? If not, edit it so that it would fit those criteria, or suggest why it is better as it is.

The dangers of mission statements

Although many organisations have mission statements, their value has sometimes been questioned. Kay (1996) asserts that visions or missions are indicative of a 'wish-driven strategy' that fails to recognise the limits to what might be possible, given finite organisational resources. He cites the case of Groupe Bull, a French computer company, which for many years sought to challenge the supremacy of IBM, particularly in the large US market. After several attempts, including entering into partnerships with two US companies, Bull finally conceded, entering into an alliance with IBM in 1992. Kay's analysis was that for 30 years Groupe Bull was:

> driven not by an assessment of what it was, but by a vision of what it would like to be. Throughout, it lacked the distinctive capabilities that would enable it to realise that vision. Bull – and other attempts at European clones of IBM – epitomises wish-driven strategy, based on aspiration, not capability. (Kay, 1996, pp. 41–3)

In a study of local government in Britain Leach (1996) found that mission statements and strategic visions had also become fashionable. While in some authorities mission statements had made a real impact in clarifying organisational values and culture, others regarded them only as symbolic public relations documents that had little effect as a management tool.

The dangers are not just that missions are unrealistic and fail to recognise an organisation's capabilities (as in the case of Groupe Bull), but also that management fails to develop a belief in the mission statement throughout the organisation. People only become to believe in, and act on, the mission statement as they see others doing so, especially senior management and other influential players. The ideas of the mission statement need to be cascaded through the structure to ensure a link between mission and day-to-day actions.

8.5 Environmental analysis

With the organisation's general purpose clearly defined, management needs to address the question 'where are we now?' This involves assessing the organisation's environments.

The external environment

Chapter 3 established that the external environment comprises forces operating at two levels: the general and competitive environments. At the macro-level, the PESTEL framework helps to identify the forces that are the major drivers of change for the organisation. At the micro-level, Porter's five forces analysis helps management to assess the state of competition within the industry. The chapter also showed that external stakeholders, such as government and pressure groups, also influence organisations. It used the power–interest matrix to identify which of those interests are likely to have most influence. If you are unsure about any of these terms, refer back to Chapter 3.

Case questions 8.2

Referring to the analytical frameworks in Chapter 3:

● What are the main external factors affecting M&S at present?
● Are there any differences between the food and clothing businesses?

Kay (1996) defined strategy as the match between the organisation's internal capabilities and its external relationships, describing 'how it responds to its suppliers, its customers, its competitors, and the social and economic environment within which it operates'. So, before devising future courses of action, management needs to look inside the organisation to establish how well it can cope with external changes in the environment.

The internal environment: resources and capabilities

Managers analyse the internal environment to identify the organisation's strengths and weaknesses. This means identifying what the organisation does well, where it might do better and whether it has the necessary resources and skills to deliver the chosen strategy. Those that are considered more than usually essential to outperforming the competition constitute critical success factors.

An **organisational capability** is an activity that an organisation can perform better than its competitors.

Resources are not very productive on their own. The term **organisational capabilities** is used to refer to a firm's capacity for undertaking a productive activity (Grant, 2002). A competence or capability is essentially an ability to undertake a particular task or perform a particular function but it can be hard to define. At a personal level, competence derives from a mix of skills, knowledge, behaviours and attitudes (Hellriegel *et al.*, 2002). Hamel and Prahalad (1996) describe an organisational competence as a 'bundle of skills and technologies', stressing the integration of people skills and business processes. Thus an organisational competence is unlikely to be held in its entirety by one individual or even a small team.

Core competencies are an organisation's major value-creating skills, capabilities and resources that shape its choice of strategy.

The value of the term **core competence** is that it draws attention towards competitive advantage (Grant, 2002). Management's task in internal analysis is to identify those particular strengths (competences and capabilities) that distinguish the organisation from its competitors in the minds of the customer and thereby underpin its competitive (or institutional) advantage. These are the organisation's core competencies (or *distinctive capabilities*), which stem from three factors (Johnson and Scholes, 2002). These are at the corporate level:

- The overall balance of activities carried out by the different business units, that is, the organisation's product/service portfolio. Does it have sufficient interests in growing rather than declining markets? Does it have too many new products (which tend to be a drain on resources) relative to longer established and more profitable ones?

At the divisional or strategic business unit level, the ability to compete effectively depends on:

- The resource base: includes physical resources (buildings and production facilities), human resources (employees' skills, knowledge, attitudes, etc.), financial resources (growth prospects, debt–equity mix, liquidity position, financial control systems, etc.) and intangibles (such as 'goodwill', or good relationships with suppliers). Each can be assessed for their adequacy in supporting a strategy.
- How the organisation performs its separate activities (or capabilities) – such as designing, producing, marketing, delivering and supporting its products or services – and manages the linkages between them. These, Johnson and Scholes argue, are the most important factors, since the key to performance often lies in the conversion of capabilities to competences, i.e. how these processes are carried out, rather than in the quantity or quality of resources at the organisation's disposal. A technique that is useful in assessing activities and linkages is value chain analysis.

Value chain analysis

The concept of the **value chain**, introduced by Porter (1985), is derived from an established accounting practice that calculates the value added to a product by individual stages in a manufacturing or service process. Porter applied this idea to the activities of an organisation as a whole, arguing that it is necessary to examine activities separately in order to identify sources of competitive advantage.

Figure 8.2 shows two categories of activity – primary activities required to transform inputs and to link with the customer (Grant, 2002), and support activities. Primary activities are:

A **value chain** 'divides a firm into the discrete activities it performs in designing, producing, marketing and distributing its product. It is the basic tool for diagnosing competitive advantage and finding ways to enhance it' (Porter, 1985).

- 'inbound logistics': focused on inputs, such as materials delivery and warehousing
- 'operations': creating the product, such as machining and packaging
- 'outbound logistics': moving the product to the buyer – storing, distribution
- 'marketing and sales': creating consumer awareness of the product
- 'service': enhancing or maintaining the product – installation, training, repairs.

The primary activities are supported by the actions of:

- 'firm infrastructure' (including organisational structure, strategic planning, and financial and quality control systems)
- human resource management: recruitment, training, rewards, etc.
- technology development: related to inputs, operational processes or outputs
- procurement: acquiring materials and other resources.

Johnson and Scholes (2002) observe that few organisations undertake all activities from product or service inception through distribution to point-of-sale themselves, but that the value chain exercise must incorporate the whole process; that is, the entire *value system*. This means, for instance, that even if an organisation does not produce its own raw materials it must nevertheless seek to identify the role and impact of its supply sources on the final product. Even if it is not responsible for after-sales service it must consider how the performance of those who deliver the service contributes to overall product/service quality.

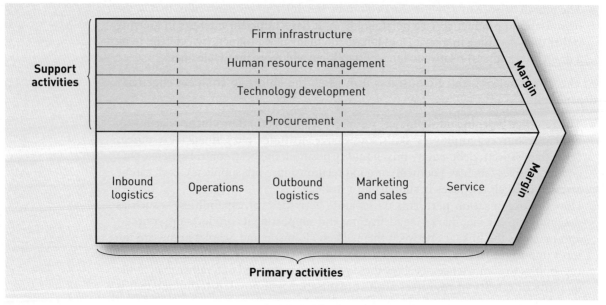

Figure 8.2 The value chain

Case questions 8.3

At the 2004 AGM, the M&S CEO indicated that management action was needed in the areas of stores (stock availability), supply chain (slow, over-committed), upstream (cut duplication), supply base (highly developed), downstream (£35m of savings) and costs (tighten procurement).

● Using the concept of the value chain, consider these remarks and give some examples of activities and linkages likely to be important to M&S in securing its commitment to managing value.

● Consider the clothing and food businesses separately.

Using the value chain

The usefulness of value chain analysis is that it recognises that individual activities in the overall production process play a part in determining the cost, quality and image of the end-product or service. That is, 'each ... can contribute to a firm's relative cost position and create a basis for differentiation' (Porter, 1985), the two main sources of competitive advantage. While a basic level of competence is necessary in all value chain activities, management needs to identify the core competences that the organisation has (or needs) to compete effectively. Analysing the separate activities in the value chain helps management do this by addressing the following issues:

● Which activities are the most critical in reducing cost or adding value? If quality is a key consumer value then ensuring quality of supplies would be a critical success factor.
● What are the key cost or value drivers in the value chain?
● What linkages do most to reduce cost, enhance value or discourage imitation? How do these linkages relate to the cost and value drivers?

Cost drivers

Porter identified the most important cost drivers:

- Economy of scale
- Pattern of capacity utilisation (including the efficiency of production processes and labour productivity)
- Linkages between activities (for example, arrangements governing the frequency and timing of deliveries affect storage costs; the 'just-in-time' system, which aims to minimise inventory costs, relies on close liaison between supplier and buyer)
- Interrelationships (for example, joint purchasing by different business units to achieve lower input costs)
- Geographical location (for example, location can affect an organisation's labour and other input costs; proximity to suppliers may also be an important inbound logistical cost)
- Policy choices (such as the choices on the mix and variety of products offered, the number of suppliers used, wages costs, skill requirements and other human resource policies)
- Institutional factors (which include the political and legal factors considered as part of the PESTEL analysis, each of which can have a significant impact on costs).

Value drivers

Value drivers are analogous to cost drivers, but relate to features, other than low price, valued by buyers. Identifying value drivers comes from understanding customer requirements (see Chapter 9), but typically include:

- policy choices (on matters such as product features and performance levels, the quality of input materials, the provision of buyer services and the skills and experience of staff)
- linkages between activities (for example, between suppliers and buyers where meeting delivery times is important to the buyer, or the links between sales and after-sales staff).

The value chain idea shows that companies can gain competitive advantage by controlling cost or value drivers and/or by reconfiguring the value chain – that is, by finding a better way of designing, producing, distributing or marketing a product or service. The cost and value drivers vary between industries, and change. The fluidity of the external environment means that organisations must also address the question of 'sustainability', by finding ways of ensuring that their competitive advantages are 'difficult for competitors to replicate or imitate' (Porter, 1985, p. 97).

As you saw in Chapter 1, Ryanair has become one of the most profitable airlines in Europe through concentrating on the parts of its value chain (turnaround, ticket transaction costs, no frills) where it could acquire and sustain competitive advantage.

Comparative analysis

Assessing organisational capability is only meaningful if contrasted with the position of competitors. Strengths and weaknesses are relative.

Nottinghamshire Healthcare Trust and the value chain

Nottinghamshire Healthcare NHS Trust (NHC) is the largest provider of mental health and learning disability services in Europe, including forensic (related to crime) mental health, adult mental health, alcohol and drug abuse and mental health for older people. The Trust was formed in 2001 by merging many separate organisations and in 2004 employed over 5000 staff, with revenue of more than £200 million. It provides services in over 100 sites, from community psychiatric services through to acute wards and secure units. NHC manages two Nottinghamshire medium secure units, as well as the high-security Rampton Hospital.

Although not in a directly competitive environment, NHC – like all Healthcare Trusts – is aware of intense stakeholder scrutiny, including local and national government, professional bodies, press, carers and users (patients). NHC has to manage the strategic tension between (a) delivering high standards of care and safety to challenging groups, whose needs are often articulated by advocacy groups; and (b) controlling costs and ensuring best value.

All of this takes place in a rapidly changing environment, where standards, targets and directives are frequently introduced or altered by national bodies or government. The Trust's Chief Executive, Jeremy Taylor, has worked in private and public healthcare environments. He recognises that strategy in mental health is often a case of 'looking back on what has already happened and realising it was strategy …'. However, he knows that the one constant for NHC is the need to control delivery standards and costs, either providing more or higher quality care (for the same input cost) or cutting the unit care cost without reducing the quality of provision. The main NHC costs are staff (80%), estate and facilities (residential, catering, offices), and drugs. Changes in the cost environment include lower-grade staff doing work previously done by doctors, using carers or volunteers, generic versions of high-volume expensive drugs becoming available, and estate management policies allowing disposal of expensive sites.

The main English monitoring authority is the Healthcare Commission. It is responsible for publishing NHS performance ratings and indicators. 'Star' rating affects how much independence trusts have and the ability to become a foundation trust. NHS organisations in England are allocated 0–3 stars based on their performance in areas such as waiting times and waiting lists, number of procedures carried out or cancelled, hospital cleanliness, death rates, financial position, and readmission rates. (Not all of these apply to NHC.)

Source: Information from the Trust, and the Trust website: **http://www.nottinghamshirehealthcare.nhs.uk/**.

Activity 8.3   Critical reflection on practice

 In July 2004, NHC was awarded three stars in the Healthcare Commission annual audit. Jeremy Taylor knows that to sustain this performance he will need to pay attention to the value chain. With the information in the case and at the website **http://www.nottinghamshirehealthcare.nhs.uk/** sketch the main primary NHC activities and the main support activities.

 Then consider which might be the most critical in reducing cost or adding value.

 For your organisation, or one for which you can gather information, use Figure 8.2 to sketch the main primary and support activities. Which are the most critical in reducing cost or adding value?

Competitive intelligence

Managers can begin to assess and develop their relative position by finding out about their competitors. Who are they? What are they doing? What are their plans and strategies? What assumptions are they making about changes in the market and the wider environment? What are their strengths and weaknesses? The answers to these questions can help organisations anticipate competitors' actions rather than merely react to them (Robbins, 2000).

Although one might think this information would be confidential, much is in the public domain. Press releases, newspaper reports, annual reports and company websites all reveal information. Research businesses provide analyses of industries and companies.

 Activity 8.4 **Explore some information websites**

The Internet is now a major resource for collecting intelligence on competitors. Look up **www.hoovers.com/global/uk/** or **www.business.com** to see what type of information is held on industries, companies and products.

Industry norm analysis

A comparative analysis will usually involve comparing performance with industry norms. These are standard sets of performance measures that allow people to compare competitors in the same industry. In the private sector, these typically take the form of measures of financial performance and market share, while in the public sector measures are often published in the form of 'league tables' – such as those used to compare local authority performance.

League tables have limitations. They report on outputs (or outcomes) but do not adjust for differences in context or degrees of operational difficulty experienced by the different organisations. Nevertheless, many see their use in public services as a spur to efficiency in the absence of market forces.

Johnson and Scholes (2002) note that a danger – in both private and public sectors – in relying solely on industry norm analysis is that 'the whole industry may be performing badly and losing out competitively to other industries that can satisfy customers' needs in different ways' (p. 172). It can, therefore, be valuable to draw comparisons with organisations in quite different businesses.

Benchmarking

A method that allows more in-depth analysis that came into fashionable use in the 1990s is benchmarking. It extends the idea of industry norm analysis by:

- encompassing not just quantitative measures of performance but also more qualitative or 'soft' dimensions, such as attitudes towards customers
- focusing on industry leaders or the 'best in class' rather than the industry as a whole
- emphasising operations or business processes rather than outputs; like Porter's value chain, this recognises the importance of the way things are done.

This form of 'process' rather than 'output' benchmarking is increasingly used as a means of improving organisational performance, often as part of a total quality management programme (Chapter 19).

NHS in England Performance Ratings 2003–2004 – Mental Health Trusts

Rating the performance of NHS trusts in England is a statutory responsibility of the Healthcare Commission, the independent inspectorate. Table 8.1 shows star ratings, performance against key targets and a 'balanced scorecard' for some Mental Health Trusts in England. The table has characteristics of an industry norm analysis but is clearly a benchmark table.

Table 8.1 Comparative benchmarking of some Mental Health Trusts

Measures of Performance / Health Trust	Rating	Key Target				Balanced Scorecard			
		Heath Team Integration	Financial Management	Hospital Cleanliness	Key Target	Clinical Focus	Patient Focus	Capacity and Capability Focus	Clinical Governance
South London and Maudsley NHS Trust	***	✓	✓	—	pass	high	high	high	✓
South Warwickshire Primary Care Trust	***	✓	✓	✓	pass	high	high	high	n/a
5 Boroughs Partnership Trust	**	✓	✓	✓	pass	medium	medium	low	n/a
Birmingham and Solihull Mental Health NHS Trust	**	✓	✓	✓	pass	medium	medium	low	✓
Bradford District Care Trust	**	—	✓	✓	pass	high	low	medium	n/a
Devon Partnership Trust	**	✓	✓	✓	pass	high	high	high	—

Source: © 2004 Commission for Healthcare Audit and Inspection, **www.healthcarecommission.org.uk**.

The **Balanced Scorecard** is a performance measure that looks at four areas: financial, customer, internal processes and people/innovation/growth that contribute to organisational performance.

The Healthcare Commission uses an approach known as the **Balanced Scorecard** (BSC). Devised for the private sector by Kaplan and Norton (1996), the BSC is a framework for defining, implementing and sustaining strategy throughout the organisation by linking it to the performance measurement system. It provides a 'dashboard' view of overall performance through successful monitoring and control of key performance indicators (KPIs) that drive and sustain organisational performance. A BSC provides greater focus on the strategic issues of customer satisfaction, organisational learning and internal business processes.

Magd and Curry (2003) point out the emphasis in today's environment on customer focus and stakeholders' interests in public sector organisational performance. Methods of assessment are employed to address these issues. Many have implemented benchmarking as one way to satisfy public expectations that they provide best-value services.

SWOT analysis

Strategy follows from finding a 'fit' between external environment and internal capabilities. Management therefore needs to identify the key issues from each analysis and draw out the strategic implications. It often uses a SWOT analysis – standing for strengths, weaknesses, opportunities and threats – to summarise the key internal and external issues. Chapter 6 discusses the technique of SWOT analysis.

The value chain and comparative analysis usually identify internal strengths and weaknesses (compared with the competition). The PESTEL and five forces analyses usually identify the opportunities and threats in the external environment (which affect the whole industry). Thus a strength might be a highly skilled workforce and a weakness might be out-of-date plant and machinery. A new line of business directed at a customer might constitute an opportunity (for the competition as well as the firm), but competition from cheaper imports could pose a threat to all current players in the industry.

Managers are usually advised to focus on identifying strengths that appear to give the company an edge over its competitors and constitute its core competences. They want to know if these can be sustained in the long term. If there is a threat from specific external factors that could erode them, can they be enhanced (e.g. through technology or training) or protected from imitation (e.g. patenting of innovation)? If erosion is inevitable then a new strategy is required. Management also needs to assess the critical success factors to ensure the organisation has the resources and competences needed to achieve a particular strategy. Management can therefore use SWOT to identify weaknesses that they need to strengthen.

Case questions 8.4

Drawing on your answers to previous questions:

- Make a summary SWOT analysis for Marks & Spencer's clothing business.
- In your opinion as a consumer, does the company now appear to be following the right strategies to restore its reputation in this market? You can see the CEO's 2004 statement at **www.marksandspencer.com/thecompany**.

8.6 Strategic choice

Analysing the factors in the previous section provides the basis for choices about strategy. These choices decide the organisation's future (Johnson and Scholes, 2002), yet are often uncertain and open to different interpretations. At the corporate level, there are fundamental questions about which business(es) the company is, or could be, in. Should it remain focused on a small range of activities or diversify? Should it remain a local or national business, or seek to operate internationally? These decisions establish the direction of the organisation. There are then choices between the alternative ways of delivering the chosen strategy. And in developing competitive strategy for individual markets a key question is what generic (or positioning) strategy to adopt – whether to compete on the basis of differentiation or cost.

Strategy directions – the product/market matrix

Figure 8.3 shows the main options in the product/market matrix. The majority (with the exception of market withdrawal) assume growth. In some parts of the public sector dependence on public resources means that growth is not an option. Instead, decisions may be about altering the service mix to use existing resources more efficiently and effectively. Similarly, for private companies, periods of economic downturn and fierce competition can precipitate contraction or restructuring.

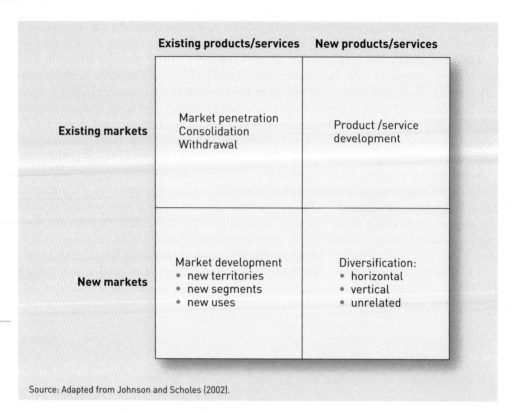

Figure 8.3

Strategy development directions – the product/market matrix

Source: Adapted from Johnson and Scholes (2002).

Existing markets, same product/service

Choice within this segment will depend on factors such as whether the market is growing, is in decline or has reached maturity. Each box contains several possible strategies:

- Market penetration is a strategy designed to increase market share. This is likely to be easier in a growing than in a mature market. Strategies may involve reducing price, increasing advertising expenditure, or improving distribution.
- Consolidation is concerned with protecting or maintaining market share in existing markets. In a growing market this means increasing the volume of business. In more mature markets firms might focus on improving cost efficiency and customer service in order to retain custom. In declining markets management might consolidate through the acquisition of other companies.
- Withdrawal from a market is a wise option in circumstances where, for instance, competition is intense and the organisation is unable to match the competence of rivals. Alternatively, changing priorities might require the redeployment of organisational resources. Health boards have withdrawn accident and emergency services from some hospitals in order to use limited resources more effectively.

Existing market, new product

A strategy of product (or service) development allows a company to retain the relative security of its present markets while altering products or developing new ones. In many retail sectors, such as fashion, consumer electronics and financial services, companies are continually changing products, usually in response to changing consumer needs and preferences. Similarly, car manufacturers compete by adding new features, improving technology and updating or extending their model range. Some new products, such as 'stakeholder pensions' in the United Kingdom, can arise out of changes in government policy. Because many new ideas do not come to fruition, new product development is a risky as well as a costly process.

New market, present product/service

Market development requires seeking new markets for existing products or services. The three main ways of doing this are by entering new geographic markets (many companies do this by internationalising their operations), targeting new market segments (new groups of customers, by age, profession, lifestyle or interests) or developing new uses for a product. New uses can often be found for manufactured materials. For example, a type of lightweight carbon originally developed for use in spacecraft is now used in the manufacture of golf clubs.

NTL and BSkyB – pay TV in the UK www.ntl.com, www.sky.com

Old loyalties to the five terrestrial TV channels are disappearing as the viewing market demands more choice in specialised areas that interest them, rather than accepting standard schedules offered by BBC and ITV programme planners. Forty-three per cent of the UK's 25m household market buy digital pay-TV (August 2004). The main competitors are the cable company NTL and the satellite-based provider Sky Digital. Both offer the same wide range of TV and radio content on a subscription basis.

NTL is the UK's biggest cable television operator. It serves the residential market through *ntl:home*, which offers telephone and Internet broadband services in addition to TV content. BSkyB (British Sky Broadcasting) operates Sky Digital, the UK's largest digital television platform. Sky also owns and operates Sky One, Sky movies and the exclusive Sky Sports channels. Sky also offers digital recording technology. The subscription-free Freeview service has quickly surpassed cable for set-top box digital TV watchers, feeding digital content through existing terrestrial household aerials.

Although the companies forecast bullish household penetration of up to 80 per cent, the growth of the market is slowing, causing the share price of both companies to fall sharply during 2004.

Sky Digital can reach all UK households via dish aerials. It has 7.4m subscribers and is targeting 10m by 2010. NTL has 3m subscribers, of whom 20 per cent take the phone and broadband products. Its cable infrastructure will allow it to reach 8m UK households by 2008 – its target is to sign up half of them.

On a product/market matrix basis, both companies want to target (a) existing markets with new products (subscription packages) and (b) new markets (terrestrial TV households) with their existing products. Both spend large amounts on marketing to attract high-volume segments. As well as attracting subscriptions, they must also satisfy the needs of advertisers. They are under constant pressure to recoup massive capital investments in cables or satellites and to pay for large call centres via a steady cash flow.

Source: *Financial Times*, 5 August 2004; and company websites.

Case questions 8.5

- Use the product/market matrix to classify the various directions of Marks & Spencer's business both before and after 2000.
- Note the methods M&S has used to deliver changes in strategic direction. Consider why these methods might have been selected.
- In the light of your reading and answers to previous questions, what kind of competitive strategy do you think M&S is following in respect of clothing and foods? Provide examples to support your answer.

Diversification

Diversification takes three forms:

- **Horizontal integration** Developing competing or complementary activities, such as when mortgage lenders move into the insurance business. With both vertical and horizontal integration there is some link between existing and new activities. Advantages include the ability to control the quality of inputs and the opportunity to expand by using existing skills. Kwik-Fit has used its database of depot customers to create a motor insurance business. Virgin has used its strong brand to create multiple complementary activities.
- **Vertical integration** Moving either backwards or forwards into activities related to the organisation's products and services. A manufacturer might decide to make its own components rather than buy them from elsewhere. Equally, it could develop forward, for instance into distribution.
- **Unrelated diversification** Developing into new markets outside the present industry. This is a strategy illustrated by the operations of conglomerate companies with a strong brand trusted by customers. The shift by some major supermarkets (e.g. Tesco) into travel insurance or other types of financial service is another example. Amongst other reasons, unrelated diversification may be undertaken as a means of spreading risk or to achieve further growth where existing markets have reached saturation or where there may be counter-cyclical demand patterns.

Alternative development directions are often not mutually exclusive and in practice most companies develop in a number of directions at the same time. Since several of the options are likely to require new organisational skills and competences, management needs to consider alternative methods for achieving a change in direction.

Alternative methods for delivering strategy

Any strategy can be delivered in one of three ways – internal development, acquisition, or through some form of alliance.

Internal development

The organisation delivers the strategy by expanding or redeploying relevant resources that it has or can employ. This enables the organisation to retain control of all aspects of the development of new products or services. This is often considered important where the product is highly technical in the design and manufacturing processes. Microsoft develops all its operating systems (e.g. Windows) in-house, rather than buying in the technology from outside. Pharmaceutical companies typically develop products in-house.

Internal development was also favoured by public service organisations in the 1990s. Many local authorities in the United Kingdom created in-house direct service organisations (DSOs) to repair and maintain council buildings. Nowadays, DSOs are usually required to compete with outside contractors. Similarly, many parts of local government and the Civil Service – for example legal services and the Stationery Office – have been privatised. The present climate for public services is not conducive to internal development. It is much more likely that attempts to meet new or growing demands will involve some form of joint venture or alliance (see below).

Acquisition (and merger)

Acquisition is where one firm takes over another. This allows rapid entry into new product or market areas and is a quick way of building market share. It is also used where the acquiring company lacks the necessary in-house skills, technology or other resources. For example, a company might be taken over for its expertise in research and development, its competences in relation to a specific production system or business process or its knowledge of a local market. Financial motives are often strong, particularly where there are opportunities to increase cost efficiency. Mergers are often undertaken for similar reasons but are more likely to come about by voluntary agreements than through contested takeover bids.

Starting in the 1990s, there have been many mergers and acquisitions in the financial services sector in the United Kingdom. Some have taken place between smaller high street institutions (e.g. the merger of the Royal Bank of Scotland and NatWest) in order to strengthen their position in a particular market, such as lending. They also achieve economies by closing branches and merging administrative processes. Others have been undertaken to extend the range of activities. Most merger and acquisition activity in the banking sector has so far been on the domestic scale. However, in other industries such as telecommunications the forces of globalisation have seen a wave of international acquisitions and mergers. For example, Vodafone of the United Kingdom has made several acquisitions, including the takeover of Germany's Mannesmann in 2000 for €145bn, in its quest to become the world's largest mobile phone company.

One of the main problems with acquisition and merger is the difficulty in merging two different organisations with different cultures and ways of doing things. Combined organisations often face a long period of disruption as a common set of procedures and operations are put in place. As long ago as 1996, Tom Peters noted that ' ... the idea of

Lookout Software

Lookout Software LLC is a small California-based software company run by the charismatic Eric Hahn and Mike Belshe. They manufacture one product: Lookout for Outlook, an email search engine for use with the Microsoft product Outlook. As Outlook users (especially corporate users with central servers) build up large histories of email in numerous folders, it is increasingly difficult for them to find and recall emails about important topics. Lookout provides a Google-like interface into which users can type keywords (e.g. 'diversification + university') to get immediate access to all emails, calendar appointments or contact information on that subject.

Lookout used a high-charm approach with its user community, responding personally to all user ideas and requests. This tactic transferred much of the debugging and development to a willing user group who felt personally involved. 'Our goal was to build simple, high-quality tools that empower people to spend less time processing email', Hahn said. 'I'm very thankful to the large community of people that provided feedback and support to our efforts, which ultimately resulted in continuous improvements to the Lookout software.'

In July 2004, Microsoft acquired Lookout Software. The press release stated that Microsoft wished '... to bring additional technology and expertise to future search efforts ... Lookout offers the critically acclaimed Lookout personal search tool for Microsoft Office Outlook [and] our vision is to take search beyond today's basic Internet search services to deliver direct answers to people's questions, and help them find information from a broad range of sources. We are thrilled to add the expertise of the Lookout team to our existing team of search experts.' Microsoft will integrate Lookout within its future offerings.

It remains to be seen how the original user community will feel about this. The Lookout Software culture could hardly be more different from that of Microsoft.

Source: **www.lookoutsoft.com/Lookout/**, Microsoft press releases, and correspondence with author.

vertical integration is anathema to an increasing number of companies. Most of yesterday's integrated giants are … de-integrating. Then they are reintegrating – not by acquisitions but via alliances with all sorts of partners … .' (Peters, 1996).

Some form of joint venture or alliance might therefore be preferable, especially where cost efficiency is not the main motive.

Joint developments and alliances

Organisations sometimes turn to partners to cooperate in developing products or services. Arrangements vary from highly formal contractual relationships to looser forms of cooperation but there are usually advantages to be gained by both parties. One attraction of this method is that it limits risk. For example, the large UK constructor John Laing announced an infrastructure joint venture in July 2004 with the Commonwealth Bank of Australia. It is a 50:50 joint venture with the bank to invest in UK hospital and European road projects, which allows both parties to limit the risk and to operate in areas in which they are strong. Rather than simply borrow from the bank, Laing shares the risk (and the reward) with the bank.

A second reason for joint ventures (JVs) is to learn about new technologies or markets. Alliances also arise where governments want to keep sensitive sectors, such as aerospace, defence and aviation, under national control. Airbus, which competes with Boeing in aircraft manufacture, was originally a JV between French, German, British and Spanish manufacturers. Alliances – such as the Star Alliance led by United Airlines of the United States and Lufthansa of Germany – are also common in the airline industry, where companies share revenues and costs over certain routes. As governments often prevent foreign ownership of airlines, such alliances are often an alternative to takeover or acquisition.

Other forms of joint development include franchising (common in many retailing activities – see the case on The Body Shop), licensing (for example, building under licence) and long-term collaboration between manufacturers and their suppliers.

management in practice   PSA Peugeot-Citroën–Toyota joint venture

In July 2001, Toyota President Fujio Cho and PSA Peugeot-Citroën CEO Jean-Martin Folz signed an agreement to develop and produce compact cars. Trading as Toyota Peugeot Citroën Automobile Czech (TPCA), the two groups believed there would be an increasing demand for compact vehicles well into the future. Total investment for this 50/50 joint venture, including research, development and business start-up costs, was €1.5bn. The plant was located in Kolin, Czech Republic, and begins operation in 2005, with annual capacity of 300,000 units and generating 3000 jobs.

By splitting the investment costs and pooling their expertise in engine and transmission technology the two firms hope to generate a better return on their investments. Moreover, selling the vehicles under two brands will make it easier to run the new plant at full capacity. For Toyota the project was seen as a cost-effective way to increase sales volumes and market share in Europe. As Europe's second largest car maker, PSA has superior knowledge of the market and a strong brand profile. For PSA, the deal was the latest in a long-running partnership policy. PSA already has technical and assembly alliances with, among others, Ford, Fiat and Mitsubishi Motors. PSA believes that a network of alliances helps the company preserve its independence (guarding against takeover bids) and allows technology transfer from one alliance to another. Diesel engines developed through PSA's joint venture with Ford, for example, could be used in the small car venture with Toyota.

Source: *Financial Times*, 9 July 2001; *Toyota News*, January 2002, April 2003.

Alliances and partnership working have also become commonplace in the public sector. In many cities alliances or partnerships have been created between major public bodies, business and community interests. Their main purpose is to foster a 'joined-up' approach to the planning and delivery of public services in an attempt to tackle social and economic problems more effectively. Public bodies also increasingly act as enablers or commissioners rather than as direct providers and have therefore developed contractual partnership arrangements with other organisations to deliver services on their behalf.

Generic competitive strategies

At the business unit level, firms face choice about how to compete with rivals. Porter (1980b, 1985) identified two basic types of competitive advantage: low cost or differentiation. From this he developed the idea that there are three generic strategies that a firm can use to develop and maintain competitive advantage: cost leadership, differentiation and focus. Figure 8.4 shows these strategies. The horizontal axis at the top shows the two bases of competitive advantage. Competitive scope, on the vertical axis, indicates whether the company competes industry-wide or within a smaller segment.

Cost leadership

Cost leadership is a strategy whereby a firm aims to deliver its product or service at a price lower than its competitors' equivalent. Overall cost leadership is achieved by the firm that is able to maintain the lowest costs of production and distribution within an industry. This strategy requires economies of scale in production and close attention to efficiency and operating costs, although other sources of cost advantage, such as prefer-

A cost leadership strategy is one in which a firm uses low price as the main competitive weapon.

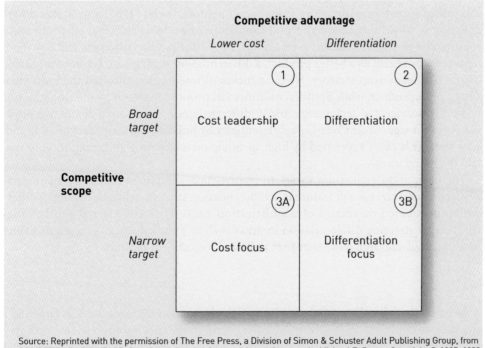

Figure 8.4

Generic competitive strategies

no-frills product and place a lot of emphasis on minimising direct input and overhead costs. A cost leadership strategy is likely to work better where industry produce is standardised, competition is based mainly on price and consumers can switch easily between different suppliers. However, a low cost base will not in itself bring competitive advantage – the product must be perceived as comparable or acceptable by consumers. Firms that have used this strategy include Costco, Somerfield, Argos and Superdrug. Firms pursuing this strategy must be effective in engineering, purchasing, manufacturing, and physical distribution. Marketing can be considered as less important, as the consumer is familiar with the product attributes. The example of Ryanair in Chapter 1 shows classic cost leadership strategy behaviour.

---

key ideas **The experience curve**

An important feature of cost leadership is the effect of the experience curve, in which the unit cost of manufacturing a product or delivering a service falls as experience increases. In the same way that a person learning to knit or play the piano improves with practice, so 'the unit cost of value added to a standard product declines by a constant percentage (typically 20–30%) each time cumulative output doubles' (Grant, 2002). This allows firms to set initial low selling prices in the knowledge that margins will increase as costs fall. The rate of travel down the cost experience curve is a crucial aspect of staying ahead of the competition in an undifferentiated market and underlines the importance of market share – if high volumes are not sold, the cost advantage is lost. Examples of products and services that are produced much more cheaply now are semiconductors, watches, cars, and travel reservations (on the Internet).

Differentiation

Differentiation strategy consists of offering a product or service that is perceived as unique or distinctive on a basis other than price.

A **differentiation strategy** is seen when a company offers a service that is distinctive – and valued as such by customers – from its competitors. Porter (1985) argued that differentiation is 'something unique beyond simply offering a low price' that allows firms to command a premium price or to retain buyer loyalty. Because customers will pay more for what they regard as a better product, a differentiation strategy can be more profitable than a cost leadership strategy. Nokia achieves differentiation through the individual design of its product, while Sony in consumer electronics achieves it by offering superior reliability, service and technology. BMW differentiates by stressing a distinctive product/service image, while Coca-Cola differentiates by building a widely recognised brand. This strategy is often supported by high spending on advertising and promotion to sustain the brand identity.

The form of differentiation varies. In construction equipment durability, spare parts availability and service will feature in a differentiation strategy, while in cosmetics differentiation is based on images of sophistication, exclusivity and eternal youth. Cities compete by stressing differentiation in areas such as a skilled workforce, good-quality housing, available land, good transport links and recreational facilities.

Focus

A **focus strategy** is when a company competes by targeting very specific segments of the market.

A **focus strategy** involves competing in a particular market segment, such as targeting a specific consumer group (e.g. teenagers, the over-60s, the medical professions) or a specific geographic market. The two variants – cost focus and differentiation focus – are simply narrower applications of the cost leadership and differentiation strategies. There

British Airways' differentiation strategy www.ba.com

After several years of poor performance British Airways has been renewing its strategy. It is seeking to differentiate itself from other airlines by focusing on business travellers rather than those travelling in economy class. Business passengers pay the full fare for their ticket, and expect a high-quality service. BA gradually reduced the number of seats available in economy class, and took fewer low-cost passengers travelling on connecting flights with other airlines. It sold GO (its low cost airline) in early 2001, as this was not consistent with the new strategy. Through this clear differentiated strategy, BA has lost passenger volume to the low-cost airlines but sustains the higher-paying business passenger who needs flexibility.

At the same time, BA has begun heavy discounting on its web-based sales – some frills (e.g. food) are still provided. In its desire to satisfy multiple segments, the company is essentially hyper-differentiating, a situation in which competitive companies must respond more rapidly to customers' changing demands.

are many examples of firms pursuing focus strategies. Saga offers travel services for the over-50s, Rolls-Royce offers luxury transport to the wealthy, many insurance companies tailor policies to the needs of particular groups (e.g. NFU Mutual caters for farmers, Female Direct offers motor insurance for women) and The Body Shop's green credentials appeal to particular consumer groups.

Moore (2001) notes that each generic strategy gives a company some kind of defence against each of the five competitive forces. For example, cost leadership, achieved through economies of scale or other cost advantage, can raise barriers to entry, and a low cost base can provide a cushion to cope with cost increases from suppliers. Differentiation, based on strong brand loyalty, can amongst other things create an entry barrier and also insulate the firm from rivalry. But firms' relative positions can always change. For instance, consumer loyalty can falter if the price premium, relative to low-cost competitors, is perceived as too great, and differentiation can be lost through imitation of a product by competitors.

Activity 8.5 Critical reflection on strategy

- Select two companies you are familiar with, and in each case gather evidence that indicates the generic strategy they are following.
- Then consider what features you would expect to see if the company decided to follow the opposite strategy.

Porter's initial argument was that a firm had to choose between the two basic strategies of cost leadership and differentiation. Many people disputed this, given that companies often appeared to follow both strategies simultaneously. By controlling costs better than competitors, companies can reinvest the savings in features that differentiate the product or service. Porter (1994) later offered some clarification: 'Every strategy must consider both relative cost and relative differentiation … a company cannot completely ignore quality and differentiation in the pursuit of cost advantage, and vice versa … Progress can be made against both types of advantage simultaneously' (p. 271). However, he notes there are trade-offs between the two and that companies should 'maintain a clear commitment to superiority in one of them'.

Options analysis

As well as identifying options, management is also faced with evaluating them. Many tools and techniques are available to aid decision making. Some, including ranking, decision trees and scenarios, assist in an initial screening process. This narrows down the number of options to a more manageable list that would be subject to a more detailed appraisal. Others, such as profitability and cost–benefit analysis, assess the feasibility of options as well as their acceptability in terms of likely risks and rates of return. Each option would be scored against the criteria set, to produce an overall rating of the attractiveness of individual options. In practice each option usually has pros and cons, and no single option emerges as a clear 'winner'. Ultimately, strategic choice is a matter of judgement about which option is most likely to best meet organisational goals.

8.7 Implementation: actions, monitoring and control

Implementing strategy

Implementation is intended to turn strategy into action, moving from the corporate to the operational levels. Many strategies fail to be implemented, or fail to achieve as much as management expected. A common mistake is to assume that strategy formulation will lead to painless implementation. Sometimes there is an 'implementation deficit', which means that either strategies are not implemented at all or they are only partially successful. The reasons for this are numerous but usually include external constraints, inadequate time, too few resources or poor communication. A common reason is also that while strategy formulation has the appearance of rationality, strategy implementation will often be a political process. Those who were content with the earlier strategy may strongly oppose the new strategy if it affects their status, power or career prospects. Implementing a major change is a complex, often conflicting process. Chapter 13 presents many ideas on the topic.

> **Strategic management** is an organisation-wide task involving both the development and implementation of strategy.

In essence, the task changes from strategic planning to that of **strategic management**. This includes all the aspects of strategic planning discussed earlier, *plus* all that is involved in managing implementation and control. In consequence, 'strategic management is characterised by its complexity ... arising out of ambiguous and non-routine situations with organisation-wide rather than operational-specific implications' (Johnson and Scholes, 2002, p. 32).

Monitoring progress

The final stage in the strategy process, as depicted in Figure 8.2, is to monitor the implementation of strategy. In order to do this satisfactorily, management needs to set standards and targets in respect of key objectives, at both strategic and operational levels. It also needs to ensure that information systems are in place.

Shareholders, analysts, management and others with an interest in the organisation's business will wish to compare performance results over time in order to reveal trends in business performance. It is only by tracking trends that a view can be taken on whether performance is in line with expectations or whether there is a need for corrective action. Many targets focus on financial and other quantitative aspects of performance, such as sales turnover, operating costs, profit margins and productivity. Some of these are the 'headline' profit and loss indicators, found in annual reports, which are of particular interest to share-holders and to industry analysts. For example, in its 2004 annual report Great Universal Stores plc (owners of Argos and Burberry) records the following 'highlights':

Indicator 12 months to March 2004	2004 (£m)	2003 (£m)	Growth (%)
Sales	7,548	7,108	6%
Profit before tax	827	642	29%
Earnings per share	60.7p	47.8p	27%
Annual dividend per share	27.0p	23.3p	16%
Dividend cover	2.25 x	2.05 x	0.20 x

Given the wide-ranging interests of stakeholders, companies do not restrict their report-ing to this type of information. In the public services, measures of quality and fairness of service outcomes may be more important to consumers and service users, but financial performance may be of greater interest to government and other funders.

Although monitoring is shown as the last stage in the strategy model, it is not the end of the strategy process. Strategy making is continuous as organisations adapt and adjust to the changes in their business environment. Regular monitoring of performance alerts management to the possibility that targets might not be achieved and that operational adjustments are needed. Equally, and in conjunction with continuous scanning of the external environment, performance monitoring can prompt wider changes to the organ-isation's corporate and competitive strategies.

Case questions 8.6

Review one of Marks & Spencer's annual reports (the most recent is on the website), including the summary financial statements (not the detailed version).

- What are the main ways in which the company measures its performance in different parts of the business?
- What measures does it use (or is it planning) in respect of its 'commitment to society' (see relevant web pages)?
- Is the emphasis on hard (quantitative) or soft (qualitative) measures?
- To whom are the measures you find likely to be of most interest?

8.8 Perspectives on the strategy process

While most managers recognise the steps outlined earlier as the basic content of strategic planning there are differing views on how the *process* actually works in practice. Some views are *prescriptive* in that they seek to explain how management *should* make strategy, while others are *descriptive* in that they try to set out how management *does* make strat-egy. Table 8.2 shows three perspectives.

Planning view

The 'planning view' is prescriptive and based on a belief that the complexity of strategic decisions requires an explicit and formalised approach to guide management through the process. In the 1960s and 1970s a wide literature, most notably the work of Ansoff (1965), espoused this structured approach. At this time, strategy was seen as a highly systematised process, following a prescribed sequence of steps and making extensive use of analytical tools and techniques. This was the 'one best way' to develop strategy that, if followed, was believed almost to guarantee corporate success. Implicit in this view are assumptions that human beings always behave rationally and that events, facts and the world in general can be viewed and interpreted in purely objective terms. However, pure rationality and objectivity rarely pertain in the real world and two alternative perspectives – the learning and the political – highlight the weaknesses of the planning view (Brews and Hunt, 1999).

Learning view

The message of the learning view is that strategy is an *emergent* or adaptive process. The idea can be illustrated by summarising Mintzberg's (1994a, b) critique of the formalised approach to strategy. In his opinion, strategic planning – which he refers to as the planning school – suffers from what he terms three 'fundamental fallacies', shown in Table 8.3.

Mintzberg's criticisms are deliberately pointed in order to emphasise his argument that, in contrast to the structured analytical approach advocated by Ansoff and others, there is no one best way to develop strategy. He regards strategic planning as 'strategic programming', a system developed during a period of stability (in contrast to the rapidly changing environment of the late twentieth and early twenty-first centuries) and

Table 8.2 Alternative perspectives on the strategy process

	Planning	Learning	Political
Approach	Prescriptive; assumes pure rationality	Descriptive; based on bounded rationality	Descriptive; based on bounded rationality
Content	Extensive use of analytical tools and techniques; emphasis on forecasting; extensive search for alternative options, each evaluated in detail	More limited use of tools and techniques and more limited search for options: time and resources don't permit	As learning view, but also some objectives and options disregarded as politically unacceptable
Nature of process	Formalised, systematic, analytical; top down – centralised planning teams	Adaptive, learning by doing; bottom up and top down	Characterised by bargaining and negotiation; use of power to impose objectives and strategies; top down and bottom up
Outcomes	Everything planned in advance; plans assumed to be achieved as set out	Plans are made but not all are 'realised'; some strategies are not planned but emerge in course of 'doing'	Plans are made but often couched in ambiguous terms to secure agreement; need interpretation in course of implementation; outcomes reflect compromises
Context/ environment	Stable environment; assumption that future can be predicted; if complex, use of more sophisticated tools	Complex, dynamic, future unpredictable	Stable or dynamic, but complex; stakeholders have diverging values, objectives and solutions

Table 8.3

Mintzberg's views on the fallacies of strategic planning

Fallacy	Description	Counter-view
Predetermination	'The prediction of ... the unfolding of the strategy formation process on schedule ... and the imposition of the resulting strategies on an acquiescent environment, again on schedule'	Internal and external environments are dynamic, so that plans rarely unfold as intended
Detachment	'The prescription is that organisations should complete their thinking before they begin to act'	'Effective strategists are not people who abstract themselves from the daily detail but quite the opposite: they immerse themselves in it [and] abstract strategic messages from it'
Formalisation	Analytical, scientific approach to strategy with a prescribed series of steps, boxes and checklists	Strategy requires insight, creativity and synthesis, all the things that formalisation discourages. It needs to function beyond checklists

Source: Mintzberg (1994a).

designed primarily for what he calls 'the machine organisation' – the classic formalised, specialised and centralised bureaucracy typically found in manufacturing industry. This style of planning, he argues, may be appropriate for certain types of organisation but not for others. Thus, what is required is a flexible approach to strategy.

To underline this point, Mintzberg makes a distinction between intended and **emergent strategy** (see Figure 8.5). He acknowledges the validity of strategy as a plan, setting out intended courses of action, and recognises that some deliberate intentions may in fact be realised. But he challenges managers to review just how closely their realised strategies mirror their original intentions. As well as the realisation of deliberate strategies, it is also likely that some plans failed to be implemented at all (unrealised strategies) and that others which he describes as 'emergent strategies' were not expressly intended but resulted from 'actions taken one by one, which converged in time in some sort of consistency or pattern'. A flexible approach to strategy is one which recognises that 'the real world inevitably involves some thinking ahead of time as well as some adaptation en route'. The essence of the learning view is this process of adaptation, the ability to react to unexpected events, to exploit or experiment with new ideas 'on the ground'. Mintzberg gives the example of a salesperson coming up with the idea of selling an existing product to some new customers. Soon all the other salespeople begin to do the same, and 'one day, months later, management discovers that the company has entered a new market'. This was not planned but learned, in a collective process. People learn in the process of implementation.

Emergent models of change emphasise that in uncertain conditions it is likely that the results of a project will be affected by unknown factors, and that planning has only a limited effect on the outcome.

Political view

The view of strategy as an emergent process has much in common with political perspectives on strategy. Both are based on the concept of 'bounded rationality'. This argues that limits on the intellectual capacity of humans, sources of information and resources are such that comprehensive rational planning, involving extensive analysis and detailed evaluation of alternative strategies, is impossible. Instead, strategists and policy makers, while seeking to be rational, are constrained into 'satisficing' behaviour – performance that is considered acceptable rather than exceptional – because of psychological, organi-

251

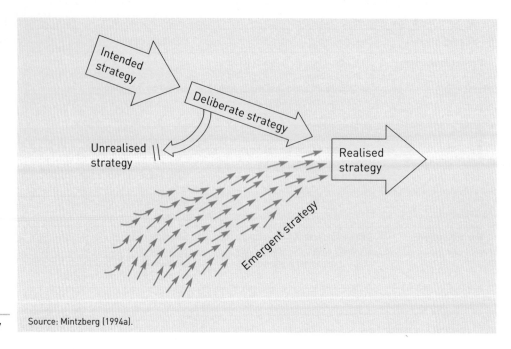

Figure 8.5

Forms of strategy

Source: Mintzberg (1994a).

sational and cost limitations. While the learning view tends to be based on the logic that 'prior thought can never specify all subsequent action' (Majone and Wildavsky in Mintzberg, 1994a, p. 289), the political view adds the further dimensions of power, conflict and ambiguity.

Drawing on his experiences in the public policy sphere, Lindblom (1959) was an early proponent of the political view (see also Chapter 7). He drew attention to the ways in which value judgements pervade and influence the planning process and pointed to the sectionalism or conflicting interests among stakeholders so characteristic of public policy, which frustrate attempts to reach agreement on objectives or on particular strategies to be pursued. He argued that the identification of values or objectives (ends) prior to the analysis of alternative strategies (means) to achieve them was an artificial construct because all strategies encompass implicit value judgements.

On the basis of these observations, Lindblom concluded that policy or strategy making was not a scientific, comprehensive or rational process, but an iterative, incremental process, characterised by restricted analysis and bargaining between the players or stakeholders involved. Lindblom labelled this the method of 'successive limited comparisons' whereby 'new' strategy is made simply by marginal adjustments to existing strategy: 'Policy is not made once and for all; it is made and remade endlessly … [through] … a process of successive approximation to some desired objectives.' Strategic choice is not a comprehensive and objective process but takes the form of a limited comparison of options, restricted to those that are considered politically acceptable and possible to implement. Lindblom's account is close to the *logical incrementalism* described by Quinn (1980) whereby 'strategy is seen to be worked through in action.'

Activity 8.6   Reviewing mission statements

Refer back to the examples of mission statements earlier in the chapter. Do you consider any of these stated intentions to be unclear or vague? If so, consider why they might have been expressed in this way.

Both the learning and the political views of strategy oppose the rigid planning view of strategy, but ultimately accept that a structured approach to strategy has its place. 'Too much planning may lead us to chaos, but so too would too little, more directly' (Mintzberg, 1994a). This view is reflected in several recent contributions to the literature on strategy that have mused upon the rise and fall, or death and reincarnation, of 1960s-style 'strategic planning'. Just as organisations adapt to the changing environment, so too do approaches to strategy. Moncrieff and Smallwood (1996) note that different planning styles emerge in response to different economic and social conditions. The planning style of the 1960s seemed to suit the relative stability that characterised the period. The highly competitive, increasingly global and fast-moving markets that characterise the present time may be better matched by a learning, adaptive or even 'real time strategy' (Taylor, 1997).

Summary

1 **Explain how the strategy process contributes to the management of organisations:**
   - Strategy is about the survival of the enterprise; the strategy process sets an overall direction with information about the external environment and internal capabilities. Defining the purposes of the organisation helps to guide the choice and implementation of strategy.

2 **Describe the main stages and elements in the strategy process:**
   - The process has three linked processes, each of which includes identifiable sub-processes. These are analysis (defining organisational purpose and analysing the environment); choice (establishing objectives, strategies and analysing options); and implementation (acting, monitoring and controlling).

3 **Explain the concept of competitive advantage and show how value chain analysis can identify its sources:**
   - Competitive advantage involves identifying the factors that distinguish an organisation from its competitors, especially its internal strengths (its capabilities and competences). Managers can do this by assessing their resource base and how the business performs the primary and support activities in the value chain.
   - The value chain enables managers to assess how individual activities help to create value for customers, in both the primary and support areas. It can then try to ensure that all the activities are performed in a way that adds most value to the final product – whether or not the organisation itself performs them.

4 **Use the product/market matrix to identify alternative strategic directions:**
   - Strategy can focus on existing or new products, and existing or new markets. This gives four broad directions, with options in each – such as market penetration, product development, market development or diversification.

5 **Explain and distinguish the main generic strategies an organisation may follow:**
   - Key strategic choices are those of cost leader, differentiation or a focus on a narrow segment of the market.

6 **Illustrate alternative methods of delivering a strategy:**
   - Strategy can be delivered by internal (sometimes called organic) development by rearranging the way resources are deployed. Alternatives include acquiring or merging with another company, or by forming alliances and joint ventures.

7 Compare planning, learning and political perspectives on strategy:

- The planning approach is appropriate in stable and predictable environments; while the emergent approach more accurately describes the process in volatile environments, since strategy rarely unfolds as intended in complex, changing and ambiguous situations. A political perspective may be a more accurate way of representing the process when it involves the interests of powerful stakeholders. It is rarely an objectively rational activity, implying that strategy models are not prescriptive but rather frameworks to guide managers.

Review questions

1 Distinguish between a corporate and an operating strategy.

2 In what ways does the concept of competitive advantage apply to for-profit organisations, non-profits, cities and countries?

3 Describe the main elements in the strategy process in your own terms.

4 Discuss with a manager from an organisation how his or her organisation developed its present strategy. Compare this practice with that set out in the model. What conclusions do you draw from that comparison?

5 Compare the strategies of Marks & Spencer and The Body Shop, and list any similarities and differences.

6 What are the main steps to take in analysing the organisation's environment? Why is it necessary to do this?

7 Can you describe clearly each of the stages in value chain analysis and illustrate them with an example? Why is the model useful to management?

8 Why do firms conduct benchmarking exercises? What difficulties can arise in external benchmarking?

9 The chapter described three generic strategies that organisations can follow. Give examples of three companies each following one of these strategies.

10 Give examples of company strategies corresponding to each box in the product/market matrix.

Concluding critical reflection

Think about the way your company, or one with which you are familiar, approaches issues of strategy. Review the material in the chapter, and perhaps visit some of the websites identified. Then make notes on these questions:

- What examples of the issues discussed in this chapter are currently relevant to your company – such as whether to follow a differentiation or focus strategy, or the balance between planning and learning?

- In responding to these issues, what assumptions about the strategy process appear to have guided what people have done? To what extent do these seem to fit the environmental forces as you see them? Do they appear to stress the planning or the learning perspectives on strategy?

- What factors such as the history or current context of the company appear to have influenced the prevailing view? Is the history of the company constraining attempts to move in new directions? How well are stakeholders served by the present strategy – how would they benefit from a significantly different one?

- Have people put forward alternative strategies, or alternative ways of developing strategy, based on evidence about other companies? If you could find such evidence, how may it affect company practice?

Further reading

Johnson, G. and Scholes, K. (2002), *Exploring Corporate Strategy* (6th edn), Financial Times/ Prentice Hall, Harlow.

The best-selling European text on corporate strategy. Although more detailed than required at introductory level, a number of sections usefully build on this chapter.

Dobson, P., Starkey, K. and Richards, J. (2004), *Strategic Management: Issues and cases*, Blackwell, Oxford.

Smith, R.J. (1995), *Strategic Management and Planning in the Public Sector* (2nd edn), Longman/Civil Service College, Harlow.

Both cover the main elements in the strategic planning process and explain, with the use of examples, some tools of strategic analysis in addition to those covered in this chapter. Smith's book also contains useful chapters on definitions and terminology and options analysis.

Kay, J. (1996), *The Business of Economics*, Oxford University Press, Oxford.

Presents a readable account of competitive strategy written from an economic perspective, illustrated by a wide range of European and other international examples.

Hamel, G. and Prahalad, C.K. (1996), *Competing for the Future*, Harvard Business School Press, Boston, MA.

Focuses on the importance of internal resources and competences in building strategic capability.

Mintzberg, H., Ahlstrand, B. and Lampel J. (1998), *Strategy Safari*, Prentice Hall Europe.

Excellent discussion of the process of strategy making from various academic and practical perspectives.

Wisniewski, M. (2001), 'Measuring up to the best: a manager's guide to benchmarking', in G. Johnson and K. Scholes (eds), *Exploring Public Sector Strategy*, Financial Times/Prentice Hall, Harlow.

A comprehensive account of benchmarking.

Moore, J.I. (2001), *Writers on Strategy and Strategic Management* (2nd edn), Penguin, London.

Summarises the work of the major contributors to the fields of strategy and strategic management – Part One contains a useful overview of the work of the 'movers and shakers', including Ansoff, Porter and Mintzberg.

Cummings, S. and Angwin, D. (2004), 'The future shape of strategy: lemmings or chimera?', *Academy of Management Executive*, vol. 18, no. 2, pp. 21–36.

Based on research among executives in Europe and Austrasia, this article develops an approach to strategy formulation that takes account of the current need to manage multiple customer groups in complex environments.

Long Range Planning and the *Strategic Management Journal* often contain new research on the topics discussed in the chapter.

Weblinks

These websites have appeared in the chapter:

www.ikea.com
www.marksandspencer.com
www.linn.co.uk
www.unilever.com
www.rspb.org.uk
www.hefce.ac.uk
www.nokia.com
www.sky.com
www.ntl.com
www.ba.com

Visit two of the business sites in the list, or any other company that interests you, and navigate to the pages dealing with news or investor relations.

- What are the main strategic issues they seem to be facing?
- What information can you find about their policies?

Annotated weblinks, multiple choice questions and other useful resources can be found on
www.pearsoned.co.uk/boddy

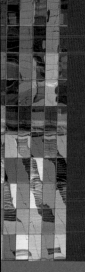

Chapter 9

Managing marketing

Aim

To explain the benefits that all organisations gain if they give a prominent role to marketing, and how they can organise the activity.

Objectives

By the end of your work on this chapter you should be able to outline the concepts below in your own terms and:

1 Compare and contrast marketing with alternative organisational orientations

2 Describe the benefits to any organisation of adopting a marketing orientation

3 Explain why marketing is an information-intensive activity

4 Identify the roles and responsibilities of the marketing manager

5 Explain market segmentation and the practice of selecting a target market

6 Describe the components of the marketing mix

7 Explain what is meant by product positioning

8 Consider whether marketing enhances consumer choice or encourages materialism and the manipulation of consumers.

Key terms

This chapter introduces the following ideas:

marketing
marketing orientation
consumer
consumer centred
marketing environment
marketing information system
market segmentation
target market
marketing mix
product life cycle

Each is a term defined within the text, as well as in the glossary at the end of the book.

Manchester United FC www.manutd.com

With over 50m fans across the globe, Manchester United Football Club (MU) is one of the best-known soccer clubs in the world. Founded in 1878, it rose to prominence in the early 1950s. Since then, the club has never been out of the sports headlines, hiring a series of almost legendary managers (including Sir Matt Busby and Sir Alex Ferguson) and buying or developing world-recognised players (including David Beckham, Ruud van Nistelrooy and Wayne Rooney).

In 1991 Manchester United became a public limited company, trading on the London Stock Exchange. The 2004 annual turnover was nearly £200m, generated from a wide range of football-related businesses (gate and TV revenues, sports clothes, etc.) and brand-related activities (MUTV, mobiles, travel, finance). Manchester United Football Club (MU) is therefore only a part of the worldwide operations. The holding company (Manchester United PLC) owns MU; Manchester United Catering (Agency Company) and Manchester United Interactive. MUTV, the club's official channel, is a joint venture between Manchester United PLC, Granada, and BSkyB.

The Club's ambition is to be the most successful team in football. Its declared business strategy is to do this by having the football and commercial operations work hand-in-hand, both in existing and new domestic markets and in the potential markets represented by the Club's global fan base, especially Asia. The marketing strategy is built on maintaining success on the field and leveraging global brand awareness through new products and partnered services designed to appeal to MU's worldwide fans. A substantial partner is Nike, whose development and marketing channels are used to generate new value from the MU trademarks (e.g. replica kits) by supplying the millions of MU fans in the UK and Asia.

Matthew Peters/Getty News and Sport

MU attempts to control and develop its own routes to market for media rights (e.g. MUTV), thereby exploiting the Club's own performance and reputation rather than relying on the collective appeal of competition football. The management believes this enhances the ability to deliver branded services to customers anywhere in the world. They rely strongly on IT-based CRM (customer relationship management) technology to convert fans to customers.

Source: Based on material from Butterworth Heinemann Case 0181, *Manchester United and British Soccer: Beautiful Game, Brutal Industry*; 'Can football be saved?, *Business Week*, 19 July 2004; and other published Manchester United material.

Case questions

- Consider the marketing implications of MU PLC's activities. What is it offering to customers?
- What groups would MU see as competitors? Are they simply other successful football clubs?
- How might MU improve its marketing?

Activity 9.1 **Describing marketing**

Before reading this chapter, write a few notes that capture your description of marketing. You might find it helpful to think of some recent purchases you have made and consider the different ways in which you came across marketing before, during or after your purchase. Keep your definition safe as you will use it again at the end of the chapter.

9.1 Introduction

Manchester United is very successful in raising awareness and favourability among fans and other customer groups. Its strategy revolves around the loyalty and trust that its customers have in the club or in the MU brand. There is a question as to what product or service customers think they are getting when they purchase an MU product. Different market segments (groups of consumers with similar needs) attribute differing benefits to the MU brand. An MU football fan might buy a season ticket to fulfil a psychological need to be part of a group with a common purpose, while a person completely uninterested in football might use an MU mobile phone because of the trust they have in that product, based on the MU reputation.

How should MU management manage the brand in these complex and sometimes unrelated markets? Might it be in the interests of the PLC to position the brand away from direct success on the football field, as that success cannot be guaranteed and the brand could be contaminated by a disaster (such as demotion from the Premier League)? How should MU promote itself? Standard advertising campaigns – based on the product's advantages over the competitor's offerings – are inappropriate. Word of mouth is vital to attract new fans, either at a young age in the home market or adults overseas. As you read above, MU are committed to a modern direct marketing system called customer relationship management (CRM), in which they treat customers as individuals (with targeted email or phone calls) rather than as members of a market segment.

Marketing is a management process that identifies, anticipates and supplies consumer requirements efficiently and effectively.

Manchester United depends on good **marketing**. Originally conceived as a local football team to keep working men occupied and interested on Saturday afternoons, it is now a worldwide business managed by trained business managers rather than by retired football players. MU marketing managers are aware that they are mainly satisfying psychological needs: when fans buy replica MU football jerseys as street-wear T-shirts, they are not simply keeping themselves warm and dry – they are making indirect statements about their persona to peer and other groups. In a highly differentiated market like this, buyers are not as price-sensitive as they are in commodity markets. A football shirt which costs less than £2 to make and deliver can sell for more than £20. Managers are able to adjust and manage the elements of the marketing management tasks, such as setting pricing points, varying the nature of the products, the way they are promoted and the channels to get them to market.

All organisations face the challenge of understanding what customers want, and ensuring that they can meet those expectations. Managers of profitable firms of any size will usually attribute much of their success to marketing; marketing is often closely tied to the business strategy. IKEA, the Swedish furniture retailer, has found and refined a formula that appeals to its target market. In 40 years it has grown from a single store to a business with over 150 outlets in over 30 countries. Virgin Direct, the financial services business founded in 1995 as a joint venture with Norwich Union, has become a major player in that sector, partly by using the telephone as its method of distributing the service to customers. Successful not-for-profit organisations such as Oxfam and the Royal Society for the Protection of Birds also demonstrate the benefits of understanding a market and communicating with it effectively.

All organisations need to deliver services or fulfil needs that their users require in order to generate revenue or retain the confidence of those who provide their funds – they have to demonstrate that they give value for money. To do so they need to be aware of their customers, sensitive to changing needs and organised to be able to deliver those needs to a level that people find acceptable. Successful organisations adopt a marketing orientation that encourages a commitment to identifying and responding to the needs, wants and demands of their consumers. Managers in such organisations have had to develop a greater focus on marketing and create systems that meet those needs of the customer.

This chapter opens by considering marketing as an organisational orientation and identifying the benefits of the marketing concept. It explains why all organisations can embrace marketing and how managers can build marketing into the structure. The chapter goes on to discuss the management of marketing information and the roles and responsibilities of marketing management – in both goods and services. It concludes with an explanation of the marketing mix and brand management.

9.2 What is marketing?

Lay people think of marketing as a range of techniques to sell goods or services better, e.g.

- Glossy brochures
- The latest promotional offer at a supermarket
- Sponsorship of popular television programmes by branded products, such as Nescafé's relationship with Channel 4's flagship teen show Hollyoaks or Cadbury's with Coronation Street
- Endorsement of products or services by celebrity names, such as Gary Lineker (broadcaster and former England football captain) advertising Walker's crisps, or Lawrence Dallaglio (former England rugby captain) promoting McDonald's
- Email messages from companies promoting travel offers or new books.

These promotional techniques illustrate the way in which marketers try to sell products or services – but there is more to marketing than promotional techniques. Definitions of marketing vary but all emphasise the need to identify and satisfy customer requirements. Kotler *et al.* (2002) define it as 'a social and managerial process by which individuals and groups obtain what they need and want through creating and exchanging products and value with others'. Peter Drucker (1999) places the activity even more firmly at the centre of business:

> Because the purpose of business is to create and keep customers, it has only two central functions – marketing and innovation. The basic function of marketing is to attract and retain customers at a profit.

The modern idiom of marketing can be described as an organisation-wide approach to managing all of the relationships shared between an organisation and its stakeholder groups. These definitions imply that marketing refers both to a marketing function within the organisation and to a more deeply embedded marketing orientation that shapes other activities of the organisation. The former view that the marketing was done by marketing people is not suitable for today's competitive environment. As David Packard, co-founder of Hewlett-Packard, said: 'Marketing is too important to be left to the marketing department', i.e. the entire organisation should be marketing the company, from the company receptionist as 'Director of First Impressions' to the Chief Executive as 'Director of Shareholder Interests'.

Consumer marketing and industrial marketing

There are two major categories of organisational marketing: (a) consumer marketing, which concerns creating and delivering products to satisfy consumers' needs, and (b) industrial or business-to-business (B2B) marketing, which is concerned with satisfying the needs of other businesses. The marketing concept is similar for both types of marketing but this chapter is mainly concerned with consumer marketing.

A marketing orientation

Marketing orientation is an organisational orientation that believes success is most effectively achieved by satisfying consumer demands.

Consumers are individuals, households, organisations, institutions, resellers and governments that purchase the products offered by other organisations.

Consumer-centred organisation is focused upon and structured around the identification and satisfaction of the demands of its consumers.

Most medium and large organisations have a marketing function – usually a department or group of people that focus on activities such as market research, competitor analysis, product strategy or promotion. Those that recognise most fully the significance of marketing incorporate marketing more deeply in the organisation, adopting not only a marketing function but a **marketing orientation**. This means that they concentrate their activities on the marketplace and the **consumer**. They are '**consumer centred**' or 'consumer driven'.

Levi have positioned themselves as a successful manufacturer of fashion clothing by making marketing a central organisational activity. With products like Levi's jeans, they respond to the changing needs, wants and demands of consumers by investing in product development and marketing communications. They watch the customers themselves to see how their clothes are worn: studies like this resulted in the popular hipster jeans, when marketers noticed that female jeans wearers were pulling the jeans down on their hips and responded with a line of products cut this way.

Charities such as Oxfam (**www.oxfam.co.uk**), Greenpeace (**www.greenpeace.com**) and Médecins sans Frontières (**www.msf.fr**) pay attention to the interests of their supporters. As well as promoting established lines of work, they survey their donors to ensure an acceptable match between the charity's campaigns and the issues that matter to those who donate the funds. Adopting a customer-focused marketing orientation enables them to continue achieving their goals (Kottasz, 2004).

management in practice

Financial services become consumer centred

Prior to the 1980s, bank and financial service providers were not noted for their customer friendliness. Customers regarded them as organisations that almost had to be persuaded to carry out their core business, such as providing a loan. Today's financial services industry has transformed itself into an aggressive and competitive market. Faced with intense competition, encouraged by deregulation and the demutualisation of many building societies, most high street retail banks adopted a more consumer-centred approach. Rather than having to be persuaded to make loans, they trumpet the advantages of taking out a loan with them and listen to the (often changing) needs of their consumers. By investing in new products and widening access to their services through telephone and electronic banking, organisations such as The Cooperative Bank (**www.cfs.co.uk**) have successfully responded to the new business and marketing environment and the competition that comes with it.

Marketing and the voluntary sector

Many staff and volunteers in charities are still uncomfortable with the idea that they are in marketing – preferring to see themselves as helpers or carers. Yet

> ... donors, local authorities, opinion formers, the media, all have the choice of whether or not to support a particular charity. They also, through exercising that choice ... can change parts of what the charity does. They make up the markets within which the charity operates. Without knowledge and understanding of those markets, the charity, quite simply, will fail. This does not mean charities operate in a value-free vacuum; rather that by knowing themselves and their mission, and by knowing the markets they exist to serve or work in, charities can match their activities to external needs and make sure that they achieve as much as possible for their beneficiaries. (p. 2)

Source: Keaveney and Kaufmann (2001).

Alternative orientations

The fact that an organisation undertakes public relations or advertising does not necessarily mean it has adopted a marketing orientation. It may in reality still have a focus on product, production or sales. Table 9.1 summarises these alternative orientations.

By identifying and understanding consumer demands, organisations with a marketing orientation can anticipate changes in consumer tastes and respond to them quickly. They do not offer products that they *assume* consumers will buy. Instead they use information about consumer demands to develop and offer products that satisfy those demands. They also anticipate future needs by studying trends in society, such as the need to be entertained during journeys, which led to the development of the Walkman type of product.

Table 9.1

Alternative organisational orientations

Organisational orientation	Focus	Benefit	Disadvantage
Product	Product features	High-quality products	Research may not have identified demand for the product and it may not sell
Production	Production	Low costs	Costs determine price and production, not consumer demands. Production may not match consumer demand
Sales	Turnover and shifting product	Sales targets met; good for cash flow in the short term	High-pressure sales techniques may meet current targets but lose future ones if users find product unsatisfactory
Marketing	Continually on consumers and consumer demands	Product offering determined by consumer demands; organisational goals achieved	Initial investment in becoming consumer centred

Source: Based on Lancaster and Messingham (1993); Dibb *et al*. (1997); Jobber (2004).

The sportswear industry provides many examples of the benefits of a marketing orientation. Aware that a wider selection of sportswear was available to men than to women at a time when women's participation rates in sport were increasing, Nike responded in a variety of ways. As well as extending their range of products to widen the choice of sportswear available to women, they sponsored the Imperial Cancer annual series of 'Race for Life' events, thereby associating the brand with issues that customers in the target market feel strongly about.

Product orientation

Organisations operating with a product orientation focus on their technological strengths and expertise. They stress the products and product features that these strengths allow them to make. They pay less attention to the demands of the market and can often find themselves in a position similar to that of the De Lorean car:

> This stainless steel car was built in Northern Ireland with government grants and Lotus expertise. Targeted for the American market, it received free publicity from its appearance in the film *Back to the Future*. When the manufacturers introduced the car to the market they found that there was no demand. Nobody wanted to buy the car. (*Car Magazine*, supplement, April 1997)

While a product orientation is focused on products for which there may or may not be demand, a marketing orientation is focused on identifying consumer demands for particular products.

The product concept works on the assumption that consumers believe in certain fixed products to satisfy their needs, so supplying organisations should simply make and offer the best that they can. The risk is that alternative ways of satisfying the demand can render a product obsolete. For example, manufacturers of slide rules (a mechanical ruler formerly used for performing calculations) did not take the approach that the consumer wanted to perform calculations – their attitude was that the consumer wanted the best slide rule. When the electronic calculator arrived, the slide rule market collapsed very quickly. The same effect can be seen today with the way in which music is purchased. Consumers do not want to satisfy a need to purchase music CDs *per se* – they want to satisfy their need to hear music. The runaway success of products like Apple's iPod portable music player (with downloadable music) is seriously threatening parts of the CD market.

Production orientation

The production orientation holds that consumers will buy products that are highly available and low-cost. Therefore, an organisation operating under the production orientation uses production efficiency and cost of materials to determine the quantity and price of goods to be produced. The production orientation focuses on efficiency and costs; it has some relevance where, for example, demand exceeds supply. If there is 10 days' rain in a seaside town, there is no need to market umbrellas, but simply to put them on the shelves before the rain stops.

Sales or selling orientation

An organisation operating under the sales orientation aims to shift as much of a product as it can as quickly as possible. Levitt (1960) provides a clear understanding of the differences between selling and marketing philosophies:

> Selling focuses on the needs of the seller; marketing on the needs of the buyer. Selling is a preoccupation with the seller's need to convert his product into cash; marketing with the idea of satisfying the needs of the consumer by means of the product and the whole cluster of things associated with creating, delivering and finally consuming it.

As Kotler *et al.* (2002) point out, the selling concept is typically practised with *unsought* goods, those that consumers do not normally think of buying, such as encyclopaedias.

Marketing orientation

Baker (1999) argues that by adopting a marketing orientation, which puts the consumer at the beginning rather than the end of the production–consumption cycle, organisations discover what consumers want. They can then decide how best to use the strengths of the organisation to meet these demands. They then *return* to the marketplace with a product for which a demand exists. They use market information about demand and the price that consumers are prepared to pay to determine how much to produce and what production costs must be to offer an price acceptable to consumers. While the sales orientation focuses on shifting products, the marketing orientation focuses on satisfying consumers and building long-term, mutually satisfying relationships with them. They focus on selling products that will satisfy consumer demands. To paraphrase Kotler *et al.* (2002), the marketing concept takes an *outside-in* perspective rather than the *inside-out* perspective of the selling concept.

Satisfying latent need

Taking the marketing approach means meeting the consumers' needs. In some instances, consumers will not be aware of the usefulness or value of a product that they do not know about or that has not been brought to market. Demand that is waiting to happen is called latent demand. Examples of widely used products that satisfy a formerly latent demand include mobile phones, electric toothbrushes and organic foodstuffs.

Activity 9.2 **Identifying consumers**

A marketing orientation suggests that organisational success is best achieved by focusing on the consumer. Identify each of the following organisations' consumers and suggest the benefits that a focus on their consumers will bring to each organisation: Microsoft, easyJet (**www.easyjet.com**), Carrefour (**www.carrefour.com**), Cancer Relief UK (formerly Imperial Cancer Research Fund).

Benefits of a marketing orientation

As an organisational orientation, marketing asserts that the most effective way of achieving organisational objectives is through consumer satisfaction. Organisations with a marketing philosophy still have to assess product features, efficient levels of production and sales targets (see the study by Shaw *et al.* (2004) of the relationship between marketers and engineers in German and UK organisations), but decisions about these matters are not the focus of organisational activities. Instead, consumer demands determine product development, levels of production and sales targets. Meeting these demands brings consumer satisfaction and organisational success.

   The adoption of a marketing orientation ensures that the whole organisation commits to achieving organisational goals by *continually* satisfying consumer demands. Aware of this objective and of their contribution towards it, different areas within the organisation are able to cooperate and coordinate their activities – for a recent comparative study of two fashion retailers, see Newman and Patel (2004). Organisations like Manchester United, Linn Products (see Chapter 8) and Sony Ericsson, which appreciate that consumer demands are continually changing, anticipate these changes and are more open and flexible in their approach to developing new products.

Kodak www.kodak.com

Kodak is the world's largest film photography company. For many years, it maintained a strong position in the film and photo development industry, fending off aggressive competition from Fuji and own-brand labels. As consumers started to move to filmless (digital) cameras, Kodak seemed slow off the mark: in 2002, it looked as though the Japanese manufacturers had stolen a march in Kodak's home US markets; Sony achieved the number 1 US market position. In 2004, digital cameras outsold film cameras in the US.

However, by listening to consumers' demands and investing in research and product development, Kodak have now recovered their market leader position by introducing products such as the latest versions of the EasyShare digital camera. This has enabled them to keep ahead of the competition, with a reputation for innovation (including a docking station for the camera) and quality.

Source: *Business Week*, 6 August 2004; *Financial Times*, 22 April 2004, 25 August 2004.

By identifying and monitoring consumer demands, marketing-oriented organisations are able to respond to these demands and ensure that the products they offer satisfy consumers. Above all else, the adoption of the marketing orientation offers stability in the marketplace (Figure 9.1).

This concept has been extended to include **network marketing**, which recognises a web of interdependencies between firms. While relationship marketing depends on managing relationships with customers, network marketing recognises that meeting their needs depends on a wider range of stakeholders – such as raw materials suppliers or delivery companies. Manchester United is a good example of multiple stakeholders and relationship marketing combining to create network marketing.

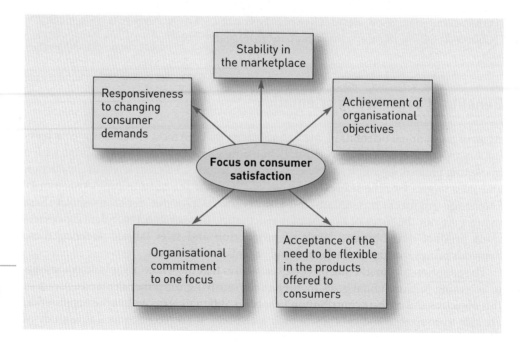

Figure 9.1

Benefits of marketing as an organisational orientation

key ideas **Transactional marketing and relationship marketing**

Researchers such as Gronroos (2000) distinguish between transactional marketing and relationship marketing. They argue that in order to ensure a stable position in the marketplace, many organisations have replaced their focus on transactions (exchange of value, e.g. a purchase) with one that seeks to develop mutually satisfying, long-term relationships with their consumers throughout the life cycle of the product. They argue that a focus on one-off transactions encourages organisations to concentrate on short-term profit maximisation and to pay less attention to their long-term position in the market-place. Organisations that move towards a relational focus have a better understanding of consumer needs. They concentrate on developing a 'long-term, continuous series of transactions' that helps them maintain stability in the market and achieve their objectives in the long term.

Others (such as Zolkiewski, 2004) argue that relationship marketing is not suitable for all organisations, and that not all long-term relationships are as beneficial or necessary as advocates of this approach claim.

A hospital develops a new approach to customer relations

The idea of building relationships with consumers has historically been most evident in industrial markets in which organisations sell to other businesses and government. Managers in public sector organisations, such as hospitals, are now using the approach. Chapman and Cowdell (1998) report the case of a hospital which had begun to explore how to improve the attention it gave to marketing. Until recently the culture in the hospital had been one in which the professional judgement of clinical staff was sacrosanct, leading to a marked 'provider focus'. Medical professionals were responsible for identifying patients' needs and supplying services to satisfy them. External policy changes had begun to change this, and more people within the hospital were beginning to be critical of the traditional approach, which had often dissatisfied increasingly articulate and demanding patients. The hospital's directorate had recognised that they needed to develop a more customer-focused orientation, including the development of relationship marketing.

> One of the trust's objectives is to maximise income. An effective way of using relationship marketing to maximise income is to use personal contact methods (to market) health services to customer groups, such as general practitioners, who are directly answerable to their patients for the quality of health services and often act as 'gate keepers' to the services provided by the trust. (p. 328)

Source: Chapman and Cowdell (1998).

9.3 What types of organisation can use marketing?

The benefits offered by the marketing orientation apply to all types of organisations. Those managing not-for-profit organisations, charities, churches and sports teams can all benefit from a marketing orientation. Writing about the health service, Moutinho (1995) states:

> ... the present day marketing concept views marketing as a social process ... [to identify] consumer needs and satisfy them through integrated marketing activities ... Marketing thinking will lead to a better understanding of the needs of different client segments; to a more careful shaping and launching of new services; to a pruning of weak services; to more flexible pricing approaches; and to higher levels of patient satisfaction.

Some healthcare organisations are now beginning to apply marketing to a broader set of problems by trying to answer critical questions such as:

- Where should the hospital locate a clinic or an ambulatory care unit?
- How can the hospital estimate whether a new service will draw enough patients?
- What should the hospital do with a maternity wing that is only 20 per cent occupied?
- How can the hospital attract more consumers to preventive care services such as annual medical check-ups and cancer-screening programmes?

The acid test for the implementation of a marketing orientation in the healthcare sector is based on the existence of an orderly, systematic and complete strategic marketing plan (Moutinho, 1995).

Saint Honoré Hospital, Brussels

Saint Honoré Hospital is situated in a suburban area of Brussels. The administrator has for some time felt that he needs to pay closer attention to the marketing aspects of the operation to ensure successful use of facilities and to help future development of the hospital. As a first step towards developing a comprehensive marketing strategy he arranged for some market research to be done. One of the questions he was particularly interested in was the factors that patients and doctors used in deciding which hospital to go to.

Amongst the data that the research produced was the following table:

Consumers' choice criteria in selecting a hospital

Aspect of the hospital	Very important (%)
Good doctors	95.7
Good nursing care	88.2
Good emergency room	86.5
Latest medical equipment	81.3
Keep patients informed about their care	71.4
Good reputation	68.7
Prices of services	59.1
Overall hospital management	56.3

Source: Moutinho (1995).

Activity 9.3   Evaluating market research

- How might the information affect the decisions taken by the management of Saint Honoré Hospital? What other information would they be wise to take into account on the views of patients?
- Can you identify another social care organisation that could use market research to assist it?

Organisations with social or charitable aims are beginning to take a marketing orientation, including those raising awareness of the dangers of smoking, increasing charitable donations and promoting the benefits of an active lifestyle. Not-for-profit organisations focus on understanding the opinions, perceptions and attitudes of people whose opinions, attitudes or behaviours they want to change, or whose support they seek.

Kotler and Andreasen (1991) have expressed the not-for-profit transaction in terms of *favourable exchange*, where one party (the marketing organisation) can induce behaviour changes in another (equivalent to the consumer) by working on the assumption that people behave in ways that they believe will leave them better off than the alternatives. The authors believe that in attempting to understand consumer behaviour, it is critical to differentiate between the exchange as a process and the exchange as an outcome. The latter is simply a transaction. The management of the exchange *process* is marketing.

A marketing orientation helps the homeless

The Big Issue was established to tackle the problem of homelessness in a progressive and entrepreneurial manner. Rather than campaigning to raise funding and donations that could be used to address homelessness, *The Big Issue* sought to challenge conventions. By adopting a marketing orientation *The Big Issue* has successfully approached the challenge of homelessness in a novel and unique manner: by developing a new product, a street magazine that homeless vendors can sell to the general public, *The Big Issue* has addressed several objectives. Vendors earn money from the magazines they sell, which highlights the extent of homelessness; the public purchase an informative magazine and also support a social cause. Using the Kotler and Andreasen model, managing the exchange process is the main task. The newspaper sale transaction is almost incidental in terms of the consumer benefits. The exchange process in contrast is to be a complex mix of a desire to reduce homelessness, a desire to help the individual vendor, assuaging of guilt at the position of someone worse off or even the reduction of mild fear at perceived aggressive selling.

9.4 Creating a marketing orientation

Michaels (1982) warned that: 'No one person, system, or technique will make a company marketing orientated' and stresses that a marketing orientation cannot be achieved overnight. Advising on the implementation of a marketing orientation, Michaels emphasises the following requirements:

- **Investment by top management** Before marketing can be instilled throughout the whole organisation, senior managers must commit themselves to the marketing orientation or other managers will not implement the necessary changes.
- **Injection of outside talent** Managements which successfully implement a marketing orientation have brought in new personnel These have helped to educate other staff about the possible benefits of the new orientation.
- **A clear sense of direction** As with any change, it is essential that management takes a planned approach to its implementation. It must set objectives and timescales to guide the introduction.

Kotler *et al.* (2002) also stress the importance of restructuring the organisation to focus on the consumer. Managers need to educate themselves and their staff about the idea and how it may support long-lasting success in the marketplace. This applies to all levels and functions who must share a common commitment if they are to work together in the interests of the consumers. Without the support of top management, the focus on consumer satisfaction advocated by the marketing orientation will not become the guiding orientation for organisational decisions.

Manchester United – the case continues

One of the challenges facing Manchester United PLC is the best organisational marketing structure to design and the internal culture to induce in managing its huge operation. At corporate level, the PLC owns football-related and non-football-related businesses and is involved with various joint ventures in TV, financial services and mobile phones. At business and product levels, management have to deal directly with their target segments. Promotional campaigns for individual products have to be sensitive to the image of sister MU products. Hoarding adverts of a noisy football crowd having a good time will be exciting to other potential fans but could be off-putting for someone who has to produce their MU credit card at local stores. Preserving the perceived value of the brand is also important: the replica jersey product manager will not want to see stores such as Tesco heavily discounting branded jerseys. This raises important questions of channel management and relationship with suppliers whose strategy might be more cost focused than differentiated. In marketing its products, MU PLC also has to take into account the needs of its nervous shareholders, who have watched the share price fall from 413p in 2000 to 130p in 2002. It has since recovered to 260p (August 2004). In a sense, the shareholders need to be treated as a market.

The structure of the organisation may have to change to allow all departments to become focused on and work together for the achievement of consumer satisfaction. Compare Figures 9.2 and 9.3. Figure 9.2 shows marketing as an important function within the organisation and Figure 9.3 is the structure required if an organisation is to become consumer centred. Such restructuring includes putting in place systems and procedures to collect, analyse and distribute data about the changing demands of consumers. It also requires that the achievement of organisational objectives through consumer satisfaction becomes the basis of decisions. An important area of organisational study is the management of the boundaries between marketing and the other functional areas, due to differences in culture. Tension can arise, for example, between the R&D team and the marketing team when new products need to be rapidly modified at concept stage to meet changing customer demands. Shortened product life cycles are a

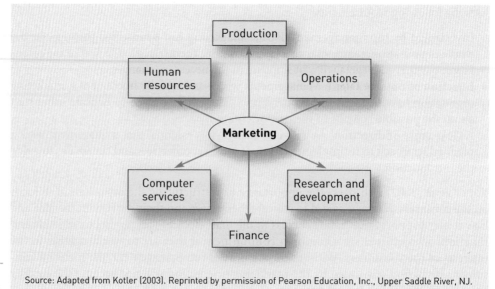

Figure 9.2

Marketing as an important function

Source: Adapted from Kotler (2003). Reprinted by permission of Pearson Education, Inc., Upper Saddle River, NJ.

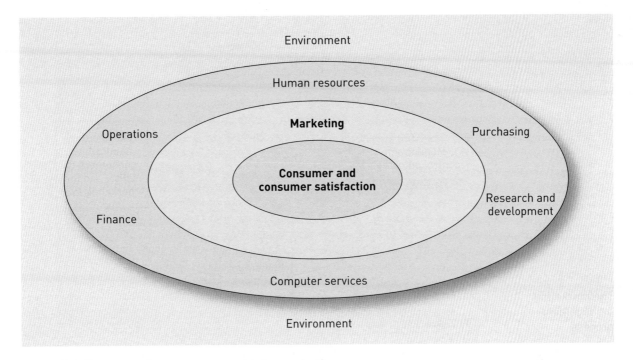

Figure 9.3 **Structure of a consumer-centred organisation**
Source: Adapted from Kotler (2003). Reprinted by permission of Pearson Education, Inc., Upper Saddle River, NJ.

feature of today's markets, which exacerbates internal tensions and highlights the need for a flexible structure and a communicative culture.

9.5 Managing the marketing function

The effective implementation of a marketing orientation requires that marketing has the central position displayed in Figure 9.3. The continual satisfaction of changing consumer demands relies upon distributing information about these throughout the organisation. For this reason, marketing professionals claim that marketing requires a central position, in which the marketing department links the consumer and the enterprise. It monitors changes in consumer demands and alerts other people to changes in the environment that may require a response. It is the responsibility of marketing to research the marketplace and decide which consumer demands the organisation can satisfy most effectively. That decision, and the marketing tools to use, are the responsibility of the marketing manager.

In common with other functional area managers, the marketing manager gathers information to plan direction, creates a marketing organisation, leads staff and other players and controls the activity by evaluating results and taking corrective action. Figure 9.4 outlines these activities.

The figure shows that the marketing function is responsible for (a) identifying those consumers whose demands the organisation can satisfy most effectively, and (b) selecting the marketing mix that will satisfy consumer demands and succeed in achieving organisational objectives.

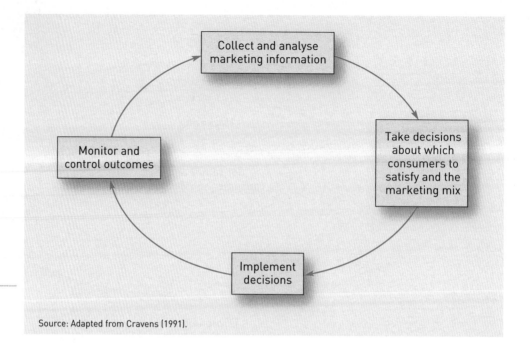

Figure 9.4

The marketing management process

Source: Adapted from Cravens (1991).

Case questions 9.1

- What customer demands were Manchester United seeking to satisfy at the time of the case study?
- What other demands does the business have to satisfy?
- What marketing tools are mentioned in the case?
- What management structure do you think would suit (a) the PLC and (b) the football club?

The **marketing environment** consists of the actors and forces outside marketing that affect the marketing manager's ability to develop and maintain successful relationships with its target consumers.

In order to take these decisions, managers need information about consumer demands, competitor strategies and changes in the **marketing environment** (Armstrong and Kotler, 2000) that are likely to impact upon consumer demands. The marketing environment contains micro and macro components. The micro-environment is that part of an organisation's marketing environment to which it is close and within which it directly operates. Each organisation will have a micro-environment unique and specific to it; as shown in Figure 9.5, it comprises the stakeholders with which the organisation regularly interacts, including employees, suppliers, distributors, consumers, competitors and publics such as pressure groups and the general public. All organisations, including small and medium-sized enterprises, have some control over changes in their micro-environment and the likely impact these will have upon their marketing activities.

The macro component of an organisation's marketing environment is more remote and will be similar for all those in the same industry. Organisations have little direct influence over their macro-environment, which consists of the PESTEL factors outlined in Chapter 3 – repeated in Figure 9.6.

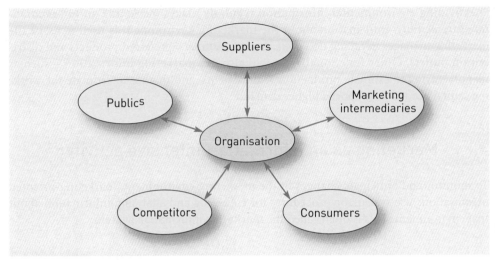

Figure 9.5

The micro-environment

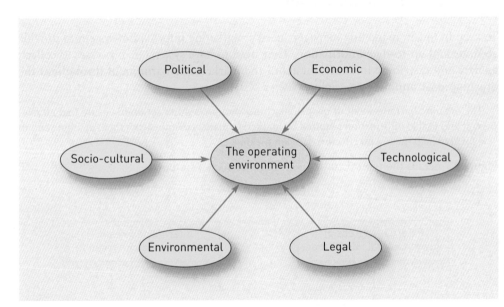

Figure 9.6

The macro-environment

Activity 9.4   Identifying the marketing environment

- Use Figures 9.5 and 9.6 to identify, for each of these organisations, those parts of their micro- and macro-environments that have most impact upon their marketing activities: Ryanair, Benetton, Médecins sans Frontières.
- How might they respond to these environmental influences?

Such frameworks are useful in identifying whether changes in the environment will have a positive or negative impact on the marketing activities of an organisation. This is because they can be useful in identifying both the *opportunities present in the environment*, such as those presented to multimedia organisations by developments in e-commerce, as well as *threats*, such as the impact of a natural disaster on a country's tourism industry.

Providing environmental information regularly makes marketing an *information-intensive activity*. Information about the marketing environment is used to assist the marketing manager in taking decisions about consumers' preferred products and distribution outlets. Other functional areas will also use marketing information – such as manufacturing to estimate production requirements, and finance to estimate the working capital needed to support a higher demand.

9.6 Marketing as an information-intensive activity

To monitor and anticipate changes in the marketing environment, marketing-oriented organisations use systematic procedures for collecting and analysing information about that environment. This is often called the **marketing information system**.

A **marketing information system** is the systematic process for the collection, analysis and distribution of marketing information.

Marketing information systems

To keep in touch, marketing managers need a marketing information system to provide accurate and up-to-date information. They need to have systematic processes to collect, analyse and distribute information about the marketing environment throughout the organisation. Cannon (1996) defines such a systems as:

> The organised arrangement of people, machines and procedures set up to ensure that all relevant and usable information required by marketing management reaches them at a time and in a form to help them with effective decision making.

Figure 9.7 details the typical component parts of such a system.

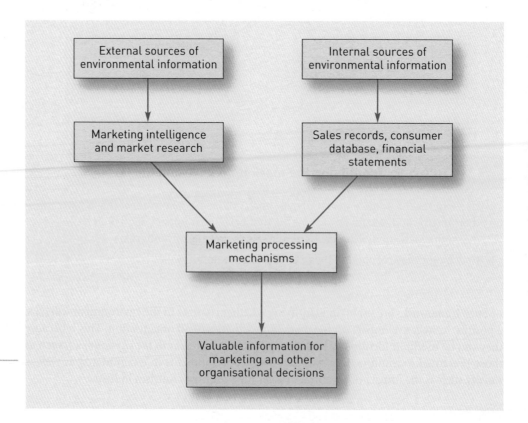

Figure 9.7

A marketing information system

A marketing information system contains internal and external sources of data and mechanisms to analyse and interpret the data. As Chapter 20 explains, data is not the same as information. Data in itself has no meaning. A company may discover that in December 2004, 59 per cent of a sample of people were aware of their product. In itself that has no value – but it does become useful information if it can be compared with similar data from earlier or later periods or with competing products. Management may then see a trend, and be able to decide if it needs to act. Table 9.2 summarises the main sources of marketing information.

Source	Description and examples
Internal records	Size and regularity of orders, cost of each level of production, customer complaints, quality statistics
Marketing intelligence	Data on micro- and macro-environments. Usually secondary data from newspapers, trade associations and industry reports. Informal sources from staff or customers are also valuable guides to, for example, competitor plans
Market research	Involves five stages: 1 specifying information required (how many people with X income, living in place Y are aware of product Z?) 2 developing hypotheses (is awareness higher or lower in area B where the product has been advertised than in C?) 3 collecting quantitative or qualitative data to refute or confirm 4 analysing the data and 5 presenting the results

Table 9.2

Sources of marketing information

Information on food shopping habits

All major supermarkets have for a long time monitored activity at point of sale so that they can order supplies close to when they will be needed. Loyalty cards keep a record of the frequency, value and type of food shopping bought by individuals, and small incentives reward customers for their store loyalty. Marketing departments use (a) the application form information (address, income bracket, family size, etc.) and (b) the regular information about buying patterns. This helps them to manage their inventory and their marketing communications, such as on sales promotions.

Figure 9.8 shows the processes involved in a market research project.

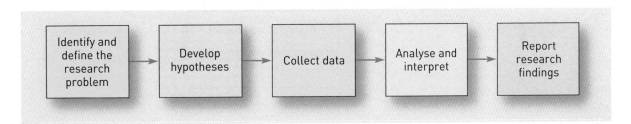

Figure 9.8 Market research process

Case question 9.2

● Suppose that Manchester United are approached by a snack food company wishing to manufacture 'Man U' breakfast bars for children and young people to have as snacks or in school lunch boxes. What type of market research would you recommend using?

9.7 Understanding the consumer – buyer behaviour

The marketing information system provides information on the marketing environment. The results of market research projects indicate solutions to precise marketing questions. Organisations with a marketing orientation also want to understand how customers decide to buy something.

Activity 9.5   Why did you buy that?

Pick a product that you buy regularly – such as a magazine, soft drink or chocolate bar. Think of the last time you bought that product and try to identify the factors which influenced your choice, such as the product features, your mood or other psychological state, your physical state (e.g. hunger), the company you were in (if any), etc.

Buyer behaviour research (Engel *et al.*, 1978; Howard and Sheth, 1969) has identified that consumers work through the series of decisions shown in Figure 9.9.

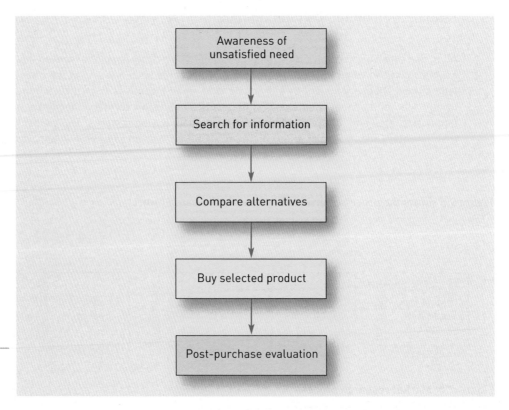

Figure 9.9

A model of consumer buying behaviour

Awareness of unsatisfied need

Consumers become aware of a need that they want to satisfy in two ways. The first is self-discovery. Stomach rumbles or a dry throat are physical signals that you are hungry and thirsty and need to satisfy these feelings. Consumers also become aware of an unsatisfied need by receiving some marketing communication from an organisation. For example, until 3M made you aware of 'Post-It pads' did you identify the need to have a small piece of paper on which you could write messages and stick to a surface? This is an example of latent need referred to earlier.

Theories of human motivation described in Chapter 15 give marketing managers guidance on the needs of potential customers. They use this to ensure that the product or service is helping consumers satisfy a need – for status, recognition, a sense of achievement and so on.

Search for information

Aware of a need, consumers search for information that will help them decide which product to buy. Many sources provide this information – personal experience is one powerful source; that of family and friends is another. A third source of information is from organisations providing products that may satisfy the need – by advertisements and other promotional activities. The information source at this stage in the buying process has great influence on the purchase decision. The poor service of a friend at a restaurant will usually dissuade a potential customer.

Activity 9.6   Reflecting on consumer information

Select from one of the following expensive products: a DVD player, a mountain bike, a round-the-world air ticket. For your selected product describe the type of information you would want before deciding which brand to buy, and why. Which of your information categories do you think would be useful for the marketing manager of that product?

The time spent on this stage of the consumer buying process depends on the type of product that consumers believe will satisfy their identified need. Buying some products is more risky than others, and customers usually seek more information on them to reduce the risk. The degree of risk depends on factors such as expense, effect on self-image and knowledge of the product. Self-image (or 'psychological closeness') is very important in some purchases such as a car or fashion clothing – or in whether to give to charity (Kottasz, 2004).

Compare alternatives

The more information a consumer has collected, the longer he or she will spend comparing different products against set criteria. For a new television, the main criteria may be brand name, surround sound, Internet access, wide screen and a reasonable price. Note that for a television, psychological closeness is less likely to be a factor. Marketing managers will take that into account in designing product ranges and variants.

Buy selected product

Having compared the alternatives and decided which will best satisfy their need, the customer makes the purchase. Even at this stage of the process other factors may intrude – out-of-stock, a price-cut on an alternative, or the advice of the salesperson may influence decisions. Note that the way a purchase is financed is a product feature, e.g. no-interest loans to purchase the product.

Manchester United – the case continues – what makes people buy?   CASE STUDY

A football game is not a tangible product. A regular and significant intangible purchase by a Manchester United football fan is the £20–30 ticket to see a home game at Old Trafford or £10 on a pay-per-view TV basis. There is no guarantee of satisfaction and no exchange or refund. No promotional advertising is needed and the ticket demand is relatively 'inelastic', i.e. prices can increase without sales volumes necessarily falling.

An important question for a marketing manager is 'how does a fan reach the decision to buy this experience and how is value measured?'. The buyer behaviour framework described above can help: domestic UK fans are typically lifelong, acquiring perceptions of and loyalty to the Club at school or in the home. Influencers would include peers and older pupils. Although football was formerly male-dominated, young females are an increasing part of the market. Most fans travel in groups of two or more, so this is a segment attribute that can be managed in raising awareness and favourability. Publicity photos can depict fans celebrating or commiserating together and the whole emphasis of attending a football match can be positioned away from 'did we win?' to 'did we have a good time?'. This approach is one of MU's declared marketing strategies.

Post-purchase evaluation

The final stage of the buying process is when the customer compares pre-purchase expectations with post-purchase reality. If expectation matches reality then the consumer is more likely to buy in the future. At this stage, consumer communications can affect future decisions. The quality of after-sales service might convince the car purchaser whether he or she made the right decision or not.

When thinking about the post-experience evaluation, marketing managers should be aware of the potential difference between how consumers think (rationally) about their product and how they feel (emotionally) about it. It is possible, for example, for football fans to think rationally that the home game they just saw was very poor but still to retain great affection and warmth for the experience and the team. This apparent dichotomy can be turned to advantage when planning promotional campaigns.

Internal and external influences shape the decisions consumers make at each stage. Table 9.3 describes these, and Figure 9.10 illustrates them.

Table 9.3 Internal and external influences on buying behaviour

Influence	Description	Example
Internal influences **Perception**	How people collect and interpret information	Affects reaction to advertisements – images, colours, words. See Chapter 16 on communication
Motivation	Internal forces that shape purchasing decisions to satisfy need	Marketers design products to meet needs. Insurers remind people of dangers against which a policy will protect them. See Chapter 15
Attitudes	Opinions and points of view that people have of other people and institutions	Marketers design products to conform. Attitudes against testing cosmetics on animals led firms to stop this practice. Similarly for environmental issues
Learning	How people learn affects what they know about a product, and hence their purchasing decisions	Marketers help people to 'learn' to associate a product with unique colours or images – such as Coke with red and white, and Nike with its 'Swoosh' symbol
External influences **Reference groups**	Other people with whom the consumer identifies	Marketers establish the reference groups of their consumers, and allude to them in promotions – e.g. sponsoring athletes in return for product endorsement
Culture	The culture to which a consumer belongs affects their values and behaviour	Subcultures associated with punk and grunge influence buying behaviour – which marketers use in positioning products for those markets
Social class	People identify with a class based on income, education, where they live, etc.	Purchase decisions confirm and reaffirm the class to which people belong, or to which they aspire. Marketers use this information in promotional material

Figure 9.10

Influences on buyer behaviour

Needs, wants and demands

A marketing orientation implies that to satisfy the consumer it is necessary to identify the products for which there is *demand* and to understand the *needs* and *wants* which the product will satisfy for the consumer. Marketers distinguish between needs, wants and demands as follows:

● **Needs** These are the core feelings that consumers 'need' to satisfy; for example, thirst is a physical need that needs to be satisfied.

● **Wants** These are the preferences that individual consumers have about the ways in which they 'want' to satisfy the needs that they share in common with others. Consumers will want different liquids to satisfy the thirst that makes them need a drink.

▶

● **Demands** The money that individual consumers have determines the types of drink which they are able to buy. An individual who needs a drink may want to buy a Red Bull energy drink. The money in their wallet determines that their demand (their actual purchasing power) is for an own-label soft drink.

To satisfy consumers, marketers need to understand their needs, wants and demands. If they define demand too narrowly they may be unable to satisfy consumers.

9.8 Taking marketing decisions

The marketing manager now has information about the marketing environment, possible opportunities and threats, and the buying behaviour of consumers. The next stage is to decide which demands to satisfy and how to do this. The first decision is about market segmentation and targeting. The second is about choosing the correct mix of marketing tools to position products and make them attractive to consumers (Figure 9.11).

Segmenting markets

Market segmentation is the process of dividing markets comprising the heterogeneous needs of many consumers into segments comprising the homogeneous needs of smaller groups.

Organisations are increasingly using **market segmentation** strategies to satisfy the different needs that exist within the marketplace. Airlines offer consumers the choice of flying first class, business class or economy class. Notice that although the basic product attribute (transport from A to B) is the same for all passengers in the plane, the total offering is not: premium passengers pay for a premium service. Universities offer degrees by full-time, part-time and distance learning study. Athletic shoe companies offer shoes specifically for running, aerobics, tennis and squash as well as 'cross' trainers for the needs of all these sports.

Segmentation is based on the fact that consumers have different needs: it is more efficient for management to treat them as homogeneous groups, for the purpose of communication, advertising and so forth. The personal computer market consists of all the individuals who need a personal computer. Within that market people with similar needs can be grouped into distinct segments: travellers needing a laptop form one distinct segment; parents wanting a low-cost personal computer with Internet connection

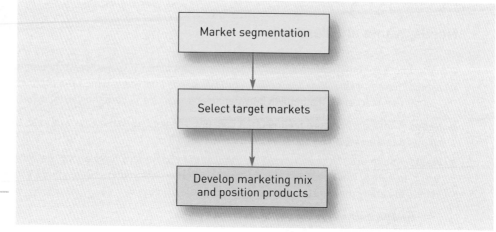

Figure 9.11

Taking marketing decisions

Segmenting markets in the public sector

The idea of segmentation is highly relevant to managers providing public services, such as further and higher education, school meals and leisure centres. They need to know who uses the services, who might use them and how provision relates to demand. To understand these questions, public sector providers need to need to understand the needs and behaviours of current and potential users. A particular feature of the public sector is that services meet two types of demand (Chapman and Cowdell, 1998, pp. 122–6):

- Non-discretionary demand – services that satisfy community demands that everyone needs, such as refuse collection, basic healthcare and street lighting
- Discretionary demand – services that people can choose to use, such as leisure and cultural services or public transport.

Market segmentation techniques apply equally to both – providers need to understand the needs of users and purchasers if they are to create value with the resources they use.

Source: Chapman and Cowdell (1998).

to help their children learn form another. Segmentation is very efficient when allocating the promotional budget. For example, the laptop ad placed in an in-flight magazine is much more likely to have an impact on the laptop-buying segment than on a parent looking for a home PC.

Segmenting the personal computer market (and any other market) relies on identifying the variables that distinguish consumers with similar needs, as follows:

- **Demography** The easiest way to segment a consumer market is by using demographic variables such as age, gender and education level. Magazine companies use gender and age variables to ensure that within their portfolio they have magazine titles that will suit the needs of females as well as males and those of different ages. Local authorities use information on age and family structures to help decide the distribution of facilities in their area.
- **Geography** This segmentation variable is commonly used by organisations competing in a global market. By segmenting markets by country, organisations such as McDonald's have been able to 'think global but act local'. While maintaining uniform global standards of service and hygiene, the company competes differently in each country by varying the menu available to suit local tastes.
- **Socioeconomic** Segmentation on the basis of socioeconomic variables – such as income, social class and lifestyle. Lifestyle segmentation includes identifying groups of consumers who share similar values about the ways in which they wish to live.

When segmenting consumer markets, marketers typically use a mix of these variables to provide an accurate profile of distinct groups. The magazine *Marie Claire*, for example,

Activity 9.7　Identifying market segments

- What market segments have the following identified: Swatch, Amazon.com, Borders Books?
- What marketing management benefits do you think their segmentation strategies offer?

uses age, gender, education, lifestyle and social class to attract a readership of educated, independently minded women between the ages of 25 and 35, in income brackets ABC1.

Having segmented a market using the variables described above, marketers have to decide which of those segments to select as **target markets** – those to be the focus for their activities. Marketing managers usually select target markets that meet the following three criteria:

A **target market** is the segment of the market selected by the organisation as the focus of its activities.

- contain demands that the resources of the organisation can satisfy
- are large enough to provide a financial return
- have growth potential.

Ultimately, segments selected as target markets are those that offer the greatest potential for achieving management goals.

Case question 9.3

- In 2002 the Manchester United website was the most visited site in China. Two hundred million Chinese regularly watch the team on TV. MU saw this as an opportunity for mail order sales to China and the rest of SE Asia. What segmentation criteria would you have recommended for MU in this burgeoning sector? As well as watching the games on TV, Asian fans frequently place bets on the outcome.

The **marketing mix** is the mix of decisions about product features, prices, communications and distribution of products used by the marketing manager to position products competitively within the minds of consumers.

9.9 Using the marketing mix

The final decision facing the marketing manager is to select the combination of price, product, promotion and place. This is known as the **marketing mix**.

key ideas The marketing mix

The marketing mix comprises four basic levers over which marketing managers have control. The mix *positions* products in the market in a way that makes them attractive to the target consumers. The **position** that a product has within a market reflects consumer opinions of that product and the comparisons that they make between it and competing products. The aim is to position products *within the minds of consumers* as more attractive, and better able to satisfy their demands, than competing products.

To position products effectively, the marketing manager develops a coordinated marketing mix. Kotler *et al.* (2002) define an organisation's marketing mix as 'a set of tools that work together to affect the marketplace'. The marketing mix has traditionally been presented as consisting of the so-called 4 Ps: product, price, promotion and place.

However, Gronroos (2000) points out that

during the last two decades marketing researchers have increasingly found that the list of 4 Ps is too restrictive and more ... variables have been suggested ... such as people, processes and physical evidence. (pp. 240–1)

He suggests that adding further categories (see, for example, Judd 2003) is a symptom of the weakness of the marketing mix approach, although it may still be useful in certain types of market such as consumer packaged goods. The main problem with the approach, in Gronroos's view, is that it restricts marketing to a limited number of decision areas, and leads to the neglect of many aspects of what he calls the 'customer relationship life cycle' (pp. 242–3).

Marketing mix – product

Decisions about which products to develop will establish the range of goods and services an organisation offers. Some are physical products; others intangible personal services. Most are a mixture of the two. Note that the product can include non-core items such as packaging, after-sales service, maintenance and insurance.

Swatch   www.swatch.com

The development and introduction of Swatch is a classic example of marketing techniques being used by a traditional industry to launch a new product. Faced with competition from low-cost producers SMH, an established Swiss watchmaker (brands included Longines and Omega) urgently needed a new product line. Its engineers developed a radically new product that was much cheaper to make than traditional models. The company worked closely with advertising agencies in the United States on product positioning and advertising strategy. In addition to the name 'Swatch', a snappy contraction of 'Swiss' and 'watch', this research generated the idea of downplaying the product's practical benefits and positioning it as a 'fashion accessory that happens to tell the time'. Swatch would be a second or third watch used to adapt to different situations without replacing the traditional 'status symbol' watch.

By 1996 it had sold over 200 million units and was the most successful wristwatch of all time. Its parent company, SMH, is the largest and most dynamic watch company in the world. Based on its brand strength, it diversified (in a joint venture with Daimler-Benz) into the **smart fortwo** car range. Daimler-Benz bought out SMH in 1998 and is producing the **formore** at the time of writing.

Source: Based on 'Swatch', Case No. 589-005-1, INSEAD-Cedep, Fontainebleau, and the Swatch web page at http://www.swatch.com.

The extent to which offerings are tangible or intangible affects how marketing staff deal with them. Services present marketing with particular challenges because of their characteristics of perishability, intangibility, heterogeneity and inseparability.

Perishability

Perishable services cannot be held in stock for even the shortest amount of time. If a plane flies with empty seats these cannot be stored for another flight – empty seats are permanently lost sales.

Intangibility

Intangible services present the marketing manager with the greatest challenge. They cannot usually be viewed, touched or tried before their purchase. One way for consumers to 'try before buy' is to be given leaflets with attractive information on the service benefits: the financial services industry relies on information packs about features and benefits of mortgages, insurance policies and bank accounts. Consumers also have little information on which to assess the product benefits relative to their demands. A common source of service information is reference groups: organisations such as health clubs encourage existing members to invite friends and family to their fitness clubs for trial memberships.

Heterogeneity and inseparability

Services are labour intensive. They rely on the skills, competences and experiences of the people who provide them, and this creates particular challenges for the marketing manager. *Heterogeneity* refers to variations in what in principle should be an identical service each time it is provided, e.g. a pedicure. *Inseparability* refers to a product or service that is consumed as it produced, e.g. a haircut. Service providers and consumers will meet for some amount of time. For a doctor's appointment, it is necessary to meet with the doctor to discuss your health.

Organisations operating through branch systems such as banks or fast-food restaurants have to overcome the hazards of inseparability and heterogeneity to ensure consistent delivery standards. Both service providers and consumers have personalities, opinions and values that make them unique. This can create differences in the levels of service and standards that consumers experience when buying services. Organisations such as Pizza Hut and UCI cinemas try to minimise differences by providing staff with company uniforms, decorating premises in a similar way and setting firm guidelines for the way staff deliver the service.

Consumer products (both goods and services) can be classified as convenience, shopping, speciality or unsought products. Each poses a different marketing challenge, which Table 9.4 summarises.

Table 9.4

Market challenges by type of product

Type of product	Examples	Marketing challenge
Convenience	Regular purchases, low price – bread, milk, magazines	Widely available, and easy to switch brands. Managers counter this by heavy advertising or distinct packaging of the brand
Shopping	Relatively expensive, infrequent purchase – washing machines, televisions, clothes	Brand name, product features, design and price are important and managers will spend time searching for best mix. Managers spend heavily on advertising and on training sales staff
Speciality	Less frequent, often luxury purchases – cars, diamond rings, houses	Consumers need much information. Sales staff vital to a sale – management invest heavily in them, and in protecting image of product by restricting outlets. Also focused advertising and distinctive packaging
Unsought	Consumers need to buy – but don't get much pleasure from – insurance, a new car exhaust pipe	Managers need to make customers aware that they supply this need, and distinct product features

The **product life cycle** suggests that products pass through the stages of introduction, growth, maturity and decline.

key ideas   Product life cycle

In managing the organisation's product decisions, marketing managers use a concept called the **product life cycle** (Figure 9.12). The central assumption upon which the product life cycle rests is that all products have a limited life, which could vary from years to decades. Depending on the stage reached by a product in its life cycle, a known set of competitive and consumer conditions exists that helps the marketing manager to specify the marketing activities required at that stage. Mapping the sales and profit generated, the product life cycle suggests that products pass through the stages of introduction, growth, maturity and decline.

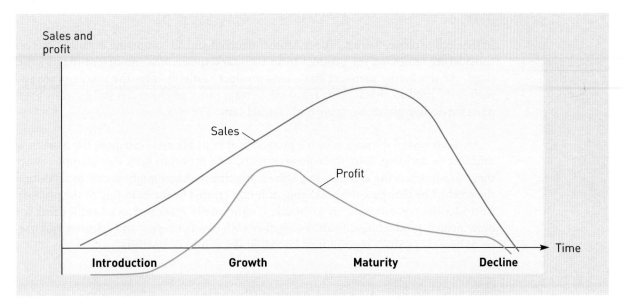

Figure 9.12 The product life cycle

Introduction

This is the stage at which products enter the marketplace. Profits are negative because sales from the early adopters have not reached the level needed to pay back investment in researching and developing the product. Few consumers are aware of – and therefore interested in – buying the product and few organisations are involved in producing and distributing it. The aim of the marketing manager at this stage is to invest in marketing communication and make as many potential consumers as possible aware of the product's entry into the marketplace.

Growth

At this stage consumers have become aware of and started buying the product. Sales rise quickly and profits peak. As people buy the product, more consumers become aware of it and the high profit levels attract new competitors into the industry. The aim of the marketing manager at this stage is to fight off existing competitors and new entrants. This can be done by (a) encouraging consumer loyalty, (b) distributing the product as widely as is demanded by consumers, and (c) cutting selling prices: production costs fall as total units increase, due to the learning curve effect. Competitors arriving later have not had time to cut costs so may balk at entering the market.

Maturity

With profits peaking during the growth stage, profit and sales start to plateau and then decline towards the end of this stage. By this stage in a product's life cycle, many consumers are aware of and have bought the product and there are many organisations competing for a decreasing amount of consumer demand for the product. The aim of the marketing manager is to fight competition by reducing the price of the product or by differentiating it by, for example, altering its packaging and design. Swatch continued to add value to its product in the later stages of its product life cycle.

At this stage product differentiation can successfully reposition products to an earlier stage in their life cycle. It is also important that the marketing manager begins to consider ideas for replacement products and to select ideas for research and development.

Decline

In the decline phase, there is little consumer demand and all competing organisations are considering removing the product from the marketplace. It is important that, by this stage, the marketing manager has a new product ready to enter the marketplace and replace the product that is being removed. Certain rarity products can still generate profits in the decline phase, e.g. spare parts for old cars.

An awareness of the stage which a product is at in its life cycle can assist the marketing manager in deciding upon the course of marketing action to take. For example, aware that a product is at the maturity stage, the marketing manager might decide to reposition the product by changing the packaging or image created by the branding of the product. Consider the repositioning of Lucozade. Traditionally marketed as a health drink for older people, product modifications together with new packaging and celebrity endorsement have successfully repositioned Lucozade as a youth sports drink.

| Activity 9.8 | Using the product life cycle |

State the stage that you believe each of the following products to be in and comment on how long, in years, you believe their life cycle to be: drawing pins, iPods, umbrellas, hand soap.

Activity 9.8 shows that some products do not have a limited lifespan and other products can be repositioned to an earlier stage. Despite these criticisms, the product life cycle offers the marketing manager a useful aid to many product decisions.

Marketing mix – price

Price is the value placed upon the goods, services and ideas exchanged between organisations and consumers. For most products, price is measured with money, though consumers do not identify all the purchases they make as having a 'price': for example, accessing BBC television programmes is the cost of a television licence, and the price of street lighting and cleaning is the community charge that individual households are responsible for paying. Not-for-profit marketing can involve a time price (driving the school hockey team bus) or a psychological price for behaviour change (ceasing physical punishment of one's children).

In selecting the price that will position a product competitively within consumers' minds, the marketing manager must be aware of the image that consumers have of the product. Consumers have expected price ranges for certain types of product. In particular, for safety products, products for children, those associated with health or connected to their self-image, consumers have a *minimum* price they expect to pay. If the price is below this, consumers will not purchase the product because they perceive such products as being of inferior quality or lower value.

The price charged must also cover the costs of producing, distributing and promoting products. It must provide the organisation with an acceptable profit yet leave an acceptable margin for distributors and retailers.

Marketing mix – promotion

Properly referred to as marketing communications, this element of the marketing mix involves taking decisions about the information that will encourage consumers to buy a product or change attitudes and behaviours in some way. Organisations can communicate with their target markets in many ways. Packaging can provide information, a company logo may transmit a particular message, and sponsoring a football team or a concert indicates an organisation's values and attitudes. The most frequent modes of encouraging consumers to buy products include advertising, sales promotions, personal selling and publicity.

A Department of Trade and Industry (DTI) advertising campaign

management in practice

The DTI is launching an online campaign to promote its new Consumer Direct telephone, online, and e-mail information service for consumers. Consumer Direct provides advice on consumer protection issues, including what rights consumers have or how to get redress for faulty goods. Run by the DTI in partnership with local authorities and existing services, including Trading Standards, there will be 11 contact centres across the UK.

Source: *Marketing Week*, 9 September 2004.

- *Advertising* is the form of communication commonly selected when an organisation wishes to transmit a message to a large audience. It is impersonal, as it does not involve direct communication between an organisation and a potential consumer. Advertising is effective in creating awareness of the offering but is less effective in persuading consumers to buy. It is, however, a cost-effective method of communicating with potential consumers in a mass market.

- Organisations typically use *sales promotions* to encourage consumers who are considering a product to take the next step and buy it. Both McDonald's and Burger King frequently offer special promotions to encourage consumers to buy their brand. Companies also use promotions to encourage repeat buys and to encourage consumers to try out new products of which advertising has made them aware.

- Marketing departments use *personal selling* when consumers require first-hand information before making a purchase. It is particularly useful for infrequently purchased products such as DVD players and cars – and in industrial marketing. Personal selling is a direct transfer of product information to potential consumers: it is able to respond to questions that consumers might have and to explain complicated or technical product features. Personal selling requires that managers train salespeople properly, especially on specific product features. It is useful for expensive or technically sophisticated products.

- *Publicity* or PR (public relations) is effective in supporting a positive image of the organisation. It involves building good working relationships with the media and using them to promote a positive image of the organisation. The aim is to ensure that positive events of media interest (such as launching a new product) are fully reported, and that negative ones do as little damage as possible.

Marketing mix – place

'Place' refers to decisions about the ways in which products can be most effectively distributed to the final consumer, either directly or through intermediaries. Decisions about marketing channels concentrate on whether the distribution of products should be owned by the producing organisation or whether products should be distributed by external parties. These decisions depend on the products involved and the costs of distribution. If product quality and image are vital to market positioning then the organisation must maintain control over distribution.

Protecting the brand

Paul Mitchell hair products maintain the image of quality that consumers attach to the name by detailing on the product packaging that authenticity cannot be guaranteed unless purchased from a Paul Mitchell approved outlet. Similarly, brands such as Calvin Klein, Nike and Clarins have expressed concerns about the distribution of their products through such stores as Tesco and Superdrug, which they believe detract from rather than add to the value of their branded products.

Distributor cost is a consideration in channel management. Having identified the price at which consumers demand to buy particular products, the costs involved in distributing products in-house relative to external providers must be considered.

A third channel decision is whether to make purchase of products available electronically through the Internet. This decision has been embraced by organisations such as easyJet, amazon.com and lastminute.com. Such organisations have decided to use electronic channels of distribution as a differentiation tool, on the grounds that consumers prefer online convenience and see this as a product feature. For many organisations, the electronic product distribution is a complementary channel used, for example, to widen product access to geographically remote markets. The major supermarkets and retailers all have busy websites, often offering discounts over store prices. This market channel also allows easy gathering of data for relationship marketing.

In developing a marketing mix that will place products competitively within the minds of consumers the marketing manager must be aware that changes in one element will create changes in other areas. For example, if the price of a product is reduced, consumer perceptions of the product might change. Creating an effective marketing mix with which to position products relies upon integration and coordination of each element.

Maintaining consistency

In positioning their products as value for money, organisations ensure that each part of the marketing mix supports and reinforces this image. This means that products must not be highly differentiated, prices should be low, and promotion messages should stress the low price and value for money. The stores in which products are distributed should be simple in design. This avoids sending a message that the costs of creating a smart place in which to buy products will be reflected in the prices.

9.10 A critical perspective on marketing

The adoption of a marketing orientation can clearly bring significant benefits to the commercial or other success of organisations. Commentators have also been critical of marketing. They argue that marketing manipulates consumer choices and encourages materialism and over-consumption. In 1996 several drinks companies introduced products known as Alcopops – fruit-flavoured carbonated drinks that taste like soft drinks but contain alcohol equivalent to a 330 ml bottle of beer. This sparked a lively debate over marketing's role in society. The manufacturers argued that they were responding to the tastes of adults who enjoy alcohol but prefer the flavour of soft rather than alcoholic drinks: they had widened the choice of alcoholic drinks available to those over the legal age. The charity Alcohol Concern argued that the fruity flavour and bright packaging manipulated under-age drinkers into possibly harmful purchases. Chapter 5 (Corporate Responsibility) also includes ideas relevant to marketing, such as the influence of ethical consumers, the success of the Fair Trade brand, and of individual products such as Café Direct which promise producers a fair return.

---

key ideas

Naomi Klein's *No Logo: Taking Aim at the Brand Bullies*

Klein (2000) presents a powerful argument against the growing dominance of some global brands in consumer markets, and how many use advertising to exploit impressionable teenagers. She argues that companies like Microsoft, Gap and Starbucks now present themselves as purveyors of lifestyles, images and dreams rather than products. In doing so they harm both the cultures in which they operate, and the workers they employ. She also reports a growing backlash by ethical shareholders, human rights activists and McUnion organisers demanding a citizen-centred alternative to the rule of the brands.

The debate on marketing's role within society will continue to run. Those concerned with environmental and public health issues will criticise organisations that they perceive to be damaging the environment or knowingly causing harm to people's health. Others argue that adopting a marketing orientation in itself is not an ethical issue, as long as it is used to inform consumers and widen their choice. Responsible marketers do not advocate that consumers should be tricked into making purchases. Where, for example, incidences of product misinformation occur and it is clear that an organisation has engaged in unethical practices, the marketing orientation would advocate that a focus on consumer satisfaction has not been adhered to. Consequently marketing thinkers would argue that such an organisation had failed to conduct its activities under the guidance of a marketing orientation. Nevertheless it is a fact that some people use marketing concepts to sell pornography, traffic drugs and invade privacy.

Activity 9.9 Revising your definition

- Having completed this chapter, how would you define marketing?
- Compare this definition with the one that you were asked to make in Activity 9.1 and comment on any changes.

Summary

1 **Compare and contrast marketing with alternative organisational orientations:**

   - Adopting a marketing orientation makes the customer the centre of attention and is different from product, production and sales philosophies. It becomes a guiding orientation for the whole organisation. If management wishes a marketing orientation to pervade the organisation, all activities are focused on meeting customer needs. Activity is monitored and controlled to ensure that work is done in a way which meets the needs of customers.

   - Implementing the approach involves precise targeting of defined market segments. It also implies restructuring to ensure that the whole organisation focuses on the customer, with organisation-wide information systems to handle marketing data.

2 **Describe the benefits to any organisation of adopting a marketing orientation:**

   - A marketing orientation implies that in major business decisions management hears a consumer perspective, through mechanisms for involving the relevant players. A firm with a consumer-centred marketing orientation focuses all activities on meeting consumer needs and is organised with that in mind.

3 **Explain why marketing is an information-intensive activity:**

   - To meet consumer needs effectively, marketing is an information-intensive activity. A major element in marketing is the management of communications, i.e. ensuring that information about external developments and customer needs is gathered, processed and transferred around the organisation. Consumers also have to be informed of the offerings and their benefits.

4 **Identify the roles and responsibilities of the marketing manager:**

   - The primacy of marketing can create organisational tension with other professional groups within the firm, whose status and position may be threatened by the primacy. Other departments are, however, expected to support and be committed to the central position of marketing.

5 **Explain market segmentation and the practice of selecting a target market:**

   - Greater consumer understanding enables a company to segment the market in various ways, and to target certain segments in the hope of meeting their distinctive needs.

6 **Describe the components of the marketing mix:**

   - The chapter then outlined the components of the marketing mix – product, price, promotion and place – that a company can use to position its offerings to consumers.

7 **Explain what is meant by product positioning:**

   - Marketing places particular emphasis on keeping in touch with external (micro and macro) developments that affect customers' needs and the organisation's objectives.

Review questions

1 What advantages does the marketing orientation have over each of the following organisational philosophies: production, product and sales?

2 Outline the benefits that the marketing orientation can offer each of the following organisations: a global brand, a football team, a university, a charity, a small firm and a high street retailer.

3 What are the key responsibilities of the marketing manager?

4 In what way is an organisation's micro-environment different from its macro-environment? Comment on these organisations' marketing environments that have greatest impact upon their marketing activities: LivingWell health clubs, McDonald's, your local library.

5 Outline various sources of marketing information and compare and contrast alternative ways of collecting and analysing information about an organisation's market environment.

6 Describe the process of buying decisions involved and identify the factors that might influence the purchase of a new car, a soft drink, a present for a friend's 30th birthday, a new clothes outfit for work.

7 What are the advantages of market segmentation and what are the variables upon which consumer markets are commonly segmented?

8 How are target markets identified and what is meant by product positioning?

9 What position does each of the following have in the marketplace and what mix of marketing tools has each used to achieve this position: Asda supermarkets, Tango soft drinks, Save the Children Fund, Surf washing powder?

Concluding critical reflection

Think about the ways in which your company, or one with which you are familiar, manages marketing. Review the material in the chapter, and perhaps visit some of the websites identified. Then make notes on these questions:

● What examples of the marketing issues discussed in this chapter struck you as being relevant to practice in your company?

● Considering the people you normally work with, what assumptions about the nature of the business and its customers appear to guide their approach – a production, sales or marketing orientation? How does this affect the way the business operates?

● What factors such as the history or current context of the company appear to influence this? Does the current approach appear to be right for the company in its context – or would a different view of the context lead to a different approach? What would the implications for people in the company be of a distinctive marketing orientation?

● Has there been any pressure to adopt a more customer-focused approach, perhaps based on evidence about similar organisations? If you could find such evidence, how may it affect company practice? What would be the obstacles to a greater emphasis on marketing?

Further reading

Judd, V.C. (2003), 'Achieving customer orientation using people power – the 5th P', *European Journal of Marketing*, vol. 37, no. 10, pp. 1301–1313.

Examines how employees can have a powerful influence on the value which the organisation delivers to customers – and complements the '4Ps' outlined in the chapter.

Newman, A.J and Patel, D. (2004), 'The marketing directions of two fashion retailers', *European Journal of Marketing*, vol. 38, no. 7, pp. 770–789.

Fascinating comparison of the recent performance of Topshop and Gap, relating the variation to their success (or not) in developing a marketing orientation throughout the business.

Kattasz, R. (2004), 'How should charitable organisations motivate young professionals to give philanthropically?', *International Journal of Non-Profit and Voluntary Sector Marketing*, vol. 9, no. 1, pp. 9–27.

An example of how research can uncover consumers' motives – in this case finding that wealthy young men were more likely to be motivated to give to charities if they received some social benefits in return – such as invitations to black tie dinners, and being associated with a well-known charity.

Tam, H. (1994), *Marketing, Competition and the Public Sector*, Longman, Harlow.

An excellent account of many applications of marketing in the public sector, with cases and examples that are still relevant.

Gronroos, C. (2000), *Service Management and Marketing: A customer relationship management approach*, Wiley, Chichester.

Highly recommended to students wishing to read more about services marketing from one of Europe's leading writers on marketing.

Jobber, D. (2004), *Principles and Practices of Marketing* (4th edn), McGraw-Hill, London.

Armstrong, G. and Kotler, P. (2000), *Marketing: An introduction* (5th edn), Financial Times/Prentice Hall, Harlow.

Both texts provide detailed introductions to marketing, the former in particular having a strong European focus.

Baker, M. (1999), *The Marketing Book* (4th edn), Butterworth/Heinemann, London.

Contains an excellent selection of classic marketing articles.

Mellahi, K., Jackson, P. and Sparks, L. (2002), 'An exploratory study into failure in successful organizations: the case of Marks and Spencer', *British Journal of Management*, vol. 13, no. 1, pp. 15–29.

Detailed empirical research into the deep-rooted internal problems that led to the difficulties which the company has experienced.

Schor, J.B. (2004), *Born to buy: the commercialized child and the new consumer culture*, Schribner, New York.

A revealing account of the ploys which some marketers use to sell products to children – turning them, she argues, into miniature consumption machines.

Weblinks

These websites have appeared in the chapter:

www.manutd.com
www.kodak.com
www.oxfam.co.uk
www.swatch.com
www.greenpeace.com
www.cfs.co.uk
www.msf.fr (Médecins sans Frontières: from the home page, go to 'contacts' and choose your country)
www.easyjet.com
www.carrefour.com

Visit two of the sites in the list (or that of another organisation in which you have an interest).

● What markets are they in? How have they segmented the market?

● What information can you find about their position in their respective markets, and what marketing challenges they face?

● Gather information from media websites (such as **www.FT.com**) which relate to the orgnanisations you have chosen. What stories can you find that relate to the marketing decisions they have made, and what the outcomes have been?

Annotated weblinks, multiple choice questions and other
useful resources can be found on
www.pearsoned.co.uk/boddy

Part 3 Case   The Virgin Group

www.virgin.com

Virgin is known all over the world and is seen by the public as fun, daring and successful. The first record shop was opened in 1971 and the record label launched in 1973. Virgin Atlantic Airways began operating in 1984, quickly followed by Virgin Holidays. In 1995 the company entered a joint venture offering financial services. By 1997 it was an established global corporation with airline, retailing and travel operations. The original record business was launched shortly after the UK government had abolished retail price maintenance, a practice that had limited competition and kept prices high. Richard Branson saw the opportunity and began a mail order business offering popular records at prices about 15 per cent below those charged by shops.

The business prospered until there was a postal strike. Branson's response was to open a retail outlet, which was an immediate success, and the start of Virgin Retail. These retail interests were later consolidated around the Megastore concept in a joint venture with a major retailer. In prestige locations in major cities Megastores began to sell home entertainment products – music, videos, and books – on a large scale. They replaced the string of small secondary retail outlets for which Virgin had become known. The success of the Megastore concept was exported to major cities throughout the world, frequently through joint ventures.

In 1973 Virgin released the hugely successful album *Tubular Bells*. The ensuing inflow of funds enabled the record business to expand but by 1990 the high annual growth was ending. This affected Virgin, which was still a relatively small player, so the record business was sold to EMI in 1992.

Rex Features

In the early 1980s Branson was approached by Randolph Fields, who was seeking additional finance for a cut-price airline he had founded. The airline business then was tightly regulated, with routes, landing rights, prices and service levels established and maintained by intergovernmental arrangements. Decisions on these and other regulations were mainly used to protect inefficient, often state-owned, national 'flag carriers'. This had kept most air fares high. After three months of intense activity Branson and Fields had gained permission to fly, arranged to lease an aircraft and recruited staff. The first flight was in June 1984. To grow, Branson needed more landing rights, and would need to persuade government ministers in order to get them (at both ends of each route). Those ministers would also be being lobbied by the established airlines, which could try to persuade them not to approve the low fares that Branson was proposing. Alternatively, they could undercut his fares and subsidise the losses from profits on other routes.

Virgin Atlantic grew successfully and by 1990, although still a relatively small player, it competed with the major carriers on the main routes from London, winning awards for innovation and service, as well as plaudits from vital business travellers. The airline was now the focus of Branson's interests and was becoming a serious threat to the established airlines, shown by an acrimonious relationship with British Airways (the UK's national carrier). It now serves 29 destinations around the world. The company is also a leading player in the low-cost airline business through Virgin Express based in Brussels and Virgin Blue in Australia. The latter was founded in 1999 with an investment of $8 million and in 2003 was valued at $2 billion. In 2004 the company announced that it would launch a 'low-cost, high frills' airline in the United States in 2005.

Research on the Virgin brand name demonstrated the impact over time of quirky advertising and publicity stunts. The brand was recognised by 96 per cent of UK consumers, and Richard Branson was correctly identified by 95 per cent as the company's founder. The Virgin name was associated by respondents with words such as fun, innovation, success and trust, and identified with a range of businesses, confirming what Branson and others had believed: in principle there were no product or service boundaries limiting a brand name, provided it was associated with a quality offering.

Encouraged by the research, Virgin began entering new sectors outside its core activities of travel and retail. Virgin businesses as diverse as radio broadcasting, book publishing and computer games found a home in the same stable as well as hotels, railways, personal computers, cola drinks, cinemas and financial services. Branson continued to work at the centre, supported by a small business development group, a press office, and key senior advisers in the areas of strategy and finance. The early Virgin style of informality and openness remains. There is not the feel of a traditional corporate head office: ties are rarely worn, denim jeans are common, and everybody is on first-name terms.

Having a centre did not mean a centralised operation. Each operating unit was expected to stand alone, having little interaction with either head office or other units. Unit managers networked informally (usually at parties or similar events), but were not obliged to follow prescriptive corporate policies; these were 'understood' rather than codified. For example, there was no common human resource policy. Managers knew that employees must be treated 'fairly' since 'that is what Richard would want', and they complied in their own way. Similarly there was no group information technol-

ogy strategist or central purchasing function, because Branson believed that those roles would constitute interference and discourage managerial creativity. Nor was there any systematic seeking out of synergy, either at the centre or by unit managers.

In 1999 a chance remark from one of his senior executives made Branson rethink his approach. The executive mentioned that the head of a rival organisation had commented that if Virgin enterprises ever decided to collaborate they would be unstoppable. To test whether this was true Branson immediately – and for the first time – brought together all his managing directors (some 30 in all) for a retreat at his hotel in Mallorca. The agenda was open, but two themes dominated – e-commerce and a proposed unifying document, the Virgin Charter.

Participants realised that, more by chance than planning, Virgin was in businesses 'that were ideally suited to e-commerce and in which growth is expected to occur – travel, financial services, publishing, music, entertainment'. To exploit this potential the participants decided to streamline their online services with a single Virgin web address: Virgin.com.

Branson believes that the Virgin name, known for its consumer-friendly image and good service, would translate well across a range of businesses – 'Virgin isn't a company, it's a brand', commented one senior manager in the company. This is attractive to partners, who provide the expertise and capital for a joint venture in their area of business (such as insurance or share trading), while Virgin provides the brand image. By putting all Virgin's business on one easily accessible site Branson hopes to cross-promote a wide range of offerings – tickets, wine, entertainment listings, financial services and many more.

Virgin is also using the web to streamline internal operations. The airline and the stores now order inventory electronically as they need it, rather than keeping it in physical form. Airline mechanics can use the Internet to source local suppliers of a required part and have it available in hours – an impossible task with earlier technologies. The Megastores only stock the most popular products. The rest are held at a fulfilment house – ready to send to customers who order them, enabling the stores to offer a wide range of products. Advertising staff in each company use the Internet to coordinate their advertising spending and strategy before booking the business with a central agency.

During the meeting in Mallorca the group also endorsed Branson's proposed Virgin Charter. Running to some 60 pages, the charter is an agreement between Virgin Management Ltd (in effect the holding company) and all the subsidiaries. It defines the role of the centre in relation to the subsidiaries in such matters as taxation, legal affairs, intellectual property and real estate. It also outlines closer links in areas previously left to individual units: IT, people, purchasing. Thus the Charter sets out ways for the many Virgin companies to tackle common activities with a common approach. Nearly all are private and owned entirely by the Virgin Group or Richard Branson's family trusts. Business should be 'shaped around people', Branson believes, citing his experience of subdividing the record company as it grew. Each new record label was given to up-and-coming managers, creating in-house entrepreneurs who were 'far more motivated to build a business' with which they and the staff identified. A natural extension of this is the notion of building a business organically, rather than by acquisition.

He believes this approach to expansion by creating discrete legal entities gives people a sense of involvement with, and loyalty to, the small unit to which they belong. This is particularly the case if he trusts the managers of subsidiaries with full authority and offers them minority share options. He is proud of the fact that Virgin has produced a considerable number of millionaires. He has said that he does not want his best people to leave the company to start a venture outside; he prefers to make millionaires within. He has created a structure of numerous small companies around the world operated quasi-independently. Both systems embody the maxims 'small is beautiful' and 'people matter'.

In 2004 one area of difficulty was its UK rail operation, where it had not yet been able to extend the Cross-Country franchise. Other parts of the company were, however, expanding rapidly with Virgin Atlantic announcing an order worth $5.5bn for 26 Airbus A340-360 aircraft, Virgin Blue flying to many new destinations in Australia, and Virgin USA scheduled to start flying in 2005. However, Virgin Express lost money in 2003, because of fierce competition in the European low-fare market, including close competition with Ryanair. Virgin Mobile, launched in 1999, had secured almost 6 million customers in Britain, the USA and Australia and Branson was contemplating issuing shares in the British part of the company. The range of products in the Virgin Megastores was being extended to include clothes, mobile phones and consumer electronics aimed at teenagers. And in 2005 a film based on Branson's best-selling autobiography (*Losing My Virginity*) will be released.

Source: Based on material from INSEAD Case 400-002-1, *The House that Branson Built: Virgin's entry into the new millennium*; 'Branson's brash new gambit', *Business Week*, 8 March 2004; and other published material.

Part case questions

- What examples does the case give of links between Branson's strategy for Virgin and the environment in which it operates?
- What environmental influences have particularly affected The Virgin Group?
- Which of these are similar to, and which are different from, those facing Marks & Spencer?
- Are the decisions mentioned in the case programmed or non-programmed? How do you sense, from the information in the case, that the company ensures the quality of those decisions?
- What common themes link the different businesses in the group?
- Which generic strategy has Virgin followed at different periods in its history?
- What factors would you suggest Virgin Atlantic should include in a benchmarking exercise?
- What other business would it need to work with to benchmark its performance?
- On balance, does the Virgin story support the planned or the emergent view of strategy?
- Why does Branson use joint ventures with other companies to realise the Virgin strategy? Are there any disadvantages in this method of working?
- To what extent has Virgin implemented a marketing orientation?
- Visit Virgin's website and comment on how it has used this to support its marketing activities.
- Where do Richard Branson's publicity stunts fit into the company's marketing strategy?

To help you develop your skills, as well as knowledge, this section includes tasks which relate the key themes covered in the Part to your daily life. Working through these will help you to deepen your understanding of the topic, and develop skills and insights which you can use in many situations.

Task 3.1 Clarifying objectives for a task

Chapter 6 pointed out that a difficulty in planning is being clear about the longer-term objectives of the project or task. A useful skill to help reconcile apparently conflicting objectives is to try to relate them to a wider set of purposes by developing a 'why/how network'. This can make it easier to relate immediate, tangible and possibly conflicting objectives to a wider, and perhaps less conflicting, set of purposes for the activity.

Select a project from your work, or perhaps concerned with your career plans. Write the name of the project at the bottom of a large sheet of paper, and then ask 'why?'. Answer by one or more sentences beginning with the phrase 'in order to ...', and write these answers above the project task. For each of these answers, repeat the process of asking 'why?', and answering with 'in order to ...', writing your answers on the sheet. Repeat this several times, until it makes sense to stop – by which time you will probably have some broad, long-term purposes which the project can serve.

Figure 6.4 illustrates the method, and you will need to work over the chart several times to ensure it is clear.

Task 3.2 Developing an outline plan for a task

If you go to the DSM website (see Chapter 6), you will see that the company authorised the investment which DSM Melamine sought in China. Use Figure 6.5 to outline (one page only) the main issues that managers in DSM Melamine should have on their agenda for managing this expansion programme.

Then use Figure 6.7 to sketch a Programme Overview Chart to show how the different projects within the programme might fit together. Check the company website to see if you can find any information about the progress of the investment.

Task 3.3 How to reach a decision

This activity allows you to practise using Vroom and Yetton's model of the different ways in which managers can involve staff in reaching a decision. Review that section of Chapter 7. Then read these four cases and decide which of Vroom and Yetton's decision-making methods would generate the most effective decision. Note your choice, and your reasons. You could then work through the decision tree and discuss your answers with other students.

Case 1

You are the manager of a small television, radio and electronics business. For some time you have had complaints from your sales staff about the need to redecorate the large shop in which they work. You recently agreed to this and you have received three tenders from reliable and well-known local contractors. They are all able to do the work to the required standard and there is little difference in the quoted costs or times for the job.

You recently asked your employees for their suggestions on suitable colour schemes and there was considerable difference of opinion. You now have to decide which tender to accept, and to tell the contractor the colour scheme.

Which decision method would you use, and why?

Case 2

You are an engineer in charge of commissioning a chemical plant. You need to estimate the rate of progress of the stages of the work to schedule the materials and equipment. You are familiar with the work and you possess all the information you need to estimate when materials and equipment will be required at the various commissioning stages. It is very important that your estimates are accurate, since if materials are not available at the right time, work will be held up. Equally, if materials and equipment arrive too soon they will be lying around idle. Your team are all committed to the plant being commissioned on time.

Which decision method would you use, and why?

Case 3

You are a training manager employed by a firm of consultants. You have to select three of your eight training advisers to work on an assignment abroad. The assignment involves a training needs analysis, preparation of training programmes and training local instructors.

The assignment is expected to last about six months. It is in a remote part of the Middle East with poor facilities and a ban on the consumption of alcohol. Your advisers are all experienced personnel and each of them is capable of performing the task satisfactorily.

Which decision method would you use, and why?

Case 4

You are a project leader and you need to decide which operators to transfer to a new plant, Line 2. Your objective is to commission this on time without adversely affecting production on the existing plant, Line 1. Most of the operatives working on Line 1 want to transfer to Line 2 because working conditions will be better and the rates of pay higher. Senior operatives working on Line 1 expect to be given preference over less senior ones, and all those on Line 1 expect to be given preference over operatives working in other departments.

You, however, want to transfer only the best operatives from Line 1 to Line 2 and make up the balance with operatives from other departments. Your reason for wanting to do this is that Line 2 will work much faster than Line 1. This means that operatives working on Line 2 will need to be much more skilled at fault rectification than those working on Line 1. The ability to react quickly to control panel and video display unit (VDU) cues is essential.

Which decision method would you use, and why?

Task 3.4   Growth through mergers

Chapter 8 showed that one popular way of implementing strategy is through a merger or acquisition. Use the Internet (such as by accessing the online versions of the *Financial Times* (**www.ft.com**) or *The Economist* (**www.economist.com**)) to identify mergers and acquisitions announced within the past month. For a selection of these, list the companies involved, the industries in which the companies worked, and how the acquiring company relates the acquisition to its broader strategy. Which of the strategic directions shown in Figure 8.3 is best represented by the stated strategy in this case? Follow the story over the coming months.

ORGANISING

Part 4

Introduction

Part Four examines how management creates the structure within which people work. Alongside planning the direction of the business, managers need to consider how they will achieve the direction chosen. A fundamental component of that is the form of the organisation. This is a highly uncertain area of management as there are conflicting views about the kind of structure to have and how much influence structure has on performance.

Chapter 10 describes the main elements of organisation structure and the contrasting forms they take. It also looks at the related idea of organisational culture – a less tangible but equally influential factor in organisational performance. Chapter 11 deals with one aspect of an organisation's structure: the human resource management policies. These are intended to ensure that employees work towards organisational objectives.

Management wants a structure that will best serve organisational goals. The main balance to strike is between tightly structured, formal arrangements, and looser ones that leave more scope for individual initiative. Chapter 12 examines these issues and describes some newer forms of organisation through which some businesses now work. Chapter 13 looks at some of the issues that arise in implementing organisational change.

The Part Case is an account of structure and change at The Royal Bank of Scotland, which has grown rapidly in recent years, most notably through its controversial acquisition of Natwest Bank in 2000.

Chapter 10

Organisation structure and culture

Aim

To introduce terms and practices that describe organisational structures and cultures.

Objectives

By the end of your work on this chapter you should be able to outline the concepts below in your own terms and:

1 Outline how the structure and culture of an organisation may affect performance

2 Illustrate structural decisions about dividing and coordinating tasks

3 Distinguish when centralised and decentralised structures may be most suitable

4 Compare the likely advantages and disadvantages of functional, divisional, matrix and network forms

5 Describe and illustrate the main forms of coordination

6 Describe the main dimensions of organisational culture, using Quinn's or Handy's typologies.

Key terms

This chapter introduces the following ideas:

organisation structure
organisation chart
formal structure
informal structure
vertical specialisation
horizontal specialisation
formal authority
responsibility
delegation
span of control
centralisation

decentralisation
formalisation
functional structure
divisional structure
matrix structure
network structure
organisation culture
power culture
role culture
task culture
person culture

Each is a term defined within the text, as well as in the glossary at the end of the book.

Oxfam GB (employing 4000 people in 80 countries) is a charity whose aim is to work with others to overcome poverty and suffering throughout the world. It organises direct humanitarian relief to those suffering the effects of war, natural disasters or poverty, and campaigns on behalf of poor people, tackling big issues such as debt, trade and the right to education. It has a visible presence in Britain through its charity shops run by volunteers, selling donated items and handicrafts from overseas. About 22,000 volunteers now work in over 800 Oxfam shops. After a trading review in 2001 shop managers were empowered to make more decisions on how best to meet local needs. Most shops sell books and music, but in addition there are now 60 specialist bookshops (the first was opened in 1987) – making Oxfam the largest second-hand book dealer in the UK. There are also specialist music and furniture shops.

The organisation began in 1942 as the Oxford Committee for Famine Relief, providing food parcels to refugees and displaced people across Europe. In 1949 members broadened the objectives to include 'the relief of suffering as a result of wars or other causes in any part of the world'. During the 1960s concern for the world's poor grew amongst the general public and Oxfam's income also grew rapidly. It began to develop

educational materials on the root causes of poverty, and the connections between rich and poor parts of the world. Field Directors focus on projects in poor countries which aim to make local communities self-supporting by improving their water supplies, farming practices and health provision. These projects are run on the principles of local involvement and control.

It also runs high-profile campaigns (through the Campaigns and Policy Division) to persuade governments and international bodies to act on the underlying causes of poverty. 'Education Now' is a global movement in partnership with other organisations to put pressure on world leaders to make education for every child a reality, while the 'Cut the Cost' campaign aims to persuade pharmaceutical companies to reduce the price of medicines in poor countries.

In 2003 Oxfam appointed Barbara Stocking as its first woman director. In an interview later that year she commented:

When I came here I said: 'I want us to be a modern, professional organisation that gets things done.' That's ended up as my motto. Oxfam is an organisation where people like to talk about ideas and they all like to be involved, and you can go round and round in circles and nothing ever happens. I was quite frustrated about that in my early days.

With the corporate management team, we really looked at getting things done. This means asking: does this activity need to be done? If it does is Oxfam the best place to do it? We're looking at outsourcing our supporter activities – so-called banking and thanking. We're taking out a minimum of 70 jobs, out of about 700 as we go into our new building in 2005. And they're concerned that I'm toughening up the organisation, particularly in Oxford.

Source: Oxfam website (www.oxfamgb.org); and *Financial Times*, 24 December 2003.

Adrian Arbib/Royal Geographical Society/Alamy

Case questions

- What examples can you find in the case of decisions about Oxfam's organisation structure?
- What developments or events may have prompted these decisions?
- From the case, what kind of 'culture' may Oxfam have?

10.1 Introduction

As in many organisations, the people running Oxfam have adapted its structure as the scale and complexity of its activities have grown. In the early days of a single group of enthusiastic volunteers it had a very simple structure, as people could easily share the tasks informally. Such informality would be risky in a company that now employs 1300 paid staff and 23,000 volunteers in the UK alone, so staff have gradually developed the structure described in the case – which continues to evolve as needs change.

Senior managers of companies that have not been performing well frequently announce structural changes. When Shell was trying to recover from the 2004 oil reserves crisis, the Board first dismissed the three senior executives involved in the failure – and then started to change the structure to prevent a recurrence. In 2003 Cadbury Schweppes announced a cost-cutting programme to save £400m annually by 2007. It had bought many other companies in recent years, but had not yet integrated them: the new structure would combine closely related businesses into fewer units and clarify reporting responsibilities. Management at Philips, the Dutch electronics group, announced in 2004 that to enhance performance they would be requiring the fiercely independent units in the company to cooperate more closely, turning the business into a single company.

When an owner-manager is running a business he or she decides what tasks are to be done and coordinates them. If the enterprise grows it usually becomes necessary to create more stability, so the entrepreneur divides the overall task amongst designated people, even if the division is flexible and informal. They can also coordinate their activities informally as people can easily communicate directly with each other. As the business grows larger, new structural questions arise. Expansion brings the possibility of confusion and misunderstanding with more people, separate units and less direct contact. Staff need to understand their responsibilities, and structures clarify what others expect.

As they create such structures managers decide how to deploy the resources of the organisation to achieve their objectives. They decide how to divide the whole enterprise into distinct units of activity, establish reporting relationships and ensure coordination between the units. What they decide reflects their theory about the best arrangement to support the current strategy.

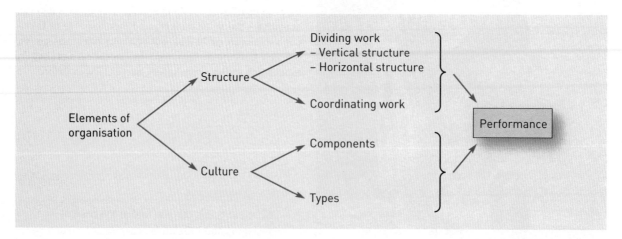

Figure 10.1 Structural and cultural elements of organisations

This chapter outlines the structural issues that managers in all organisations need to resolve, and which Figure 10.1 illustrates. Managers create a formal structure when they decide how to divide the work of the organisation. They create a vertical structure that shows the reporting relationships throughout the organisation, and a horizontal structure as they allocate work to departments. Having divided work, they need to decide how best to coordinate the parts so that they work together. Finally, the chapter introduces ideas about the components and types of organisational culture. Together with many informal arrangements, these decisions shape the distinctive nature of an organisation.

10.2 Dividing work – creating the vertical structure

Organisation structure describes the way tasks are divided, supervised and coordinated. The **organisation chart** shows this in picture form. When people join a department or take a job within the structure the organisation chart gives a fairly clear signal about what they should do. The director of marketing is expected to deal with marketing, not finance. Various 'operating policies' reinforce the signal from the basic structure. These cover matters such as selection, development, appraisal and reward, which managers design to influence employee behaviour that supports their objectives. Operating policies shape the kind of people managers select, what behaviour they reward and what career moves they encourage.

> **Organisation structure** 'The structure of an organisation [is] the sum total of the ways in which it divides its labour into distinct tasks and then achieves coordination among them' (Mintzberg, 1989).

The organisation chart

This is a diagram showing the main departments and positions within the organisation. Lines link senior executives to the other departments or people for whose work they are responsible. It shows to whom each department or division reports, and clarifies four features of the **formal structure**:

> An **organisation chart** shows the main departments and senior positions in an organisation and the reporting relations between them.

- **Tasks** – the major tasks or activities the organisation undertakes
- **Subdivisions** – how the major tasks are further divided
- **Levels** – the position of each post within the management hierarchy, and the reporting links
- **Lines of authority** – the lines linking the boxes show who has formal authority over whom.

> **Formal structure** is the official guidelines, documents or procedures setting out how the organisation's activities are divided and coordinated.

Such charts are always changing, but provide a convenient summary of the current allocation of tasks and who is responsible for them. Figure 10.2 shows the organisation chart for an aircraft factory within what is now BAE Systems, a large UK manufacturing business. The factory has six main departments – design, production engineering, purchasing, inventory, production and human resources. The chart shows the chain of command within the plant and the tasks of the respective departments (only some of which are shown). In this case the chart includes direct staff such as operators and engineers, and shows the lines of authority throughout the factory. It does *not* show the **informal structure** – the many patterns of work and communication that are part of organisational life.

> **Informal structure** is the undocumented relationships between members of the organisation that inevitably emerge as people adapt systems to new conditions and satisfy personal and group needs.

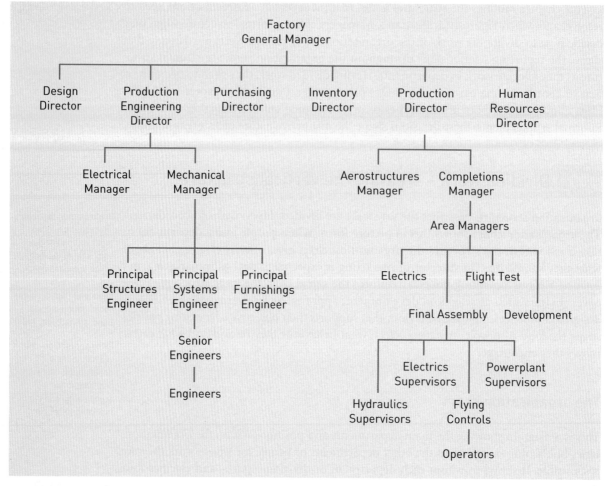

Figure 10.2 The structure within a BAE aircraft factory

Source: Information provided by the company.

Dividing tasks

One person working as an independent owner-manager has no need for an organisation structure. He or she decides what to do, and how they will plan and coordinate the different activities. Growth increases the problems of coordination, though in small businesses staff usually handle these issues informally by mutual give-and-take. People usually (not always) begin to experience more difficulties with informal structures if the business starts to grow. The dangers of informality begin to outweigh the benefits.

'Job specialisation ... is an inherent part of every organisation, indeed every human activity' (Mintzberg, 1979, p. 69). Management divides work into smaller tasks, with people or departments specialising in one or more of these. They become more expert in one task than they could be in several and save time by not moving between them. By concentrating on one, they are more likely to come up with improved ideas or methods. Taken too far, specialisation leads to the negative effects noted in Chapter 15.

Multi-show Events

Multi-show Events employs 11 people, providing a variety of entertainment and promotional services to large businesses. When Brian Simpson created the business in 1990 with a full-time staff of two the company obviously had no formal structure. He reflected on the process of growth and structure:

> While the company was small thinking about a structure never occurred to me. It became a consideration as sales grew and the complexity of what we offered increased. There were also more people around and I believed that I should introduce a structure so that clear divisions of responsibility would be visible. It seemed natural to split sales and marketing from the actual delivery and production of events as these were two distinct areas. I felt that by creating 'specialised' departments we could give a better service to clients as each area of the company could focus more on their own roles. [Figure 10.3 below shows the structure.]
>
> We had to redesign the office layout and introduce a more formalised communication process to ensure all relevant information is being passed on – and on the whole I think this structure will see us through the next stage of business growth and development.

Source: Private communication.

The principle applies at all levels and in all but the very smallest companies. Figure 10.2 shows the specialisation of work in the BAE factory. At the top is specialisation between design, production, purchasing and so on. It shows a **vertical specialisation** in that people at different levels deal with distinct sets of activity. It also shows a **horizontal specialisation** throughout. Within production engineering the chart shows that some specialise in electrical problems and others in mechanical. Within the latter it shows that separate groups specialise in structures, systems and fittings. Although Multi-show Events is still a very small company, they too have begun to create a structure to clarify who is responsible for which tasks.

Vertical specialisation refers to the extent to which responsibilities at different levels are defined.

Horizontal specialisation is the degree to which tasks are divided among separate people or departments.

Lines of authority

The lines of authority show the links between people in the organisation, by showing everyone whom they report to and who reports to them. It shows whom they can ask to do a piece of work, whom they can go to for support – and who will be expecting results from them. In Figure 10.2 the production director can give instructions to the aerostructures or completions manager, but not to the electrical manager in production engineering. The powerplant foreman reports to the final assembly manager, who in turn reports to the completions manager. Figure 10.3 shows the lines of authority in the comparatively tiny Multi-show Events. In both cases there are many informal contacts in the course of normal human activity. These bring extra life to the organisation and help it cope with unplanned events, with which the formal system cannot deal.

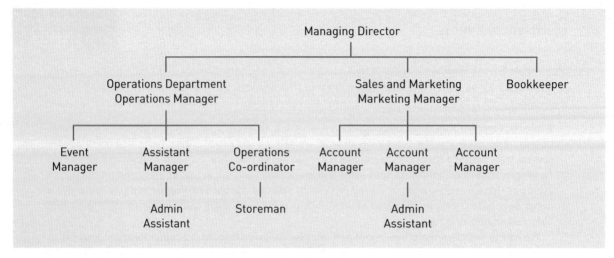

Figure 10.3 The organisation structure at Multi-show Events

Authority, responsibility and delegation

Formal authority is
the right that a person in
a specified role has to
make decisions, allocate
resources or give
instructions.

The lines of authority show the allocation of formal power within the organisation. **Formal authority** is the right that a person has to make decisions, allocate resources or give instructions. It is based on the position, not the person. The production engineering director at BAE has formal authority over a defined range of matters – and anyone else taking over the job would have the same amount of formal authority.

Subordinates – those below someone else in the hierarchy – comply with instructions or requests because they accept that the person has the formal (sometimes called legitimate) authority to make that request. An operator in the hydraulics area of final assembly would accept an instruction from the hydraulics foreman, but probably not from the powerplant foreman (he or she may do something as a personal favour for the latter, but that is different from accepting formal authority). If managers attempt to give instructions or do things that are beyond their area of formal authority, they are likely to meet resistance – they have no formal authority over those areas.

Responsibility refers
to a person attempting to
meet the expectations
others have of them.

Responsibility is a person's duty to perform a task that has been assigned to them. The production director and the hydraulics foreman are responsible for the tasks that go with those positions. To fulfil those responsibilities they require the formal authority over the relevant resources, including the right to deploy them. A person who has been given responsibility for a task, but not the authority to match it, will be in a difficult position. He or she will need to rely on other sources of power (Chapter 14) to influence people to get things done.

Accountability means that people with authority and responsibility for an area are required to report on, and justify, their work to those above them in the chain of command. The principal systems engineer is responsible for that area of work, and has authority over certain resources. He or she is accountable to the mechanical manager for the way they have used those resources, by comparing what they have achieved with what was expected. The measures could include the cost, quantity, quality or timeliness of the work.

Oxfam GB – the case continues

The main aspects of the Oxfam organisation structure are:

- **The Council** – the governing body which meets seven times a year. It is made up of between 10 and 12 unpaid Trustees and is ultimately accountable for the overall management of Oxfam.
- **The Director** is the Chief Executive and is responsible to the Trustees for the management of Oxfam.
- **Six Deputy Directors** each responsible for a Division:

  - Marketing (fundraising, communications and campaigns)
  - International (developing and implementing Oxfam's programmes in over 70 countries)
  - Trading (shops and recycling in Britain, and the Fair Trade operation)
  - Finance and Information Systems (finance and IS throughout the organisation)
  - Corporate Human Resources (advises other divisions on HR matters)
  - Campaigns and Policy (advocacy of policies to promote lasting change).

Each Division has HR and Finance teams responsible for those matters.

Source: Oxfam website.

Delegation is the process by which people transfer responsibility and authority for certain parts of their work to people below them in the chain of command. While the production director is responsible and accountable for all the work in that area, they are only able to do this by delegating the work downwards. They are still accountable for the results, but they pass the responsibility, and the necessary authority, to subordinates – and this continues down the hierarchy. If managers delegate more to their subordinates this enables quicker decisions and more rapid responses to new conditions. However, delegation is not a straightforward process, and some managers are reluctant to delegate in case it reduces their power (see Chapter 14).

> **Delegation** occurs when one person gives another the authority to undertake specific activities or decisions.

Line and staff authority

Chapter 1 distinguished between line managers and staff managers. Line departments are those that have direct responsibility for delivering the products or services of the organisation. People in those departments have line authority over their direct subordinates – as the production director in Figure 10.2 has line authority over the completions manager. Staff departments have an advisory relationship in support of the line departments, in matters such as human resources or finance. Their authority is more of an advisory one. The human resources director has no line authority to instruct the production director how to design an appraisal system – but can offer help and advice on how to do this.

The span of control

The **span of control** refers to the number of subordinates reporting to a supervisor. Where staff are closely supervised then there is a narrow span of control – as shown in the top half of Figure 10.4. Other organisations have wider spans of control, by introducing more autonomy and team working – producing broader spans of control and flatter organisation structures. Managers have more people reporting to them, implying that subordinates will have more freedom to use their initiative.

> A **span of control** is the number of subordinates reporting directly to the person above them in the hierarchy.

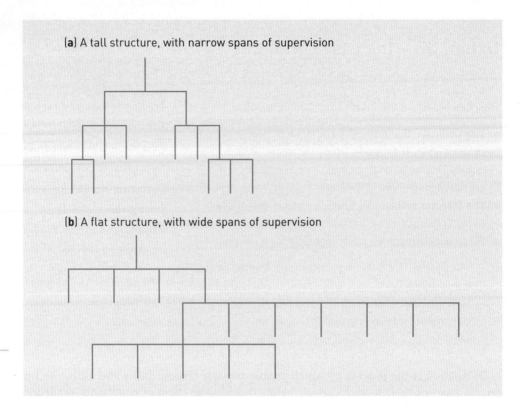

Figure 10.4

Tall and flat organisation structures

Centralisation and decentralisation

When an organisation grows beyond the smallest operation, management divides work vertically, as those at the top delegate more of their work to those below them – and so begin to create a hierarchy such as that shown in Figure 10.4. As the business grows the hierarchy becomes more complex, but behind the detail it is often possible to see three levels – corporate, divisional and operating – such as at Cadbury Schweppes (**www.cadburyschweppes.com**):

- **Corporate** The most senior group, such as the Board of Cadbury Schweppes, who are responsible for managing the overall direction of the organisation. This includes not only guiding and monitoring the performance of subordinate levels of the organisation but also maintaining links with significant external institutions such as banks and political bodies.
- **Divisional** Responsible for implementing broad areas of policy and for securing and allocating budgets and other resources. Cadbury Schweppes is organised geographically so the managers in, for example, the Europe, Middle East and Africa (EMEA) Division are responsible for meeting the targets which the Board sets for that division. Divisional managers represent the division's interests to the Board and also monitor and control the performance of the operating units within their area.
- **Operating** The level responsible for doing the technical work of the organisation – making products, catching thieves, caring for patients or delivering services. Within EMEA there is a team responsible, for example, for the Dairy Milk brand in the UK – ensuring it is produced and sold successfully in that market. Other teams will be responsible for the day-to-day delivery of other products in the range.

Joan Woodward's research

Joan Woodward's study of 100 firms in Essex found great variety between them in the number of sub-ordinates managers supervised (Woodward, 1965). The number of people reporting directly to the Chief Executive ranged from two to 18, with the median span of control being six. The average span of control of the first-line supervisors varied from 10 to 90, with a median of 37. Woodward explained the variation by the technological system used (discussed more fully in Chapter 12).

A key issue in designing the vertical hierarchy is establishing what decisions people at each of the levels can make. **Centralisation** is when those at the top make most of the decisions. The divisional level ensures that those at operating level follow the policy.

Centralisation is when a relatively large number of decisions are taken by management at the top of the organisation.

Philips www.philips.com

management in practice

After a period of heavy losses during the 1990s Philips, the Dutch electronics company, appointed a new Chief Executive in 2001 – Gerard Kleisterlee. He acted quickly to restructure the company, including reducing staff by 25 per cent. The company has a rich 113-year history of innovation and pioneered electric shavers, medical X-rays and compact discs: it symbolised European technical prowess.

But the same engineering culture has also produced failures (such as an early rival to the now-standard VCR) and revenues now are little higher than they were 10 years ago. To pick up the pace, Kleisterlee has reorganised the company – selling unprofitable areas, outsourcing much electronics manufacture (see Section 10.6). Now he is refocusing the company around the most profitable sectors, especially medical systems, and pushing all products to a digital format. This focus is backed up by breaking down the walls separating the fiercely independent divisions and getting them to communicate. 'We're transforming ourselves into a single company', says Mr Kleisterlee. Under the 'One Philips' slogan, he is centralising functions such as marketing and human resources to eliminate duplication.

Source: *Business Week*, 3 May 2004.

Decentralisation is when a relatively large number of decisions are taken in the divisions or operating units. People in the operating units work as they think best, provided they deliver the results expected by the corporate level and keep within some broad guidelines. Branch managers in ATMays, a chain of retail travel agents (since absorbed into Going Places), had considerable freedom over pricing and promotional activities, but were required to follow very tight financial reporting routines.

Decentralisation is when a relatively large number of decisions are taken lower down the organisation in particular operating units.

Johnson & Johnson www.jnj.com

This leading healthcare products company is organised into three divisions – drugs, medical devices and consumer products. Although most widely known for established consumer products like medical plasters and baby powder, its deeper strength lies in its scientific research and innovation. 'J&J's success has hinged on its unique culture and structure . . . Each of the far-flung units operates pretty much as an independent enterprise. Businesses set their own strategies; they have their own finance and human resources departments, for example. (While this is costly) Johnson & Johnson has been able to turn itself into a powerhouse precisely because the businesses it buys, or the ones it starts, are given near-total autonomy. That independence fosters an entrepreneurial attitude that has kept J&J intensely competitive as others around it have faltered.'

Source: *Business Week*, 5 May 2003.

A political analogy

The same issue arises in the wider political world. European nations vary in how they divide power between central, regional and local government. France and the United Kingdom are relatively centralised, while the Netherlands and probably Spain are more decentralised, with strong provincial or regional governments. Much of the controversy over the UK's relationship with the European Union relates to the similar question of subsidiarity: what matters should those in Brussels decide, and what should individual member states decide? As in business, pressures for changes in the current balance are always present – and the solutions reflect both rational and political influences.

In practice, organisations display a mix of both. Many companies have moved towards more decentralised structures in the belief that those who are closest to the action will make better decisions. Others have done the opposite, limiting the power of divisions

Table 10.1

Advantages and disadvantages of centralisation

Factor	Advantages	Disadvantages
Response to change	Can ensure thorough debate taking account of all issues	Slower response to local variations in conditions
Use of expertise	Concentration of expertise at the centre makes it easier to develop new services and promote best practice methods	Less likely to take account of local knowledge
Cost	Economies of scale in purchasing supplies and facilities, and less administrative cost if using common systems	Centralised systems may be wasteful when applied locally – local suppliers may be better value than corporate suppliers
	Retains control over major/costly decisions	May lack relevant knowledge for good decisions
Policy implications	Less risk of local managers breaching legal requirements	More risk of local managers breaching legal requirements
Staff commitment	Backing of centre ensures wide support	Staff motivated by greater local responsibility
Consistency	Provides consistent image to the public – less variation in service standards	Local staff discouraged from taking responsibility – problems can be blamed on the centre
	Able to compare performance on common measures	Common measures may not be appropriate locally

and taking more decisions at the centre. Hewlett-Packard had a tradition of local auton-omy ('The HP Way'). The company founders believed that 'smart people will make the right choices if given the right tools and authority' – and so pushed strategic decisions down to the managers most involved in each business. The company appointed a new chief executive, Carleton Fiorina, in 1999. She created a Strategy Council that advised her on strategy and allocated resources across the company – a big change from 'The HP Way' – until she left the company in 2005 after disagreements over policy.

There is always a tension between centralising and decentralising (Table 10.1). The profile at any point reflects the shifting power of these forces, as managers weigh the ben-efits of a move in one direction or the other (including their personal career interests).

Case questions 10.1

- What clues are there in the case about the balance between centralisation and decentralisation in Oxfam?
- What are the advantages of having strong central control over campaigns? Are there any disadvantages?

Formalisation

Formalisation is the practice of using written or electronic documents to direct and con-trol employees. Documents include rule books, procedures, instruction manuals, job descriptions – anything that sets out what people must do in designated circumstances. They include the scripts that operators in most call centres must use to guide their con-versation with a customer. The intention of these formal methods (consistent with the ideas of Max Weber discussed in Chapter 2) is to bring more consistency and predictabil-ity to organisational work.

Formalisation is the practice of using written or electronic documents to direct and control employees.

There is always tension between formality and informality. If people are to be more responsive to individual needs, and able to adapt to local conditions, they favour infor-mal arrangements with few rules. The informal organisation appears to be the most responsive and effective approach. Yet many organisations introduce more formal meth-ods in the shape of detailed procedures and guidelines to meet the requirements of industry regulators or consumer legislation. They need to protect customers against unsuitable selling methods or to protect staff against unfounded complaints. This often leads managers to introduce more formal systems and recording procedures.

Activity 10.1   Critical reflection on structures

Gather information on how your college or university is structured, focusing on the parts most directly involved in delivering your education.
- How have the various parts of the task been divided up?
- Are all the teaching staff you see in one department or in several?
- Do you have a separate management library or computing suite, or do you share a wider facility?

Answers to such questions reflect how the overall task has been divided. If you work in an organisation, similarly reflect on the vertical structure – such as:
- Which aspects are centralised and which are decentralised?
- Have senior managers acted in a similar way to those at Philips?

10.3 Dividing work – creating the horizontal structure

A highly visible aspect of structure is the way an organisation's work is divided into smaller units or departments. There are five approaches to this aspect of structural design, which Figure 10.5 illustrates in summary form. The functional, divisional and matrix forms are widely used, each using the chain of command within whichever form is chosen. Two forms that are becoming more common use teams and networks as the basis of structure.

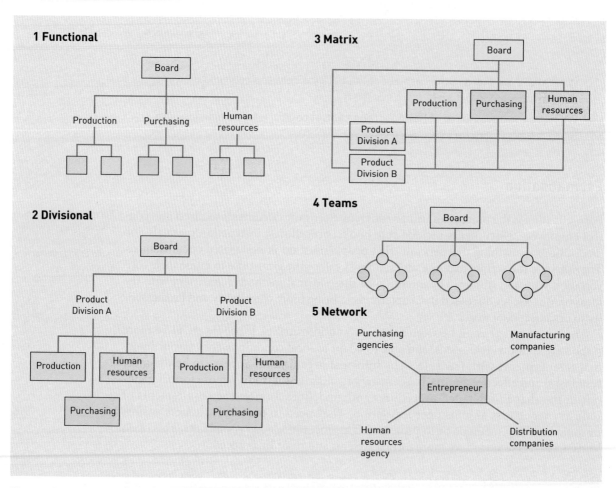

Figure 10.5 Five types of structure

The five approaches to structure are:

1. **Functional** People work in departments made up of those with a common technical or professional expertise, such as purchasing or legal affairs.
2. **Divisional** People work in departments that are themselves part of a division delivering a product or service to a distinct group of customers. These are sometimes called strategic business units, and have their own profit and loss account.
3. **Matrix** People are based in a functional group, and then work for a divisional group or project on distinct tasks.
4. **Teams** The team is the basic building block, with teams forming to complete tasks and coordinate their work with others, at all levels.

5 Networks The organisation acts as a broker between independent organisations that contract to provide services as required.

Each has advantages and disadvantages – and organisations often combine elements of more than one type. Each form also has different implications for those managing and working within them.

Specialisation by function

In a **functional structure** managers group activities and employees according to their professional or functional specialisms, such as production, finance, marketing or information services. The BAE factory has a functional approach, with staff working in design, production engineering, purchasing, inventory, production or human resources. Figure 10.6 shows the main structural division of a hospital. The chart at senior levels shows a clear functional division into nursing and quality, medical, finance and human resources.

Functional structure is when tasks are grouped into departments based on similar skills and expertise.

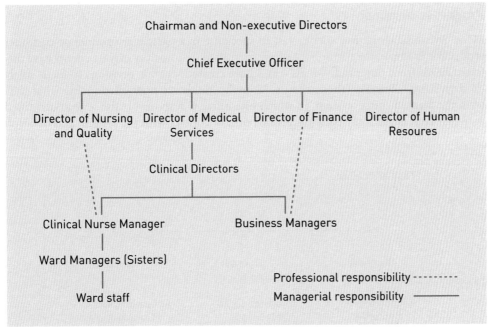

Chairman and Non-executive Directors

Chief Executive Officer

Director of Nursing and Quality | Director of Medical Services | Director of Finance | Director of Human Resoures

Clinical Directors

Clinical Nurse Manager | Business Managers

Ward Managers (Sisters)

Ward staff

Professional responsibility --------
Managerial responsibility ————

Figure 10.6

Partial organisation structure in a hospital

The functional approach can be efficient. Management creates a separate department for each major task, and people with expertise in that task work together. They share skills and can see a professional career path in their department.

Problems arise when an organisation grows and diversifies into a range of different products, markets or geographical areas. Managers responsible for achieving results in these areas expect functional staff to give priority to what they need. If a sales executive makes a commitment to a customer, he or she will expect the manufacturing facility to meet that commitment. The manufacturing unit may have equally pressing orders from other sales staff. Units compete with each other for functional services such as information systems – which can never meet all the demands for systems development. The focus of staff tends to be inward, towards the interests of the function, rather than outward towards the whole business. Table 10.2 summarises the advantages and disadvantages.

Table 10.2

Advantages and disadvantages of functional specialisation

Factor	Advantages	Disadvantages
Staff careers	Clear career paths and professional development	Isolation from wider issues damages promotion prospects
Resources	Specialisation leads to high standards and efficiency	Conflict over priorities
Working relations	Common professional interests support good internal relations	Lack of wider awareness damages external relations

Divisional approach

A **divisional structure** is when tasks are grouped in relation to their outputs, such as products or the needs of different types of customer.

Managers create a **divisional structure** when they arrange the organisation around its main products, services or customer groups. They create separate units and make them responsible for all the functions necessary to deliver services to the customer. The units focus on defined groups of customers with distinct requirements.

Product or customer

Many divisional structures enable staff to specialise in a particular product or customer group. For example, the major banks have identified that wealthy private clients have different needs from other individuals – and have created separate divisions to focus solely on delivering services to those clients. Many hospitals are now introducing what they term the 'named-nurse' system, in which one nurse is responsible for several identified patients. That nurse is the patient's prime point of contact with the system, and their job

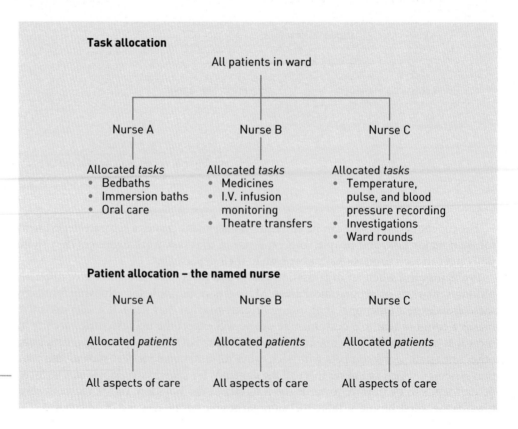

Figure 10.7

Task and named-nurse structures

is to manage the delivery of services to the patient from other (functional) departments. Figure 10.7 contrasts the task and named-nurse approaches.

In a divisional structure senior managers give each unit the authority to design, produce and deliver the product or service, using resources under its control or bought from outside suppliers. The advantages are that they can focus all resources on the one product. Separate areas of functional expertise are more likely to cooperate as they all depend on satisfying the same set of customers. It is probably more expensive, as each product group may have a wide range of specialisms, duplicating provision. The problems of cooperation between departments that beset functional structures may still arise, though in different forms.

Geographic divisions

Here managers divide the organisation geographically, usually according to the location of customers. They group all the tasks required under the management of that geographic region rather than having them divided amongst functions at the centre. For example, large companies with many service outlets – supermarkets, hotels, breweries – often divide the business into regions. This allows management to focus on identifying and meeting different customer requirements in the region, or on meeting different environmental conditions. A geographical management structure also makes it easier for the centre to monitor and control the many relatively small outlets. Table 10.3 summarises these points.

Factor	Advantages	Disadvantages
Staff focus	Functional staff focus on product and customer needs	Isolation from wider professional and technical developments
Resources	Dedicated facilities meet customer needs quickly	Costs of duplication across the organisation (e.g. distribution networks, computer systems)
Working relations	Common customer focus supports good internal relations	Potential conflict with other divisions over priorities, and no incentive to support other divisions
Control	Regional divisions use autonomy to meet local needs	Divisions develop policies independently of wider organisational interests

Table 10.3

Advantages and disadvantages of a divisional structure (product or geographic)

Matrix organisation

A **matrix structure** combines functional and divisional structures. On one axis of the matrix is a range of functional groups and on the other are the products or projects, with a manager responsible for each. Staff from the functional areas work on one or more projects. When a project no longer needs their expertise they are allocated by their functional boss to work on another. Subordinates have two bosses – a long-term, functional head, and a temporary head of the project currently being worked upon. Table 10.4 shows that while the approach has advantages it can also raise some serious management problems.

A **matrix structure** is when those doing a task report to both a functional and a projector divisional boss.

Table 10.4

Advantages and disadvantages of a matrix structure

Factor	Advantages	Disadvantages
Staff focus	Staff gain variety of work experience, and develop understanding of customer needs	Isolation from wider professional developments in functional base
	Functions develop professional expertise	Conflicting demands of project and functional boss
Resources	Dedicated facilities can be arranged to meet customer needs as required	Costs of duplication across the organisation as demands vary
Working relations	Project focus supports good internal relations	Potential conflict with functional divisions over priorities

Product development at Toyota   www.toyota.com

Toyota used to organise its product development in a matrix form. The product planning division employed about 7000 people working on 16 current projects. Each represented a new model and employed a chief engineer and several hundred staff. There were also 16 functional engineering divisions.

> A chief engineer had to coordinate people in 48 departments in 12 divisions to launch a new product ... In addition, relatively young chief engineers did not always get sufficient cooperation from senior functional managers . . . For their part, functional managers found it difficult to spend the time on managing details on so many projects. Most of these managers had to oversee work for about 15 different projects at the same time.

Source: Cusumano and Nobeoka (1998), pp. 22–4.

Mixed forms

Especially in large organisations, practice is more complex than these simple categories suggest. Such businesses typically use a variety of methods for dividing tasks – The Body Shop example shows functional, product and geographical structures within the same company – see Figure 1 in Part 1 Case. The structure of Unilever, the Anglo-Dutch conglomerate that produces a vast range of consumer products throughout the world, is another example.

Teams

In their search for more flexibility, lower costs and faster response, more managements use teams as a way of organising work. This is particularly true in companies that depend on a steady flow of scientific developments to create new products – such as Johnson & Johnson or Philips. Management delegates significant responsibilities and authority not to individual workers but to an identifiable team, which is then mutually accountable for the results. The team may be from across functions or from within a single area – in which case it looks like a small department. The difference is that there is probably less hierarchical division amongst the members and more mutual accountability for results. They are sometimes called 'self-managing teams' to emphasise the relative absence of hierarchical relationships (Manz and Sims, 1993). The many potential advantages are balanced by disadvantages, such as a tendency to take on their own purpose and to spend time in debate rather than action (see Chapter 17).

Mixed structure at Unilever www.unilever.com

During the year ended 31 December 2003 Unilever was organised on both a product and a regional basis.

> Our operations are organized into two global divisions – Food and Home and Personal Care (HPC) – each headed by a Divisional Director. This structure allows the appropriate focus on food and HPC products at both global and regional level and allows us to optimize synergies across the product portfolio.
>
> The two divisional operations are organized into business groups on a regional basis, with certain exceptions (such as the global business of Prestige, our fragrance business). The regional and global businesses are headed by Business Presidents. These businesses remain the driving force behind Unilever, comprising the operating companies which provide the key interface with customers and consumers, allowing quick response to the needs of local markets.

Source: *Unilever Annual Report*, 2003.

Networks

A **network structure** can take countless forms – essentially they refer to increasingly common situations in which organisations remain independent but agree to work together to deliver products or services. Sometimes this happens when managers arrange for other companies to undertake certain activities on their behalf, usually those that they do not see as being core to the business. The remaining organisation concentrates on setting strategy direction and managing the core units. Abbey (a UK bank) has an agreement with computer services company Unisys to process and manage the 1.5m insurance policies it has sold. Large electronics producers such as Dell and Sun Microsystems have many of their products made under contract by companies that specialise in such work. The arrangement is becoming common in personal services – such as when Care UK runs homes for mentally ill elderly patients and schools for disturbed children on behalf of local authorities.

A similar structural form is when managers sell one of their services to another company, but still deliver the service to customers under their own name. Abbey sold its credit card business to MBNA as the cost of updating its systems to compete effectively in the card business was too high. However, the company will continue to offer cards – designed and operated by MBNA but showing the Abbey logo.

This section has described five alternative ways of dividing tasks. Most enterprises adopt a mix of forms and continually adapt to changing circumstances. They seek to achieve a balance between the advantages and disadvantages of each type in their circumstances. Structures are transitional rather than permanent forms. Networks enable small firms to grow rapidly with limited capital expenditure, if they can secure services from suppliers, and the boundaries of organisations become harder to identify. Arrangements with suppliers to provide services that were available within the company raise new challenges of coordination.

A **network structure** is when tasks required by one company are performed by other companies with expertise in those areas.

321

10.4 Coordinating work

The division of work must be coordinated to achieve the intended results – without it there will be confusion and poor performance. Effective coordination becomes more essential as customers expect higher quality and shareholders expect higher profits. Yet it is difficult to coordinate large, widely dispersed businesses, operating and changing at great speed.

Direct supervision

This is where a manager ensures coordination by directly supervising his or her staff to ensure they work together in line with company policy. The limitation lies in the idea of the span of control – the number of people whom a manager can effectively supervise directly. Chapter 12 shows that spans of control vary with circumstances.

Hierarchy

If disputes or problems arise between staff or departments, they can be reconciled by putting the arguments to their common boss in the hierarchy. It is the boss's responsibility to reach a solution. At the BAE aircraft factory (Figure 10.2), if the engineer responsible for structures has a disagreement over some work problem with the systems engineer, they can ask the mechanical manager to adjudicate. If that fails they can escalate the problem to a higher level – the production engineering director. The weakness of this method is that it takes time to get a response, and meantime the issue is unresolved. In rapidly changing circumstances the hierarchy cannot cope with the volume of issues requiring attention, and becomes slow at making decisions.

Standardising inputs and outputs

This involves making sure that what goes into the system, and what managers expect it to produce, are standardised. This makes coordination with other stages easier. If the purchaser of components specifies accurately what is required, and the supplier meets that specification, coordination between those who use the parts will be easier. Similarly, if staff work to precise specifications, coordinating with the next stage of the process becomes easier. If staff all receive the same training in how to do a task they will need less direct supervision, as their manager can be more confident that they will be working consistently.

Rules and procedures

Another way to coordinate the activities of people or departments is to prepare rules or guidelines on how they should perform.

Safety procedures in a power station

The following instructions govern the steps that staff must follow when they inspect control equipment in a nuclear power station:

1 Before commencing work you must read and understand the relevant Permit-to-Work and/or other safety documents as appropriate.
2 Obtain keys for relevant cubicles.
3 Visually inspect the interior of each bay for dirt, water and evidence of condensation.
4 Visually inspect the cabling, glands, terminal blocks and components for damage.
5 Visually check for loose connections at all terminals.
6 Lock all cubicles and return the keys.
7 Clear the safety document and return it to the Supervisor/Senior Authorised person.

Organisations have procedures for approving capital expenditure. To compare proposals on a common basis they give strict guidelines on the questions a bid should answer, how people should prepare a case, and to whom they should submit it. Companies developing new computer software have major problems in coordinating the work if several designers are working on different parts of the same project. People can easily duplicate work that others have done, or work on an older version, not realising that someone has produced a new version. To overcome this, companies use strict change control procedures to ensure that the sub-projects fit together efficiently.

Information systems

Information systems help to ensure that people who need to work in a consistent way have common information about what is happening. Sharing information makes it easier to coordinate the different activities within a company. The Internet offers a radical solution to the problem of moving information and knowledge between organisations, as the Siemens example shows.

Internet coordination at Siemens www.siemens.com

Mr von Pierer, Chief Executive of Siemens until 2005, is enthusiastic about the way the company is using the Internet to coordinate different parts of the company. One example is online purchasing which enables the company to save huge amounts of money by pooling the demands of several purchasing departments, using a company-wide system called click2procure.

Another way is to encourage customers to buy online. They can click on 'buy from Siemens' on the website home page and place orders for most Siemens products. The automation and drives division, for example, generates some 30 per cent of its sales online. The strategy also helps to improve internal administrative processes – such as by handling 30,000 job applications a year online, or expecting employees to book their business travel arrangements over the Internet.

There is more to this than paperless administration. The idea is to make sure that the whole supply chain – from customers, through Siemens, and then on to its suppliers – runs smoothly. Different bits of Siemens had previously developed Internet applications independently, which has caused problems:

it was almost impossible to connect all these different systems in order to get information to flow from your customer to your supplier.

Mr von Pierer also wants customers to have a single, coordinated view of the company:

I don't think that in the future customers will tolerate four or five different views about Siemens. They want one view of our capabilities. Even if a customer is buying things from several different Siemens divisions, it should deal directly with only one, which should act as a lead manager within the company. Inside Siemens, the customer should be identified by only one code.

However, he acknowledged that reorganising all the internal processes would be a major task.

Source: Boddy *et al.* (2005) and company website.

Another example is IBM, which has changed its purchasing processes so that they are now conducted almost entirely over the Internet. This ensures that new instructions to hundreds of suppliers flow almost automatically as the manufacturing programme changes to match current orders. This was previously a laborious activity in which people easily made mistakes. Modern information systems have transformed it into a much more tightly coordinated activity.

Direct personal contact

This is the most human form of coordination: people talking to each other. Mintzberg (1979) found that people use this method in both the simplest and the most complex organisations. There is so much uncertainty in the latter that information systems cannot cope with all eventualities. Only direct contact can coordinate these.

Structure in a social service

The organisation cares for the elderly in a large city. Someone who had worked there for several years reflected on the structure:

Within the centre there was a manager, two deputies, an assistant manager, five senior care officers (SCOs) and 30 officers. Each SCO is responsible for six care officers, allowing daily contact between the supervisor and the subordinates. While this defines job roles quite tightly, it allows a good communication structure to exist. Feedback is common as there are frequent meetings of the separate groups, and individual appraisals of the care officers by the SCOs. Staff value this opportunity for praise and comments on how they are doing.

Contact at all levels is common between supervisor and care officers during meetings to assess the needs of clients – for whom the care officers have direct responsibility. Frequent social gatherings and functions within the department also serve to enhance relations and satisfy social needs. Controls placed on the behaviour of the care officers come from the highest positions in the hierarchy, especially those derived from legislation such as the Social Work Acts and the Health and Safety Executive. Performance measures also exist. For example, outsiders regularly assess how the Quality of Practice code is working, along with those established in the department on absenteeism and lateness.

Structure certainly plays a major role in the effectiveness of employees at work by encouraging and motivating them. However, in a department such as this the need to improve quality of service has to come from the desire of the individual to do better for clients.

| Activity 10.2 | Critical reflection on coordination |

- How are the separate activities typically coordinated in an organisation you know? You may want to focus on coordination between one or two specific groups or departments. List the main methods that are used, taking the headings above as a point of reference.
- How effectively does this structure support people's work towards the objectives?

Oxfam – the case continues   CASE STUDY

Oxfam GB has adopted a divisional approach to its organisation, but within that divides its international programmes into regions – such as South America, East Asia, Horn, East and Central Africa and South Africa.

It is also a member of Oxfam International, which consists of 12 similar organisations in other countries, such as Oxfam America and Oxfam France. They also carry out extensive campaigning and humanitarian work.

Source: Oxfam website.

Case questions 10.2

- What issues of coordination are likely to arise:
  - within Oxfam GB?
  - between the members of Oxfam International?
- Which of the methods of coordination listed are they likely to use to deal with these, and why?

10.5 Organisational cultures

The idea of organisational culture has been part of the management vocabulary since the early 1980s. Academics and managers frequently refer to it as one of the reasons for the success or failure of an organisation. In 2000 British Nuclear Fuels introduced a programme of culture change designed to win back the confidence of its customers after a series of damaging safety failures. The safety watchdog, the Nuclear Installations Inspectorate, concluded that the company was guilty of systematic management failure and had a serious safety culture problem. The company's response was a programme of cultural change designed to instil openness and self-discipline. The company has imposed, and is rigorously enforcing, practices designed to reduce vehicle speeds on internal roads, 'the mis-use of site passes, abuse of the e-mail system, sloppy time-keeping and eating in active areas' (*Financial Times*, 9 February 2001, p. 13). Mergers sometimes experience difficulties over a clash of cultures.

Cap Gemini and Ernst & Young

When the French company Cap Gemini merged with the information technology consultancy of Ernst & Young (E&Y) they found significant cultural differences. Cap Gemini's chief operating officer commented that accurate statistics from E&Y were scarce: 'They changed their figures repeatedly. We said we needed audited accounts. They said: "Do you really need audited accounts from a third party?" For them that was somehow traumatic.'

Source: Based on an article by Caroline Daniel, *Financial Times*, 5 February 2001, p.15.

Organisation culture is the collection of relatively uniform and enduring values, beliefs, customs and practices that are uniquely shared by an organisation's members and which are transmitted from one generation of employees to the next.

Interest in **organisation culture** has grown as academics and managers have come to believe that it influences behaviour. Several claim that a strong and distinct culture helps to integrate individuals into the team or organisation (Deal and Kennedy, 1982; Peters and Waterman, 1982; Ouchi, 1981). They claim that creating the right culture is a key element in high-performing organisations – provided the culture is the right one for the situation.

Others question the link between a strong culture and economic performance. Kotter and Heskett (1992) studied 207 companies and attempted to relate the strength of their culture to economic performance. Although the two variables were positively correlated, the relationship was much weaker than the advocates of organisational culture as an influential variable have predicted. Some also doubt the ability of managers to change an organisation's culture.

Edgar Schein (1985) believed that as people work together they develop a distinctive culture, reflecting what they perceive to be the correct way to approach and deal with organisational problems. He believed that culture develops as group members share enough experiences to form a view of what works and what does not. This then shapes how members expect each other to behave, and these common assumptions and beliefs can exert a profound influence on how a group performs. The main beliefs that Schein identified were those concerned with:

- **mission and strategy** – beliefs about the overall mission and its reason for being;
- **goals** – what the operational goals should be so as to meet the broader mission;
- **means** – how the group is to meet its goals;
- **criteria for measuring results** – consensus on how performance is to be measured;
- **remedial strategies** – the prevailing assumptions about how to put things right.

Schein believed that cultures act as a filter for coping with information and provide members with a common set of guidelines that they use to work out how to make a contribution. The more clearly members work through these issues to develop a common understanding, the better the group will perform.

Schein, and most other writers on culture, approach the topic from a managerialist or functionalist perspective, seeing culture as something which can be managed as a tool for improving organisational performance. Others take a more critical view, and the Key Ideas feature gives an example.

Martin Parker – a critical perspective on culture

Parker (2000) offers a very readable critique of the way some writers have marketed the idea of organisational culture as a route to improved performance, while at the same time he acknowledges that their work 'begins to put forward a valuable language which can be used to represent organization and organizing' (p. 10). His book is an attempt to rescue culture from 'managerialism', and includes a valuable chapter on the history of studies of organisational culture, and some extended case studies.

He reviews three popular managerialist works (Deal and Kennedy, 1982; Peters and Waterman, 1982; Ouchi, 1981), and comments critically on their methods (such as their lack of counter-examples, or of companies with strong cultures which also failed); the limited range of economic sectors from which they were drawn; and the ceaseless sales promotion. He also points out that one of the attractions of their work may have been that readers saw it as a counter to earlier views which stressed bureaucratic, quantitative and rational methods for controlling staff. Yet promoting the use of culture as an organisational tool, while apparently a more humane, soft, approach, may have exactly the same intention – 'to intervene in the identity of the employee just as all organizational control strategies . . . have done' (p. 25).

Having set out the cases from his research he concludes that rather than the single strong culture advocated by the managerialist writers, organisations have multiple cultures, which cut across each other. He identifies three types of division which people use to identify themselves and others – a means of grounding the distinctiveness of the individual or group – based on space/function, generational, and occupation/profession. While these frequently overlap, they provide a robust way of understanding the perspectives from which members will view events around them, and which are likely to hinder attempts to develop unified, consensual or organisation-wide cultures intended as a means of employee control.

Source: Parker (2000).

Components of organisational cultures

Deal and Kennedy (1982) refer to culture as 'the way we do things around here' and Hofstede (1991) sees it as the 'collective programming of the mind', which distinguishes one group from another. While the idea of culture appears vague, it reflects some identifiable components – practices, customs, beliefs and values.

- **Practices.** These represent the surface level of a culture – the visible elements such as language, etiquette, form of greeting and clothing. They include also the artefacts of the business – the physical layout (open-plan or closed offices).
- **Customs.** These are the accepted modes or norms of behaviour within the organisation, reflecting its values and beliefs, that provide guidelines for the way people and groups are expected to behave towards each other. These often shape aspects of the physical appearance of the organisation – the artefacts.
- **Beliefs.** The assumptions that members hold about the organisation and the situation within it – about what practices work well in this business, for example how people make decisions, how teams work together and styles of problem solving.
- **Values.** Deeply held ideas of members about what is right or wrong, fair or unfair – anything that has personal worth or meaning. These values are expressed in operating beliefs and norms of behaviour.

Figure 10.8 illustrates how cultures develop – as people come to share a set of beliefs they use these to establish norms about the way they should behave towards each other and to outsiders. If the outcomes are positive this reinforces their shared belief in the values underlying their behaviour. In this way organisations develop deep-seated values and beliefs about the way that staff should run things. What degree of direction should there be? Should people have job titles? How should they dress at work? What is the expected pattern of behaviour in meetings – confrontational and challenging, or cooperative and supportive? Do bosses expect staff to defer to them, or to challenge prevailing practices and attitudes? How important is time-keeping, or meeting commitments to colleagues? Should they follow the rules or use their initiative?

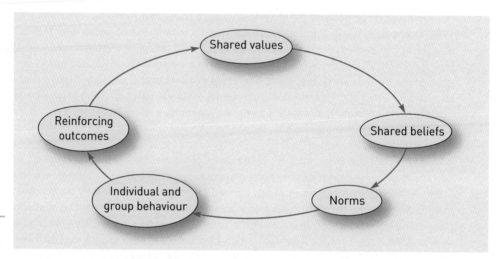

Figure 10.8

The stages of cultural formation

You can sense and observe the distinctiveness of organisational cultures once you have been in a few different departments or organisations. They feel different; receive visitors differently; people work together differently; the pace is different – some buzz with life and activity, others seem asleep. Some feel as if rules guide behaviour while others use procedures as little as possible. The same is true of departments and groups within organisations. Some are welcoming and look after visitors and those from outside, while others seem inward looking. Some stick to the rules, others are entrepreneurial and risk taking. Some have regular social occasions while in others staff rarely meet except at work.

Types of organisational culture

The competing values model developed by Quinn *et al.* (2003) – introduced in Chapter 2 – offers a way of describing cultures and of comparing one with another. The model is based on two inherent tensions – flexibility/control and internal/external. The four cultural types shown in Figure 10.9 express competing views on how organisations should be managed, and staff motivated.

Open systems

This represents an open systems view, in which people recognise that the external environment plays a significant role, and is seen as a vital source of ideas, energy, resources, etc. It also sees the environment as complex and turbulent, requiring entrepreneurial, visionary leadership and flexible, responsive behaviour. Key motivating factors are growth, stimulation, creativity and variety. Examples are start-up firms and new business units – organic, flexible operations.

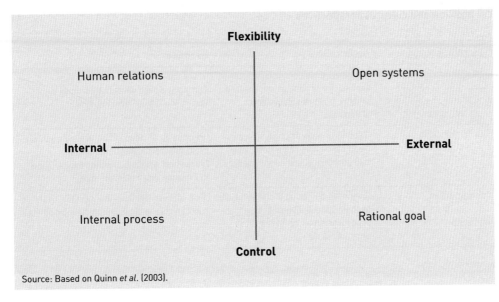

Source: Based on Quinn *et al.* (2003).

Figure 10.9

Types of organisational culture

Rational goal

Members see the organisation as a rational, efficiency-seeking unit. They define effectiveness in terms of production or economic goals that satisfy external requirements. Managers create structures to deal with the outside world. Leadership tends to be directive, goal-oriented and functional. Key motivating factors include competition and the achievement of predetermined ends. Examples are large, established businesses – mechanistic.

Internal process

Here members pay little attention to the external world, having instead an inward focus. Their goal is to make the unit internally efficient, stable and controlled. Goals are known, tasks are repetitive, and methods stress specialisation, rules and procedures. Leaders tend to be conservative and cautious, emphasising technical issues. Key motivating factors include security, stability and order. Examples include utilities and public authorities – suspicious of change.

Human relations

People emphasise the value of informal interpersonal relations rather than formal structures. They place high value on maintaining the organisation and the well-being of its members, and define effectiveness in terms of developing people and their commitment. Leaders tend to be participative, considerate and supportive. Motivating factors tend to be attachment, cohesiveness and membership. Examples are found in professional service firms and some internal support functions.

Multiple cultures

Building on work by Martin (1992, 2002), Ogbonna and Harris (1998, 2002) provide a useful insight into the diversity of cultures within organisations. Much of the discussion of culture has been in terms of identifying the components and nature of a single, unified culture within an organisation. Martin suggested three perspectives:

Table 10.5 Hierarchical position and cultural perspectives

Position in hierarchy	Cultural perspective	Description	Example
Head office managers	Integration	Cultural values should be shared across the organisation. Unified culture both desirable and attainable	'If we can get every ... part of the company doing what they should be doing, we'll beat everybody.'
Store managers	Differentiation	Reconciling conflicting views of head office and shop floor. See cultural pluralism as inevitable	'People up at head office are all pushing us in different directions. Jill in Marketing wants customer focus, June in Finance wants lower costs.'
Store employees	Fragmented	Confused by contradictory nature of the espoused values. See organisation as complex and unpredictable	'One minute it's this, the next it's that. You can't keep up with the flavour of the month.'

Source: Based on Ogbonna and Harris (1998).

A **power culture** is one in which people's activities are strongly influenced by a dominant central figure.

A **role culture** is one in which people's activities are strongly influenced by clear and detailed job descriptions and other formal signals as to what is expected of them.

A **task culture** is one in which the focus of activity is towards completing a task or project using whatever means are appropriate.

A **person culture** is one in which activity is strongly influenced by the wishes of the individuals who are part of the organisation.

- **Integration** – the emphasis here is on identifying consistencies in the data that is observed, and using those common patterns to explain the events.
- **Differentiation** – the focus is on conflict, and on identifying the different and possibly conflicting views of members towards events.
- **Fragmentation** – here the emphasis is on the fluid nature of organisations, and on the interplay and change of views about events.

Ogbonna and Harris conducted in-depth interviews with staff in three retailing companies and concluded that positions in the hierarchy determined their perspective on organisational culture, as shown in Table 10.5.

They conclude that cultural perspective depends on place in the hierarchy. This implies that attempts to introduce cultural change based on head office values and perceptions are likely to be ineffective. Since complete consensus across an organisation will be unlikely, it may be better for managers to pursue policies which recognise subcultural differences, and only seek to reconcile those differences that are essential to policy. They also observe that culture remains a highly subjective idea, which is largely in the eye of the beholder – 'and is radically different according to an individual's position in the hierarchy' (p. 45). The next Management in Practice feature uses quantitative survey data from a different industrial setting to confirm this idea.

key ideas   Charles Handy's cultural types

Charles Handy, developing an idea of Roger Harrison, also distinguished four cultures, which he designated **power**, **role**, **task** and **person culture**.

- **Power** A dominant central figure holds power: others follow the centre's policy and interpret new situations in the way the leader would. Many entrepreneurial firms operate in this way, with few rules but with well-understood, implicit codes on how to behave and work. The firm relies on the individual rather than on seeking consensus through discussion. It can respond quickly as, once the centre approves, staff implement ideas. The main problem is size since, as it grows, it becomes harder for the person at the centre to maintain the required degree of close control. He or she may be unwilling to let go and remain involved in detail, slowing the response to new situations.

- **Role** Typical characteristics are the job description or the procedure. Managers define what they expect in clear, detailed job descriptions. They select people for a job if they meet the specified requirements. Procedures guide the way people and departments interact. If all the parts follow the rules coordination is straightforward. People's position in the hierarchy determines their power. A role culture works well in a stable predictable environment. Problems arise when things change, and it becomes hard for the role culture to adapt.

- **Task** This focuses on completing the task or project rather than the formal roles that people occupy. People value each other for what they can contribute and expect everyone to help as needed. The emphasis is on getting the resources and people for the job and then relying on their commitment and enthusiasm. People will typically work in teams, to combine diverse skills into a common purpose. Expertise is typically the source of power – the person with the evident knowledge taking the lead for that part of the task. Groups can re-form quickly around new tasks, so task cultures are highly adaptable. They are hard to control and may waste resources. Staff may develop less professional or technical knowledge than they would in a role culture, as they are moving between different projects too quickly for full specialisation.

- **Person** Here the individual is at the centre and any structure or system is there to serve the individual. The form is unusual – places such as small professional and artistic organisations are probably closest to it. These organisations exist to meet the interests of the professional stars rather than some larger organisational goal. Various forms of experiment in communal or cooperative living may also take this form. People do things to satisfy the needs of the members rather than an external market. Handy also points out that while the full form of personal culture is rare, many technically specialised individuals in conventional organisations aspire towards that form of environment.

Source: Handy (1993).

Cultures and subcultures in an electronics plant

In 1999 staff in the UK plant of a major semiconductor company completed a well-established survey instrument, intended to measure the cultural pattern within an organisation. The instrument can be used to identify the dominant culture, and any subcultures, within an organisation. The study showed that there were significant differences between departments – a dominant culture, several subcultures and a counter-culture within the organisation. The latter was very security oriented and appeared to be misaligned with the objectives of the organisation.

The most obvious subcultures found were:

- **Dominant culture** The organisation is dominated by a competitive/oppositional style, indicating that it is a driven, task-oriented 'Theory X' place to work (see Chapter 15 for 'Theory X an Y').
- **Process Development Group** The survey identified that this department was heavily weighted towards achievement, self-actualising, humanistic-encouraging and affiliation – essentially a 'Theory Y' group of staff.
- **The Fab 3 Management Team** Broadly competitive/oppositional, but expressed cautiously (low scores on the factors).
- **Manufacturing operators** A different and intense culture, focused on opposition, defensiveness, avoidance and dependence – very security conscious. Management believed this would reduce organisational effectiveness.

The Process Development Group and the Fab 3 Management Team had subcultures that management concluded were broadly complementary to the dominant culture and aligned to the overall business objectives. However, management was deeply concerned to discover the existence of a strong counter-culture within the Manufacturing Operator group that made up 700 of the 1400 employees at the plant.

Source: Private information from a manager within the company.

Summary

1 **Outline how the structure and culture of an organisation may affect performance:**

- People create structures to signify people's tasks and responsibilities towards the current objectives, and to provide incentives for work that supports them. The structure signals what people are expected to do within the organisation, and is intended to support actions that are in line with performance goals.

2 **Illustrate structural decisions about dividing and coordinating tasks:**

- The vertical dimension indicates the balance between centralised and decentralised decisions; decisions about how to divide tasks at each level creates the horizontal structure; creating mechanisms to ensure that people working on these divided tasks work coherently creates a system of coordination.

3 **Distinguish when centralised and decentralised structures may be most suitable:**

- Centralised structures are when most major decisions are taken by those at the top of the organisation or unit, while decentralisation leaves more scope for autonomy by those in the operating units. Centralisation brings consistency and efficiency, but also brings the danger of being slow and out of touch with local conditions. People in decentralised units can respond quickly to local conditions but risk making the company appear inconsistent.

4 **Compare the likely advantages and disadvantages of functional, divisional and matrix forms:**

- Functional forms allow people to specialise and develop expertise and are efficient, but they may be inward looking and prone to conflicting demands.
- Divisional forms allow focus on particular markets of customer groups, but can duplicate facilities, thus adding to cost.
- Matrix forms try to balance the benefits of functional and divisional forms, but can again lead to conflicting priorities over resources.
- Networks of organisations enable companies to draw upon a wide range of expertise, but may involve additional management and coordination costs.

5 **Describe and illustrate the main forms of coordination:**

- Direct supervision, hierarchy, standardising inputs, rules and procedures, information systems and direct personal contact.

6 **Describe the main dimensions of organisational culture, using Quinn's or Handy's typologies:**

- Quinn *et al.* (2003) – open systems, rational goal, internal process and human relations.
- Handy (1993) – power, role, task and person.

Review questions

1 Describe what is meant by a model of an organisation, and compare two organisations using any model from the chapter.

2 Draw the organisation chart of a company or department that you know. Discuss it with people in one or more of the positions shown, and compare their account of the structure with that shown on the chart.

3 What factors are encouraging companies to (a) centralise, (b) decentralise organisational functions?

4 Summarise the advantages and disadvantages of the various forms of horizontal specialisation outlined.

5 Several forms of coordination are described. Select two that you have seen in operation and describe in detail how they work – and how well they work.

6 Describe an educational or commercial organisation that you know in terms of the competing values model of cultures.

7 What is the significance of the idea of 'fragmented cultures' for those who wish to change a culture to support performance?

Concluding critical reflection

Think about the structure and culture of your company, or one with which you are familiar. Review the material in the chapter, and perhaps visit some of the websites identified. Then make notes on these questions:

- What examples of the themes discussed in this chapter are currently relevant to your company? What type of structure do you have – centralised or decentralised, functional or divisional, etc.? Which of the methods of coordination identified do you typically use? Which form of culture best describes the one in which you work? What structural or cultural issues arise that are not mentioned here?

- In responding to issues of structure, what assumptions about the nature of organisations appear to guide your approach? If the business seems too centralised or too formal, why do managers take that approach? What are their assumptions, and are they correct?

- What factors in the context of the company appear to shape your approach to organising – what kind on environment are you working in, for example? To what extent does your structure involve networking with people from other organisations – and why is that?

- Have you seriously considered whether the present structure is right for the business? Do you regularly compare your structure with that in other companies? How do they do it?

Further reading

Peters, T.J. and Waterman, D.H. (1982), *In Search of Excellence*, Harper & Row, London.

Deal, T.E. and Kennedy, A.A. (1982), *Corporate Culture: The rites and rituals of corporate life*, Addison-Wesley, Reading, MA.

Two works from a strongly 'managerialist' perspective which brought ideas about culture to a receptive audience, selling millions of copies. Worth reading either, for a flavour of the original works.

Hall, W. (1995), *Managing Cultures*, Wiley, Chichester.

Gives a clear and practical introduction to the topic of culture, based on extensive empirical work within major European companies.

Martin, J. (2002), *Organizational Culture: Mapping the terrain*, Sage, London.

Parker, M. (2000), *Organizational Culture and Identity: Unity and division at work*, Sage, London.

Two scholarly and critical texts, which give insights into organisational culture that are likely to be more valuable to future managers than texts which take a more simple pre-scriptive approach.

Ogbonna, E. and Harris, L.C. (2002), 'Organizational culture: a ten-year, two-phase study of change in the UK food retailing sector', *Journal of Management Studies*, vol. 39, no. 5, pp. 673–706.

Reviews the background to continuing theoretical and practical interest in the topic, and the feasibility, based in part on the author's primary empirical research, of planned cultural change.

Weblinks

These websites have appeared in the chapter:

www.oxfam.org.uk

www.baesystems.com

www.cadburyschweppes.com

www.philips.com

www.jnj.com

www.toyota.com

www.unilever.com

www.siemens.com

Visit two of the business sites in the list, and navigate to the pages dealing with corporate news, investor relations or 'our company'.

● What organisational structure issues can you identify that managers in the company are likely to be dealing with? Can you find any information about their likely culture from the website?

● What kind of environment are they likely to be working in, and how may that affect their structure and culture?

Annotated weblinks, multiple choice questions and other
useful resources can be found on
www.pearsoned.co.uk/boddy

Chapter 11

Human resource management

This case study traces some of the developments in human resource management in BMW's operations in Germany and the UK over the last few years as part of its strategic response to competitive pressures. The case starts with some background information on the organisation and maps out issues (throughout the chapter) that have arisen from the introduction of teamworking since the pilot stage in the early 1990s through to full implementation.

BMW was established in 1916 and by 1964 was producing almost 150,000 cars each year; it has grown substantially since then. By the late 1980s it employed some 54,000 people, was the seventh largest automobile manufacturing company in the world, and had subsidiaries in many European countries, New Zealand, South Africa, the United States, Canada and Japan. In 2004 BMW employed almost 100,000 people – 60,000 in Germany alone. In 2003 BMW sold a record of over 1.1 million cars (930,000 BMWs and 180,000 Minis), up 8.0 per cent on the previous year. Western Europe is the major market for the group, accounting for 59 per cent of all BMW cars sold.

BMW needs to be placed in the larger context of growing concerns about the loss of competitiveness in the German motor industry. A 1996 report by the German Motor Industry Association identified increased wage costs, higher non-wage labour costs, shorter agreed working time than many competitor countries and the continuing strength of the Deutschmark as being major sources of concern in this regard. These concerns have lowered employment in the industry, stimulated investments abroad and resulted in a high priority being given to initiatives to improve productivity.

Diversification has been central to BMW's competitive strategy, while the HRM policies derive from, and are consistent with, the company's 'six inner values': communication, ethical behaviour to staff, achievement and

BMW Great Britain

remuneration, independence, self-fulfilment and the pursuit of new goals. This value-oriented policy dates back to the early 1980s, arising out of a scenario-planning exercise among senior managers. This underlying philosophy is important in shaping the design of any new BMW plant (an 'open design' that advances the visual management of the process) and the process of introducing any new or reformed HRM practices. In the latter case much emphasis is placed on extensive consultation, information sharing and seeking to establish positive interrelationships between individual changes.

Case questions

- What issues concerning the management of people are likely to be raised in a group such as BMW that has rapidly expanded its production and distribution facilities?

- How have these issues been affected by domestic developments in Germany?

- How is the increased competition likely to affect the people who work for BMW?

11.1 Introduction

BMW is a large and successful business in a growing area of the world economy – automobile production. Yet it faces competitive problems stemming in part from high employment costs in its German operations, and competition from new sources. Management is attempting to retain the company's position by diversifying the product range and the number of countries in which it manufactures. The company believes that its business strategy has to be matched by its HRM strategy – and is adapting this to bring about a better-trained and more flexible workforce suited to the new conditions.

Such activities are part of a broader change taking place in many western companies, as managers try to align the way they deal with people with broader strategies. Management influences other people through both personal and institutionalised practices. It seeks to be less reactive, less focused on grievances and the routine aspects of personnel administration. Instead it wants to be more proactive in developing a labour force at all levels that will support the organisation's strategy. It also seeks greater coherence between the main aspects of HRM – especially in the areas of selection, development, appraisal and rewards.

This chapter focuses on some institutionalised practices intended to influence the attitudes and behaviour of employees. These practices are commonly referred to as **human resource management** (HRM). The chapter begins by discussing the basic purpose and objectives of HRM, and the reasons for its greater prominence in management discussions. The chapter subsequently focuses on particular HRM policies and practices. HRM covers four main areas (Beer and Spector, 1985):

> **Human resource management** is the effective use of human resources in order to enhance organisational performance.

- Employee influence (i.e. employee involvement in decision making)
- Human resource flow (i.e. recruitment, selection, training, development and deployment)
- Work systems (i.e. work design, supervisory style)
- Reward systems (i.e. pay and other benefits).

Employee influence and work systems are discussed elsewhere, particularly in Chapters 14 and 15. Consequently discussions surrounding HRM policies within this chapter centre on human resource flow and reward management. Human resource flow is concerned with the flow of individuals into and through the organisation – human resource planning, job analysis, employee recruitment and selection. Management designs these practices to ensure that the organisation has the right people available to help it achieve strategic objectives. Reward management aims to attract, retain and acknowledge employees within an organisation. A number of systems are available to achieve these goals, many of which will be highlighted in this chapter. HRM, however, is more than a sum of institutionalised policies and it is not simply the case of selecting the 'right' policy to ensure a highly motivated workforce and their subsequent high performance. The complexities of managing people are well known and it is important to return to a broader picture of HRM to avoid solely focusing on individual policies. It is from this standpoint that the chapter ends by presenting critical perspectives and emerging themes in the field.

11.2 Emergence and meaning of human resource management

At its broadest level, HRM refers to all aspects of managing people in the workplace. This section seeks to expand and clarify this definition and to outline why this field has become vital to organisational success.

Historical development

The term 'human resource management' is relatively new, gaining prominence in US companies and business schools from about 1980 (Brewster, 1994) and it is now widely used in the business world. Traditionally, managers had tried to institutionalise the way they managed staff by creating separate personnel departments. Partly stimulated by the human relations model (see Chapter 2), management believed they could ensure a committed staff by paying attention to employee grievances and looking after their general welfare. Growing trade union power also led management to create departments that specialised in conducting negotiations and monitoring the agreements reached.

Such personnel management departments typically had limited power, and found it difficult to show that they contributed to financial or any other measures of organisational performance (Legge, 1978; Tyson and Fell, 1985). Senior management saw personnel as reactive, self-contained and obsessed with procedures. It was overwhelmingly concerned with managing employee grievances, discipline and relations with trade unions. The main aim was to minimise costs and avoid any disruption of production. The consequence was that personnel departments typically had little influence on the strategic decisions of organisations.

Greater competition, and changes in the nature of that competition, led to change. Guest (1987) attributes this wider use to the following factors:

- The emergence of more globally integrated markets in which competition is more extensive and severe. Product life cycles are shorter, with innovation, flexibility and quality often replacing price as the basis of competitive advantage.
- The economic success during the 1980s of countries that had given employee management a relatively high priority, such as Japan and (West) Germany.
- The highly publicised 'companies of excellence' literature (Peters and Waterman, 1982) which suggested that high-performance organisations were characterised by a strong commitment to human resource management.
- Changes in the composition of the workforce, particularly the growth of a more educated staff.
- The decline in trade union membership and collective bargaining in many advanced industrialised economies.

Management came to believe that HRM was too important to be left exclusively to personnel specialists who were characterised as reactive and who focus on the minutiae rather than the bigger picture of organisational performance. They took the view that *line* management needed to be more actively involved in managing people: only then would HRM issues receive senior management attention (Fombrun *et al.*, 1984). In particular, the early advocates of HRM argued that the approach would be very distinct from personnel management. Consequently the key themes of HRM would be 'integration', 'planning', a 'long-run' orientation, 'proactive' and 'strategic'.

Writers on HRM have argued that the more effective management of people will lead to improved organisational effectiveness and performance. This is based on theories of sustained competitive advantage that emphasise the importance of firm-specific, valuable resources which are difficult to imitate (Pfeffer, 1994). Table 11.1 highlights the HRM policies that are likely to affect HRM outcomes and wider organisational outcomes.

Table 11.1

A human resource management model

HRM policies	HRM outcomes	Organisational outcomes
Organisation/job design		High job performance
Management of change	Strategic integration	High problem solving, change and innovation
Recruitment, selection and socialisation	Commitment	High job performance, low turnover
Appraisal, training, development	Flexibility/adaptability	High cost effectiveness
Reward systems	Quality	Low turnover, absence, grievances

Source: Guest (1988).

Case questions 11.1

- When did HRM policies begin to be seriously developed at BMW?
- What led management to take this initiative?

Activity 11.2 Assessing the changes needed

An organisation has decided to pursue a quality-enhancement strategy in which teamworking arrangements will be a central feature. It recognises the need to enhance its level of workforce training and to replace its individual performance-related pay arrangements. Are there any other changes in the HRM area that it needs to consider? (Use Table 11.1 to assist you.)

key ideas Features of an organisation committed to HRM

- The firm competes on the basis of quality and differentiation as well as price.
- Human resource considerations weigh heavily in corporate strategic decision making and governance processes. Employee interests are represented through the voice of human resource staff and/or senior executives consult with employee representatives on decisions that affect HRM policies and employee interests. In either case, employees are treated as legitimate stakeholders in the organisation.

- Investments in new hardware or physical technology are combined with the investments in human resources and changes in organisational practices required to realise the full potential benefits of these investments.

- The firm sustains a high level of investment in training, skill development and education, and personnel practices are designed to use these skills fully.

- Compensation and reward systems are internally equitable, competitive and linked to the long-term performance of the firm.

- Employment continuity and security are important priorities and values to be considered in all corporate decisions and policies.

- Workplace relations encourage flexibility in the organisation of work, empowerment of employees to solve problems, and high levels of trust amongst workers, supervisors and managers.

- Workers' rights to representation are acknowledged and respected. Union or other employee representatives are treated as joint partners in designing and overseeing innovations in labour and human resource practices.

Source: Kochan (1992).

HRM: the philosophy

Many managers and academics now stress the advantages of adopting what has been variously labelled a 'high commitment', 'best practice' or 'mutual gains' human resource management model. HRM, in contrast to personnel management, adopts a strategic perspective and contributes to organisational performance by effective management of staff. The philosophy through which this is pursued seeks to gain a win–win situation for both employer and employee; the organisation ultimately gains profitability and employees gain not only economically (through remuneration) but also intrinsically through having a satisfying and challenging job. This approach assumes that employees and employer have one goal, the long-term success of the organisation, and in essence they have one voice. This is also known as a unitary perspective. However, some authors doubt the extent to which the two parties have one voice in reality; this debate will be revisited at the end of this chapter.

There are different emphases within the broad HRM approach. One distinction is between 'hard' and 'soft' approaches (Storey, 1992, pp. 26–8; Legge, 1995, pp. 66–7). The former takes a rational, planning, business-led perspective. The latter sees people as valuable assets whose motivation, involvement and development should have priority. Another theme is that if HRM is to support performance, management needs to balance external and internal fit (Beer and Spector, 1985).

External fit

External fit refers to the link between wider strategy and HRM strategy. Ideally management tries to establish a close and consistent link between the two so that HRM activities encourage people to act in ways that support the wider competitive strategy. Chapter 8 distinguished low-cost and differentiation strategies. These require different employee attitudes and behaviours, which HRM policies can encourage. Extensive training, team-working and shop-floor problem-solving arrangements are likely in an organisation committed to a differentiation strategy.

External fit is when there is a close and consistent relationship between an organisation's competitive strategy and its HRM strategy.

341

Such HRM practices are unlikely in an organisation that follows a low-cost strategy, paying low wages to a casual labour force. Indeed, a US review (Greer, 2001, p. 292) suggested that in general there is a greater performance impact when HRM policies match particular competitive strategies. In addition, the study showed that some human resource practices appear to increase performance in almost any setting, including cognitive tests in selection, staffing selectivity and training.

Case questions 11.2

- What is your image of BMW cars? What words would you use to describe them?
- In order to meet the image you expect, what kind of behaviour would you expect of employees?
- What HRM practices will encourage/discourage that behaviour?

Activity 11.3 Comparing HRM policies

List the major differences in HRM policies that you would expect to observe between two organisations, one pursuing a low-cost strategy and the other a quality enhancement strategy. (Use the previous Key Ideas to assist you.)

Internal fit

Organisations also benefit if they have HRM policies that are internally consistent. The individual measures need to complement and reinforce each other by sending a *consistent* set of signals to the workforce. An organisation that encourages teamworking can support this through the payment system. It is likely to fail if this rewards people mainly for their individual contribution, encouraging people to compete rather than cooperate. Achieving **internal fit** may require particular competencies among HRM professionals, with knowledge not only of HRM issues but of business issues as well. Research at the University of Michigan highlighted five leading competency domains (Becker *et al.*, 2001, pp. 158–61):

Internal fit is when the various components of the HRM strategy support each other and consistently encourage certain attitudes and behaviour.

- Knowledge of the business
- Delivery of HR practices
- Management of change
- Management of culture
- Personal credibility.

This section has introduced and defined the field of HRM and highlighted the strategic nature of this discipline and ways in which it contributes to wider organisational performance. The starting point for this is human resource planning.

11.3 Human resource planning

Human resource planning involves a detailed analysis of the size and nature of the workforce required to fulfil the organisation's strategy. It requires forecasting the broad number and type of employees required, and then a more precise job analysis to ascertain skills and competencies necessary to guide recruitment. This is followed by effort to recruit and select the most appropriate person. This section summarises key issues in these three areas.

Forecasting

In the 1960s and 1970s (at a time of labour shortage) researchers tried to develop techniques for forecasting the demand and supply of labour in organisations. They expected the demand for labour to follow from the organisation's business plan, as an estimate of the numbers and types of employees to meet financial and output objectives. The ability to meet forecast staffing needs (in terms of overall numbers and types of workers) depends on existing staffing levels in the various job categories at the beginning of the planning period, adjusted for (a) the outflow of staff over the planning period (e.g. retirements, dismissal, resignations), (b) the inflow of staff during the planning period (i.e. new recruits), and (c) the internal movement of staff between job categories (e.g. promotions). Two broad strands are important:

- *Forecasting human resource demands*: refers to the number of staff required to fulfil future needs of the organisation.
- *Forecasting human resource supplies*: examines skills required within the portfolio of jobs and analyses whether current staff can meet these demands.

A number of techniques are associated with these forecasting approaches and are presented in Table 11.2.

Table 11.2

Forecasting techniques

Forecasting human resource demands		
Judgemental forecasting	Delphi technique	Involves obtaining independent estimates of future staffing needs through successive distribution of questionnaires to various levels of management. The expectation is that some four or five iterations should produce a convergence in the estimates.
Statistical projection	Simple linear regression	A statistical calculation in which projected future demand is based on a past relationship between the organisation's employment level and a variable such as the level of sales.
Forecasting human resource supplies		
Judgemental forecasting	Succession planning	This involves developing charts indicating present jobholders and the names of possible replacements.
Statistical projection	Markov matrix analysis	This approach can model or simulate human resource flows by examining the rates of movement between job categories over time.

Source: *Business 2.0*, November 1999.

A major limitation of human resource planning models is the uncertainty of the business environment. Uncertainty may, paradoxically, make comprehensive planning a waste of time. Operating in a highly volatile environment might seem like a strong incentive to engage in human resource planning. Yet these same circumstances make sophisticated planning extremely difficult. The forecasts are likely to be of limited accuracy and value because of rapidly changing circumstances. This has led to changes in the practice of human resource planning, namely reduced planning horizons, more line management involvement, more qualitative forecasting techniques and more attention to the process, as opposed to the outcomes, of planning.

Uncertainty and human resource planning

This computer manufacturing plant operates in a very competitive product market, characterised by short product life cycles (i.e. six months) and strong, unpredictable shifts in product demand. It forecasts future sales and estimates a corresponding demand for labour each year. These figures are then adjusted each month. However, it solely 'produces to order' (i.e. holds virtually no stock) and has found that sales, output and hence its demand for labour vary a great deal each week. It has therefore established a pool of 40 people in the area (generally unemployed) upon which it can draw to meet sudden increases in demand. Currently some 15–20 per cent of its workforce are temporary staff, many on monthly contracts.

Source: Interview with manager.

11.4 Job analysis

Job analysis is the process of determining the characteristics of an area of work according to a prescribed set of dimensions.

The previous section outlined methods of forecasting the number and nature of the workforce. In order to move to the final stage, recruitment, it is frequently necessary to analyse specific aspects of roles through job analysis. This section discusses approaches to job analysis.

Job analysis evaluates the principal constituents of a role, including skills and level of responsibility. It typically leads to a written job description that has important implications for employee selection, training and performance appraisal.

A job description

The appointment
Title: Assistant General Manager, Mills
Reports to: General Manager, Mills

Main functional role
To provide a strategic focus and overview of production optimisation issues, constraints and development opportunities equally for both mills.

Responsibilities
- To work with established mill management teams to proactively address matters of plant future developability and resolution of current problems through line management.

- To improve the overall performance of the mill management teams through example and leadership.
- To liaise with UK and International Sales in order to ensure the needs of the customer are met by anticipating and overcoming production challenges through research and comprehension of key issues.
- To assist with all administrative tasks of the General Manager, in particular ensuring that all reports to Head Office of mill performance are completed accurately, on time and with such elaboration as required on trend deviations from budget, and plans to overcome.
- To deputise for the General Manager in his absence and to attend senior managers' and other meetings as necessary on mills' performance.

The candidate

Experience and qualifications

A graduate of chemical/mechanical engineering or chemistry with subsequent experience in paper science. Should have 8–10 years in the paper (ideally, but not exclusively) or other process industry as a production manager or engineer. Strong production focus and proven ability to solve production problems that have a technical origin.

Skills

- Able to take a broad overview with the initiative and judgement to identify the optimum route for implementation.
- Able to maintain several activities without losing perspective or priority.
- Able to identify with and champion corporate focus and direction for the mills.
- Strong interpersonal and leadership skills in influencing mill management teams.
- Presentation skills.

Future prospects

Candidates must possess potential for further career development with the Group to General Manager or equivalent.

The literature on job analysis is largely concerned with these steps:

- How is the data for the job description collected? Possibilities include interviewing the job incumbent, observing people doing the job, and distributing questionnaires.
- Who should collect this information or data? Should it be the job incumbent, the supervisor, or a specialist from inside or outside the organisation?
- How should the job information be structured and put into a standardised format?

The job analysis process aims to describe the purpose of a job, its major duties and activities, the conditions under which it is performed and the necessary knowledge, skills and abilities. Jobs are broken into *elements*, such as information input, mental processes, work output, relationship with other people, and job context. These elements are rated along various dimensions such as extent of use, importance, amount of time involved or possibility of occurrence.

Job analysis in an electronics plant

This example outlines how management in an electronics plant produced a job analysis. In this plant teamworking operations (eventually without any supervisory personnel) are all important and a new job, of manufacturing team member, was created. To help identify the key competences of the job, a work profiling questionnaire was completed by people such as the managers of production, engineering and HR, as well as some production supervisors. This produced the key tasks for the position, and the participants then ranked these in order of importance. The skills identified were:

- Hard skills: visual checking, technical understanding, fault-finding skills, and mechanical comprehension
- Soft skills: attention to detail, data rational, practical, and sociable/supportive in a team environment.

Source: Personal interview with manager.

Competences

In recent years there has been a move away from thinking about jobs as a set of tasks towards thinking about the set of competences an individual must have to successfully fulfil requirements of a job. The aim here has been to identify and develop the behavioural competences required for the satisfactory and/or high performance of individual jobs. The subtle change reflects demands made by the external environment for organisations to be flexible. The use of competences enables the use of employee skills flexibly, where individuals can adapt to new requirements and situations rather than rigidly imposing a 'static' set of tasks.

Competences in an international business

This organisation, which has plants in five different countries, has a long-standing performance management system, centred around the notion of employee competences. However, these competences had not been updated for some 12 years which, in conjunction with other issues concerning the performance management systems, had resulted in some of the individual plants developing their own approaches. Such local initiatives were seen to put at risk the achievement of certain corporate-wide objectives, and made it difficult to compare performance appraisal information and results between plants. To address these problems the organisation in 2000 established a seven-person, multi-functional performance management team. The consultations and deliberations of this team resulted in the establishment of the following eight key competences for the organisation as a whole:

- Results orientation (achievement and initiative)
- Teamwork
- Leadership
- Quality and process focus
- Influence and interpersonal skills
- Personal adaptability
- Technical and business skills
- Management and supervision.

Fuller definitions and associated metrics have been established for each of the competences.

Source: Personal interview with manager.

The changing scope of work

Smaller workforces mean that management often broadens the job descriptions of the staff who remain. The move towards teamworking in many organisations, as discussed in Chapter 17, also has implications for job analysis:

> [In] a team situation individual tasks may be quite fluid. Further, team effectiveness often asks for team members to develop a wide variety of skills so that they are capable of providing an assortment of inputs. Thus cross-training is becoming more common and narrow job descriptions are giving way to individual contributions being driven by dynamic relationships within the team. The fluidity of tasks and the flux of individual inputs as a function of interdependency on the inputs of other team members mean that a snapshot of the work activities for individual employees may be difficult to take and would likely soon be limiting and out of date in a team environment. Thus, the traditional job analysis assumption of continuing tasks for individuals appears to be incorrect when in team situations. (Academy of Management, 1996, p. 11)

The continuation of the BMW case study below illustrates the teamworking arrangements introduced amongst production employees in the German operations of the group.

BMW – the case continues – new work structures

CASE STUDY

In response to increased competition, market over-capacity and substantial reductions in collectively agreed working hours in Germany (a 35-hour week in the metal/electrical industries from October 1995), BMW sought greater efficiency through increased employee performance. Following a 1991 agreement on a 'pilot phase for future work structures', and with the agreement of the works council, the company introduced in 1995 new forms of work organisation. Employees were arranged into self-managing groups (each with 8–15 workers), with a high degree of autonomy but with clearly defined tasks. Members of the group decide upon each individual's responsibility and the rotation of jobs, as well as making on-the-spot suggestions and decisions about product improvement.

Each group elects a spokesperson as an activity coordinator and representative of the group, although they have no power to give orders or take disciplinary action. Supervisors remain as the group's immediate superior in technical and disciplinary matters, but play more of an advisory/facilitating role. The supervisor is responsible for proposing and agreeing objectives, presenting progress figures, helping progress continuous improvements and ensuring the improvement of qualifications of group members. The company has to ensure that adequate training is available, goals are agreed upon and results circulated. Improved product quality and job satisfaction are the aims, leading in turn to greater productivity. BMW was hoping for a 4 per cent annual increase in productivity, compared with 2 per cent previously.

Source: *European Industrial Relations Review*, issue 271 (1996), pp. 23–4.

Case questions 11.3

- How will the introduction of teamworking help to improve the external fit between HRM and broader strategy?
- To achieve internal fit, what other changes will BMW need to make to support teamworking?

11.5 Employee recruitment and selection

A job analysis exercise is intended to produce a comprehensive and accurate job description. The next part of the HRM process is recruitment and selection. The goal of recruitment is to produce a good pool of applicants and select the best of these to fit the job. The selection process aims to minimise (a) *false positive errors*, whereby the selection process predicts success in the job for an applicant, who is therefore hired, but who fails; and (b) *false negative errors*, whereby an applicant who would have succeeded in the job is rejected because the process predicted failure. As the costs of the latter are not directly experienced by the organisation, managers are more concerned about the former.

Studies of the selection process have mainly centred on the **validity** of the process, in the sense of its ability to predict future performance. Additional criteria in the selection process include fairness and cost. There are many selection procedures and processes open to human resource managers. However, it is beyond the scope of this chapter to analyse all of these in detail; consequently the three most commonly used techniques – interviews, selection tests and assessment centres – will be discussed in this section.

Validity occurs when there is a statistically significant relationship between a predictor (such as a selection test score) and subsequent measures of on-the-job performance.

Interviews

Management traditionally relies on application forms, references and interviews for selecting employees. The interview remains popular (because of low direct costs and applicability to a wide range of jobs) despite research showing the low validity of the method (Robertson, 1996; Newell and Tansley, 2001). Interviewer ratings correlate poorly with measures of subsequent on-the-job performance of the candidates hired (i.e. they generate far too many false positive errors). The reason for this is that many interviewers are not good at seeking, receiving and processing the amount and quality of information that is necessary to make an informed hiring decision. Problems with the interview as a selection device are:

- Decisions are made too quickly.
- Information in the early stage of the interview has a disproportionate influence on the decision.
- Interviewers compare applicants with an idealised stereotype.
- Appearance and non-verbal behaviour strongly shape decisions.
- Interviewers are poorly prepared and ask too many questions of limited value.
- 'Good' responses to certain questions are given undue weight.

Activity 11.4 Interviewing interviewees

- Arrange to talk to some friends or colleagues who have recently been interviewed for jobs. Ask them to describe the overall process and to identify any features or aspects of the experience that they particularly liked or disliked. Ideally you should talk to at least one person who was offered the job and to one who was not.
- As background work for this exercise, compile a checklist of the key features of 'good practice' interviews that should help inform the way you ask questions. A useful reference here is Rebecca Corfield's (1999) *Successful Interview Skills*. As well as practising your own interviewing skills you should compare the experience of the interviewees with best practice techniques.

Aware of these difficulties, more organisations are systematically training people in good interview techniques. Others use standard interview schedules in which all applicants are asked the same set of questions in roughly the same order. The membership of interview panels is also changing. Organisations using teamworking arrangements often include team members in the selection process as well as personnel staff and line management. There is evidence that structured interviews, such as 'situational' or 'behavioural' approaches, have a higher predictive validity than unstructured ones (Heffcutt and Arthur, 1994). Nevertheless the latter are widely used, possibly because of their perceived flexibility.

Selection tests

The weaknesses of the interview method and the changing nature of jobs have encouraged more managements to use formal methods of selection tests such as ability tests and personality questionnaires (*People Management*, August 1996, p. 22). Psychometric tests are more popular in Sweden and Portugal than in the United Kingdom, although they are less used in France, Switzerland and the Netherlands (Sparrow and Hiltrop, 1994, p. 341).

Slimming down the selection process

management in practice

This organisation's selection process originally involved applicants visiting the site on four separate occasions: for personality testing, for two separate interviews and then a medical examination. However, in a very tight labour market environment, and with a leading local competitor only requiring a single visit for interview/medical examination purposes, it has tried to streamline the process by combining the personality testing and the first interview on a single day. The number of individual tests has also been reduced. This was because the tests were resulting in the hiring of individuals who were 'overqualified' relative to the needs and demands of the job, which was leading to employee dissatisfaction and relatively high turnover rates.

Source: Personal interview with manager.

There are many long-established tests available, for both abilities and personality. In recent years it has been the growing use of personality tests that has been particularly noticeable, and at the same time controversial. Organisational psychologists hold varying opinions about the accuracy and value of personality tests. Some of the concerns and criticisms of this form of testing are:

- They should only be used and interpreted by qualified and approved experts.
- Candidates can fake the answers to some questions, to give the answers they think the organisation is looking for.
- An individual's personality may vary with their circumstances.
- Good performers in the same job may have different personalities.

The feature below shows the personality test score of a company director's secretary, based on the commonly used 16 PF test.

management
in practice

A personality profile (16 PF test)

	(1	2	3	4	5	6	7	8	9	10)	
Reserved								8			Outgoing
Concrete thinking								8			Abstract thinking
Affected by feelings							7				Calm, unruffled
Not assertive								8			Assertive, dominant
Serious, reflective						6					Happy-go-lucky
Expedient						6					Conscientious
Shy					5						Venturesome
Tough minded							7				Tender minded
Trusting						6					Suspicious
Practical						6					Imaginative
Forthright					5						Shrewd
Self-assured										10	Apprehensive
Conservative						6					Experimenting
Group oriented								8			Self-sufficient
Undisciplined								8			Self-disciplined
Relaxed								8			Tense

There is a growing concern that the misuse of tests may breach equal opportunities legislation and regulations. In addition there is the potential problem of managing employee expectations. One long-standing criticism of the employee selection process is that the organisation is 'over-sold' to those hired. If employees' expectations are then not met on the job they are likely to leave. There is a danger of creating a sense of an elite labour force that will be well looked after when 2000 applicants are reduced to fewer than 300 who are offered a job. Extensive testing risks adding to the 'over-sell' problem.

Assessment centres

Assessment centres are multi-exercise programmes designed to identify the recruitment and promotion potential of personnel.

Assessment centres use many systematic tests and several assessors to arrive at a comprehensive picture of a candidate's abilities and potential. They have been used for many years to help select candidates for positions at senior levels, but their use is becoming more widespread. Industrial Relations Services (IRS, 1997) reports that in the United Kingdom the use of assessment centres is increasing more rapidly than any other selection procedure, with 65 per cent of large firms (over 1000 employees) using them.

Assessment centres appear to have much higher levels of validity for selection purposes than interviews and employee tests. To some this is a positive finding. That is, the package approach of assessment centres (with their multiple tests and multiple assessors) comes closest to being a reasonable simulation of what the actual job will involve. Other commentators offer a more critical explanation for the relatively high validity of the results from assessment centres – they involve a self-fulfilling prophecy. Knowing that someone has succeeded in an assessment centre, their managers and colleagues act in ways that ensure that the person subsequently does well. Other concerns about assessment centres include:

- Their relatively high cost
- Their tendency to become a 'paper factory', with a huge amount of documentation being generated and analysed

- The ethical and practical problems of providing feedback to individuals whose performance was not impressive
- The possibility of producing 'clones' who are very similar to the present job incumbents, which may not be appropriate in rapidly changing circumstances.

E-recruitment is a more recent development in recruitment and selection processes. Technology can save huge amounts of time and money in the first stages of shortlisting and interviewing candidates. According to a Reed Executive report (Reed, 2000) cost savings are the biggest advantage of e-recruitment. It predicted that within five years up to 30 per cent of job adverts will be placed on the Internet.

Do individuals fit the organisation?

This essentially narrow, technical task of achieving an 'individual employee/individual job fit' has been questioned by some writers on strategic human resource management. For instance, research on cultural change programmes has emphasised the need to recruit and select employees who fit well with the larger direction of change in the organisation. A specific instance of change along these lines is the attempt to identify individuals who will work well in teams. Research here has concentrated on identifying the competences necessary to contribute in, for example, multi-disciplinary teams (West and Allen, 1997).

Such an orientation will have important implications for job analysis, and may result in changes in selection methods and in the individuals involved in selection processes. Indeed there is now a growing body of literature which argues that individuals should be hired for the organisation, not the job. As Bowen *et al.* (1996) write:

> Diverse firms ... are using the approach to build cultures that rely heavily on self-motivated, committed people for corporate success. New, often expensive, hiring practices are changing the traditional selection model. An organisational analysis supplements a job analysis, and personality attributes are screened in addition to skills, knowledge and abilities. (p. 139)

The *organisational* analysis mentioned here is concerned with the leading components of the larger work *context*, such as the longer-term goals and values of the organisation, rather than simply the content of the individual job.

Hiring for the organisation rather than the job

key ideas

Potential benefits

- More favourable employee attitudes (e.g. greater organisational commitment)
- More desirable individual behaviours (e.g. lower absence and turnover)
- Reinforcement of organisational design (e.g. support for desired organisational culture)

Potential problems

- Greater investment of resources in the hiring process
- Relatively undeveloped and unproven supporting selection technology
- Individual stress
- May be difficult to use the full model where payoffs are greatest
- Lack of organisational adaptation

Source: Bowen *et al.* (1996), p. 146.

Case questions 11.4

- In what ways are developments in BMW already encouraging a 'hire for the organisation, not for the job' approach?
- What implications will that have for achieving internal fit in the company's HRM policies?

This section has examined three aspects of human resource planning: forecasting, job analysis and selection. The next section turns to some issues of reward management.

11.6　Reward management

Changes in reward management have been at the heart of developments in HRM and aim to align employer and employee objectives. While merit/performance pay has been highly visible in many countries, there has been a more recent shift towards more flexible and variable reward systems. This change has been driven by clear government support for greater employment flexibility. According to the Department of Trade and Industry (1996), 'Britain's deregulated labour market now allows employers considerable freedom to choose pay systems that meet their own needs and those of the workforce ... flexible pay is an integral part of the pay agenda' (p. 3). A Towers Perrin (1999) study of 460 European organisations found that, in the previous three years, 94 per cent had made significant changes to pay systems, while 96 per cent planned further changes. The key developments in UK remuneration policies appear to be:

- A shift away from collectively bargained pay towards more individual performance or skills-driven systems
- An attempt to link pay systems more directly to business strategy and organisational goals
- An emphasis on non-pay items, such as life assurance and childcare vouchers
- The developments of more flexible pay components and individualised reward packages.

Developments in pay policies are also linked to changes in work organisation. The case study shows the new bonus payment arrangements for production employees in the German operations of BMW and recent developments in BMW's UK operations. These team-based payment arrangements fit the new work structures outlined earlier.

BMW – the case continues – changes to reward structures

CASE STUDY

The new work structures, with their emphasis on multi-skilled workers, quality objectives and the individual's contribution to group performance, were accompanied by new payment arrangements. A bonus system applied to all 36,000 production employees who operated with defined performance targets.

Basic remuneration consists of the minimum pay rate agreed in the metalworking industry collective agreement plus a 10 per cent BMW supplement. The previous six wage groups were expanded to nine. This allowed for finer gradations determined by the demands placed on the employee. These reflected the criteria of function, difficulty and variety of activities, and scope for decision making. If a worker regularly performed a higher value activity then movement up the groups was possible.

On top of the basic remuneration a fixed 25 per cent *additional bonus* was paid to all employees for meeting prearranged quotas. This quota involved producing a set number of units to the company's quality standards by a workforce of an agreed size. Employees in each group were consulted and invited to comment on whether the quotas were realistic and achievable.

Employees could also earn extra pay through a *personal supplement*, which was payable if an individual contributed to the group results. Expectations and specific goals were discussed and agreed in talks between the employee and the supervisor. An individual's contribution to the group was discussed every year and this assessment determined the personal supplement received.

More recent developments in BMW's UK operations further underline the linkage between pay and the drive for increased worker flexibility and efficiency. In early 2001 new pay agreements emphasising flexible working arrangements and performance-related pay were introduced. In the new Hams Hall plant the two-year pay deal contains a performance bonus that will deliver up to 5

per cent of production workers' annual pay. This will be calculated on an individual basis rather than on the site's performance. A similar deal was initially rejected by workers at the Cowley, Oxford plant, where pay was not the stumbling block. Instead, workers and unions were opposed to the new flexible working arrangements that included an extended working week. Further flexibility gains are expected at the Oxford plant following the recruitment of temporary workers, which will allow flexibility in production systems, including the abolition of traditional shutdown periods for holidays.

Source: *European Industrial Relations Review*, Issue 271 (1996), p. 24; *Financial Times*, 26 January 2001; *The Times*, 8 February 2001.

Case questions 11.5

- What external business factors have prompted this review of the payment system at BMW?
- How will it affect the management of the appraisal system?
- How will it affect the demands on the management information system (see Chapter 20)?

Types of remuneration system

This section seeks to outline different methods or systems for addressing reward management. Table 11.3 summarises some common types before discussing the increasingly popular methods of performance-related pay and flexible benefit packages.

Type of system	Explanation
Time rate	Reward is related to the number of hours worked
Payment by results	Reward is related to quantity of output
Skill-based pay	Reward is based on the employee's level of knowledge and skills
Performance-related pay	Reward is based on individual performance in relation to agreed objectives
Flexible benefits packages	Reward is based on selection of benefits (for example, healthcare or company car) to suit the individual's preferences and lifestyles

Table 11.3

Approaches to reward management

Performance-related pay

Performance-related pay arrangements involve a linkage between a human resource flow activity (i.e. performance appraisal) and reward systems. To some observers this is an unfortunate linkage to make because it risks 'overloading' the appraisal process. That is, it is asking the appraisal process to achieve too many objectives, risks making awkward interviews even more difficult and will ultimately cause the training/development objectives of appraisal to take second place to money considerations.

That said, there are some positive points to be made about performance-related pay arrangements, in that (a) such arrangements do have some theoretical or conceptual underpinnings in expectancy theory (see Chapter 15), and (b) some organisations have used such arrangements for many years and report positive effects on both individual and organisational performance.

However, there are many other organisations where the track record of performance-related pay is less impressive. Either there has been little positive impact on organisational performance or the arrangements have been counter-productive for other reasons (Beer and Cannon, 2004). Research by Purcell (2000) finds that 'reward management does more harm than good in building trust, commitment and motivation'. A Towers Perrin (1999) survey found that 84 per cent of companies that linked pay and performance experienced operating difficulties, including ineffective communication and inadequate support from senior management. Lawson (2000) notes, 'the amount of work being undertaken in organisations to modify, change and improve individual performance pay schemes indicates a trend of unhappiness with them. In short, the record of performance-related pay arrangements has been highly variable' (p. 315). There are various possible reasons for this:

- The expectancy theory of employee motivation that underpins such arrangements does not apply universally or at all times.
- Performance-related pay arrangements have not been well received by employees because of inadequate prior discussion, consultation and explanation.
- Performance-related pay fits the circumstances of some organisations much better than others. For instance, introducing performance-related pay arrangements into an organisation characterised by 'low trust' relationships between employees and management is a certain recipe for creating further problems.
- Performance-related pay arrangements have multiple goals or objectives, but not all of these can be achieved by the one set of arrangements. For instance, individual performance-related pay is most successful in demonstrating to employees that performance affects their pay – but may inhibit cooperation within the workforce.
- There is an embedded assumption that companies are rationally directed organisations and that managers have the foresight to know what is needed for the forthcoming year. In reality, change is quicker and messier than that.

 **Performance-related pay in a not-for-profit organisation**

This not-for-profit organisation has 23 separate grades of employees, with annual salary increases being related to changes in the cost of living, and incremental payments occurring (within grades) every three years. In 1995 a new chairman (with a private sector background) was appointed, with some other individuals (also from the private sector) being appointed to the finance committee. The chairman and other new appointees were highly critical of the existing salary/grading arrangements.

They viewed them as 'very old-fashioned, with little capacity to motivate staff'. In particular, the absence of performance-related pay was viewed as highly undesirable. Although the personnel manager could point to no employee dissatisfaction with the existing arrangements or give examples of tangible organisational difficulties, a senior working party was established to 'move things along' and a consultancy firm engaged to help introduce some changes.

Source: Personal interview with manager.

Activity 11.5 When is performance-related pay suitable?

Identify some of the key features of an organisation where performance-related pay arrangements are likely to be appropriate.

One of the major growth areas of performance-related pay in recent years has been in the public sector of many advanced industrialised economies.

Common problems with performance-related pay in the public sector

key ideas

- A lack of differentiation in performance ratings.
- A clustering of managers at the top of the salary range in merit pay schemes where they are no longer eligible for merit increments.
- Dissatisfaction among staff who are rated fully satisfactory but who, under quotas and other restrictive guidelines for some schemes, receive either a smaller pay award than their colleagues or no award at all in a given year.
- Relatively low levels of funding that make schemes highly competitive and, in some countries, cutbacks in funds during times of economic restraint.
- A narrowing of the range and a reduction in the average size of bonuses paid.

Source: OECD (1993).

Flexible reward system

More flexible mechanisms for calculating remuneration are becoming popular. These approaches come under labels such as cafeteria benefits, flexible benefits and package compensation. Essentially remuneration is calculated in terms of an overall compensation package that may include life insurance, medical care or a company car.

For the employer, benefits include aligning total reward strategy to both the HR and business strategies, ensuring benefits match the requirements of a diverse workforce, value for money, and the creation of an employer brand. From the employee perspective a choice of benefits means that work–life issues can be balanced more successfully.

management in practice The demographic pension time bomb

In recent years pensions have become a real source of debate in the boardroom. There has been a move away from employers providing defined benefits plans for new employees into money purchase schemes, this trend having been embraced by companies such as Safeway, Barclays and British Airways. Employers contend that there has been a short-term rise in scheme costs due to increased cost of compliance with legislation following the 1995 Pensions Act. However, demographic changes also have had an impact:

> Fewer people contributing less to state and occupational schemes that have to pay out to more elderly pensioners for longer periods of time simply doesn't add up. According to the Pensions Policy Institute, in the 1960s a 25-year-old saving 11% of salary would have earned a maximum two-thirds of final salary pension after 40 years. Today the Institute estimates it will take 47 years to generate the same pension. (CIPD, 2002, p. 15)

CIPD state that HR's contributions include: a requirement for clear communication of reward and pension policies; ensure a flexibly designed pension policy; and the education of managers and employees enabling the workforce to take responsibility for retirement provision.

Source: CIPD (2002).

BMW – the case continues – outcomes of teamworking

CASE STUDY

The previous section of the case reported the initial rejection of new flexible working proposals by employees and unions at the BMW Cowley, Oxford plant. But some two years later this plant won the 2003 CIPD People Management Award where it was reported: 'with self-directed teamworking, they have managed to do what the British and Japanese could not do at Cowley. A decade ago, no one would have thought that they had a chance of delivering high performance, but it seems they've succeeded against all the odds. The judges were impressed with the emphasis on unlocking the creativity of shopfloor operators. We had the sense that teams were really shaping the self-directed teamwork, and this is changing the business from the inside out'.

What has produced such a dramatic change in such a short period of time? Individual HR changes need to be seen in the larger context of more than £230 million invested since 2000 to refit and upgrade the plant, which has underpinned a sense of enhanced employment security (employees have risen from 2500 to 4500 to allow a seven-day operation, although many are tempo-

rary workers). This major organisational change programme has had three major aims: to upgrade the site and processes to world-class standards, to integrate the different BMW and Rover cultures, and to launch a new vehicle (the 'mini').

The two 'high-profile' HRM initiatives within this larger context have been, firstly, the establishment of hundreds of self-directed teams of 8–15 employees right across the site. Teams have been extensively trained, and given the authority to tackle production problems directly, and to rotate tasks among members. The use of teams is intended, amongst other things, to strengthen identity, improve communication, integrate support functions, improve training and be part of reward management. The second high-profile HRM initiative is that of continuous process improvement via an employee suggestion scheme. Individual bonus payments are given in return for suggestions that save costs or improve production. Workers must come up with an average of three suggestions and save £800 each to qualify for the full £260 annual bonus.

The benefits of these HRM changes are visible: (a) in 2002, production targets were exceeded by more than 60%; (b) the programme of continuous process improvement saved £10.5 million in 2002–2003; and (c) in 2003, there were 14,333 employee suggestions of which 11,064 (80%) were implemented.

Source: *People Management*, 6 November 2003; *FT Intelligence*, 19 March 2003.

Case questions 11.6

● In light of the prior discussion of the notion of internal fit, what would you conclude about the changes discussed here?

● What themes of employee motivation (see Chapter 15) have BMW apparently tapped into in achieving such results?

● How might you go about investigating whether a 'Hawthorne' or 'novelty' effect has been influential in these circumstances?

11.7　Critical perspectives on HRM

Although the philosophy and terminology of HRM has spread widely in the management literature, there are questions about how widely management has applied it, whether it can show results when it has been applied, and its effects on power relations within organisations, involving a set of techniques and practices that are potentially contradictory (Blyton and Turnbull, 1994). It is with this mindset that we move away from discussion of specific HRM policies and return to a broader perspective to evaluate some fundamental questions which HRM specialists face.

More rhetoric than reality?

One argument is that while many managers talk about human resource management a much smaller number use it in the fullest sense of the term. It may not suit the circumstances of all countries. For example, an economy that typically follows a low-wage strategy, has a limited tradition of planning and works to short-run financial measures will not provide a suitable place in which to develop advanced HRM policies. Even within a more benign national system HRM is likely to be confined to a relatively small and atypical group of organisations. Foreign-owned, non-union, greenfield site operations have often been identified as the most natural homes for such an employment approach (Guest, 1987). Another point is that, while organisations may adopt certain HRM practices, few will do so in a comprehensive, strategic manner. In other words, there will be little evidence of internal fit; rather, a more *ad hoc*, reactive, piecemeal approach will be apparent (Storey, 1992).

Does it work?

The second line of questioning in relation to HRM is the limited evidence that the use of the approach has enhanced organisational effectiveness and performance. That is, the quantity and quality of evidence supporting a strong, positive relationship between HRM and organisational performance is far from impressive (Legge, 1995).

Nonetheless, significant development has occurred in recent years in this area in order to unravel the complex relationship between HRM and organisational performance. For example, an important study in the United States involving some 1000 firms reported a strong relationship between a set of high-performance work practices and certain measures of firm performance, such as employee turnover, productivity and financial performance (Huselid, 1995). Similarly, Boselie and Dietz's (2003) recent review concluded that practices related to employee development and training, empowerment, information sharing and reward systems are likely to yield tangible returns for employers, a view congruent with Delaney and Huselid (1996), Wright *et al.* (2003) and Batt (2002).

There are now some useful reviews of this body of research, which has been one of the most important in the HRM area in recent times (Ichniowski *et al.*, 1996; Wood, 1999; Becker *et al.*, 2001; Boselie and Dietz, 2003). In general the findings emphasise that a bottom-line payoff will only come about if a more strategic orientation is adopted towards the introduction and operation of HRM, i.e. the notions of external and internal fit are more strenuously observed.

Despite these optimistic results, many of these studies suffer from methodological and conceptual limitations (Wood and Wall, 2002). From a methodological standpoint, the studies are reliant on cross-sectional and self-reporting data and future research would benefit from longitudinal research. In addition, a number of conceptual questions remain unanswered: it is not clear as to the relative importance of a single policy as opposed to a 'bundle' of policies, the precise mechanisms linking HR policy and practice, and the extent to which outcomes are universal or dependent on additional variables.

Does it shift the power balance?

Finally there is a line of criticism that HRM can have negative effects on employees and unions. The underlying contention here is that HRM embodies a unitary view of organisations. This view (see Chapter 2) rejects the legitimacy of employees/management conflict in the employment relationship and seeks to align the aims and objectives of individual employees with those of owners and their agents (i.e. senior management). To some commentators HRM is simply the latest in a long line of attempts to shift the terms of the wage/effort bargain in favour of management. Others stress that HRM practices are designed to help organisations to be run on a non-union basis, or at least that they will have the effect of reducing the role, strength and presence of unions. However, in the United Kingdom, HRM practices seem to be more a feature of the union rather than the non-union sector, probably because there are more small firms in the non-union sector (Beaumont, 1996). This being said, the relevance of HRM practices to small firms should not be ignored, as one UK survey indicates:

> the larger the organization, the more chance there was that each of the new employment initiatives had been launched. The reasons are fairly obvious: the larger organizations had more expertise at their disposal, and the relevance of some of the initiatives was clearly tied to size. However, there was an interesting and important new finding. When we looked at the degree to which certain initiatives had been sustained, we found that smaller organizations had enjoyed the greater success. The reason for this is presumably that once the head of a small enterprise decides to introduce a new approach, it is more likely to be followed through. (Storey, 1995, p. 20)

11.8   Emerging themes

This chapter has described a range of strategies and policies associated with HRM that are intended to influence the attitudes and behaviour of employees to facilitate a loyal and committed workforce. However, in the last 20 years the business landscape has been transformed; employers no longer have the capacity to offer long-term job security, thus the employment relationship has been dramatically altered. In short, the cultural foundations of HRM are somewhat shaky and the extent to which employees identify with organisations has been questioned. The nature of the workforce has also changed in recent years and statistics suggest that the workforce is now more diverse than ever before. Such diversity has frequently been cited as a source of competitive advantage, although the extent of empirical work in this area is sparse. Organisational identity and workforce diversity are two important emerging themes in the HRM literature and worthy of discussion in this final section.

Organisational identity

Changes in the business environment over the last two decades have been well documented. Businesses have encountered mounting competition and senior managers have been forced to meet the dual demands of cost effectiveness and innovation in order to remain competitive. As a result of these pressures many organisations have followed a 'lean and mean' strategy and reduced staff. In addition, and due to the uncertainty of the business environment, employers have not been able to offer job security. These macro changes have had lasting results on the way employees feel about their job, their occupation and their employers.

The old employment 'deal' or psychological contract was founded on mutual trust between employee and employer. Employees offered loyalty and commitment while employers ensured job security, career prospects and training (Rousseau, 1995). Under the new arrangement the employment relationship has become more calculative on both sides: employees consent to working longer hours and taking on added responsibility, while offering a broader skills base and tolerating ambiguity and change. In turn employers promise higher pay and skills development.

The concept of a committed and loyal workforce who identify with their employer has often been regarded as being at the heart of HRM. Nevertheless, this is now under threat as a result of changing circumstances and consequently organisational identity has become an important area of research for both academics and practitioners.

Organisational identity has been defined as 'a cognitive linking between the definition of the organization and the definition of self' (Dutton *et al.*, 1994, p. 242). In essence, it can be described as 'who am I' and to what extent do I define myself through my employer (Sparrow and Cooper, 2003). Research has outlined potential causes or factors that enhance organisational identity. Employees are more likely to identify with their employer when:

- Employees work for high-status groups
- Others in the group are similar to themselves
- They are part of a smaller work group
- Employees work for an organisation for a long period of time
- Employee and employer values are congruent.

If organisational identity has been eroded through changes to the employment relationship, what are the implications? From an organisational perspective, studies suggest that the loss of employee identity has a number of negative consequences:

- Reduced employee performance and thus organisational performance
- Reduced job satisfaction
- Withdrawal of organisational citizenship
- Increased intentions to leave the organisation, resulting in higher labour turnover.

From an employee point of view, the demise of emotional identification with their employer has signified a loss of a sense of meaning, belonging and control. As a result of this bereavement, individuals have sought alternative sources of identity, including their profession, the work group, or indeed the project they are currently working on (Cappelli, 2000; Van Knippenberg and van Schie, 2000). Further empirical research is required to explore the full implications of this loss of identity and will be a significant challenge for HR practitioners.

Workforce diversity

The workforces in many advanced economies are becoming increasingly diverse. This can be simply illustrated: for example in the UK, in 1984 58 per cent of women were in employment, a figure that had risen to 70 per cent in 2003, while the proportion of workplaces with employees from ethnic minority groups has risen from 36 per cent in 1980 to 48 per cent in 1998. For individual organisations in a competitive labour market context, the challenge is to achieve a diverse workforce, both for reasons of legal compliance and to gain the maximum possible business advantage from such a 'macro-level' change – the latter interest is, as we still see, the essence of the so-called 'business case' for diversity.

Gender and ethnic origin are but two examples of diversity. Anti-discrimination legislation has largely concentrated on demographic or visible diversity, spreading beyond gender and race to embrace disability, age and sexual orientation. This increasing scope has increased the number of organisations that seek to meet legal requirements.

However, alongside compliance there is interest in a more proactive stance, based on the business case for diversity (John *et al.*, 1999). The contention is that organisations gain in business terms from seriously embracing the case for diversity by:

- Greater access to a wider range of individual strength, experiences and perspectives
- A greater understanding of the diverse groups of potential and existing customers represented within a workforce
- Better communication with these diverse groups of potential and existing customers (Anderson and Metcalf, 2003, p. 1x).

key ideas **A case for diversity**

Diversity is a reality in labour markets and customer markets today. To be successful in working with and gaining value from this diversity requires a sustained, systematic approach and long-term commitment. Success is facilitated by a perspective that considers diversity to be an opportunity for everyone in an organisation to learn from each other how better to accomplish their work and an occasion that requires a supportive and co-operative organizational culture as well as group leadership and process skills that can facilitate effective group functioning. Organizations that invest their resource are taking advantage of the opportunities that diversity offers and should outperform those that fail to make such investments.

Source: Kochan *et al.* (2003), p. 18.

Conclusions that support this line of argument include one that the top 100 companies, ranked in terms of their equal opportunities, outperformed the bottom 100 in terms of their return on investment (Howard, 1999). However, reviews of the evidence (Anderson and Metcalf, 2003; Kochan *et al.*, 2003) conclude that:

- The amount of systematic research evidence is very limited.
- What systematic evidence is available does not clearly and continuously support the straightforward business case.
- The 'potential impacts' (listed earlier) can be offset by increased communication and conflict costs and difficulties.
- It may be less diversity as such that matters, but rather having the essential mix of HRM policies in a supportive organisational context to maximise benefits and minimise costs.
- The nature of the outcomes and results might vary with the different dimensions of diversity that are being studied.

While the traditional business case for diversity is plausible, it still requires further monitoring and systematic gathering of information to support the argument.

Calls for increased diversity in the Civil Service

Diversity initiatives have been high on the agenda in the civil service; the Chairman of the Inland Revenue, Sir Nicholas Montagu, commented 'nothing less makes moral, business and social sense'. Diversity targets state that by 2004–2005, 35% of senior civil servant jobs should be held by women (from the current level of 26%). In addition, the number of senior posts held by individuals from ethnic minorities should be increased from 2.8% to 3.2% and by employees with disabilities from 1.7% to 3%. Nonetheless, inclusiveness goes beyond merely employment figures and 'diversity is about creating a culture change where people feel valued and where talents are going to be fully utilized'. As a consequence of this broader cultural challenge, the public sector has expended time, money and energy on training, for example on the topics of communication, leadership and effective networking.

FT

Source: *Financial Times*, 10 May 2004.

Summary

1 Understand the potential links between HRM practices and organisational strategy and performance:

- The rise of HRM can be explained by issues such as more globally integrated markets, highly publicised 'companies of excellence', changing composition of the workforce and the decline of trade union membership.
- The importance of external fit by linking the wider business strategy and HRM strategy.
- Internal coherence among HRM policies is crucial, as is that between organisational strategy and HRM strategy. For example, a differentiation strategy will usually require sophisticated HRM practices such as training, teamworking and shop-floor problem solving.

2 Discuss how the wider context shapes the ability to change HRM practice:

- Wider contexts impinge upon the implementation of HRM practices, for example the relative availability of skills in the labour market.

3 Understand the main difficulties of a longer-term approach to HRM:

- The pace of change in the business environment means that future planning is difficult as fundamental issues may change quickly.

4 Describe and analyse the changing nature of job requirements:

- In recent years, due to the need for flexibility, there has been a move away from viewing jobs as a set of tasks to thinking about the set of competences a person requires to accomplish a job successfully.

5 As a potential job seeker, recognise some of the important issues that will face you at the recruitment/selection stage:

- Choices are open to HRM practitioners in the recruitment/selection process, for example selecting the best technique to choose the correct person.
- Each technique has a number of strengths and weaknesses and it is important to be aware of these.

6 Understand and identify contemporary emerging themes in the HRM literature:

- Issues and challenges facing HRM continually change; contemporary emerging themes include the changing composition of the workforce, where managing diversity is an important topic. In addition, the changing employment relationship has also triggered a query surrounding the relative worth of organisational identity.

Review questions

1 What do the terms internal and external fit mean in an HRM context?

2 What are the arguments put forward in favour of an organisation adopting a deliberate HRM strategy?

3 Summarise the criticism of HRM that it is based on a unitary perspective (see Chapter 2) of organisations.

4 There is little evidence that HRM has achieved the business objectives claimed for it. What evidence would you look for, and how would you show the link between cause and effect?

5 How can the concept of organisational analysis support the recruitment process?

6 What are the main criticisms of personality testing?

7 What are the advantages and disadvantages of performance-related pay?

8 What lessons can you draw from the way BMW has used the payment system to support other aspects of the HRM policy? More generally, summarise the lessons you would draw from the BMW case.

Concluding critical reflection

Think about the way your company, or one with which you are familiar, deals with HRM. Review the material in the chapter, and make notes on these questions:

- Which of the issues discussed in this chapter are most relevant to your approach to HRM? Is there a clear and conscious attempt to link HRM with wider strategy? Can you give examples of issues where the two support, or do not support, each other? How did those arise, and what have been the effects?

- What assumptions do people make in your business about the role of HRM? Is it, for example, seen as mainly a topic for the specialist, or as part of every manager's responsibility? Does the workforce as a whole buy in enthusiastically to the policies adopted, or do they perceive a gap between the rhetoric and the reality?

- What is the dominant view about how changes in the business environment will affect staff commitment, and the need for new HRM policies to cope with this? Why do they think that? Do people have different interpretations?

- Can you compare your organisation's approach to HRM with that of colleagues on your course, especially those in similar industries? If there are differences in approach, can you establish the likely reasons? How open is your organisation to innovation in this area?

Further reading

Beardwell, L. and Holden, L. (2004), *Human Resource Management: A contemporary approach* (4th edn), Financial Times/Prentice Hall, Harlow.

A comprehensive collection of readings covering strategic issues, key practice areas and an international perspective.

Price, A. (2004), *Human Resource Management in a Business Context* (2nd edn), Thomson, London.

A comprehensive coverage of the field and specifically connects HRM and the business context in all its guises.

Redman, T. and Wilkinson, A. (2001), *Contemporary Human Resource Management: Texts and cases*, Financial Times/Prentice Hall, Harlow.

An up-to-date collection of texts and case studies in human resource management covering key practice areas.

Legge, K. (1995), *Human Resource Management: Rhetorics and realities*, Macmillan, London.

A highly critical examination of many of the leading, individual themes in HRM, emphasising the gap between the theory and practice of HRM.

Burke, R. and Cooper C. (2004), *Reinventing HRM*, Sage, London.

Harzing, A. and Van Ruysseveldt, J. (2003), *International Human Resource Management* (2nd edn), Sage, London.

An explicitly international perspective on the topic.

Weblinks

These websites have appeared in this and other chapters:

www.bmw.com

www.the-body-shop.com

www.marksandspencer.com

www.ba.com

www.rbs.com

www.oticon.com

Visit two of the business sites in the list, or any other companies which interest you, and navigate to the pages dealing with 'our staff', recent news or press releases.

- What information can you find about the way the company treats its staff – is there evidence that they are following a modern approach to HRM?
- What impression does it give you of how they see staff contributing to the core strategy of the business?
- Compare and contrast the issues you identify on the two sites.

Annotated weblinks, multiple choice questions and other
useful resources can be found on
www.pearsoned.co.uk/boddy

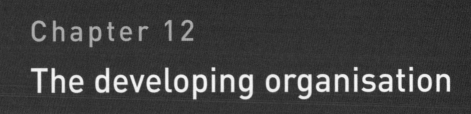

Chapter 12
The developing organisation

Aim

To contrast mechanistic and organic forms of organisation structure, and outline the factors that influence management choice between them.

Objectives

By the end of your work on this chapter you should be able to outline the concepts below in your own terms and:

1 Explain the evolving nature of organisation structures

2 Compare the features of mechanistic and organic structures and describe the 'contingencies' believed to influence managers' choice between them

3 Summarise the work of Woodward, Burns and Stalker, Lawrence and Lorsch and John Child, showing how they contributed to this area of management theory

4 Contrast contingency and managerial choice perspectives on structure

5 Outline empirical research on current patterns of change in the structures, processes and boundaries of organisations

6 Describe some alternative ways of organising economic activity and compare them with conventional structures.

Key terms

This chapter introduces the following ideas:

mechanistic structure
organic structure
contingencies
technology
flexible manufacturing
differentiation
integration
interdependence
strategic alliance
virtual organisation
complementarities
contingency approach
determinist
structural choice

Each is a term defined within the text, as well as in the glossary at the end of the book.

Oticon www.oticon.com

Oticon www.oticon.com

Oticon, a Danish company, is the world's second-largest producer of hearing aids with about 1200 staff in Denmark (the parent company, William Demant Holdings, has about 4400 employees worldwide). Oticon has its own basic research and production facilities and stresses the high engineering and design quality of its products. Competition intensified during the 1980s and the company began to lose market share to larger rivals like Siemens. Lars Kolind was appointed chief executive in 1988. In 1990 he concluded that a new approach was needed to counter the threats from larger competitors who were becoming stronger. Oticon's only hope for survival and prosperity was to be radical in all aspects of the business. Kolind intended the changes to turn Oticon from an *industrial* organisation producing hearing aids into a *service* organisation with a physical product.

He organised product development work around projects. The project leader was appointed by the management team and recruited people to do the work. Employees chose whether or not to join – and could only do so if their current project leader agreed. Previously most people had a single skill; they were now required to be active in at least three specialisms – one based on professional qualification and two others unrelated to the first. A chip designer could develop skills in customer support and advertising, for example. These arrangements allowed the company to respond quickly to unexpected events and to use skills fully.

Previously Oticon had a conventional hierarchical structure, and a horizontal structure of separate functional departments. The only remnant of the hierarchy is the 10-person management team, each member of which acts as an 'owner' to the many projects through which work is done. Kolind refers to this as 'managed chaos'. The company tries to overcome the dangers of this by developing a very strong and clear purpose and mission 'to help people with X problem to live better with X', and a common set of written values. Examples include 'an assumption that we only employ adults (who can be expected to act responsibly)', and 'an assumption that staff want to know what and why they are doing it', so all information is available to everyone (with a few legally excepted areas).

There are no titles – people do whatever they think is right at the time. Again the potential for chaos is averted by building underneath the flexible organisation a set of clearly defined business processes, setting out how they are to be carried out. 'The better your processes are defined, the more flexible you can be.' The absence of departments avoids people protecting local interests and makes it easier to cope with fluctuations in workload.

Oticon was one of the earliest companies to redesign the workplace to maximise disturbance. It referred to this as the mobile office, in which each workstation consisted of a desk without drawers (nowhere to file paper). There were no installed telephones, though everyone had a mobile. The workstations are equipped with powerful PCs through which all work was done (staff had a small personal trolley for personal belongings which they wheeled to wherever they were working that day). Although common today, this arrangement was revolutionary at the time.

Source: Based on Bjorn-Andersen and Turner (1994), Rivard *et al.* (2004) and company website.

Oticon

Case questions

- What factors persuaded management to change the structure at Oticon?
- How would you expect staff to react to changes of this sort?

12.1 Introduction

Lars Kolind was taking a big risk with the changes he made at Oticon. Yet the previous organisation was not working, and he needed to change the way people worked together. Changing the structure towards a team-based operation was the way he chose to go, hoping that this would make better use of scarce resources and mean a faster response to customer needs. Chapter 10 showed the components of structure that are present in all kinds of businesses. This chapter shows how managers try to shape those structural components to achieve their objectives.

They regularly restructure their organisations in the hope of improving performance. Some try to centralise decisions, to ensure greater control over local operations – as happened at Hewlett-Packard after it took over Compaq. In 2000 Littlewoods, a large UK retail chain, merged its three businesses – Index stores, Littlewoods stores and its large home shopping division – into one operation. In 2001 Ford of Europe placed its transmissions operations in a joint venture with Getrag, a German transmissions group, to help reduce costs and improve its use of assets (*Financial Times*, 1 February 2001).

Others do the opposite. After mounting criticism of its performance, British Telecom announced in 2000 that it would divide its business into five separate units. GlaxoSmithKline has grouped its research activities into five autonomous divisions – for similar reasons to those that encouraged Oticon to make its changes. These are just a few of the many examples in which companies reshape the chain of command or the way departments are grouped together to help improve performance.

The reason for such activity is the view that a strategy is more likely to succeed if the organisation has a structure that encourages people to act in ways that support it. In shaping their department or organisation managers use the components examined in Chapter 10. They decide how to divide work vertically and horizontally, and how best to integrate those separated activities. They decide which decisions those at the centre should take, and how much formality there should be. They also decide whether to adjust these features as circumstances change.

This chapter reviews how managers resolve these questions, and what lessons they can draw from research on the topic. Figure 12.1 shows the themes of the chapter. It begins by comparing mechanistic and organic forms of organisation – two broad types that

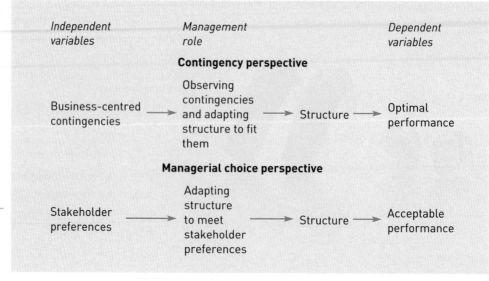

Figure 12.1

Comparing contingency and managerial choice perspectives

reflect the accumulation of decisions on particular components. It then reviews the factors that one line of research ('contingency' theory) suggests will influence these decisions. Research has identified three convergent themes in contemporary change, relating to the structure, processes and boundaries of organisation, and each of these is explained and illustrated. The chapter then contrasts contingency theories with an alternative view which emphasises the wider scope for 'managerial choice' of structure than contingency theorists imply. A final section introduces some alternative forms of organisation to those conventionally operating in capitalist economies.

12.2 Mechanistic and organic structures

Chapter 10 indicated that the purpose of structure is to support organisational goals – the right structure is a powerful management tool, as it encourages people to behave in ways that management hopes will support its objectives. That chapter also outlined the elements of the structure – the vertical and horizontal division of work, and the coordination of that work – that give formal shape to an organisation.

Some people develop a structure that emphasises the vertical hierarchy to achieve coordination. They define responsibilities clearly, take most decisions at the centre, delegate tightly defined routine tasks and have rigorous reporting requirements. This enables those at the centre to know what is happening lower down the organisation. They ensure that policies are applied consistently, that a uniform image is presented to the outside world, that customers receive consistent treatment and that best practice passes rapidly around the organisation. Communication is likely to be mainly vertical, as the centre passes down instructions and staff send queries to those above them in the hierarchy. The vertical aspects of the structure dominate and control the organisation. This is very similar to what Burns and Stalker (1961) called a **mechanistic structure**.

A mechanistic structure means there is a high degree of task specialisation, people's responsibility and authority are closely defined and decision making is centralised.

Oticon – the case continues – a mechanistic past

CASE STUDY

Before the change the company had six distinct hierarchical levels, with privileges based on rank:

Not only was there a specific company car assigned to each management level, but other material signs existed . . . prestige and reward were very apparent: in the length of the curtains, the type of carpet . . . the size of people's desks. It all gave status. And that was what people strove for. (Rivard *et al.*, 2004, p. 181)

Horizontal boundaries were also strong, as the two main divisions – Electronics (product development) and

International (sales) – communicated poorly. Within these divisions work was organised round specific departments and tasks.

People were locked into specific roles and responsibilities and were rewarded only for those – nobody took initiatives. (Rivard *et al.*, 2004, p. 180)

Source: Based on Bjorn-Andersen and Turner (1994), and Rivard *et al.* (2004).

Others develop a structure with more emphasis on the horizontal aspect. They use broadly defined, flexible tasks, frequently set up cross-functional teams to work on problems (such as Oticon has done) and expect authority to reflect expertise rather

An **organic structure** is one where people are expected to work together and to use their initiative to solve problems; job descriptions and rules are few and imprecise.

than position in the hierarchy. Management accepts that those at the centre cannot know all the answers, and must depend on those nearest the action to find the best solution to problems. Communication is likely to be horizontal amongst those familiar with the task. There may not even be an organisation chart, so fluid is the division of labour and departmentalisation. This approach corresponds to what Burns and Stalker (1961) called an **organic structure**. Table 12.1 compares the features of mechanistic and organic organisations.

A more organic structure at Philips www.philips.com

The Dutch Group Philips is the world's third-largest consumer-electronics company – renowned for its innovative products. It has faced many crises in recent years, and in 2002 was trading at a heavy loss. Gerard Kleisterlee became chief executive in 2001 and has made radical changes in the company's structure. He reduced the many separate divisions to just five, and is breaking down long-established internal divisional barriers to communication, so that expertise in one can be used in another. For example, the lighting group is working with the consumer electronics division to produce a room-lighting system that changes colour according to what is being shown on the TV.

Source: *The Economist*, 12 June 2004.

Table 12.1

Characteristics of mechanistic and organic systems

Mechanistic	Organic
Specialised tasks	Contribute experience to common tasks
Hierarchical structure of control	Network structure of contacts
Knowledge located at top of hierarchy	Knowledge widely spread
Vertical communication	Horizontal communication
Loyalty and obedience stressed	Commitment to goals more important

Source: Based on Burns and Stalker (1961).

Within a company some units or activities will correspond to mechanistic forms and others to organic – the distinction is not so much between wholly mechanistic or wholly organic organisations, as between which activities take which form. A company may have a centralised information system and tightly controlled policies on capital expenditure – while also allowing divisions considerable autonomy on, say, research and development or advertising policy.

Case questions 12.1

- What was the role of strategy and technology in encouraging the change at Oticon?
- What features of the present form correspond to the organic model?
- How does management hope that the new structure will support their strategy?

12.3   Contingencies shaping the choice of form

Why do managers favour one form of structure rather than another? A widely held (though disputed) view is that it depends on certain **contingencies** – 'the essence of the contingency paradigm is that organizational effectiveness results from fitting characteristics of the organization, such as its structure, to contingencies that reflect the situation of the organization' (Donaldson, 2001, p. 1). Successful organisations appear to be those in which managers maintain a good fit between contingent factors (such as strategy, technology, size/life-cycle and environmental uncertainty) and the structure through which people deploy and manage organisational resources. Figure 12.2 illustrates these contingent factors, which the following sections examine.

Contingencies are factors such as uncertainty, interdependence and size that reflect the situation of the organisation.

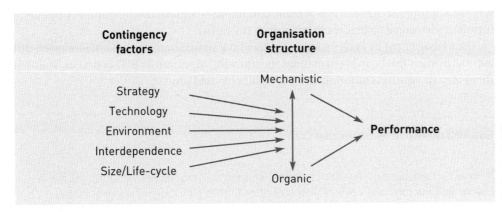

Figure 12.2

Contingent factors shaping organisation structures

An alternative perspective is that this is too rational a view of organisational life, and that managers develop structures that reflect other factors – such as fashion or personal ambition supported by political empire building. After outlining the contingency factors the chapter presents the managerial choice perspective.

Strategy

Chapter 8 outlined Porter's view that firms adopt one of a small number of alternative generic strategies – cost leadership, differentiation or focus. With a cost leadership strategy managers concentrate on increasing efficiency to bring their costs below those of competing firms. A differentiation strategy focuses on innovation – on developing new products or services more rapidly and imaginatively than competing firms. Contingency theory suggests that each strategy requires people to behave in a different way, and therefore a structure which supports that behaviour.

A cost leadership strategy is likely to be best supported by a clear functional structure. This uses task specialisation and a strict chain of command to ensure that people work efficiently. The structure sets out clear roles and performance targets, encouraging people to focus on their part of the task. Powergen, a privatised electricity utility, initially followed a cost-leadership strategy, aiming to keep costs low in the face of tougher competition in the electricity generating business. It adopted a tight functional structure, with detailed rules and performance measures governing power station operations. There is evidence of more companies moving towards centralised, tightly controlled structures – a move that often appears to be driven by a need to cut costs.

A differentiation strategy, on the other hand, requires innovation and flexibility – with ideas flowing easily between people with something to contribute, wherever they work. A matrix or team-based structure is most likely to work best, since it encourages the mixing of people from across functional boundaries to work together on projects to develop innovative solutions to customer problems. Oticon moved towards this team-based structure, as has Microsoft in its efforts to maintain high levels of innovation in its research organisation. As Powergen diversified into many different businesses it tried to support this with a new structure – based on three autonomous product divisions.

The idea is that teams or autonomous divisions enable organisations to differentiate themselves by being able to respond more quickly than competitors to new demands. A study by Hill and Pickering (1986) of divisionalised companies supported this idea. It showed that companies in which business units had relatively high decision-making authority were more successful than those which had not. The decentralised structure was the appropriate structure in volatile conditions – and many companies continue to introduce divisional structures to support that strategy.

The Management in Practice feature shows how GlaxoSmithKline (GSK) followed this approach when the board restructured its critically important R & D activities, splitting them into six relatively autonomous but tightly focused units.

GlaxoSmithKline www.gsk.com

In February 2001 Tachi Yamada, head of Research and Development at GlaxoSmithKline (GSK), set out the company's plan to split the company's research organisation ('the engine room of any pharmaceutical company') into six 'internal biotechnology companies'. These units will compete for resources. Divided along therapeutic lines, they will operate autonomously. The company is the world's second-largest drugs company, and employs 15,000 scientists with an annual budget of £2.5 billion. Jean-Paul Garnier, chief executive, said that organising this research group required a radical new structure. Early research, where scarce skills and expensive equipment are applied across a range of diseases, needed to stay big. So did late-stage development where huge dossiers of clinical trial data were prepared for regulators. However, the section in the middle, where bright ideas were honed into drugs, would work best as competing, autonomous units:

> We start big, we move to small and then back to big again. Nobody has attempted this before.

The job of the six autonomous units is to deliver drugs with 'proof of concept' – after small-scale clinical tests on patients – to GSK's development organisation. That will put drugs through full clinical trials, aimed at winning regulatory approval and maximising sales potential.

The business units, called Centres of Excellence for Drug Discovery, can deliver molecules invented at GSK or brought in from academia or external biotech groups. Dr Yamada said:

> They have complete autonomy. They can have 100 chemists per project, or five. It doesn't matter to me how they do it, so long as they produce drugs.

Clinical trials are undertaken on a massive scale, often across continents, and must comply with strict regulatory conditions. Thus corporate control, uniformity and economies of scale are pre-eminent. The other area where scale will be leveraged is early research, where hundreds of millions of pounds are spent on platform technology. Two divisions, Genetics Research and Discovery Research, will work on understanding basic biology and on producing leads to set drug discovery units on their way. Figure 12.3 illustrates the new structure.

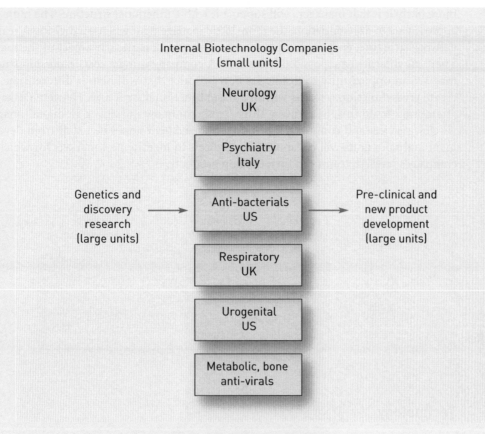

Internal Biotechnology Companies
(small units)

Neurology
UK

Psychiatry
Italy

Genetics and
discovery
research
(large units) → Anti-bacterials
US → Pre-clinical and
new product
development
(large units)

Respiratory
UK

Urogenital
US

Metabolic, bone
anti-virals

Figure 12.3 The structure introduced at GlaxoSmith Kline

'The merger provided us with huge scale, so I had to design something that would take advantage of that', says Dr Yamada. 'But we know that big can sometimes mean bad. So we had to design something that could maintain agility, entrepreneurial spirit and individual accountability.' Dr Yamada describes the hybrid structure as 'six biotech companies nested within a full array of platform technologies'. In an effort to attract talent and emulate biotech's entrepreneurial culture, GSK scientists will have incentives. Big share option packages will be reserved for teams that come up with drugs. More radically still, scientists will receive royalties on the sale of medicines they helped invent. 'If you can become a millionaire by joining a biotech company, why shouldn't you do that by joining GSK?' asks Dr Yamada. 'What we are aiming for is a step change in productivity. I believe we've been as productive as any other company. It's just that we need to do much, much better.'

Allen Oliff, who ran one of the research units, commented in 2002 that scientists were enthused by the independence and flexibility they now enjoyed:

At other companies scientists have to think about 45 different things, about getting published in academic journals and building their own research infrastructure. Here we focus exclusively on the area from drug discovery to early drug development – bureaucracy and time-wasting have been drastically reduced.

Source: Based on *Financial Times*, 23 February 2001 and 24 October 2002.

Figure 12.4 expresses the idea that different strategies require different structures, by showing on one axis the structural types described in Chapter 10, with the strategic goals from Chapter 8 on the other. The more the strategy corresponds to cost leadership, the more likely it is that managers will support it with a functional structure. The more they approximate to differentiation, the more likely management will use a divisional, team or network structure, enabling people to concentrate on a particular aspect of the market. There are intermediate possibilities as well. A company using a cost-leadership strategy may see an opportunity to develop a new product that will help it differentiate – so create cross-functional teams within a basic functional structure. Hewlett-Packard is attempting to do this, by creating three 'cross-company initiatives' in digital imaging, wireless services and commercial printing. Management hopes that staff from development and sales units will collaborate on projects to identify new markets for which the company's research teams can then develop products.

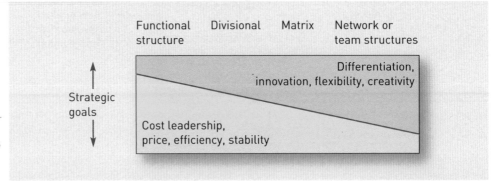

Figure 12.4

Relationship between strategies and structural types

Technology

Technology is the knowledge, equipment and activities used to transform inputs into outputs.

Technology includes the knowledge, tools and techniques used to transform organisational inputs into outputs. It includes buildings, machines, computer systems and the knowledge and procedures associated with them. Just as structure needs to fit the strategy of a firm, so it also needs to fit the technology of the firm – whether in manufacturing or services.

Woodward's manufacturing technology

Joan Woodward's study of organisations and their structure (Woodward, 1965) had a great influence on thinking about management. When she conducted the research the dominant view was that there were certain principles (see, for example, Brech, 1957) that managers should apply, irrespective of the business they were in. These principles were based on the work of writers in the scientific management and human relations traditions discussed in Chapter 2. In either case the emphasis was on identifying the 'one best way', which would apply universally. However, Woodward questioned this prescriptive approach, choosing instead to conduct empirical research into current organisational practice.

She gathered information from 100 British firms to establish whether basic structural features such as the span of control, the number of levels in the hierarchy or the degree of formalisation varied between them. The research team could see no pattern until they analysed the companies by their manufacturing process, which they grouped into 11 categories, of three broad types. These formed a scale of increasing technical complexity. The researchers then observed a relationship between the degree of technical complexity and the structural arrangements in the company:

- **Unit and small batch production** Firms in this group produce goods in small numbers, often to a customer's unique order. It is similar to craft work, as people and their skills are deeply involved in the process. Examples of such products are custom-built cycles, designer furniture, Aston Martin sports cars and luxury yachts.
- **Large batch and mass production** This form is typified by the production of large quantities of standard products. All customers receive the same product, supplies of which are placed in stock until customers need them. Machines, typically a production line of some kind, do most of the physical work, with people complementing the machinery as they produce things such as computer discs, cigarettes, Ford cars and Electrolux washing machines.
- **Continuous process** Here the entire workflow is mechanised, in a sophisticated and complex form of production technology. The machinery does the production work, with operators in a supporting role – monitoring it, fixing faults and generally overseeing the process. Examples include the Guinness Brewery in Dublin, an Esso oil refinery and a Corus steel plant.

The difference between them is what Woodward called technical complexity – the degree to which machinery is involved to the exclusion of people. Figure 12.5 shows one of the structural characteristics associated with each type – the span of control of first-line supervisors. The span of control is greatest for mass production work, with the median span of control being lower in the other forms of technology.

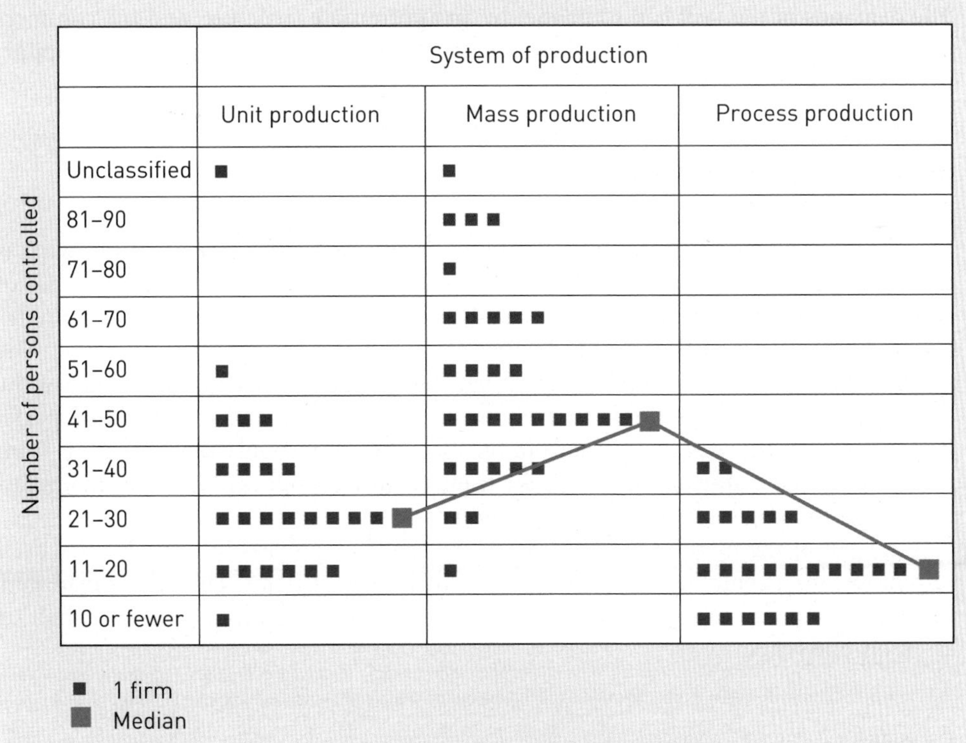

Number of persons controlled	System of production		
	Unit production	Mass production	Process production
Unclassified	■	■	
81–90		■ ■ ■	
71–80		■	
61–70		■ ■ ■ ■ ■	
51–60	■	■ ■ ■ ■	
41–50	■ ■ ■	■ ■ ■ ■ ■ ■ ■ ■ ■ ■	
31–40	■ ■ ■ ■	■ ■ ■ ■ ■	■ ■
21–30	■ ■ ■ ■ ■ ■ ■ ■	■ ■	■ ■ ■ ■ ■
11–20	■ ■ ■ ■ ■ ■	■	■ ■ ■ ■ ■ ■ ■ ■ ■ ■
10 or fewer	■		■ ■ ■ ■ ■ ■

■ 1 firm
■ Median

Figure 12.5

Span of control of first-line supervision in three production systems

Source: Woodward (1958, p. 15), Crown copyright, reproduced with permission of the Controller of Her Majesty's Stationery Office.

Activity 12.1 **Describing the pattern**

Describe the patterns shown in Figure 12.5. What differences does the diagram show between the structures most commonly found in the different types of production system?

Woodward explained this by observing that different manufacturing techniques impose different demands on people and organisations. Unit production technology requires close supervision as this enables managers to ensure that staff meet the unique requirements. They can communicate directly with those working on different parts of the task and so manage the uncertainties and changes involved in designing and producing 'one-off' items. Firms with large batch or mass production systems face less uncertainty, and more of the necessary knowledge has been incorporated into the design of the plant and its procedures. On an assembly line the work is so routine that a supervisor can oversee many employees – a wider span of control.

The research team also asked whether a particular kind of structure ensured business success. They found that firms which conformed to the median organisational structure for their 'technology group' were more successful financially than those that deviated from it. Firms that had adopted the classic management principles, such as formal definitions of responsibility, were not always financially successful. These principles worked well in large batch and mass production, but not in unit or process production systems. The demands of the task had to be met by an appropriate structure, and the commercially successful firms were those where the structure provided the right kind of support to the work of employees.

Flexible manufacturing

Flexible manufacturing is a manufacturing technology using computers to automate and integrate manufacturing components such as robots, machines, design and engineering.

Manufacturing firms such as Rolls-Royce or European Airbus now often use what is termed a **flexible manufacturing** system (Bessant, 1991) to produce small batches of components. Such systems depend on highly automated systems, in which a computer system holds details of the parts to be manufactured and the resources available. The system plans the order in which different batches will be manufactured, and drives the computer-aided machine tools that physically transform metal into finished parts. Robotic vehicles move parts to and from the machines, in response to instructions from the computer. Operators usually work as a team, ensuring supplies of material, maintaining and positioning tools and removing products.

A variant of the method is when managers divide employees into small 'cells' each responsible for assembling one product or a small range of items. This allows managers to change manufacturing plans more easily than with a traditional conveyor-belt or assembly line system.

Service technologies

The companies that Woodward studied were engaged in manufacturing – activities which physically change materials. Service activities are different – they relate to the transaction of intangibles (hairdressing, theatre performances, holidays) or they support the production and delivery of physical products (the financial, human resources or advertising staff in a business manufacturing cars or compact discs).

More employees in the developed economies work in service jobs than in manufacturing. Advances in production technologies mean that manufacturing companies employ fewer people to make the things they sell – and employ many more people on internal service activities such as marketing and human resources. At the same time there has been a steady growth in the number of people working in organisations that sell or provide intangible products – banks, bars, retailing, healthcare, etc.

Technology plays as central a role in delivering services as it does in delivering manufactured goods. Managers can use technology to shape the way staff interact with customers. Staff at branches of Barclays Bank (or any other retail bank) used to handle many cash transactions with customers, and for security reasons sat behind protective glass screens. These necessary precautions made banks seem remote and unwelcoming to customers. Technological developments in payment systems mean that much less cash is now handled in bank branches – which are now designed to bring staff and customers closer together.

More generally, developments in information technology (IT) have great implications for the structuring of service activities – as the Management in Practice feature shows.

The Royal Bank of Scotland – centralised manufacturing

The Royal Bank of Scotland Group (RBS) Manufacturing Division is responsible for the operations that support the income-generating business areas. It has three functional areas: Technology (IT operations and development), Operations (Account management, Lending, Telephony, Payments), and Services (Purchasing, Property, other support units). As the primary back-office 'engine room' for the world's fifth-largest bank, Manufacturing provides operational services to over 20 brands serving 20m customers across a variety of delivery channels (branches, Internet, ATMs, telephone, etc.).

Since 1999 RBS income has increased by an average of 14 per cent a year while the number of staff in Manufacturing has remained static (at about 20,000). This efficiency gain has in part been achieved by an IT strategy of 'build once, use many times'. This means developing a single IT platform to support the many different financial brands and delivery channels across RBS. By building newly acquired business areas into the same IT platform, Manufacturing has established a very large system with big economies of scale. By developing common processes for the different brands, this large platform operates very efficiently while meeting the different demands of the businesses.

Manufacturing's scale has allowed it to develop large information processing centres specialising in account management, lending, telephony, payments or credit cards, and handling large volumes of transactions from low-cost buildings.

Source: Adapted from Boddy et al. (2005).

Companies use information technology to rationalise processes and ensure consistent quality to the customer wherever he or she is receiving the service – as happened at The Royal Bank of Scotland. Another example is when service companies such as Airtours (one of the UK's largest holiday groups) use information technology to change their distribution system. In 2002 the company closed many of the shops through which it sold holidays, since most people now prefer to book their holidays by telephone. The company now takes these calls at low-cost call centres that use advanced communications and IT to manage the way staff handle calls. Many companies have used information technology in this way to rationalise services and cut costs – consistent with the cost-leadership strategy described earlier (see Boddy et al., 2005).

Other service companies, such as Oticon, use the technology in a different way, to support a more decentralised, organic structure. Consulting companies such as PricewaterhouseCoopers have introduced information systems designed to encourage staff to share knowledge and expertise directly amongst themselves. These 'groupware' systems capture information from staff as they work on projects, and then store in a database information about the methods used and lessons learned. Other staff can search the database for other people with similar interests, and seek their advice on the consulting problems they face. This spreads good practice around the organisation and encourages people to form teams that can learn from each other.

The technology of the Internet further illustrates this. Some companies use it to cut costs very significantly. EasyJet, the low-cost airline, only accepts reservations over the Internet, and the savings this brings help towards the company's low-cost strategy. Others use it to offer a highly differentiated service. Amazon.com uses data about customers to build a profile of products likely to interest them, and then alerts them to new goods or services that are likely to be of interest to that individual customer. It is using the technology to support a differentiation strategy.

Environment

Classical organisation theories specified, broadly, that management should exercise control over employees through practices such as tight job descriptions, clear rules and a defined hierarchy. Research over many years, such as that by Hage and Aiken (1967), Gerwin (1979) and Hill and Pickering (1986), showed that performance depends on having a structure that is suitable for the particular environment in which a firm is operating. Burns and Stalker (1961) from the University of Edinburgh compared the structure of a long-established rayon plant in Manchester with the structures of several new electronics companies then being created in the east of Scotland. Both types of organisation were successful – but had different structures.

The rayon plant had clearly set-out rules, tight job descriptions and clear procedures, and coordination was primarily through the hierarchy. In this mechanistic form of organisation management creates a high degree of specialisation by dividing tasks into small parts. The boundaries of responsibility and authority are clearly defined, and people are discouraged from acting outside their remit. Decision making is centralised, with information flowing up the hierarchy, and instructions flowing down.

The small companies in the newly created electronics industry were completely different. They had very few job descriptions and their rules and procedures were ambiguous and imprecise. Staff were expected to use their initiative in deciding priorities. They worked together to solve problems. Communication was largely lateral, rather than through the hierarchy. Burns and Stalker termed this an organic form of organisation. Table 12.1 summarises the contrasts between the mechanistic and organic forms.

Burns and Stalker (1961) concluded that both organisational forms were appropriate for their particular circumstances. The rayon plant was operating in a stable environment. It was the production unit of a larger business, and its sole purpose was to supply a steady flow of rayon to the company's spinning factories. Delivery schedules rarely changed; the technology of rayon manufacture was well known and fully documented in printed manuals.

The electronics companies were in direct contact with their customers, the largest of which was the Ministry of Defence. The demand for both commercial and military

Oticon – the case continues – communication and technology

While the company uses advanced information systems for many functions it believes that dialogue is better than email, and has designed the building to support face-to-face dialogue between staff. The problem owner will usually use email or personal contact to bring two or three people together and have a stand-up meeting. Decisions are noted in the computer (accessible by everyone). By 1994 the company had halved product development time and more than doubled sales. It employed half as many administrative staff as in 1990, but double the number on product development. Financial performance improved dramatically in the years following the change.

Hardware companies have organisations that look like machines: a company that produces knowledge needs an organisation that looks like a brain, i.e. which looks chaotic and is un-hierarchical. (Lars Kolind)

Source: Based on Bjorn-Andersen and Turner (1994).

Case questions 12.2

- Oticon has had both mechanistic and organic structures: what prompted the change?
- Why has the new structure improved business performance?

products was volatile, with frequent changes in delivery requirements. The technology was new, often applying a recent discovery from a research laboratory. Contracts were often taken in which neither the customer nor the company knew what the end product would be: it was likely to change during the course of the work.

Burns and Stalker concluded that neither mechanistic nor organic structures were appropriate in all situations. Stable, predictable environments were likely to encourage a mechanistic structure. Volatile, unpredictable environments were likely to encourage an organic structure. This recognition that environmental conditions place different demands upon organisations was a major step in understanding why companies adopt contrasting structures – an idea illustrated in Figure 12.6.

		Structure	
		Mechanistic	*Organic*
Environment	*Uncertain (unstable)*	**Incorrect Fit:** Mechanistic structure in uncertain environment Structure too tight	**Correct Fit:** Organic structure in uncertain environment
	Certain (stable)	**Correct Fit:** Mechanistic structure in certain environment	**Incorrect Fit:** Organic structure in certain environment Structure too loose

Figure 12.6 Relationship between environment and structure

379

Activity 12.2 **Critical reflection on a structure**

● Is your college or university a mechanistic or an organic organisation? What about the department in which you study? Look for evidence of the characteristics in Table 12.1 to help you assess whether it is closer to one form than the other.

● If you work in an organisation, is the department or unit in which you work mechanistic or organic? Why has that form developed, and is it suitable? How does it compare with other departments in the business?

Organic problem solving in a mechanistic structure

The organisation I work for has just come through a short-term cash-flow crisis. The problem arose because, while expenditures on contracts are relatively predictable and even, the income flow was disrupted by a series of contractual disputes.

The role culture permeates the head office, and at first the problem was pushed ever upwards. But faced with this crisis all departments were asked for ideas on how to improve performance. Some have been turned into new methods of working, and others are still being considered by the 'ideas team', drawn from all grades of personnel and departments. This was a totally new perspective, of a task culture operating within a role culture – that is, we developed an organic approach. What could be more simple than asking people who do the job how they could be more efficient?

To maintain the change in the long run is difficult, and some parts have now started to drift back to the role culture.

Source: Private communication.

Organisations do not face a single environment. People in each department try to meet the expectations of other players in their part of the wider environment, and gradually develop structures which support the required behaviours. An organisation's payroll section has to meet strict legal requirements on, amongst other things, salary entitlements, taxation and pensions records. This implies that staff will be expected to follow rules and procedures strictly, with little scope for using their initiative. They will work in a relatively mechanistic structure. The product development and advertising departments, for example, face quite different requirements – and so will have evolved structures that encourage creativity and innovative thinking; they will have a relatively organic form.

key ideas   Lawrence and Lorsch: differentiation and integration

Two American scholars, Paul Lawrence and Jay Lorsch, developed Burns and Stalker's work. They observed that organisations typically contain distinct subunits (departments). If these subunits are doing different tasks each will face a separate segment of the total environment. These will place different demands on each subunit – some being relatively stable, others unstable. Lawrence and Lorsch predicted that in order to cope with this demand subunits will develop different structures and ways of working, appropriate to their respective environments. Those in stable environments would move towards mechanistic forms, while those in unstable environments would move towards organic forms.

How would that diversity affect the task of coordinating their efforts? The authors examined these issues through a study of six organisations facing stable, moderately stable and unstable environments respectively. One firm in each was chosen as a successful operation, the other as an unsuccessful one.

Lawrence and Lorsch concluded that the subunits did indeed differ from each other, and in ways they had predicted. Those facing unstable environments (research and development) had less formal structures than those facing stable ones (production). The greater the **differentiation** between departments the more effort managers needed to devote to integrating their work. Successful firms achieved more **integration** between subunits than the unsuccessful ones. They used a variety of integrating devices such as task forces and project managers with the required interpersonal skills. The less effective companies in the uncertain environment used rules and procedures.

Source: Lawrence and Lorsch (1967).

An important implication of this is that coordination between such departments will be difficult, as they will work in different ways. Paul Lawrence and Jay Lorsch explored this issue, and their contribution is in the Key Ideas feature.

Differentiation The state of segmentation of the organisation into subsystems which develop attributes relevant to their external environment.

Integration is the process of achieving unity of effort amongst the various subsystems in accomplishing the organisation's task.

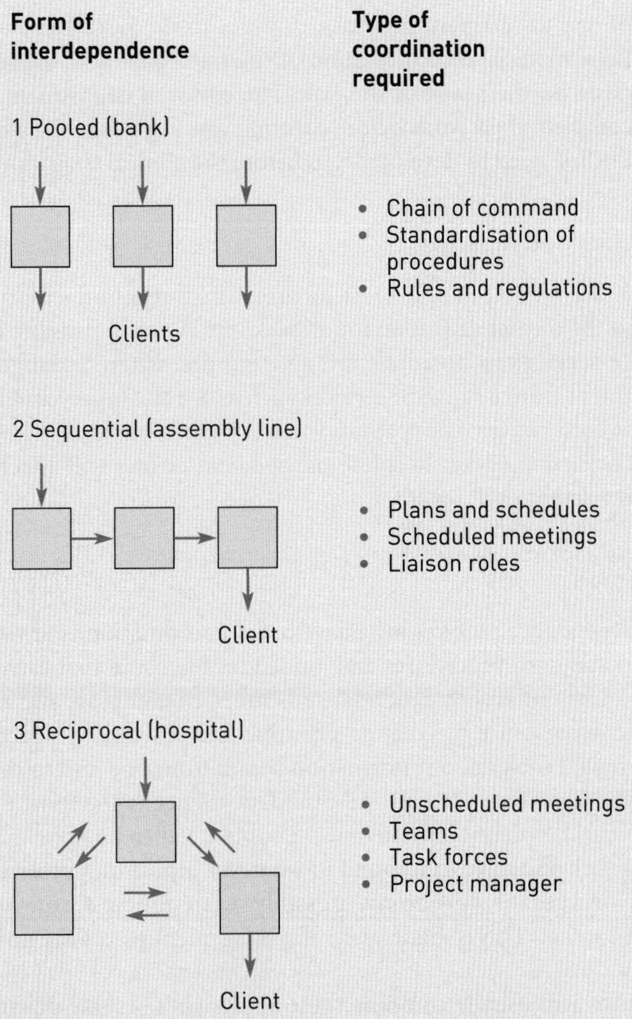

Form of interdependence | **Type of coordination required**

1 Pooled (bank)

Clients

- Chain of command
- Standardisation of procedures
- Rules and regulations

2 Sequential (assembly line)

Client

- Plans and schedules
- Scheduled meetings
- Liaison roles

3 Reciprocal (hospital)

Client

- Unscheduled meetings
- Teams
- Task forces
- Project manager

Figure 12.7

Types of co-ordination required for different forms of interdependence

Source: From *Management*, 4th edition by Daft (1997). Copyright © 1997. Reprinted with permission of South-Western, a division of Thomson Learning. www.thomsonrights.com. Fax 800 730-2215.

Task interdependence

Interdependence is
the extent to which
departments depend on
each other for resources
or materials to
accomplish their tasks.

A further characteristic influencing structure is the degree of interdependence between the departments. **Interdependence** is the extent to which departments rely on each other for resources (including information) or materials to perform their tasks (Thompson, 1967). A low level means they can work independently with little need for contact; a high level implies constant exchanges while working on a task. These imply different structural forms, as shown in Figure 12.7.

Pooled interdependence

Departments work relatively independently because the work does not flow between units. The branches of Pret A Manger or Lloyds TSB are examples of pooled interdependence. They draw on some common resources such as advertising and finance but have little need for day-to-day interaction with each other.

Sequential interdependence

The output of one department provides an input to the next. Departments depend on others to provide material or information of the right quality at the right time for them to begin working on their part of the task. The editorial departments of *The Financial Times* must complete their work before printing can begin; the drug development units at GlaxoSmithKline need to develop drugs before the clinical trials can begin.

Reciprocal interdependence

The degree of interaction here is most intense. The output of activity A is the input to activity B, and the output of B is an input back into A – and possibly into several others as well. Acute services in hospitals are an example, where a dangerously ill patient requires treatment from a range of services such as X-ray, surgery and blood transfusion. The output of each activity is uncertain when it begins, but affects what the others then need to do. The structure that hospital management creates will affect how smoothly or otherwise these activities fit together.

Structural implications

Pooled interdependence requires little day-to-day coordination, and what is required can be handled by standard procedures and guidelines to ensure that each branch offers the same service. Sequential interdependence is more challenging, and management supports this interdependence by creating planning and scheduling structures. They intend these to ensure that material or information passes from one unit to the next at the right time and in the right form. Reciprocal interdependence is the most difficult to coordinate, as little can be planned in advance. People need to be able and willing to work flexibly, using their initiative to respond to whatever inputs they receive. This implies relatively high degrees of autonomy, possibly with much teamworking and direct interpersonal contact. This is made easier if management places the units physically close to each other.

Organisations will usually combine these approaches – some departmental activities are pooled while others are reciprocal. Departments can work independently on many tasks, but need to work more closely on other tasks. Suppliers and customers may also be part of this interdependence, so structures need to be such that they provide relevant information to them. At GlaxoSmithKline the three phases of basic research, drug development and clinical trials are pooled – though in the case of an individual drug they will be sequential. At the point of handover between the stages there may be a great deal of reciprocal interdependence. The Centres of Excellence operate with a high degree of interdependence amongst the members of a team.

Size and life cycle

Size, as measured by the number of employees, affects the structure of organisations. Small organisations tend to be less formal with less division of labour – people take part in a wide range of tasks to get the work done. Weber (1947) noted that larger organisations tended to have more formal, bureaucratic structures. Research by the Aston group (Pugh and Hickson, 1976) showed that size of organisation was positively related to increasingly formal structures. Blau (1970) argued that size leads to more levels in the hierarchy, and more separate specialised units. In small organisations the necessary coordination between the parts can be achieved informally by face-to-face contact or direct supervision. Like the head of Multi-show Events (see Chapter 10), as managers divide a growing business into separate units, perhaps over a wide geographical area, they need to install more formal controls. These include detailed job descriptions, formal reporting relationships and tighter control systems.

This implies that organisations go through distinct stages in their life, with a structure suited to that stage.

Birth stage

The entrepreneur creates the business alone, or with a few partners or employees. They operate informally with little division of labour – tasks overlap. There are few rules or formal systems for planning and coordination. Decisions are made by the owner so in that sense they are a centralised form.

Youth stage

If the business survives and thrives it will probably need to raise more capital to finance growth. As at Lily O'Brien's (see the Management in Practice feature), Mary Ann O'Brien no longer has sole control, but shares decisions with members of the team she recruited as the business grew. Tasks become divided (such as by creating the positions of Design, Finance and Development Managers) as the work grows. Separate departments will be created, and controls will therefore become more formal to ensure coordination. Many small companies fail when they expand rapidly without imposing tight controls and systems for managing risks – as an executive of a publishing company which got into difficulties recalled:

> We were editors and designers running a large show, and we were completely overstretched. Our systems were simply not up to speed with our creative ambitions.

The growth of Lily O'Brien's www.lilyobriens.ie

Lily O'Brien's is a small Irish company run by Mary Ann O'Brien who began the business in her kitchen in 1992. She gained the idea for the handcrafted chocolate business quite by chance during a visit to South Africa, and when she returned to Ireland began experimenting with different recipes to see what worked:

> Initially, I just worked in the kitchen of our flat, and drove round delivering chocolate to our customers . . . I was the MD, operations manager, quality controller, production staff and Chief Taster, while my daughter Lily, to whom the company owes its name, was in charge of staff entertainment.

She took chocolate-making lessons in Belgium and Switzerland, developing the skills of a highly precise craft. In 1993 she borrowed £30,000 for her first 'industrial-scale' chocolate machinery and moved into a catering kitchen. Slowly a business started to emerge – but it was still being run as a cottage industry. Later, a friend from the meat industry invested in the business and encouraged her to stop thinking in kilos and to start thinking in tonnes. She soon won a contract from one of Ireland's supermarket chains – and now supplies retailers in Europe, America, Asia and Africa. The company now employs 150 people, and in 2004 moved into new premises in Co. Kildare.

She knew from the start that her skills were in sales – and that chocolate making is a scientific, complicated process. So as the business grew she hired the best food technologists, designers, production, operational, financial and development staff that she could find. Recalling a successful bid to win a contract to supply British Airways:

> I asked the team to come up with a range of beautiful contemporary designs for packaging, and our R&D department to come up with a range of 'dessert-like' sweets.

Source: *Financial Times*, 20 April 2004, and company website.

Midlife stage

If growth continues, it begins to resemble a formal bureaucracy. There is extensive division of responsibility and many formal rules to ensure coordination among the parts. There are more professional and specialist staff, performing support functions in areas such as finance and human resources. There are common systems for budgeting, financial control and rewards. This leads to the growth of stronger functional departments, which take over responsibility for their areas from top management.

Maturity stage

Here the organisation is large and mechanistic, with a strong vertical system and well-developed controls. There are rules and policies for most things, with large specialist staff carrying out defined tasks. More decisions are made at the centre – bringing the danger of slow response to new conditions. To overcome these barriers to innovation and to encourage cross-functional communication, managers may change the structure. One approach is to decentralise the organisation by creating separate divisions with profit responsibility – as Microsoft did in 2002 when it created seven business units with a relatively high degree of autonomy.

Microsoft's midlife crisis? www.microsoft.com

management in practice

Although still highly profitable, some observers are asking whether the world's second-largest company by market value is becoming too slow to act. Growth is slow, and Linux is challenging the core software business. The next version of the Windows operating system (code-named Longhorn) is not now expected until 2006, five years after the previous update – the longest ever gap between Windows updates. To meet even that date, the company is believed to be cutting back on some of the features originally planned.

The original businesses (Windows, Office and Server Software) are growing only at the rate of the overall software industry, while the new business areas (games, Internet applications, business software and mobile phones) are growing too slowly to give a major boost to revenues.

To encourage innovation, Chief Executive Steve Balmer divided the company into seven business units, each with profit and loss responsibility. But this independence is not complete – they are still expected to coordinate their activities and align with the core Windows strategy. One ex-manager commented:

> In the past, the system was optimized for people who could get things done. Now everybody is always preparing for a meeting.

Microsoft says these frustrations are just part of the growing pains of becoming a mature organisation. Balmer gives the new management system an A–:

> I know it's absolutely the right thing for the long-term health of the company.

Source: Reprinted from 19 April 2004 *Business Week* by special permission, Copyright © 2004 by the McGraw-Hill Companies, Inc.

Others, like Siemens, discard older, slow-growing businesses, or create new management boards to speed decision making. GlaxoSmithKline is another example of a mature company making radical changes to encourage innovation in research and development, and so increase the output of commercial products. As Christensen and Raynor (2003) point out, mature companies face daunting challenges in trying to meet investors' expectations of continued, profitable growth – and in most cases fail to meet those expectations.

Oticon – the case continues – return to innovation

CASE STUDY

The dramatic change in structure at Oticon was not achieved without pain. Kolind launched a direct attack on the established culture, on privileges tied to seniority and titles, and on work processes. In moving to an organisation in which there were only project members, project leaders and project owners, he knew that many would not easily accept losing the power they derived from controlling information. He used his power to drive the change, announcing: 'I am 100 per cent sure that we will try this. There's enough time so that you can make a choice – whether you are going to try it with us or whether . . . you find another job' (quoted in Rivard *et al.*, 2004, p. 174).

The Board of the firm also became concerned about profitability in the early years, as the new structure was creating so many initiatives and new products that it was difficult to manage them all effectively. They therefore appointed Neils Jacobsen as co-Chief Executive in 1992, to place more emphasis on financial discipline and performance. Jacobsen took over from Kolind as Chief Executive in 1998.

Source: Based on Rivard *et al.* (2004).

Moving through the life cycle

Organisations do not go through these stages in an orderly fashion – they move at their own pace, and the transition stages are not necessarily clear at the time. Some do not progress beyond the early stages, while for others the attempt to move from one to the next is a source of tension and disagreement. People who have been comfortable with the earlier stages may resent the increasing distance and formality that size often brings. 'Young' organisations that prematurely impose a 'mature' structure probably have the wrong structure, and their performance will suffer. Conversely, organisations that grow without putting in place appropriate controls and systems are also likely to suffer economically (as the publishing company example showed). In times of rapid external change and uncertainty, a major management challenge in large organisations is to create a structure that allows the organisation to recover the advantages of flexibility it once had, and which its younger competitors now have.

Growth and structure in a housing association

A manager in a housing association, which was created to provide affordable housing for those on low incomes, describes how its structure changed as it grew.

> Housing associations have to give tenants and their representatives the opportunity to influence policy. In the early days the association had few staff, no clear division of labour and few rules and procedures. It was successful in providing housing, which attracted more government funds, and the association grew. As more houses came into management this activity required an organisational structure to support it. The association no longer served a single community, but a number of separate geographical areas. Staff numbers grew significantly and specialised departments were created to provide specific and separate functions. The changes have led to concerns amongst both staff and committee that the organisation is no longer responsive to community needs and that it has become distant and bureaucratic.

Source: Private communication from the manager.

key ideas · Donaldson's integration of contingency approaches

Donaldson (2001) offers a model which integrates the several contingency approaches outlined in this section, arguing that they can be integrated by identifying two main contingencies. These are task and size, with the task contingency reflecting uncertainty and interdependence. In terms of the authors included in this section the relationship is:

Task uncertainty	Burns and Stalker (1961)
	Lawrence and Lorsch (1967)
	Woodward (1958)
Task interdependence	Lawrence and Lorsch (1967)
	Thompson (1967)
Size	Blau (1970)
	Pugh and Hickson (1976)

Source: Donaldson (2001), pp. 17–21, 29.

12.4　Organisations in transition

Warren Bennis predicted over three decades ago that since most organisations now face turbulent environments, mechanistic, bureaucratic structures would soon disappear:

> The social structure of organisations of the future will have some unique characteristics. The byword will be 'temporary'. There will be adaptive, rapidly changing temporary systems. There will be task forces organised around problems to be solved by groups of relative strangers with diverse professional skills. The group will be arranged on an organic rather than mechanical model; it will evolve in response to a problem rather than to programmed role expectations. The executive thus becomes co-ordinator or 'linking pin' between various task forces … As no catchy phrase comes to mind, I call these new style organisations adaptive structures. (Bennis, 1969, p. 34)

Writers continue to predict the demise of traditional forms, and their replacement by 'boundaryless' (Ashkenas, 1995), 'self-controlling' (Champy and Nohria, 1996), 'flexible' (Volberda, 1998) or 'individualized' (Ghoshal and Bartlett, 1998) forms. Such accounts often generalise from the experience of individual firms and may overstate the scale of change in the economy as a whole. New business forms do not suddenly replace existing ones, but coexist alongside them, as managers in each adapt to their perceptions of changing conditions.

The reason for the many changes in organisational form which are undoubtedly taking place is the accumulating and converging effects of the PESTEL factors introduced in Chapter 3. Political forces have encouraged the deregulation of protected industries and the removal of barriers to international trade. This increased competition encourages managers to seek more economical means of production – further adding to globalisation and to organisational changes to support this shift. Social and educational developments mean that many people seek different forms of working arrangement, with organisations needing to adapt their form to provide it. Rapid developments in information technologies enable not only new businesses to develop but also new forms for existing ones. Together these add up to a shift in many businesses from producing commodities to delivering services (Heydebrand, 1989).

While each developing organisation has unique characteristics, Fenton and Pettigrew (2000) found that three linked themes permeated research:

- The globalising firm and its changing boundaries – referring to the widespread tendency for companies operating globally to focus on a small number of core tasks, while outsourcing the remaining tasks to other firms. This in turn leads to internal changes to the organisation.
- The knowledge firm in the knowledge economy – recognising that competitive performance in many sectors no longer depends on good use of physical assets, but on the way in which highly mobile intellectual talent can be developed, motivated and retained. Such firms pay great attention to innovative ways of creating and using knowledge both within and beyond their boundaries.
- Networks and the socially embedded firm – which refers to the way in which firms increasingly deliver their goods and services by developing alliances, joint ventures and other forms of relationship with other businesses. They do so in the belief that this enables them to acquire access to relevant knowledge and information more quickly than if they were to build that capability themselves.

Pettigrew *et al.* (2003) led the major INNFORM research programme to map empirically the extent of these changes in organisations in Europe, Japan and the USA. They grouped the many individual forms of change under the 'headings of changing structures, changing processes and changing boundaries' (p. 11), each of which embodies three more specific forms of change – shown in Figure 12.8.

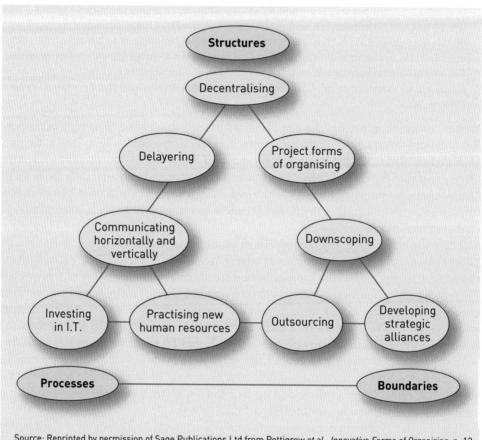

Figure 12.8

New forms of organising: the multiple indicators

Source: Reprinted by permission of Sage Publications Ltd from Pettigrew *et al.*, *Innovative Forms of Organizing*, p. 12 Copyright © Pettigrew *et al.* 2003.

Changing structures

Harsher competition has put traditional hierarchies under growing pressure, as their many layers are both expensive and inflexible. Many companies have sought to decentralise their structures, removing layers of management and giving more authority over both strategic and operational decisions to business units or cross-functional project teams. The trend is not all one way, as other managers have used the power of modern IT to enhance the degree of central control. The technology that makes it possible for managers to decentralise structures also enables them to centralise them. Mergers often lead to attempts to impose greater central control on the merged businesses, and modern information systems make such control possible. They can collect data as transactions occur in the most distant locations of the company, giving the centre greater insight into events and greater possibilities of tighter control.

This may be because, while the Internet reduces transaction costs of doing business in markets, 'it also reduces co-ordination costs within companies' (Carr, 2004, p. 12). It makes management itself more efficient, so that more activities can be conducted internally. Companies such as Wal-Mart and IBM use sophisticated IT systems to manage complex supply chains, by imposing rigid standards for processes, data and systems. Imposing these standards may be quicker and cheaper in many kinds of business than waiting for free markets to produce them.

A trend to centralise?

Research by the Institute for Personnel and Development shows that after years of decentralising control to individual business units and allowing them to operate almost as independent companies, many organisations are changing direction. They are taking personnel, finance and other specialist functions away from business units and national subsidiaries and setting up shared service centres for the whole organisation. Almost all organisations in the survey have responded to external pressures by creating a coherent product or service image. Based on telephone interviews with 153 chief executives from across UK industry, the survey also found that 85 per cent of organisations are providing more leadership direction from the centre, while a third are taking decision making away from divisional business units. The survey concluded that recentralisation is firmly on the agenda.

Source: *People Management*, 6 May 1999.

Changing processes

The flexibility and responsiveness required in many parts of the economy requires information to pass quickly both vertically and horizontally – i.e. between the different activities which make up an organisation's 'value chain' (see Chapter 8). Many organisations use IT to promote these changes, and support them with HRM practices that support cooperation between distinct units of the business. A smoother flow of information means, for example, that information about orders can be automatically transmitted through each stage of the chain, enabling a quicker and more efficient response to customers. That same information can also be used to update personnel, salary and financial information, again almost instantly. Many companies use Enterprise Resource Planning systems, which combine previously separate information systems into a single, consistent database for the whole company. These are notoriously difficult to implement, and many fail to meet expectations. The Management in Practice feature indicates a relatively successful example to indicate their potential links with organisation structure.

ERP at Elf Atochem

Elf Atochem North America is a chemicals subsidiary of the French company Elf Aquitaine. Following a series of mergers in the early 1990s, managers were hampered by the fragmentation of critical information systems among its 12 business units. Ordering systems were not integrated with production systems. Sales forecasts were not tied to budgeting systems or to performance measurement systems. Each unit was tracking and reporting its financial data independently. The many incompatible systems meant that operating data was not flowing smoothly through the organisation, and top management was not getting the information it needed to make sound and timely business decisions.

   The company's executives saw that an enterprise system would be the best way to integrate the data flows. Looking beyond the technology, the executives saw that the real source of Elf Atochem's difficulties was not the fragmentation of its systems but the fragmentation of its organisation.

Although the 12 business units shared many of the same customers, each unit was managed autonomously.

Management decided to focus on four processes: materials management, production planning, order management and financial reporting. These cross-unit processes were the ones most distorted by the fragmented organisational structure. Moreover, they had the greatest impact on the company's ability to manage its customer relationships in a way that would both enhance customer satisfaction and improve corporate profitability.

Elf Atochem also made fundamental changes to its structure. In the financial area, for example, all accounts receivable and credit departments were combined into one. This enabled the system to consolidate all of a customer's orders into a single account and issue a single invoice. It also allowed managers to monitor overall customer profitability – something that had been impossible to do when orders were fragmented across units.

Source: Based on Davenport (1998).

Clearly people can use IT to change the way they perform any of these functions, and Henry Lucas has put forward some radical ideas in this area (*see* Key Ideas).

key ideas Lucas and electronic design variables

Henry Lucas coined the phrase 'electronic design variables' to reflect the opportunities for structural change that information technology provides. He proposed that managers can now consider basing much more of their organisation on electronic means. Rather than start with the structure and ask how technology can support this, they may consider how objectives can best be served by electronic means, and then build a structure to support that.

'Electronic design variables', as Lucas calls them, such as networked computing and telecommunications systems, can be used to change structures by:

- Restructuring work so that parts can be outsourced to other companies, easily linked by electronic means.

- Automating information processes in the vertical hierarchy, thus removing layers of management and giving wider spans of control.

- Improving coordination of work by using electronic links of various kinds to ensure smoother flow within and between organisations.

Source: Lucas (1996).

Changing boundaries

A **strategic alliance** is an arrangement in which two firms agree to cooperate to achieve specific commercial objectives.

The third widespread form of change is when managers redraw the boundaries of their business by concentrating on their core competencies, contracting with other businesses to provide non-core functions. This implies that managers reduce the scope of the firm's activities, outsourcing many activities – often through a **strategic alliance**. Managers consider which parts of the value chain need to be performed within the firm, and which can be done by someone else.

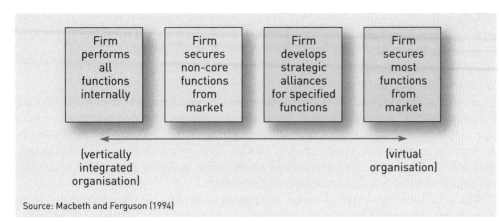

| Firm performs all functions internally | Firm secures non-core functions from market | Firm develops strategic alliances for specified functions | Firm secures most functions from market |

(vertically integrated organisation)

(virtual organisation)

Source: Macbeth and Ferguson (1994)

Figure 12.9

A continuum of inter-organisational relations

Transaction cost theory predicts that the choice will reflect the relative costs of the alternatives. Doing business in a market incurs some transaction costs quite apart from the purchase price of the item – such as evaluating potential vendors, agreeing terms, drawing up and monitoring contracts and evaluating supplier performance. If a company does the work itself, with its own staff, it avoids these costs – and so will expand to take in any activities that it can carry out more cheaply 'than the total of the market price for performing the activity plus the attendant transaction costs. More generally, companies will get bigger as external transaction costs increase and to shrink as they decrease' (Carr, 2004, p. 12).

One effect of the Internet is to reduce transaction costs, particularly those that relate to the cost of information. Companies can use the Internet to advise potential suppliers all over the world of their requirements, and invite competitive bids. Suppliers can equally make their presence known very cheaply. Many of the costs associated with creating and managing a business relationship are reduced by cheap and instant communications.

This implies (if correct) that companies will be less inclined to do things themselves, and more inclined to use the market. Many Western companies outsource some activities to companies in countries with significantly lower costs. Some deal with physical manufacturing processes or labour-intensive support processes like Human Resource Management.

Outsourcing examples – HRM and BMWs

management in practice

Since 1999 several large firms such as BT, BP and BAE Systems have outsourced the human resources (HR) function to external providers on long-term contracts. These deals are made feasible by IT systems which automate HR processes such as administering benefits, payroll, recruitment and training. Specialised companies develop highly automated processes which they run for many companies from a single location, at very low cost.

In 2003 *Business Week* reported that the new BMW X3 compact sports utility model to be released in January 2004 was engineered and produced by the Austrian auto supplier Magna Steyr. To monitor the changeover BMW dedicated a team of just 30 engineers to monitor development engineering, processes and production. Magna's engineers trained for four weeks at BMW plants and research centres, immersing themselves in BMW's culture and products. The company adapted its information systems to fit with BMW's, to handle the orders for these custom-built cars.

Source: (BMW) *Business Week*, 8 December 2003.

Others depend on the Internet to carry the core communication systems of the business – such as telephone contact or software development centres in south-east Asia. Companies like Wipro Technologies, Tata Consultancy and Infosys have encouraged many Western, especially US, technology companies to take advantage of skilled, relatively low-cost staff in India.

A more radical prospect is that the process of outsourcing goes beyond a traditional company buying more functions in the market, towards a situation where a company consists largely of agreements with other organisations. They use the power of the Internet to identify outside expertise to provide the services they need in (say) design, manufacture, testing or distribution and restrict their in-house activities to a very few core skills which give a distinct competitive advantage.

Virtual organisations are those that deliver goods and services but have few, if any, of the physical features of conventional businesses.

The Internet offers a radical means of creating such networked organisations. Some predict that the work of temporary companies can be coordinated with little or no central direction and control – though brokers, venture capital firms, suppliers and contractors could all play a role. Industries would then begin to resemble the 'Hollywood model' of film production, in which teams of specialists come together to create a product, and then disperse once it is complete. This is sometimes referred to as the '**virtual organisation**,' though often this is just a new term for an old practice: most organisations have some degree of physical separation within their value chain – see the Key Ideas feature.

---

key ideas — The process of becoming virtual

Venkatraman and Henderson (1998) propose that the virtual organisation is not so much a state as a process. Organisations differ in the degree to which they are 'virtual', rather than either being so or not. Venkatraman and Henderson suggest that virtualness is a characteristic of any organisation, based on its position along three vectors – customer interaction, asset configuration and knowledge leverage. This idea allows us to consider how IT developments enable managers to physically separate some organisational activities:

- **Customer interaction** Here consider how IT makes it easier for customers to experience products and services remotely and perhaps engage in some dynamic customisation.
- **Asset configuration** Here the focus is on the extent to which a firm coordinates resources and activities within a network: it does not depend only on assets that it physically controls.
- **Knowledge leverage** This means gaining access to wider sources of expertise, including that in other organisations.

In all these respects organisations can be to a greater or lesser extent virtual, measured by the number and importance of cross-boundary transactions. The authors argue that moving along the spectrum needs a new set of management skills, as opposed to when most assets are within the organisation.

Complementary changes

Complementarities Practices are said to be complementary when doing more of one increases the returns from doing more of another.

Several studies of organisational performance (Milgrom and Roberts, 1990; Miles and Snow, 1994; Whittington *et al.*, 1999) have drawn attention to the benefits of complementary changes. This is similar to contingency theory in that it shows that performance depends on the fit between key organisational variables (such as having an organic structure in a volatile environment). The idea of **complementarities** goes further in proposing that 'high-performing organizations are likely to be combining a number of practices at the same time and that the payoffs … are greater than the sum of the parts'

(Pettigrew *et al.*, 2003, p. 17). As Whittington *et al.* (1999) observed, higher-performing European firms achieved 'whole system' change: 'the ... benefits of ... new organisational practices depend on the context of other changes in which they are set, and are especially strong when combined within comprehensive organisational change' (p. 598).

Conclusions of the INNFORM programme

key ideas

The INNFORM project studied the extent to which companies in Europe, Japan and the United States had made the changes shown in Figure 12.9 between 1992 and 1997. Their main conclusions were that in this period:

● There was strong evidence of change, with delayering, decentralised structures and project-based organisation

● There were considerable process changes, especially in developing closer horizontal and vertical links, and investment in IT

● There were significant increases in outsourcing activities and in forming alliances

● While many organisations are changing structures, these are supplementing, not replacing, older forms – 'The new is emerging alongside and within the old, rather than replacing the old' (Pettigrew *et al.*, 2003, p. 32).

Source: Pettigrew *et al.* (2003).

Activity 12.3   Critical reflection on change

Compare recent changes in your organisation with the model in Figure 12.8.

● What changes in structure have there been?

● What changes in process?

● What changes in boundaries?

● To what extent have the various changes complemented each other (such as a change in structure being accompanied by a supporting change in HR practice)?

12.5   Contingencies or management choice?

The contingency approach

The ideas discussed in Section 12.3 are collectively referred to as the **contingency approach** to organisation structure. This says that the most effective structure will depend (be contingent) upon the situation in which the organisation is operating:

> The organization is seen as existing in an environment that shapes its strategy, technology, size and innovation rate. These contingent factors in turn determine the required structure; that is, the structure that the organization needs to adopt if it is to operate effectively. The effectiveness of the organization is affected by the fit between the organizational structure and the contingencies. This leads the organization to adapt its organization structure so that it moves into fit with the contingency factors. In this way organizational structure is determined by the contingencies. (Donaldson, 1996, p. 2)

Contingency approaches to organisational structure are based on the idea that performance depends on having a structure that is appropriate to the environment.

Hence contingency theorists take the view that successful organisations adopt a structure which is right for their strategy and for the environment in which they are working. Effective management involves formulating an appropriate strategy and developing a structure which supports that strategy by encouraging appropriate behaviour. The emphasis is **determinist** (the form is determined by the environment) and functionalist (the form is intended to serve organisational effectiveness) (Donaldson, 1995).

The appropriate form develops incrementally as management observes some misfit in its present arrangements. It makes what it hopes will be appropriate adjustments in aspects of the structure – altering the degree of, say, formalisation by introducing some new procedures or rules as the company grows, as happened at Lily O'Brien's. Others, like GSK, introduce greater divisional autonomy to encourage creativity or responsiveness to local conditions.

> **Determinism** is the view that an organisation's structure is determined by its environment.

Management choice

The contingency approach has become the mainstream theory attempting to explain the shape of organisations, and it has obvious practical implications. However, it has been criticised on several grounds by writers such as Child (1972, 1984). He argues that the determinism of contingency theory has been overstated and that contingency theorists ignore the degree of **structural choice** which managers have. The process of organisational design is not only a technical, rational matter but one shaped by political processes. These political considerations (reflecting the values and interests of influential groups) are able to influence the structure that emerges for these reasons:

> **Structural choice** approaches emphasise the scope management has for deciding the form of structure, irrespective of external conditions.

- The standards of performance against which organisational performance is assessed are not always rigorous. Some degree of under-performance caused by an inappropriate structure may be tolerated if there is sufficient 'slack' within the system.
- There is evidence that a degree of choice is available between different modes of organisation without serious diseconomies being incurred. So managers can choose from the available range, in view of their own or their staff's preferences, rather than be required to adopt the form implied by contingency theory for their environment.
- To the extent that political interests are pursued in organisational life, structures will reflect the interests of politically powerful groups within the organisation. They will try to secure organisational structures that protect or advance their positions. This approach rejects the functionalism of contingency approaches.

Overall, writers of this view argue that contingency theory reduces managers almost to automatons, or puppets, able to exercise little influence on their own actions. In practice, they argue, managers do have choice over the structure they design. The contrasting ways in which leading grocery companies have used the Internet seem to support that view.

 **Retailers' response to the Internet**

The Internet makes it possible for supermarket chains to create a website on which customers can order their shopping, which the company then delivers to their home. Sainsbury's responded by creating a new division to handle this business, with a separate management structure, warehouses and distribution system. Tesco chose to integrate its Internet shopping business with existing stores – staff pick the customer's Internet order from the shelves of a conventional store. Other chains, such as Somerfield and Morrison's, do not (in 2005) offer an online service. So while the technology is available to all, only some have chosen to use it and they manage it with different structures.

Those favouring a contingency approach reject these criticisms. They concede that managers exercise choice, but argue that this choice is constrained by the need to adapt the structure to ensure acceptable performance:

> As an organization grows it must bureaucratize and structurally differentiate. Similarly as an organization diversifies it must adopt a more decentralized structure, shifting from functional to multi-divisional. Organizations are under pressure to perform from several sources: from competitors, from stakeholders such as owners and employees, and from the aspirations of their own managers. Therefore organizations will seek to avoid the performance loss that comes from retaining structures that are in misfit with the contingencies. [They] will move from misfit into fit by adopting the structure which fits. There will typically be one particular structure, or a narrow band of structural alternatives, out of all the various conceivable types of structure. Hence the discretion exercised will be severely limited. (Donaldson, 1996, p. 51)

This implies that while managers go through the motions of choosing, the direction they can follow is substantially set. Nevertheless their role remains significant. It includes, for example, interpreting the contingencies correctly, selecting a form of structure appropriate for those contingencies, implementing it and continuing to adapt it. They add value by choosing and implementing a structure which will be effective in those circumstances.

Activity 12.4 Critical reflection – contingency or choice?

Recall some significant changes in the structure of your organisation.
- Try to establish the reasons for them, and whether they had the intended effects.
- Do those reasons tend to support the contingency or management choice perspectives?

Case questions 12.3

- Does the Oticon example support contingency or management choice approaches?
- Does the role of management in the company support either of these approaches?

12.6 Alternative forms of economic organisation

This book examines economic activity which is organised within capitalist forms of enterprise (of any size) or through established public bodies. These 'conventional' forms of organisation provide almost all of the world's traded goods, and employ most people in transforming resources into outputs which others value. They are not the only way to conduct productive activity and this section presents examples of these alternative forms. While some of the management challenges are similar to those people face in conventional businesses, others are different.

Consumers' or workers' cooperatives

A cooperative is a business that is wholly or substantially owned and controlled by those who work in it – they run it for their benefit and that of other members (as in retail cooperatives). A well-known early example is provided by textile workers in Rochdale, England, in the 1840s, who created a cooperative to supply food and other daily requirements. They set out some principles which are still common to most cooperatives:

- Open, voluntary membership
- Democratic control
- Limited return, if any, on equity capital
- Surplus belongs to users/owners
- Education matters – the co-op should educate people in cooperative principles
- Cooperation with other cooperatives.

Interest in setting up and working in cooperatives is intermittent: trade unions and socialist political parties give them little practical encouragement. Some public bodies support them as a way of providing local services in remote areas, and some communities, especially in deprived areas, have created them as means of providing both services and employment. Most remain very small, providing local services requiring little capital investment such as catering, printing, wholefoods and bookshops.

The Mondragon Cooperative in Spain www.mondragon.mcc.es

In 1956, inspired by a young priest, workers in the Basque region of Spain established a cooperative enterprise, initially making domestic heaters. The venture has flourished (though at times has suffered severe problems when the wider economy has been weak) and is now the world's largest workers' cooperative. At the end of 2003 the business included 218 companies in three business groups – Finance, Industrial and Distribution. It is the seventh largest group in Spain by sales value (10bn euros in 2003) and employs 68,000 people. The original industrial group expanded rapidly, as did a retail venture which now operates widely throughout Spain.

The original regional grouping of cooperatives was restructured in 1990 into a divisional model based on products – Finance, Distribution and Industrial. The latter has seven business areas within it such as Automotive, Components, and Household Goods. The Bank (Caja Laboral) was initially conceived as a way of channelling the public's savings into the cooperatives, enabling them to grow.

The Mondragon mission combines the basic objectives of a business organisation competing in international markets with the use of democratic organisation, job creation, promotion of its workers in human and professional terms and developing the social environment. The workers elect the directors, and they are accountable to an annual general assembly of all workers. The governing council (equivalent to the Board in conventional organisations) is also elected by the workers.

Source: Company website.

Profit sharing and share ownership schemes

Profit sharing schemes enable employees to share some of the risks and rewards of enterprise by taking some of their income in a form that depends on company profits. There is a potential incentive effect, if employees can see how their activities contribute to profits, in which they will share.

Share ownership means that employers acquire a share of the assets of the firm. The purpose of this approach is to enable workers to develop a sense of belonging in the company, by owning a share of it. Employees in Asda (a UK retailer owned by Wal-Mart) can put money into a savings scheme and receive a share of company profits in proportion to their savings. In 2004 some 3.5 million people in the UK belonged to such schemes, which the government encourages through tax incentives.

The evidence of the effects of such schemes on productivity and profitability is mixed. Keef (1998), for example, found that employee ownership did not result in the expected changes in employee attitudes – probably because the stake held by an individual in relation to the total capital of the firm is very small. Opportunities to participate in decision making were found to be more important than equity ownership as such in raising commitment and satisfaction (Pendleton *et al.*, 1998).

The open source movement

The familiar story of the way the Linux software system developed illustrates a new approach to organisation structure (Markus *et al.*, 2000). Linus Torvalds, who developed the initial version, made it available on the Internet, and invited other software developers to download it freely, and then to test and modify it. It gradually attracted enthusiastic software developers, until the Linux community involved thousands of developers around the world, all sharing their work. Within a few years this informal group, working through the Internet, has created a highly successful piece of software that many corporate IT departments use.

The community (and other 'open source' communities) have evolved mechanisms and processes to ensure order, despite the potential for chaos. These include:

- High intrinsic motivation and self-management amongst developers, ensuring they deliver high-quality work and appropriate social behaviour. Receiving payment for contributing to a software project is important, but so also is the development and maintenance of reputation.
- Membership is fluid, but managed. Development teams typically have a core community, with additional members brought in for particular tasks.
- Control is exercised through a few simple rules, designed to ensure appropriate conduct and fair play.
- Self-governance is achieved formally through discussion and voting amongst community members, and informally through social control by other members.

Enthusiasts of the open source movement reject the model of organisation represented by Microsoft, which they see as a technologically closed world in which one company develops and controls access to the product. The open source movement has spread far beyond Linux to embrace a wide range of software programs that run on corporate computer systems and networks. Microsoft itself recognised the challenge in a memo to staff in June 2003:

> Non-commercial software products in general, and Linux in particular, present a competitive challenge for us and for our entire industry, and they require our concentrated focus and attention. (*Financial Times*, 18 June 2003, p. 15)

Although these examples are from different contexts, they share a common theme of being attempts to resolve some of the seemingly paradoxical aspects of managing a value-adding enterprise in democratic societies, especially the balances between:

- efficiency and democracy
- economic and social concerns
- equality and hierarchy
- identifying with an experimental model and cooperating with other business models.

Summary

1 Explain why managers regularly change the structure of their organisation:

- Structure helps to influence behaviour by the way it divides and coordinates tasks (e.g. by encouraging focus on a particular task or group of customers) and through the operating mechanisms of selection and rewards.

2 Compare the features of mechanistic and organic structures:

- Mechanistic – people perform specialised tasks, hierarchical structure of control, knowledge located at top of hierarchy, vertical communication, loyalty and obedience valued.
- Organic – people contribute experience to common tasks, network structure of contacts, knowledge widely spread, horizontal communication, commitment to task goals more important than to superiors.

3 Describe the 'contingencies' believed to influence managers' choice between mechanistic and organic forms:

- Strategy, environment, technology, interdependence, age and size.

4 Summarise the work of Woodward, Burns and Stalker, Lawrence and Lorsch, and John Child, showing how they contributed to this area of management theory:

- Woodward: appropriate structure depends on the type of production system ('technology') – unit, small batch, process.
- Burns and Stalker: appropriate structure depends on uncertainty of the organisation's environment – mechanistic in stable, organic in unstable.
- Lawrence and Lorsch: units within an organisation face different environmental demands, which implies that there will be both mechanistic and organic forms within the same organisation, raising new problems of coordination.
- John Child: contingency theory implies too great a degree of determinism – managers have greater degree of choice over structure than contingency theories implied.

5 Outline empirical research on current patterns of change in the structures, processes and boundaries of organisations:

- The INNFORM project studied the extent to which companies in Europe, Japan and the United States had changed their structures during the 1990s. The main conclusions were that there was more decentralised and project-based organisation, closer horizontal and vertical links, investment in IT and more outsourcing and alliances.
- These new forms are supplementing, not replacing, older forms.

6 Contrast contingency and structural choice perspectives on structure:

- Contingency theories stress that performance depends on managers developing a structure that is suited to their environment. However, John Child observed that:
  - the standards against which organisational performance is assessed are not always rigorous, and some degree of under-performance caused by an inappropriate structure may be tolerated;
  - some choice is available between different modes of organisation without incurring serious diseconomies;
  - structures will reflect the interests of politically powerful groups within the organisation, who will secure a form that protects their position.

7 Describe some alternative ways of organising economic activity and compare them with conventional structures:

- These include cooperatives, profit-sharing and share ownership schemes, the open-source movement for software design, and radically managed businesses like Semco.

Review questions

1 How does the structure of an organisation support or hinder its strategy?

2 Explain the difference between a mechanistic and an organic form of organisation.

3 Give an example to illustrate each of the factors that influence management's choice between mechanistic and organic structures.

4 What is meant by the term 'a contingency approach'?

5 If contingency approaches stress the influence of external factors on organisational structures, what is the role of management in designing organisational structures?

6 What is the main criticism of the contingency approaches to organisation structure?

7 What do you understand by the term 'virtual organisation', and what is the contribution of Venkatraman and Henderson to our understanding of the term?

8 What did the INNFORM project show to be the main characteristics of organisational change during the 1990s?

9 How does the open source movement attract people to contribute to software development projects?

Concluding critical reflection

Think about the changing structure of your company, or one with which you are familiar. Review the material in the chapter, and perhaps visit some of the websites identified. Then make notes on these questions:

- What examples of the themes discussed in this chapter are currently relevant to your company? Do you have a mainly mechanistic or mainly organic structure? Which of the themes of organisational change have you experienced in your organisation?

- If the business seems too mechanistic or too organic, why is that? What assumptions appear to have shaped managers' approach? In what ways does the recent evolution of your structure support the contingency or managerial choice perspectives?

- What assumptions about the most important contextual contingencies seem to shape your approach to organising? Do you agree that account has been taken of the most influential contingencies? If not, what other factors may have shaped the decisions?

- Have managers considered whether the present structure is right for the business? Do they regularly compare your structure with that in other compannies? How do they do it?

Further reading

Woodward, J. (1965), *Industrial Organization: Theory and practice*, Oxford University Press, Oxford. Second edition 1980.

Burns, T. and Stalker, G.M. (1961), *The Management of Innovation*, Tavistock, London.

Lawrence, P. and Lorsch, J.W. (1967), *Organization and Environment*, Harvard Business School Press, Boston, MA.

> The research by these writers who initiated the contingency approaches to organisation was published almost 40 years ago. They are short and accessible accounts of the research process, and it would add to your understanding to read at least one of them in the original. The second edition of Woodward's book (1980) is even more useful, as it includes a commentary on her work by two later scholars.

Christensen, C.M. and Raynor, M.E. (2003), *The Innovator's Solution*, Harvard Business School Press, Boston, MA.

> Absorbing analysis of the dilemmas managers face in creating the disruption needed to enable growth in mature companies. A major work from a leading researcher on developing organisations.

Donaldson, L. (2001), *The Contingency Theory of Organizations*, Sage, London.

> A comprehensive and up-to-date account by one of the leading scholars of contingency theory. Outlines the underlying principles of the theory and the controversies surrounding it, as well as offering valuable guidance on emerging research possibilities.

Ostroff, F. (1999), *The Horizontal Organisation: What the organisation of the future looks like*, Oxford University Press, Oxford.

Ashkenas, R. (1995), *The Boundaryless Organisation: Breaking the chains of organisation structure*, Jossey-Bass, San Francisco.

> These two books recount how some organisations (mainly GE in the Ashkenas book) have attempted radical new forms of structure.

Steinbock, D. (2001), *The Nokia Revolution: The story of an extraordinary company that transformed an industry*, McGraw-Hill, London.

> Excellent account of the evolution of Nokia, its evolving strategy, and how it has adapted the structure to support that.

Rivard, S., Bennoit, A.A., Patry, M., Pare, G. and Smith, H.A. (2004), *Information Technology and Organizational Transformation*, Elsevier/Butterworth-Heinemann, Oxford.

> As well as being the source of some information on the Oticon case, this book includes other examples of the way in which information technology is enabling managers to develop new forms of organisation. A coherent theoretical structure makes the book a useful addition to this area.

Galbraith, J.R. (2002), *Designing Organisations: An executive guide to strategy, structure and process*, Jossey-Bass, San Francisco.

> A practical guide to managing some of the issues covered in the chapters, with useful diagnostic instruments.

Whittington, R. and Mayer, M. (2002), *Organising for Success in the Twenty-First Century*, Chartered Institute of Personnel and Development, London.

> This preliminary report from a major research project into the capabilities which help organisations to change provides a valuable overview of the topic.

Hamm, S. (2005), Linux Inc., *Business Week*, 31 January 2005, pp. 50–7.

> A detailed insight into the way the Linux community is developing, and the insight it offers into the potential of new forms of organising.

Weblinks

These websites have appeared in the chapter:

www.oticon.com

www.philips.com

www.gsk.com

www.lilyobriens.ie

www.microsoft.com

www.mondragon.mcc.es

Visit two of the business sites in the list, and navigate to the pages dealing with corporate news, investor relations or 'our company'.

● What kind of environment are they likely to be working in, and how may that affect their structure?

● Is there evidence on the site (perhaps on the news pages) of changes to the company structure? Does it indicate possible contingencies to explain the change, or may it reflect the 'structural choice' perspective?

Annotated weblinks, multiple choice questions and other useful resources can be found on
www.pearsoned.co.uk/boddy

Aim

To outline theories of change in organisations and show how these relate to practice.

Objectives

By the end of your work on this chapter you should be able to outline the concepts below in your own terms and:

1 Assess whether change is a continual rather than an episodic part of managing
2 Explain the meaning of organisational change and give examples
3 Explain the interaction between change and context, and the implications
4 Compare life cycle, emergent, participative and political theories of change
5 Use a technique to identify the most potentially difficult aspects of a change
6 Evaluate systematically the possible sources of resistance to change
7 Compare the relative roles of front-stage performance and back-stage activity in managing change, and the contribution of individual skills and formal structures
8 Explain the meaning of organisational development, its values and techniques.

Key terms

This chapter introduces the following ideas:

external context
perceived performance gap
performance imperatives
internal context
organisational change
interaction model
receptive contexts
non-receptive contexts
life cycle

emergent perspective
participative perspective
political perspective
counterimplementation
organisation development
sensitivity training
process consultation
survey feedback

Each is a term defined within the text, as well as in the glossary at the end of the book.

Vodafone/Ericsson   www.vodafone.com, www.ericsson.com

In 2004 Vodafone offered mobile services to subscribers in 28 countries and was the world's largest mobile network operator, with about one quarter of the market. Ericsson was the world's largest supplier of mobile network infrastructure, and Vodafone its largest customer. Vodafone has achieved its strong market position partly by internal growth and by acquiring other operators – such as AirTouch (USA) in 1998 and Mannesmann (Germany) in 2000. Many of these acquisitions also had shareholdings in other mobile operators, meaning that in some countries Vodafone operates through partially rather than wholly owned subsidiaries.

As demand for mobile services grew, Vodafone extended the network on a country-by-country basis, with local management teams running the business. They usually ordered network equipment from Ericsson, negotiating terms with Ericsson staff in that country. Although Vodafone's in-country managers communicated with their counterparts in other countries, Vodafone did not attempt to coordinate the way they operated. Ericsson operated in a more centralised fashion, though with some scope for local managers to establish terms of business that reflected their market or competitive environment.

This had the following consequences:

- Terms and conditions for purchasing network equipment varied between countries
- Communication between the two companies in each country was direct, through meetings, telephones, letters, fax and email
- Communication about Ericsson products between Vodafone operators in different countries was ad-hoc
- Sharing of product information between Ericsson and Vodafone was in-country, mainly through written documents
- Ordering and order tracking was done by local systems in each country
- Configuration of network equipment varied between countries, as did service and support arrangements.

In early 1998, before the merger with AirTouch, Vodafone management had begun to assess what synergies they may be able to gain from the merger, especially over the supply of network equipment. They expected to make big savings if they could aggregate their worldwide requirements for network equipment, and source this from common global suppliers. The later acquisition of Mannesmann increased the scope for synergy – and claims about the potential savings in this area were made to shareholders and the financial markets.

© Vodafone

Vodafone therefore began a project with Ericsson to develop new ways of managing the relationship. The intention was to find ways of aggregating Vodafone's global requirements so that the companies would manage their relationship in a unified way. They realised that managing a change of this scale would raise difficult issues about:

- the degree of planning to undertake
- the scale and value of the synergies from a new global relationship
- the attitudes of those managing Vodafone operations in the various countries
- the resources which would be needed to manage the change.

Source: Based on material from Ibbott and O'Keefe (2004).

Case questions

- How may the structure of Vodafone's in-country operations affect the project?
- Will a new global relationship mean a more centralised or a more decentralised company?
- Should the two companies put significant resources into planning the change in advance?

13.1 Introduction

The manager whom Vodafone appointed to manage this significant change faces a problem that is familiar to many managers. The chief executive has put him in charge of implementing a major change that the board has decided on. Many people will be affected, and some may be uneasy about how the change will affect them. The change from a country to a global structure will have major implications for the way they run the business in their country, and change the relationship they have with their main equipment supplier.

Managers initiate or experience change so regularly that in many organisations change is seen as the normal state of affairs, interrupted by occasional periods of relative stability. In the most innovative areas of the economy some senior managers see one of their primary tasks as being to challenge current practices, hoping in that way to foster a climate of exploration and innovation. They want people to see change as the norm – merely one further intervention in a continuing flow of events, rather than something which will be followed by a return to normal stability. At BP, for example, the challenge to successive senior managers has been that of continuing to transform the business from a relatively small (for that industry), diversified business into the second-largest oil company in the world. Mergers, such as that between Chrysler (US) and Daimler (Germany), usually bring with them the need to make major internal changes. Small businesses make radical changes too – as when Hindle Power, an engineering company with 30 employees, faced the loss of a valuable distribution contract unless it changed the way it worked. It embarked on a radical programme of change that returned the company to profit, and grew the business (*People Management*, 3 February 2000, p. 52).

The external environment described in Chapter 3 is the main source of change. Political, economic, social and technical developments change what people expect of a business – which can then persuade its managers to change the way they operate to meet these new expectations. Research by the Institute of Personnel and Development (IPD) into 151 large organisations found that the major reasons for organisational changes were a need to create closer customer relations, significant financial pressure to improve performance, or intensifying competition (IPD, 1999). Anecdotal evidence is that while most managers accept the need for change, many are critical of the way their organisations introduce it. Managers still experience great difficulty in implementing major organisational changes successfully.

This chapter presents theories about the nature of change in organisations. It begins by explaining current external pressures for change, and how these prompt internal change to one or more elements of the organisation. The chapter then outlines a model that shows how change depends on the interaction between the external and internal environments of the organisation. It then presents four complementary perspectives on how people try to manage that interaction, each with different management implications. Further sections deal with diagnosing the characteristics of a change, managing resistance, skills and structures, and Organisation Development.

TQM and BPR

key ideas

Though Total Quality Management (TQM) appears to be central to the success of Japanese companies, the experience of Western companies has been that it is difficult to introduce and sustain. Indeed, one of the founders of the TQM movement, Philip Crosby (1979), claimed that over 90 per cent of TQM initiatives fail. Though a 90 per cent failure rate seems incredibly high, studies of the adoption of TQM by companies in the UK and other European countries show that they too have experienced a similarly high failure rate – perhaps as much as 80 per cent. (Economist Intelligence Unit, 1992)

Business process re-engineering (BPR) has been hailed as 'the biggest business innovation in the 1990s' (Mill, 1994, p. 26). Wastell *et al.* (1994, p. 23) concluded from the available evidence that 'BPR initiatives have typically achieved much less than promised'. Other studies have come to similar conclusions (Coombs and Hull, 1994).

Therefore even well-established change initiatives, for which a great deal of information, advice and assistance is available, are no guarantee of success.

Source: Burnes (1996), pp. 172–3.

Activity 13.1   Recording a major change

From discussion with colleagues or managers, identify a major attempt at change in an organisation. Make notes on the following questions and use them as a point of reference throughout the chapter.

- What was the change?
- Why did management introduce it?
- What were the objectives?
- How did management plan and implement it?
- How well did it meet the objectives?
- What lessons have those involved taken from the experience?

13.2   Initiating change

Chapter 1 introduced the idea that managers work within a context that shapes what they do, and which they may also change. This chapter explains the interactive nature of that process, and Figure 13.1 illustrates the themes it will cover. A particular episode of change begins when enough people perceive a gap between desired and actual performance – usually because the internal context of the organisation is unable to meet the external demands upon it. Using their implicit or explicit theory of change, they initiate a project to change one or more aspects of the internal context in the hope of closing the performance gap. The outcomes of the change effort will be affected by practical issues of design and implementation – but whatever the outcomes they will in turn affect the subsequent shape of the external and internal contexts, providing the starting point for future changes.

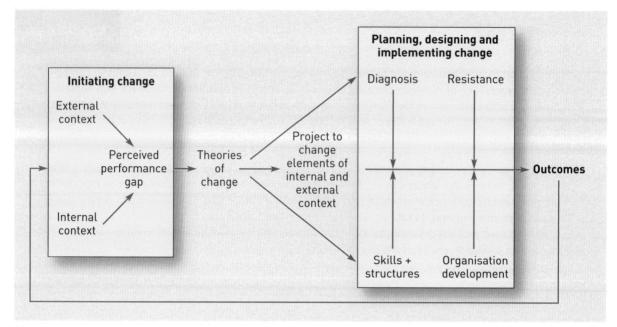

Figure 13.1 A model of the change process

The external context

The **external context** consists of elements beyond the organisation such as competitors, or the wider PESTEL factors.

Chapter 3 described the **external context** of business and Chapter 12 showed how these contexts place new demands on organisations. Foremost amongst these are the spread of globalisation and rapid development of information and communication technologies. Together with deregulation and the privatisation of former state businesses, these are transforming the competitive landscape in which firms operate. They face competition from unexpected quarters, threatening their prosperity or even their survival. Managers at British Airways and KLM have had to respond to the pressure of new competition from low-cost airlines such as Ryanair and easyJet. Established banks face competition from new entrants such as retailers (Sainsbury's) or conglomerates (Virgin) offering financial services. The growth of the Internet has enabled companies offering high-value/low-weight products to open new distribution channels and invade previously protected markets.

Major change at Siemens www.siemens.com

In 2001 the Siemens division that makes car parts was in poor shape, having lost almost €260m in the previous financial year. A senior manager said:

> We realized we had to set ourselves more demanding goals . . . We had to do more to increase our commercial performance in an economic environment that was becoming more difficult.

Siemens' first task was to set up a new global structure for the division, based on 15 product groups – such as dashboard electronics. The job of heading each group was given to a manager who would look for growth opportunities and run their operations as though they were mid-sized businesses. They were also given cost-cutting targets in six main categories, such as materials, production, and administration.

One aspect of the change programme is a quarterly conference of the top managers from each product group. At these meetings a team of 20 internal auditors present the managers with charts recording their performance on 15 variables, such as product quality, and how well they have introduced ideas agreed at previous meetings. A director commented:

> The review is very open. It's a bit like seeing where each part of the business is on a football league table. If you are close to the bottom, there's no hiding from it. People don't like it if they come out badly in the scoring system, but it's a challenge for them to try to improve.

FT

Source: *Financial Times*, August 19 2003.

These forces have collectively meant a great shift of economic power from producers to consumers, many of whom now enjoy greatly enhanced quality, choice and value. This implies that managers wishing to retain customers need continually to seek new ways of adding value to the resources they use, if they are to retain or extend their position in the market against new or existing competitors. Unless they act they will experience a dangerously widening performance gap.

Perceived performance gap

A **perceived performance gap** arises when people believe that the actual performance of a unit or business is out of line with the level they desire. If those responsible for transforming resources into outputs do so in a way that falls below what customers expect, there is a performance gap. Cumulatively this will lead to other performance gaps emerging – such as revenue from sales being below the level needed to secure further resources. If uncorrected this would eventually cause the business to fail.

In the current business climate, two aspects of performance dominate discussion – what Prastacos *et al.* (2002) call '**performance imperatives**': the need for flexibility and the need for innovation. In a very uncertain business world the scope for long-term planning is seriously limited. Successful businesses are likely to be those that develop a high degree of strategic and organisational flexibility, while also (Volberda, 1997) maintaining efficient and stable processes. This apparent paradox (of combining flexibility and stability) reflects the fact that while companies need to respond rapidly they also need to respond efficiently. This usually depends on having developed a degree of stability and predictability in the way they transform resources into goods and services.

The other imperative identified by Prastacos *et al.* (2002) is innovation – 'the ability to generate a variety of successful new products or services (embedding technological innovation), and to continuously innovate in all aspects of the business' (p. 58). In many areas of business, customers expect a constant flow of new products, embodying the latest scientific and technological developments: companies which fail to meet these expectations will experience a performance gap. Delivering, say, an advanced mobile phone to the market depends not only on the quality of the applied research which goes into a better screen display, but also on being able to turn that research into a practically useful object, and to produce and distribute enough devices at a price which is attractive to customers. Meeting performance expectations depends on the organisation – the **internal context** of management.

A **perceived performance gap** arises when people believe that the actual performance of a unit or business is out of line with the level they desire.

Performance imperatives are aspects of performance which are especially important for an organisation to do well, such as flexibility and innovation.

The **internal context** consists of elements within the organisation such as its technology, structure or business processes.

The internal context

Chapter 1 introduced the internal context (Figure 1.3, repeated here as Figure 13.2) as the set of elements within an organisation that shape behaviour. Change begins to happen when sufficient influential people believe, for example, that outdated technology or a confusing structure is causing a performance gap – by inhibiting flexibility or innovation. They notice external or internal events and interpret them as being a threat to the performance that influential stakeholders expect. This interpretation, and their implicit theory of change, encourages them to propose a change to one or more aspects of the organisation, shown in Figure 13.2.

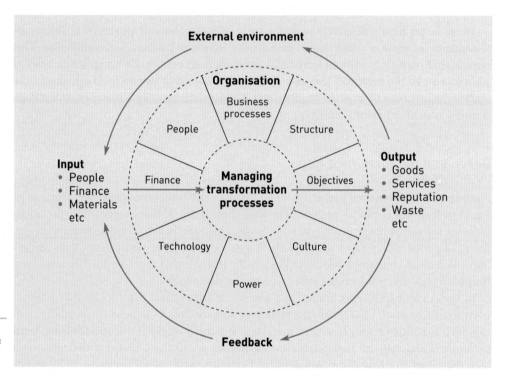

Figure 13.2

Elements of the internal context of management

They then have to persuade enough other people that the matter is serious enough to earn a place on the management agenda. People in some organisations are open to proposals for change, others tend to ignore them – BP faced new competitive pressures throughout the 1980s, but it was only around 1990 that sufficient senior people took the threats seriously enough to initiate a period of rapid change.

People initiate organisational change for reasons other than a conscious awareness of a performance gap – fashion, empire-building or a powerful player's personal whim can all play a part. Employees or trade unions can propose changes in the way things are done to improve working conditions. The need for change is a subjective matter – what some see as urgent others will leave until later. People can affect that process by managing external information – magnifying customer complaints to make the case for change, or minimising them if they wish to avoid change.

Whatever the underlying motivations, **organisational change** is an attempt to change one or more of the elements shown in Figure 13.2. Table 13.1 illustrates specific types of change that people initiate under each element, including some which appear elsewhere in this book.

Organisational change is a deliberate attempt to improve organisational performance by changing one or more aspects of the organisation, such as its technology, structure or business processes.

Table 13.1

Examples of
change in each
element of the
organisation

Element	Example of change to this element
Objectives	Developing a new product or service
	Changing the overall mission or direction
	Oticon's new strategic objectives as a service business (Chapter 12 case)
Technology	Building a new factory
	Creating a website on the Internet
	The Student Loan Company implementing a new computer system (Chapter 20 case)
Business processes	Improving the way maintenance and repair services are delivered
	Redesigning systems to handle the flow of cash and funds
	Benetton's new system for passing goods to retailers (Chapter 19 case)
Financial resources	A set of changes, such as closing a facility, to reduce costs
	New financial reporting requirements to ensure consistency
	The Royal Bank of Scotland reducing costs after the NatWest merger (Part 4 case)
Structure	Reallocating functions and responsibilities between departments
	Redesigning work to increase empowerment
	Vodafone/Ericsson moving to a global structure (Chapter 13 case)
People	Designing a training programme to enhance skills
	Changing the tasks of staff to offer a new service
	Changes at the Benefits Agency to encourage staff to be more innovative (Chapter 15 case)
Culture	Unifying the culture between two or more merged businesses
	Encouraging greater emphasis on quality and reliability
	GSK creating a more entrepreneurial research culture (Chapter 12)
Power	An empowerment programme giving greater authority to junior staff
	Centralising decisions to increase the control of HQ over operations

It is rare for any significant change to consist of only one of these elements. The systemic nature of organisations means that a change in any of these areas is likely to have implications for others. When Tesco introduced its Internet shopping service alongside its established retail business the company needed to create a website (technology). In addition, managers needed to decide issues of structure and people (would it be part of the existing store business or a separate business unit with its own premises and staff?) and about business processes (how exactly would an order on the website be converted to a box of groceries delivered to the customer's door?). They had to manage these ripples initiated by the main decision. Managers who ignore these consequential changes achieve less than they expected.

Once they have perceived a need for change, those promoting it then use their implicit or explicit theory of change (Sections 13.3 and 13.4) to set up a formal or informal change process, which they then implement (Sections 13.5–13.8) in the relevant organisational unit. How well people manage the steps in this process determines the effect on the performance gap, which in turn feeds back to the context of the organisation.

Case questions 13.1

Identify the possible ripple effects that may need to be managed in the Vodafone/Ericsson change, using the elements in Figure 13.2 as a guide. Start by entering the move to a global relationship in the structure area. Then think of the possible implications that this change could have for other elements. These begin to form the management agenda for this project. Which of these are likely to cause most difficulty?

13.3 The interaction of context and change

How managers implement change depends on their theory about the nature of organisational change. This section presents an 'interaction model', describing the way a change interacts with its context. The next section outlines four complementary perspectives on managing that interaction.

The interaction model is a theory of change which stresses the continuing interaction between the internal and external contexts of an organisation, making the outcomes of change hard to predict.

People introduce change to alter the context

Management attempts to change elements of its context to encourage behaviours that support its objectives (this is, to close the performance gap). Vodafone wanted to change the context within which it worked with Ericsson. By moving from country relationships with Ericsson to a more unified global structure, management hoped to create a structure which enabled people in both companies to reduce the cost to Vodafone of expanding the network. When Tesco introduced online shopping, management needed (at least) to change technology, structure, people and business processes to enable staff to deliver the new service. When people plan and implement a change they are creating new 'rules' (Walsham, 1993) that they hope will guide the behaviour of people involved in the activity.

People do not necessarily accept the new arrangements without question, or without adapting them in some way. They may themselves make further changes to the context. As people begin to work in new circumstances – with a new technology or a new structure – they make small adjustments to the original plan. As they use a new information system or website they decide which aspects to ignore, use or adapt.

As people become used to working with the new system their behaviours become routine and taken for granted. They become part of the context that staff have created informally. These new contextual elements may add to, or replace, the context that those formally responsible for planning the change created. These informally created aspects of the context may or may not support the original intentions of those who initiated the project. The interaction between people and context continues into the future.

Sun Microsystems and a supplier

Boddy *et al.* (2000) studied Sun Microsystems and one of their suppliers as they moved towards a more cooperative supply chain relationship. Managers in both companies introduced changes to the context of work – technology, processes and roles. These were designed to create a context that encouraged more cooperation, and closer interpersonal links, between people in the two companies. For example, the supplier's sales coordinator:

> There is a close relationship with my opposite number in Sun. We speak several times a day, and he tries to give me as much information as he possibly can.

Sun staff echoed this:

> What makes them different is that you're talking to them daily . . . The relationships are a bit different – it is a bit closer than an ordinary supplier where you don't have that bond. Dealings are more direct. People are becoming more open with each other.

Both groups came to appreciate the other's requirements and tried to make things easier for them. Sun staff learned about the supplier, and vice versa. Both spoke of 'harmonising expectations'.

Source: Boddy *et al.* (2000).

The context affects the ability to change

While the project aims to change the context, elements in the context itself will help or hinder that attempt. All of the elements of Figure 13.2 will be present as the project begins, and some of these will influence how people react to the proposal. Managers who occupy influential positions in an existing structure will review a proposal to change it from the perspective of their careers, as well as of the organisation. At Tesco the existing technology (stores, distribution systems, information systems) and business processes would influence managers' decisions about how to implement the Internet shopping strategy.

The prevailing culture (Chapter 10) – the shared values, ideals and beliefs that hold a unit together – has a strong influence on how people view a change. Cultures develop as members work together to deal with problems, and in so doing develop shared assumptions about the external world and their internal processes. As firms grow, subcultures develop within them. Members are likely to welcome a project that they believe fits the culture or subculture. They are likely to resist one that conflicts with or challenges the culture.

Culture and change at a European bank

While teaching a course to managers at a European bank, the author invited members to identify which of the four cultural types identified in Chapter 10 best described their unit within the bank. They were then asked to describe the reaction of these units to an Internet banking venture that the company was introducing.

Course members observed that colleagues in a unit which had an internal process culture (routine back-office data-processing) were hostile to the Internet venture. They appeared to be 'stuck with their own systems', which were so large and interlinked that any change was threatening. Staff in new business areas of the company (open systems) were much more positive, seeing the Internet as a way towards new business opportunities.

Source: Data collected by the author.

The prevailing culture is a powerful influence on the success or failure of innovation. Some support and encourage change: a manager in Sun Microsystems commented on the culture within that successful and fast-moving business:

Receptive contexts are those where features of the organisation (such as culture or technology) appear likely to help change.

Non-receptive contexts are those where the combined effects of features of the organisation (such as culture or technology) appear likely to hinder change.

A very dynamic organisation, it's incredibly fast and the change thing is just a constant that you live with. They really promote flexibility and adaptability in their employees. Change is just a constant, there's change happening all of the time and people have become very acclimatised to that, it's part of the job. The attitude to change, certainly within the organisation, is very positive at the moment.

At Sun (and many other companies) the culture encourages change. At other organisations the culture encourages people to resist change, or at least be cautious towards it. Such cultures, especially the deeper values and beliefs, have a force and momentum that reflects fundamental assumptions about the nature of people, the organisation and the environment. These values and beliefs are hard to change, and yet are a crucial factor in determining the organisation's response to change. 'Managers learn to be guided by these beliefs because they have worked successfully in the past' (Lorsch, 1986, p. 97).

key ideas Receptive and non-receptive contexts

Pettigrew *et al.* (1992) sought to explain why managers in some organisations were able to introduce change successfully, while others in the same sector (the UK National Health Service) found it very hard to move away from established practices. Their comparative research programme identified the influence of context on ability to change: **receptive contexts** are those where features of the context 'seem to be favourably associated with forward movement. On the other hand, in **non-receptive contexts** there is a configuration of features which may be associated with blocks on change' (p. 268).

Their research identified eight such contextual factors, which provide a linked set of conditions that are likely to provide the energy around change. These are:

● Quality and coherence of policy
● Availability of key people leading change
● Long-term environmental pressure – intensity and scale
● A supportive organisational culture
● Effective managerial–clinical relations
● Cooperative interorganisational networks
● The fit between the district's change agenda and its locale.

While some of these factors are specific to the health sector, they can easily be adapted to other settings. Together these factors give a widely applicable model of how the context affects ability to change.

Source: Pettigrew *et al.* (1992).

The distribution of power also affects receptiveness to change. Change threatens the status quo, and is likely to be resisted by stakeholders who benefit from the prevailing arrangements. Innovation depends on those behind the change developing political will and expertise that they can only attempt within the prevailing pattern of power.

The context has a history, and several levels

The present context is the result of past decisions, and is usually focused on one of several 'levels' of context. Both features influence the process of change. Management seeks to implement change against a background of previous events. Past decisions shaped the organisation context as it is today, and its ability to change. As a manager introducing a change observed:

> There are so many changes taking place, they are more or less numb, and this is simply another change which they are just going to have to take on board. The result is that they are somewhat passive and neutral, and when I ask what their requirements might be, the response is usually 'you tell me'. (Boddy, 2002, p. 38)

The promoter of a major project in a multinational also experienced the effects of history, as he tried to raise enthusiasm amongst his colleagues:

> They were a little sceptical and wary of whether it was actually going to enhance our processes. Major pan-European redesign work had been attempted in the past and had failed miserably. The solutions had not been appropriate and had not been accepted by the divisions. Europe-wide programmes therefore had a bad name. (Boddy, 2002, p. 38)

Beliefs about the future also affect how people react to a proposal. Optimists are more receptive and open to change than those who feel threatened and vulnerable.

Vodafone/Ericsson – the case continues   CASE STUDY

Vodafone conducted business in each country in partnership with other operators, with Vodafone often having a minority shareholding in the company. For example, in the UK it owned 100 per cent of the equity, in Germany 99 per cent and in Australia 91 per cent. In the Netherlands, Portugal and Spain this fell to 70, 50 and 22 per cent respectively.

This meant that 'considerable political skill and discussion was required to handle the attitudes of the various operating companies with regard to Ericsson's local in-country operations. Some countries had acquired very favourable terms and conditions that would not necessarily be matched by the global agreements, while others had key skills that would now be "given up" to the global effort.'

Source: Ibbott and O'Keefe (2004), p. 226.

The context represented by Figure 13.2 occurs at several levels of the organisation – such as operating, divisional and corporate. People at any of these levels will be acting to make changes in their context – which may help or hinder the manager of a particular change. For example, a project at one level will often depend on decisions at other levels about the resources available. The manager leading a refinery team experienced this:

> One of the main drawbacks was that commissioning staff could have been supplemented by skilled professionals from within the company, but this was denied to me as project manager. This threw a heavy strain and responsibility on myself and my assistant. It put me in a position of high stress, as I knew that the future of the company rested upon the successful outcome of this project. One disappointment (and, I believe, a significant factor in the project) was that just before commissioning, the manager of the pilot plant development team was transferred to another job. He had been promised to me at the project inception, and I had designed him into the working operation. (Boddy, 2002, pp. 38–39).

Acting to change an element at one level will have effects at this and other levels, and elements may change independently. The manager's job is to create a coherent context that encourages desired behaviour, by using their preferred model of change.

Activity 13.2 Critical reflection on reactions to context

- What aspects of the contemporary context, shown in Figure 13.2, have had most effect on a project you are familiar with?
- How have historical factors affected people's reactions?
- Were the effects positive or negative for the project?
- To what extent is the context receptive or non-receptive to change?

Case questions 13.2

- How may the existing context of Vodafone and Ericsson affect how in-country managers react to the proposed change?
- How may that affect the way the project leader manages the change?

13.4 Four perspectives on change

There are four complementary perspectives on change, each with different implications for managers. These are the life cycle, emergent, participative and political perspectives.

Life cycle perspective

> **Life cycle** models of change are those that view change as an activity which follows a logical, orderly sequence of activities that can be planned in advance.

Much of the advice given to those responsible for managing projects uses the idea of the project **life cycle**. Projects go through successive stages, and results depend on conducting the project through these stages in an orderly and controlled way. The labels vary, but major themes are:

1 Define objectives
2 Allocate responsibilities
3 Fix deadlines and milestones
4 Set budgets
5 Monitor and control.

This approach (sometimes called a 'rational–linear' approach) reflects the idea that a change can be broken down into smaller tasks, and that these can be done in some preferred, if overlapping, sequence. It predicts that people can make reasonably accurate estimates of the time it will take to complete each task and when it will be feasible to start work on later ones. People can use tools such as bar charts (sometimes called Gantt charts after the American industrial engineer Henry Gantt who worked with Frederick Taylor), to show all the tasks required for a project, and their likely duration. These help to visualise the work required and to plan the likely sequence of events – as illustrated in Figure 13.3.

Task	Week ending																	
	January			February				March					April				May		
	11	18	25	1	8	15	22	1	8	15	22	29	5	12	19	26	3	10	17
Find site	███	██	██	██	██	██	██	██	██										
Acquire site											██	██	██	██					
Gain planning permission															██	██			
Begin construction																		██	

Figure 13.3 **A simple bar chart**

In the life cycle model successfully managing a project depends on specifying these elements at the start and then monitoring them tightly to ensure the project stays on target. Ineffective implementation is due to managers failing to do this. For example, Lock (2003), in his authoritative and highly regarded text on project management, identifies the 'key stages' of a manufacturing project, shown in Figure 13.4. He advises project managers to ensure that the stages are passed through in turn, 'until the project arrives

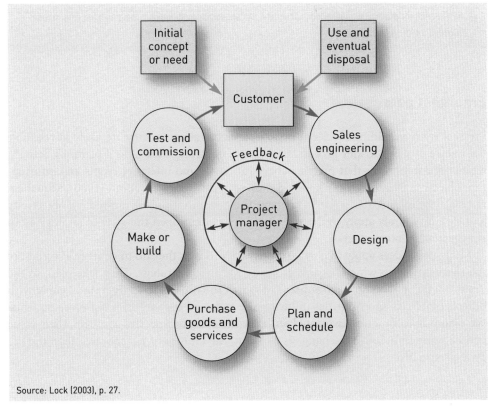

Source: Lock (2003), p. 27.

Figure 13.4
A project life cycle

415

back to the customer as a completed work package'. Emphasising the iterative, cyclical nature of the method, he writes that 'Clockwise rotation around the cycle only reveals the main stream. Within this flow many small tributaries, cross-currents and even whirlpools are generated before the project is finished' (p. 26).

Many books on project management, such as Woodward (1997) and Lock (2003), present advice on tools and techniques for each stage of the life cycle. Those advising on changes to information systems usually take a similar approach, recommending a variety of 'system development life cycle' approaches (see, for example, Chaffey, 2003). For some projects, and for some parts of other projects, the project life cycle approach gives valuable guidance to those introducing change. It is not necessarily a sufficient approach in itself and those managing change may need to use additional methods. One difficulty is that people may not be able to specify the end point of the change at the start – or the subtasks that will lead to that result. Many changes have uncertain outcomes that cannot be planned in detail but which emerge as the change unfolds.

Activity 13.3   Critical reflection on the project life cycle

You may be able to gain some insight into the project life cycle by using it on a practical task. For example:

- If you have a piece of work to do that is connected with your studies, such as an assignment or project, sketch out the steps to be followed by adapting Figure 13.4; alternatively do the same for some domestic, social or management project.

- If you work in an organisation, try to find examples of projects which use this approach, and ask those involved when the method is most useful, and when least useful.

- Make notes summarising how the life cycle approach helps, and when it is most likely to be useful.

Emergent perspective

Projects are the building blocks of organisational strategy, so they are likely to resemble the nature of that broader process. Early views of strategy saw it as a planning activity, based on assumptions that people behave rationally and interpret events and information objectively. However, as Chapter 8 showed, writers such as Quinn (1980), Mintzberg (1994a, 1994b) and Stacey (1994) believe these assumptions of rationality, objectivity and certainty rarely apply in the real world. They developed the view of strategy as an *emergent* or adaptive process.

Emergent models of change emphasise that in uncertain conditions a project will be affected by unknown factors, and that planning has little effect on the outcome.

Mintzberg's ideas apply to change projects as much as they do to strategy. Projects are the means through which organisations deliver broad strategy. They take place in the same volatile, uncertain environment in which the organisation operates. People with different interests and priorities influence the ends and the means of a project. So while the planning techniques associated with the life cycle perspective can help, their value will be more limited if the change is closer to the emergent perspective than the life cycle perspective.

Vodafone/Ericsson – the case continues

The globalisation strategy was developed and implemented through the Global Supply Chain Management (GSCM) forum which first met in 1999. Initially it was attended by representatives from both companies in those countries where Vodafone had a majority shareholding in the local operating company, though membership gradually expanded to include most countries in which Vodafone operated. The initial meeting resolved that all joint activities should be conducted in an open and transparent way.

It would be a process of learning through experience; there would be no requirement to produce plans that formed a rigid basis of change control. (Ibbott and O'Keefe, 2004, p. 224).

The members believed that a planned project approach would not have worked, as it was important to be able to cope with rapid change.

Both the end point and direction were uncertain, and fundamental process changes had to be agreed within and between companies. The acquisition of Mannesmann of Germany, unplanned at the start of the transformation, provided an opportunity for further benefits (p. 229).

The forum also recognised that the two sides would benefit in different ways, but there was no attempt to plan how to share the benefits – either party would retain whatever benefits they secured. Vodafone's equity-based structure in the different countries meant that those leading the project had to sell the concept of the global endeavour to the management teams of each entity. Ericsson's more unified structure of wholly owned subsidiaries gave them less scope for resisting proposals.

GSCM meetings set up several work streams that would move the relationship towards global collaboration. The leadership of each work stream was assigned to one or other of the participating countries. The teams leading them had to secure resources for the project from within their country operations, working as they saw fit. Examples of work streams were:

- Creating a global price book for all products bought from Ericsson (UK team)
- Agreeing a standard base station design (UK team)
- Agreeing a common procedure for software design and testing (Australia)
- Developing a computer-based information system linking the parties for information sharing – initially called Groupware (The Netherlands).

While the groupware project was at first intended to support communications between the teams working on the globalisation project, it later evolved into a system through which both parties conducted routine transactions – such as ordering products. The simple communication system emerged, without any formal plan, into a system for handling all orders from Vodafone to Ericsson that had a global price.

Source: Ibbott and O'Keefe (2004).

Boddy *et al.* (2000) show how this emergent process occurred when Sun Microsystems began the partnering project described earlier. Sun's initial intention from the partnership was to secure a UK source for the bulky plastic enclosures that contain their products, while the supplier was seeking ways to widen the customer base. There were few discussions about a long-term plan. As Sun became more confident of their supplier's ability the work became more complex. Initially they only supplied the plastic enclosure, into which Sun fitted components such as cables and power supplies. The supplier later took on this work, delivering a more valuable product. They also began to supply Sun's US factory as well as that in the United Kingdom, and have taken more responsibility for managing inventory.

Both have gained from this emerging relationship. They acknowledge that in 1991 they did not foresee the amount and type of business they would eventually be undertaking. A sales coordinator:

It's something we've learnt by being with Sun – we didn't imagine that at the time. Also at the time we wouldn't have imagined we would be dealing with America the way we do now – it was far beyond our thoughts. (Boddy *et al.*, 2000, p. 1010)

Mintzberg's point is that managers should not expect rigid adherence to 'the plan'. Some departure from it is inevitable, due to unforeseeable changes in the external environment, the emergence of new opportunities, and other unanticipated events. A flexible approach to change is one which recognises that 'the real world inevitably involves some thinking ahead of time as well as some adaptation en route' (Mintzberg, 1994a, p. 24).

Case questions 13.3

● Were those leading the change taking a life cycle or an emergent view?

● Which of those views does the evidence of later events seem to support?

Participative perspective

The **participative perspective** is the belief that if people are able to take part in planning a change, they will be more willing to accept and implement the change.

The **participative perspective** is a familiar theme in the management literature. The term indicates feelings of personal involvement in, and contribution to, events and outcomes. The underlying belief is that if people can say 'I helped to build this', they will be more willing to live and work with it, whatever it is. Many texts offer advice on how to involve employees in implementing change effectively. This applies to the 'quality of working life' movement of the 1960s and 1970s, to the 'quality circle' movement of the 1970s and 1980s and to 'high involvement management' practices (Lawler, 1986).

---

key ideas **Enid Mumford's Ethics approach to participation**

A well-known example of the participative approach in the field of systems design is Mumford and Weir's (1979) Ethics approach, summarised in Figure 20.7. Here the key ingredients include user involvement in system development, recognising the social issues in implementation and using sociotechnical principles to redesign work. Several other methodologies are available for involving users in the system design process, for understanding users' needs more effectively and for giving them wider influence in design decisions that will affect their work.

 **Staff participation in planning the CGU merger**

One of the UK's biggest mergers in 1998 was that of Commercial Union and General Accident to form CGU. The merger involved many changes throughout the new organisation, and management decided to involve employees very widely in planning the change, mainly through three large meetings of hundreds of staff at all levels, nominated by their colleagues:

1 Two hundred staff conducted a culture survey of the two companies. They were paired, one from each company, and escorted each other into the other's company, where they used a set format to build a culture map – how the firms were similar and how they were different.

2 Five hundred managers and technical specialists attended a two-day conference to work in teams on the results of the Discovery programme and other survey data. Their task was to form a view about what would make CGU Insurance the best place to work for its employees. Video cameras captured the action and displayed it overhead on giant television screens around the hall, giving the two days the feel of a vibrant sporting event. Amongst the priorities the delegates agreed were clear boundaries of authority, the freedom to take decisions within those boundaries, clear expectations, feedback, access to opportunity, and support for development.

3 Eighty people attended a four-day structured design workshop. Their task was to start designing a new organisation to meet the needs of shareholders, customers, employees and business partners. They produced a design that included principles of access (such as ensuring all brokers would have easy entrance to their new offices), size of business units (30 to 50 people), and size of teams (between 10 and 12).

Tony Clarry commented:

> The roll-out in the 51 locations so far has been smooth, which we attribute to the degree of commitment to the integration teams and to the conscientiousness of our people. Of course, there has been pain ... but involving people in decision making continues to be at the heart of what we do. We believe our approach has proved the value of real consultation.

Source: Based on an article by Tony Clarry, who led the integration of the two companies, in *People Management*, 2 September 1999.

While the approach is consistent with democratic values, it is not free. It takes time and effort, and may raise unrealistic expectations. There are circumstances in which it may be inappropriate or unworkable, such as where any of the following apply:

- There is already full agreement on how to proceed
- The scope for change is limited, because of decisions made elsewhere
- Those taking part in the exercise have little knowledge of the topic
- Decisions are needed urgently to meet deadlines set elsewhere
- Management has decided what to do and will do so whatever views people express
- There is fundamental disagreement and inflexible opposition to a change.

Participative approaches assume that a sensitive approach by reasonable people will result in the willing acceptance and implementation of change. For some changes that is the case, and a participative approach will help people to manage the change successfully. Other situations contain issues or conflicts that participation alone cannot solve.

Activity 13.4   Critical reflection on participation

Have you been involved in, or affected by, a change in your work or studies?

If so:

- What evidence was there that those managing the change agreed with the participative approach?
- In what way, if any, were you able to participate?
- How did that affect your reaction to the change?

If not:

- Identify three advantages and three disadvantages for the project manager in adopting a participative approach.
- Suggest how managers should decide when to use the approach.

Political perspective

The perspectives described so far offer little guidance where a change challenges established interests, or where powerful players have opposing views. Whipp *et al.* (1988) argue that change often involves several actors, representing different levels and sections of the organisation. They will probably be pulling in different directions, in the pursuit of personal as well as organisational goals:

> Strategic processes of change are now more widely accepted as multi-level activities and not just as the province of a . . . single general manager. Outcomes of decisions are no longer assumed to be a product of rational . . . debates but are also shaped by the interests and commitments of individuals and groups, forces of bureaucratic momentum, and the manipulation of the structural context around decisions and changes. (p. 51)

The **political perspective** reflects the view that organisations are made up of groups with separate interests, goals and values, and that these affect how they respond to change.

Several sociological analyses of organisational change emphasise a **political perspective** on change (Pettigrew, 1985, 1987; Pfeffer, 1992a; Pinto, 1998; Buchanan and Badham, 1999). Pettigrew (1985) was an early advocate of the view that decisions on strategic change combine political as well as rational factors. In Pettigrew's view change is a complex mix of seemingly rational assessment mixed with differential perceptions and quests for power. People who bring about successful change spend time creating a climate in which people accept the change as legitimate – often by manipulating apparently rational data about the business context to build support for their ideas.

---

key ideas **Tom Burns on politics and language**

Tom Burns (1961) observed that political behaviour in the organisation is invariably concealed or made acceptable by subtle shifts in the language that people use:

Normally, either side in any conflict called political by observers claims to speak in the interests of the corporation as a whole. In fact, the only recognised, indeed feasible, way of advancing political interests is to present them in terms of improved welfare or efficiency, as contributing to the organisation's capacity to meet its task and to prosper. In managerial and academic, as in other legislatures, both sides to any debate claim to speak in the interests of the community as a whole; this is the only permissible mode of expression. (p. 260)

Pfeffer (1992a) also argues that power is essential to get things done in organisations. His point is that decisions in themselves change nothing. It is only when someone implements them that anyone notices a difference. He proposes that projects require more than people able to solve technical problems. Projects frequently threaten the status quo: people who have done well in the past are likely to resist them. Innovators need to ensure the project is on the agenda, and that senior managers support and resource it. Innovators need to develop a political will, and to build and use their power.

Many observers now stress the importance of power and political behaviour for those managing change. Buchanan and Badham (1999) consider why political behaviour occurs, and conclude that:

Henry Kissinger on politics in politics

In another work Pfeffer (1992b) quotes Henry Kissinger:

Before I served as a consultant to Kennedy, I had believed, like most academics, that the process of decision-making was largely intellectual and all one had to do was to walk into the President's office and convince him of the correctness of one's view. This perspective I soon realised is as dangerously immature as it is widely held. (p. 31)

Its roots lie in personal ambition, in organisation structures that create roles and departments which compete with each other, and in major decisions that cannot be resolved by reason and logic alone but which rely on the values and preferences of the key actors involved.

Power politics and change are inextricably linked. Change creates uncertainty and ambiguity. People wonder how their jobs will change, how their workload will be affected, how their relationships with colleagues will be damaged or enhanced. Change in one organisational dimension can have knock-on or 'ripple' effects in other areas. As organisations become more complex, the ripple effects become harder to anticipate. (p. 11)

Reasonable people are likely to disagree about means and ends, and to fight for what they believe to be the appropriate line of action.

Politics and change in the public sector

These views of change as a fluid process find support in a contemporary account of project management in the public sector, based on research amongst a group of managers implementing major change projects:

The powerful influence of the political process on organisational and cultural change is transparent for local authorities, but this may also be relevant in other non-elected organisations. Competing values and interests between different stakeholders are often less overt but none the less powerful factors championing or blocking processes of change.

Source: Hartley *et al.* (1997) p. 71.

This implies that successful project managers will be those who understand that their job consists of more than being technically competent, and who are able and willing to engage in political actions.

The political perspective recognises the messy realities of organisational life. Major changes will be technically complex and will often challenge established interests. These will pull in different directions and pursue personal as well as organisational goals. The practical implication of this is that political tensions are likely to arise in projects where people disagree about ends and means, and where resources are scarce. Managers will need political skills as well as those implied by rational or participative models of change.

In politically charged situations those managing change need to be sensitive to the power and influence of key individuals in the organisation, and to how the change

Political action in hospital re-engineering

A major hospital responded to a persistent performance gap (especially unacceptably long waiting times for certain treatments) by 're-engineering' the way patients moved through and between the different clinical areas. This included creating multi-functional teams responsible for all aspects of the flow of the patient through a clinic, rather than dealing with narrow functional tasks. The pro-gramme was successful, but was also controversial. One of those leading the change recalled:

> I don't like to use the word manipulate, but ... you do need to manipulate people. It's about playing the game. I remember being accosted by a very cross consultant who had heard something about one of the changes and he really wasn't very happy with it. And it was about how am I going to deal with this now? And it is about being able to think quickly. So I put it over to him in a way that he then accepted, and he was quite happy with. And it wasn't a lie and it wasn't totally the truth. But he was happy with it and it has gone on.

Source: Buchanan (2001), p. 13.

will alter the pattern of influence. They will need to be able to negotiate and sell ideas to indifferent or sceptical colleagues. They may have to filter information to change perceptions, and do things that make the change seem legitimate within the organisation.

Pensco

Pensco was a medium-sized life insurance business. Changes to pensions legislation brought new opportunities in the market for personal and group pensions, and also brought more competition. The industry changed and so did the company. A new general manager arrived, who immediately began to move the organisation vigorously in the direction of a market-led, sales-maximising approach. He recruited a colleague from his previous company as head of information systems (IS), who had a repu-tation as an autocratic and aggressive manager. The changes to the pensions products depended on changing the information systems to process the new business.

In response to new legislation managers began developing new pensions products. The initial pro-posals came from the Actuarial Department (AD). Staff in sales and marketing (S&M) were dismissive of the AD proposals and had a different interpretation of market requirements. They actively lobbied for their view. S&M also believed that the IS Department had 'too much power in the organisation ... We are working to change that. S&M should drive the organisation ... But I can't get away from the view that IS still dictate what the company can and can't do' (Knights and Murray, 1994, p. 187).

For their part, IS had trouble finding out what the business requirements were – partly because of unresolved conflicts between AD and S&M over the product range. In part also the head of IS was seen to be keen to gain favour with the general manager. He did so by appearing to accept all requests for systems developments – which they were unable to deliver.

The company maintained the public position and despite the many difficulties the project was suc-cessful. The authors of the case reported different views from the clerical staff who were processing new proposals (without adequate IS support). As a team leader commented: 'They [the managers] don't have a grasp of what's going on. They just want the figures. They don't appreciate our problems. I wish they'd acknowledge there is one' (p. 162).

Source: Based on Knights and Murray (1994).

These perspectives (life cycle, emergent, participative and political) are complementary in that successful large-scale change, such as that at Vodafone/Ericsson, is likely to require elements of each. Each perspective can be linked to management practice, as illustrated in Table 13.2.

Table 13.2 Perspectives on change and examples of management practice

Perspective	Themes	Example of management practices
Life cycle	Rational, linear, single agreed aim, technical focus	Measurable objectives; planning and control devices such as Gantt charts and critical path analysis
Emergent	Objectives change as learning occurs during the project, and new possibilities appear	Open to new ideas about scope and direction, and willing to add new resources if needed
Participative	Ownership, commitment, shared goals, people focus	Inviting ideas and comments on proposals, ensuring agreement before action, seeking consensus
Political	Oppositional, influence, conflicting goals, power focus	Building allies and coalitions, securing support from powerful players, managing information

13.5 Diagnosing the characteristics of a change

When implementing a specific organisational change the management task depends on the unique features of that process. Research into a variety of changes has indicated the factors that make a change more or less difficult to manage, and this section outlines these.

Driving and restraining forces

Lewin (1947) observed that any social system is in a state of temporary equilibrium. Driving forces are trying to change the situation in directions that they favour. Restraining forces push the other way to prevent change, or to move it in another direction. This equilibrium 'can be changed either by adding forces in the desired direction, or by diminishing the opposing forces' (p. 26). Figure 13.5 illustrates the idea.

Driving forces encourage change from the present position. They encourage people and groups to give up past practice and to act in ways that support the change. They take many forms – such as a newly available technology, an inadequate business process or the support of a powerful player. Conversely factors such as the already-installed technology, shortage of finance, the opposition of powerful players or the company culture can be restraining forces. In many small companies, managers are said to be so absorbed in day-to-day matters that they are unable to put time and energy into major changes that would help the business to grow. They become committed to maintaining existing practice.

Those advocating a change can, in Lewin's terms, 'add forces in the desired direction' by stressing the advantages of the change, emphasising the threat from competitors or making the benefits seem more attractive. Mr Yun Jong-yon, chief executive of Samsung

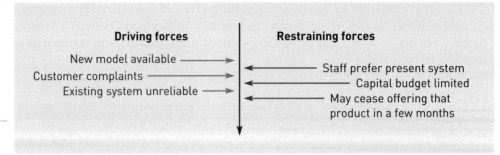

Figure 13.5

Driving and restraining forces

Electronics, was credited with transforming the company from a struggling producer of cheap electronics into one of the world's best-performing and most respected IT companies. He explained part of his approach:

> I'm the chaos-maker. I have tried to encourage a sense of crisis to drive change. We instilled in management a sense that we could go bankrupt any day. (*Financial Times*, 13 March 2003, p. 15)

Alternatively they can seek to 'diminish the opposing forces' by showing that the problems will not be as great as people fear, or pointing out that difficulties will be temporary.

Lewin observed that while increasing the driving forces could produce change in the desired direction, it could also increase tension amongst those 'forced' to change. The change may then be short-lived, or offset by the negative effects of the tension. Since these secondary effects may go against the interests of those promoting change, he suggested that trying to reduce the forces restraining change is usually the wiser route.

External events can trigger and drive change: new competition, a change in legislation, the activities of a pressure group, a chance conversation. Information from any of these sources can trigger change. People with sufficient power can use these and countless other external signs to justify a proposal.

The power of the visual image

John Kotter's most recent book on change (Kotter and Cohen, 2002) includes several examples of the use of dramatic visual images to overcome inertia. In one case, showing a video of an angry customer to employees sparked a sense of urgency that helped to overcome long-standing resistance to improving the product. Another explains how a taskforce handling poor investment planning made a light-hearted video with spoof characters who mimicked the damaging behaviour of senior executives. The video apparently shocked the executives into changing their behaviour. Kotter believes that the main reason why change efforts of any size fail is that there is not a great enough sense of urgency about the need to change – and that visual shocks can help break that barrier.

Source: Kotter and Cohen (2002).

In the same way, forces within the organisation – changing management priorities, the availability of funds, opposition from groups who see their privileges threatened – can drive change, or restrain it. The degree and direction of change in an organisation reflect the shifting balance and direction of the driving and restraining forces.

Diagnosing the change

Change projects vary in their difficulty, and research reported by Boddy (2002) identified those features that distinguished projects and affected the change management challenge they represented.

Core/margin

Some changes aim to change an activity that is marginal to the business or is in a background, supporting role – changing the way pensions are paid, or relocating administrative functions. Others are such that their success or failure is critical to the business. They are part of a broader strategy – such as a new online service for a bank or creating a website for an established retailer. They affect core operating processes, basic technologies or visible aspects of the business and its reputation. An example would be the series of projects that The Royal Bank of Scotland initiated to merge the operations of NatWest Bank with its own (see Part 4 case), or the doomed project to automate the settlement process at the London Stock Exchange (Drummond, 1996).

Novel/familiar

Some changes introduce novel, untried solutions and so depend on much learning and discovery during the project itself – both the problem and the solution are uncertain. The ideas floated are novel and highly uncertain – such as when Sainsbury's and Tesco set up their Internet retailing operations. Other projects centre on systems that others have used in similar situations. People understand the setting and the likely solution at the start of the project – as when Sainsbury's or Tesco refurbish a branch. They have done it many times before and both the problem and the solution are familiar.

Figure 13.6 shows these two critical dimensions of change projects. Those in quadrant 4 are likely to be most challenging to those responsible for implementing them. They are core to the business, and at the same time involve designing novel solutions.

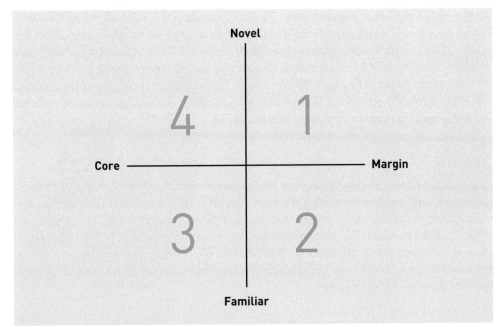

Figure 13.6

Critical dimensions of change projects

Rapid/gradual

Senior managers usually expect rapid change. They expect the project manager to achieve quick results and become impatient with requests for more time for design, testing, training or consultation. Pressure to implement a project rapidly inevitably leads to a search for short-cuts. Others are able to make the change at a more leisurely pace, with adequate time for pilot schemes, revisions and training.

Controversial/uncontroversial

Some changes are vigorously opposed from the start by one or more parties, who seek to undermine the project by overt or covert means. Major production or administrative reorganisations threaten established interests that may disagree fundamentally about the direction of the change. The Pensco change studied by Knights and Murray (1994) and described earlier in this chapter is an example of this. Other changes arouse no such controversy as everyone concerned accepts the desirability of the change.

Changing goals

As the discussion on emergent projects implied, goals typically evolve in dialogue between senior management and project management. Sometimes these changes reflect poor initial planning; at other times they reflect the fact that the business environment is volatile and that the project is best seen from an emergent perspective. Even if sponsors set clear goals at the outset, changing circumstances make it necessary to change them. This is a feature of the world in which business operates, and which shapes the job of the project manager. Projects in which the priorities and goals are frequently questioned will be harder to manage than ones in which they are stable.

Outside links

A feature of business life is the significant growth in cooperation between organisations – such as that between Vodafone and Ericsson – so that projects then involve working with people from other organisations. These will contain the same elements shown in Figure 13.2 but in a different form. Some differences may be of no consequence, but others, such as incompatible technologies or cultures, will cause severe difficulties. Some will have cultures that are receptive to change and keen to move ahead quickly; others need longer to adjust. They have different priorities, reflecting their part of the business and other demands on them. Changes that are entangled with changes in other units are harder to manage than those that are self-contained.

Senior stance

The attitude of top managers towards the project is critical. They cannot give detailed guidelines, and may not even set out a clear blueprint for change. But their actions and words affect the ability of the project manager to influence other people. They shape part of the context in which the project manager works. Are they visibly behind the idea of change, willing to give it the resources it needs, and with reasonable expectations of what the project can achieve? How demanding are they, how tolerant of risk and delay? Will there be pressure for short-cuts?

Other changes

Volatile environments mean that change is more frequent, and so comes in clusters. Most changes take place at the same time as other major changes. The turbulent environment of organisations prompts management to initiate simultaneous responses – and multi-project situations bring more uncertainty. There will be more competition for resources, and more scepticism as staff observe yet another change being launched. Table 13.3 summarises the features presented so far.

Table 13.3 **Project profile tool**

Significance:	Margin	1	2	3	4	5	Core
Solution:	Familiar	1	2	3	4	5	Novel
Pace:	Gradual	1	2	3	4	5	Rapid
Intentions:	Uncontroversial	1	2	3	4	5	Controversial
Changing goals:	Rare/minor	1	2	3	4	5	Often/major
Outside links:	Few	1	2	3	4	5	Many
Senior stance:	Supportive	1	2	3	4	5	Unsupportive
Other changes:	Few	1	2	3	4	5	Many

Source: Boddy (2002).

Activity 13.5 Identifying the pitfalls of change

Review a project against these features, by drawing a circle round the number on each of the scales that most accurately describes the project. High scores indicate where trouble is most likely to arise.

13.6 Forms and sources of resistance to change

Most managers are expected to implement change in the context in which they work. In doing so they use their power to influence others to act in a particular way. Chapter 14 outlines theories of power and influence, so this and the following sections examine just three aspects of this activity – understanding resistance to change, using front-stage and back-stage tactics, and supporting individual activity with formal structures.

Resistance to change

Much of the management literature presents resistance to change in pejorative terms as something to be overcome, but this discussion takes a more neutral stance. Some changes are clearly of general benefit to the organisation and all or most of its members. There is also much anecdotal evidence of managers who have introduced change mainly to further their local interests – to build a personal reputation or extend the influence of a department. Since organisations are made up of political and career systems as well as working systems, this is inevitable. Even when people intend to support organisational interests they sometimes misinterpret signals from the outside world and propose misguided changes.

For all these reasons people at all levels in an organisation will sometimes resist change. They may see it as a threat to their interests or status. Or they may believe that the change proposed will damage rather than benefit the organisation.

Forms of resistance

Overt and public resistance is often unnecessary. There are many other ways in which those opposed to a change can delay it, including:

- Refusing to use new systems or procedures
- Making no effort to learn
- Using older systems whenever possible
- Not attending meetings to discuss the project
- Excessive fault finding and criticism
- Deliberate misuse
- Saying it has been tried before and did not work
- Protracted discussion and requests for more information
- Linking the issue with pay or other industrial relations matters
- Not releasing staff for training.

These delaying tactics come from anywhere in the organisation – they are as likely to come from managers who see a change as a threat to their interests as they are to come from more junior staff. Change creates winners and losers, and potential losers are apt to engage in what Keen (1981) termed the tactics of **counterimplementation**.

Counterimplementation refers to attempts to block change without displaying overt opposition.

Sources of resistance

Johnston et al. (1967), in one of the earlier papers on the topic, distinguished between change that people can choose to accept or reject, and change over which they have little influence or control. The authors propose that people resist the latter form of change only if they see it as a threat to economic security or job status, or if it brings uncertainty and increased complexities. As well as the individual reaction in isolation, they also suggest that resistance may stem from changes in group relations, especially if the importance of these informal social relationships in the workplace is underestimated. If change means that the superior exercises closer control over the subordinate, the subordinate is likely to resist it.

---

key ideas **Peter Keen on counterimplementation**

Keen (1981) suggested that overt resistance to change is often risky, and may not in practice be necessary. He identified several ways in which those wanting to block a change can do so – even while appearing to support it. They include such tactics as:

- *Divert resources*. Split the budget across other projects; give key staff other priorities and allocate them to other assignments; arrange for equipment to be moved or shared.
- *Exploit inertia*. Suggest that everyone wait until a key player has taken action or read the report or made an appropriate response; suggest that the results from some other project should be monitored and assessed first.

- *Keep goals vague and complex*. It is harder to initiate appropriate action in pursuit of aims that are multidimensional and specified in generalised, grandiose or abstract terms.
- *Encourage and exploit lack of organisational awareness*. Insist that 'we can deal with the people issues later', knowing that these will delay or kill the project.
- *'Great idea – let's do it properly'*. And let's bring in representatives from this function and that section, until we have so many different views and conflicting interests that it will take for ever to sort them out.
- *Dissipate energies*. Have people conduct surveys, collect data, prepare analyses, write reports, make overseas trips, hold special meetings ...
- *Reduce the champion's influence and credibility*. Spread damaging rumours, particularly among the champion's friends and supporters.
- *Keep a low profile*. It is not effective openly to declare resistance to change because that gives those driving change a clear target.

Source: Based on Keen (1981).

Activity 13.6 Critical reflection on resistance

Discuss with someone who has tried to introduce change in an organisation what evidence there was of resistance.

- Which of the forms listed by Keen (in Key Ideas above) were in evidence?
- Can they identify any other forms?

Then consider these questions:

- Have you ever resisted a proposed change?
- What form did your resistance take?

Kotter and Schlesinger (1979) also identified individual sources of resistance, such as self-interest, misunderstanding and lack of trust: 'people also resist change when they do not understand its implications and perceive that it might cost them much more than they will gain' (p. 108). Employees assess the situation differently from their managers and may see more costs than benefits for both themselves and the company. Recardo (1991) made similar points from a study of new manufacturing systems. Change requires learning and exposure to uncertainty, insecurity and new social interactions. It is often marked by poor communication and management of the change process. Additional factors that Recardo identified as engendering resistance were reward systems that did not reward the desired behaviour and a poor fit between the change and the existing culture.

These views can be brought together by using the elements of the organisation shown in Figure 13.2. People can base their resistance on any of these contextual elements, as shown in Table 13.4.

Table 13.4

Sources of
resistance to
change

Element	Source of resistance
Objectives	Lack of clarity or understanding of objectives, or disagreement with those proposed
People	Change may threaten important values, preferences, skills, needs and interests
Technology	May be poorly designed, hard to use, incompatible with existing equipment, or require more work than is worthwhile
Business processes	As for technology, and may require unwelcome changes to the way people deal with colleagues and customers
Financial resources	Scepticism about whether the change will be financially worthwhile, or less so than other competing changes; lack of money
Structure	New reporting relationships or means of control may disrupt working relationships and patterns of authority
Culture	People likely to resist a change that challenges core values and beliefs, especially if they have worked well before
Power	If change affects ownership of and access to information, those who see they will lose autonomy will resist

In addition to these substantive or content reasons for resisting change, people may also resist because of the way others manage the change. They object to the process of change, irrespective of the specific change being made. Change is disturbing, and people are likely to resist if they do not feel they have been able to participate in discussions about the form it should take.

13.7 Individual skills and formal structures

Individual skills

Boddy (2002, pp. 94–5) suggests that two strategies are necessary to implement large changes. Those promoting the change have to produce a 'public/front-stage performance' of logical and rationally planned change linked to widespread and convincing participative mechanisms. They also have to pursue 'back-stage activity'. They have to exercise power skills, influencing, negotiating, selling, searching out and neutralising resistance.

Front-stage performance

Change processes within organisations have to conform to organisational 'theatre' to be successful. People affected have to be convinced that they are genuinely involved in the change and have some influence over its outcome. Top management and expert staff have to be convinced that the change is technically rational, logical and also congruent with the strategic direction of the organisation. Established project management techniques such as network planning and control techniques, cost–benefit analysis and technological appraisals are useful in themselves (see, for example, Lock, 2003); so are bar and Gantt charts, cumulative spending curves and scheduling tools. Such techniques are widely recognised as appropriate tools for managing change projects. They are also valuable in sustaining the image of the project manager. They reassure senior managers that the right things are being done in their name.

Back-stage activity

While the literature on participative management advises that manipulation and threats are counterproductive, management does use them in situations when there is a lack of time, resources and expertise as well as according to the scale and complexity of the project. Back-stage activities include establishing who can damage the project, co-opting likely opponents early, providing clear incentives to people to support the new system, and trying to create a 'bandwagon' effect. This is a 'back-stage' political strategy that depends heavily on the presence of a 'fixer' with prestige, visibility and legitimacy. Boddy and Gunson (1996) cite several examples of such moves based on mobilising coalitions. Some led from the front and put strong political pressure on sometimes reluctant managers to push a project through. While the front-stage activities of technical and strategic logic and user-participation strategies are important in providing organisational credibility at all levels, the back-stage activity is key to success or failure.

Formal structures

Change depends on someone being able and willing to influence others to plan and implement. Yet as Hartley *et al.* (1997) observed, a 'recurring theme [amongst the internal change agents] was how best to mobilise programmes of organisational and cultural change ... when they lack direct access to the traditional levers of line-management power ... and the role depends on influence rather than direct command' (p. 67). Project managers usually have little formal authority – yet the key part of their job is to influence others to do certain things. Personal skills alone will often be insufficient. More formal structures and institutions need to support them.

Vodafone/Ericsson – the case continues   CASE STUDY

The Global Supply Chain Management (GSCM) forum both created, and provided leadership for, the virtual work streams. These aimed to redesign business activities, processes and structures. Processes emerged from these work teams, that were then implemented through the information system. While the forum set their strategic direction, the virtual work teams experimented within the direction set, and then generated business requirements for the IS. The GSCM reviewed the work of the virtual teams.

The virtual work teams had to staff and resource their activities as appropriate. Each virtual team, led by a country and including local members from Vodafone and Ericsson, leveraged resources and interacted with other teams and colleagues in their base companies. In doing so, these multi-level global virtual teams created varied horizontal relationships between Vodafone and Ericsson, and between Vodafone operating interests.

Vodafone regarded the project as having been a success, in that it contributed to the cost savings arising from the mergers and acquisitions which the company had made, commenting in its interim report for 2002 that global supply chain management was now generating significant synergy savings for the group.

Source: Ibbott and O'Keefe (2004).

Without some human agency, without someone putting personal effort into the problem, nothing will change. Kanter (1983) and Buchanan and Boddy (1992) identify the attitudes and skills that the change agent requires – and these include the skills required by the practices listed in Table 13.2. There are, however, limitations to what people acting on their own to manage change can achieve. As individuals they have limited power. This can to some extent be overcome by supporting individual action with appropriate structures, such as clearly establishing their role, establishing links to the board or senior managers, and creating project teams with the expertise and power to support the work of the individual manager. These all serve to enhance the power sources available to someone managing a change.

Roles with and without formal authority

A number of interesting things have happened. I personally have been legitimized by my division's management team as the Customer Service and Order Fulfilment Manager. I have also been legitimized as the European Programme Manager for order scheduling. (Boddy, 2002, p. 74)

My role was not properly set up, and clearly it was my mistake that I would be subordinate to the Board, and not a member of it. In hindsight I really needed to operate at the highest level to carry the necessary 'clout', and to keep the Board itself properly informed. (p. 74)

Source: Boddy (2002).

Case questions 13.4

- How are the companies balancing the needs for individual action and formal structures?
- Was the GSCM forum expected to take on that role when it was established?

13.8 Organisation Development

Organisation Development is a systematic process in which applied behavioural science principles and practices are introduced with the goal of increasing individual and organisational performance.

This final section introduces a comprehensive and still widely used approach to managing change. Known as **Organisation Development** (OD), its methods reflect a clear set of values about people and work, many of which relate to ideas on organisation culture (Chapter 10), human resource management (Chapter 11), and work design (Chapter 15).

A fundamental dilemma in managing is how to balance the needs and aspirations of the individual with the behaviour required for high organisational performance. OD practitioners believe that 'the conflicting interests of organizations and their members can be reconciled through appropriate interventions' (Buchanan and Huczynski, 2004, p. 578). It can be used to resolve these conflicts within a single unit of a business, or for the organisation as a whole, aiming for both individual development and organisational effectiveness. Practitioners try to achieve these mutually supporting goals through deliberate and systematic interventions, using knowledge from the social and behavioural sciences.

Robbins (2001, p. 553) outlines the values which underlie most OD activities:

- The individual should be treated with respect and dignity
- The organisation climate should be characterised by trust, openness and support
- Hierarchical authority and control are de-emphasised
- Problems and conflicts should be confronted, not disguised or avoided
- People affected by change should be involved in its implementation.

Some practitioners believe that this agenda is worth pursuing in its own right, though others stress that implementing practices based on these values will make a business more efficient and effective.

A common theme in OD is that bureaucracy is an obstacle to performance, and that an organisation in which staff have more freedom and flexibility in the way they work will also show a better financial performance. Table 13.5 summarises how OD practitioners tackle these problems in both private and public sector organisations (Bate, 2000).

Table 13.5

Bureaucratic diseases and OD cures

Bureaucratic disease	Symptoms	OD cures
Rigid functional boundaries	Conflict between sections, poor communications	Team building, job rotation, structural change
Fixed hierarchies	Frustration, boredom, narrow specialist thinking	Training, job enrichment, career development
Information only flows down	Lack of innovation, minor problems escalate	Process consultation, management development
Routine jobs, tight control	Boredom, absenteeism, conflict with supervisors	Job enrichment, job rotation, supervisory training

Source: Buchanan and Huczynski (2004), p. 581.

OD practitioners have developed a range of interventions. The most common techniques are listed below, and more detail on each is contained in Buchanan and Huczynski (2004), pp. 586–94.

- **Sensitivity training** Conducted in small groups, the aim of **sensitivity training** is to allow participants to discuss themselves, to observe and discuss how the members interact with each other and to exchange feedback on each other. The intention is that through such discussions participants become more sensitive to their behaviour, the effects they have on others, and how others see and relate to them.

  Sensitivity training is a technique for enhancing self-awareness and changing behaviour through unstructured group discussion.

- **Changing structure** Many of the approaches to structural change described in Chapters 10 and 12 have become part of the OD toolkit. These include efforts to decentralise organisations by giving more decision-making power to local units, or changing the horizontal structure of the organisation through business process redesign. Structural changes signify which areas of the organisation are becoming more significant, and which are in decline.

- **Process consultation** A consultant undertakes **process consultation** to help members of the organisation to develop a clearer insight into the problems facing the organisation, as distinct from an external consultant doing the analysis. It is consistent with one of the core OD values that people are ultimately responsible for their own development.

  Process consultation is an OD intervention in which an external consultant facilitates improvements in an organisation's diagnostic, conceptual and action planning skills.

- **Survey feedback** This refers to the technique of conducting a survey of employee attitudes, and providing managers or supervisors with anonymous analyses of the results – hence the term **survey feedback**. Respondents may also be invited to suggest themes or questions to include in the survey, and to take part in group discussions of the results.

  Survey feedback is an OD intervention in which the results of an opinion survey are fed back to respondents to trigger problem-solving on the issues which the survey identifies.

- **Team building** Attempts are made to develop more effective teams, which are becoming more critical to organisational performance. There are many approaches, such as that developed by Meredith Belbin (1993) in which members work to identify the distinctive roles they play in teams, and can then plan how to ensure that more of the roles which should ideally be present in a team are covered (see Chapter 17 for a full discussion of Belbin's work).

- **Intergroup development** This helps overcome the boundaries that can arise between groups that are expected to work together. Functional boundaries and diverse experiences lead groups to develop a strong internal identity – but with the possible disadvantage that they develop negative feelings towards other groups. Intergroup development helps to break down assumptions, and encourage more cooperative working across team boundaries.
- **Grid organisation development** This is an application of Blake and Mouton's (1969) managerial grid, described in Chapter 14. The grid assumes that leadership styles vary on two dimensions – concern for production and concern for people. Managers can be assessed on the extent to which they are high, medium or low on each dimension. The prescription is that ideally they should be high on both, and the technique is intended to help managers reflect on their style, and move their style closer to the ideal type.

Summary

1 **Assess whether change is a continual rather than an episodic part of managing:**
   - Especially in innovative parts of the economy, change is the normal condition as people intervene in a continually shifting external business environment. It will be rare for change to be followed by a return to stability.

2 **Explain the meaning of organisational change and give examples:**
   - Organisational change refers to deliberate attempts to change one or more elements of the internal environment, such as technology or structure. Change in one element usually stimulates change in other areas.

3 **Explain the interaction between change and context, and the implications:**
   - A change programme is an attempt to change one or more aspects of the internal context, which then provides the context of future actions. The prevailing context can itself help or hinder change efforts.

4 **Compare life cycle, emergent, participative and political theories of change:**
   - Life cycle: change projects can be planned, monitored and controlled towards achieving their objectives.
   - Emergent: reflecting the uncertainties of the environment, change is hard to plan in detail, but change emerges incrementally from events and actions.
   - Participative: successful change depends on human commitment, which is best obtained by involving participants in planning and implementation.
   - Political: change threatens some of those affected, who will use their power to block progress, or to direct the change in ways that suit local objectives.

5 **Use a technique to identify the most potentially difficult aspects of a change:**
   - The project profile tool is a research-based technique which enables change managers to evaluate project risks on eight dimensions (Table 13.4).

6 **Evaluate systematically the possible sources of resistance to change, and their implications for gaining commitment:**
   - Reasons can be assessed using the internal context model, as each element (objectives, people, power, etc.) is a potential source of resistance. Analysing these indicates potential ways of overcoming resistance.

- The force-field analysis model allows players to identify the forces driving and restraining a change, and implies that reducing the restraining forces will help change more than increasing the driving forces.

7 **Compare the relative roles of front-stage performance and back-stage activity in managing change, and the contribution of individual skills and formal structures:**

- Front-stage performance includes the activities of planning, enabling participation, etc., to reassure others that the project is being managed in a professionally acceptable way. In addition, change managers are likely to need to engage in back-stage activities of threats and manipulation to overcome significant resistance, especially when the problem is urgent and time is short.

- Individual skills to perform the activities implied by the analysis need to be supported by formal structures or mechanisms. These can provide forums in which issues can be addressed, and progress related to wider organisational changes.

8 **Explain the meaning of organisational development, its values and techniques:**

- OD refers to a set of techniques which practitioners use to reconcile the conflicting interests of people and organisations, both to satisfy human needs and to improve organisational performance. Typical values include treating individuals with respect, a trusting, open and supportive climate, flat rather than hierarchical structures, confronting conflict, and involving those affected by change in implementation.

Review questions

1 What does the term 'performance gap' mean, and what is its significance for change?

2 Explain what is meant by the inner context of management, and give examples of attempts to change one or more elements.

3 What are the implications for management of the systemic nature of major change?

4 Review the change that you identified in Activity 13.1 and compare its critical dimensions (Table 13.1) with those at The Royal Bank of Scotland.

5 Can managers alter the receptiveness of an organisation to change? Would doing so be an example of an interaction approach?

6 Outline the life cycle perspective on change and explain when it is most likely to be useful.

7 How does it differ from the 'emergent' perspective?

8 What are the distinctive characteristics of a participative approach, and when is it likely to be least successful?

9 What skills are used by those employing a political model?

10 Is resistance to change necessarily something to be overcome? How would you advise someone to resist a change to which he or she was opposed?

11 What are likely to be the benefits and disadvantages of using an OD approach to a major change project?

12 Evaluate an example of change management in view of the models in this chapter.

Concluding critical reflection

Think about the way people handle major change in your company, or one with which you are familiar. Review the material in the chapter, and perhaps visit some of the websites identified. Then make notes on these questions:

- What examples of the themes discussed in this chapter are currently relevant to your company? What performance imperatives are dominant, and to what extent do people see a performance gap? What perspectives do people have on the change process – life cycle, emergent, participative or political?

- In responding to issues of structure, what assumptions about the nature of change in organisations appear to guide your approach? Is any one of the perspectives dominant, or do people typically use several methods depending on circumstances? Does the approach typically used generally work? If not, why do managers take that approach? What are their assumptions, and are they correct?

- What factors in the context of the company appear to shape your approach to managing change – is your organisation seen as being receptive or non-receptive to change, for example, and what lies behind that?

- Have there been any serious challenges to the way people manage major change in your organisation – for example by comparing your methods systematically with those of other companies?

Further reading

Pettigrew, A.M. and Whipp, R. (1991), *Managing Change for Competitive Success*, Blackwell, Oxford.

Pettigrew, A., Ferlie, E. and McKee, L. (1992), *Shaping Strategic Change*, Sage, London.

Both of these books provide detailed, long-term analyses of major changes – the first in four commercial businesses and the second in several units within the UK National Health Service. The theoretical approach of these works has informed the development of this chapter, emphasising the interaction of change and context. Although the cases are old, they still provide useful empirical insights into the task of managing change.

Burnes, B. (2000), *Managing Change* (3rd edn), Financial Times/Prentice Hall, Harlow.

Long case studies supplement an up-to-date treatment of theory in the area.

Mabey, C. and Mayon-White, B. (eds) (1993), *Managing Change* (2nd edn), The Open University/Paul Chapman Publishing, London.

Collection of readings, including some classic articles in the area of change management.

Lock, D. (2003), *Project Management* (8th edn), Gower, Aldershot.

An excellent source of information on conventional project management techniques.

Buchanan, D. and Badham, R. (1999), *Power, Politics and Organizational Change: Winning the turf game*, Sage, London.

A modern approach to politics in organisations, offering a theoretical and practical guide, based on extensive primary research.

Clark, J. (1996), *Managing Innovation and Change*, Sage, London.

A study of change at Pirelli, the multinational tyres and cables group. By examining a major change in one division over several years it emphasises the long-term, evolutionary nature of change. Each chapter begins with a review of relevant theory that is then used to guide the analysis of events in the company.

Weblinks

These websites have appeared in the chapter:

www.vodafone.com

www.ericsson.com

www.siemens.com

Visit two of the business sites in the list, and navigate to the pages dealing with corporate news, investor relations or 'our company'.

- What signs of major changes taking place in the organisation can you find?
- Does the site give you a sense of an organisation that is receptive or non-receptive to change?
- What kind of environment are they likely to be working in, and how may that affect their approach to change?

Annotated weblinks, multiple choice questions and other useful resources can be found on
www.pearsoned.co.uk/boddy

The Royal Bank of Scotland

The Royal Bank of Scotland Group, founded in 1727, is one of Europe's leading financial services groups. During the economic recession of the early 1990s the bank was in trouble. It had had to make heavy provisions for bad debts and was losing customers to the new building society banks. The share price of just over £1 in 1992 reflected investors' critical view of recent performance. The cost:income ratio (a key measure of bank performance) was over 70 per cent.

In 2004 the share price was over £15 and observers regarded RBS as one of the most innovative and best-performing banks in the United Kingdom. It was by then (on market capitalisation) the UK's seventh largest company, and the fifth largest bank in the world. In 2003 pre-tax profits rose 29 per cent to over £6 billion. In the UK alone the enlarged Royal Bank of Scotland Group has more than 15 million customers and more than 2200 branches. At 31 December 2003 the Group had assets of £455 billion, over 120,000 staff worldwide and a cost:income ratio of 42 per cent.

What happened to bring about this change? Much of the credit is due to a series of major internal changes during the 1990s, followed by some successful acquisitions. The early internal changes took place between 1992 and 1997 during what was called Project Columbus. This drove a series of radical changes throughout the retail division, including:

- Segmenting customers into three new streams – retail, commercial and corporate
- Creating new management roles and organisation structures

The Royal Bank of Scotland

- New human resource policies to base appointment and promotion on achievement and ability.

This transformed the bank's business, and provided the base for further acquisitions.

Over the years the bank has become more centralised. Initially banks operated as decentralised operations, as branch managers had considerable autonomy. With the first wave of IT in the 1960s many functions were centralised. Now the balance may be switching again, as customers complain they cannot get decisions from remote regional offices. Control brings more centralised decisions over products, margins, risk management, etc. Against that, the customer relationship managers press for more local flexibility to override the system.

The Manufacturing Division, which deals with routine functions such as clearing cheques, account opening and various other paper processes, is a very mechanistic structure. The bank created the Manufacturing

Division by transferring most administrative tasks from the branches to a central location. To select staff for the new division from those working in the branches, they used psychometric tests to draw out those more comfortable with processes and systems. Those who were more interested in people remained in the branches.

The branches themselves had been mechanistic, with tellers having strictly defined tasks. Now the branches are much more organic, with tellers trying to interest customers in other products, and the physical layout is more open. The bank tries to be organic at the customer-facing areas, with customer relationship managers trying to improve service quality.

The bank was quick to exploit the opportunities that new technology offers. It was an early innovator when it launched Direct Line as one of the first examples of delivering financial services by telephone, and now one of the United Kingdom's largest private motor insurers. It has launched an online bank (**www.rbsdigital.com**), complementing the services offered by the traditional bank.

The formal structure in 2005 was that it had eight 'customer-facing' divisions:

- Retail (The Royal Bank of Scotland and NatWest)
- Wealth management
- Retail direct
- Corporate banking and financial markets
- RBS Insurance
- Ulster Bank Group
- Citizens (United States).

These were supported by six Group divisions – Manufacturing, Legal, Strategy, Finance, Risk and Internal Audit, Communications, and Human Resources.

Amongst its alliances it includes a strategic alliance with BSCH of Spain, which provides scope to develop financial service activities across Europe. It also has a joint venture with Tesco – Tesco Personal Finance, one of the main supermarket banking brands in the United Kingdom.

RBS has developed a reputation for acquiring other financial institutions and integrating them profitably. Most notable was the acquisition of NatWest Bank in 2000, not least because NatWest was three times the size of RBS at the time. To win the bank RBS had to demonstrate its ability to extract major cost savings from the combined operations, and to drive greater income from the combination of brands, customers, products and skills. The RBS bid promised to deliver a 'new force in banking' with the scale and strength to exploit new opportunities in the UK, Europe and the USA. Some industry analysts doubted the ability of RBS to deliver on its bid promises, so the company was under pressure to complete the integration process on time and to meet the cost savings and income benefits quoted during the bid.

The Integration Programme was quickly established following the takeover, dividing the task into 154 integration initiatives to be completed in three years. These were expected to yield £1.1 billion in annual cost savings and reduce staff by 18,000. Programme Management teams were established in each affected business and technology area, and control and reporting procedures were set up. The key elements of the integration strategy were agreed and widely communicated:

- To use RBS information systems as the single platform for operations across the merged bank
- To migrate customer-facing systems such as credit cards, ATMs and Internet screens to RBS systems early
- To transfer the NatWest customer and accounting data to the RBS systems in a single weekend.

The early stages of the integration programme involved some challenging decisions about the structure of the programme teams.

- *Centralised versus decentralised control.* Once the initial programme strategy had been devised, the individual parts of the integration programme were allocated to local business areas to deliver. At this stage it would have been easy to devolve control and monitoring of the programme to the individual areas. However, management decided to maintain close central control of the change process, as this would increase efficiency by developing a standard set of control procedures to be used by all areas. These simplify the process of compiling progress updates for the whole programme, and develop a common level of rigour to be applied by all areas. This ensures that progress updates and issues are communicated effectively to the senior executive, and that appropriate levels of prioritisation are applied across the whole programme.
- *Business versus technology control.* While much of the work of the integration programme was IT-related (i.e. the transfer of NatWest data to the RBS systems

platform), it was critical for the business areas to have a strong say in what could be done when. Programme Steering Groups therefore contained a mix of representatives from the affected business areas and the appropriate Technology teams. Project plans were required to contain an appropriate selection of both Business and Technology activities and milestones. Key steps in the systems transfer process were assessed for impact on business areas and customers prior to acceptance.

The programme had well-developed control procedures. A monthly reporting process compared the achievement of actual costs and benefits against budget, summarising the progress made so far and the main achievements and difficulties being encountered. Processes for controlling the programme and reporting on progress were put in place. In particular, procedures for tracking the financial performance were established, requiring regular financial reports on each project. The overall baseline figures for the whole programme were broken down into monthly figures to be achieved by each business area. As well as financial reporting, other controls included:

- *High-level plans*. These consisted of a set of milestones covering the most important steps towards the completion of the initiatives. High-level plans were expected to contain approximately one milestone per month in order that progress could be assessed with sufficient regularity.
- *Project 'RAG' status*. Project teams were required to report the status of their work using a 'traffic light' system of Red, Amber or Green (RAG): Green – satisfactory; Amber – difficulties that may affect time, quality or costs; Red – serious problems requiring changes to the agreed deliverables.
- *Change control*. Once the initial plans and financial targets were established, they were fixed and could only be changed through a formal process at a defined level of seniority.
- *Dependencies*. When one project depends on another, both parties must agree what is to be delivered and when. A dependency management process recorded and monitored these.

Monthly reports were presented to senior management, giving a clear view on progress being made against plans. The monthly reports were therefore designed to include a view of the progress planned for the next three months, with an indication of confidence in achieving this progress.

The largest integration task was that of moving all NatWest data onto the RBS computer systems and shutting down the NatWest systems. This was an enormous programme in itself, involving the migration of 18 million customer accounts worth £158 billion and with huge daily transaction volumes. The preparation work would take over two years to complete, so the transfer itself could not take place until well into 2002.

To create a shared vision for the integration programme across all staff in the new RBS Group, including those 80,000 or so NatWest staff members who felt vulnerable following the hostile takeover, a series of steps were undertaken. For example:

- 'Creating a New Force in Banking' was a key message used by RBS during the bid process to describe the positive outcome of the integration. This was also used during the early stages of the integration programme in staff and public communications. Use of a simple catchphrase gave a focus and sense of purpose to the programme for all staff to follow.
- Early communications to staff included statements on the key elements of the integration strategy. Sharing this level of information with staff gave a common understanding of what was being done and how individual projects fitted with the overall approach. Throughout the programme, a regular set of communications were made to staff by directors, describing the achievements to date and the plans for the future.

The integration programme was completed in early 2003 – within three years of the acquisition date as originally planned and promised. The biggest single event in the programme – the transfer of NatWest customer and account data to the RBS computer platform – happened over one weekend in October 2002. RBS is now operating on a large-scale, stable technology platform which can handle multiple businesses, and with proven experience in managing major integration programmes. This has enabled it to continue acquiring and integrating other financial services companies – seven in 2003 alone, and continuing in 2004.

Part case questions

- Is RBS becoming more centralised or more decentralised?
- What form(s) of structure has the bank used to divide the business? Since it is also necessarily a geographically dispersed organisation, what methods of coordination is it likely to use?
- Which type of culture would best describe RBS?
- What are the main issues of an HRM nature that are likely to be topical within RBS?
- From your understanding of the material in Chapter 11, what aspects of HRM should RBS be focusing its efforts upon?
- How will the merger with NatWest have affected this?
- Does RBS have a mechanistic or an organic structure?
- What contingency factors have probably shaped that structure?
- What are the main features of the way in which RBS managed the NatWest integration programme?
- Which model(s) of change did RBS management use to implement its new policies? What management practices did it use?

Part 4 Skills development

To help you develop your skills, as well as knowledge, this section includes tasks which relate the key themes covered in the Part to your daily life. Working through these will help you to deepen your understanding of the topic, and develop skills and insights which you can use in many situations.

Task 4.1 Analysing a department or organisation

While every organisation is unique, all are made up of the elements shown in Figure 13.2 (p. 408). These form the internal context within which managers operate, and shape the demands which the manager faces. A useful skill is that of being able to use this model to identify and analyse significant features of an organisation or business unit. This exercise invites you to analyse just four of the elements – select more if they seem relevant to the situation.

Analyse a department or organisation with which you are familiar by making a few notes in response to these questions:

- What is the main objective or mission of the department or organisation?
- What is the structure?
- What are the main characteristics of the people?
- What technologies (and in what layout) do people use to meet the objectives? This includes all kinds of physical facilities, including computer systems.

Consider a recent large change. What were the direct and indirect effects on each of these components? What difficulties, if any, had to be managed?

Compare your answers with those prepared by another student, to further increase your skills of analysis, and of identifying key organisational features.

Task 4.2 Distinguishing mechanistic from organic structures

Chapter 12 distinguished between mechanistic and organic forms. Since these greatly affect how people work, a manager needs to be able to identify each type, and the practices which can, whether intended or not, lead an organisation towards one or the other.

Analyse a department or organisation with which you are familiar by making a few notes in response to these questions:

- Identify a department that is mainly mechanistic, and indicate the features or practices that illustrate that.
- Identify a department that is mainly organic, and indicate the features or practices that illustrate that.
- Why do you think each takes the form they do?

- Is that form the appropriate one for the work being done?
- If not, what specific features or practices would you recommend that management change to move towards the form you think most suitable?
- Are there any examples of problems in the working relationships between units which may be attributed to their having mechanistic and organic characteristics?

Task 4.3   Analysing stakeholders

A valuable skill in managing any kind of organisational change (such as in strategy, structure or technology) is that of managing those with a stake in the project, and who can affect its success. This exercise enables you to practice using a tool which helps to understand and manage stakeholders constructively.

Select a major organisational change project with which you are familiar, or which you can ask someone about. Write the name of the project in a circle at the centre of a sheet of paper. Draw other circles around the sheet, each identifying an individual or group with a stake in the project. Place the most significant nearer the centre, and others around the edge.

Use a scale such as that shown below to assess the 'present' (X) and 'hoped for' (Y) level of commitment of each stakeholder to the project.

Key stakeholder	Vigorous opposition	Some opposition	Indifferent towards it	Will let it happen	Will help it happen	Will make it happen
				X		Y
				X	Y	
			X		Y	
				X		Y
		X			Y	

Rate each stakeholder on whether their power to affect the project is high or low.

Use a grid like that shown below to note your answers to these questions for the main (powerful) stakeholders:

Stakeholder	Their goals	Current relationship	What is expected of them?	Positive or negative to them?	Likely reaction?	Ideas for action

- What are their priorities, goals and interests?
- What is the general tone of our present relationship with them?
- What specific behaviour is expected of them, in relation to this project?
- Are they likely to see this as positive or negative for them?
- What is their likely action to defend their interests?
- What actions can we consider to influence them?

Compare your answers with those prepared by another student for their project, to further increase your skills of analysis, and of identifying ideas for managing stakeholders.

LEADING

Part 5

Introduction

Generating the effort and commitment to work towards objectives is central to managing any human activity. One person working alone, be it in private life or in business, has only him or herself to motivate. As an organisation grows, management activities become, in varying degrees, separated from the core work activities. The problem of generating effort changes its nature: now one person, or one occupational group, has to secure the willing cooperation of other people and their commitment to the task. Those other people may be subordinates, peers or superiors whose support, and perhaps approval, needs to be generated and mobilised.

The quality of that commitment is as important as whether or not it is secured. Staff are often in direct contact with customers. They are aware of their unique and changing requirements, and have an immense effect on the view the customer forms of the organisation. Others are in creative roles, with a direct impact on the quality of the service delivered to the final customer, whether they are contributing to a core R&D project or a TV programme. Others need to work reliably and flexibly in order to meet changing external or internal customer needs.

Throughout a business, customers' expectations of service quality and efficiency translate into expectations from staff. Unwilling or grudging commitment damages the service offered and eventually the business itself. How does management secure the motivation it needs from others? Part Five offers several perspectives on the dilemma. Chapter 14 examines ideas on influencing others, while Chapter 15 presents a range of theories about what those others may want from work. Communication is central to most management functions and activities, and Chapter 16 examines this topic. Finally, teams are an increasingly prominent aspect of organisations, and the motivation and commitment generated within them is often central to performance – so they are the subject of Chapter 17.

The Part Case is W.L. Gore and Associates, an organisation renowned for its use of teams.

Chapter 14

Influence and power

Aim

To examine how people influence others by using personal skills and/or power.

Objectives

By the end of your work on this chapter you should be able to outline the concepts below in your own terms and:

1 Distinguish leading from managing, and explain why each is essential to performance

2 Explain why leading and managing both depend on being able to influence others

3 Compare trait, behavioural and contingency perspectives on influencing

4 Outline theories that focus on power (both personal and organisational) as the source of influence

5 Contrast the style and power perspectives, and explain why sharing power may increase it

6 Outline a model of the tactics which people use to influence others, including the use of cooperative networks.

Key terms

This chapter introduces the following ideas:

influence
leadership
traits
behaviour
initiating structure
consideration
situational models
contingency models
power
transactional leaders
transformational leaders
political behaviour
delegating
networking

Each is a term defined within the text, as well as in the glossary at the end of the book.

Semco

Semco is a Brazilian company that employs 3000 people in three countries, working in manufacturing, professional services and software. The main offices are in Såo Paolo, where Antonio Semler founded the company in 1954 to make industrial equipment such as pumps and centrifuges. He ran it in a traditional way, but in 1982 his son Ricardo Semler took over as chief executive. The company has survived a turbulent Brazilian economy, and by 2004 the annual revenue of what is in effect a federation of about 10 companies exceeded $200 million.

Ricardo Semler has unusual ideas about business and has gradually dismantled the management structure he inherited, moving Semco towards a very flexible form with profit sharing, employee participation and a free flow of information. Under the profit-sharing plan employees (known as Associates) receive one quarter of the profits of their respective division. The scheme is run by an elected committee, which reflects Semler's trust in his employees' abilities to make decisions.

Employees are free to agree their working hours with their co-workers – coming in and leaving work at times to suit their domestic or other commitments. Many were sceptical of this innovation – but Semler argues that provided people are committed to their job and the company, they will (and do) manage their time responsibly – 'they're the best judges of the amount of time and the proper place necessary to get the work done . . . do we really believe that responsible adults . . . would simply not show up after promising to do so? That a journalist who understands the urgency of deadlines would go to the movies while the presses are standing still, waiting for his submission?' (Semler, 2003, pp. 27–8).

The Brazilian economy was in poor shape during the early 1990s, with many companies going bankrupt. Semco survived, though only by cutting costs sharply. The workers themselves proposed the solutions, such as having people do several jobs rather than one. This developed a workforce that was cross-trained in several skills, and with a deep knowledge of the business. Most work is now done by units that perform all the necessary support functions such as marketing and finance themselves. For many years the company has organised work in self-managed teams, whereby groups of six to eight manufacturing employees take responsibility for

James Leynse/Corbis

all aspects of a production task. They set their targets and production goals, and decide what they should be paid. The teams vote on hiring and firing members and managers.

The management structure is like three concentric circles. The inner core has six Counsellors who determine general policy and strategy, each acting as CEO for six months. Two seats at meetings are reserved for employees – the first there take the seats. The second circle consists of Partners – the leaders of each division. All remaining Associates make up the outer circle. Team leaders are within this outer circle – such as engineers, marketers and production supervisors. Associates are encouraged to openly oppose and reject proposals by upper management.

Sources: Based on material from Thunderbird, The American School of International Management, Case A15-98-0024, *Ricardo Semler and Semco S.A.*; Semler (2003); and other published material.

Case questions

- What examples are there of senior managers influencing associates?
- What examples are there of associates influencing senior managers?
- What assumptions about people lie behind Semler's management style?

14.1 Introduction

When Ricardo Semler took over Semco from his father, he faced challenges typical of many managers today. The Brazilian economy was in trouble, and employee morale was threatened by the danger of losing their jobs or of not earning an adequate wage. While he could have used conventional means of authority and control to influence his staff, he took a radically different approach of delegating increasing amounts of power to employees, later commenting that:

> Semco managers are concerned with the essence of what employees do for the company, nothing more. (Semler, 2003, pp. 28–9)

All managers face this challenge of influencing others – such as when Sari Baldauf became head of Nokia's network division, and built it up to become one of the world's leading suppliers of network equipment. When the market collapsed in 2000, she had simultaneously to cut back that division (reducing staff by 7500 in three years) while still influencing the company and its staff to invest for future growth in other areas. Ron Eddington at British Airways faces these issues as he seeks to change the way people work, to reduce the company's costs in the face of competition from low-cost airlines. Carlos Ghosn, now CEO of Renault (see Chapter 16), faced the challenge of influencing staff at Nissan to make unprecedented changes in the way they worked – changes which transformed it from a loss-making to a profitable business.

 **Jorma Ollila of Nokia, and Bob Ayling of BA**

Jorma Ollila is chief executive of Nokia, the world's biggest supplier of mobile phones. He became chief executive in 1992 and led the transformation of the company from an undistinguished business into a world leader in the industry. In contrast, Bob Ayling resigned in March 2000 after four years as chief executive of British Airways. The precise reasons for his departure were unclear, but probably included the fact that profits and share price had fallen sharply. While commentators regard Ollila as one of the most successful leaders of the time, Ayling had failed. He was unable to influence staff, unions, customers and investors about the wisdom of his approach to the business.

Whatever their role in the organisation, managers can only add value to the resources they use by influencing others. In terms of Figure 1.2, the tasks of planning, organising, leading and controlling depend on securing the cooperation of other people to act in a particular way. People throughout an organisation do their jobs by influencing others, and their performance depends on how well they do so. The targets of influence will often be in more senior positions.

In that sense the work of the manager is not that of the careful analyst, working out precisely the best solution to a problem. It is closer to that of an entrepreneur, determined to get things done in an often hostile, indifferent or political setting. Managers typically operate across established functional or departmental boundaries, working with many different people who have other priorities and interests.

This chapter explores the topics shown in Figure 14.1. It begins by clarifying what influence means in the context of managing and then presents three perspectives on the topic – traits, behavioural and contingency. It then examines theories on how people can use their power to influence others, power which can come from both personal and organisational sources. Finally it presents a model of the tactics people can use to influence, including that of networking. The figure also indicates that the outcomes of an influence attempt depend not only on the choice of method but on the circumstances in which it is used. Those outcomes in turn affect the influencer's power – a successful result is likely to further increase it, and *vice versa*. The chapters on motivation, communication and teams are closely linked to influence and power.

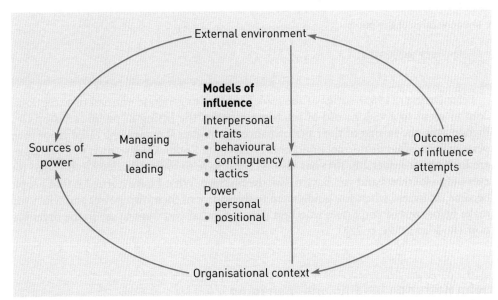

Figure 14.1

A model of the influencing process

14.2 Managing and leading

People continually **influence** each other throughout any organisation. Research and commentary on influencing use the terms 'manager' and 'leader' (and their derivatives) interchangeably. There is no accepted or definitive distinction between them and this book does not seek to establish one. However, it is worth spending a few lines considering the meaning behind the terms.

Influence is the process by which one party attempts to modify the behaviour of others by mobilising power resources.

Chapter 1 defined a manager as someone who gets things done with the support of others. Most commentators view an 'effective manager' as someone who 'gets things done' to ensure order and continuity. They maintain the steady state – keeping established systems in good shape and making incremental improvements. People generally use the term 'effective leader' to denote someone who brings innovation, moves an activity out of trouble into success, makes a worthwhile difference. They see opportunities to do new things, take the initiative to raise the issue and do something about it.

 Leif Beck Fallesen, chief executive of *Borsen*

Borsen is a Danish business newspaper, equivalent to the *Financial Times*. During the early 1990s circulation and profitability declined. In 1996 the board appointed Leif Beck Fallesen as chief executive, with a brief to improve the position. The paper's circulation has grown by about 15 per cent a year since 1997, while that of similar papers has remained static or declined. The leadership actions he took included creating:

- regular features aimed at growing market segments (such as small businesses, family-owned businesses and younger readers)
- a joint venture providing business content to Danish Television
- an innovative online version of the paper.

Source: Company presentation and other sources.

Leadership refers to the process of influencing the activities of others toward high levels of goal setting and achievement.

Peter Drucker (1985) writes of the leader's ability to generate unusual or exceptional commitment to a vision, and of **leadership** being 'the lifting of people's vision to a higher sight, the raising of their performance to a higher standard, the building of their personality beyond its normal limitations'. And Anita Roddick has written that: '[People] are looking for leadership that has vision ... You have to look at leadership through the eyes of the followers and you have to live the message. What I have learned is that people become motivated when you guide them to the source of their own power and when you make heroes out of employees who best personify what you want to see in the organisation' (Roddick, 1991, p. 223).

key ideas John Kotter on leading and managing

Kotter (1991) distinguishes between the terms leadership and management – while stressing that organisations need both, and that one person will often provide both. He regards good management as bringing order and consistency to an activity – through the tasks of planning, organising and controlling. He observed that modern management developed to support the large companies which developed from the middle of the nineteenth century. These complex enterprises tended to become chaotic, unless they developed good management practices to bring order and consistency to key dimensions of performance, such as quality and profitability. The early pioneers of management created the discipline

'to help keep a complex organization on time and on budget. That has been, and still is, its primary function. Leadership is very different. It does not produce consistency and order . . . it produces movement.'

Individuals whom people recognise as leaders have created change – whether for the better or not. Good leadership is that which

'moves people to a place in which they and those who depend on them are genuinely better off, and when it does so without trampling on the rights of others.'

It does so through establishing direction and strategy, communicating it to those whose cooperation is needed, and motivating and inspiring people. Managing and leading are closely related, but differ in their primary functions – the one to create order, the other to create change. Organisations need both if they are to prosper.

Source: Kotter (1991).

Many people work to create change and to create order in varying degrees, so there is no value in a sharp distinction between managing and leading (John Adair quotes a Chinese proverb: 'What does it matter if the cat is black or white, as long as it catches mice' (Adair, 1997, p. 2)). Managing and leading both depend on being able to influence others to put effort and commitment to the task – whether that is to create order or to create change. People such as Carlos Ghosn of Renault-Nissan (see Chapter 16) can only succeed with the support of others.

People at all levels who want to get something done need to influence others. The effectiveness of senior managers in influencing others has the most visible effects on performance. They shape the overall direction of the business, moving it into new areas or changing the way it operates. Yet they depend on people lower down the organisation also being able and willing to exercise influence – whether to bring stability or to initiate change in their respective areas of responsibility.

Managers (and leaders) often influence people who are equally powerful – as Lesley Macdonagh testifies. She is managing partner of Lovell's, an international law firm, and was the first woman to take the top management job at a leading City of London legal practice:

> The hardest things in management ... are complicated people issues. Sometimes you realise you can't solve everything. Our assets are the brains and personalities of some highly intelligent people, so there are a huge number of relationship issues. Most of these 250 people are very driven. If you get it right, the commitment is already sorted out. But you've got to take a lot of people with you a lot of the time. (*Financial Times*, 15 February 2001, p. 17)

So managing and leading require people to influence colleagues on the same organisational level, those formally above them in the hierarchy and people outside the organisation. Figure 14.2 illustrates this.

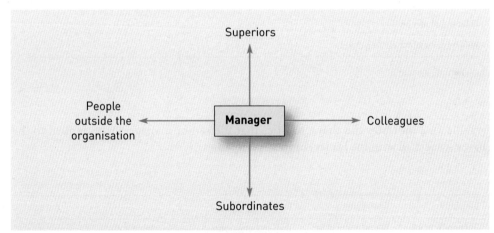

Figure 14.2

Influencing in four directions

How do managers and leaders ensure that others do what they want them to do? The sections which follow present alternative answers to that question.

14.3 Traits models

Early studies focused on the individual rather than the situation in which he or she worked. They tried to identify the **traits** that prominent leaders possessed, on the assumption that some people had attributes which made it more likely that they would be effective. These attributes include both traits and skills, both of which combine

Traits are a variety of individual attributes, including aspects of personality, temperament, needs, motives and values.

heredity and learning. People inherit aspects of temperament such as energy or personal drive, while experiences and what they learn from them shape their values. Early researchers on leadership believed that they could identify the traits and skills of effective leaders, which could be used to help select future leaders. Stogdill (1974) reviewed 163 trait studies published between 1949 and 1970, and Table 14.1 presents his results.

The *Financial Times*/PriceWaterhouseCoopers Annual Survey of the world's most respected companies continues this tradition of identifying the traits of effective leaders. Common traits included vision, ability to forecast trends, speed, decisiveness, courage, tenacity, optimism and enthusiasm.

Table 14.1

Traits and skills found most frequently to be associated with successful leaders

Traits	Skills
Adaptable to situations	Clever (intelligent)
Alert to social environment	Conceptually skilled
Ambitious and achievement oriented	Creative
Assertive	Diplomatic
Cooperative	Fluent in speaking
Decisive	Knowledgeable about group task
Dependable	Persuasive
Dominant (desire to influence others)	Socially skilled
Energetic	Well organised
Persistent	
Self-confident	
Tolerant of stress	
Willing to assume responsibility	

Source: Stogdill (1974).

Table 14.2 indicates the characteristics that the senior managers who replied to the survey associated with the leaders of these companies.

Table 14.2

Traits of those leading some of the world's most respected companies

Leader	Company	Traits
Jurgen Schremp	DaimlerChrysler	'daring behaviour'
Michael Dell	Dell Computers	'listening to customers and employees'
Richard Branson	Virgin	'a maverick, encouraging people to do things differently'
John Browne	BP	'taking lead on environment and social responsibility'

Source: *Financial Times*, 15 December 2000, 15 November 2004.

FT

Limitations

One limitation of the traits model is the large number of factors that researchers have identified. Lists of desirable traits look like impossible ideals, which are rarely present in one person. Another difficulty with this line of research is to take account of the intervening variables that affect whether a particular trait contributes to performance. Whatever traits Phillip Watts had that led to his appointment as Head of Exploration at Shell were still there when he resigned in 2004 after a scandal over the way their oil reserves were reported. Other factors intervened to make his tenure less successful than those who appointed him had expected. Having certain traits is probably necessary for effective leadership, but will not be sufficient. Their relative importance is likely to depend on other factors, including the situation in which the manager is operating – which may have contributed to the inconclusive results of much research which attempted to relate the possession of certain traits to performance. Thus the board of BP regarded Bob Horton as such a successful leader when he was running the North American operation that they appointed him as chairman and chief executive of the whole company in 1990. In 1992 they replaced him with David Simon. Traits that were valuable in North America seemed less suitable in the United Kingdom.

Contributions

Despite these limitations the traits model may help to explain why some people get to positions of great influence and others do not. Some items in Stogdill's list have been found to recur in many empirical studies linking traits and effectiveness, such as high energy levels, tolerance of stress, emotional maturity and at least a moderately high need for achievement (Yukl, 2001). Baum and Locke (2004) note a revival of interest in the personal characteristics of potential leaders, such as entrepreneurs creating new ventures. Management selection practices reflect this belief, and the criteria often include traits that are thought to be relevant for success. Table 14.3 lists the traits which the UK National Health Service Leadership Qualities Framework identifies as distinguishing 'effective and outstanding leaders'.

Table 14.3

NHS Leadership Qualities Framework

Personal qualities	Setting direction	Delivering the service
Self-belief	Seizing the future	Leading change through people
Self-awareness	Intellectual flexibility	Holding to account
Self-management	Broad scanning	Empowering others
Drive for improvement	Political astuteness	Effective and strategic influencing
Personal integrity	Drive for results	Collaborative working

Source: Based on Department of Health (2002), *NHS Leadership Qualities Framework*, NHS Leadership Centre, London.

As two of the foremost scholars of leadership concluded, 'There is no one ideal leader personality. However, effective leaders tend to have a high need to influence others, to achieve; and they tend to be bright, competent and socially adept, rather than stupid, incompetent and social disasters' (Fiedler and House, 1994, p. 111).

Activity 14.1 Which traits do employers seek?

Collect some job advertisements and recruitment brochures. Make a list of the traits that the companies say they are looking for in those they recruit.

14.4 Behavioural models

Another set of theories sought to identify the behaviours or styles of effective managers. What did they do to influence subordinates that less effective managers did not? Scholars at the Universities of Ohio State and Michigan respectively developed their models at about the same time. Their research identified two major categories of **behaviour**: one concerned with interpersonal relations, the other with accomplishing tasks.

Behaviour is something a person does that can be directly observed.

Ohio State University model

Researchers at Ohio State University (Fleishman, 1953) developed questionnaires that subordinates used to describe the behaviour of their supervisor, and concluded that they viewed their manager's behaviour on two dimensions – 'initiating structure' and 'consideration'.

Initiating structure is a pattern of leadership behaviour that emphasises the performance of the work in hand and the achievement of production or service goals.

Initiating structure refers to the degree to which a leader defines and organises their role and the role of followers, is oriented towards goal attainment and establishes well-defined patterns and channels of communication. Those using this approach focused on getting the work done, ensuring that everything was properly planned and worked out. They asked subordinates to follow the procedures, and made sure that they were working to full capacity. Typical behaviours included:

- Allocating subordinates to specific tasks
- Establishing standards of job performance
- Informing subordinates of the requirements of the job
- Scheduling work to be done by subordinates
- Encouraging the use of uniform procedures.

Consideration is a pattern of leadership behaviour that demonstrates sensitivity to relationships and to the social needs of employees.

Consideration refers to the degree to which a leader shows concern and respect for followers, looks for their welfare and expresses appreciation and support (Judge *et al.*, 2004). Such leaders assume that subordinates want to work well and try to make it easier for them to do so. They place little reliance on their formal position and power, typical behaviours including:

- Expressing appreciation for a job well done
- Not expecting more from subordinates than they can reasonably do
- Helping subordinates with personal problems
- Being approachable and available for help
- Rewarding high performance.

Surveys showed that supervisors displayed distinctive patterns – some scored high on initiating structure and low on consideration, while others were high on consideration and low on initiating structure. Some were high on both, others low on both. Research into the effects on performance were often inconclusive, but a recent review of over 130 such studies (Judge *et al.*, 2004) concluded that there was evidence that consideration tended to be more strongly related to follower satisfaction, while initiating structure was slightly more related to measures of leader performance.

University of Michigan model

Researchers at the University of Michigan (Likert, 1961, 1967) conducted similar studies and found that two types of behaviour distinguished effective from ineffective managers: job-centred and employee-centred behaviour.

- *Job-centred supervisors* ensured that they worked on different tasks from their subordinates, concentrating especially on planning, coordinating and supplying a range of support activities. These correspond to the initiating structure measures at Ohio.
- *Employee-centred supervisors* combined the task-oriented behaviour with human values. They were considerate, helpful and friendly to subordinates, and engaged in broad supervision rather than detailed observation. These behaviours were similar to what the Ohio group referred to as considerate.

From numerous studies, Likert (1961) concluded that:

> Supervisors with the best records of performance focus their primary attention on the human aspects of their subordinates' problems and on endeavouring to build effective work groups with high performance goals. (p. 7)

Managerial grid model

Blake and Mouton (1969, 1979) developed the managerial grid model to extend and apply the Ohio State research. It identifies various combinations of concern for production (initiating structure) and concern for people (consideration), as shown in Figure 14.3.

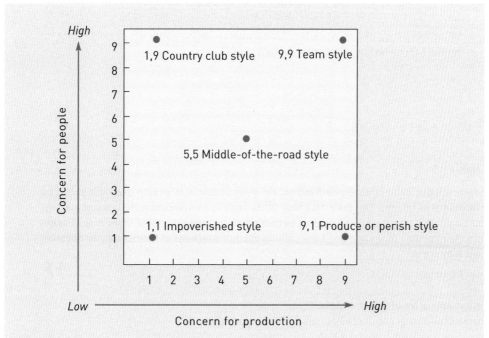

Figure 14.3

The managerial grid

The horizontal scale relates to concern for production, which ranges from 1 (low concern) to 9 (high concern). The vertical scale relates to concern for people, also ranging from 1 (low concern) to 9 (high concern). At the lower left-hand corner (1,1) is the impoverished style: low concern for both production and people. The primary objective of such managers is to stay out of trouble. They merely pass instructions to subordinates, follow the established system, and make sure that no one can blame them if something goes wrong. They do only as much as is consistent with keeping their job.

At the upper left-hand corner (1,9) is the country club style: managers who use this style try to create a secure and comfortable family atmosphere. They assume that their subordinates will respond productively. Thoughtful attention to the need for satisfying relationships leads to a friendly atmosphere and work tempo.

High concern for production and low concern for people is found in the lower right-hand corner (9,1). This is the produce or perish style. These managers do not consider subordinates' personal needs. All that matters is achieving the organisation's objectives. They use their formal authority to pressure subordinates into meeting production quotas. They believe that efficiency comes from arranging the work so that employees merely have to follow instructions.

In the centre (5,5) is the middle-of-the-road style. These managers obtain adequate performance by balancing the need to get the work done with reasonable attention to the interests of employees. In the upper right-hand corner (9,9) is the team style which, according to Blake and Mouton, is the most effective approach, aiming for both high performance and high job satisfaction. The manager fosters performance by building relationships of trust and respect.

Activity 14.2 Critical reflection on the managerial grid

- Reflect on two managers you have worked with, one effective and one ineffective from your point of view.

- Which of the positions in the Blake and Mouton grid most closely describe their style? Note some of their typical behaviours.

- What were they like to work for? Does your reflection support or contradict the model? If the latter, what may explain that?

 Two leaders' styles

Jorma Ollila of Nokia

'He is extremely ambitious and extremely demanding. He gives authority to people to do things but he demands performance in return.' The main risk that Ollila sees is complacency. He talks of a 'daily, continuous fight against bureaucracy and against becoming an incumbent, stable institution. People easily move into their comfort zones and don't ask chilling enough questions of themselves, or question the environment they are in.'

Source: *Financial Times*, 8 December 2000, p. 16.   **FT**

David Michels, chief executive of Hilton Hotels

Argument is an essential part of the success of any business, he says:

'You have to talk to staff and you can't insulate yourself by getting in first-class limos all the time. You have to get on the Tube and you have to get people to argue with you. I argue so much with my staff I sometimes wonder who is in charge. I enjoy [life as chief executive], I really do. But sometimes I sit back and think "bloody hell, this is difficult".'

Source: *Financial Times*, 6 June 2003.   **FT**

Many trainers have used the Blake and Mouton model to help managers develop towards the '9,9' style. Implicit in the approach is the idea of flexibility. The '9,9' manager would be successful not by applying the same behaviour in every situation but by using task- or relationship-centred behaviours in a way that was appropriate to the situation at hand.

Others have questioned whether showing a high level of concern for both production and people is always the best approach. Sometimes a concern for production may be more important than concern for people – such as in a sudden crisis that requires swift action. Situational or contingency models offer a possible answer.

Semco – the case continues · CASE STUDY

Employees have gradually taken greater responsibility over everything from cafeteria menus to new product designs and plant relocations. They are always free to develop new skills in other areas of the business, and to transfer to different units if they are accepted by their new colleagues. Another innovation is that workers set their own production quotas and come in on their own time to meet them if necessary, without pressure from management and without overtime pay. Their managers have considerable autonomy over the strategy for their business unit, including setting levels of pay.

Employees can see all company financial information, and Semco developed a unique way of presenting financial information in a clear, simplified way. They also developed a course to teach everyone to read balance sheets and cash-flow statements. Employees in each business group use this financial information to develop their business plan for the next six months, deciding what staff they will need and fixing their salaries. There are eleven compensation options (such as fixed salaries, royalties or stock options), which employees can choose between.

Anyone who requests too large a salary . . . runs the risk of being rejected by their colleagues. So self-interest almost always prevents them from asking for excessive paycheques. We also encourage people to set their own salaries without creating a deficit in their departments.

That's why monthly revenue reports, budgets, costs, salaries, profit-sharing, and transparent numbers (publishing salaries) are so important at Semco. If workers understand the big picture, they'll know how their salaries fit. (Semler, 2003, p. 197)

All meetings, including those of the counsellors, are open to all employees who wish to attend. This gives staff the information they need to make informed decisions, and reinforces the democratic nature of the decision-making process.

Moving an organization or business ahead by virtue of what its people stand for means removing obstacles like official policies, procedural constraints and relentless milestones, all of which are set up in the pursuit of quarterly or otherwise temporary success. It means giving up control, and allowing employees to manage themselves. It means trusting workers implicitly, sharing power and information, and celebrating true democracy. (Semler, 2003, pp. 112–13)

Case questions 14.1

- Where would you place Ricardo Semler on Blake and Mouton's managerial grid?
- Does the Semco story support or not the prescriptions of that model?

459

key ideas — Does style affect performance?

Bass (1990) reviewed research to assess the effects of the leader's style on performance and found them inconclusive. In some cases subordinates were more satisfied with a structuring leader, while others failed to find any significant relationships. It is also possible that the direction of the cause/effect relationship is unclear. It is usual to assume that the relationship is from leader behaviour to subordinate behaviour. It may be that leaders behave in a considerate style to subordinates who are performing well.

14.5 Situational (or contingency) models

Situational models of leadership attempt to identify the contextual factors that affect when one style will be more effective than another.

Situational (or contingency) models present the idea that managers influence others by adapting their style to the circumstances. Three such models are set out below (a fourth, developed by Vroom and Yetton (1973) featured in Chapter 7).

Tannenbaum and Schmidt's continuum of leader behaviour

Unlike the 'one best way' model implied by the behavioural models, Robert Tannenbaum and Warren Schmidt (1973) saw that leaders worked in different ways, which they presented as a continuum of styles, ranging from autocratic to democratic. Figure 14.4 illustrates these extremes and the positions in between. Which of these the leader uses should reflect three forces:

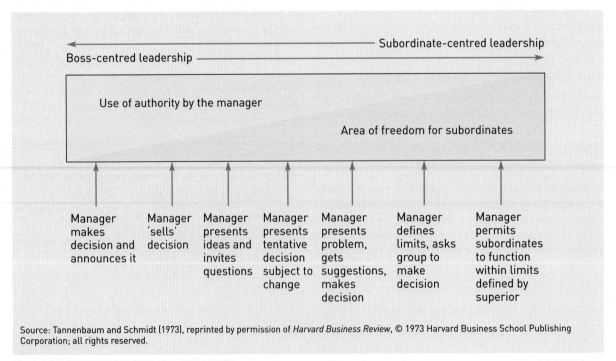

Source: Tannenbaum and Schmidt (1973), reprinted by permission of *Harvard Business Review*, © 1973 Harvard Business School Publishing Corporation; all rights reserved.

Figure 14.4 The Tannenbaum–Schmidt continuum of leadership behaviour

- **Forces in the manager:** personality, values, preferences, beliefs about participation and confidence in subordinates
- **Forces in subordinates:** need for independence, tolerance of ambiguity, knowledge of the problem, expectations of involvement
- **Forces in the situation:** organisational norms, size and location of work groups, effectiveness of team working, nature of the problem.

House's path–goal model

House (House and Mitchell, 1974; House, 1996) argued that effective leaders are those who clarify their subordinates' path to the rewards available, and ensure that rewards which the subordinates value are available. They help subordinates to identify and learn behaviours that will help them complete the task and so secure the rewards for doing so. The model identifies four styles of leader behaviour:

- **Directive:** letting subordinates know what the leader expects; giving specific guidance; asking subordinates to follow rules and procedures; scheduling and coordinating their work
- **Supportive:** treating them as equals; showing concern for their needs and welfare; creating a friendly climate in the work unit
- **Achievement oriented:** setting challenging goals and targets; seeking performance improvements; emphasising excellence in performance; showing confidence that subordinates will attain high standards
- **Participative:** consulting subordinates; taking their opinions into account.

House suggested that the appropriate style would depend on the situation – the characteristics of the subordinate and the work environment. For example, if an employee has little confidence or skill then the leader needs to provide coaching, training and other support. If the subordinate is one who likes clear direction then they will respond best to a leader who acts in that way. Highly skilled professionals will usually expect to work on their own initiative and resent a directive style – they will be influenced more if the leader uses a participative or achievement-oriented style.

The work environment includes the degree of task structure (such as whether it is routine or non-routine), the formal authority system (the extent to which rules and procedures guide activities) and the work group characteristics (the amount and quality of teamwork within the group). Figure 14.5 summarises the model.

The model predicts that a directive style would work best when the task is ambiguous and the subordinates lack flexibility – the leader absorbs uncertainty for the group and shows them how to achieve the task. A supportive style works well in highly repetitive tasks or those that are frustrating or physically unpleasant – subordinates respect the leader who joins in an unpleasant or difficult task. An achievement-oriented style works when the group faces non-repetitive ambiguous tasks, which will challenge their ability – so they need encouragement and pressure to raise their ambitions. The leader using this style urges subordinates to use their abilities to the full and encourages them by showing confidence in those abilities. A participative approach is likely to work best when the task is non-repetitive and the subordinate(s) are confident that they can do the work.

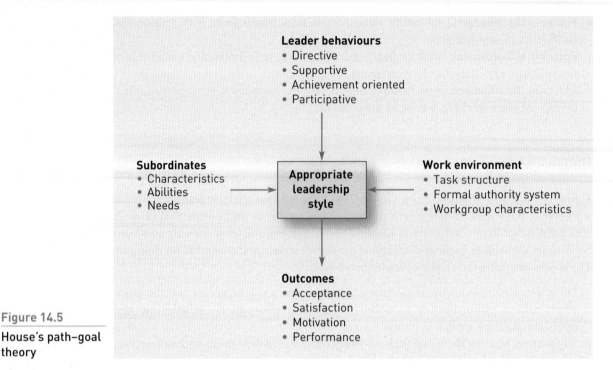

Figure 14.5

House's path–goal theory

Helmut Panke, chief executive of BMW www.bmw.com

Helmut Panke became CEO of Bavarian Motor Works (BMW) in 2002, since when he has overseen a rapid expansion of the model range. Sales, and the company's share price, have risen strongly in the two years since he took charge of the company. Panke demands top performance from staff, and from himself. He first demonstrated his skills at building BMW's global business as head of North American operations in the mid-1990s, during which time the US became BMW's largest market.

> Panke's management style could be called Socratic. He loves to pose questions and lead debates with groups of managers – a practice that reflects his academic training (he has a doctorate in nuclear physics) and gets results . . . By encouraging debate, Panke has forged a performance-driven culture that isn't afraid to send tough questions up the ranks. 'Panke takes a huge amount of time to discuss with people, then he lets them manage on their own. That way he gets 120% from everyone', says a manager who has seen Panke rise up the ranks over 20 years. . . . 'My biggest challenge is saying "no" to projects that are exciting but don't fit BMW's strategy', comments Panke (p. 48).

Source: *Business Week*, 7 June 2004.

The path–goal model does not provide a formula for the best way to lead, and House stressed that it was in the early stages of development. Reviews of empirical work to test the theory (such as that by Indvik, 1986, who reviewed 48 empirical studies) have on balance supported the central proposition – that effective leaders select the style most appropriate to the situation and the subordinates. Contingency models indicate that participative leadership styles are not necessarily the most effective, and that, as Table 14.4 shows, there will be situations where a directive style is appropriate.

Participative style most likely to work when:	Directive style most likely to work when:
Subordinates' acceptance of the decision is important	Subordinates do not share the manager's objectives
The manager lacks information	Time is critically short
The problem is unstructured	Subordinates accept top-down decisions

Table 14.4

Conditions favouring participative or directive styles

key ideas John Adair and Action Centred Leadership

Over 2 million people worldwide have taken part in the Action Centred Leadership approach pioneered by John Adair, a widely recognised authority on leadership training. He proposes that people expect leaders to fulfil three obligations – to help them achieve the task, to build and maintain the team and to enable individuals to satisfy their needs. These three obligations overlap and influence each other – if the task is achieved that will help to sustain the group and satisfy individual needs. If the group lacks skill or cohesion it will neither achieve the task nor satisfy the members. Figure 14.6 represents the three needs as overlapping circles in what is almost a trademark for John Adair's work. To achieve these expectations the leader performs the eight functions shown in the figure – similar to those shown in Chapter 1.

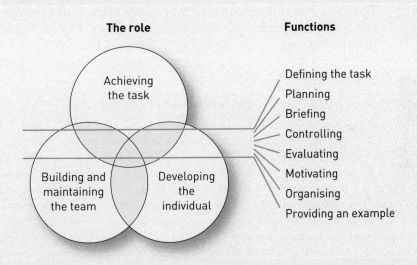

Figure 14.6 Adair's model of leadership functions

Source: Adair (1997), p. 21.

14.6 Sources of power to influence others

Earlier sections have centred on the personal skills that people can use to influence others, including their ability to adapt their methods to the situation in which they are working. Another perspective shows that people can also influence others by using their **power**.

Power concerns 'the capacity of individuals to exert their will over others' (Buchanan and Badham, 1999).

Sources of power

What are the bases of one person's power over another? French and Raven's (1959) widely quoted classification identifies five sources of power:

- **Legitimate power** flows from the person's formal position in the organisation, and derives from the job that he or she holds. This position gives the job holder certain forms of power, for example to make capital expenditures, to offer overtime, to choose a supplier or to recruit staff.
- **Reward power** is the ability of someone to reward another. It is visible when one person complies with another person's request or instruction because they expect some reward in return. The reward itself can take many forms – a pay rise, time off or more interesting work.
- **Coercive power** is the ability to obtain compliance through fear of punishment. It is the capacity to harm or restrict the actions of others, which they try to avoid. It may take the form of reprimands, demotions, loss of a job – or the threat of physical force. Aggressive language and a powerful physical presence are other forms of coercive power.
- **Referent power**, also called *charismatic* power, is visible when some characteristics of the manager are attractive to the subordinate. They want to identify with him or her, and this gives the manager power over them.
- **Expertise power** is visible when people acknowledge someone's specialised knowledge and are therefore willing to follow their suggestions. During a problem-solving activity it often becomes clear who knows most about particular aspects of the problem. The leadership of the group may temporarily move to that person. This knowledge and skill may be either *administrative* (how an organisation operates) or *technical* (how to do a task).

> A **transactional leader** is one who treats leadership as an exchange, giving followers what they want if they do what the leader desires.

> A **transformational leader** is a leader who treats leadership as a matter of motivation and commitment, inspiring followers by appealing to higher ideals and moral values.

---

key ideas **James Burns and transformational leadership**

James Burns (1978) distinguished between **transactional** and **transformational leaders**. Transactional leaders influence subordinates' behaviour by way of a bargain. The leader enables followers to reach their goals, while at the same time contributing to the goals of the organisation. If subordinates behave in the way desired by the leader they will receive rewards that they value.

Burns contrasted this approach with that of transformational leaders. They work in ways that lead subordinates to change their goals, needs and aspirations. Transformational leaders raise the consciousness of followers by appealing to higher ideals and moral values. They do this by displaying a number of identifiable behaviours, such as articulating 'transcendent goals, demonstration of self-confidence and confidence in others, setting a personal example for followers, showing high expectations of followers' performance, and the ability to communicate one's faith in one's goals' (Fiedler and House, 1994, p. 112).

The degree to which a leader is transformational depends on the effect on his or her followers. Fiedler and House (1994) claim that empirical research supports the claims for the successes of charismatic leaders. Followers and superiors see them as more effective than transactional leaders.

Table 14.5 develops the French and Raven list, by showing that each type of power can have both a personal and a positional source. The most significant change to the French and Raven model is to show that referent (charismatic) power is not just personal but can also have a positional source (Hales, 2001). Chapter 10 showed how distinctive cultures and sub-cultures develop within organisations, which can exert a strong influence on how people act. When people refer to this prevailing culture in an attempt to influence behaviour ('what I'm asking you to do is consistent with our culture') they are drawing on a positional form of referent power.

Power resource	Personal	Positional
Coercive	Forcefulness, insistence, determination	Authority to give instructions, with the threat of sanctions or punishment available
Reward	Credit for previous or future favours in day-to-day exchanges	Authority to use organisational resources, including the support of senior people
Expertise: **Administrative**	Experience of the business, whom to contact, how to get things through the system	Authority to use or create organisational policies or rules
Technical	Skill or expertise relevant to the task	Authority to access expertise, information and ideas across the business
Referent	Individual beliefs, values, ideas, personal qualities	Authority to invoke norms and values of the organisational culture

Source: Based on Hales (2001)

Table 14.5

Personal and positional sources of power

Someone who has little access to these sources of power will have less influence than someone with much access. People continually defend their present power sources, and try to gain new ones.

Perceptions of power

Power is only effective if the target of an influence attempt recognises the power source as legitimate and acceptable. If they dispute the knowledge base of a manager, or challenge their positional authority over a matter, the influence attempt is likely to fail.

Managers who are successful influencers ensure that their power sources are sustained, and take every opportunity to enhance them.

Marketing brand Me

People should manage their reputation like a brand. The most effective candidates [for promotion] do not leave their image to chance. They work at it, and massage its growth. They know that the best publicists they can have are their immediate staff. They are aware that team members talk about them more than anyone else. So they provide evidence to feed that grapevine ... Staff need stories about their leader.

Another way to manage your reputation is to manage your boss ... People keen to manage their reputation should find out what motivates the boss and try to satisfy those goals. If your boss likes punctuality and conscientiousness, turn up on time and work hard. If he or she needs reassurance, give it. If it is power, respond as someone who is less powerful. Why irritate a person who can influence your career path?

Source: John Hunt, 'Marketing brand Me', *Financial Times*, 22 December 2000.

FT

Responses to the use of power

People respond to influence attempts in three ways – resistance, compliance and internalisation. Table 14.6 describes the alternatives. Resistant staff will have no commitment to the work. They do what is required grudgingly, and without enthusiasm or imagination. While it may be possible to overcome resistance by using threats or coercion, this may not be the most useful reaction in the longer term. Compliance too has limitations, especially if long-term success depends on further innovation. Only when staff are fully committed because they have internalised the influencer's goals, and see themselves as part of the creative process, is the influencing task complete.

Table 14.6
Three outcomes of influence attempts

Outcome	Description	Commentary
Resistance	Target is opposed to the request and actively tries to avoid carrying it out	Target may make excuses or try to dissuade the influencer from persisting. May also seek support from higher authority or undermine the influencer's efforts
Compliance	Target willing to do what is asked, but is apathetic, unenthusiastic and makes minimal effort	For a complex task, an unsatisfactory outcome. For routine tasks it may be enough for the influencer to accomplish their goals
Internalisation	Target internally agrees with a decision or request and makes a great effort to meet it successfully	Usually the most successful outcome from the point of view of the influencer, especially on a difficult task

Grudging compliance is unlikely to lead to satisfactory performance. The complexities of work processes often require people to work with imagination and flexibility. In service industries employee behaviour directly influences customer perceptions, such as whether they see employees working responsibly and with concern for what they are doing. This is not likely to happen if managers have used their power in ways that have secured only compliance, not the commitment that comes from internalisation.

Activity 14.3   Critical reflection on sources of power

- Try to identify at least one example of each of the personal and positional power sources. Examples could come from observing a manager in action (including people in your university or college) or from your reading of current business affairs.
- Can you identify what the person concerned has done to develop their power?
- Have other events helped to build, or to undermine their power?

Case questions 14.2

- Which of the sources of power in Table 14.5 has Ricardo Semler used?
- What has he done to increase his power in the eyes of those he is trying to influence?
- What other forms of authority has he acquired?
- Which of the sources of power in Table 14.5 could the Associates use?

14.7   Using positional power to influence others

Those who want to be effective influencers can increase their chances of doing so by building up those sources of power that come from their position within the organisation. Kanter (1979) observed that people are more likely to be influenced by strong and powerful managers than by weak and isolated ones. She identified many ways in which a manager's position in the organisation affects their power, such as:

- Approvals needed for non-routine decisions (fewer approvals means more power)
- Relation of job to current organisational priorities (central relation means more power)
- External contact (more opportunities for this means more power)
- Senior contact (more opportunities for this means more power).

The nature of the job and the pattern of contacts that come with it give the manager access to three 'lines of power':

- **Supply**: money and other resources that can be used to bestow status or rewards on others in return for their support
- **Information**: being in the know, aware of what is happening, familiar with plans and opportunities that are in the making
- **Support**: able to get senior or external backing for what he or she wants to do.

The more of these lines of power the manager has, the more will subordinates cooperate. They do so because they believe that the manager has the power to engage in **political behaviour** and make things happen: they have 'clout' – weight or political influence in the organisation. A person's position in the organisation gives them access to one or more of the sources of power shown in Table 14.5.

> **Political behaviour** is 'the practical domain of power in action, worked out through the use of techniques of influence and other (more or less extreme) tactics' (Buchanan and Badham, 1999).

Coercive

This is the ability to give instructions or threaten penalties, derived from a person's formal position in the hierarchy. While this appears to give someone in that position great coercive power over subordinates, this may be an illusion. At best it may only produce compliant behaviour; at worst it may foster active resistance or attempts to undermine the manager's position.

Reward

This is the ability that position gives to use the financial and other resources of the organisation to give rewards in return for support. Managers with large budgets and valuable networks of contacts use these resources, or the promise of them, to exert influence. Managers who choose to be remote and isolated in back-room work will not have that power – and so will have little influence on people or events.

Expertise

Administrative expertise

This is the power that the holder of a position has to create formal policies which support their influence attempts. They can create rules, procedures or positions that sustain their power – especially if they can also appoint loyal supporters, or those in their debt, to those positions. In this way they encourage others to act in the way they prefer – as when the new chief executive of Centrica persuaded his staff to improve customer service.

Structures and rewards at Centrica www.centrica.co.uk

Centrica inherited severe customer relations problems when it demerged from British Gas, so restoring customer trust was an important part of the new chief executive's job. He changed the structure of Centrica to influence other managers to give it priority. Customer service satisfaction targets were included in an executive bonus scheme covering its top 200 people. Also, a senior board executive was made responsible for all customer services.

Source: Based on *Financial Times*, 24 February 2001.

Sir John Harvey-Jones's leadership at ICI

In a classic study of ICI under Sir John Harvey-Jones, Pettigrew paid particular attention to the link between the leadership of the company and the change process. Sir John Harvey-Jones was clearly instrumental in initiating and implementing immense and fundamental change. Pettigrew's study shows that Harvey-Jones did not achieve this by a few dramatic acts or decisions. Rather it depended heavily on actions that he took over many years to change the structure of the organisation so that managers had more access to sources of power with which to influence others in the direction of radical change. For example, greater power was given to divisional directors to reward staff according to their performance.

This research led to the conclusion that studies of leadership should not focus only on the actions of individuals, important though they are. Rather they should view leadership as a continuous process taking place within a particular organisational context. The leader exerts influence by shaping that context and providing others with more positional power to initiate change.

Source: Pettigrew (1985, 1987).

Too much internal focus

A department of a local authority consisted of a director, two senior officers, three officers and 14 staff. The director's style was to involve himself in operational matters, and he rarely found time to work with other senior managers. He normally met only with the senior officers within his department and rarely involved others in these discussions. He took the view that officers should not be involved in policy matters. He saw himself as the only competent person in the department and was comfortable in this operational role.

Staff consider themselves to be capable and professional. They expect to be involved more fully and are used to taking initiatives in both the routine and innovative aspects of the work. The fact that the director becomes involved in operational detail affects the officers in two ways. They are annoyed at the lack of trust this displays in their own abilities. They also suffer from the relatively low status of the department, caused by the director not being active externally and so lacking influence outside the department.

Technical expertise

This is the power a person gains from holding a position that gives them access to information, of being in the know, aware of what is happening and of opportunities which are emerging. They can use their position, and the contacts that go with it, to build their image as a competent person. This credibility adds to their power to influence others. It is a contentious area, since people compete for access to information, and the power that goes with it – as the 'flowering of feudalism' feature indicates.

The flowering of feudalism

'Knowledge is power' has become such a managerial cliché that many at the top of big companies tend to forget that the principle can work both ways. Those lower down the management hierarchy also have an interest in husbanding information – and the power that goes with it. According to a recent survey of large European companies by the management consulting arm of KPMG, an accounting firm, the vast majority have found it impossible to establish pan-European management information systems for the simple reason that middle-ranking managers in different countries do not want those at headquarters to know what they are up to.

By 1993 few companies had succeeded in taking the first step by collecting information on their own far-flung European operations in a uniform way. After interviewing the chief executives or financial officers of 153 large European companies, KPMG found that only 8 per cent had established common information systems across their European subsidiaries. And this was not because of glitches with computers. 'Technically, of course, anything is possible with information systems these days', observed the boss of a Danish tobacco firm. 'It is not the technical aspect that we find daunting; it's the time and energy we have to spend explaining it to people and persuading them to accept it.'

When they try to introduce the computers and procedures to gather such information, reported Alistair Stewart, who conducted the survey, European firms meet 'Ghandhi-like' resistance from their subsidiaries. European HQs may be sending mixed signals to subsidiary managers: preaching autonomy and responsibility while trying to computerise all aspects of their business so that staff at headquarters can monitor their every move. 'People are reluctant to share their information', complained the head of one French company, which manufactures industrial equipment. 'Managers in particular seem to think it gives them extra power.' Clever chaps.

Source: Based on an article in *The Economist*, 27 February 1993, © The Economist, London, 1993.

Referent

This is where managers use their position to influence others by showing that what they propose is consistent with the accepted values and culture of the organisation. They invoke wider values in support of their proposal. The effectiveness of the influence attempt depends on the other people having a similar view of the culture.

The more of these sources of power the manager has, the more others will cooperate. They do so because they believe that the manager has the power to make things happen. Such a manager has weight or political influence in the organisation, which encourages others to accede to their wishes.

'To increase power, share it'

Delegation occurs
when one person gives
another the authority to
undertake specific
activities or decisions.

Kanter (1979) also proposed that managers can increase their power by, paradoxically, **delegating** some of it to subordinates. By sharing power with subordinates managers can further increase their own power. As subordinates carry out tasks previously done by the manager, the manager has more time to build the external and senior contacts – which further boost his or her power. By delegating not only tasks but also lines of supply (such as giving subordinates a generous budget), lines of information (inviting them to attend high-level meetings) and lines of support (giving visible encouragement to subordinates' work), managers develop subordinates' confidence, and at the same time enhance their own power.

The major benefit of delegation is that it reduces the manager's workload. Relieved of the need to deal with the detail of a task, the manager has more time to concentrate on major planning and creative work. More time can be spent on external matters, making contacts, keeping in touch with what is happening in the firm or the industry. This builds the visibility and reputation of the manager's unit. A manager who fails to delegate, and who therefore looks inward rather than to the world outside, will become increasingly isolated from external events.

Semco – the case continues   CASE STUDY

The offices are open plan (like those at Oticon), and managers have none of the minor privileges often associated with the role, like parking spaces, executive dining rooms or secretaries. There are very few rules, as Semler believes in treating employees like adults.

We have absolute trust in our employees . . . (and) we are proving that worker involvement doesn't mean that bosses lose power. What we do is strip away the blind, irrational authoritarianism that diminishes productivity. We're thrilled that our workers are self-governing and self-managing. It means that they care about their jobs and about their company, and that's good for all of us. (Semler, 1994, pp. 4–5)

A major innovation occurred when some engineers offered to develop new products and lines of business, working with Semco equipment and facilities in return for a share of the royalties or savings from their ideas. They would report to senior management after six months – who would extend or revoke the mandate. The group was successful, and senior managers have encouraged this 'satellite' system throughout the group. These have become highly innovative divisions within Semco, and some two-thirds of the company's new

products come from satellites. Workers thrived on having complete accountability and responsibility, understanding that failure to perform would result in the unit being discontinued.

This way of developing the business has enabled it to develop from the original industrial machinery unit, which has evolved into high-tech mixing equipment used in, for example, the pharmaceutical industry. Another unit (SemcoBAC) makes cooling towers for commercial properties, and a third (Semco Johnson Controls) manages large properties like hospitals and airports. Other units are in environmental consulting, inventory management, HRM outsourcing and several other diverse businesses. The common theme which links them is that they are all in markets in which the solutions are highly engineered (and therefore difficult), in which Semco can be a market leader, and in which they can charge a high price for their services. Underlying all of the transformation that has taken place, Semler identifies a common core value:

If you ask people what Semco is, their answer will be the same as it was two decades ago . . . People will talk about shared ideas . . . and that comes from the freedom to ask, Why? (Semler, 2003, p. 8)

14.8 Choosing tactics to influence others

Another approach to the study of influence has been to identify directly how managers tried to influence others. An early example of this was work by Kipnis *et al.* (1980), who identified a set of influencing tactics that managers used in dealing with subordinates, bosses and co-workers. Yukl and Falbe (1990) replicated this work in a wider empirical study, and refined the categories. Table 14.7 defines the Yukl and Falbe influence categories.

Table 14.7

Influence tactics and definitions

Tactic	Definition
Rational persuasion	The person uses logical arguments and factual evidence to persuade you that a proposal or request is viable and likely to result in the attainment of task objectives
Inspirational appeal	The person makes a request or proposal that arouses enthusiasm by appealing to your values, ideals and aspirations or by increasing your confidence that you can do it
Consultation	The person seeks your participation in planning a strategy, activity or change for which your support and assistance are desired, or the person is willing to modify a proposal to deal with your concerns and suggestions
Ingratiation	The person seeks to get you in a good mood or to think favourably of him or her before asking you to do something
Exchange	The person offers an exchange of favours, indicates a willingness to reciprocate at a later time, or promises you a share of the benefits if you help accomplish the task
Personal appeal	The person appeals to your feelings of loyalty and friendship towards him or her before asking you to do something
Coalition	The person seeks the aid of others to persuade you to do something, or uses the support of others as a reason for you to agree also
Legitimating	The person seeks to establish the legitimacy of a request by claiming the authority or right to make it or by verifying that it is consistent with organisational policies, rules, practices or traditions
Pressure	The person uses demands, threats or persistent reminders to influence you to do what he or she wants

Source: Based on Yukl and Falbe (1990).

The nine tactics cover a variety of behaviours that people can use as they try to influence others – whether subordinates, bosses or colleagues. Yukl and Tracey (1992) extended the work by examining which tactics managers used most frequently with different target groups. They concluded that managers were most likely to use:

- rational persuasion when trying to influence their boss
- inspirational appeal and pressure when trying to influence subordinates
- exchange, personal appeal and legitimating tactics when influencing colleagues.

14.9 Influencing through networks

An important way to influence others is the ability to draw on a network of informal relationships. **Networking** refers to 'individuals' attempts to develop and maintain relationships with others [who] have the potential to assist them in their work or career' (Huczynski, 2004, p. 305). Table 14.8 shows several types of network.

Table 14.8

Some types of network

Practitioners	Joined by people with a common training or professional interest, and may be formal or informal
Privileged power	Joined by people in powerful positions (usually by invitation only)
Ideological	Consisting of people keen to promote political objectives or values
People-oriented	Formed around shared feelings of personal warmth and familiarity – friendship groups which people join on the basis of identity with existing participants
Strategic	Often built to help develop links with people in other organisations

The ability to influence can be greatly enhanced by being connected to many such networks, giving access to contacts and information. They help people to know what is happening in their business and to extend their range of contacts in other organisations. Strong anecdotal evidence that networking influences career progression was supported by Luthans' (1988) research described in Chapter 1, which showed that people who spent a relatively large amount of time networking received more rapid promotion than those who did not. As Thomas (2003) observed: 'in management what you know and what you have achieved will seldom be sufficient for getting ahead. Knowing and being known in the networks of influence, both for what you have achieved and for who you are may be essential'.

key ideas Art Kleiner and Core Groups

Kleiner suggests that organisations, despite the rhetoric about customers and stakeholders, exist to serve the interests of what he calls their Core Group – 'the people who really matter'. The nature of the Core Group varies from place to place – sometimes concentrated amongst senior managers, at others widely dispersed – but every organisation is continually acting to fulfil the perceived needs and priorities of its Core Group – the organisation goes wherever people 'perceive the core group needs and wants to go' (p. 8). 'If we are going to act effectively in a society of organizations, we need a theory to help us see organizations clearly, as they are' (p. 6).

Source: Kleiner (2003).

Kotter (1982) observed that general managers rely heavily on informal networks of contacts to get things done. This is especially necessary to influence those in other organisations – to make a sale, to gain access to a country's market or to set up a joint venture. The same general principles apply, with the added complexity of having to establish what forms of influence will work best in dealing with different organisational or national cultures.

Influence in China and Taiwan

Star TV (a subsidiary of Rupert Murdoch's News Corporation) developed close links with the Chinese authorities, in the hope of expanding the delivery of its entertainment channel on Chinese TV. This paid off in 2003, when it became the first foreign-owned company to receive permission for a limited nationwide service.

> 'Everything in China is about relationships and mutual benefit', said Jamie Davis, head of Star TV in China. 'I think Rupert Murdoch has a very good relationship with the Chinese Government . . . and we work hard at it.' **FT**

Source: *Financial Times*, 9 January 2003

> The sudden elevation of Ho-chen Tan to the top job at Chunghwa Telecom last month was demonstration of the value of having friends in high places. He was in charge of transport in Taipei in the mid-1990s, when the Taiwanese President, Chen Shui-bian, was mayor of the city. Mr Ho-chen says his contacts in the administration will help Chunghwa to win a voice in how the government handles the company's privatization: 'I hope our company can win the right to make suggestions. Perhaps my network in the current government and the faith put in me will help the company to get more opportunities.' **FT**

Source: *Financial Times*, 21 February 2003.

Whichever methods are used, the outcome of an influence attempt will depend not only on the tactics used but on how well the influencer is able to meet the needs of the influencee, as discussed in Chapter 15.

Summary

1 **Distinguish leading from managing, and explain why each is essential to performance:**

- Although both are essential and the difference can be overstated, leading is usually seen as referring to activities that bring change, whereas managing brings stability and order. Many people both lead and manage in the course of their work.

2 **Explain why leading and managing both depend on being able to influence others:**

- Achieving objectives usually depends on the willing commitment of other people. How management seeks to influence others affects people's reaction to being managed. Dominant use of power may ensure compliance, but such an approach is unlikely to produce the commitment required to meet innovative objectives.

3 **Compare trait, behavioural and contingency perspectives on styles of influence:**

- Trait theories seek to identify the personal characteristics associated with effective influencing.
- Behavioural theories distinguish managers' behaviours on two dimensions, such as initiating structure and consideration.
- Contingency perspectives argue that the traits or behaviours required for effective influence depend on factors in the situation, such as the characteristics of the employee, the boss and the task.

4 **Outline theories that focus on power (both personal and organisational) as the source of influence:**

- The more power a person has, the more they will be able to influence others. Table 14.5 identified sources of power as coercion, reward, expertise (administrative and technical) and referent – all of which can have both personal and organisational dimensions.

5 **Contrast the style and power perspectives, and explain why sharing power may increase it:**

- Sharing power with subordinates may not only enable them to have more satisfying and rewarding work, but by enabling the manager to have more time to develop senior and external contacts, he or she can then enhance their power more than if they focused on internal matters.

6 **Outline a model of the tactics which people use to influence others, including the use of cooperative networks:**

- Yukl and Falbe have identified these tactics in attempts to influence others: rational persuasion, inspirational appeal, consultation, ingratiation, exchange, personal appeal, coalition, legitimating and pressure. They have also found that effective influencers vary their tactics depending on the person they are trying to influence. A further line of research identifies the value of building collaborative networks as part of effective influencing.

Review questions

1 Why is the ability to influence others so central to the management role?

2 What evidence is there that traits theories continue to influence management practice?

3 What are the strengths and weaknesses of the behavioural approaches to leadership?

4 What is meant by the phrase a '9,9 manager'?

5 Discuss with someone how he or she tries to influence people (or reflect on your own practice). Compare this experience with one of the contingency approaches.

6 Evaluate that theory in the light of the evidence acquired in review question 5 and other considerations.

7 Explain in your own words the main sources of power available to managers. Give examples of both personal and institutional forms of each.

8 List the lines of power that Kanter identifies and give an example of each.

9 What does the network perspective imply for someone wishing to be a successful influencer?

Concluding critical reflection

Think about the ways in which you typically seek to influence others, and about how others in your company try to exert influence. Review the material in the chapter, and then make notes on these questions:

- What examples of the issues discussed in this chapter struck you as being relevant to practice in your company?
- Thinking of the people you typically work with, who are effective and who are less effective influencers? What do the effective people do that enables them to get their way? What interpersonal skills do they use? What sources of power, or what networks, do they use? Do the prevailing assumptions fit with Kanter's view that 'to increase power, share it'? On balance, do their assumptions accurately reflect the reality you see?
- What factors such as the history of the company or your personal experience have shaped the way you manage your attempts at influencing? Does your current approach appear to be right for your present position and company – or would you use a different approach in other circumstances? (Perhaps refer to some of the Management in Practice features for how different managers exert influence.)
- Have people put forward alternative approaches to influencing, based on evidence about other companies? If you could find such evidence, how may it affect company practice?
- How do you and your colleagues react to the Semco approach, which appears to have helped create a successful, profitable business?

Further reading

Yukl, G.A. (2001), *Leadership in Organizations* (5th edn), Prentice Hall, Upper Saddle River, NJ.

Combines a comprehensive review of academic research on all aspects of organisational leadership with clear guidance on the implications for practitioners.

Buchanan, D. and Badham, R. (1999), *Power, Politics and Organizational Change: Winning the turf game*, Sage, London.

A modern approach to politics in organisations, offering a theoretical and practical guide, based on extensive primary research.

Huczynski, A.A. (2004), *Influencing Within Organizations* (2nd edn), Routledge, London.

Draws on a wide range of academic research to provide a practical guide to being an effective influencer – from how to conduct yourself at a job interview to coping with organisational politics.

Branson, R. (1999), *Losing My Virginity*, Virgin Books, London.

Roddick, A. (2000), *Business as Unusual*, Thorsons, London.

Semler, R. (2003), *The Seven Day Weekend: Finding the work/life balance*, Century, London.

Accounts of their approach to management by three charismatic leaders.

Kleiner, A. (2003), *Who Really Matters: The core group theory of power, privilege and success*, Doubleday, New York.

Absorbing perspective of the realities of corporate power, with many practical implications for career planning.

Adams, S. (1998), *The Dilbert Principle*, Boxtree, London.

Light relief from your studies.

Pedler, M., Burgoyne, J. and Boydell, T. (2004), *A Manager's Guide to Leadership*, McGraw-Hill. Maidenhead.

A highly practical book, based on the philosophy that leadership is defined by what people do when faced with challenging situations. The authors use their well-established self-development approach to encourage readers to act on situations requiring leadership, and then to reflect and learn from the experience.

Weblinks

Visit these websites (or others of similar companies of which you learn):

www.oticon.com

www.gore.com

www.semco.locaweb.br (in Portuguese in 2004)

www.thebodyshop.com

www.mondragon.mcc.es

Each of these organisations has tried to develop new approaches to managing and influencing staff, and have, despite periods of difficulty, survived and in most cases prospered. They are still quite rare, as relatively few entrepreneurs have successfully followed their example.

● Use the House model to analyse what conditions may explain their success.

● Why do you think so few others have adopted the same approach?

> Annotated weblinks, multiple choice questions and other
> useful resources can be found on
> www.pearsoned.co.uk/boddy

Chapter 15

Motivation

The Benefits Agency was responsible for delivering a range of state benefits to the public. Most Agency staff worked in a network of local offices organised into district management units. The 159 districts were organised into 13 area units. Each area director was accountable to the Agency's top management team.

The Agency used to form part of a large government department (dealing with social security matters) and, like most of the European public sector, provided permanent employment. Staff usually joined after leaving school and could expect a secure job, a predictable career path and a guaranteed pension when they retired. The work was routine, and staff were expected to follow precisely defined rules to ensure equal treatment to all citizens. Managers valued staff who followed the rules, and discouraged innovation. The management structure was hierarchical and staff passed any unusual problem to those above them in the Agency.

Alamy

A change in public policy brought radical change, as the Benefits Agency became a separate organisation within the government service. It would conduct the same functions on behalf of government but would be managed differently.

A chief executive was appointed on a three-year contract (which in itself gave a clear signal about the end of the previous 'job for life' culture). He defined a new vision: 'To provide the right money to the right person at the right time and the right place'. To deliver this more customer-centred service he gave district managers more control over their budget, thereby reducing control by senior managers. Management in some areas ignored the new freedoms and continued to manage in the old, hierarchical way.

The management of the area described in this study interpreted the freedoms as giving them authority to make very wide changes. The management board defined their vision as: 'To be the leading provider of social security services in the country'. District managers were encouraged to give more decision-making power to staff when dealing with the public, and staff were encouraged to be innovative in their approach. A critical factor in achieving this vision was to have the right number of skilled and motivated staff.

Case questions

- What attracted staff to work in the Benefits Agency before these changes?
- How are they likely to have reacted to the changes introduced?

15.1 | Introduction

Motivation refers to the forces within or beyond a person that arouse and sustain their commitment to a course of action.

The problem for managers in the Benefits Agency is that they cannot meet the expectations of the public unless they maintain and increase the **motivation** of the employees. Unmotivated employees will not provide good service, will make mistakes, and the reputation of the Agency will suffer. How will staff react to the changes prompted by the move away from a secure government job? Many joined the Agency or its predecessors because they valued the public service aspect of the work, and the secure, predictable work. How they react will affect the success or otherwise of the changes that senior management is planning.

All businesses need enthusiastic and committed employees who work in a way that supports organisational goals. When Centrica attempted to improve customer satisfaction and trust (see Chapter 14), management depended on staff being motivated to deliver better service. Microsoft and Dell depend on their engineers being motivated to develop a constant flow of innovative products. Hospitals depend on medical and nursing staff being willing to work there, and to work in a way that provides good patient care.

Yet motivation arises within people – so managers need to ensure that people can satisfy their needs through work. People have different motivations, so a reward that is attractive to one may be unimportant to another.

 **Terry Green of Debenhams**

'What is it you dream of when you're young?' Terry Green, chief executive of Debenhams, posed the question . . . He is sitting in his shirt sleeves . . . behind a massive desk in his rooftop office in London's West End.

'I'll tell you', says Green, before I have a chance to answer. 'Having a flash car, a sexy girlfriend and a house in the country. And this', he continues, pulling out a book of photos of his new home, a 10-bedroomed mansion set in 22 acres of countryside, . . . 'is my boyhood dream realised.'

If he has realised his dreams, will the hunger go? 'No', he says, 'that's the brilliance of it.' Because since he took on [the new house] he's personally more in debt than he's ever been. He has to keep earning more money, making Debenhams a huge success, to pay off his mountainous mortgage.

Source: The Davidson Interview, *Management Today*, January 1999, p. 40.

Money is evidently a major motivator for Terry Green (who no longer works for Debenhams) – as it is for many on very low incomes too. Others find deep satisfaction in the work itself – like Theresa Marshall, who is a classroom assistant in a city primary school:

> I've found my niche and couldn't be happier – it's no exaggeration to say that I absolutely love my job. My favourite part is helping the children with their reading skills and seeing the pleasure that they can get out of books.

Some enjoy working with physical things or the challenge of designing an innovative product – while others enjoy working directly with other people.

With people having such diverse needs and interests, how can managers motivate them to work in ways that meet the manager's priorities? In small organisations the relationship between an owner-manager and a few employees is close and direct. Each can develop a good idea of what the other expects and adjust the pattern of work and the pattern of rewards to meet changing requirements. As the organisation grows the links become less personal. Motivation increasingly depends on more formal approaches, based on managers' theories of motivation – what they believe will influence employees. They make working assumptions about how staff are likely to respond to different inducements. Staff evaluate what is on offer and respond according to how well it meets their needs.

This chapter outlines and illustrates the main theories of human needs, as shown in Figure 15.1. How managers interpret the wider context shapes the behaviour which they expect from people – who also have needs and expectations of the organisation. The next section examines the psychological contract that expresses these mutual expectations. The following sections then present three main groups of theories about motivation at work – content, process and work design. Content theories help explain why people work, by identifying human needs that work may satisfy. Process theories help explain the thought processes that people go through as they decide which of several possible actions will best satisfy their needs. Work design theories connect the content and process approaches to workplace practice.

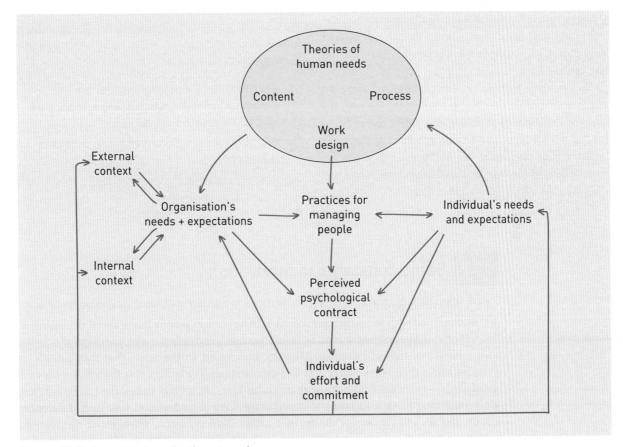

Figure 15.1 A model of motivation at work

The Benefits Agency – the case continues

Behaviour that had been valued was now a barrier to promotion. Staff who had hoped to gain promotion by following the rules now found they had little chance of moving up. Some became disillusioned but continued to deliver – at a reduced level of productivity. Some could not adapt, and left. Others applied their efforts to a new goal – to resist the changes.

Another group enthusiastically embraced this new culture where innovation, creativity and risk taking were valued. Districts introduced the 'one-stop' approach, so that one member of staff (rather than several) could deal with all the benefits that a person claimed. This led to the creation of multi-function teams, and to big changes in the way staff worked. Staff responded enthusiastically to these changes, even though pay awards were still strictly controlled and promotion opportunities had become fewer.

New policies brought further change, including the appointment of a new chief executive. In line with the government's policy of controlling public expenditure the Agency's budget was sharply reduced. At the same time the body responsible for auditing public organisations criticised the inaccuracy of benefit payments and the scope the system offered for fraud.

The new chief executive amended the Agency's vision to 'pay the right money to the right person at the right time every time'. The top management team became uneasy about the increased freedom of the area directors. Examples of a return to the older structure began to appear, such as introducing centrally controlled checking teams and increases in the number of mandatory management checks. Staff in the region reacted with dismay, and management again has the problem of how to create a skilled and motivated staff.

Case questions 15.1

- What rewards did management of the Benefits Agency use when it was operating as part of the government service?
- How were these different after the change in approach?
- How did staff react to the changes?

15.2 Some constants in motivation

Much behaviour is routine, based on habit, precedent and unconscious scripts. This chapter is concerned with the larger, precedent-setting choices people make about behaviour at work. For some people work is an occasion for hard, enthusiastic and imaginative activity, and a source of rich satisfaction. They are motivated, in the sense that they put effort (arousal) into their work (direction and persistence). For others it is something they do grudgingly – work does not arouse their enthusiasm, or merely passes the time until they find something more interesting to do. Managers try to understand why such differences occur, and seek to encourage the former rather than the latter. Theories of motivation, which try 'to explicate with increasing precision' (Steers *et al.*, 2004, p. 379) the factors that energise, channel and sustain behaviour, can inform that consideration.

Targets of attempts to motivate

Who are managers trying to motivate? Theories of motivation originally concentrated on how managers motivate subordinates, but they need to influence many other people:

colleagues, their own senior managers, people in other organisations. They also try to influence consumers – marketers also use theories of human motivation. In all of these cases people try to understand human needs in the belief that doing so accurately makes it easier to influence what they do.

Those with a more critical perspective argue that 'workers need to be influenced to cooperate because of their essential alienation from the productive process' (Thompson and McHugh, 2002, p. 306). In addition they suggest that management typically uses motivation theories to maintain the established power relations between employer and employee. Management often imposes schemes on a relatively passive workforce to make work more interesting. The latter accept these in the absence of realistic alternatives. Staff may even express greater satisfaction with a new arrangement as a way of coming to terms with the inherent stability of the power structure. As always in management, people see the topic from different perspectives: motivation is not a neutral or value-free subject.

Figure 15.2 illustrates a simple model of human motivation. We all have certain needs, such as for food, social contact or a sense of achievement, which motivates behaviours aimed at satisfying that need. If the action leads to an outcome that satisfies the need we experience a sense of reward. The feedback loop shows that we then decide whether the behaviour was appropriate and worth repeating.

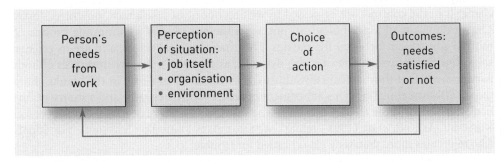

Figure 15.2

Human needs in context – the situational perspective

Individuals do not act in isolation, but within a social context that includes:

- The job – how interesting, varied or responsible it is
- The organisation – supervision, career and promotion prospects, pay systems
- The environment – the chances of getting another job.

These contextual factors, some of which management can influence, affect the behaviours people choose to satisfy a need.

In using Figure 15.2 to organise the discussion, remember that:

- Needs can only be inferred: we make assumptions about which needs a person values.
- Needs will change, and people sometimes experience conflicts between them.
- The effect of satisfying a need on the strength of that need in future is uncertain.

The psychological contract

Managers have expectations of the people who work for them. At the same time employees have expectations of managers – not just on pay, but also on such things as fairness, trust and opportunities for self-development. This set of mutual expectations makes up the **psychological contract**.

A **psychological contract** is the set of understandings people have regarding the commitments made between themselves and their organisation.

The psychological contract expresses the idea that each side has expectations of the other regarding what they will give and what they will receive in return. Employers offer rewards in the hope of receiving certain types and levels of performance. Employees contribute effort in the expectation of reward. Rousseau and Schalk (2000) refer to psychological contracts as 'the belief systems of individual workers and their employers regarding their mutual obligations' (p. 1). These arise from the promises made by each as the employment relationship begins and is sustained through daily interaction. Some elements in the contract are expressed in writing but most take a tacit, unwritten form. The current state of a psychological contract is the outcome of a continuing process of mutual adjustment between the parties. They have no legal status, and are in essence subjective and informal. They are also dynamic, as changes in the circumstances of both parties mean that they continually adjust the contract – people fill in the blanks along the way (Rousseau, 1995). This adjustment process is both inevitable and a source of difficulty, especially if the employer changes the contract in a way that makes employees feel worse off. As Kolb *et al.* (1991) remarked, 'a company staffed by "cheated" individuals who expect far more than they get is headed for trouble' (p. 6).

While the psychological contract is enacted between the individual and the employer, this negotiation takes place within a national and then a global context (see Figure 15.3). As Chapter 4 showed, nations develop distinct management systems which shape what players in the wider society expect of the employment relationship. Some societies are typified by a close and long-term affinity between employer and employee, while others see the relationship as a temporary transaction which will last only as long as both

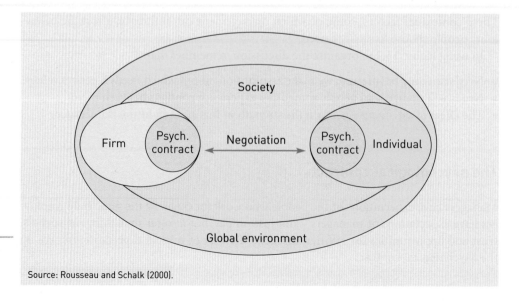

Figure 15.3

Key contexts for psychological contracting

Source: Rousseau and Schalk (2000).

parties require it. This means that the nature of an acceptable contract varies widely between countries, with significant implications for those managing beyond national boundaries (Rousseau and Schalk, 2000).

Guest and Conway (2001) studied how a sample of employees viewed the state of the psychological contract with their employer by asking them for their **perceptions** of delivery of promises, fairness, and trust. 'Delivery' covered such matters as having kept their promise to provide:

Perception is the active psychological process in which stimuli are selected and organised into meaningful patterns.

- A reasonably secure job
- Fair pay for the work you do
- A career
- Interesting work
- Fair treatment by managers and supervisors
- Help with problems outside work.

Thirty-three per cent of respondents answered 'a lot', and 50 per cent 'somewhat'. The study provided empirical support for the view that a positive psychological contract is a good predictor of work satisfaction and commitment. Those who felt they had been treated fairly were more satisfied than those who had not.

Best workplaces in Europe www.greatplacetowork.co.uk

The Great Place to Work Institute conducts an annual survey identifying the best workplaces in Europe and around the world. Table 15.1 indicates some of the top European firms in the 2004 survey.

Table 15.1 Some of the 'Best Places to Work in Europe' 2004 (in alphabetical order)

Name, country and business	Comments
Danone (Spain, food and beverages) www.danone.com	Pioneering role in corporate responsibility, rapid growth in number of female managers, development opportunities to young professionals and managers; holds a free summer camp for staff children
Kanal 5 (Sweden, media)	Lively atmosphere, employees and managers discuss mutual concerns openly; offers parental leave ('best leadership training you can get'); contacts with a service company to take care of errands such as shopping
Kraft Foods (Germany, Greece, food and beverages) www.kraft.com	Every year 15 manual staff are selected for a five-day visit to a Kraft facility in another country; selected young professionals spend 12–18 months working for Kraft in another country; a diversity council encourages promotion and integration of disadvantaged people
MBNA (Ireland, financial services) www.mbna.com/europe	Managers are expected to have regular one-to-one meetings with employees to give feedback; regularly celebrates successes; £300 for accepted employee suggestions
Pfizer (Denmark, pharmaceuticals) www.pfizer.com	All employees receive over 150 hours of training a year; arranges shopping etc. to be done for employees; bonus for recommending new employees; half of managers are women
Technogym (Italy, fitness equipment)	Culture places high value on fitness – free medical checks, gyms, food education courses; vision project involves focus groups and team meetings
Timpson (UK, service retailing) www.timpson.co.uk	'The people who serve our customers run the business – everyone else is there to help'; elaborate training; all managers swap jobs for six weeks; constant internal communications; area managers are expected to praise 10 times as much as they criticise

Source: *Financial Times*, and **www.greatplacetowork.co.uk**.

'Employees leave managers, not companies'

From the employee's point of view, there is clear evidence that good management rests squarely on four foundations:

- Having a manager who shows care, interest and concern for each of them
- Knowing what is expected of them
- Having a role that fits their abilities
- Receiving positive feedback and recognition regularly for work well done.

In a Gallup study of performance at unit level, covering more than 200,000 employees across a dozen or more industries, teams that rated managers highly on these four factors were more productive and more profitable. They also had lower staff turnover and higher customer satisfaction ratings.

Source: *People Management*, 17 February 2000, p. 45.

At a time of great change in the business world previously stable psychological contracts are easily broken. Technological changes and increased competition lead senior management to change employment policies and working conditions, or put staff under great pressure to meet demanding performance targets. The Benefits Agency is an example of this.

Case questions 15.2

- In the 1980s what were the main elements of the psychological contract between the government service and its employees? List what each was expecting of the other.
- How did that change in the early 1990s?
- How did staff respond?
- Are there possible links between that response and later events in the organisation?
- Are there any lessons which that suggests?

The following section outlines an early theory of motivation, which some companies use to influence staff behaviour. Subsequent sections look at theories about the content of human needs at work.

15.3 Behaviour modification

Behaviour modification is a general label for attempts to change behaviour by using appropriate and timely reinforcement.

Behaviour modification refers to a range of techniques that were developed to help treat various psychological conditions such as eating disorders and heavy smoking. They have also been used in organisational settings to deal with issues such as lateness and absenteeism. The techniques have developed from Skinner's (1971) theory that people learn to see relationships between actions and their consequences, and that these relationships guide future behaviour. If we receive rewards for doing something, we tend to repeat that behaviour. If we experience something unpleasant after an action, we tend not to repeat it.

Behaviour modification techniques focus on specific observable behaviours rather than on attitudes and feelings. 'In promoting safety, for instance, we did not dwell on accident-prone workers or probe for personality or demographic factors, none of which can be changed. Instead we focused on the organization and what it can do to rearrange the work environment' (Komaki, 2003, p. 96). This includes specifying what people need to do, measuring behaviour and identifying the consequences that people experience from it. If the influencer sees the behaviour as undesirable, he or she may try to influence the person to change by affecting the consequences (rewards or punishments).

Komaki (2003) gives an example of how she and her colleagues used the method in a bakery which had begun to experience a sharp increase in injuries. To encourage safe working practices, the research team worked with management on these steps:

- *Step 1: Specify desired behaviour*. This included defining very precisely the safe working practices that were required – such as walking round conveyor belts, how to sharpen knives, and using precise terms when giving instructions.
- *Step 2: Measure desired performance*. Trained observers visited the site and recorded whether workers were performing safely by following the specified behaviours.
- *Step 3: Provide frequent, contingent, positive consequences*. In this case, the positive consequence was feedback, in the form of charts on walls showing current accident figures, which were much lower than previous levels.
- *Step 4: Evaluate effectiveness*. Collecting data on accident levels after the event, to compare with those before. In this case people were found to be performing safely for a much higher proportion of the time than previously, and injuries fell from 53 a year to 10.

Practitioners emphasise several principles used in the approach, which is claimed to be effective (see, for example, a survey by Komaki *et al.*, 2000).

- Payoffs (benefits) must be given only when the desired behaviour occurs.
- Payoffs must also be used as soon as possible after the behaviour, so that the link between behaviour and reward is evident.
- Desirable behaviour is likely to be repeated if reinforced by rewards.
- Reinforcement is more effective than punishment, as punishment only temporarily suppresses behaviour.
- Repeated reinforcement can lead to permanent change in behaviour in the desired direction.

Attempting behaviour modification in a call centre

In our call centre staff are rewarded when behaviour delivers results in line with business requirements. Each month staff performance is reviewed against a number of objectives such as average call length, sales of each product and attention to detail. This is known as Effective Level Review and agents can move through levels of effectiveness ranging from 1 to 4, and gain an increase in salary after six months of successful reviews. Moving through effective levels means that they have performed well and can mean being given other tasks instead of answering the phone. The role can become mundane and repetitive so the opportunity to do other tasks is seen as a reward for good performance. Thus it reinforces acceptable behaviour.

Conversely staff who display behaviour that is not desirable cannot move through these levels and repeated failure to do so can lead to disciplinary action. This can be seen as punishment rather than behaviour modification. People can become resentful at having their performance graded every month, particularly in those areas where it is their line manager's perception of whether or not they have achieved the desired results.

Source: Private communication from the call centre manager.

Above all, proponents of the approach stress the need to reward desirable behaviours rather than to treat them with indifference. These rewards can result from individual action by a manager (a word of praise or thanks) or from organisational practices (shopping vouchers for consistently good timekeeping). Advocates of the method believe that it encourages management to look directly at what is likely to make a particular person act in a desirable way, and to ensure those rewards are available and can be sustained. The method depends on identifying rewards that the person will value (or punishments they will try to avoid). Theories that attempt to understand these are known as content theories of motivation.

15.4 Content theories of motivation

Most writers on this topic have been attempting to identify the needs people have that are likely to influence their behaviour. For example, Frederick Taylor (see Chapter 2) believed that people worked for money. Employees would follow the strictly laid down methods if management rewarded their output with more money. The work of Frank Gilbreth helped to develop the systems for introducing such payment-by-results systems widely.

Activity 15.2 Was Taylor wrong?

Many managements believe that money is a powerful incentive.

- Find someone who works for an organisation where incentives or commissions make up a significant part of that person's pay and ask how that affects his or her behaviour.
- Are there are any negative effects?

Chapter 2 described how writers such as Mary Parker Follett and Elton Mayo emphasised aspects of motivation other than money, especially the need for acceptance by other people. Evidence for this is when groups agree the level of output they will produce. If people value membership of the group more than the financial incentive they will conform to the group. Mayo drew attention to the social motivations of people at work, and advised managers to foster these rather than counter them by individual incentives.

Abraham Maslow – a hierarchy of needs

Maslow was a clinical psychologist who developed a theory of human motivation to help him understand the needs of his patients. He stressed the clinical sources of the theory and that it lacked experimental verification. He also observed that Douglas McGregor (1960, see Section 15.5) had applied the theory to industrial situations and had found it useful in ordering his data and observations.

Maslow proposed that individuals experience a range of needs, and will be motivated to fulfil whichever need is most powerful at the time (Maslow, 1970). What he termed the lower-order needs are dominant until they are at least partially satisfied. Then, Maslow predicted, normal individuals would turn their attention to satisfying the needs at the next level, and so on, so that the higher-order needs would gradually become dominant. He referred to these needs as being arranged in a hierarchy:

Self-actualisation
Esteem
Belongingness and love
Safety
Physiological

Physiological needs are the needs which must be satisfied to survive – food and water particularly. Maslow proposed that if all the needs in the hierarchy are unsatisfied then the physiological needs will dominate. People will concentrate on activities that enable them to obtain the necessities of life. Until they have these, they will not attempt to satisfy the higher needs.

Once the physiological needs were sufficiently gratified a new set of needs would emerge, which he termed *safety needs* – the search for 'security; stability; dependency; protection; freedom from fear, anxiety and chaos; need for structure, order, law, limits … and so on' (Maslow, 1970, p. 39). People concentrate on satisfying these needs, to the exclusion of other considerations. If this need is dominant for a person they can satisfy it by seeking a stable, regular job with secure working conditions and access to insurance for ill-health and retirement. They resent sudden or random changes in job prospects.

Belongingness needs would follow the satisfaction of safety needs:

> [If] both the physiological and the safety needs are fairly well gratified, there will emerge the love and affection and belongingness needs … now the person will feel keenly the absence of friends … and will hunger for affectionate relations with people in general. (p. 43)

These needs include a place in the group or family, and at work they would include wanting to be part of a congenial team. People object when management changes work patterns or locations if this disrupts established working relationships. They welcome change that brings them closer to people they know and like.

Maslow observed that most people have *esteem needs* – self-respect and the respect of others. Self-respect is the need for a sense of achievement, competence, adequacy and confidence. People also seek the respect of others, what he called a desire for reputation in the eyes of other people – prestige, status, recognition, attention. They try to satisfy this need by taking on challenging or difficult tasks which will show that they are good at their job and can accomplish something worthwhile. If others recognise this they earn status and respect.

Lastly, Maslow used the term *self-actualisation* needs to refer to the desire for self-fulfilment and for realising potential. He pointed out that the specific form this takes will vary: 'At this level, individual differences are greatest. The clear emergence of these needs usually rests upon some prior satisfaction of the physiological, safety, love, and esteem needs' (pp. 46–7). This implies that people seeking to satisfy self-actualisation needs will look for personal relevance in their work. They may value new responsibilities that help them realise their potential or discover unknown talents.

To illustrate Maslow's hierarchy with a practical example, a member of staff at the Benefits Agency summarised the ways in which the organisation had traditionally satisfied the different needs (Table 15.2).

Table 15.2

How the traditional system at the Benefits Agency enabled people to satisfy the needs identified by Maslow

Needs	How they were met
Self-actualisation	Promotion opportunities (steady and fast track)
	Funding and time off for further education
Esteem	Regarded in society as a good job
	Grade prestige
	Promotion
Belongingness and love	Sports and social clubs (local and national)
	Office parties/outings
	Permission for informal activities
Safety	Attractive non-contributory pension
	Safe working conditions
	'No redundancy' policy
	Payment for absence due to illness
Physiological	Good working conditions
	Steady incremental salary

Case question 15.3

● Which needs were being met, and in what ways, under the new policy at the Benefits Agency?

Maslow did *not* claim that the hierarchy was a fixed or rigid scheme. His clinical experience suggested that most people with whom he had worked had these needs in about this order. He had also seen exceptions. There had been people for whom self-esteem was more important than love. For others creativeness took precedence, in that they did not seek self-actualisation once they had satisfied their basic needs, but in spite of these *not* being satisfied. Others had such permanently low aspirations that they experienced life at a very basic level.

Maslow also cautioned against the impression that as people satisfy one need completely another emerges. Rather he proposed that most normal people are partially satisfied and partially unsatisfied in their needs. This implied that a more accurate description of the hierarchy would be in terms of decreasing percentages of satisfaction at successive levels. So a person could think of himself as being, say, 85 per cent satisfied at the physiological level and 70 per cent at the safety level (the percentages are, of course, meaningless). Moreover, the emergence of a higher-level need was not a sudden event. Rather a person would gradually become aware that a higher need could now be attained.

In summary, Maslow believed that people are motivated to satisfy those needs that are important to them at that point in their life, and offered a description of those needs. The strength of a particular need would depend on the extent to which needs lower in the hierarchy had been met. In particular, he stressed the importance of the physiological needs, which he believed most people would seek to satisfy first, before the others became operative. Self-actualisation was fulfilled last and least often, although he had observed exceptions.

A new manager at a nursing home

management in practice

Jean Parker was appointed manager of a nursing home for the elderly. Recent reports by the Health Authority and Environmental Health inspectors had been so critical that they threatened to close the home. Jean recalls what she did in the first eight months:

> My task was to make sweeping changes, stabilise the workforce and improve the reputation of the home. I had no influence on pay, and low pay was one of the problems. To motivate staff I had to use other methods. Staff facilities were appalling – the dining areas were filthy, showers and some toilets were not working, there were no changing rooms and petty theft was rife. Given the lack of care and respect shown to staff it is little wonder that care given to residents was poor, and staff were demotivated. They turned up to work, carried out tasks and went home. There had been little communication between management and staff. My approach was to work alongside the staff, listen to their grievances, gain their trust and set out an action plan.
>
> The first steps were easy. The staff room was cleaned and decorated, changing rooms and working showers and toilets were provided. Refreshments were provided at meal breaks. Police advice was sought to combat petty theft and lockers were installed in each area. The effect of these changes on staff commitment was astounding. They felt somebody cared for them and listened. In turn, quality of care improved and staff started to take pride in the home, and bring in ornaments and plants to brighten it.
>
> I then started to hold monthly meetings to give management and staff an opportunity to discuss expectations. Policies and procedures were explained. Noticeboards displaying 'news and views' were put up. A monthly newsletter to residents and relations was issued. Staff took part enthusiastically in fund-raising activities to pay for outings and entertainment. This gave them the chance to get to know residents in a social setting, and was a break from routine. A training programme was introduced.
>
> Some staff did not respond and tried to undermine my intentions. Persistent unreported absence was quickly followed by disciplinary action. By the end of the year absenteeism was at a more acceptable level, many working problems were alleviated, and the business started to recover.

Source: Private communication and discussions with the manager.

Activity 15.3 Critical reflection on the theory

- Which of the needs identified by Maslow did Jean Parker's changes at the nursing home help staff to satisfy?
- Do your studies and related activities on your course satisfy needs identified by Maslow?
- What evidence can you gather from your colleagues on the relative importance to them of these needs?

How does Maslow's approach compare with Skinner's? Skinner believed that by providing positive reinforcement (or punishment) people would be motivated to act in a particular way. The rewards they obtained would satisfy their needs. Maslow took the slightly different position that people would seek to satisfy their needs by acting in a particular way. Both believed that to change behaviour it would be necessary to change the situation. Skinner emphasised that this would take the form of positive reinforcement to satisfy needs after an activity. Maslow implied that influencers should provide conditions that enable to people to satisfy their needs from the activity.

Clayton Alderfer – ERG theory

Doubtful about the empirical support for the hierarchy of motives proposed by Maslow, Alderfer developed another approach (Alderfer, 1972). His work both built on Maslow's ideas and presented an alternative. He developed and tested his theory in questionnaire and interview-based studies carried out in five organisations – a manufacturing firm, a bank, two colleges and a school. He aimed to identify the primary needs – those that an organism possesses by the nature of being the creature it is. Satisfaction refers to the internal state of someone who has obtained what he or she is seeking. Frustration is the opposite – when someone seeks something but does not find it.

Existence needs reflect a person's requirement for material and energy exchange with his or her environment. They therefore include all the material and physiological desires – hunger and thirst represent deficiencies in existence needs. Pay and benefits of various kinds represent ways of satisfying material requirements.

Relatedness needs involve relationships with significant other people – family members, colleagues, bosses, subordinates, team members, regular customers and so on. This includes groups and individuals. People satisfy their relatedness needs by sharing thoughts and feelings. Acceptance, confirmation and understanding are elements in this process of satisfying relatedness needs.

Growth needs are those that impel a person to be creative or to produce an effect on themselves and their environment. People satisfy these needs by engaging with problems that call upon them to use their skills fully or require them to develop new ones. People experience a greater sense of completeness when they have satisfied their growth needs. That satisfaction depends on finding the opportunity to exercise talents to the full.

Existence needs reflect a person's requirement for material and energy.

Relatedness needs involve a desire for relationships with significant other people.

Growth needs are those which impel people to be creative or to produce an effect on themselves or their environment.

---

key ideas **Seven major propositions of Alderfer's theory**

P1 The less that existence needs are satisfied, the more they will be desired.

P2 The less that relatedness needs are satisfied, the more existence needs will be desired.

P3 The more that existence needs are satisfied, the more relatedness needs will be desired.

P4 The less that relatedness needs are satisfied, the more they will be desired.

P5 The less that growth needs are satisfied, the more relatedness needs will be desired.

P6 The more that relatedness needs are satisfied, the more growth needs will be desired.

P7 The more that growth needs are satisfied, the more they will be desired.

Source: Alderfer (1972).

Alderfer showed how his formulation of needs compared with that put forward by Maslow. Figure 15.4 summarises his discussion of the point.

Alderfer proposed that his three categories of need are active in everyone, although in varying degrees of strength. Unlike Maslow, he found no evidence of a hierarchical relationship between needs. However, he did find that if higher needs are frustrated, lower needs will become prominent again, even if they have already been satisfied, and offered propositions relating lower-level need satisfaction to higher-level desires, and *vice versa* – see Key Ideas.

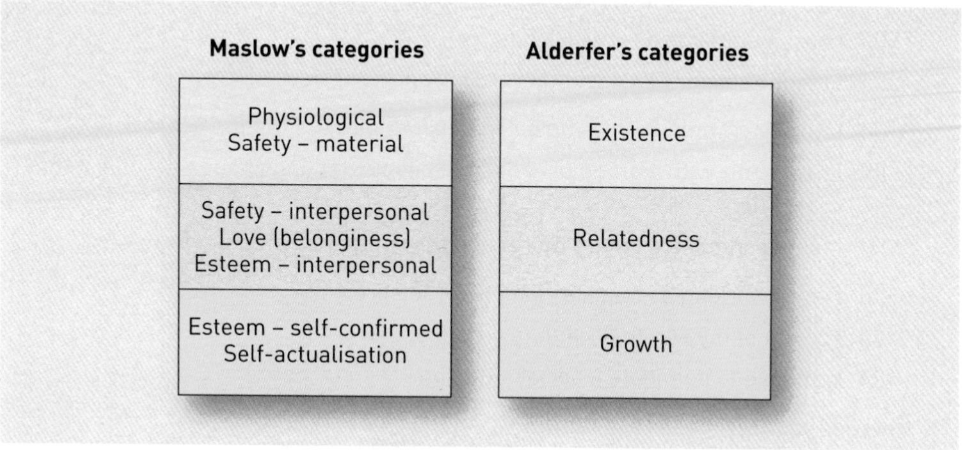

Figure 15.4

Comparison of the Maslow and Alderfer categories of needs

Both theories are hard to test empirically as it is difficult to establish operationally whether a person has satisfied a need. Their value is that they integrate earlier ideas that had concentrated on single needs, and show the variety of needs which people may seek to satisfy at work.

David McClelland

McClelland (1961) and his colleagues have examined how people think and react in a wide range of situations. This work led them to identify three categories of human need, which individuals possess in different amounts:

- Need for affiliation – to develop and maintain interpersonal relationships
- Need for power – to have control over one's environment
- Need for achievement – to set and meet standards of excellence.

McClelland believed that, rather than being arranged in some form of hierarchy, individuals possess each of these possibly conflicting needs, which motivate their behaviour when activated. McClelland used the Thematic Apperception Test to assess how significant these categories were to people. The subjects of the research were shown pictures with a neutral subject and asked to write a story about it. The researchers coded the stories and claimed these indicated the relative importance to the person of the affiliation, power and achievement motives.

You can assess your scores on these motives by completing Activity 15.4.

Activity 15.4   Assessing your needs

- From each of the four sets of statements below choose the one that is most like you.

  1 (a) I set myself difficult goals, which I attempt to reach.

     (b) I am happiest when I am with a group of people who enjoy life.

     (c) I like to organise the activities of a group or team.

  2 (a) I only completely enjoy relaxation after the successful completion of exacting pieces of work.

▶

(b) I become attached to my friends.

(c) I argue zealously against others for my point of view.

3 (a) I work hard until I am completely satisfied with the result I achieve.

(b) I like to mix with a group of congenial people, talking about any subject that comes up.

(c) I tend to influence others more than they influence me.

4 (a) I enjoy working as much as I enjoy my leisure.

(b) I go out of my way to be with my friends.

(c) I am able to dominate a social situation.

- Now add your responses as follows:

The number of (a) responses ( ) Achievement

The number of (b) responses ( ) Affiliation

The number of (c) responses ( ) Power

This simple exercise will give you an insight both into the differences between McClelland's three types of motive and into your preference. The larger your score in an area, the more likely your preference is in that area. Compare your answers with others whom you know in the class. Discuss whether the results are in line with what you would have expected, given what you already know of each other.

Source: Based on Jackson (1993).

Frederick Herzberg – two-factor theory

While Maslow and McClelland focused on individual differences in motivation, Herzberg (1959) related motivation to the nature of a person's work. He developed his theory following interviews with 200 engineers and accountants about their experience of work. The researchers first asked them to recall a time when they had felt exceptionally good about their job, and then asked about the events that had preceded those feelings. The research team then asked respondents to recall a time when they had felt particularly bad about their work, and the background to that. Analysis showed that when respondents recalled good times they frequently mentioned one or more of these factors:

- achievement
- recognition
- work itself
- responsibility
- advancement.

They mentioned these much less frequently when describing the bad times. When talking about the bad times they most frequently recalled these factors:

- company policy and administration
- supervision
- salary
- interpersonal relations
- working conditions.

They mentioned these much less frequently when describing the good times.

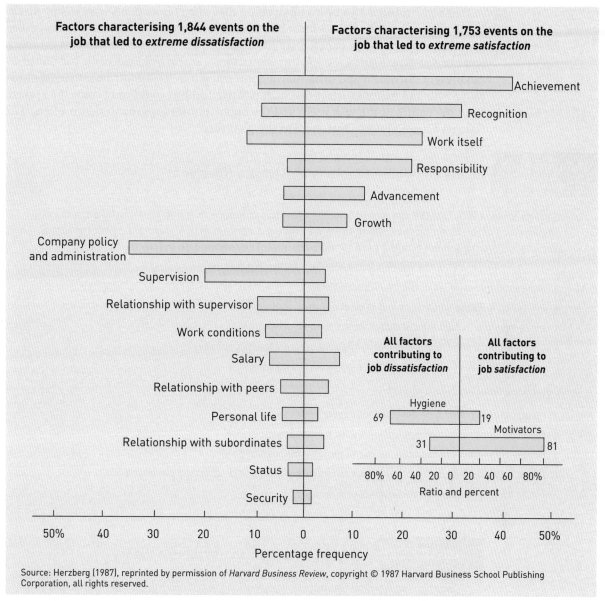

Figure 15.5 Herzberg's comparison of job satisfaction and job dissatisfaction scores

Herzberg concluded that the factors associated with satisfaction describe people's relationship to what they were doing. They included the nature of the task, responsibility carried or recognition received. He renamed these satisfiers 'motivator factors', as they seemed to influence the individual to superior performance and effort. The second set, associated with dissatisfaction, related to conditions surrounding the work. He named these the 'hygiene' or ('maintenance') factors as they served mainly to prevent dissatisfaction, not foster high performance. Figure 15.5 illustrates the results.

In summary, Herzberg concluded that the factors which produce job satisfaction are separate and distinct from those that lead to job dissatisfaction, hence the term 'two-factor' theory. He suggested that satisfaction and dissatisfaction are not opposites: they are separate dimensions influenced by different factors. The dissatisfiers (company policy and administration, supervision, salary, interpersonal relations and working conditions) contribute little to job satisfaction. The factors that lead to job satisfaction (achievement, recognition, work itself, responsibility and advancement) contribute little to job dissatisfaction if they are absent.

Motivator factors are those aspects of the work itself that Herzberg found influenced people to superior performance and effort.

Hygiene factors (or maintenance factors) are those aspects surrounding the task which can prevent discontent and dissatisfaction but will not in themselves contribute to psychological growth and hence motivation.

495

Herzberg explained this by his observation that when respondents were feeling dissatisfied, this was because management had treated them unfairly. When they were satisfied it was because they were experiencing feelings of psychological growth and gaining a sense of self-actualisation. So the hygiene factors – an environment with fair policies – can prevent discontent and dissatisfaction but will not in itself contribute to psychological growth and hence satisfaction. Such positive feelings could only come, he argued, from the nature of the task itself, and the opportunities for growth that it offers. The Gamma Chemical story illustrates Herzberg's theory.

Focus on hygiene factors at Gamma Chemical

Gamma Chemical purchased the site of another chemical company that had recently failed, and re-employed 30 of the 40 employees. While there was no overt dissatisfaction, during the first two years of ownership management found it hard to motivate staff. They showed no initiative or creativity, and no commitment to the new company or its goals. Yet the company had:

- increased the salaries of the re-employed staff
- improved working conditions and provided better equipment
- placed people in positions of equal status to their previous jobs
- operated an 'Open Door' policy, with supervisors easily approachable
- offered security of employment and a no-redundancy policy.

Other aspects of practice included:

- no structured training or development programmes
- the small unit restricted opportunities for career advancement
- people had little responsibility as management imposed decisions
- there was no clear connection between individual work and company performance.

Source: Private communication and discussions with the manager.

Activity 15.5 Critical reflection on Herzberg's theory

- Comment on Gamma Chemical's assumptions about motivating the re-engaged staff.
- Evaluate the empirical base of Herzberg's research. What reservations do you have about the wider applicability of the theory?
- Gather other evidence of changes in working practice, and decide whether it supports or contradicts Herzberg's theory.

Herzberg argued that work motivation is largely influenced by the extent to which a job is intrinsically challenging and provides opportunities for recognition and reinforcement. As such he linked thinking about motivation with ideas about job design, and especially the motivational effects of job enrichment. There are many examples where management has redesigned people's jobs with positive effects: few if any of these experiments were the result of knowing about Herzberg's theory, but their effects are often consistent with its predictions. Section 15.8 has more on this.

15.5 Management assumptions – Theory X or Theory Y

As a manager attempts to influence others he or she must make assumptions about how they will react to different incentives. These assumptions will guide the organisational arrangements they put in place. Douglas McGregor (1960) developed this idea in his book *The Human Side of Enterprise*. In this he argued that 'every managerial act rests on assumptions, generalisations and hypotheses – that is to say, on theory' (p. 6).

Such assumptions are often implicit and unconscious – but nevertheless shape managers' predictions that if they do *a*, then *b* will occur. The theories may or may not be adequate but it is impossible to reach a managerial decision, or take a managerial action, uninfluenced by them. 'The insistence on being "practical" really means "Let's accept my theoretical assumptions without argument or test"' (p. 7).

McGregor went on to present two contrasting sets of assumptions underlying management policy and practice. *Theory X*, which he called the traditional view of direction and control, expresses the following assumptions:

- The average human being has an inherent dislike of work and will avoid it if at all possible.
- Because of this human characteristic, most people must be coerced, controlled, directed and/or threatened with punishment to get them to put forth adequate effort towards the achievement of organisational objectives.
- The average human being prefers to be directed, wishes to avoid responsibility, has relatively little ambition, and wants security above all.

McGregor was critical of these assumptions. He believed that they led to a management strategy towards people which ignored the full range of possible human needs. Theory X assumptions concentrated on the lower-level needs that Maslow had identified. He believed that managers who accepted a Theory X view would fail to discover, let alone use, the potentialities of the average human being.

 **Recognising potential at 3M**

Although you may not have heard of the company, you will have used some of its products such as sandpapers, 'Scotch' brand sellotape, masking tape and Post-it notes. The company is regarded by many as one of the most innovative in the world, and the secret of their success over many years is attributed by Ghoshal and Bartlett (1998) to a 'deep, genuine and unshakeable belief in the ability of the average individual' (p. 43). For over 80 years the company has nurtured unconventional people, creating a climate that stimulated ordinary people to produce extraordinary performances. It was a management philosophy that focused more on recognising the potential of each individual employee than on harnessing the power of new structures and systems.

Source: Ghoshal and Bartlett (1998).

He then pointed out that accumulating knowledge about human behaviour made it possible to suggest a 'modest beginning for new theory about the management of human resources' (p. 47). This he termed *Theory Y* – the integration of individual and organisational goals – which expressed a different set of assumptions:

- The expenditure of physical and mental effort in work is as natural as play or rest.
- External control and the threat of punishment are not the only means of bringing about effort towards organisational objectives. People will exercise self-direction and self-control in the service of objectives to which they are committed.
- Commitment to objectives is a function of the rewards associated with their achievement.

- The average human being learns, under proper conditions, not only to accept, but also to seek, responsibility.
- The capacity to exercise a relatively high degree of imagination, ingenuity and creativity in the solution of organisational problems is widely, not narrowly, distributed in the population.
- Under the conditions of modern industrial life the intellectual potentialities of the average human being are only partially utilised.

The practical implications of the two sets of assumptions are clear. Those who hold to Theory X will tend to advocate using time-recording systems, close supervision, quality checked by someone other than the person doing the work, narrowly defined jobs and precise job descriptions. The central principle of Theory X is that of external control, by systems, procedures or supervision.

The central principle of Theory Y is integration. It advocates 'the creation of conditions such that the members of the organisation can achieve their own goals *best* by directing their efforts towards the success of the enterprise' (p. 49). Managers who hold to Theory Y see their job as being to create conditions in which people accept responsibility, and apply imagination, ingenuity and creativity to organisational problems. For example, Kevin Smith took over as Chief Executive of GKN, a large engineering business, in 2003. He recalled his first job in a textile mill:

> [The people there] were held back by an environment ill-suited to helping them reach their potential. I learned about the pent-up capabilities of people inside organisations. If you can unleash those capabilities, and give people the possibility to realise their hopes and dreams in their work, then you can create enormous power. (*Financial Times*, 20 December 2002)

McGregor argued that a problem of the modern organisation is that it does not tap the creative ability of its staff. To take advantage of these hidden assets managers should be more willing to provide employees with scope to use their talents. They should be less prescriptive and directive. They should create the conditions that integrate individual and organisational goals.

management in practice
Motivating sales teams

I work as a sales manager for a medium-sized pharmaceutical company with a team of six. My role is to achieve maximum sales using the resources available. The company sets activity targets – 'more calls mean more sales' is a favourite slogan. This produces a problem, as there are doctors who are readily available but who are unlikely to produce business: others are less available but have more potential. Do we follow the company strategy or do things the way our experience tells us will work better?

Management has structured the company on Theory X assumptions. We are told what we are expected to achieve, and how we are expected to achieve them. There are few opportunities for us to express a view. We meet the senior people about twice a year. The meetings usually have a rushed agenda, and seem to be a way of telling us what will happen rather than encouraging discussion on what should happen. They ask us to write two-monthly reports, but the points we raise seldom get a reply.

Another company in the industry is now taking a different approach. This involves each salesperson developing his or her business plan. They have considerably more autonomy to use their ideas. The trade-off is that the consequences of failure are more severe, and this will not suit everyone – it is a different psychological contract with which they are working. The curious thing is that that company had been very successful with an earlier approach, which was like ours. But the market is experiencing its biggest ever change, and shifting responsibility to salespeople who are in constant contact with customers has a considerable advantage.

Source: Private communication and discussions with the manager.

Activity 15.6   Critical reflection on Theory X and Theory Y

- Write down the Theory X assumptions demonstrated in the first company in the 'Motivating sales teams' Management in Practice, and the Theory Y ones in the second.
- Make a list of management practices that you have experienced which reflect the assumptions of Theory X and Theory Y respectively. What were their effects?
- Can you identify someone who behaves in a way consistent with Theory X, and someone else who behaves according to Theory Y? Did this reflect the way they themselves were managed, or some other reason?

key ideas   Morse and Lorsch, 'Beyond Theory Y'

Although McGregor expressed the view that Theory Y assumptions were the most appropriate ones for effective management, others have challenged this. They argue that Theory Y assumptions may be as inappropriate in some circumstances as Theory X assumptions are in others. Morse and Lorsch (1970) first raised this prospect following their comparative study of management practices in four companies. Two were in routine operations, at which one was successful and one was not. The other two were in highly creative businesses, and again one was successful, the other not. They concluded that the successful company in the routine business used a consistent Theory X style. The successful company in the creative business used a consistent Theory Y style.

15.6   Individual and national differences

The patterns of needs differ significantly between people, and any attempt to understand motivation must take account of this. The relative importance of a need is likely to change with a person's commitments and interests. Young people or those with high-earning partners give security a low priority. People rate it more highly as they take on mortgage or family commitments. People also experience conflict between their needs. For example, a need for security because of family circumstances may challenge a need for recognition that could imply a risky job change or a move to another town.

People also vary in how they translate their needs into work behaviour. One person with a high need for responsibility or advancement may satisfy it by seeking a transfer to a different department. Another may decide to move to a different type of work. How do people react when they fail to satisfy a need? Do they try harder or give up?

A final point of growing significance in the international business world is that the theories outlined were all developed in the United States. Do they apply to people working in other countries? Hofstede (1989) articulated what he believed were the 'unspoken cultural assumptions' present in both Theory X and Theory Y. He writes:

> … in a comparative study of US values versus those dominant in ASEAN countries, I found the following common assumptions on the US side and underlying both X and Y:

1 Work is good for people.
2 People's capacities should be maximally utilised.
3 There are 'organisational objectives' that exist apart from people.
4 People in organisations behave as unattached individuals.

These assumptions reflect value positions in McGregor's US society; most would be accepted in other western countries. None of them, however, applies in ASEAN countries. Southeast Asian assumptions would be:

1 Work is a necessity but not a goal in itself.

2 People should find their rightful place in peace and harmony with their environment.

3 Absolute objectives exist only with God. In the world, persons in authority positions represent God so their objectives should be followed.

4 People behave as members of a family and/or group. Those who do not are rejected by society.

Because of these different culturally determined assumptions, McGregor's Theory X and Theory Y distinction becomes irrelevant in Southeast Asia. (p. 5)

Hofstede's work that was presented in Chapter 4 showed marked differences in national cultures. These are likely to influence the relative importance that people in those countries attach to the various motivational factors. People in Anglo-Saxon countries tend to display a relatively high need for achievement, strong masculinity scores and low uncertainty avoidance. This is not the norm in other cultures. Harris and Moran (1991) also suggest that cultures emphasise different life goals, and contrast East Asian with western cultures. This implies people will attach different importance to motivational factors.

---

key ideas **Prevailing cultural norms and beliefs**

East Asia	Western
Equity	Wealth
Group	Individual
Saving	Consumption
Extended family relations	Nuclear and mobile family
Highly disciplined and motivated	Decline in work ethic and hierarchy
Protocol, rank, status	Informality and personal competence
Avoid conflict	Conflict to be managed

Source: Harris and Moran (1991).

15.7 Process theories of motivation

Process theories try to explain why people choose one course of action towards satisfying a need rather than another. A person who needs a higher income could satisfy it by, say, moving to another company, applying for promotion or investing in training. What factors will influence their choice?

Expectancy theory

Expectancy theory argues that motivation depends on a person's belief in the probability that effort will lead to good performance, and that good performance will lead to them receiving an outcome they value (valence).

Vroom (1964) developed one attempt to answer that question with what he termed the **expectancy theory** of motivation. It focuses on the thinking processes people use to achieve rewards. Stuart Roberts is studying a degree course in Chemistry and has to submit a last assignment. He wants an A for the course, and so far has an average of B+. His motivation to put effort into the assignment will be affected by (a) his expectation that hard work will produce a good piece of work, and (b) his expectation that it will receive a grade of at least an A. If he believes he cannot do a good job, or that the grading system is unclear, then his motivation will be low.

The theory assumes that individuals:

- have different needs and so value outcomes differently
- make conscious choices about which course of action to follow
- choose between alternative actions based on the likelihood of an action resulting in an outcome they value.

There are, then, three main components in expectancy theory. First, the person's expectation (or **subjective probability**) that effort (E) will result in some level of performance (P):

$$(E \rightarrow P)$$

This will be affected by how clear they are about their roles, the training available, whether the necessary support will be provided and similar factors. If Stuart Roberts understands what the assignment requires and is confident in his ability to do a good job, his $(E \rightarrow P)$ expectancy will be high.

The second component is the person's expectation that performance will be **instrumental** in leading to a particular outcome (O):

$$(P \rightarrow O)$$

This will be affected by how confident the person is that achieving a target will produce a reward. This reflects factors such as the clarity of the organisation's appraisal and payment systems and previous experience of them. A clear grading system, which Stuart understands and knows that staff apply consistently, will mean he has a high $(P \rightarrow O)$ expectancy. If he has found the system unpredictable this expectancy would be lower.

The third component is the **valence** that the individual attaches to a particular outcome:

$$(V)$$

This term is best understood as the power of the outcome to motivate that individual – how keen Roberts is to get a good degree. It introduces the belief that people differ in the value they place on different kinds of reward. So the value of V varies between individuals, reflecting their unique pattern of motivational needs (as suggested by the content theories). Someone who values money and achievement would place a high valence on an outcome that was a promotion to a distant head office. He or she would try to work in a way which led to that. Such an outcome would be much less welcome (have a much lower valence) to a manager who values an established pattern of relationships or quality of life in the present location.

In summary:

$$F = (E \rightarrow P) \times (P \rightarrow O) \times V$$

in which F represents the force exerted, or degree of motivation a person has towards an activity. Two beliefs will influence that motivation, namely the expectation that:

- making the effort will lead to performance $(E \rightarrow P)$
- that level of performance will lead to an outcome they value $(P \rightarrow O)$.

Adjusting these beliefs for valence – how desirable the outcome is to the person – gives a measure of their motivation. The beliefs that people hold reflect their personality and their experience of organisational practices, as shown in Figure 15.6.

The use of the multiplication sign in the equation signifies that both beliefs influence motivation. If a person believes that however hard they try they will be unable to perform to a required standard then they will not be motivated to do so (so $E \rightarrow P = 0$). The

Subjective probability (in expectancy theory) is a person's estimate of the likelihood that a certain level of effort (E) will produce a level of performance (P) which will then lead to an expected outcome (O).

Instrumentality is the perceived probability that good performance will lead to valued rewards, measured on a scale from 0 (no chance) to 1 (certainty).

Valence is the perceived value or preference that an individual has for a particular outcome.

same applies for (P → O). A low score in either of these two parts of the equation, or in V, will lead to low effort, regardless of beliefs about the other part.

A criticism of the theory is that it implies a high level of rational calculation, as people weigh the probabilities of various courses of action. It also implies that managers estimate what each employee values, and try to ensure that motivational practices meet them. Neither calculation is likely to be made that rationally, which may diminish the model's practical value.

However, the model is useful in recognising that people vary in their beliefs (or probabilities) about the components in the equation. It shows that managers can affect these beliefs by redesigning the factors in Figure 15.6. If people are unclear about their role, or receive weak feedback, the theory predicts that this will reduce their motivation.

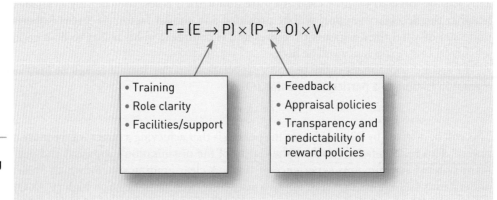

$$F = (E \rightarrow P) \times (P \rightarrow O) \times V$$

- Training
- Role clarity
- Facilities/support

- Feedback
- Appraisal policies
- Transparency and predictability of reward policies

Figure 15.6

Organisational practices affecting subjective probabilities

Hindle Power

In 2000 this family-owned engineering company employed 50 people, selling and servicing Perkins engines in the east of England. In 1996 Perkins told all its distributors that they would need to meet tougher customer service targets, or lose their contracts. Graham Hughes, Hindle's general manager, realised that long-term change would not occur unless people were trained to do their jobs better. Staff were given considerable scope in setting their own training needs. A new appraisal system was designed to help people clarify their career goals and request training to achieve them. The company's training manager Steve Widdrington believes the appraisal system encourages people to stretch themselves, rather than looking back and focusing on past results: 'People are taking more responsibility. I believe that works when you give staff the chance to develop.'

In 1996 the company was losing money on a turnover of £6 million. In 1999 it was profitable and hoped to turn over £15 million in 2000: 'Rarely has the link between training and the bottom line been so clear.'

Source: *People Management*, 3 February 2000, pp. 52–3.

As at Hindle Power, managers can influence motivation by practical actions such as:

- Establishing the rewards people value
- Identifying and communicating performance requirements
- Ensuring that reasonable effort can meet those requirements
- Providing facilities to support the person's effort

- Ensuring a clear link between performance and reward
- Providing feedback to staff on how well they are meeting performance requirements.

The theory links insights from the content theories of motivation with organisational practice.

Equity theory – J. Stacey Adams

Equity theory is usually associated with J. Stacy Adams (a behavioural scientist working at the General Electric Company) who put forward the first systematic account (Adams, 1963) of the idea that fairness in comparison with others influences motivation. People like to be treated fairly and compare what they put into a job (effort, skill, knowledge, etc.) with the rewards they receive (pay, recognition, satisfaction, etc.). They express this as a ratio of their input to their reward. They also compare their ratio with the input-to-reward ratio of others whom they consider their equals. They expect management to reward others in the same way, so expect the ratios to be roughly equal. The formula below sums up the comparison:

$$\frac{\text{Input (A)}}{\text{Reward (A)}} : \frac{\text{Input (B)}}{\text{Reward (B)}}$$

Person A compares the ratio of her input to her reward to that of B. If the ratios are similar she will be satisfied with the treatment received. If she believes the ratio is lower than that of other people she will feel inequitably treated and be dissatisfied.

The theory predicts that if people feel unfairly treated they will experience tension and dissatisfaction. They will try to reduce this by one or more of these means:

- Reducing their inputs, by putting in less effort or withholding good ideas and suggestions
- Attempting to increase their outcomes, by pressing for increased pay or other benefits
- Attempting to decrease other people's outcomes by generating conflict or withholding information and help
- Changing the basis of their comparison, by making it against someone else where the inequity is less pronounced
- Increasing their evaluation of the other person's output so the ratios are in balance.

Case questions 15.4
- What evidence was there at the Benefits Agency of perceived inequity?
- How did people react?

As individuals differ, so will their way of reducing inequity. Some will try to rationalise the situation, suggesting that their efforts were greater or lesser than they originally thought them to be, or that the rewards are reasonable. For example, a person denied a promotion may decide that the previously desired job would not have been so advantageous after all. Members may put pressure on other members of the team whom they feel are not pulling their weight. Some may choose to do less, so bringing their ratio into line with that of other staff.

Perceived inequity and theft

Greenberg (1990) studied the occasion of a temporary 15 per cent pay cut in two factories to see whether employees' reactions were consistent with equity theory predictions. Both plants were owned by the same company, but were in different places. The company lost a contract, and management decided to reduce pay by 15 per cent temporarily, rather than make some staff redundant. A third plant (C) was unaffected by these events.

In Plant A, care was taken to explain the reasons for the cut, answering questions and expressing regret at the decision. In plant B managers merely announced the decision in a short meeting, gave no explanation and expressed no regrets.

Greenberg monitored changes in employee theft rates and turnover after the pay cut. As predicted by equity theory, employees in Plant B now felt unrewarded and unfairly treated relative to Plant A. Employees in Plant A felt the same, but less severely than in Plant B. Theft and turnover increased significantly in Plant A, but by a much greater amount in Plant B. There was no change in Plant C. When the temporary pay cut ended, theft and turnover returned to normal levels.

The research highlights that perceptions of equity are affected not only by substantive things (such as the amount of pay), but by how changes are made – a procedural comparison. In this case, the substantive cuts were the same in both plants, but the procedures followed led to those in Plant B feeling unfairly treated, and acting accordingly.

Source: Greenberg (1990).

Clearly the focus and the components of the comparisons are highly subjective, although the theory has an intuitive appeal. The subjective nature of the comparison makes it difficult to test empirically, and there has been little formal research on the theory in recent years (though see Mowday and Colwell, 2003). There is, however, abundant anecdotal evidence that people compare their effort/reward ratio with that of other people or groups.

Goal-setting theory – Edwin A. Locke

Goal-setting theory argues that motivation is influenced by goal difficulty, goal specificity and knowledge of results.

Goal-setting theory refers to a series of propositions designed to help explain and predict work behaviour. Its best-known advocate is Edwin Locke (Locke, 1968, 1996; Locke and Latham, 1990) and the theory is supported by a growing body of evidence. There are four main propositions:

1 *Challenging goals* lead to higher levels of performance than simple or unchallenging goals. Difficult goals are sometimes called 'stretch' goals because they encourage us to try harder, to stretch ourselves. However, beyond a point this effect fades – if people see a goal as being impossible, their motivation declines.

2 *Specific goals* lead to higher levels of performance than vague goals (such as 'do your best'). We find it easier to adjust behaviour when we know exactly what the objective is, and what is expected of us.

3 *Participation* in goal setting can improve commitment to those goals, since people have a sense of ownership and are motivated to achieve the goals. However, if management explains and justifies the goals, without inviting participation, that can also increase motivation.

4 *Knowledge of results* of past performance – receiving feedback – is necessary to motivation. It is motivational in itself, and contains information that may help people attain the goals.

The main attraction of goal theory is the directness of the practical implications, including:

- *Goal difficulty*: set goals that are hard enough to stretch employees, but not so difficult as to be impossible to achieve.
- *Goal specificity*: set goals in clear, precise and if possible quantifiable terms.
- *Participation*: allow employees to take part in setting goals, to increase ownership and commitment.
- *Acceptance*: if goals are set by management, ensure they are adequately explained and justified, so that people understand and accept them.
- *Feedback*: provide information on past performance to allow employees to use it in adjusting their performance.

Goal theory has many implications for appraisal schemes and other performance management techniques, at all levels of an organisation.

Self-efficacy

One contingency which influences the effects of goal theory is the self-confidence of the workers concerned. Self-efficacy refers to a person's belief in their ability to perform a task. The higher your level of self-efficacy, the more confident you are in your ability to succeed in a task. This implies that in difficult situations or where goals are challenging, people with low self-efficacy are likely to reduce their effort or give up altogether, whereas those with high self-efficacy will welcome the challenge of a demanding goal, which they are confident they will reach. As Bandura observes: 'substandard performances diminish effort in individuals who doubt their capacity but lead self-assured individuals to redouble their efforts to succeed' (Bandura, 1997, p. 461). Moreover those with high self-efficacy seem to respond to negative feedback with increased effort and motivation, whereas those with low self-efficacy reduce their efforts. The same principles apply to teams and organisations – the higher the sense of collective efficacy, the better the team performance. Research by Bandura (1997) into the performance of schools concluded that:

> Schools in which the staff members have a strong sense of collective efficacy flourish academically. Schools in which the staff members have serious doubts about their collective efficacy achieve little progress or decline academically (p. 469).

Self-efficacy is an individual's belief that he or she is capable of performing a task.

15.8 Motivation as a form of social influence

People value both intrinsic and extrinsic rewards. Extrinsic rewards are those that are separate from the performance of the task, such as pay, security and promotion possibilities. Intrinsic rewards are those that people receive from the performance of the task itself – using skills, feeling a sense of achievement, doing work that is in itself satisfying. Recall that a central element in Frederick Taylor's doctrine of scientific management was the careful design of the 'one best way' of doing a piece of manual work. Experts carefully analysed how people did the job and identified the most efficient set of tasks, usually by breaking down the task into many small parts. Such work provided few if any intrinsic rewards – and Taylor's system concentrated on providing clear extrinsic rewards.

A problem with Taylor's approach is that jobs which are broken into small parts are boring to many people, making them dissatisfied, careless and frequently absent. As these limitations became clear managers looked for ways to make jobs more intrinsically

Intrinsic rewards are valued outcomes or benefits that come from the individual, such as feelings of satisfaction, achievement and competence.

Extrinsic rewards are valued outcomes or benefits provided by others, such as promotion, a pay increase or a bigger car.

rewarding – so that the work itself brought a reward of interest or challenge. The work of writers such as Maslow, Herzberg and McGregor prompted many experiments aimed at increasing the opportunities for people to satisfy their 'higher' needs at work. The idea was that staff would work more productively if management offered intrinsic rewards (motivators in Herzberg's terms) as well as extrinsic ones (Herzberg's hygiene factors). A series of research projects indicated the potential of this approach, and led to the development of the job enrichment model.

Job enrichment model

A **job enrichment model** represents the idea that managers can change specific job characteristics to promote job satisfaction and so motivate employees.

The **job enrichment model** formulated by Hackman and Oldham (1980) extended the work of earlier motivation theorists by proposing that managers could change specific job characteristics to motivate employees and promote job satisfaction. Doing so would enable staff to satisfy more of their higher-level needs and so lead to greater motivation and performance.

The model identifies three critical *psychological states* that must be present to achieve high motivation. If any are low, motivation will be low. The three states are:

- *Experienced meaningfulness*: the degree to which employees perceive their work as valuable and worthwhile. If workers regard a job as trivial and pointless, their motivation will be low.
- *Experienced responsibility*: how responsible people feel for the quantity and quality of work performed.
- *Knowledge of results*: the amount of feedback employees receive about how well they are doing the job. Those who do not receive feedback will care less about the quality of their performance.

These psychological states are influenced by five *job characteristics* that contribute to experienced meaningfulness of work:

- *Skill variety*: the extent to which a job makes use of a range of skills and experience. A routine administrative job is low in variety, whereas that of a marketing or customer support assistant is likely to require a wide variety of analytical and interpersonal skills.
- *Task identity*: whether a job involves a complete operation, with a recognisable beginning and end. A nurse who organises and oversees all the treatments for a hospital patient has more task identity than one who provides a single treatment to many different patients.
- *Task significance*: how much the job matters to others in the organisation or to the wider society. People who can see that their job contributes directly to performance, or that it is a major help to others, will feel they have a significant task.
- *Autonomy*: how much freedom and independence a person has in deciding how to go about doing the work. A sales agent in a call centre following a tightly scripted (and recorded) conversation with a potential customer has much less autonomy than a sales agent talking face to face to a customer.
- *Feedback*: the extent to which a person receives feedback on relevant dimensions of performance. Modern manufacturing systems can provide operators with very rapid information on quality, scrap, material use and costs. Operators can then receive a high level of feedback on the results of their work. Staff redesigning a product will have to wait much longer before they find out whether their design meets customer needs.

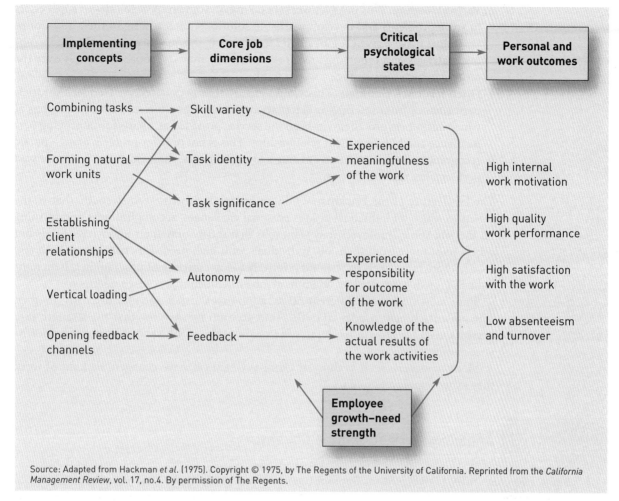

Source: Adapted from Hackman *et al.* (1975). Copyright © 1975, by The Regents of the University of California. Reprinted from the *California Management Review*, vol. 17, no.4. By permission of The Regents.

Figure 15.7 The job characteristics model

The extent to which a job contains these elements can be calculated using a tested instrument, and then using the scores obtained to calculate the *motivating potential* score for the job. Figure 15.7 presents the model schematically.

The model also shows how management (or staff) can increase the motivating potential of jobs by using five implementing concepts:

- **Combine tasks** Rather than divide the work into small pieces, as Taylor recommended, staff can combine them so they use more skills and complete more of the whole task. An order clerk could receive orders from a customer and arrange transport and invoicing instead of having these done by different people.
- **Form natural workgroups** In order to give more responsibility and enable sharing of skills, groups could be created that carry out a complete operation. Instead of a product passing down an assembly line, with each worker performing one operation, a group may assemble the whole product, sharing out the tasks amongst themselves.
- **Establish customer relations** This would bring home to employees the expectations of the people to whom their work goes, whether inside or outside the organisation, enabling them to see how their job fits into the larger picture. Instead of people doing part of the job for all customers, they can look after all the requirements of some customers. They establish closer relationships and gain a better understanding of their customers' needs.

- **Vertical loading** This involves workers taking on some responsibilities of supervisors to solve problems and develop workable solutions, thus adding to their autonomy. Operators may be given responsibility for checking the quantity and quality of incoming materials and reporting any problems. They may use more discretion over the order in which they arrange a week's work.
- **Open feedback channels** This would ensure that people receive feedback on their performance from internal or external customers. Operators can attend meetings at which customers give their views on the service provided as a basis for improving performance and building client relationships. This is not only for problem areas – public recognition of achievement contributes to a positive psychological state and improved performance and satisfaction.

The last feature of the Hackman–Oldham model is growth–need strength, that is, the extent to which an individual desires personal challenges, accomplishment and learning on the job. Some employees may want jobs that satisfy only their lower-level needs but others want more from their job. Individuals with high needs for challenge, growth and creativity are more likely to respond positively to job enrichment programmes. If an individual's growth needs are low, attempts at job enrichment may cause resentment.

Since individuals have different needs, a job that satisfies one may dissatisfy another. The job enrichment model takes this into account by showing that the strength of a person's need for growth moderates the relationship of job characteristics to performance and/or satisfaction.

Many managers, such as those at Gamma Chemical, have changed the kind of work they expect employees to do.

Changing work at Gamma Chemical

Some two years after taking control, Gamma Chemical had made these changes to working arrangements:

- They introduced a cross-training programme to improve job diversity and individual growth.
- They created problem-solving teams from natural work units to give operators a sense of ownership and achievement.
- They expected operators to make more decisions, increasing individual authority and accountability.
- They introduced an appraisal system that shows operators how their function affects company performance.

Management believed these changes had resulted in 20 per cent more output and 50 per cent less wastage.

Source: Private communication and discussions with the manager.

Managers have not usually introduced changes such as these to provide more interesting jobs for staff. They have usually been a response to more demanding business conditions and a need to cut costs and increase responsiveness. They can do this if more junior staff do a wider range of tasks, often beginning to work as a team that is jointly responsible for an area of work. Nevertheless the results of such changes often support what the theory predicts. Another approach is to give staff more responsibility for decisions, without referring to supervisors above them in the hierarchy. This is usually called empowerment.

15.9 Empowerment

People use the term 'empowerment' to refer to a range of practices that give more responsibility to less senior staff. Clutterbuck (1994) concluded that the common features of such approaches are that they are intended to help people to take more control of their job and working environment, and enhance the contributions they make as individuals and members of a team. They also provide opportunities for personal growth and self-fulfilment. Advocates of empowerment claim several advantages, including:

- Quicker responses to customer queries, since answers can be given or decisions made by staff over issues they previously had to refer to a more senior manager.
- Employees feel more satisfied as they are doing more responsible work and developing new skills.
- Employees welcome the chance to deal more intensely with customers.
- This in turn can encourage employees to come up with more practical ideas for service improvement than managers who are less directly involved with customers.
- The improved service builds customer loyalty and repeat business.

Such advantages in themselves are persuasive to managers and many have introduced programmes with the stated aim of empowering employees. Bowen and Lawler (1992) define empowerment in terms of the degree to which four ingredients of the organisation are shared with front-line employees:

- Information about the organisation's performance
- Rewards based on the organisation's performance
- Knowledge that enables employees to understand and contribute to organisational performance
- Power to make decisions that influence organisational direction and performance.

They argue that the extent to which these are present distinguishes the degree of empowerment employees have. If they remain at the top of the organisation, management still exercises fairly direct control. If they are pushed down the organisation so that front-line employees have more information and more power to make decisions, then this indicates that management is trying to adopt an empowering approach. The more that staff exercise self-control and self-direction, the more they are empowered.

Empowering nurses at Western General Hospital

management in practice

A nurse manager at the Western General Hospital in a large city commented on the empowerment of nurses at the hospital:

> The service has been trying to be more responsive to the needs of patients by delegating power and responsibility to local level. Nurses have recognised the benefits to patients if nurses carry out their work by patient allocation rather than by task allocation. This has developed into the 'named nurse' concept, which intriguingly incorporates four of the five core dimensions of the job characteristics model. The nurse assesses needs, plans, implements and evaluates the care of his or her patients, so having skill variety, task identity, task significance and autonomy.
>
> Perhaps even the feedback element is provided from the evaluation stage of each patient's care. The empowerment approach fits with the organisation's unpredictable environment, the individualised service relationship and staff needs and characteristics. The recently appointed nurse managers are

enthusiastic, and this has filtered down to staff. They are gradually becoming aware of the move from Theory X to Theory Y style of management. They appreciate that at last their skills and experience are being recognised and used.

Information flows more freely and openly. Decisions are made only after discussion with the staff who will be affected by the outcome. Nurses in the wards are aware of their allocated budgets and what they are spending. Recruitment of staff is now done by existing staff on the ward, where previously managers decided whom to appoint.

Source: Private communication from a senior nurse in the hospital.

Bowen and Lawler go on to suggest a model of levels of empowerment. At one extreme management takes a control orientation towards staff, while at the other extreme it takes an involvement orientation. Figure 15.8 summarises the range of options, and those embodying some degree of empowerment are described below:

- *Suggestion involvement*: staff are encouraged to submit ideas to improve ways of working and are rewarded for doing so. Control remains with management, which chooses whether or not to accept an idea.
- *Job involvement*: staff are able to develop and use more skills, have greater autonomy and receive more feedback. Supervisors' jobs change from direction to support.
- *High involvement*: occurs when organisations give their lowest-level employees a sense of involvement in the total organisation's performance. All of the four ingredients listed above are designed to support that condition.

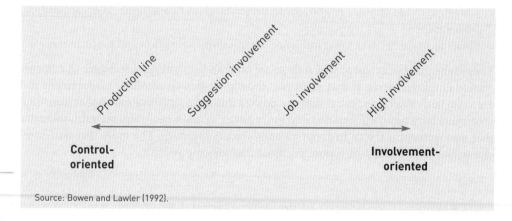

Figure 15.8

Levels of empowerment

Source: Bowen and Lawler (1992).

management in practice | ## Air Asia: Allowing people to think

Air Asia is a rapidly growing discount airline based in Malaysia and run by CEO Tony Fernandes. It keeps costs down by selling tickets only over the Internet and offering no free meals. Fernandes grills ground crews on how to shorten turnaround times between landing and take-off, and confers with mechanics on how to coddle spare parts so they last longer. His chief engineer, Wan Hasmar, once told Fernandes the tyres on the landing gear, which cost $6000 a set, would last longer if pilots took a shallow approach on landing. Fernandes immediately issued orders for pilots to sweep in low, short-circuiting the airline's chain of command. 'We allow people to think', says Fernandes – and the tyres now last 180 landings, up from 70 before the change.

Source: *Business Week*, 1 September 2003.

Increasing empowerment can be difficult, with some initiatives experiencing:

- the usual problems of introducing any significant change (see Chapter 13)
- resistance from some staff who value familiar ways, which give certainty and predictability to their working lives
- resistance from middle managers who fear losing parts of their role (Ezzamel *et al.* 1994)
- the risks of losing control (Simons, 1995).

Empowerment is about power and is bound to be controversial. This may imply redistributing power from an over-concentration at the centre of the organisation. Alternatively, management may remove the constraints that prevent people using the power which they already have, for example through their knowledge of customers or processes.

15.10 Work and careers in a time of change

Major forces such as globalisation, deregulation, privatisation, developments in information technology, as well as changing lifestyles, have major implications for understanding motivation at work. Companies are both downsizing and expanding – often at the same time in different divisions or at different levels. Workforces are increasingly diverse with divergent needs and demands. Information technology is often associated with changes in the nature and location of work, as well as enabling the creation of new organisational forms. Many organisations employ temporary staff or workers on short-term contracts, rather than on relatively secure lifetime careers. These changes have profound effects on how companies attract retain and motivate staff – making a deeper understanding of motivational issues more pressing than ever. The expectations of both organisations and people keep changing, implying that new kinds of psychological contract will be emerging.

The organisational world that McGregor and Herzberg observed was a place of large manufacturing organisations operating in relatively stable markets. Western organisations and values dominated the business world, natural resources seemed plentiful, and computers were novelties. In 1969 at least one major bank still kept customer records in handwritten books. Today the same company offers banking services on the Internet. Most employees were men, worked full-time until retirement, and expected to stay with the same employer for many years – often for most of their career. All these features have changed, and will continue to do so.

Many organisations are operating internationally and face severe competition not only on price but also on quality, innovation and responsiveness. Most employees work in service occupations, where the quality of interpersonal interaction with the customer is an important part of the transaction. Information technology is having dramatic effects on the availability of information. This affects both organisational structures and what people delivering goods or services are expected to do. Another change is that many organisations employ other firms to provide functions that their own staff previously performed.

Many who joined the public sector find that their organisation has been sold to the private sector. This usually requires managers and staff to work in a radically different way if they want to keep their jobs. Those who remain in the public sector face new pressures (Flynn, 2002). They are more likely to face conflicts with members of the public who know their entitlements and are willing to argue for them. At the same time local and national governments require staff to work within tight budgets. They probably need to work more closely with private-sector agencies that provide many services previously provided internally, and manage the shifting balance between central control and local autonomy. The psychological contract for many is very different from the ethos of public service prevailing when they joined. Then, many who joined the service may have been motivated by a sense of service to other people and of doing some good. This is different from being motivated by the prospect of making a profit and receiving some personal financial benefit.

Organisations are less likely to offer long-term or full-time careers. Competition is used to justify keeping staff costs low by minimising the number of regular jobs on offer and meeting extra demand by employing temporary or casual staff. Work is increasingly part time, done at what used to be regarded as unsociable hours. Standard procedures often structure the work processes tightly to fit the requirements of information systems that link all parts of the organisation. At the same time staff are expected to work together cooperatively in teams and build good relationships with customers. They must follow procedures, but also use their imagination and initiative as required to solve unusual problems.

People have different expectations of their organisations either because of wider social trends or in response to what organisations themselves are doing. As many women as men are in paid employment; both have to manage 'dual careers' in conjunction with family commitments, particularly the care of young children and elderly relatives.

How Littlewoods offers a work–life balance

Barry Gibson, Group Chief Executive of Littlewoods, a UK retail business:

Many employees have responsibilities for young children or elderly parents that conflict with responsibilities at work. Life is about much more than work . . . Companies that support the work/life balance of their employees gain a committed and innovative workforce, which then provides a better service than their competitors. At Littlewoods we have found that the highest quality contributions have come from employees who feel they have real balance in their lives. We have worked hard to develop policies that are family friendly. Flexible working is a business reality for us. Sixty-two per cent of our employees work flexibly. Wherever it is operationally possible, people work part time, reduced hours, job share and work from home. It is essential to review your employees' needs regularly. Employee surveys provide good feedback. On the basis of our surveys we have introduced childcare information services in all of our business units, regular holiday play schemes for the children of employees in some areas, a pre- and post-school club and subsidised places at a nursery. But making such policies work in practice can only be achieved by regular top-level commitment. Our executive board formally discusses equal opportunities each quarter and twice a year we have a strategy committee to consider the issues.

Source: *Management Today*, October 1999, p. 14.

More people are setting up their own business rather than work for an employer, although it is unclear whether this is from genuine preference or the lack of an alternative. It does mean that more employment is now in small organisations.

People differ in their commitment to work as a full-time career and expect very different things from an organisation. Work is central for many, but not for everyone, especially as the hours of work and the length of working life decline. Many do not expect self-fulfilment from their work. They seek it instead through a hobby, through social activities or perhaps by running a pressure group. New generations seek different things from life and from work, and many are less committed to conventional work patterns. Identifying the rewards that people seek from their work has always been a matter of intelligent guesswork and inference. It is likely to become more so as people come to expect more diverse rewards from fulfilling their side of the psychological contract.

Hiltrop (1995) reviewed the changes taking place in the psychological contract as both organisations and people change their expectations. Elements of the new contract include:

- Organisations are becoming more demanding places in which to work.
- The paternalism of earlier times, in which both sides expected a long-term career together, is gone.
- Roles and responsibilities are much more fluid and ambiguous.
- Increasingly, companies expect people to contribute their skills through specific, short-term tasks, not through long-term employment. In order to maintain their income people need to plan their development and careers, and build their reputation.
- Security, income and status derived from an employer are less available, implying people need to develop other sources of psychological reassurance.
- Opportunities to improve employability (by movement to another project) are more likely to be the reward for good work than promotion.
- People are increasingly paid on the basis of contribution rather than level or status.

Table 15.3 presents Hiltrop's summary of the main characteristics of the old and new psychological contracts.

Characteristic	Old	New
Focus	Security	Employability
Format	Structured	Flexible
Duration	Permanent	Variable
Scope	Broad	Narrow
Underlying principle	Tradition	Market forces
Intended output	Loyalty and commitment	Value added
Employer's key responsibility	Fair pay for good work	High pay for high performance
Employee's key responsibility	Good performance in present job	Making a difference
Employer's key input	Stable income and career advancement	Opportunities for self-development
Employee's key input	Time and effort	Knowledge and skills

Source: Hiltrop (1995).

Table 15.3

Changing psychological contracts

Summary

1 Understand the significance of work motivation, including the psychological contract, to the task of managing:

- People depend on others within and beyond the organisation to act in a particular way, and understanding what motivates them is critical to this. Motivation includes understanding the goals which people pursue (content), the choices they make to secure them (process) and how this knowledge can be applied to influence others (including through work design).

● The relationship between employer and employee is expressed in the psychological contract, which needs to be in acceptable balance for effective performance.

2 Understand theories which focus on the content and process of motivation, and those which relate these ideas to issues of work design and empowerment:

● Content theories seek to understand the needs which human beings may seek to satisfy at work and include the work of Maslow, Alderfer and Herzberg as well as of earlier observers such as Taylor and Mayo.

● Expectancy theory explains motivation in terms of valued outcomes and the subjective probability of achieving those outcomes.

● Equity theory explains motivation in terms of perceptions of fairness by comparison with others.

● Goal-setting theory believes that motivation depends on the degree of difficulty and specificity of goals.

● Self-efficacy theory may moderate the predictions of goal-setting theory, by suggesting that how people respond depends on their level of personal confidence in being able to complete a task successfully.

3 Explain the significance of understanding the assumptions which managers use in motivating staff, and how these vary between national cultures:

● McGregor's Theory X and Theory Y set out different assumptions which managers have about their staff, which has implications for how they seek to motivate them. These appear to vary between nations and cultures.

4 Use the models presented to diagnose motivational problems and recommend areas of possible action:

● Most of the models can be used to analyse the likely effects of organisational practices on motivation, and to indicate areas for possible management action.

● People are only motivated if the job meets a need which they value – providing appropriate content factors leads to satisfaction and performance.

● Herzberg suggests that motivation depends on paying attention to motivating as well as hygiene factors.

● Jobs can be enriched by increasing skill variety, task identity, task significance, autonomy and feedback.

● Expectancy theory predicts that rewards motivate high performance when the organisational practices support performance, and when the links between performance and rewards are clear – provided that individuals have strong growth needs.

● Setting high and specific goals will enhance performance, provided that employees have high levels of confidence in their abilities to do the task.

5 Relate these ideas to current developments in the environment of managing:

● As educational levels rise and staff become more informed, they expect to have more opportunities to meet higher-level needs at work, in addition to lower-level needs.

● Changing competitive conditions mean that critical performance indicators for many organisations stress responsiveness, creativity and innovation – which can only be encouraged by motivational policies that encourage these behaviours. Economic and predictable performance also remain important for many organisational functions, which raises possible dilemmas for organisation-wide motivational policies.

Review questions

1 Outline the idea of the psychological contract. What are you expecting (a) from a future employer in your career; (b) from an employer who provides you with part-time work while you are studying?

2 What are the three things that are pinpointed when using behaviour modification?

3 How does Maslow's theory of human needs relate to the ideas of (a) Frederick Taylor and (b) Elton Mayo and the human relations movement?

4 How does Alderfer's theory differ from Maslow's? What research lay behind the two theories?

5 How did you score on the McClelland test? How did your scores compare with those of your fellow students?

6 Explain the difference between Herzberg's hygiene and motivating factors. Give at least three examples of each.

7 Explain the difference between E → P and P → O in expectancy theory.

8 Outline the basic assumptions of Theories X and Y that Douglas McGregor used to characterise alternative ways in which managements view their workers. List three management practices associated with each.

9 What are the five job design elements that are expected to affect people's satisfaction with their work?

10 Give an example of an implementing concept associated with each element.

Concluding critical reflection

Think about the ways in which you typically seek to motivate other people (staff, colleagues or those in other organisations) and about your company's approach to motivation. Review the material in the chapter, and then make notes on these questions:

- What examples of the issues discussed in this chapter struck you as being relevant to motivational practice in your company?

- Thinking of the people you typically work with, who are effective and who are less effective motivators? What do the effective people do that enables them to motivate others? Do they seem to take a mainly Theory X or mainly Theory Y approach? Do their assumptions seem to be broadly correct, or not? To what extent does the work people do have a high Motivational Potential Score?

- What factors such as the history of the company or your personal experience have shaped the way you motivate others, and your organisation's approach to motivation? Does your current approach appear to be right for your present position and company – or would you use a different approach in other circumstances? (Perhaps refer to some of the Management in Practice features for how different managers motivate others.)

- Have people put forward alternative approaches to motivating, based on evidence about other companies? If you could find such evidence, how may it affect company practice?

Further reading

Roethlisberger, F.J. and Dickson, W.J. (1939), *Management and the Worker*, Harvard University Press, Cambridge, MA.

Herzberg, F. (1959), *The Motivation to Work*, Wiley, New York.

McGregor, D. (1960), *The Human Side of Enterprise*, McGraw-Hill, New York.

Maslow, A. (1970), *Motivation and Personality* (2nd edn), Harper & Row, New York.

The original accounts of these influential works are unusually readable books showing organisations and research in action. Roethlisberger and Dickson's account of the Hawthorne experiments is long, but the others are short and accessible.

Clutterbuck, D. and Dearlove, D. (1996), *The Charity as a Business*, Directory of Social Change, London.

For those interested in management in the voluntary sector and charities, this has chapters on motivation and leadership in such organisations.

Brown, R. (ed.) (1997), *The Changing Shape of Work*, Macmillan, London.

A selection of papers on current trends and changes in the labour market.

Heil, G., Bennis, W. and Stephens, D.C. (2000), *Douglas McGregor Revisited*, Wiley, New York. A review of McGregor's ideas, which the authors argue are more in tune with modern organisational needs than when he wrote *The Human Side of Enterprise* in 1960.

Rousseau, D.M. and Schalk, R. (2000), *Psychological Contracts in Employment: Cross-national perspectives*, Sage, London.

A collection of essays by experts from 13 countries, providing a rich insight into the varying national circumstance within which individuals and firms develop acceptable contracts.

Weblinks

Visit the websites of companies that interest you, perhaps as possible places to work. Or you could visit the websites of some of those that appeared in Table 15.1 (Europe's Best Places to Work) such as:

www.greatplacetowork.co.uk

www.mbna.com/europe

www.timpson.co.uk

www.danone.com

www.kraft.com (then choose country)

www.pfizer.com

Navigate to the pages dealing with 'about the company' or 'careers'.

● What do they tell you about working there? What seem to be the most prominent features?

● What needs do they seem to be aiming to meet? Would they meet your needs?

Annotated weblinks, multiple choice questions and other useful resources can be found on
www.pearsoned.co.uk/boddy

Chapter 16

Communication

Aim	**To describe and illustrate the main aspects of communication in organisations, and how these can help or hinder performance.**
Objectives	By the end of your work on this chapter you should be able to outline the concepts below in your own terms and: 1 Explain the role of communication in managing 2 Identify and illustrate the elements and stages in the communication process 3 Use the concept of information richness to select a communication channel 4 Compare the benefits of different communication networks 5 Describe how new technologies support communication 6 Outline some essential interpersonal communication skills 7 Consider how aspects of the wider context affect communication.
Key terms	This chapter introduces the following ideas: communication message coding decoding noise feedback non-verbal communication selective attention stereotyping channel information richness information overload Internet intranet extranet groupware *Each is a term defined within the text, as well as in the glossary at the end of the book.*

Carlos Ghosn, CEO of Nissan www.renault.com

In 1999 Renault bought a controlling stake in the struggling Japanese car maker Nissan. The Renault board immediately sent one of their senior managers, Carlos Ghosn, to Japan as head of the newly acquired business. The company was deeply in debt and losing market share in both Japan and the US and was doing little product development. On taking over as boss, Ghosn promised that if Nissan was not profitable by 2000, he and his entire management team would quit.

In 2004 the company reported that sales had risen by 8 per cent over the previous year, and that profits had also risen strongly. Nissan had overtaken Honda within Japan, had the highest operating profit of any of the world's auto companies and was no longer in debt.

Paul Sancya/Associated Press

This rapid improvement in company performance was even more remarkable because it involved a Westerner operating in Japan's closed, tradition-bound business environment. He rapidly transformed a traditional Japanese company, whose business culture valued a slow, methodical search for consensus before taking decisions. His cost-cutting was controversial as it meant closing surplus plants, making 23,000 employees redundant and ending long-established, but very expensive, purchasing contracts. He reorganised the company and replaced a promotion system based on seniority with one based on performance. As well as cutting costs, Ghosn revived the company's design, innovation and quality processes, and initiated the design and launch of an ambitious range of new vehicles.

Carlos Ghosn was born in Brazil of Lebanese parents, though raised as a French citizen. He speaks five languages fluently, and has transformed ailing companies in the United States, South America, France and now Japan. In an interview he said:

The basic objective of management is to create value. It's very important never to forget why we're here, and the higher you are in management, the more obvious it has to

be. At the heart of all this is how you get the attention of people and how you get people motivated to what you are doing. How do you get people thrilled in a certain way about what's going on in the company? There's a lot of doubts and a lot of scepticism. But you know it's a competition and if you do better than your competition you're going to get better results. Motivation is the ultimate weapon. My management style is inspired by this.

His approach to management stresses:
- the importance of transparency in all business dealings
- extensive use of cross-functional teams
- breaking cultural barriers between employees
- sparking innovation through empowerment.

Sources: *Business Week*, 4 October 2004, and other published sources.

Case questions
- What examples can you find in the case of potential areas of communication difficulty?
- What clues can you find about Ghosn's beliefs about communicating?

16.1 Introduction

When Carlos Ghosn began the task of saving Nissan, there were many who doubted whether he could succeed. While he had an acknowledged record of success in vigorously and quickly rebuilding companies, these had been in Western economies and cultures. Would his methods be acceptable in Japan, where the business culture has been a much more secretive, slow-moving and consultative style? How would he convince managers and staff at Nissan of the need to change established practices? How could he bridge the gap between what his directors at Renault expected him to do, and the interests of the Japanese employees? How would it be possible to communicate his vision and reach a mutual understanding about the future of the company?

Most managers experience similar communication issues, though in less challenging circumstances. Those in companies like W.L. Gore and Associates and Oticon want research teams to communicate ideas and results within and between research projects. Those in service organisations such as Forté Hotels want staff to communicate ideas and suggestions – and to understand company policy. The final assembly of the Airbus A380 at Toulouse depends on intense communication between staff at hundreds of suppliers around the world.

Even with the advanced communications technologies now available, people continue to experience ineffective communication. Computer-based systems provide useful tools, but do not replace the need for human communication. Email now dominates communication channels in many organisations, and other computer-based systems enable people to exchange data and information quickly, accurately and over great distances. These benefits are considerable, yet they bring with them communication problems of their own. People typically receive, or can easily obtain, more information than they need or want – and waste time selecting or discarding from the abundance available. Company-wide information systems make it easy for geographically separated people to exchange messages – but how they interpret those messages depends on their relationship: 'Technology won't make messages more useful unless we build personal relationships first. The message will get through more easily if the recipient has some pre-existing relationship with the sender' (Rosen, 1998). If people have never met, they will not yet have the mutual trust and shared knowledge which is necessary for true communication.

Some managers underestimate the communication problems. Someone who works with a major utility business recently wrote to the author:

> The majority of managers within [the business] consider themselves to be effective communicators. Staff have a different perspective, and a recent staff survey rated communications as being very poor, with information being top down, no form of two-way communications and managers only hearing what they want to hear.

This chapter begins by showing how communication is essential to the management role of adding value to resources. Securing the mutual understanding which is the aim of communication involves navigating the stages of a generic communication process. People send and receive messages through one or more distinct channels (or media), passing along formal and informal organisational networks. While developments in technology can support communication, that still depends on people developing some identifiable interpersonal skills. People exercise these within an organisational context of culture, structure and power, which will affect both the choice of communication methods and whether communication leads to mutual understanding. Figure 16.1 provides an overview of these themes.

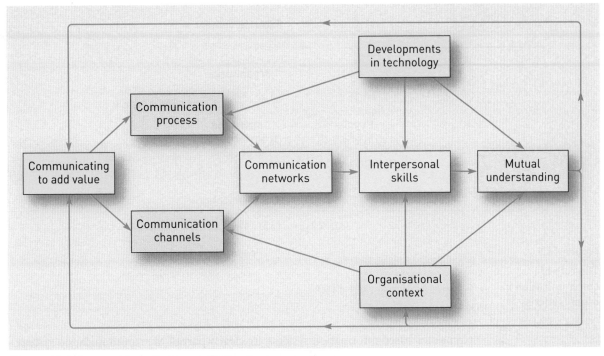

Figure 16.1 An overview of communication in organisations

16.2 Communicating to add value

We base our understanding of the world on information and feelings that we receive and send. People at all levels of an organisation need to add value to the resources they use, and to do that they need to communicate with others – about inputs, about the transformation process and about outputs. Information about inputs could include the availability of materials or equipment; information relevant to the transformation process may be about capacity or quality; output information could include complaints from customers or advertising a new product. Information about a customer's order needs to flow accurately to all the departments that will help to satisfy it – and then between departments as the task progresses. People communicate information up and down the vertical hierarchy, and horizontally between functions, departments and other organisations. Figure 16.2 shows how communication supports these fundamental processes intended to add value to resources.

Those responsible for managing an activity aim to add value by planning, organising, leading and controlling the work of themselves and other people – which they can only do through communicating. Stewart (1967) and Mintzberg (1973) showed that formal and informal communication was central to the management job. This is most evident in the informational role – but equally managers can only perform their interpersonal and decisional roles by communicating with other people. In the liaison role the manager receives emails and phone calls, and holds conversations with people working on different aspects of a project. At the same time he or she is sending messages to those involved.

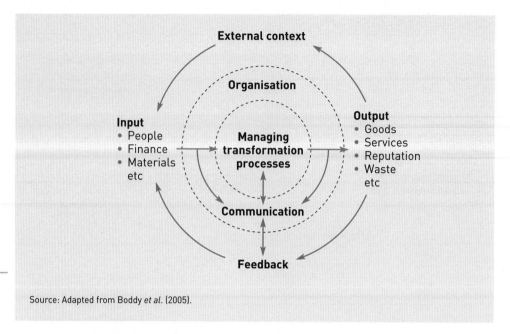

Figure 16.2

The role of communication in organisations

Source: Adapted from Boddy *et al.* (2005).

Computer-based information systems are clearly part of the communication system – but only part. They deal very efficiently with structured, explicit data and information – but much less so with the unstructured, tacit information and knowledge which is so crucial to our understanding of the world. A current challenge is to ensure that technology supports, rather than disrupts, human communication.

What is communication?

Communication is the exchange of information through written or spoken words, symbols and actions to reach a common understanding.

Communication happens when people share information to reach a common understanding. Managing depends on conveying and interpreting messages clearly so that people can work together. While speaking and writing are easy, achieving a common understanding is not. Different backgrounds and personal needs affect our ability to absorb messages from those with different histories, but until those involved in the exchange reach a common understanding, communication has not taken place.

Activity 16.1   Collecting symbols and actions

The definition of communication refers to words, symbols and actions. Try to identify examples of symbols and actions that intentionally or unintentionally communicate a message to you. Some clues:

● *Symbols*: someone's style of dress or manner, or the appearance of the entrance to your college or university

● *Actions*: someone taking time to offer directions to a visitor or looking bored during a meeting; interrupting someone.

How communicating adds value

Communication features in some way in every chapter – influencing others, working in teams, giving marketing information to senior management, interpreting financial data or posting a job vacancy on the company website. It is through communication that people add value in areas such as innovation, quality, delivery and cost. *Innovation* depends on having good information about changing customer demands, and on being able to use scientific discoveries – which depends on effective communication between those in the scientific and business communities. Embodying such ideas in usable products involves close communication within cross-functional project teams and probably with suppliers and customers. Efforts to enhance *quality* depend on everyone in the organisation and its suppliers playing their part – understanding how their work affects others, advising people of difficulties or understanding what quality means to the customer. Without communication there is no quality.

Communication failure in a small Dutch company

The company was founded in 1881 and the present owner is one of the fourth generation of the family. The company trades and manufactures packaging machines and employs 16 people. Someone who has recently joined the company said:

> Last year was difficult. Five people left the company and took with them much knowledge and experience. The company really consists of one person – the owner. He does not delegate much and there is little communication between him and the rest of the organisation. The only part of the company that interests him is the game of selling machines. He describes the rest of his tasks as annoying. The result is that, for example:
>
> 1 When we sell a machine, Operations do not know exactly what Sales has promised a customer. The customer expects the machine they specified, but do not always get it.
> 2 There is lack of internal communication – people in the company do not know their precise responsibilities or who is responsible for which tasks.
> 3 There is no time planning for ordered machines. No one knows the delivery date that we have promised a customer.
> 4 There is no budget system for a machine project. When we sell a machine we do not know if we will make a profit or a loss.
>
> All together, the company faces serious problems because of a lack of policy, management, information and communication.

Source: Private communication from the manager.

Another measure of performance is *delivery* – supplying the customer with what they expect, when they expect it. This depends on all stages in the process operating reliably and speedily. People at each stage need information about orders, capacity and potential bottlenecks to adjust the production plan – which means communicating accurate, reliable and timely information up and down the supply chain. The quality of communication is especially critical in rapidly changing, stressful circumstances where people can easily misinterpret information and make wrong decisions. The competitive requirement to continually reduce the *cost* of goods and services puts pressure on all areas – people need to understand the factors that drive their costs and seek ways to reduce them. So they need systems that provide them with information about current performance, and they need to communicate with others to find ways to remove waste.

Forté's Commitment to Excellence Programme

In 1999 Forté launched a pilot Commitment to Excellence Programme at 26 of its hotels, which the company claims has transformed communication between managers and staff. One junior employee commented that she was full of ideas, but until recently few members of staff, especially those in the 'back of house' jobs, would have dared to make any suggestions. There was a culture of fear, in which people were afraid to make decisions, or make mistakes. James Stewart is a regional general manager whose territory includes Burford Bridge, one of the hotels chosen to pilot the Commitment to Excellence Programme. He recalled that in the past there was 'no communication with head office, which was seen as being there not to help, but to find people out'.

When Granada took over Forté, Tracy Robbins, worldwide customer service director, and Stephanie Monk, group human resources director for Granada, commissioned research by MORI (a market research consultancy) into customer and staff perceptions. Interviews with more than 500 customers and 300 employees in seven countries revealed inconsistencies in service standards across and within the various Forté Hotel brands. There was a stronger focus on completing tasks than on looking after customers, while weak internal communication meant that hotels did not work effectively with head office. The research also drew attention to low staff morale: 'We knew that one of the key ways to improve staff satisfaction, which then clearly triggers customer satisfaction, was to address that [communication] issue.'

Source: *People Management*, 14 October 1999.

16.3 The communication process

The **message** is what the sender communicates.

We communicate whenever we send a **message** to someone and as we think about what he or she says in return. It sounds a simple process, but is subtle and complex, with great scope for sending and receiving the wrong message. Whenever someone makes a comment such as 'That's not what I meant' or 'I explained it clearly, and they still got it wrong' they are indicating a communication failure. We waste time when we misunderstand directions, or cause offence by saying something that the listener misinterprets.

We infer meaning from words and gestures and then from the person's reply to our message. We continually interpret their messages and create our own in turn. A manager and a colleague have a conversation. Each listens to the other's words, sees their gestures, reads the relevant documents or looks over the equipment to understand what the other means. When they achieve a mutual understanding about what to do they have communicated effectively. To understand why communication problems occur we need a model of the steps in the process, shown in Figure 16.3.

Communication requires at least two people – a sender and a receiver. The *sender* initiates the communication when they try to transfer ideas, facts or feelings to the *receiver* – the person to whom they send the message. The sender **codes** the idea they wish to convey into a message by using symbols such as words, actions or expressions. Deciding how to code the message is an important choice, and depends in part on the purpose:

Coding is translating information into symbols for communication.

- Is it to convey specific and unambiguous information?
- Is it to raise an open and unfamiliar problem, and a request for creative ideas?
- Is it to pass on routine data, or to inspire people?

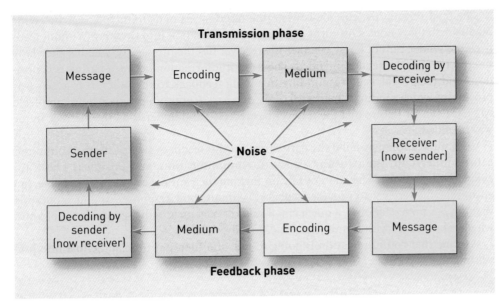

Figure 16.3

The communication process

Accurate coding

Hellriegel and Slocum (1988) suggest five principles for coding a message accurately:

- **Relevancy** Make the message meaningful and significant, carefully selecting the words, symbols or gestures to be used.
- **Simplicity** Put the message in the simplest possible terms, reducing the number of words, symbols or gestures used.
- **Organisation** Organise the message as a series of points to facilitate understanding. Complete each point in the message before proceeding to the next.
- **Repetition** Restate key points of the message at least twice. Repetition is particularly important in spoken communication because words may not be clearly heard or fully understood the first time.
- **Focus** Concentrate on the essential aspects of the message. Make the message clear and avoid unnecessary detail.

The message is the tangible expression of the sender's idea. The sender chooses one or more channels (sometimes called the communication medium) – such as an email, a face-to-face meeting or a letter to transmit the coded message to the receiver. The receiver **decodes** the symbols contained in the message, and tries to reconstruct the sender's original thought. Coding and decoding are potential sources of communication failure as the sender and receiver have different knowledge, experience and interests. Receivers also evaluate a message by their knowledge of the sender, which affects the extent to which 'the individual perceives information received from a sender to be valuable' (Maltz, 2000, p. 114). These 'filters' interfere with the conversion of meaning to symbols and *vice versa* and, along with other distractions and interruptions that disrupt any stage in the communication process, are referred to as **noise**, and 'arise within individuals (psychological filters), within the message (semantic filters) and within the context (mechanical filters)' (Dimbleby and Burton, 1992, p. 221).

Decoding is the interpretation of a message into a form with meaning.

Noise is anything that confuses, diminishes or interferes with communication.

Feedback (in communication) occurs as the receiver expresses his or her reaction to the sender's message.

The final stage in the episode is when the receiver responds to the message by giving **feedback** to the sender. This turns one-way communication into two-way. Without feedback the sender cannot know whether the receiver has the message or whether they have interpreted it as the sender intended. The flow of information between parties is continuous and reciprocal, each responding by giving feedback to the other. It is a two-way process, of which sending a message is only one part. Communication is only completed when the sender knows that the receiver has received and understood the message in the way intended.

Communication may fail if the parties neglect this feedback stage. Effective communicators understand the two-way aspect of communication, and positively check for evidence of feedback. They do not rely on making their message as clear as possible, but encourage the receiver to provide feedback. Without some response – a nod, a question that implies understanding, a quick email acknowledgement – the sender does not know whether he or she has communicated successfully.

Assume that communication is going to fail, and then put time and effort into preventing that.

Non-verbal communication

Non-verbal communication is the process of coding meaning through behaviours such as facial expression, gestures and body postures.

An important type of interpersonal communication is **non-verbal communication**, which some people refer to as body language. Experts in the field (such as Knapp and Hall, 2002) claim that the words in a message have less impact on the sender than the accompanying non-verbal signals. These include the tone of voice, facial expression, posture and appearance, and provide most of the impact in face-to-face communication (Beall, 2004).

Small changes in eye contact, such as raising eyebrows or a directed glance while making a statement, add to the meaning that the sender conveys. A stifled yawn, an eager nod, a thoughtful flicker of anxiety gives the sender a signal about the receiver's reaction. Gestures and body position give equally vivid messages – leaning forward attentively, moving about in the chair, hands moving nervously, gathering papers or looking at the clock. Whether intended or not, these send a signal to the receiver.

Positive non-verbal feedback helps to build relations within a team. A smile or wave from the manager to the staff members at least acknowledges that they exist. Related to a task it indicates approval in an informal, rapid way that sustains the subordinates' confidence. Negative feedback can be correspondingly damaging. A boss who looks irritated by what the staff member sees as a reasonable enquiry is giving a negative signal. So too is one who looks bored or distracted during a presentation.

 **Virtual teams at Cisco** www.cisco.com

Cisco Systems supplies much of the physical equipment which supports the Internet, and most of its design teams are formed of staff who work in different facilities throughout the world. Says a member of one such team:

> It means you have to be a bit more careful when it comes to communication. Most of the time you have to use email and instant messaging to discuss issues, which means there can be misunderstandings if you're not careful. When you interact in person you use things like facial expression and hand gestures – none of these are available when emailing so you have to state your arguments more clearly.

Source: Chapter 17 case.

As with any interpersonal skill, some people are better at picking up clues from non-verbal behaviour than others. The sender of a spoken message can benefit by noting the non-verbal responses to what he or she says. If they do not seem appropriate (raised eyebrows, or a hint of anxiety), the speaker should pause and check that the receiver has received the intended message, and not misinterpreted it.

Perception

When a receiver hears a message he or she tries to decode and interpret it. Perception is the process by which individuals make sense of their environment by selecting and interpreting information. Perceptions of reality and its meaning influence what people say and do, not some objective or factual reality.

We receive a stream of information beyond our capacity to absorb, and a process called **selective attention** helps us to remain sane. We actively notice and attend to only a small fraction of the available information, filtering out what we do not need. Factors such as the strength of the signal and the reputation of the sender influence what we select.

Even when people observe a common piece of information they interpret it, and react to it, in different ways. This 'perceptual organisation' arranges incoming signals into patterns that give some meaning to the data – relating it to our interest in the topic, the status of the sender or the benefits of attending to it. Experience, social class, education or career plans influence this process of perceptual organisation, which leads people to attach different meanings to the same information. Effective communicators understand this, and are alert to the way it will affect how people react to a message.

A common form of perceptual organisation is known as **stereotyping**. 'They always complain' or 'You would expect people from marketing to say that' are signs that someone is judging a message not by its content but by the group to which the sender belongs. An inaccurate stereotype means that we misinterpret the meaning because we are making inaccurate assumptions about the sender.

Perceptual differences are natural, but interfere with communication. Our unique personalities and perceptual styles affect how we interpret a message, so senders cannot assume that receivers attach the same meaning to a message as they intended.

> **Selective attention** is the ability, often unconscious, to choose from the stream of signals in the environment, concentrating on some and ignoring others.

> **Stereotyping** is the practice of consigning a person to a category or personality type on the basis of their membership of some known group.

Case questions 16.1

- As Carlos Ghosn began work at Nissan, he would have needed to try to secure common understandings on, amongst other things, issues of innovation, quality, delivery and cost.
- Review the model of the communication process and identify how each of the steps could have been a source of difficulty in achieving common understanding on the action required. Also consider the possible effects of selective attention and stereotyping.

16.4 Selecting communication channels

The model of communication in Figure 16.3 shows the steps that people need to take to communicate effectively. The process fails if either sender or receiver does not encode or decode the symbols of the message in the same way. Selecting the wrong communication

A **channel** is the medium of communication between a sender and a receiver.

channel can also lead to difficulty – for example, sending a sensitive message that requires subtle interpretation as a written instruction with no chance for feedback.

Activity 16.2 Understanding communication practices

- Think of an example where communication between two or more people failed. Note down why you think that happened, using the model in Figure 16.3.
- Email is widely used in business: list the advantages and disadvantages of that medium compared with face-to-face communication.

Information richness refers to the amount of information that a communication channel can carry, and the extent to which it enables sender and receiver to achieve common understanding.

Channels have different capacities to convey information and this is known as their 'information richness'. Channel richness is the amount of information that can be transmitted during a communication episode. Lengel and Daft (1988) developed a contingency model using the idea of information richness, which is the capacity of a medium to convey information and to promote common understanding between sender and receiver. Figure 16.4 shows a range of media varying in richness from high to low.

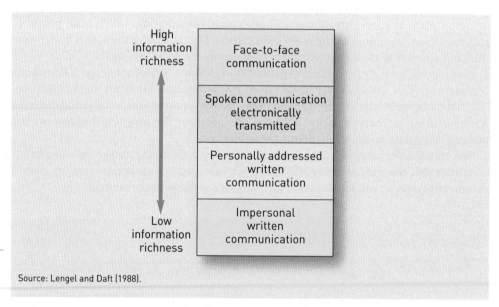

Figure 16.4

The Lengel–Daft media richness hierarchy

Source: Lengel and Daft (1988).

The richness of a medium (or channel) depends on its ability to:

- handle many cues at the same time
- support rapid two-way feedback
- establish a personal focus for the communication.

Face-to-face communication

Face-to-face discussion is the richest medium, as both parties can pick up many information cues (concentration, eye contact, body movements, facial expression) in addition to the spoken words. This enables them to gain a deep understanding of the nuances of meaning.

Most managers prefer to talk rather than write. All studies of how they use their time show that most is spent in face-to-face contact with other people. They prefer oral communication because it is quick, spontaneous and enriched by non-verbal signals. It takes place in one-to-one conversation (face-to-face), through meetings of several people or when someone communicates to many people at a conference. Management by wandering around is a widely used and effective communication technique. Rather than having formal meetings, managers go into the work areas and talk to employees informally about the issues that concern them. They can gain valuable insights into what is actually going on, which may often be filtered out in formal reports from supervisors or other managers.

Despite the benefits, few managers rely entirely on this method. It takes time and becomes progressively less practical as managers and their staff become more geographically dispersed. Another disadvantage is that there is no written record of what was discussed or agreed. For important issues, it is useful to combine face-to-face communication (where that is feasible) with a written communication soon afterwards confirming what was agreed, to check for mutual, durable understanding.

Advances in technology are helping in this area with applications which give some of the advantages of face-to-face meeting without the disadvantages. Videoconferencing is a technology which allows people from widely dispersed locations to communicate face to face (and so see each others' facial expressions and gestures) without the time and cost of travel.

 **Videoconferencing at W.R. Grace** www.grace.com

WR Grace manufactures speciality chemicals and has facilities in 40 countries. To improve communications between its staff, and with customers, it installed videoconferencing for both training and meetings in its larger premises around the world. It uses the system to integrate audio, video, telephone calls and interactive web access to documents. A third of calls now involve customers who typically have their own dedicated facilities.

Electronic collaboration is used to present new products and to answer technical support issues. In one case the engineers diagnosed the cause of a fault at a South American refinery from still pictures uploaded into the web conferencing facility. This saved the customer vital time and saved Grace the expense of flying an engineer to the site.

The company's manager of global collaborative services said:

> With a video call you can tell much more about the person by their gestures and body language than by what they are saying over a telephone. You can tell if you are going in the right direction or if you are coming to an agreement.

Electronic collaboration allows people to work as a more integrated team. In the past managers used to fly to headquarters for discussions and take the results back to their staff:

> We now get input from more junior staff who would never be able to fly to a meeting. They have a valuable contribution because they are dealing with the issue every day. This gives them a vested interest, so they take ownership and move it forward.

FT

Source: *Financial Times*, 21 January 2004.

Spoken communication electronically transmitted

This is the second highest form of communication in terms of media richness. Although when we speak over the telephone we cannot see the non-verbal signals of expression or body language, we can pick up the tone of voice, the sense of urgency or the general manner of the message, as well as the words themselves. It is also easy to get quick feedback, as both sides can check that the other has understood what has been said, thus promoting the chances of mutual understanding.

Voicemail systems and answering machines can supplement telephone systems, by allowing people to record messages by both the sender and the intended receiver if the latter is unable to answer the phone at the time of the call. Many companies now use message recording systems to pass customers to the right department, by offering them several options to which they respond by pressing the relevant buttons on their keypads. These undoubtedly reduce costs but are frequently complex and badly designed, in which case the customer experiences an irritating communication failure.

Personally addressed written communication

Personally addressed written communication has the advantage of face-to-face communication in that, being addressed personally to the recipient, it tends to demand their attention. It also enables the sender to phrase the message in a way that they think best suits the reader. If both parties express their meanings accurately and seek and offer feedback, a high level of mutual understanding can be reached, and is also recorded. Even if people reach their understanding by communicating face to face, they will often follow it up with a written email, fax or letter.

Email has grown rapidly as a means of communication within and between organisations. It has the advantages of the letter, and the instant delivery allows an interchange to be completed in minutes that could have taken days. People use it to send written messages quickly from wherever they have access to a computer, enabling more to work from home for at least part of the time. Mobile phones that receive emails and text messages make it easier for people to exchange personally addressed written communication. However, the disadvantages include:

● lack of the body language that adds meaning to words in a face-to-face conversation
● adding many recipients to the 'copy' box, leading to email overload
● using the technology to distribute unsolicited email messages.

Activity 16.3 | **Critical reflection on communication methods**

Think of a task you have done with a small group of people, either at work or during your studies. How did you communicate with each other? List all the methods used, and any advantages or disadvantages they had.

Impersonal written communication

This is the medium with the lowest amount of information richness – but it is suitable for sending messages to large numbers of people. Newsletters and routine computer reports are lean media because they provide a single cue, are impersonal and do not encourage response.

Managers often use them to send a simple message about the company and developments in it to widely dispersed employees and customers. They also use them to disseminate rules, procedures, product information, and news about the company, such as new appointments. The medium also ensures that instructions are communicated in a standard form to people in different places, and that a record of the message is available. Electronic means such as emails or company websites, either Internet sites that are open to the public, intranet (open only to company employees) or extranet (open only to designated customers or suppliers), supplement paper as a way of transmitting impersonal information. As with email, the ease with which electronic messages can be sent to large numbers of people leads to **information overload**, when people receive more information than they can read, let alone deal with adequately. The danger is that the volume of information distracts people from other things.

> **Information overload** arises when the amount of information a person has to deal with exceeds their capacity to process it.

Each channel has advantages and disadvantages. If the message is to go to many people and there is a significant possibility of misunderstanding, some relatively structured written or electronic medium is likely to work best. If it is an unusual problem which needs the opinion of several other people, then a face-to-face discussion will be more effective.

In a study of 95 executives in a petrochemical company Lengel and Daft (1988) found that the preferred medium depended on how routine the topic was:

> Managers used face-to-face [communication] 88 per cent of the time for non-routine communication. The reverse was true for written media. When they considered the topics routine and well understood, 68 per cent of the managers preferred … written modes. (p. 227)

management in practice — Communication during a merger

When two insurance companies merged, management used a variety of channels for different kinds of communication. As soon as the merger was agreed they wanted all staff to receive the same message very quickly. They told all branch managers to be in their office by 7 a.m. on the day of the announcement to receive a fax, which branch managers used to brief their staff (personal static media).

When the company sought the views of staff on the kind of organisation that the company should create to meet customer needs, they arranged large gatherings of staff to debate these issues in small groups for several days (physical presence).

Source: Based on an article in *People Management*, 2 September 1999.

Carlos Ghosn – the case continues   CASE STUDY

Five years after arriving from France's Renault to run Nissan, CEO Ghosn is still . . . mobbed for autographs during plant tours, and generally heaped with national adulation for saving a car company once given up for dead. At glitzy auto shows from Paris to Beijing, his cosmopolitan air . . . and sterling track record make him a star attraction. He's as smooth as Thai silk in public, and his colleagues marvel at his personal magnetism, his 24/7 work ethic, and his rigorous attachment to benchmarks and targets. But . . . there is another side . . .; if you miss a number or blindside the boss with a nasty development, watch out. 'To people who don't accept that performance is what is at stake, he can be ruthless', says Dominique Thormann, a senior vice-president with Nissan Europe.

Ghosn explains his approach:

I'm very demanding on myself, and I'm very demanding on the people around me. But I know that to be able to be demanding you have to empower people. You can't be demanding of someone who isn't empowered, it isn't fair. If you would put two words around the management style, I would say value and motivation. If you show the pain, but not the vision, you're not going to get what you want from anybody.

One of his early visions was simply expressed – 1 million cars sold, top level of profitability in the industry, and no debt. He explained:

When people see this, they say: 'Yeah, I'm ready to fight for this.' If you eliminate the benefit, why will people want to work 14 hours a day?

He reaches deep into the organisation by constant – and often unannounced – visits to dealerships, test tracks, assembly plants and parts suppliers. On a recent visit to Nissan's Iwaki engine plant, 180 km north of Tokyo, he was mobbed by eager factory hands. He doubtless enjoyed the attention, but at each stop it was evident he was looking for nuggets that would help him squeeze yet another ounce of productivity from the plant. He worked the floor, chatting to assembly workers, drilling foremen, all to get that extra fact that would edge the company forward. The visit clearly paid off for Ghosn,

who knows he is nothing without an inspired workforce. 'The only power that a CEO has is to motivate', he says. Speaking of his approach he advises:

Be transparent and explain yourself in clear, lucid terms. Do as you say you are going to do. Listen first: then think.

Source: Business Week, 4 October 2004; and other published sources.

Case questions 16.2

● What evidence is there in the case about the communication channels which Ghosn prefers to use?

● What are their advantages and disadvantages in the circumstances at Nissan, and what other methods will the company use?

Activity 16.4 Assessing university communications

List the communications channels that your university or college uses to send you information about these aspects of your course:

● changes to rooms, timetables, or dates

● reading lists and other study materials

● ideas and information intended to stimulate your thinking and to encourage discussion and debate

● your performance so far and advice on what courses to take.

Were the methods appropriate or not? What general lessons can you draw?

16.5 Communication networks

Communicating in groups and teams

Different tasks require different forms of interpersonal communication. Figure 16.5 illustrates this. The figure shows two types of communication pattern within a group. In the centralised pattern information flows to and from the person or group at the centre. In the decentralised pattern more of the messages pass between those away from the centre. If the task requires communication between people in a group, but is relatively straightforward, the star pattern of communication will work adequately. An example would be to prepare next year's staff budget for the library when there are to be no major changes. The person at the centre can give and receive familiar, structured information from section heads in an efficient way.

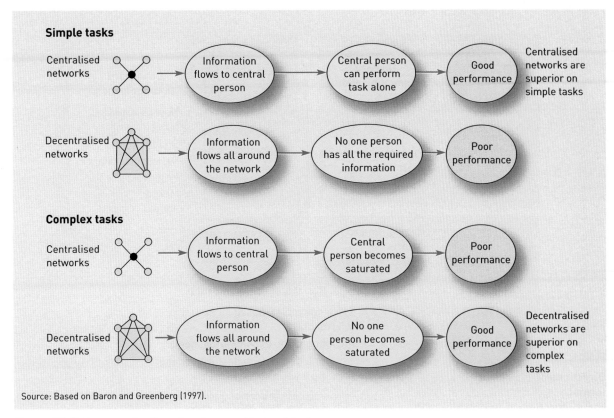

Source: Based on Baron and Greenberg (1997).

Figure 16.5 Communication structure and type of task

This centralised structure will obstruct performance if the task is uncertain, and when those away from the centre have information that will help the work. An example would be a team developing a new product rapidly in conjunction with suppliers and customers. Because of the novelty of the task, unfamiliar questions or situations will arise. Group members can deal with these only by exchanging information rapidly amongst each other. That changes the situation for others who then have to change what they do in response to constantly changing circumstances. If all information has to pass through the centre, the centre will not be able to handle unexpected difficulties. That will lead to unacceptable delays while those away from the centre await a decision on their next move. So a web form of communication is more suitable, in which people communicate as required – amongst themselves and with the centre.

Communicating across the organisation

As organisations grow they need to supplement informal communication methods with more formal arrangements. At first these are quite simple, such as a list of current orders and what stage they have reached. Then there may be a system for setting budgets for the different parts of the activity and for collecting information on what they cost. Later people probably develop some rules or guidelines about passing information to other departments so that they know about changes that affect them. These systems are the basis of the formal or institutionalised communication system. As Figure 16.6 shows, they pass information downward, upward or horizontally.

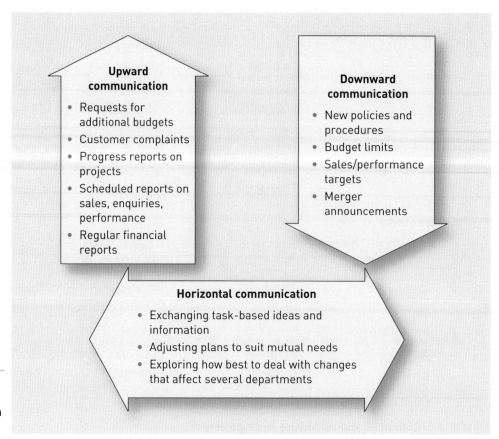

Figure 16.6

Directions of formal communications in organisations

Downward communication

Management uses downward communication when they try to ensure coordination by issuing a plan and expect those lower in the hierarchy to follow it. Examples include information about:

- New policies, products or services
- Orders received, as a signal to relevant departments to start planning their part
- Budget changes or any changes in financial reporting and control systems
- New systems and procedures
- New appointments and reorganisations
- Changes to roles or job descriptions.

If the downward communication inhibits comments or responses, the sender will be unclear how receivers reacted to the message. If downward communication is rare, so that subordinates are unclear about policy or changes, it usually indicates that managers do not trust subordinates to understand the information or use it responsibly.

Team briefings

Team briefings are a popular way of passing information rapidly and consistently throughout the organisation – Blakstad and Cooper (1995) quote the results of a survey of 915 companies in which 57 per cent of respondents rated team briefings as the most common method of communicating with employees. Under this method senior management provides a standard message and format, and briefs the next level in the hierarchy. Those managers then brief their subordinates following the same standard format, and this process continues down the organisation. Team briefings are a way of communicating company issues to all staff through line managers. Addressing small groups with a common structure enables management to:

- deliver a consistent message
- involve line managers personally in delivering the message
- deliver the message to many people quickly
- reduce the possible distortions by 'the grapevine'
- enable staff to ask questions.

Planning a team briefing

Management needs to agree and follow the timing of a team briefing, otherwise some departments will hear before others and the grapevine will become active. The following steps help ensure an effective briefing:

- *Step1 – What to communicate.* Senior management agrees what information to communicate to staff, then draws up a briefing outline.
- *Step 2 – How it will be communicated.* The senior managers agree to hold individual team briefing sessions with the managers reporting to them on an agreed date.
- *Step 3 – Delivering the message.* On the appointed day the senior managers gather their line managers, explain the purpose of the session, read through the brief and expand upon it as appropriate. The line managers receive a copy of the brief and are given time for questions and to make notes.
- *Step 4 – Spreading the word to staff.* Each line manager conducts a team briefing – using the same briefing outline – to those reporting directly to them. This should take place within two to four hours. This process should continue until everyone in the organisation has attended a session.
- *Step 5 – Feedback.* Line managers should provide brief comments to their senior managers using a standard format. This highlights problems raised by staff.

Upward communication

Upward communication refers to systematic methods of helping employees to pass on their views and ideas to management. Managers try to ensure coordination by encouraging feedback. In small organisations this is usually fairly easy. The owner-manager is likely to be in close touch with what employees are thinking, so information and ideas reach the boss quickly. As the business grows the layers of the hierarchy can easily break the flow. Unless they create mechanisms to allow information to move upwards, their boards may be acting on the wrong information.

key ideas Why businesses ignore vital information

Sidney Finkelstein has studied the causes of corporate failure – one of which is when managers fail to recognise and act on vital information. He found that this was not usually due to incompetence or idleness, but to a combination of circumstances that made them unreceptive to information that mattered. These included:

- **Undirected information** when staff are slow to recognise the importance of new information, because they have not been shown that they need to take the implied danger seriously. It may also be that there is no one who is able to act on the information: as when a research laboratory has a discovery whose potential no-one in the business can recognise.
- **Missing communication channels** when companies cannot act on vital information because there are no communication channels between people receiving the information and those who need to act on it. This also happens if the channels exist, but are blocked – if a subordinate reports a problem to a boss, but cannot pass it elsewhere if the boss takes no action.
- **Missing motives** when employees are reluctant to share vital information because there is no incentive to do so – such as fearing ridicule or the boss's displeasure if they bring bad news. If the payment system encourages competition between divisions, there will be no incentive to share information across those boundaries.
- **Missing oversight** when senior managers assume that the information they receive is correct, without checking that this is the case. It is easy to accept good news unquestioningly, but that carries the danger that someone may be deliberately hiding news of severe problems.

Source: Finkelstein (2003).

management in practice Hinckley and Rugby Building Society

A new chief executive of this long-established building society introduced an open management style, together with a belief in giving employees a genuine part in running the organisation. One example arose when the board recognised the need for a new computer system. There were only two potential suppliers and in many organisations senior operational managers or IT specialists would have decided between them. At the Hinckley and Rugby a working group including staff from all levels investigated the options and recommended its choice to the board. This willingness to listen to staff was characteristic of the new culture.

When the decision on the software was made, all staff were informed through team briefings and via the first issue of *Summit News*, a newsletter that would be published monthly during the project. This set out who was going to be involved in the steering committee, the timetable and the reasons for the change. The project involved intense communication between staff at all levels, and over half the employees were involved in some aspects of design and planning.

The new system went into operation very smoothly, and amongst the reasons for the success was the attention given to effective and sustained communications – the 'glue' of the process. Regular team briefings and a monthly newsletter kept people up to speed. With the society's open culture and so many people involved in the project, informal communications also worked effectively, relaying first-hand information rather than rumour.

Source: Based on an article in *People Management*, 20 January 2000.

Employee opinion surveys

Some companies conduct regular surveys amongst their employees to gauge their attitudes and feelings towards company policy and practice. They may also seek views on current issues, or about possible changes in policy or practice. The surveys can be valuable both as a general indicator of attitudes and as a way of highlighting particular issues that need attention, such as a growing demand for childcare facilities.

Suggestion schemes

These are devices by which companies encourage employees to suggest improvements to their job or other aspects of the organisation. Employees usually receive a cash reward if management accepts their idea.

Activity 16.5   Researching opinion surveys

Gather some evidence from a company about its experience of using employee opinion surveys or suggestion schemes. What are their purposes? Who designs them and interprets the results? What have the benefits been?

Formal appeal or grievance procedures

These set out the steps to be followed when an individual or group is in dispute with the company. For example, an employee who has been penalised by a supervisor for poor timekeeping may disagree with the facts as presented or with the penalty imposed. The grievance procedure states how the employee should set about pursuing a claim for a review of the case. Similar procedures now exist in colleges and universities, setting out how a student with a grievance about their assessment can appeal against their results to successively higher levels of the institution.

Horizontal communication

Horizontal communication crosses departmental or functional boundaries, usually connecting people at broadly similar levels within the organisation. Computer-based information systems have greatly increased the speed and accuracy with which routine information can pass between departments. As a customer places an order, modern systems can quickly pass the relevant information to all the departments that will play a part in meeting it, making production a much smoother and predictable process.

Much horizontal communication is about less routine, less structured problems: when different parts of the organisation cooperate on projects to introduce new products or systems, people communicate frequently. They need to pass information to each other on the current state of affairs so that each distinct unit can be ready to contribute to the project as required.

As management creates a structure for the organisation it influences how much horizontal communication will take place. In a hierarchical, mechanistic organisation (see Chapter 10) most information passes vertically between managers and subordinates. In organic structures, where managers delegate more decisions to lower levels, there is more horizontal communication. Instead of referring problems up the hierarchy to a common boss, staff in the respective departments sort out problems themselves.

Managing knowledge at Ebank

Ebank is a large European bank that was created by merging two separate banks. It has grown by acquiring other banks, and now operates in 70 countries. Separate divisions deal with different types of business, such as domestic, international and investment banking. It received a shock when a major global client left the bank because it was not providing an integrated service across countries. Despite Ebank calling itself a 'global bank', the reality was different. Each country and department operated independently and had its own systems and processes. While the vision from the top was to create a truly networked global bank, there was little knowledge sharing across internal boundaries.

Members of the corporate business strategy group wrote a paper recommending that Ebank develop a worldwide communication network connecting all the businesses, using intranet technology. The paper recognised that the true competitive advantage of the bank was not in financial transactions but in providing knowledge to customers. For example, it may be able to advise a client (a European supermarket chain) to buy a similar business in China based on its global knowledge of economic trends and financial conditions. However, to offer such advice the bank needed to integrate knowledge from a range of departments and countries. At the time this was not possible because staff did not share such knowledge. So the vision was to develop a global communication system – a knowledge management system – to integrate the knowledge within the bank.

Source: Based on Newell (1999).

Informal communication

The grapevine is the spontaneous, informal system through which people pass information and gossip. It happens throughout the organisation and across all hierarchical levels as people meet in the corridor, by the photocopier, at lunch, on the way home. The information that passes along the grapevine is usually well ahead of the information in the formal system. It is about who said what at a meeting, who has applied for another job, who has been summoned to explain their poor results to the directors, or what orders the company has won.

The grapevine does not replace the formal system, but passes a different kind of information around – qualitative rather than quantitative, current ideas and proposals rather than agreed policies. As it is uncensored and reflects the views of people as a whole rather than of those in charge of the formal communications media, it probably gives a truer picture of the diversity of opinions within the company than the formal policies will. Nevertheless, the rumours and information on the grapevine might be wrong or incomplete. Those passing gossip and good stories of spectacular disasters in department X may also have their own interests and agendas, such as promoting the interests of department Y. The grapevine is as likely to be a vehicle for political intrigue as any of the formal systems.

The grapevine can be a source of early information about what is happening elsewhere in the organisation. This allows those affected but not yet formally consulted to begin preparing their position. Put the other way round, someone preparing proposals or plans can be quite sure that information about them will be travelling round the grapevine sooner than they expect. Sometimes it is useful to deliberately let the matter slip out and begin circulating information to be able to gauge reaction before going too far with a plan.

16.6 Developments in communication technology

Information technology is radically changing many aspects of communication within and between organisations, though the technology does not alter the fact that communication is a human process.

Convergence of telephone, television and computers

The most dramatic changes are the result of the rapid convergence of three communication technologies that developed independently of each other – telephone, television and computers. The ability of the telephone to send signals along glass fibre-optic cables has increased capacity and reduced cost so dramatically that the cost of carrying additional calls is virtually zero, irrespective of distance. This has encouraged people to use it not only for speech communication, but also to pass data and pictures between fixed computers and between them and various mobile communication devices (Cairncross, 2001).

The use of satellites to communicate television images, and the use of digital technology, increased the television capacity available and enabled the convergence of televisions and computers. By fitting more power into the microchips which are at the heart of a computer, engineers are able to roughly double computing power every two years. As the power of each microchip multiplies, so the price of computing falls, leading to smaller computers and greater capacity. From being standalone calculators, computers, and their ability to communicate pictures, are now embedded in many other fixed and mobile products. Mobile data systems allow staff to receive information when away from the office much more accurately than by verbal messages over radio or telephone.

Internet, intranets and extranets

Another technical development with immense implications for communication was the creation of the **Internet**, which enables telephone networks, cable-television networks and networks of computers to connect with each other as if they were a single network. Linking mobile phones to the Internet has led to the explosive growth of the 'Wireless Internet', which liberates much computing from the desk top, enabling people to communicate wherever they are. People use the Internet to support a wide range of business communications. Another important communication development is the World Wide Web, which allows users to communicate with remote locations via a web address, again vastly increasing the amount of information being communicated.

The management importance lies in applying Internet technologies to support business processes, communications and transactions. This includes selling a product or service over the Internet using the company's website, and using the Internet to communicate information about the sale throughout an organisation's processes from suppliers through to the customer. Another relevant term is an **intranet**, a private computer network, operating within an organisation, often used to communicate information to, from and among staff. This can include relatively static information like contacts and payment procedures, but it can also be used to set up online exchanges of information around the company (Sinickas, 2004). The opposite is an **extranet**, a closed collaborative network that uses the Internet to link businesses with specified suppliers, customers or other trading partners. Another technology that supports communication is **groupware** (also known as a 'workflow system'), which supports communication among people working in teams. The components of such systems typically include:

The **Internet** is a web of hundreds of thousands of computer networks linked together by telephone lines through which data can be carried.

An **intranet** is a version of the Internet that only specified people within an organisation can use.

An **extranet** is a version of the Internet that is restricted to specified people in specified companies – such as major customers or suppliers.

Groupware systems provide electronic communication between members of geographically dispersed teams.

- electronic communication and messaging
- information sharing
- collaborative writing, authoring and design
- workflow management and coordination
- decision support and meeting systems
- scheduling systems, calendars and diaries
- conference systems
- administration of documents.

Greater accuracy and mutual understanding?

These developments in technology have clearly transformed many aspects of communication between people in organisations, and between them and their customers. Using computer technologies to transmit data automatically between different stages of a production or service process generally ensures that it is transmitted more accurately, consistently and quickly than was possible with manual methods. Computer networks with multimedia capabilities enable people to transmit messages, documents, video images and sound around the world. Customers and employees routinely expect information technology to function smoothly and the information it manages to be reliable. Sound decisions and competitive advantage depend on such accuracy.

However, as Whetten and Cameron (2002) point out,

> ... comparable progress has not occurred in the interpersonal aspects of communication. People still become offended at one another, make insulting statements and communicate clumsily. The interpersonal aspects of communication involve the nature of the relationship between the communicators. (p. 219)

Although modern communication technologies greatly aid the transmission of data and information between people, they do not in themselves ensure communication which, as the definition states, requires the parties to achieve mutual understanding. That depends on people combining appropriate communication technologies with interpersonal communication skills.

Activity 16.6 Critical reflection on Internet systems

Discuss the implementation of an internet, intranet or extranet system with someone who has experienced it in a working organisation. Ask them about matters such as:

(a) the advantages and disadvantages compared with previous communication methods

(b) how it affected the way people communicate with each other

(c) whether it was a satisfactory substitute for face-to-face or spoken communication.

16.7 Interpersonal communication skills

If communication was perfect the receiver would always understand the message as the sender intended. That rarely happens, as people interpret information from their perspectives, and their words fail to express feelings or emotions adequately. Power games affect how people send and receive information, so we can never be sure that the message sent is the message received. Breakdowns and barriers can disrupt any communication chain.

Using groupware at PwC www.pwc.com

PricewaterhouseCoopers (PwC) is one of the world's leading advisory organisations whose member firms employ 122,000 people in over 140 countries. The company, founded 150 years ago, traditionally operated as a collection of national or regional groups, further divided into functions. These worked in relative isolation from colleagues, especially those in other countries.

PwC realised that clients (especially large multinationals) required it to handle bigger and more complex jobs. Staff would have to offer a wider range of experience – which was largely available in the collective but unorganised experience of the consultants. How could management gather and communicate this valuable information quickly? The solution was to install a groupware system incorporating database management, email, spreadsheets and other functions.

The system enables staff to share information quickly worldwide. They use their PCs to communicate and work on the same electronic files. The company has invested heavily in knowledge databases, containing details on:

> . . . all the projects we've done in particular industries and topics. So I can find out from my desk where our knowledge base is. I can have a set of case studies on our client's desk in a few hours. Other databases contain what the company has learned from those projects. Consultants on a project use the database as a source of ideas and information. The system is central to communications between offices and consultants across time zones. This is essential in a global business and the system allows much easier internal communication, irrespective of location.

A senior manager in the company reflected on their experience with the groupware product:

> The ability to manage globally in a people-business depends on good communications. Our groupware has helped us to move as quickly as we have. We've been able to respond to opportunities partly because we had the systems in place. Virtually everyone in the practice is now a groupware user.

Source: Private communication from a manager in the company.

Communication practices

The ideas presented in this section suggest some practices which are likely to help improve anyone's interpersonal communication skill.

Send clear and complete messages

The subject, and how the sender views it, is as much part of the communication process as the message itself. The sender needs to compose a message that will be clear to the receiver, and complete enough to enable both to reach a mutual understanding. This implies anticipating how others will interpret the message, and eliminating potential sources of confusion.

Encode messages in symbols the receiver understands

Senders need to compose messages in terms that the receiver will understand – such as avoiding the specialised language (or jargon) of a professional group when writing to an outsider. Similarly, something which may be read by someone whose native language is different should be written in commonplace language, and avoid the clichés or local sayings that mean nothing to a non-native speaker.

Select a medium appropriate for the message

The sender should consider how much information richness a message requires, and then choose the most appropriate of the alternatives (such as face to face, telephone, individual letter or newsletter), taking into account any time constraints. The main factor in making that choice is the nature of the message, such as how personal it is or how likely it is to be misunderstood.

Select a medium that the receiver monitors

The medium we use greatly affects what we convey. Receivers prefer certain media and pay more attention to messages that come by a preferred route. Some dislike over-formal language, while others dislike using casual terms in written documents. Putting a message in writing may help understanding, but others may see it as a sign of distrust. Some communicate readily by email, others are reluctant to switch on their system.

Be a good listener

Communication experts stress the importance of listening. While the person sending the message is responsible for expressing the ideas they want to convey as accurately as they can, the receiver also has responsibilities for the success of the exchange. Listening involves the active skill of attending to what is said, and gaining as accurate a picture as possible of the meaning the sender wished to convey.

Many people are poor listeners. They concentrate not on what the speaker is saying but on what they will say as soon as there is a pause.

---

key ideas | **Six practices for effective listening**

- **Stop talking**, especially that internal, mental, silent chatter. Let the speaker finish. Hear them out. It is tempting in a familiar situation to complete the speaker's sentence for them and work out a reply. This assumes that you know what they are going to say, when you should instead be listening to what they are actually saying.
- **Put the speaker at ease** by showing that you are listening. The good listener does not look over someone's shoulder or write while the speaker is talking. If you must take notes, explain what you are doing. Take care, because we all rely on the other person's facial expression while we are speaking to them. The speaker will be put off if you look away or concentrate on your notes instead of nodding reassuringly.
- Remember that your **aim is to understand** what the speaker is saying, not to win an argument.
- Be aware of your **personal prejudices** and make a conscious effort to stop them influencing your judgement.
- Be alert to **what the speaker is not saying** as well as what they are. Very often what is missing is more important than what is there.
- **Ask questions**. This shows that you have been listening and encourages the speaker to develop the points you have raised. It is an active process, never more important than when you are meeting someone for the first time – when your objective should be to say as little and learn as much as possible in the shortest time.

Avoid noise

Noise refers to anything that interferes with the intended flow of communication, which includes multiple – sometimes conflicting – messages being sent and received at the same time. If non-verbal signals are inconsistent with the words, the receiver may see a different meaning in your message from what was intended. Noise also refers to the inclusion in a message of distracting or minor information that diverts attention from the main business. Communication suffers from interruptions that distract both parties and prevent the concentration essential to mutual understanding.

Supportive communication

Whetten and Cameron (2002) argue that ineffective communication leads people to dislike each other, and to become defensive, mistrustful and suspicious. That in turn leads to a further decline in the quality of communication, and a further decline in relationships: a cycle that harms personal satisfaction and organisational performance. To break out of this cycle they advocate the use of supportive communication – communication that seeks to preserve a positive relationship between the communicators while still dealing with the business issues. There are eight principles in the model, illustrated in Key Ideas.

Whetten and Cameron – supportive communication
`key ideas`

- **Problem oriented, not person oriented**
  A focus on problems and issues that can be changed rather than people and their characteristics.

  Example: 'How can we solve this problem?'   *Not*: 'Because of you there is a problem.'

- **Congruent, not incongruent**
  A focus on honest messages in which verbal messages match thoughts and feelings.

  Example: 'Your behaviour really upsets me.'   *Not*: 'Do I seem upset? No, everything's fine.'

- **Descriptive, not evaluative**
  A focus on describing an objective occurrence, your reaction to it, and offering an alternative.

  Example: 'Here is what happened, here is my   *Not*: 'You are wrong for doing what you did.'
  reaction, here is a suggestion that
  would be more acceptable.'

- **Validating, not invalidating**
  A focus on statements that communicate respect, flexibility and areas of agreement.

  Example: 'I have some ideas, but do you have   *Not*: 'You wouldn't understand, so we'll do it
  any suggestions?'   my way.'

- **Specific, not global**
  A focus on specific events or behaviours, avoiding general, extreme or vague statements.

  Example: 'You interrupted me three times   *Not*: 'You're always trying to get my attention.'
  during the meeting.'

- **Conjunctive, not disjunctive**
  A focus on statements that flow from what has been said and facilitating interaction.

  Example: 'Relating to what you've just said,   *Not*: 'I want to say something (regardless of what
  I suggest . . .'   you have just said).'

- **Owned, not disowned**

  A focus on taking responsibility for your statements by using personal ('I') words.

  Example: 'I have decided to turn down your request because . . .'

  Not: 'Your suggestion is good, but it wouldn't get approved.'

- **Supportive listening, not one-way listening**

  A focus on using a variety of responses, with a bias towards reflective responses.

  Example: 'What do you think are the obstacles standing in the way of improvement?'

  Not: 'As I said before, you make too many mistakes: you're just not performing.'

Source: Whetten, David A. and Cameron, Kim S., *Developing Management Skills*, 6th edition (2002), © 2002. Reprinted by permission of Pearson Education, Inc., Upper Saddle River, NJ.

They argue that following these principles ensures greater clarity and understanding of messages, while at the same time making the other person feel accepted and valued. As such they can be effective tools for achieving the mutual understanding, as well as the accuracy, of whatever is being communicated.

16.8 The organisational context of communication

While good interpersonal skills will improve communication, their effect on achieving mutual understanding will be affected by factors in the organisational context – such as cultures, structures and power.

Carlos Ghosn – the case continues   CASE STUDY

Ghosn has created many cross-company teams to study urgent problems such as product planning, vehicle engineering, power trains and purchasing – even when two companies with such different values have to work together. Asked about his experience of managing Nissan's largely Japanese workforce, he said:

It's interesting to see how human beings handle difference. People have always had problems with what is different from them. Different religion, race, sex, age, training – human beings have always had a challenge confronting what is different.

You feel more comfortable, more secure, with somebody who is like you. You feel insecure with someone who is different from you – younger, or a foreigner. But I recognize that even if someone is different, I'm going to learn a lot. We have a tendency to reject what is different – and yet we need what is different. Because what is different is the only way we can grow by confronting ourselves.

I have no doubt that cultural influences can affect the outcomes of discussions among multi-cultural teams, contributing much richer solutions than those teams' members would have developed on their own.

Generally speaking, my impression is that Japanese people are naturally process-oriented thinkers. French people are conceptual, ingenious and innovative. Americans are direct, get-to-the-point, bottom-line driven. The mix of those traits can be a tremendous asset during problem-solving or brainstorming sessions.

Sources: *Business Week*, 4 October 2004; and other published sources.

Culture

Differences in culture (as well as differences in language skills) can clearly impede efforts to communicate in multinational teams – though another view is to stress the learning benefits of such teams, as the Carlos Ghosn case study indicates.

Structure

Organisations are typically divided into separate units, focusing on their particular part of the total task. As explained in Chapter 12, this segmentation often leads to people focusing too much on their interests and priorities and not enough on other players. They forget that others will have an interest in what they are doing, or will be affected by it – and fail to communicate information that would be relevant to both parties. Finkelstein (2003) quotes the example of Nissan's US operation:

> Nissan, for example, operated for years with a rigid bureaucratic culture that required its sales, manufacturing and R&D divisions in the US to report separately to Japan, and not interact with each other. In effect all the corporate communication channels led only to Tokyo. To make matters worse, there was no direct interaction between regional managers in America and top corporate executives in Japan. This meant that if the Nissan sales people discovered customers were rejecting an automobile because of a small but irritating design feature, the design department was unlikely ever to hear about it. (p. 197)

Conversely, people in a structure which encourages and rewards cooperation and teamwork (such as those at Oticon or W.L. Gore) will experience freer communication.

Power

Information has great value. Those who possess it have something others do not have and may need or want. Sole ownership of information can also be used to boost or protect a person's status or the significance of his or her role. Chapter 14 showed that access to information and the means of communicating it to others is a source of power. People may hoard it rather than share it, and use it at the most opportune moment. Those with access to inside information have both prestige and power.

 **A further look at PwC** www.pwc.com

The manager also made the following comment, which illustrates how information can be seen as 'currency', and how the company dealt with it.

> We had to overcome a number of issues to encourage (groupware) use because some of the consultant managers think they're competing with each other. The competition still exists in practice units. So we've 'incentivised' them to share. If they're not meeting the culture, not sharing, that's not going to help them. We have a peer recognition system and an upward appraisal system. So if a consultant thinks a manager is not applying the culture, that will show up. And the peer recognition system allows people who have been sharing and helping others to be acknowledged and rewarded. We apply peer recognition throughout the business. It also needs certain disciplines – people must see it as part of their job to maintain information and record details of their projects. It's part of how they manage a client.

Source: Private communication from a manager in the company.

16.9 Communication from a critical perspective

Information is not neutral. People can use it to legitimise particular sets of values and to exclude discussion of others. Communication affects the distribution of power. Those with power can try to maintain it by managing what is communicated, encouraging some types of information or discussion and suppressing others. Alvesson and Wilmott (1996) argue that most official company language uses terms that legitimise the idea of organisations as models of rationality and especially of instrumental rationality. Management typically encourages communication that supports instrumental rationality – a concern with means, not ends. Arguments presented as supporting a rational analysis or solution often hide the self-interest of those presenting the information. Messages are labelled as containing 'rational' data and arguments and are used to support a particular course of action.

However, what is communicated as 'rational' may in fact be highly contentious or 'irrational'. Management may propose to concentrate production in larger factories on the rational grounds of lower costs. Opponents may argue that this ignores other costs such as extra traffic pollution or the effects on communities if plants are closed.

If these criteria are used, the decision to concentrate production may be irrational. At the root of the issue is whether communication is used instrumentally to reach particular ends (low costs to one company) or to encourage critical reflection (the possibility that company goals could include avoiding pollution and supporting smaller communities). Alvesson and Wilmott (1996) argue that the prevailing management wisdom would be to belittle as unreal idealists those who attempted to challenge some of the goals of business organisations:

> Critical analysis subjects the rationality of such understandings and objectives to close scrutiny, arguing that the espoused rationality of conventional management theory and practice takes for granted the prevailing structure of power relations and is preoccupied with preserving the status quo. (p. 51)

Summary

1 Explain the role of communication in managing:
- People at all levels of an organisation need to add value to the resources they use, and to do that they need to communicate with others – about inputs, the transformation process and the outputs. It enables the tasks of planning, organising, leading and controlling.
- It also enables managers to perform their informational, decisional and interpersonal roles.

2 Identify and illustrate the elements and stages in the communication process:
- Sender, message, encoding, medium, decoding receiver and noise.

3 Use the concept of information richness to select a communication channel:
- In descending order of information richness, the channels are
  - face-to-face communication
  - spoken communication electronically transmitted
  - personally addressed written communication
  - impersonal written communication.

4 Compare the benefits of different communication networks:

- Centralised networks work well on structured, simple tasks, but are less suitable for complex tasks as the centre becomes overloaded.
- Decentralised networks work well on complex tasks, as information flows between those best able to contribute. On simple tasks this is likely to cause confusion.

5 Describe how new technologies support communication:

- The convergence of vision, voice and data technologies has greatly enhanced the ability to communicate data and information with little regard to distance, especially of structured, explicit data.
- However, mutual understanding of information and knowledge depends on senders and receivers having a shared context. Using information systems to support mutual understanding still depends on dealing with the human context of the process.

6 Outline some essential interpersonal communication skills:

- Send clear and complete messages.
- Encode messages in symbols the receiver understands.
- Select a medium appropriate for the message.
- Include a feedback mechanism in the message.
- Pay attention.
- Be a good listener.

7 Consider how aspects of the wider context affect communication:

- However good the interpersonal skills, mutual understanding will also be affected by cultural, structural and political factors in the situation.

Review questions

1 Explain why communication is central to managing.

2 Draw a diagram of the communication process, showing each of the stages and elements. Then illustrate it with a communication episode you have experienced.

3 How does feedback help or hinder communication?

4 What is non-verbal communication, and why is it important to effective communication?

5 What do you understand by the term 'information richness', and how does it affect the choice of communication method?

6 What is team briefing?

7 Name three practices that can improve interpersonal communication skill.

8 What limits the ability of computer-based systems to solve communication problems?

9 Give examples of the way that the context of an organisation can affect communication.

Concluding critical reflection

Think about the ways in which you typically communicate with others, and about communication in your company. Review the material in the chapter, and then make notes on these questions:

- What examples of the issues discussed in this chapter struck you as being relevant to practice in your company?
- Thinking of the people you typically work with, who are effective and who are less effective communicators? What do the effective communicators do? What interpersonal communication skills do they use? How have modern communications systems supported communication in your company? On balance, have assumptions about their value been supported? Can you see examples of structural, cultural and political factors affecting the degree of mutual understanding?
- What factors such as the history of the company or your personal experience have shaped communication practices? Does your current approach appear to be right for your present position and company – or would you use a different approach in other circumstances? (Perhaps refer to some of the Management in Practice features for how different managers communicate.)
- Have people put forward alternative approaches to communicating, based on evidence about other companies? If you could find such evidence, how may it affect company practice?

Further reading

Goffman, E. (1959), *The Presentation of Self in Everyday Life*, Doubleday, New York.

> A classic (and short) work that gives many insights into interpersonal communications.

Whetten, D.A. and Cameron, K.S. (2002), *Developing Management Skills*, Prentice Hall International, Upper Saddle River, NJ.

> Extended discussion of interpersonal communication skills, with useful exercises.

Hargie, O.D.W. (1997), *Handbook of Communication Skills*, Routledge, London.

> A collection of papers covering all aspects of interpersonal communications skills, including non-verbal behaviour, explaining, listening, humour, and the selection interview.

Beall, A.E. (2004), 'Body language speaks: reading and responding more effectively to hidden communication', *Communication World*, vol. 21, no. 2, pp. 18–20.

> A well-illustrated article about body language, which also lists some further resources.

Finkelstein, S. (2003), *Why Smart Executives Fail: and what you can learn from their mistakes*, Penguin, New York.

> Fascinating account of the sources of communication failure in public and private organisations.

Weblinks

Visit these websites (or those of companies which interest you, or of where you are studying):

www.renault.com

www.shell.com

www.bp.com

- In what ways is the company using the website to communicate information about inputs, outputs and transformation processes?
- Is it providing a one-way or a two-way communication process?

Annotated weblinks, multiple choice questions and other
useful resources can be found on
www.pearsoned.co.uk/boddy

Chapter 17

Teams

Aim

To outline the significance of teams and how they develop.

Objectives

By the end of your work on this chapter you should be able to outline the concepts below in your own terms and:

1 Explain why organisations use teams for a wide range of tasks

2 Distinguish the stages of development through which groups pass

3 Explain Belbin's theory of team roles

4 Evaluate the effectiveness of a team and identify possible reasons for variations in performance

5 Outline the organisational factors that influence team performance

6 Describe the meaning of 'groupthink', and give some examples of its symptoms

7 Use a theory to decide whether a team is always appropriate.

Key terms

This chapter introduces the following ideas:

team
structure
working groups
formal teams
informal groups
team-based rewards
preferred team role
observe
content
groupthink

Each is a term defined within the text, as well as in the glossary at the end of the book.

Cisco Systems is a company at the heart of the Internet. It is a leading developer and supplier of the physical equipment and software that allow digital data to travel around the world over the Internet, and also provides various support services that enable companies to improve their use of the network. It was founded in 1984 by a group of scientists from Stanford University, and its engineers have focused on developing Internet Protocol (IP)-based networking technologies. The core areas of the business remain the supply of routing and switching equipment, but it is also working in areas such as home networking, network security and storage networking.

The company employs 34,000 staff working from 70 offices around the world, developing new systems and working with customers to implement and enhance their network infrastructure. Most projects are implemented by staff from several sites working as virtual teams, in the sense that they are responsible for a collective product but work in physically separate places.

In March 2004 the company created a team to coordinate the testing and release of Version 4 of Cisco's Element Management Framework (EMF), a highly complex piece of software that monitors the performance of large numbers of elements in a network. The product was to be released in November 2004, when the members of the team would be free to work on other projects. The team had eight members, drawn from four sites and three countries:

Name	Location	Role
Steve	Raleigh, North Carolina	Project Coordinator
Richard	Cumbernauld, Scotland	Development Manager
Graham	Cumbernauld, Scotland	Development Engineer
Eddie	Cumbernauld, Scotland	Development Engineer
Rai	Austin, Texas	Test Engineer
Silvio	Austin, Texas	Test Engineer
Jim	Raleigh, North Carolina	Network Architect
Gunzal	Bangalore, India	Release Support Engineer

The role of the coordinator was to ensure the smooth operation of the team and to monitor actual progress against the challenging delivery schedule. The software was developed in Cumbernauld, by engineers writing the code and revising it as necessary after testing by the test engineers. They are responsible for rigorously testing all software and reporting all problems concisely and accurately to the development engineers.

The network architect has extensive knowledge of the network hardware that the software would manage, and supervised the development and testing of the software to ensure that it worked as efficiently as possible with the hardware. The release support engineer deals with the logistics of software release, such as defining each version and ensuring deliverables are available to the manufacturing departments at the appropriate times.

Each member worked full-time on the project, though they never met physically during the life of the project. All members took part in a weekly conference call, and also a daily call attended by the coordinator, development manager and a member of the test team. Communication throughout the team was mainly by electronic mail, together with instant messaging.

Source: Communication from members of the project team.

Case questions

- What challenges would you expect a team which never meets will face during its work?
- In what ways may it need to work differently from a conventional team?

17.1 Introduction

Cisco is an organisation where management uses teams extensively to deliver its products and services to customers. The people with the skills it needs for a particular project will be widely dispersed around the organisation but need to work together to meet customer needs. Teams are a way of bringing them together for the duration of a project – they then disperse and re-form in different combinations to work on other projects. The company also uses teams for internal development projects, where staff from a variety of functions and geographical areas work together on a part-time basis to deal with a pressing management problem, such as improving a financial or marketing system.

People at work have always developed loyalties amongst small groups of fellow workers and there are well-documented examples of industries where work was formally organised in small, self-managing teams (Trist and Bamforth, 1951). This is now happening much more widely, with teams rather than individuals becoming the basic building block of many organisations. This is most evident in research-based organisations such as Microsoft (Cusumano, 1997), W.L. Gore and Associates or GlaxoSmithKline, where scientists or engineers from different disciplines come together to work on a common project and then disband when the work is complete. There are many cross-organisational teams – such as when Sun Microsystems and one of their major suppliers created a range of teams to manage the flow of components between the two businesses (Boddy *et al.*, 2000, and see Management in Practice in Section 13.3). Teams bring together people with different ideas and perspectives to solve difficult problems. Most economic and social problems require the contribution of several disciplines or organisations. Creating a team draws people from these areas together to work on the problem.

However, putting people together as a group does not in itself ensure either performance or satisfaction. Some teams, such as that at Cisco, work to very high standards and levels of achievement. They are conspicuously successful and achieve more than was expected. Others fail, wasting both time and opportunity. The differences in performance – in meeting business goals or in satisfying members – reflect how the members managed the team.

The diversity of backgrounds that makes a team worthwhile also makes it harder for the team to work. Creating a team (or 'group', 'section', 'task force' or 'working party') is only the start. Members then need to learn to work together collaboratively to reach a target. The greater the diversity, the greater the challenge it will be to make the team work.

This chapter examines the use of teams in organisations, and the management issues that they raise, as shown in Figure 17.1. The chapter begins by outlining why more organisations now use teams and introduces a way of evaluating how well a team performs. It then discusses the different types of teams and the stages through which an effective team must pass. This leads to a theory about the sources of team effectiveness, which forms the structure for the rest of the chapter – the motivation, composition and working methods of teams. For all their potential advantages, teams have costs as well as benefits, and are not appropriate for all kinds of work. Deciding to invest in teams can follow a conscious decision rather than current fashion, so the chapter concludes with a way of reaching that decision in a particular situation.

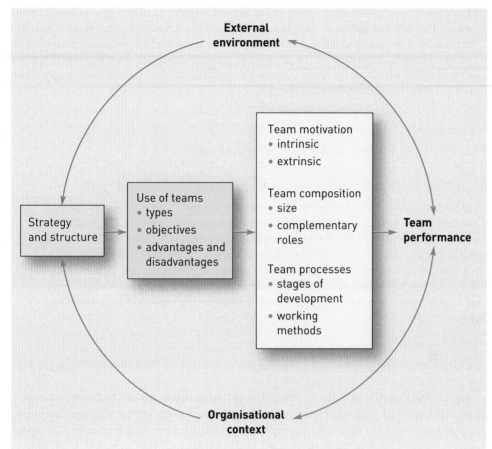

Figure 17.1
A model of team performance

17.2 Advantages of teams

There are both motivational and business reasons for the widespread use of teams.

Motivational reasons

The Hawthorne studies described in Chapter 2 showed that a supportive work group had more influence on performance than physical conditions. People have social needs that they seek to satisfy by being acknowledged and accepted by other people. This can be done on a person-to-person basis (mutual acknowledgement or courteous small-talk on the train), but most people also put some effort into being a member of several relatively permanent cooperative groups. These provide an opportunity to express and receive ideas and to reshape one's views by interacting with others. Acceptance by a group meets a widely held human need.

Follett and Barnard developed these ideas on the social nature of people and on the benefits of cooperative action. They saw the group as an intermediate institution between the solitary individual and the abstract society, and argued that it was through the institution of the group that people organised cooperative action. In 1926 Follett wrote:

Early psychology was based on the study of the individual; early sociology was based on the study of society. But there is no such thing as the 'individual', there is no such thing as 'society'; there is only the group and the group-unit – the social individual. Social psychology must begin with an intensive study of the group, of the selective processes which go on within it, the differentiated reactions, the likenesses and the unlikenesses, and the spiritual energy which unites them. (Quoted in Graham, 1995, p. 230)

key ideas   Mary Parker Follett and Japanese management

According to Tokihiko Enomoto, Professor of Business Administration at Tokai University, Japan:

Follett's work has become part of our teaching on management, and is well known to quite a number of ... managers in our government institutions and business organisations. Much of what Follett says about individuals and groups reflects to a substantial extent our Japanese view of the place of individuals in groups, and by extension their place in society ... She sees individuals not as independent selves going their separate ways, but as interdependent, interactive and interconnecting members of the groups to which they belong. This is something close to the Japanese ethos. We can fully agree with Follett when she writes that 'the vital relation of the individual to the world is through his groups'.

Source: Quoted in Graham (1995), pp. 242–3.

Likert (1961) developed this theme of the potential of groups as a basis for organising work. He observed that while effective managers used many of the traditional tools of scientific management they did not emphasise compliance by using hierarchical and economic pressures. Instead they encouraged participation by group members in all aspects of the job, including setting goals and budgets, controlling costs and organising work. Effective managers developed staff into a working team with high group loyalty. They used participation and other leadership practices to ensure that staff developed high levels of teamworking skill.

Why were these groups effective? Likert suggested the explanation lay in the *principle of supportive relationships*. He agreed with Maslow that people value receiving a positive response from others, as this helps to build and maintain their self-esteem. The relationships people experience within an organisation serve the same purpose, especially when they spend much of their time with their work group.

People value these supportive relationships, and Likert found that effective organisations had developed a system of interlocking groups with a high degree of group loyalty amongst the members. Their managers had deliberately built and linked such groups by ensuring people had overlapping membership of more than one group. He advocated that management should ensure that 'each person ... is a member of one or more functioning workgroups that have a high degree of group loyalty, effective skills of interaction and high performance goals' (Likert, 1961, p. 104). Figure 17.2 shows the idea of supportive relationships.

These ideas continue to influence practice. Katzenbach and Smith (1993b) observed that members of a team who surmount problems together build trust and confidence in each other. They benefit from the buzz of being in a team, and of 'being part of something bigger than myself'.

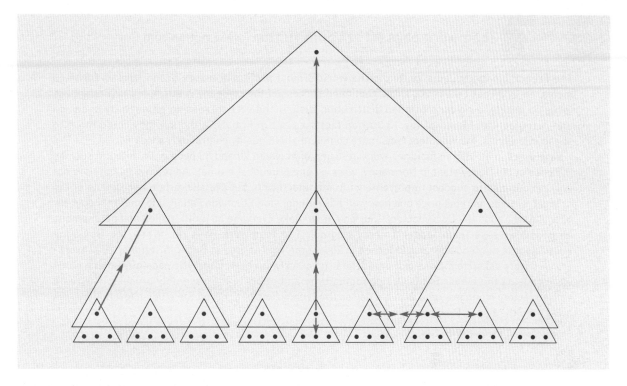

Figure 17.2 Likert's principle of supporting relationships
Note: The arrows indicate the linking pin-functions, both vertical and horizontal – as in cross-functional teams.
Source: Adapted from Likert (1967), p. 50.

Business reasons

As scientific and technical knowledge grows it becomes more fragmented between different professional groups. Solving many technical, production, social, health and other types of problem is therefore likely to involve several disciplines. Even if staff remain within their separate hierarchical structures, management will often create multidisciplinary teams to work together to deliver a service or resolve some common problem. Teams can bring complementary skills beyond those that any of the individual members could bring.

In the area of healthcare there is a long tradition that professional groups work independently and autonomously – and 'each has its own view of the patient, and its own view of the solution. Each profession has been given its own spectacles through which to view the world' (Soothill *et al.*, 1995, p. 6). Yet there is growing interest in developing collaborative and teamworking practices between the various professions involved in delivering patient care. One reason has undoubtedly been the unnecessary suffering caused by different groups failing to pass on information. Another has been the need to improve the quality of care and make better use of resources. Many believe that these can best be achieved by encouraging independent professionals to work as teams. Teams can also reduce costs and blur expensive demarcation lines between professional staff.

Teams are also used when organisations need to make large improvements in performance quickly, or to enhance permanently their flexibility and responsiveness. They seem especially attractive where an organisation faces great uncertainty. Top management cannot have all the knowledge and information that is needed to specify in advance

Teamwork pays off at Louis Vuitton www.vuitton.com

The French company Louis Vuitton is the world's most profitable luxury brand, whose earnings increased by 30 per cent in 2003. The continued success of the company is attributed to a relentless focus on quality, a rigidly controlled distribution system and ever-increasing productivity in design and manufacture. Eleven of the 13 Vuitton factories are in France: although they could move to cheaper locations, management feels more confident about quality control in France.

Employees in all Vuitton factories work in teams of between 20 and 30 people. Each team, such as the ones at the Ducey plant in Normandy, work on one product at a time, and team members are not only encouraged to suggest improvements in manufacturing, but are also briefed on details of the product, such as its retail price and how well it is selling, says Stephane Fallon, a former manager for Michelin who runs the Ducey factory. 'Our goal is to make everyone as multi-skilled and autonomous as possible', says team leader Thierry Nogues. The teamwork pays off. When the Boulogne Multicolour (a new shoulder bag launched in 2004) prototype arrived at Ducey in summer 2003, workers who were asked to make a test production run quickly discovered that the decorative metal studs were causing the zipper to bunch up, adding time and effort to the assembly process. The team alerted factory managers, and within a day or two technicians had moved the studs a few millimetres away from the zipper. Problem solved.

Source: *Business Week*, 22 March 2004.

how an issue should be managed. Creating a group allows it to benefit from the insights and enthusiasm of people across the organisation – who are more likely to produce a solution than managers or professional staff working on their own. Creating a team with appropriate authority gets talent working on organisational problems much more quickly than hierarchical structures could (Druskat and Wheeler, 2004). So teams are often seen by management as a way of using the talent and resources within the company more effectively than through more prescriptive, individual-centred styles.

Teams can also cut costs, as the Management in Practice feature on Coats Ltd shows.

Teams at Coats

Coats Ltd (a textile company) decided to introduce self-managed work teams into its manufacturing operations. This was a result of the need for improved quality and efficiency from the plant. The aim was to replace the traditional manufacturing set-up with teams of highly trained employees fully capable of managing themselves and completing a whole piece of work. The members of each team would be able to perform a wide variety of tasks, have more decision-making power and access to more information. The teams would perform roles traditionally performed by supervisors such as scheduling, setting priorities and monitoring quality. A manager from the plant later commented:

We started with some pilot groups, and after some initial difficulties over the composition of the groups they are working well. The performance of the teams has reached, and in some cases exceeded, expectations, especially in three key performance measures of machine efficiency, wastage and absence.

The role of individuals has also evolved as they became more at ease with the team set-up. They were more flexible, committed and also willing to act in different team roles. An attitude survey was carried out after six months and 85 per cent of staff said they preferred working in teams.

Source: Communication from a manager in the plant.

Teams do not always work, however, and the next Management in Practice example is a cautionary tale.

A community mental health team

The management of a unit in a healthcare organisation decided to reduce radically the number of hospital places available. It would also increase the resources available for community care. As part of the change a resource centre was established in one area containing multidisciplinary teams, each with about 30 staff. These teams would provide a round-the-clock service for the severely mentally ill in the community. The service was to be patient centred and would use a team approach with a flattened hierarchy and greater mutual accountability. A nurse became general manager. There were many team-building and similar activities.

Problems soon arose, and it was clear that many staff could not cope with the extra responsibility and shared decision making. The job is difficult and sometimes dangerous, and one in which people's lives are at stake. Management changed the system to give a stronger role definition to each member of staff and a clearer structure of authority and management. It also recognised that, while team-working may be an ideal to aim for, it has limitations. It needs to be supported by broader management structures and practices.

Source: Communication from a manager in the service.

Case questions 17.1

- What were the business reasons that have led Cisco to use teams, especially virtual ones?
- On the information you have on the case so far, does the team meet the definition of a 'real team'? (See Table 17.1, page 560.)

Why effective teams contribute to business performance

Many managers, especially in sectors facing severe competition, see teams as a way of reaching a new synthesis between high efficiency and high-quality jobs (Wickens, 1995). Faced with complex problems, managers use teams to:

- provide a structure within which people with a wide range of technical skills and different perspectives can come together
- provide a forum in which issues or problems can be raised and dealt with – rather than being left unattended
- enable people to extend their roles, so possibly improving responsiveness and reducing costs
- encourage acceptance and understanding by staff of a problem and the solution proposed
- promote wider learning by encouraging reflection, and spreading lessons widely.

> ### Activity 17.1   Gathering data on teams
>
> Gather some original information on how at least two organisations have used teams to get work done, or where an organisation has abandoned teamwork. Use the questions below as a starting point for your enquiry. The data you collect may be useful in one of your tutorials, as well as adding to your knowledge of teams.
>
> - What is the main task of the organisation or department?
> - How are the staff in the area grouped into teams?
> - Use the definition of a 'real team' (Table 17.1 below) to describe the team.
> - What type of team is it? (Use the ideas in Section 17.5 as a guide.)
> - What do management and team members see as the advantages and disadvantages of teamworking in this situation?
> - Have there been any recent changes in the organisation of the teams, such as members taking on new tasks? If so, why?

17.3   Crowds, groups and teams

A **team** is 'a small number of people with complementary skills who are committed to a common purpose, performance goals, and approach for which they hold themselves mutually accountable' (Katzenbach and Smith, 1993b).

Structure is the regularity in the way a unit or group is organised, such as the roles that are specified.

A group (or **team**) is not just any collection of people. A crowd in the street is not usually a group: they are there by chance, and will have little if any further contact. Are 150 students in a lecture theatre a team? What about the staff in a supermarket? In a take-away restaurant? In the same section of a factory? They are not a crowd: they have some things in common, and people may refer to them as a group. Compare them with five people designing some software for a bank, each of whom brings distinct professional skills to their collective discussions of the most suitable design, or with seven students working together on a group assignment. They have a **structure** to handle the whole process, work largely on their initiative, and move easily between all the tasks, helping each other as needed.

> ### Activity 17.2   Crowds, groups and teams
>
> Note down a few words that express the differences between the examples given. Do some sound more like a group than others?

One difference is in the extent to which they share a common purpose. Groups or teams aim to produce some outcome to which all members have contributed, and for which they share some collective responsibility. A second difference is in the extent to which members share ideas and activities to get the job done. Teams can add value to individual work by exchanging ideas, information and effort. There is some continuing interdependence, which leads to a sense of membership, and of being (temporarily) distinct from outsiders.

Teams or not?

Consider a Davis Cup tennis or Ryder Cup golf team, in which most of the action takes place between individual participants from either side. No significant coordination occurs between the members during each of the matches.

- In what ways would such teams meet the above definition?
- Can you think of other examples of people who work largely on their own but are commonly referred to as a team?

In normal conversation people typically use the words 'group' and 'team' interchangeably – they mean the same thing. This book follows that common usage, but it is essential to be aware that the words can mean different things. Some work effectively and others do not. Becoming an effective group or team costs time and effort. That cost is not necessary if the task could be done by well-motivated and cooperative individuals. It is worth taking a few sentences to clarify the meaning behind the terms.

Katzenbach and Smith (1993b) define a team as 'A small number of people with complementary skills who are committed to a common purpose, performance goals, and working approach for which they hold themselves mutually accountable' (p. 45). A group of people that works together is not necessarily a team on this definition. The essential point is that groups (or teams) differ in what they produce.

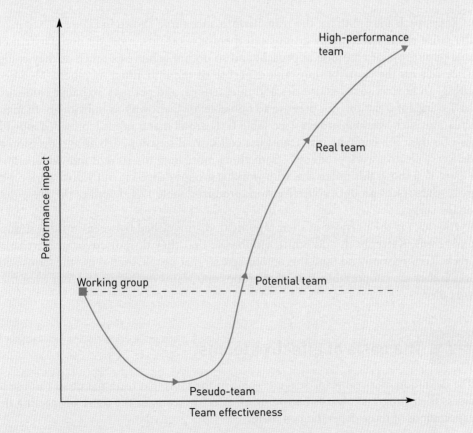

Figure 17.3

The team performance curve

Table 17.1

Description of the points on the team performance curve

Point	Description
Working group	There is no significant need to become a team. The focus is on individual effort. Members interact mainly to share information and best practices. They help each other to perform within their area of responsibility. There is no strong common purpose or joint work product for which they are all accountable
Pseudo-team	There are opportunities for collective performance, but members have not focused on trying to achieve it. No interest in shaping a common purpose or set of performance goals, though it may call itself a team. Time in meetings detracts from individual performance, without any joint benefits. Whole is less than potential sum of parts
Potential team	There are opportunities for collective performance, and members are trying to achieve this. They still need to develop clarity over purpose, goals or joint work products. They may require more discipline in working out a common approach or to establish collective accountability
Real team	A small number of people with complementary skills who are equally committed to a common purpose, performance goals and working approach for which they hold themselves mutually accountable
High-performance team	Meets all the tests of a real team, and in addition members are deeply committed to one another's personal growth and success

Source: Katzenbach and Smith (1993b), pp. 90–2. Reprinted by permission of *Harvard Business Review*, copyright © 1993 Harvard Business School Publishing Corporation, all rights reserved.

Katzenbach and Smith use the 'team performance curve' shown in Figure 17.3 to make the point clear. While many groups call themselves teams, most do not clarify their shared purpose or common approach, and so do not achieve as much as they could. They rely on the contributions and expertise of the individual members. Members engage in normal social courtesies and interactions, and perhaps exchange some task advice and information. But they are accountable for their work as individuals. In many situations such 'working groups' (see Table 17.1) are all that is needed, provided individuals do their job competently. Teams use collective discussion, debate and decision to deliver 'collective work products' – something more than the sum of individual effort. Figure 17.3 shows this difference, with working groups delivering individual work products, while teams produce collective work products. Table 17.1 describes the five points on the curve.

A **working group** is a collection of individuals who work mainly on their own but interact socially and share information and best practices.

Having, for the purpose of their argument, distinguished between working groups and teams, Katzenbach and Smith emphasise that they do not advocate particular labels. They recommend (and this author agrees) that people should use the terms with which they are comfortable. It is what groups and teams *do* that matter, not what they are called.

17.4 The basis of effective teams

The definition of a 'real team' suggests some of the tools that team members can use to assess their progress towards becoming an effective team, in the sense of meeting the expectations of those depending on them.

Small number

Groups of more than about 12 people have great difficulty operating as a coherent team. It becomes harder for them to agree on a common purpose and the logistical problems of finding a place and time to work together increase. Most teams have between two and ten people – with between four and eight probably being the most common range. Larger groups usually divide into subgroups.

Complementary skills

Teams benefit from having members with three types of skill between them. First, there are *technical*, *functional* or *professional skills*, relevant to the subject of the group's work. A group implementing a networked computer system will require at least some members with appropriate technical skills, while one developing a new strategy for a retailer will contain people with strategic or business development skills.

Secondly, a team needs to include people with *problem-solving and decision-making skills*. These enable the team to approach a task systematically, using appropriate techniques of analysis. These include SWOT analysis, project management methods, cost–benefit analysis, diagramming techniques, and flowcharting.

Finally, a team needs people with adequate *interpersonal skills* to hold it together as a human institution. Members' attitudes and feelings towards each other and to the task change as work continues. The changing degree of commitment may generate irritation and conflict and someone needs to have the skill to manage these disagreements constructively.

Common purpose

Teams cannot work to a common purpose unless members spend time and effort clarifying that purpose. They need to express it in clear performance goals. These focus members' energy on activities that support their achievement. A common purpose helps communication between members, since they can interpret and understand their contributions more easily.

Common approach

Teams need to decide how they will work together to accomplish their common purpose. This includes deciding who does which jobs, what skills members need to develop, and how the group should make and modify decisions. The common approach includes supporting and integrating new or reticent members into the team. Working together on these tasks helps to promote the mutual trust and constructive conflict necessary to team success.

Mutual accountability

A team cannot work as one until its members willingly hold themselves to be collectively and mutually accountable for the results of the work. As members do real work together towards a common objective, commitment and trust usually follow. If one or more members are unwilling to accept this collective responsibility, the team will not become fully effective.

17.5 Types of team

Teams have to cope with different issues, depending on their type of work, formality, permanence and physical separation.

Type of work

Hackman (1990) distinguished seven types of team in terms of the functions they perform, and the risks and opportunities associated with each. Table 17.2 summarises these.

Table 17.2 Hackman's classification of team types and their associated risks and opportunities

Type	Risks	Opportunities
Top management teams – to set organisational directions	Underbounded; absence of organisational context	Self-designing; influence over key organisational conditions
Task forces – for a single unique project	Team and work both new	Clear purpose and deadline
Professional support groups – providing expert assistance	Dependency on others for work	Using and honing professional expertise
Performing groups – playing to audiences	Skimpy organisational supports	Play that is fuelled by competition and/or audiences
Human service teams – taking care of people	Emotional drain; struggle for control	Inherent significance of helping people
Customer service teams – selling products and services	Loss of involvement with parent organisation	Bridging between parent organisation and customers
Production teams – turning out the product	Retreat into technology; insulation from end users	Continuity of work; able to hone team design and product

Source: Hackman (1990), p. 489.

Case questions 17.2

- What kinds of team do Cisco use, in Hackman's typology?
- What other kinds of team from the list have you experienced?

Formality

A **formal team** is one that management has deliberately created to perform specific tasks to help meet organisational goals.

Formal teams

Formal teams are created by the organisation as part of the business's basic structure. There are both vertical and horizontal teams, as shown in Figure 17.4.

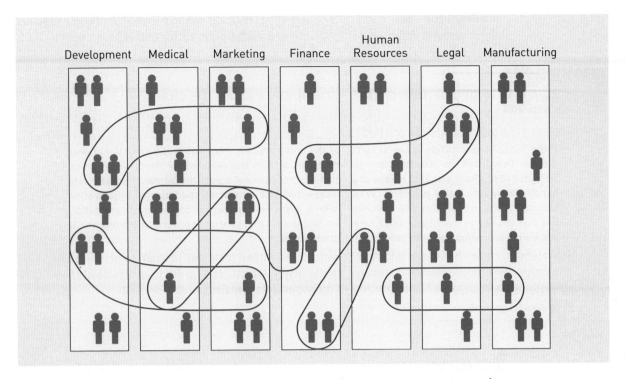

Figure 17.4 Horizontal and vertical teams within Eli Lilley (a pharmaceutical company)
Source: *Business Structures* (video), TV Choice Productions, Bromley, Kent, UK, 2004.

Vertical teams consist of a manager and his or her subordinates within a single department or function. The manager and staff in the Treasury Department of a bank, and the senior nurse, nursing staff and support staff in a unit of the Western General Hospital, are formally constituted vertical teams. So is a team leader and his or her staff in an ING Bank call centre in The Netherlands. In each case management created them to support broader goals by meeting the requirements in the earlier team definition.

Horizontal teams consist of staff from roughly the same level, but in various functional departments. The Cisco EMF team is an example, being brought together to release the new software. In Hackman's typology, task forces would be an example. They are often called cross-functional teams, frequently created to deal with a non-routine problem that requires several types of professional knowledge. Managers create them to take advantage of opportunities, such as to develop a new product or process, especially where these raise issues across a global enterprise (Govindarajan and Gupta, 2001).

Informal groups

Although not created by management, **informal groups** are a powerful feature of organisational life. They develop as day-to-day activities bring people into contact with each other – who then discover common interests or concerns. These may be unrelated to work – people find they share a common sporting or social interest with others in the organisation, and form a set of relationships with them through arranging outings or competitions. Informal groups form directly during work when people in different formal groups start exchanging information and ideas. Staff using a software package may begin to pass around problems or tips. Staff in separate departments dealing with a customer may start passing information to each other to avoid misunderstandings, even though this is not part of the specified job. Informal groups may also develop in opposition to

An **informal group** is one that emerges when people come together and interact regularly.

563

management – as when people believe they are being unfairly treated, and come together from across groups to express a common dissatisfaction with a management policy.

key ideas **Informal networks: the company behind the chart**

According to Krackhardt and Hanson (1993):

> If the formal organization is the skeleton of the company, the informal is the central nervous system. This drives the collective thought processes, actions and reactions of the business units. Designed to facilitate standard modes of production, management create the formal organization to handle easily anticipated problems. When unexpected problems arise, the informal organization becomes active. Its complex web of social ties form every time colleagues communicate and solidifies over time into surprisingly stable networks. Highly adaptive, informal networks move diagonally and elliptically, skipping entire functions to get work done.

The authors argue that these informal networks can either foster or disrupt communication processes. They recommend that managers try to understand them in order to make use of their strengths, or even adjust aspects of the formal organisation to complement the informal.

Source: Krackhardt and Hanson (1993), p. 104.

Permanence

Permanent teams give shape to the structure of an organisation even though individual members come and go. Functional or departmental teams are examples – they provide regular professional support (such as a legal group) or deliver customer services such as healthcare or concerts. Others are top teams responsible for the overall direction and strategy of the business.

Temporary teams are created to deal with a one-off project such as a new product, service or organisational structure. Hackman refers to these as task forces, which disband when the task is complete. Such teams face particular problems, which Boddy (2002) identified as follows:

- The next job the team members hope to be working on may distract them from completing the current, temporary, assignment.
- Varied technical skills: those less familiar with the technical aspects, perhaps because they come from a user department, will usually be reluctant to air their questions in the public forum.
- The members have other jobs to do, because in most cases they will only be part-time members of the project team.
- The members may have political and possibly personal agendas, being there as representatives of a department or function rather than as individuals.

Physical separation

Modern communications technologies enable and encourage people to create teams in which the members are physically distant for most of the time, even though they are expected to deliver high-quality collective outcome. Many of the teams in Cisco are like this. The growing internationalisation of management means that people frequently work in teams drawn from different nations and cultures, as well as working remotely, raising new teamwork challenges (Govindarajan and Gupta, 2001; Robey et al., 2003).

Companies such as British Airways (at their headquarters near Heathrow airport) and most large consulting companies such as PricewaterhouseCoopers encourage staff to work from home or on clients' premises, reserving space in the office only as required (known as 'hot-desking'). They expect staff to communicate with other team members electronically or by telephone. While the method saves money, it requires careful management to ensure the benefits of teamworking are retained. Practices include ensuring that some regular (or at least initial) face-to-face contact occurs, and that members resolve issues of roles, working methods and conflict management (Maruca, 1998).

17.6 Stages of group development

Putting people into a group does not mean they perform well immediately, as teams need to go through stages of growth. Some never perform well. Tuckman and Jensen (1977) developed a theory that groups can potentially pass through five fairly clearly defined stages of development. Figure 17.5 shows these.

Teams need to have the chance to grow up and to develop trust amongst the members. As the work makes progress people learn about each other, and how they can work well together. The closer they get, the easier it becomes to develop mutual trust.

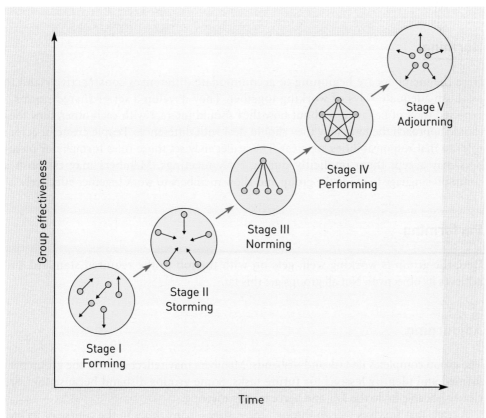

Figure 17.5

Stages of group development

Forming

Forming is the stage at which members choose, or are told, to join a team. Managers may select them for their functional and technical expertise or for some other skill. They come together and begin to find out who the other members are, exchanging fairly superficial information about themselves, and beginning to offer ideas about what the group should do. People are trying to make an impression on the group and to establish their identity with the other members.

Storming

Conflicts may occur at the storming stage, so it can be an uncomfortable time for the group. As the group begins the actual work members begin to express differences of interest that they withheld, or did not recognise, at the forming stage. People realise that others want different things from the group, have other priorities and, perhaps, have hidden agendas. Different personalities emerge, with contrasting attitudes towards the group and how it should work. Some experience conflicts between the time they are spending with the group and other duties. Differences in values and norms emerge.

Some groups never pass this stage. Open conflict is not the only signal of problems. Members may believe the group is performing well – but may be deluding themselves. If the group does not confront disagreements it will remain at the forming or storming stage. It will do no significant work, and fall behind more successful teams. Eventual performance depends on someone doing or saying something that moves the group to the next stage.

Norming

Here the members are beginning to accommodate differences constructively and to establish adequate ways of working together. They develop a set of shared norms – expected ways of behaving – about how they should interact with each other, how they should approach the task, how they should deal with differences. People create or accept roles so that responsibilities are clear. The leader may set those roles formally or members may accept them implicitly during early meetings. Members may establish a common language to guide the group and allow members to work together effectively.

Performing

Here the group is working well, gets on with the job to the required standard and achieves its objectives. Not all groups get this far.

Adjourning

The group completes its task and disbands. Members may reflect on how the group performed and identify lessons for future tasks. Some groups disband because they are clearly not able to do the job, and agree to stop meeting.

A team that survives will go through these stages many times in the course of its life. As new members join, as others leave, as circumstances or the task change, new tensions arise that take the group back to an earlier stage. A new member implies that the team needs to revisit, however briefly, the forming and norming stages. This ensures the new member is brought psychologically into the team and understands how they are expected to behave. A change in task or a conflict over priorities can take a group back to the storming stage, from which it needs to work forward again. The process will be more like that in Figure 17.6 than the linear progression implied by the original theory.

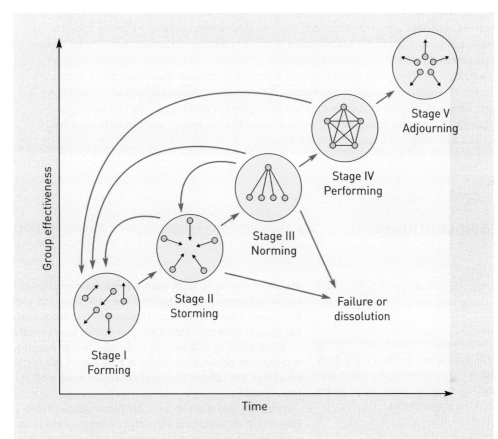

Figure 17.6

Modified model of the stages of group development

The evolution of a project team

A local authority created a project team to select and implement a computer-based housing management system. The chief executive appointed the assistant head of the information technology department as project leader, who then asked some members of the housing department to join the team. The director of the housing department allocated some project duties to his staff without reference to the project leader. The housing department believed the IT department was invading its territory. Both incidents caused relationship problems until managers clarified roles and expectations. To help gain the group's commitment the project leader explained the plan to the team. They discussed and agreed it in principle.

The group members pointed out that they could not work on the project as well as on their normal duties. They believed that working in their normal open-plan offices alongside other housing staff would distract them. The chief executive agreed to a limited amount of time off for the project, and ▶

allocated a separate room for those working on it. One member still refused to commit to timescales. The other members told him forcefully that they were equally busy but able to comply, implying his behaviour was affecting team performance. This was enough to persuade him to participate more fully. There was another early conflict when members of two functional groups put forward opposing system requirements and were reluctant to specify in writing what their joint requirements would be. The team, with the encouragement of the project leader, established some guidelines on the working practices they would use.

Members contacted suppliers and other sites that had installed similar systems to gather information about potential systems. The project leader noted that team members enjoyed these visits, and she used them as a motivator to encourage the completion of more boring but essential tasks such as systems documentation. Performance improved as the project continued. Each member had prepared a checklist for meetings with suppliers and users. As they learned how each other worked this process improved, with each evaluation increasing their effectiveness as a team. They completed document preparation, evaluation and recommendation on time and to the level of performance required. The group adjourned once they had implemented the project.

Cisco – the case continues

Members of the team commented on the way the team developed. A common issue was the problem of scheduling meetings:

I've always found in virtual teams that when the team is first formed it isn't really getting any serious work done (unless we're under severe time pressure), it's about getting everyone together so they at least have some knowledge of the others in the team. (Steve)

Another said:

It was strange when we first started working together, because we didn't push on and get any testing or fixing done straight away. Steve was really pushing for us all to spend a few hours in conference calls getting to know each other and how we were all going to work together. We took our time to get into the actual work that was required. (Graham)

Other reflections included:

I had a few discussions with Steve . . . he wanted us to spend most of our time in conference meetings with the rest of the team, while my engineers already had a good understanding of the work that was needed and just wanted to get on with it. But Steve is the team lead so we had to go along with his approach. (Richard)

It's weird having to form such a close relationship with someone [when] you don't even know what they look like. But as we're using IM [Instant Messenger] just about every day you get used to it. I think you sometimes have to make an extra effort to talk directly to people, just to keep the relationship going. Sometimes it'd be easier for me to email Rai, but I phone him, just so we can have a bit of a chat. (Eddie)

It means you have to be a bit more careful when it comes to communication. Most of the time you have to use email and IM to discuss issues, which means there can be misunderstandings if you're not careful. When you interact in person you use things like facial expression and hand gestures – none of these are available when emailing so you have to state your arguments more clearly. (Jim)

Source: Communication from members of the project team.

Case questions 17.3

- Relate these accounts to the stages of team development.
- What examples of forming, storming and norming does it contain?

17.7 A model for team effectiveness

What models of team development can managers use to build a team that moves towards meeting one or more of these measures of success? Based on the work of Hackman (1990), Table 17.3 summarises three long-term measures of team effectiveness. These are necessarily subjective, and a team may succeed on some and fail on others. Judgement must also reflect the conditions in which the team is working.

Criteria	Description
Has it met performance expectations?	Is the group completing the task managers gave to it – not only the project performance criteria, but also measures of cost and timeliness?
Have members experienced an effective team?	Is it enhancing their ability to work together as a group? Have they created such a winning team that it represents a valuable resource for future projects?
Have members developed transferable teamwork skills?	Are members developing teamwork skills that they will take to future projects? This indicates a team meeting the needs of the business and the team members

Source: Based on Hackman (1990).

Table 17.3

Criteria for evaluating team effectiveness

Based on research with 27 teams of different types (including 'task forces' – equivalent to project teams), Hackman proposed that to perform well a group must surmount three hurdles. The members must:

- be willing to exert sufficient effort to accomplish the task to an acceptable level
- bring adequate knowledge and skill to the task
- use group processes that are appropriate to the work and the setting.

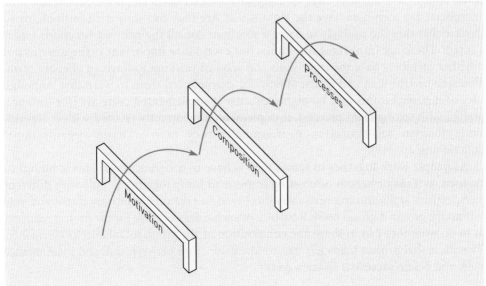

Figure 17.7

Hurdles in the way of team effectiveness

These hurdles (see Figure 17.7) show how well a group is doing and where possible difficulties are arising.

To overcome each of these hurdles, Hackman argues that a team needs both internal and external support. The manager cannot rely on internal team practices (or personal enthusiasm) alone. He or she should also attend to wider organisational conditions such as the availability of team-based rewards. If both are in place it is more likely that the group will put in the effort, have the skill and use good team processes. Table 17.4 summarises these points.

Team-based rewards are 'payments or non-financial incentives provided to members of a formally established team and linked to the performance of the group' (IPD, 1996).

Table 17.4 Points of leverage for enhancing group performance

Requirements for effectiveness	Internal conditions	Organisational context
Effort (see Chapter 15)	Motivational structure of task	Remedying coordination problems and rewarding team commitment
Knowledge and skill	Team composition	Available education and training, including coaching and guidance
Performance strategies	Working processes that foster review and learning	Information system to support task and provide feedback on progress

Source: Based on Hackman (1990), p. 13.

Securing adequate effort is essentially a matter of motivation and so draws on the ideas in Chapter 15 – such as the intrinsic nature of the task and whether adequate extrinsic rewards are available. The present chapter deals with the other two hurdles – team composition and team processes.

17.8 Team composition

In a mechanical sense, team composition includes questions of size and membership. Is it too large or too small? Is there an acceptable balance between part-time and full-time members? Do members have the right skills? Are they too similar in outlook, or so diverse that they are unlikely to agree a solution? Are all the relevant functions represented? These are important questions, but even more important is the question of whether members have the right skills and ways of working to form an effective team. Research by Uhl-Bien and Graen (1998), for example, led them to warn that 'Although cross-functional teams may be highly effective if implemented correctly (for instance, staffed with strong team players), if implemented incorrectly (staffed with independently focused self-managing professionals) they may ... harm organizational functioning' (p. 348).

As people work together in teams they behave in different ways. This is bound to happen, as a major benefit of creating teams is to bring together people with different perspectives, skills and interests. Members tend to take on a relatively distinctive role within the group. A group needs a balance of such roles, so a task for the project manager is to do what they can to shape the composition of the group to enhance performance. Two ideas that project managers use are the distinction between task and maintenance roles and Belbin's research on team roles.

Task and maintenance roles

Some people focus on the project task, on getting the job done, on meeting deadlines. Others put most of their energies into keeping the peace, and ensuring the group stays together – they help to maintain the project team. Table 17.5 summarises the typical activities of people in the two roles.

Table 17.5

Summary of task and maintenance roles

Emphasis on task	Emphasis on maintenance
initiator	encourager
information seeker	compromiser
diagnoser	peacekeeper
opinion seeker	clarifier
evaluator	summariser
decision manager	standard setter

Teams need both roles, and skilful project managers try to ensure this happens.

Meredith Belbin – team roles

Belbin, of Oxford University, conducted a series of studies in which colleagues systematically observed several hundred small groups while they performed a task. From these observations he concluded that each person working in a group tends to behave in a way that corresponds closely to one of nine distinct roles. The balance of these roles in a group affects how well or badly it performs.

Belbin's research method

key ideas

The research arose from the practice at the Henley School of Management of basing much of their training on work done by managers in teams. Groups of up to 10 managers worked on exercises or business simulations. The organisers had long observed that some teams achieved better financial results than others – irrespective of the abilities of the individual members as measured by standard personality and mental tests. The reasons for this were unclear. Why did some teams of individually able people perform less well than teams that appeared to contain less able people?

Belbin therefore undertook a study in which observers, drawn from the course members, used a standard procedure to record the types of contribution that members made. Team members voluntarily took the psychometric tests, and the researchers recorded quantifiable results of the team performance. The researchers formed teams of members with above-average mental abilities, and compared their performance with the other teams. The 'intelligent' teams usually performed less well. Of 25 such teams only three were winners, and the most common position was sixth in a league of eight. The explanation lay in the way such teams behaved during the task. Typically they spent much time in debate, arguing for their point of view to the exclusion of other opinions. These highly intelligent people were good at spotting flaws in other members' arguments. They then became so engrossed in these arguments that they neglected other tasks. Failure led to recrimination. The lesson was that behaviour (rather than measured intelligence) affected group performance.

Source: Belbin (1981).

The researchers identified the types of behaviour that people displayed in teams – their preferred team roles. Some were creative, full of ideas and suggestions. Others were much more concerned with detail, ensuring that the team had dealt with all aspects of the situation and that quality was right. Others again spent most of their time keeping the group together. Table 17.6 lists the nine roles identified in Belbin (1993). Belbin and his colleagues observed that the composition of teams was crucial to their success, as members played a range of roles. Winning teams had members who fulfilled a balance of roles that was different from the less successful ones.

Table 17.6

Belbin's team roles

Role	Typical features
Implementer	Disciplined, reliable, conservative and efficient. Turns ideas into practical actions
Coordinator	Mature, confident, a good chairperson. Clarifies goals, promotes decision-making, delegates well
Shaper	Challenging, dynamic, thrives on pressure. Has the drive and courage to overcome obstacles – likes to win
Plant	Creative, imaginative, unorthodox – the 'ideas' person who solves difficult problems
Resource investigator	Extrovert, enthusiastic, communicative – explores opportunities, develops contacts, a natural networker
Monitor–evaluator	Sober, strategic and discerning. Sees all options, judges accurately – the inspector
Teamworker	Cooperative, mild, perceptive and diplomatic. Listens, builds, averts friction, calms things – sensitive to people and situations
Completer	Painstaking, conscientious, anxious. Searches out errors and omissions. Delivers on time
Specialist	Single-minded, self-starting, dedicated. Provides scarce knowledge and skill

Source: Based on Belbin (1993).

Winning teams had an appropriate balance, such as:

- A capable chairman
- A strong plant – a creative and clever source of ideas
- At least one other clever person to act as a stimulus to the plant
- A monitor–evaluator – someone to find flaws in proposals before it was too late.

Ineffective teams usually had a severe imbalance, such as:

- A chairman with two dominant shapers – since the chairman will almost certainly not be allowed to take that role
- Two resource investigators and two plants – since no one listens or turns ideas into action
- A completer with monitor–evaluators and implementers – probably slow to progress, and stuck in detail.

Belbin did *not* suggest that all teams should have nine people, each with a different **preferred team role**. His point was that team composition should reflect the task:

> The useful people to have in a team are those who possess strengths or characteristics that serve a need without duplicating those that are already there. Teams are a question of balance; what is needed is not well-balanced individuals but individuals who balance well with one another. In that way human frailties can be underpinned and strengths used to full advantage. (Belbin, 1981, p. 77)

Preferred team roles are the types of behaviour that people display relatively frequently when they are part of a team.

Trainers use the model widely to enable members to evaluate their own preferred roles. They also consider how the balance of roles within a team affects performance. Some managers use it when filling vacancies. A personnel director joined a new organisation and concluded that it employed few 'completer–finishers'. Management started initiatives and programmes but left them unfinished as they switched to something else. She resolved that in recruiting new staff she would try to bring at least one more 'completer–finisher' to the senior team.

Using Belbin's roles in film-making teams

management in practice

Hollywood had experienced a shift from long-term jobs to short-term project teams. With their highly skilled freelance staff who come together for a brief period to carry out specific tasks and then disband, film making offers a model for the future of work in the wider world. Angus Strachan has been using Belbin's model to help film directors manage expensive production teams more effectively:

> Managing film teams requires a mature coordinator who can handle creative people with delicate egos and strong opinions . . . A good unit production manager is a strong monitor–evaluator, someone who can carefully analyse the overall situation and make the big calls. The second assistant director needs to be a strong completer–finisher, passing on accurate information that enables the unit production manager to keep abreast of the situation . . . A successful assistant director also needs to be a good communicator and organizer who has the flexibility to adjust schedules – in Belbin's terms to take on the resource investigator role.

Source: Angus Strachan, 'Lights, camera, action', *Personnel Management*, 16 September 2004, pp. 44–6.

However, there is little evidence that companies deliberately use the model when forming teams from existing staff. Managers typically form teams on criteria of technical expertise, departmental representation, or simply who is available. How the team processes will work is a secondary consideration. This is understandable, but in doing so managers make the implicit assumption that people will be able and willing to cover roles if one seems to be lacking.

Whether the theory is widely used or not, it implies that a manager responsible for a team may find the work goes better if they put effort into securing the most suitable mix of members.

Cisco – the case continues

Recalling the roles within the team, Steve said:

My job was mainly to ensure that everything in the virtual team runs smoothly – often just a matter of arranging and coordinating meetings, but also encouraging some kind of creative spark that'll help discussion along. Gunzal takes his time to make decisions, but when he does, he's usually correct. Eddie is very systematic in his work, and very hard working.

Another commented:

I'd say Graham is often the one who comes up with original ideas, while Jim has an incredible range of contacts within the company, and can usually find the right person to go to. Rai is very precise in everything he does and it's very

important that he receives the correct information from the engineers. If they don't explain something properly he's good at going back to ask for more information.

Source: Communication from members of the project team.

Case questions 17.4

- Which of the Belbin roles can you identify among the members of the team?
- Are any of the roles missing, and how may that have affected team performance?

Activity 17.4 Critical reflection on team composition

Evaluate a team you have worked with using Belbin's team roles.
- Which roles are well represented, and which are missing?
- Has that affected the way the team has worked?
- Which of the roles most closely matches your own preferred role?
- What are the strengths and weaknesses of Belbin's model to the manager?
- Have you any evidence of managers using it to help them manage teams? If so, in what way was it used, and with what effect?

17.9 Team processes

Teams need to decide the process that they will use to help them work together to accomplish their common purpose. This common approach includes some mechanical but vital aspects of planning meetings and identifying communication patterns.

Common approach

A primary outcome of an effective 'norming' stage is that members agree both the administrative and social aspects of working together. This includes deciding who does which jobs, what skills members need to develop, and how the group should make and modify decisions. In other words the group needs to agree the work required and how it will fit together. It needs to decide how to integrate the skills of the group and use them cooperatively to advance performance.

The common approach includes supporting and integrating new or reticent members into the team. It also includes practices of remembering and summarising group agreements and discussions. Working together on these tasks helps to promote the mutual trust and constructive conflict necessary to team success. Groups need to spend as much time on developing a common approach as they do on developing a shared purpose.

Team members need to control their meetings effectively – whether face to face or at a distance. That involves ensuring they are conducted in a way that suits the purpose of the task, without participants feeling they are being manipulated. Table 17.7 is an example of the advice widely available to managers about effective and ineffective meetings.

Table 17.7 Five tips for more effective meetings

Meetings are likely to succeed if:	Meetings are likely to fail if:
● they are scheduled well in advance	● they are fixed at short notice (absentees)
● they have an agenda, with relevant papers distributed in advance and invite additions at the start	● they have no agenda or papers (no preparation, lack of focus, discussion longer)
● they have a starting and finishing time and follow prearranged time limits on each item	● they are of indefinite length (discussion drifts), time is lost and important items are not dealt with (delay, and require a further meeting)
● decisions and responsibilities for action are recorded and circulated within 24 hours	● decisions lack clarity (misunderstanding what was agreed, delay, reopening issues)
● they keep subgroups or members of related teams informed of progress	● the team is not aware of work going on in other teams that is relevant to its work

Content of communication

Group members depend on information and ideas from others to help them perform the group task; a useful skill is to be able to identify the kind of contribution that people make (Chapter 16 illustrated patterns of group communication), and whether this helps the group to manage the task. To study and learn how people behave in groups we need a precise and reliable way to describe events. There are many such models and you can develop one depending on the particular focus of interest. Table 17.8 illustrates one list of behaviours. The point is that if, for example, a group spends a lot of time proposing ideas and disagreeing with them, it will not progress far. A more effective group will spend more time proposing and building, which of course implies developing better listening skills.

Table 17.8 Categories of communication within a group

Category	Explanation
Proposing	Putting forward a suggestion, idea or course of action
Supporting	Declaring agreement or support for an individual or their idea
Building	Developing or extending an idea or suggestion from someone else
Disagreeing	Criticising another person's statement
Giving information	Giving or clarifying facts, ideas or opinions
Seeking information	Seeking facts, ideas or opinions from others

Observing the team

Observation is the activity of concentrating on how a team works rather than taking part in the activity itself.

Content is the specific substantive task that the group is undertaking.

Members can develop the skill of assessing how well a team is performing a task. There are many guides to help them do this, and anyone can develop their ability to **observe** groups by concentrating on this aspect rather than on the **content** of the immediate task. They work slightly apart from the team for a short time and keep a careful record of what members say or do. They also note how other members react, and how that affects the performance of the team. At the very least, members can reflect on these questions at the end of a task:

- What did people do or say that helped or hindered the group's performance?
- What went well during that task, which we should try to repeat?
- What did not go well, which we could improve?

With practice, and of course in the reality of the workplace, skilled members of a team are able to observe what is happening at the same time as they work on the task itself. They can do this more easily and powerfully if they focus their observations on certain behaviour categories, such as those shown in Table 17.8 – but suited to the purpose of the observation.

17.10 The disadvantages of teams

For all the undoubted benefits of teams, they also have disadvantages and costs.

Take on their own purpose

Some groups take on a life of their own, and become too independent of the organisation that created them. As members learn to work together they generate enthusiasm and commitment – and become harder to control. The team may divert the project to meet goals that they value, rather than those of the sponsor. As experts in the particular issue they can exert great influence over management, by controlling or filtering the flow of information to the organisation as a whole, so that their goals become increasingly hard to challenge. Their work becomes relatively isolated from other parts of the organisation, and they focus on what they see to be key issues.

Use too much time

The benefit of wider perspectives comes from discussion. This inevitably takes longer than if an individual made the decision. Time spent in discussion may encourage participation and acceptance – but only if the group manages this well. If discussion strays over unrelated issues, or goes over matters that they have already dealt with, the team loses time. This can also be an opportunity for members opposed to the project to prolong group discussion and to use the search for agreement as a blocking tactic. Some members will complain about the time spent. In fast-moving situations they may simply not be able to afford the time and so withdraw their support.

Allow an individual to dominate

Some teams allow one member to dominate. This may be the formal leader of the group in a hierarchical organisation, where people do not challenge those in a position of authority. It may be a technical expert who takes over, when others hesitate to show their lack of knowledge or to ask for explanations. In either case the group will not draw on the experience available, and it will probably be a dissatisfying and unproductive experience. It may produce a worse result, and be more costly, than if one person had dealt with the issue.

Succumb to groupthink

An influential analysis of how **groupthink** occurs was put forward by the social psychologist Irving Janis. His research began by studying some major and highly publicised failures of decision making, looking for some common theme that might explain why apparently able and intelligent people were able to make such bad decisions – such as President Kennedy's decision to have US forces invade Cuba in 1961. One common thread he observed was the inability of the groups involved to consider a range of alternatives rationally, or to see the likely consequences of the choice they made. Members were also keen to be seen as team players, and not to say things that might end their membership of the group. Janis termed this phenomenon 'groupthink', and defined it as:

> **Groupthink** is 'a mode of thinking that people engage in when they are deeply involved in a cohesive in-group, when the members' striving for unanimity overrides their motivation to realistically appraise alternative courses of action' (Janis, 1972).

> . . . a mode of thinking that people engage in when they are deeply involved in a cohesive in-group, when the members' striving for unanimity overrides their motivation to realistically appraise alternative courses of action. (Janis, 1972, p. 9)

He identified eight symptoms of groupthink, shown in Key Ideas.

---

key ideas

Irving Janis on the symptoms of groupthink

Janis (1977) identified eight symptoms that give early warning of groupthink developing – and the more of them that are present, the more likely it is that the 'disease' will strike. The symptoms are:

- **Illusion of invulnerability** The belief that any decision they make will be successful.
- **Belief in the inherent morality of the group** Justifying a decision by reference to some higher value.
- **Rationalisation** Playing down the negative consequences or risks of a decision.
- **Stereotyping out-groups** Characterising opponents or doubters in unfavourable terms, making it easier to dismiss even valid criticism from that source.
- **Self-censorship** Suppressing legitimate doubts in the interest of group loyalty.
- **Direct pressure** Strong expressions from other members (or the leader) that dissent to their favoured approach will be unwelcome.
- **Mindguards** Keeping uncomfortable facts or opinions out of the discussion.
- **Illusion of unanimity** Playing down any remaining doubts or questions, even if they become stronger or more persistent.

Source: Based on Janis (1977).

Groupthink in medicine

An experienced nurse observed three of the symptoms of groupthink in the work of senior doctors:

- **Illusion of invulnerability** A feeling of power and authority leads a group to see themselves as invulnerable. Traditionally the medical profession has been very powerful and this makes it very difficult for non-clinicians to question their actions or plans.
- **Belief in the inherent morality of the group** This happens when clinical staff use the term 'individual clinical judgement' as a justification for their actions. An example is when a business manager is trying to reduce drug costs and one consultant's practice is very different from those of his colleagues. Consultants often reply that they are entitled to use their clinical judgement. This is never challenged by their colleagues, and it is often impossible to achieve change.
- **Self-censorship** Being a doctor is similar to being in a very exclusive club, and none of the members want to be excluded. Therefore doctors will usually support each other, particularly against management. They are also extremely unlikely to report each other for mistakes or poor performance. A government scheme to encourage 'whistle-blowing' was met with much derision in the ranks.

Source: Private communication.

Activity 17.5 Critical reflection on teams

Recall some teams of which you have been a member.

- Which of the advantages and disadvantages have you observed?
- When teams have performed well, or badly, can you relate that to ideas in this chapter, such as the stages of group development, or to Belbin's team roles?

17.11 Are teams worth the investment?

Katzenbach and Smith (1993b) raise the question of whether teams as they have defined them are always necessary for effective performance. Individuals can handle many tasks as well as a group – and perhaps better. An example is where a task requires someone to use their expertise on a narrowly defined technical issue with no wider implications. For such purposes someone who is part of an effective working group can meet the performance required. There is no need to invest the extra effort needed for team performance. Indeed it could be counter-productive. Off-site team development activities can be exciting and motivating. If members then find that the task to be done involves little real interaction, beyond normal interpersonal cooperation, they will feel let down by the wasted effort. In other projects the task clearly requires people to work together to create joint work products besides individual contributions. Then the risk and cost of creating a team will be worthwhile.

Critchley and Casey (1984) raised the same dilemma. Reviewing the many teams with which they had worked, they concluded that teams were not always necessary, and may have represented an expensive solution to simple problems. They concluded that the expense of developing a high level of skill in teamworking is often unnecessary. The answer depended on the nature of the task being undertaken:

- *Simple puzzles of a technical nature* could be done quite effectively by members working independently of each other, on the basis of their technical expertise, with a reasonable degree of polite social skills.
- *Familiar tasks with moderate degrees of uncertainty* need some sharing of information and ideas, but the main requirement is reasonable cooperation between the people concerned using skills of negotiation and coordination.
- *A high degree of uncertainty and relatively unknown problems* require high levels of information sharing and deep interpersonal skills to cope with the 'shared uncertainty'. Such tasks require a high level of team skills.

Summary

1 Explain why organisations use teams for a wide range of tasks:

- As management faces new expectations about cost and quality many see teams as a way of using the talents and experience of the organisation more fully to meet these tougher objectives.
- Teams also meet important motivational needs – for social contact and to be part of a collective achievement.

2 Distinguish the stages of development through which groups pass:

- Forming, storming, norming, performing and adjourning. Note also that these stages occur iteratively as new members join or circumstances change.

3 Explain Belbin's theory of team roles:

- Belbin identified nine distinct roles within a team and found that the balance of these roles within a team affected performance. The roles are: Implementer, Coordinator, Shaper, Plant, Resource investigator, Monitor–evaluator, Teamworker, Completer, Specialist.

4 Evaluate the effectiveness of a team and identify possible reasons for variations in performance:

- Criteria include meeting performance expectations, members having experienced an effective team, and members developing transferable teamwork skills.
- Team performance depends on effort, knowledge/skill and performance strategies – each of which can be affected by the team itself *and* by wider organisational factors.

5 Outline the organisational factors that influence team performance:

- Effort can be encouraged by removing coordination problems and rewarding teamwork.
- Knowledge/skill can be fostered by education, training and coaching.
- Performance strategies can be encouraged by relevant technologies being available and by providing feedback.

6 Describe the meaning of 'groupthink', and give some examples of its symptoms:

- When members become so committed to maintaining group cohesiveness, they may no longer look critically at alternatives. Symptoms include illusion of invulnerability, belief in the inherent morality of the group, rationalisation, stereotyping out-groups, self-censorship, direct pressure, mindguards, and an illusion of unanimity.

7 Use a theory to decide whether a team is always appropriate:

- An effective team is an investment, and that is only worthwhile if the task is one which will benefit from being treated as a collective work product. This is most likely when the task is highly uncertain, so it depends on a high level of interaction within the team to produce a solution.

Review questions

1 Why has the balance shifted recently in favour of teamwork? What are the main business and motivational reasons?

2 Katzenbach and Smith distinguish between working groups and real teams. Describe the differences, and suggest when each form is appropriate to a task.

3 W.L. Gore and Associates (see Part Case) is beginning to form more distant teams. What management issues are likely to arise in this form of team?

4 How many stages of development do teams go through? Use this model to compare two teams.

5 List the main categories of behaviour that can be identified in observing a group.

6 Compare the meaning of the terms 'task' and 'maintenance' roles.

7 Evaluate Belbin's model of team roles. Which three or four roles are of most importance in an effective team? What is your preferred role?

8 Give examples of the external factors that affect group performance. Compare the model with your experience as a group member.

9 What are the potential disadvantages of teams?

Concluding critical reflection

Think about your experience of teams, and about the ways in which your organisation uses teams. Review the material in the chapter, and then make notes on these questions:

- Which of the issues discussed in this chapter struck you as being relevant to practice in your organisation?

- Thinking of the teams in which you have worked, which are effective and which ineffective? What happens in the effective teams that does not happen in the less effective ones? What team-building skills do people use, and to what extent are they supported or hindered by wider organisational factors? Are teams supported by specific coaching or guidance? Are teams sometimes created unnecessarily – such as when the task would be better done by an individual or a working group?

- What factors such as the history of the company or your personal experience have shaped the way you use teams? Does your current use of teams appear to be right for your present position and company – or would you use a different approach in other circumstances?

- Have people put forward alternative approaches to teams (such as introducing more self-managing teams), based on practice in other companies? If you could find such evidence, how may it affect company practice?

Further reading

Belbin, R.M. (1993), *Team Roles at Work*, Butterworth/Heinemann, Oxford.

An account of the experiments that led Belbin to develop his model of team roles.

Hayes, N. (1997), *Successful Team Development*, International Thomson Business Press, London.

A lively and well-referenced account of many of the issues covered here.

Hackman, J.R. (1990), *Groups that Work (and Those that Don't)*, Jossey-Bass, San Francisco.

Katzenbach, J.R. and Smith, D.K. (1993), *The Wisdom of Teams*, Harvard Business School Press, Boston, MA.

Both books contain many good examples of the use of teamwork.

Sandberg, A. (ed.) (1995), *Enriching Production*, Avebury, Aldershot.

A very wide range of perspectives on the use of teams at Volvo, and of the wider forces that affected the fate of the Volvo experiments.

Druskat, V.U. and Wheeler, J.V. (2004), 'How to lead a self-managing team', *MIT Sloan Management Review*, vol. 45, no. 4, pp. 65–71.

Govindarajan, V. and Gupta, A.K. (2001), 'Building an effective global business team', *MIT Sloan Management Review*, vol. 42, no. 4, pp. 63–72.

Two contemporary articles based on empirical research in a manufacturing plant and a series of global businesses respectively.

Weblinks

Visit these websites (or others of similar companies of which you learn):

www.cisco.com

www.vuitton.com

www.microsoft.com

www.oticon.com

www.bmw.com

www.gore.com

www.mondragon.mcc.es

Each of these organisations has tried to develop new approaches to using teams – encouraging staff to share ideas and experience, as well as gaining personal satisfaction from them. Try to gain an impression from the site (perhaps under the careers/working for us section) of what it would be like to work in an organisation in which teams are a prominent feature of working.

> Annotated weblinks, multiple choice questions and other
> useful resources can be found on
> www.pearsoned.co.uk/boddy

Part 5 Case W.L. Gore and Associates in Europe

W.L. Gore and Associates is a remarkable example of a business organised around team principles. While working as a scientist at Dupont Corporation, Bill Gore became convinced of the potential value of polytetrafluoroethylene (PTFE), commonly known as Teflon, as an insulating material for wire. This led him and his wife Vieve to begin W.L. Gore and associates in Newark, Delaware, in 1958. The company has grown to the extent that in 2004 the plants in Livingston and Dundee, Scotland, were ranked by *The Sunday Times* as 'Britain's Best Company to Work For' and the company also featured in *Fortune* magazine as one of America's 100 Best Companies to Work For (ranking twelfth in the list). The company is owned by the Gore family and the associates (see below).

In 1969 their son, Bob Gore, discovered that PTFE could be stretched to form a strong porous material, which enabled the company to broaden the range of its electronics products to include new applications such as medical implants, high-performance fabrics and solutions to environmental pollution. The business is well known for the GORE-TEX® brand, under which many of their products are marketed. GORE-TEX® fabric works in a wide range of temperatures, does not age, is weather durable, porous and strong.

The focus of the business is the development, manufacture and engineering of products and technologies based on PTFE and other fluoroplastics for a wide range of applications. It has four product divisions:

- *Electronic products*: special cables and cable assemblies for the aviation, aerospace, automation, telecommunication, medical and IT industries
- *Medical products*: vascular grafts, implants, patches and dental implants
- *Fabrics*: branded high-performance fabrics for sportswear, leisurewear, work and protective wear
- *Industrial products*: filter media and gaskets in environmental technologies, and in the food, fibre and textile industries.

The company has a tradition of valuing close and direct personal contact amongst people, which is seen as essential to the success of this kind of innovative business. There are no job titles in the company – all

© 2005 W.L. Gore and Associates

employees are known as 'associates'. Associates are hired for general work areas, and with the guidance of their sponsors, and a growing understanding of opportunities and team objectives, commit to projects that match their skills. Teams organise around opportunities and leaders emerge based on the needs and priorities of a particular business unit – some would provide technical leadership, others business leadership and so on. Leaders usually emerge naturally by demonstrating special knowledge, skill or experience that is in line with business objectives.

Since its inception in 1958 the company has avoided traditional hierachy, opting instead for a team-based environment which fosters personal initiative, encourages innovation and promotes direct communication amongst associates. The business philosophy reflects the belief that given the right environment thare are no limits to what people can accomplish, provided these are consistent with the business objectives and strategies.

Associates work to four principles:

- Fairness to each other and everyone with whom they come in contact
- Freedom to encourage, help and allow other associates to grow in knowledge, skill and scope of responsibility
- The ability to make one's own commitments and keep them
- Consultation with other associates before undertaking actions that could affect the reputation of the company – this is known as the waterline principle.

The last principle is intended to balance the risks of innovation: while associates are encouraged to be innovative, they are not expected to make significant financial commitments without thorough review and participation by other associates and in line with business objectives.

A new associate at Gore is assigned one or more sponsors who help them become acquainted with the company and its ways of working, ensure they receive credit and recognition for their work, and ensure that they are fairly paid. One person can fill all roles.

To ensure a fair and effective pay structure, the company asks associates to rank their team members each year in order of contribution to the enterprise. This includes an associate's impact and effectiveness, as well as past, present and future contributions. In addition to the numerical ranking, associates are invited to comment on the rationale behind their ranking, as well as on the particular strengths or potential areas for improvement for each associate reviewed. The company also ensures that pay is competitive by taking part in extensive benchmarking. Each year they compare the pay of Gore associates from various functions and roles with their peers at other companies to ensure that pay reflects market conditions.

The benefit plan consists of core benefits and flexible benefits. Core benefits are provided to all eligible associates and include pay, holidays, sick pay, life insurance and the Associate Stock Option Plan (ASOP). The purpose of ASOP is to provide equity ownership in the company, and through that a degree of financial security in retirement. All associates can acquire a share in the company, in which the Gore family holds a major stake.

The company has several plants in Europe. An associate from the United Kingdom commented:

Leadership probably happens in three different ways. We still have the concept of natural leaders emerging through followership. There are then some areas of the business where leaders are appointed, and we probably find that more in this plant where we have a large production operation. We need associates with operational expertise which meets our business needs.

Decisions to take on additional staff are made on a consultative basis. At the moment it's very much project driven in certain areas. So a group would be working on a specific new product development, and they'll look at the resources they require for that work – and if they haven't got the resources a decision will be taken to go outside. What therefore tends to happen is that people are brought into the business with a specific area of work in mind. Not necessarily a job description, but a role description. That would then settle that person into the business. Once that work commitment has finished they'll then try to seek an alternative role in the business, with another dedicated team.

We have about 140 associates in this plant, organised according to what we call the three-legged principle. The legs consist of sales, product management and manufacture, and these legs are bound together in areas such as marketing, administration, inside sales and vendor support. We also have a position called product specialist, and that person is typically someone with a technical background, who is perhaps working in sales. They are in effect sales people, developing very close links with our customers. They work very closely with our customers on current products, but also to identify customer requirements and move with them to research and develop new products. And we have a team of them in each plant. All of them take an industry sector. Say, for example, in the fabrics plant, we have a product specialist looking after the fire industry, one looking after police, one military, one ski. Each group covers customers throughout Europe.

Associates tend to be committed to one area of work. So, for example, here in industrial filtration we are working on products for office automation technology – basically photocopiers – and we then assemble a team to develop that product. There'd be some production people, engineers, admin support: somebody will have seen a need, researched the product, brought together a team.

The focus is very much on the R&D. One challenge is to retain the team-working ethos while working globally. There is a danger of duplication if the interests of separate teams in different parts of the world evolve in such a way that they are working on similar products. Yet at the same time we don't want to create structures or processes that stifle creativity. We don't want to say that people should focus on specific areas of research. We need to find ways of sharing expertise globally.

Freedom of choice is not total. People will be asked at some point to go on a work commitment by the leader of the business group. When there is a pressing business objective, someone leading a commitment will find the right person for the job, in a way that is best for them and the company. Leaders might be appointed because people recognize that they have exercised leadership within their function (say as a chief chemical engineer). It could also be that each plant has an overall business leader. We have a business leader for industrial filtration and, if there was a particular skill needed on an area of work, he may decide to ask somebody to commit to that.

Balance between procedures and guidelines, and human initiative

We do have standard procedures and rules and regulations. The underpinning principle is to keep them to the minimum, and it's about questioning why we need them. If there's a business reason why that is the best way to deal with it then we're not afraid to put in policies and procedures, for example ISO 9000. There is a mentality that people understand the need for processes when there's something tangible. So, in manufacturing, people accept that that is required. Less so in areas like HR, where there is a reluctance to do anything that people would see as a limiting structure. So if people can readily see the need, we put in procedures; but when it's not tangible we are very questioning about whether it's required. We are very flexible in the way we introduce things. If it increases profits, protects health and safety, and if people can see the tangible results, then there really isn't too much of a problem. The buy-in is absolutely essential.

How do you go about getting that buy-in?

You go and speak to key people and influence people, and you make a judgement as to who is key to get this project

through, trying to see where opposition might come from, and trying to deal with it before you actually impose the procedure. You don't need everyone fully committed – apart from those who actually have to do something. Commitment in Gore is very much when you personally have to deliver something, so a commitment in Gore is when you commit to doing XYZ on a certain project. It's not in terms of 'you've got my support', it's 'I have to deliver for a certain project'. Buy-in is willingness to accept and to put the effort in on behalf of the team.

Balance between people and institutions

Our main focus is on people, and we try to ensure that is effective by this emphasis on commitment. So somebody starts a project, and it's so much ingrained into our culture that if you commit to do something then you make sure you see it through. So part of our culture enables us to be more successful through the people route than might be the case in a more traditional structure. We really have very few institutional structures. The one I mentioned is very recent and came about from a recognition that we wanted to start working towards global teams, and we're starting to try to create centres of excellence within plants. In order to do that we need to have some way of getting knowledge transferred between plants.

That really is a big issue for us at the moment. We just had a big international conference which looked at what sort of processes we have, and how we could introduce them without compromising the elements of our culture that have been so successful for us. For me that is a fascinating dilemma. We need to stop duplication of effort, and that's not something we've done in the past. Plants have grown because somebody's had a project which has taken off, and that team has developed the plant from that project. Given the commonality of the core technology, several plants could be developing in similar directions at the same time. At some point the duplication becomes wasteful. How do we control that in R&D without stifling people's creativity? The centre of excellence and economy of resources is raising the issue of some degree of global integration between teams as top priority.

Sources: Company website, discussion with associate, and published information. Copyrighted material reproduced with the permission of W.L. Gore and Associates. © 2005 W.L. Gore and Associates.

Part case questions

- How does W.L. Gore and Associates influence staff to work on vital projects?
- How do research staff influence each other? Compare the way that people at Gore and at Semco influence other members of the company.
- How is W.L. Gore and Associates balancing personal and institutional sources of power and influence?
- How does management ensure that associates are motivated to work on projects that are important to the company's future prosperity?
- If you were a talented research scientist, what would be the attractions and rewards of working for Gore?
- Which theories of human needs appear to be supported by the reported policies and attitudes at W.L. Gore and Associates?
- In what ways are the associates at Gore empowered?
- Why do teams seem to work so well for Gore? What benefits do you think they bring both to the business and to the individuals? What if teams compete, rather than cooperate?
- What, if any, differences are there between Gore's approach and that used by Cisco?

To help you develop your skills, as well as knowledge, this section includes tasks which relate the key themes covered in the Part to your daily life. Working through these will help you to deepen your understanding of the skills and insights wich you can use in many situations.

Task 5.1   Acquiring power to influence others

Power is a feature of any group or organisation, and to work effectively people need to acquire and use power – the capacity of individuals to exert their will over others. Chapter 14 identified the personal and organisational sources of power – coercive, reward, expertise and referent. It also showed that a person's position in the organisation can affect their access to power. Using some or all of these behaviours, based on the ideas in the book, will help you become more familiar with ways of increasing your power, and hence your ability to influence others.

1 Use tactics to influence others
Draw on the Yukl and Falbe research to select the right tactics to use when influencing others:

- Use rational persuasion – logical arguments backed up with convincing information – when influencing your boss.
- Use exchange, personal appeal and legitimating tactics (e.g. relating your request to organisational policy) when influencing colleagues.
- Use inspirational appeal and pressure when influencing subordinates.

2 Gain control over organisational resources
To use the power which comes from being able to offer something to others you want to influence, seek out opportunities that give you control over budgets, information, expertise, facilities – anything which others may value and which you can use in return. The investment and trouble in gaining that control will usually be worthwhile.

3 Manage your reputation – be visible
Try to understand what the culture of your organisation most values in successful staff, and what images it is best to avoid. Do they prefer those who are risk-takers or those who play safe? Do the important things get agreed during social occasions or in formal meetings? How are people expected to behave with colleagues? Also:

- Ensure that your achievements are known about, and that people talk about them.
- Manage your boss – find out what is important to them, and try to help them achieve their goals – why irritate a person who can affect your career?

4 Build your network
Research clearly shows that networking pays – by giving contacts, sources of information, sources of rewards and so on. Networks take time to develop, so don't waste time before you start. They also need maintaining – do people favours that they will remember when you want something from them.

5 Develop your expertise
Ensure that the skills and knowledge you have are relevant to the organisation, and that you keep them up to date. Concentrating on significant new areas of technical or administrative knowledge will soon mean that you are acknowledged as the local expert, so that others seek out your views and opinions.

6 Be ready to share power with subordinates
They will probably be more committed to working for you, and more importantly, delegating will give you more time to cultivate the external and senior contacts you need to develop your power.

Motivating others

Being able to motivate others (colleagues as well as subordinates) will be one of the keys to your performance as a manager. While there is no single answer to this managerial challenge, the theories in Chapter 15 give some clues about the practices and skills you can use.

1 Recognise individual differences
Individuals have unique interests and needs, and all motivational theories need to be used with that in mind. They help to indicate likely motives and processes, but motivating people depends on recognising their diversity.

2 Enable people to pursue their goals through their work
If responsible, informed people are able to do work that satisfies their needs, they will be more committed and motivated to it than if it does not satisfy them. People who seek challenge and achievement will thrive in jobs that enable them to set goals, have autonomy in how they do the work and receive feedback on performance.

3 Use goals imaginatively
Goal-setting theory includes some clear prescriptions about the motivational effects of goals – such as setting goals that are clear and challenging, but achievable; allow staff to participate in setting goals or explain the reasons for them convincingly; provide feedback on performance. Also try to build and maintain people's self-confidence in their abilities, as this affects how they react to challenging goals.

4 Ensure that effort will lead to performance
People will be more motivated if they see a predictable link between effort and performance – which can be done by ensuring they are clear about what is expected, have adequate training opportunities, have competent colleagues, and have adequate facilities and technologies.

5 Ensure that performance is clearly linked to rewards
People will also be more motivated if they are confident that performance will be rewarded – so ensure that appraisal and reward schemes are seen to be well designed and fairly administered.

6 Check for equity
While equity theory is hard to test empirically, strong anecdotal evidence shows the dangers of inadvertent management action leading to a sense of inequity and therefore a loss of motivation. Ensure that perceived differences in the ratio of inputs to rewards can be justified, and also that people are using appropriate bases of comparison.

7 Ensure extrinsic rewards are satisfied as well as intrinsic ones

People value extrinsic rewards as well as intrinsic ones. Money matters to most people, and ensuring that they see their pay is adequate, and fair for the work they do, provides an essential basis on which to build other motivational practices.

Task 5.3 Interpersonal communication

Interpersonal communication skills are a vital management skill. This activity helps you develop your awareness and understanding of listening.

Answer *True* or *False* to each of these statements:

1 People's thoughts can interfere with their listening.
2 People may resist listening to others who blame or get angry with them.
3 People are more likely to talk to those with whom they feel safe than to those with whom they do not.
4 People who have something they are keen to say are good at listening.
5 Some people listen too much because they are afraid of revealing themselves.
6 Talking is more important than listening.
7 People who feel very emotional about issues make good listeners.
8 People who are very angry are rarely good listeners.
9 People are less likely to hear messages which agree with their view than messages which challenge those views.
10 Fatigue never affects the quality of people's listening.

How did you score?

The correct answers to the good-listening test are:

1 True	2 True	3 True	4 False	5 True
6 False	7 False	8 True	9 False	10 False

Give yourself two points for each correct answer. Most accomplished listeners will score 16 or more. A score under 10 suggests you can benefit by improving your listening skills, as you are probably missing a lot of useful information.

Task 5.4 Observing a group

A useful skill to develop is that of observing the processes within a group – that is, how the members work together. This can give you a new insight into the successful and unsuccessful group practices, which you can then use to improve future groups.

One method is to observe the behaviours within the group, noting how other members react and how that affects the performance of the team – perhaps using the list in Chapter 17:

Proposing	Putting forward a suggestion, idea or course of action
Supporting	Declaring agreement or support for an individual or their idea
Building	Developing or extending an idea or suggestion from someone else
Disagreeing	Criticising another person's statement
Giving information	Giving or clarifying facts, ideas or opinions
Seeking information	Seeking facts, ideas or opinions from others

Alternatively you could assess how well a team is performing a task by asking, at the end of a meeting:

- What did people do or say that helped or hindered the group's performance?
- What went well during that task which we should try to repeat?
- What did not go well, which we could improve?

Another idea is to rate the team using these scales – circle the number which best reflects your opinion of the discussion in a group.

1 How effectively did the group obtain and use necessary information?

1	2	3	4	5	6	7
Badly						Well

2 To what extent was the group's organisation suitable for the task?

1	2	3	4	5	6	7
Unsuitable						Suitable

3 To what extent did members really listen to each other?

1	2	3	4	5	6	7
Not at all						All the time

4 How fully were members involved in decision taking?

1	2	3	4	5	6	7
Low involvement					High involvement	

5 To what extent did you enjoy working with this group?

1	2	3	4	5	6	7
Not at all						Very much

6 How well was time used?

1	2	3	4	5	6	7
Badly						Well

CONTROLLING

Part 6

Introduction

Any purposeful human activity needs some degree of control if it is to achieve what is intended. From time to time you check where you are in relation to your destination. The sooner you do this, the more confident you are of being on track. Frequent checks ensure you take corrective action quickly to avoid wasting effort and resources.

An owner-manager can often exercise control by personal observation, reference to limited paperwork and then a decision about corrective action. As the organisation grows so does the complexity. It becomes increasingly difficult to know the current position as work goes on in many separate places at the same time. People in those separate places may differ about their precise objectives and targets.

To help them exercise control, management is able to use a range of systems and techniques. Financial control is clearly of major interest – how does management try to keep the financial score while all around it everything is changing? Chapter 18 introduces the main issues in this area. Financial measures reflect what has been happening in the operations of the organisation. The more information management has about actual progress compared with intended performance, the easier it is to adjust, so Chapter 19 reviews the main concepts in operations management. Control depends on information, and Chapter 20 reviews key aspects of information systems. Rapid technological developments are transforming this aspect of management – but only when managers attend to organisational as well as technical aspects.

The Part Case is Airbus, a consortium of European aircraft manufacturing companies based at Toulouse, France. It became an independent commercial company in 2001 and has steadily gained market share in the world civil aviation market, competing strongly with Boeing. It has begun building the Airbus 380 range, which is due to enter service in 2006. The complex logistical arrangements raise many issues of finance, operations and information systems.

Chapter 18

Finance and budgetary control

Aim

To show why organisations need finance, where it comes from, how its use should be controlled and why financial measures are critical indicators of performance.

Objectives

By the end of your work on this chapter you should be able to outline the concepts below in your own terms and:

1 Understand the role of the finance function in management
2 Be able to interpret basic financial reports
3 Know the difference between profit and cash
4 Know what a simple financial plan contains and its purpose
5 Understand the importance of financial results to evaluate performance
6 Know the basic steps in calculating the financial consequences of a management decision
7 Be able to explain how budgets aim to ensure internal activities are directed at meeting external financial requirements.

Key terms

This chapter introduces the following ideas:

capital market
limited liability company
shareholders
cash flow statement
assets
profit and loss statement
balance sheet
shareholders' funds
fixed assets
current assets
liabilities

Each is a term defined within the text, as well as in the glossary at the end of the book.

BASF is one of the world's leading chemical companies with production sites in 41 countries and customers spread across the world. The head office and main chemical processing complex is located at Ludwigshafen, Germany. The group comprises more than 160 subsidiaries and affiliates. Its main product groups are chemicals, plastics, products for the agricultural industry and 'performance products' designed in conjunction with customers to meet specific needs. It also engages in oil and gas exploration and production.

A main objective of the company is to earn a premium on its cost of capital in order to ensure profitable growth, thereby giving it a competitive advantage in gaining access to international capital markets. The pursuit of profit has to be achieved whilst recognising the importance of the principles of sustainable development, combining economic success with environmental protection and social responsibility. Its shares are listed in the Dow Jones Sustainability Index. Research and development has to be at the heart of the group's efforts to retain its competitive position: in 2003 R&D expenditure was €1.1 billion, or 3.3 per cent of sales.

BASF has successfully developed highly integrated processing plants to use resources and materials to maximum advantage. Waste and by-products are fed directly into other processes where they are important materials. Pipe networks facilitate efficient, safe and environmentally friendly transfer of resources. BASF describes this integration as 'Verbund'.

The hazardous nature of the industry demands the highest safety standards amongst employees. Risk identification, measurement and control are most important. The *Verbund* system minimises undesirable emissions, but also benefits BASF customers. The group maintains close relationships with its customers to find mutually beneficial solutions to their problems. Reward systems for employees are as closely related to corporate objectives as possible, especially by using a measure known as earnings before interest on capital and taxation (EBIT).

A summary of the BASF operating (profit) report for year ended 31 December 2003 is:

		Euros millions
Sales		33,361
Less Cost of sales		23,333
Gross profit on sales		10,028
Selling expenses	4,519	
General and administrative expenses	706	
Research and development expenses	1,105	
Other items	1,040	7,370
Operating profit before tax (EBIT)		2,658
Losses from financial assets		267
Interest expense		223
		2,168
Less Taxation		1,192
Minority interests		66
Net income		910

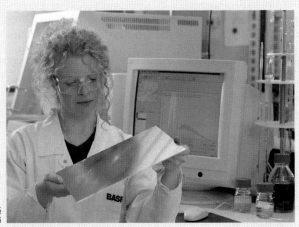

BASF

18.1 Introduction

In the financial year that ended in December 2003 BASF made a profit of €910 million from its activities during the year. This 'headline' figure is a very crude measure of the effectiveness with which the managers have run the company over the year. The problem for investors is how to assess this performance. How does it compare with other firms in similar businesses? Is it consistent with the stated targets of the company? Does the way it has been achieved bode well for the future by, for example, investing in research and development that will bring returns in later years? Investors will also want to know how these broad summary figures relate to the work of managers and staff within the firm – are they motivated and organised in ways that encourage them to produce good returns in the future?

Similar questions arise about the annual report of any public firm – you can read commentaries on these every day in the financial pages of your newspaper. Investors and financial analysts continually evaluate a company's financial performance against its objectives and against comparable businesses. They try to judge its prospects, and how effectively managers are doing their jobs. The Part 1 Case presented information about The Body Shop. This is an interesting company, which has a strong sense of social responsibility. This is what the Chairman and the Chief Executive Officer said in the 2004 annual report: 'The Body Shop built its strong values heritage in 2003 by launching a global campaign against domestic violence. The success of the campaign has demonstrated that this is an issue of high concern to both customers and staff.' The Body Shop can only pursue this and similar objectives so long as it continues as a business, and that requires that it should be profitable. Otherwise it will fail.

Chapter 1 described organisations as aiming to add value to the resources they used. It is crucial to the success of an organisation that it has the appropriate resources and that these are managed to achieve the results that stakeholders expect. Whatever the nature of the organisation or its line of business, it will need financial resources to operate. It needs to manage these well if it is to prosper. Most companies depend on people in the external environment for the funds they need to grow the business. The main source of information for people outside the business who wish to assess its performance and prospects is the company's annual report to shareholders. This contains a great deal of financial and other data – but is more subjective than it first appears. It is important to know how financial performance is measured, and the assumptions that people make in constructing the figures. It is also important to know how these financial measures relate to the performance of those working within the firm.

The chapter begins by explaining why companies need the capital market and how they communicate with it. A major link in that process is the annual report, so the chapter then explains important parts of that document. The chapter goes on to show how these figures, which are intended mainly for investors outside the organisation, influence and are themselves influenced by processes of internal planning and control.

18.2 The pressures on companies to perform

Many people reading this book will be expecting to start a career that they hope will provide an income to support an attractive lifestyle. Few will be thinking about retirement or the need to support themselves after their working lives have ended. This may be a sombre subject to introduce, but it is fundamentally important to understanding the financial environment in which organisations operate. Governments are increasingly concerned about the ability of traditional public pension schemes to support people in their old age. Individuals are expected to take more responsibility for their pension.

Activity 18.1   Identifying shareholders

Find a copy of the annual report and accounts for 2004 for Mothercare PLC or The Body Shop International PLC. What can you discover about the shareholders in the company?

Pension funds and life assurance companies expect to pay their investors an acceptable income or lump sum when they retire. The funds can only do this if they invest contributions successfully, and investors naturally expect their premiums to be invested profitably by pension fund managers. These pension fund and life assurance companies compete with each other, and the rewards for success, and consequent growth in contributions from investors, are high. There is pressure on the fund managers to perform well by identifying good investment opportunities, which is also in the investors' best interests as eventual pensioners. The fund managers will be looking for good investment opportunities in companies that are profitable and well managed.

This is where the discussion comes full circle, back to the investor. In order to attract money into its business to enable it to expand, management needs to demonstrate to the capital market that it is a profitable and successful business.

The fund managers in the **capital market** expect managements to operate their businesses profitably. So this pressure from the external capital market directly affects the organisation and all employees. There may be bad years or periods of low or negative profitability (losses) and the capital markets know that. But continual losses will eventually lead to failure. The business will simply run out of money and not be able to meet its financial obligations. So the pressures to perform that managers and employees feel originate outside the organisation. However, as future pensioners, dependent on the performance of fund managers, those pressures serve their long-term interests (Coggan, 2002).

The **capital market** comprises all the individuals and institutions that have money to invest, including banks, life assurance companies and pension funds and, as users of capital, business organisations, individuals and governments.

Within an organisation it is unlikely that managers, apart from those at the top, will feel the direct pressure from outside. Yet, as the chapter shows, this external pressure does affect the expectations that top managers have of those below them. These expectations are gradually transmitted down the organisation, so that all staff experience them in some way, even if indirectly. The pressures can be considerable as the senior managers expect to be rewarded with the opportunity to purchase shares in the company at a favourable price at some future time (share or stock options). Sometimes this pressure leads to dubious practices and alleged fraud designed to enhance the share price, as in the cases of Enron and WorldCom. This has brought considerable pressure from regulators to improve corporate governance and the quality of financial reporting.

18.3 The world outside the organisation

Raising capital

If you have looked at the annual report of Mothercare or The Body Shop you will have discovered that life assurance companies and pension funds are major shareholders. Most reports do not show such detail, and it is often difficult to discover because the shares are not necessarily ultimately owned by the company named in the share register. They are just one of the many sources from which large organisations raise capital.

A large public company can raise money by issuing shares to people and institutions that respond to a share issue. The main benefit is to enable companies to finance large-scale activities. The shareholders appoint the directors who are ultimately responsible for managing the company. A shareholder is entitled to vote at general meetings in accordance with the number of shares owned. Once the shareholders have paid for their shares in full they cannot generally be required to pay more money into the company, even if it fails.

The affairs of companies are governed by company law, in some countries administered by a government body such as the Securities and Exchange Commission in the United States, and by the body governing the share market, such as the Bourse in France and the Stock Exchange in the United Kingdom. Before a company can invite the public to subscribe for shares it has to be registered with the national financial regulators and fulfil a number of requirements. The first step after registration in order to raise money is to issue a prospectus. Again there are many rules and legal matters that have to be satisfied. In essence, the prospectus explains the history of the company, what it plans to do as a business, and what it plans to do with the money raised.

If the business is small it will not invite the public to buy shares. The promoters will contribute their own money, most likely in sufficient amount to ensure that they have control (more than 50 per cent of the shares). The amount of capital available to the company in these circumstances will be limited by the money the founders can afford to contribute. They may go to a bank to seek finance, but the willingness of a bank to lend will also depend on the amount subscribed by the shareholders.

Banks, fund managers and investors at large will contribute only if they believe that there is a good, sound, well-managed business that is likely to make a profit. The investors have many investment opportunities. They will not invest in a company that will not reward them, as by investing they are taking a risk. The amount of return they expect will be related to the risk – the greater the risk the greater the required return.

A **limited liability company** has an identity and existence in its own right as distinct from its owners (shareholders in Europe, stockholders in North America). A shareholder has an ownership right in the company in which the shares are held.

Shareholders are the principal risk takers in a company. They contribute the long-term capital for which they expect to be rewarded in the form of dividends – a distribution from the profit of the business.

Activity 18.2 Borrowing money

Find out the interest rate at which you could borrow money to (a) buy a car, (b) buy a house, (c) spend on your credit card. Can you explain what you discover?

A **limited liability company** gives a business access to large amounts of capital, but at the same time allows some protection to the **shareholders**, as they cannot be held liable for the debts of the business in the event of its financial failure. This limited liability means that investors can contribute capital knowing that their private and personal assets are not at risk. Of course they could lose all their investment in the shares. This is the risk they take, and is why they expect a higher return than they would receive if they put their money in a bank or in government securities, where the risk of default is virtually zero.

Because a company has access to capital in this form there has to be regulation. The Companies Act is the principal instrument of control, with the addition of the Stock Exchange for those listed as public companies within the United Kingdom. A most important requirement is to provide information about the performance of the business from time to time (Sutton, 2003; Elliott and Elliott, 2003). This is done most comprehensively in the company's annual report. Amongst other things the annual report includes detailed financial information of three distinct types. There is a cash flow statement, a profit and loss statement and a balance sheet.

| Activity 18.3 | Reading an annual report |

Obtain a copy of a company annual report and list the kinds of information that you find in it, for example financial, product, management. You will find some website references at the end of the chapter.

Cash flow statement

The easiest to understand of the three types of statement is the cash flow, as it states just that. It shows where cash has come from and how it has been spent. The following is a simplified summary of the **cash flow statement** for The Body Shop International PLC for the year ended 28 February 2004.

Cash flow statement shows the sources from which cash has been generated and how it has been spent during a period of time.

		£ millions
Net cash inflow from operating activities		41.4
Interest paid on loans		(1.8)
Payment of taxation		(7.3)
Investments (including property and equipment)		(13.8)
Acquisitions and disposals		(1.0)
Dividends to shareholders		(11.6)
Cash inflow from the above activities		5.9
Financing: short-term debt	12.6	
share capital	2.4	
loan repayments (net)	15.0	–
Increase in cash for the year		5.9

Reproduced with kind permission of The Body Shop International PLC.

In the ordinary course of successful business it might be expected that the cash received from trading (selling products or services) should be greater than the cash spent to purchase components, supplies, labour, energy and all the other resources combined to make, promote, distribute and secure the sales. The cash surplus could then be reinvested to help finance expansion and some of it paid to the shareholders by way of dividend to recompense them for their investment. Their original contribution remains in the company, however, as part of the continuing capital base. In the case of The Body Shop there was an increase in cash of £5.9 million after paying dividends and investing in some new **assets**.

Assets are the property, plant and equipment, vehicles, stocks of goods for trading, money owed by customers and cash: in other words, the physical resources of the business.

The idea of a cash surplus as being the essential requirement from operations is appealing but unfortunately too simplistic. Taking as an example a motor vehicle manufacturer, a car has to be designed and tested, components sourced from suppliers, production lines prepared, cars distributed to dealers, and motoring journalists and publicity agents organised in preparation for a major launch promotion. All of this before any of the cars can be sold – so there will be very heavy cash outflows before cash starts to come in. This process may take a couple of years. In the pharmaceutical industry there is a large investment in continuing research and development that may take 10 years or longer before cash begins to flow back, and then only if the research is successful. Heavy investment in product development in the electronics industry has to be made before any products emerge.

Much the same thing occurs in new technology-based service companies such as ebay.com or lastminute.com. They, like all new dot.com companies, have to invest heavily in building their website and in advertising to make people aware that it exists before cash begins to flow in. It would be highly unlikely in these conditions for the business to show a cash surplus in periods when it is making such heavy investment. Indeed it may be necessary to raise additional capital from shareholders or banks to finance the investment in equipment and in training the people who will operate it.

> ### Activity 18.4   Measuring R&D expenditure
>
> Look at the annual report for BASF (**www.basf.com**), Siemens (**www.siemens.com**), Solvay (**www.solvay.com**) or any large manufacturing business, and find out what it tells you about research and development. List the projects that the report mentions. What does the report say about the length of time before the projects will be profitable?

It is impossible to draw sensible conclusions about the company's financial performance on the basis of cash flow alone. Not only is the annual surplus or deficit influenced by major investment, but other infrequent events, such as a major restructuring exercise following a new strategy, could also distort the impression.

The profit and loss statement

Profit and loss statement reflects the benefits derived from the trading activities of the business during a period of time.

The **profit and loss statement** is designed to overcome the limitations of a cash flow statement, although cash has the important characteristic of complete objectivity. Cash flows can be observed, measured and verified. Profit measures are subjective.

The profit after taxation and the profit retained in the business are quite different from the cash surplus reported in the cash flow statement. This is because the profit statement is not based on cash but on business transactions that (a) may result in cash transactions in the future, or (b) reflect cash transactions from previous periods.

Sales may be credit sales that approved customers may pay for later. Cost of goods sold may include the purchase of goods that will be paid for in the next financial year. Operating expenses will include depreciation which, with other terms, is explained below.

Here is a simplified summary of the profit statement for The Body Shop International PLC for the year ended 28 February 2004.

	£ millions
Sales of products	381.1
Cost of goods sold	(140.7)
Gross profit (or gross margin)	240.4
Operating expenses (shops, administration and distribution)	(210.1)
Operating profit	30.3
Payment of interest on loans	(1.8)
Taxation on profit	(6.8)
Profit after taxation	21.7
Dividends to shareholders	(11.6)
Retained profit	10.1

Reproduced with kind permission of The Body Shop International PLC.

Case question 18.1

Refer to the summary profit statement of the BASF Group.

- Calculate the gross profit as a percentage of sales.
- Calculate the profit before tax as a percentage of sales.

Activity 18.5 Calculating and comparing profit

Look at the annual report of a company that interests you, probably in a similar line of business to BASF.

- Calculate the gross profit in a recent year as a percentage of sales.
- Calculate the profit before tax as a percentage of sales.
- How does the company compare on these measures against BASF?
- Is there a major difference in the items in the profit statements of the two companies?

Depreciation

Depreciation is a major cause of the difference between cash flow and profit. Think about the investments mentioned in relation to motor vehicle production. Apart from occasional modifications, the same basic model may be produced and sold for several years, perhaps as many as 10 for a small-volume producer. So the initial investment to develop the design and make the cars should be spread over the life of the investment and will be subtracted from sales revenue in each year. This process is called depreciation. The idea is simple, but there are several estimates required before the annual amount can be measured. Depreciation is based on the original cost of the investment, including set-up and training, less the expected scrap value at the end of its life. It may also be necessary to add the expected cost of decommissioning: think about a nuclear power generator in this respect. Hence an estimation must be made of the life of the investment, the residual value and the initial cost, which itself is open to conjecture. To make matters worse there are at least four methods of spreading the cost over the life-span. The simplest is to allocate an equal amount each year. Assets may also be periodically revalued to take account of changes in their fair value which then becomes the base for calculating depreciation. In both circumstances, if the fair value (the present value of expected future cash flows, or the expected market price less selling costs if it were to be sold) is less than the amount already allowed for depreciation, then the difference must be charged as an expense and subtracted from revenue. This diminution in value is described as impairment.

Credit

Most products are not sold for cash but on credit, sometimes for an extended period of time, possibly many months. A retail store might offer generous credit terms in order to promote sales – 'nothing to pay for six months' or 'easy terms over nine months' are familiar promotional devices. Creditworthiness will be checked before the customer is given credit. However, even the most careful checks cannot ensure that the customer may not become redundant or fall ill and not be able to work. As an example, suppose that the company's financial year ends on 31 December and that a customer is buying a personal computer at the end of October on nine months' credit of equal monthly payments. Should the company report the full value of the sale, the three instalments that the customer has paid, or nothing until the PC has been paid for in full? It is usual practice to report the full amount, as the business has a legal contract to force the customer to pay. The idea is fine, but experience shows that not all customers will pay in full. There will be bad debts. An estimate of doubtful debts has to be made before arriving at profit.

Warranty claims

If a problem arises with a product sold under warranty it will be replaced or fixed, but at a cost to the manufacturer. The cost of repairing under warranty has to be estimated because warranty claims may not be made within the same financial year as the sale.

These are simple examples of subjectivity in profit measurement. There are many more, but these suffice to illustrate the point that the measure of profit cannot be said to be accurate. It is an approximation. Nevertheless, it is the main indication of trading performance measured in financial terms. The question remains, how well does profit reflect good performance? To evaluate this, profit needs to be related to the amount of investment in the business.

18.4 Measuring periodic performance

Both the cash flow and the profit statements relate to a period of time – conventionally to a financial or trading year. It is usual for large organisations also to produce brief reports on their performance quarterly or half-yearly.

Just how much profit is desirable has to be considered in relation to the investment in a business. Therefore a measure of investment is needed with which to compare periodic profit. When you think that an investor (fund manager) could invest in risk-free government securities for a guaranteed minimum return known in advance, an investment in a risky company that did not offer at least the same expectation of reward would not be contemplated. So the return, or ratio of profit to investment, would be expected to be higher for a risky investment than for a risk-free opportunity. The rate of return required for a particular investment has to be assessed by comparing alternative investment opportunities and their rates of return.

Measuring the investment base

How can the investment base be measured? The obvious base is the amount of the initial investment. If you deposit money in a bank deposit account it will attract interest. At the end of the year you can measure the rate of return by expressing the interest earned for the year as a percentage of the initial investment. If you leave the interest in the account the following year, the investment base would be increased by the amount of interest reinvested. The initial investment plus the interest you earned in the first year now becomes a part of the capital base, as you chose not to withdraw it. The investment base can grow over time. Much the same happens in a business. Profit is generated, some is distributed as a cash dividend and the balance, usually the larger proportion, is retained in the business to finance expansion.

A simple measure of the capital base with which to compare profit appears to be the amount of capital originally contributed, plus profit that is retained and added each year to the base.

Another way to look at it, for companies listed on the Stock Exchange, is to relate the profit or earnings per share to the share price. This approach recognises that a successful business will grow and develop a good reputation and image that will reflect the results of good, professional management and reliable, high-quality products and service. If you own shares in such a company, you would expect the value of those shares to increase to reflect the success of the business, for example from customer loyalty, brand reputation and reliability, loyal relationships with suppliers of components and services, and good design. You would continue to hold the shares only as long as the return based on the price at which you could sell the shares in the market is at least equal to that from an alternative investment with similar risk. This topic is revisited later in the chapter.

18.5 The balance sheet

The report that shows the capital base of a business is the **balance sheet**. The Body Shop PLC balance sheet as at 28 February 2004 showed the following information on page 604.

The balance sheet reveals two separate but related aspects of the business. First it shows the total assets of the business. These include the physical resources such as property, buildings, machinery, computers, stocks (or inventories) of raw materials, work in progress and completed products, money owed by customers, and cash. The other dimension is the sources of the finance that have enabled the business to acquire its assets. Finance (or capital) comes from shareholders by way of contributions for shares when they are first issued, together with retained profits from successful operations as previously explained. This is the shareholders' capital (or **shareholders' funds**). In addition there will usually be money borrowed from a bank and possibly from other sources

Balance sheet shows the assets of the business and the sources from which finance has been raised.

Shareholders' funds are the capital contributed by the shareholders plus profits that have not been distributed to the shareholders.

603

Fixed assets are the physical properties that the company possesses – such as land, buildings, production equipment and vehicles – and which are likely to have a useful life of more than one year. There may also be intangible assets such as patent rights or copyrights.

Current assets can be expected to be cash or to be converted to cash within a year.

Liabilities of a business as reported in the balance sheet are the debts and financial obligations of the business to all those people and institutions that are not shareholders, e.g. a bank, suppliers.

		£ millions
Property, plant and equipment (tangible **fixed assets**)		61.9
Intangible assets		31.7
Investments		6.1
Stocks of goods for resale (**current assets**)	52.4	
Money owing from customers (debtors in the UK, or accounts receivable)	42.1	
Cash and bank accounts	17.6	112.1
		£211.8
These resources were financed by shareholders (including retained profit)	135.4	
Money owing to suppliers, banks and tax	76.4	£211.8

Reproduced with kind permission of The Body Shop International PLC.

as well. These are the **liabilities** of the organisation. The sum total of the shareholders' funds and liabilities will equal the amount of assets. The former represents the source from which the finance has been raised. The latter shows the destination or the physical resources in which the capital has been invested.

The balance sheet of BASF Group is presented as another example.

BASF Group – the case continues   CASE STUDY

Group balance sheet as at 31 December 2003

Assets		Euros millions
Intangible (patents, licences, goodwill)		3,793
Property, plant and equipment (at cost after depreciation deducted)		13,070
Financial assets		2,600
		19,463
Current assets		
Inventories	4,151	
Accounts receivable from customers and others	9,360	
Liquid assets (including cash)	628	14,139
		33,602
Shareholders' equity		
Issued shares and retained profit		15,878
Liabilities		
Pension fund and other commitments	9,187	
Loans	3,907	
Accounts payable and other short-term obligations	4,630	17,724
		33,602

The shareholders are the main risk takers and the profit is attributable to them, so the measure of the rate of return is profit after tax divided by shareholders' funds, commonly known as the *return on equity*. However, there are many imperfections in the measure, one of which is the fact that goodwill will not usually be included as an asset unless it appears following the purchase of another business. Brand names such as the title of a newspaper or the name of a consumer product may be valued by the directors and included as assets. This apparent inconsistency may be surprising. Accountants argue that newspaper mast-heads, or brand names, could be sold separately from the business, whereas goodwill can only be sold with the business as a whole. Many companies only include brands if they have purchased them from another company or, in the case of goodwill, taken over another company for a price greater than the value of the tangible assets minus the liabilities (net worth). Further difficulties in measuring a rate of return arise from problems in measuring depreciation and, consequently, asset values, changes in price levels and share values.

Case question 18.2

Refer to the summary financial information for the BASF Group. Calculate the rate of return (after tax) on equity (shareholders' funds).

Depreciation

The discussion of the profit statement explained that depreciation in particular was an expense item that was difficult to measure. It represents an attempt to estimate the proportion of the cost of using long-term assets that is attributable to a particular accounting period. Any of the cost that has not already been subtracted in the profit statements remains to be subtracted in the future.

Measuring depreciation at The Body Shop www.thebodyshop.com

In The Body Shop annual report for 2004 the assets, plant and equipment were shown in note 12 as having cost £153.9 million. The depreciation for the year that was included in the profit statement as an item of expense (within the figure of £210.1 million) amounted to £6.8 million. When added to depreciation charged in earlier years, and allowing for the sale of some assets, the book value in the balance sheet as at 28 February 2004 was £61.9 million. This means that of the £153.9 million, there remains an amount of £61.9 million to be charged against sales revenue in future years. This remaining balance is the value that appears in the balance sheet for long-term assets (fixed or non-current assets).

If the value in the market – either buying price or selling price – is similar to the balance sheet figure, that is purely coincidental. The balance sheet figure is simply original cost minus the proportion so far depreciated.

The estimate of doubtful debts subtracted from customers' outstanding accounts (debtors or accounts receivable), estimated warranty claim costs, estimated pension fund liabilities, the value of goodwill, brands or other intangible assets are all highly subjective measures. Furthermore, the accounting policies may well differ between companies even though they are in the same industry. So the aggregate amount shown in the balance sheet for assets is not necessarily a reflection of market values.

> **Activity 18.6** **Comparing accounting policies**
>
> Look at the annual reports for two or three companies in the same industry, or in similar industries, and read the section called accounting policies. Make a list of practices that seem to be different.

Changes in price levels

There is a further complication to measuring performance, especially in periods of unstable prices. An asset is recorded at its original cost less depreciation. Suppose there are two companies involved in much the same business with similar assets, but one company purchased its equipment when prices were much lower than was the case for the second company. Although they may have similar physical assets, the costs showing for one may be quite different from those for the other. Traditionally accountants do not make allowances for differences in price levels through time. Money amounts at different times are added together as though they represented the same values, which is clearly nonsense. Consequently, during a period of changing prices it is difficult to compare the rate of return on equity between companies based on the profit statement and balance sheet. These days in most Western economies the rate of inflation is very low, so this is not a problem, although the prices of some commodities, components and products will frequently change.

Share values

There is another way of approaching the question of performance measurement. If you were thinking of buying shares in the market through the Stock Exchange, you would consider the likely future returns in relation to the price you would have to pay for the shares. You will therefore be comparing different investment opportunities and will attempt to choose the one that offers the best return for whatever degree of risk you are prepared to accept. The return you expect would be an estimate of future dividends plus the likely growth in the share price, and you would relate this to the price you would have to pay to buy the shares. If the potential investment offered a greater expected return than shares you already hold (assuming the same degree of risk), not only would you be interested in buying the new shares, but you would also be inclined to sell your existing shares to buy more new ones to increase your return. It would be rational for all investors in this position to behave in the same way. The consequence of this action should be clear. Selling pressure for the shares of one company would drive the price down to the point at which investors would be indifferent as to which company's shares they purchased, as they would tend to offer the same expected return. This process, known as arbitraging, is likely to happen in a well-organised and efficient market (Ross *et al.*, 2002).

So the measure of performance that shareholders are likely to adopt will not be directly related to the company's financial reports, but more to the financial markets. They will be comparing expected returns with the prices of securities (shares) in the market. This does not mean that financial reports from companies do not serve any useful purpose. They do, because they provide some of the information that helps the traders in shares to assess the likely returns from these companies in the future and, above all, provide information about past performance and recent financial position. While share prices in the market are directly influenced by buying and selling pressure, the expectations that give rise to those pressures come in part from the financial reports.

Companies whose shares do not offer returns consistent with those of competitors are likely to become takeover targets with bids from stronger, more efficient performers. Figure 18.1 shows the comparative changes in the share price for two companies in the banking business – Bank of Scotland and Halifax – at the time they were merging. The graph shows clearly how the share price for the Bank of Scotland had performed better than that for the Halifax. This may have enhanced the bargaining power of the Bank of Scotland.

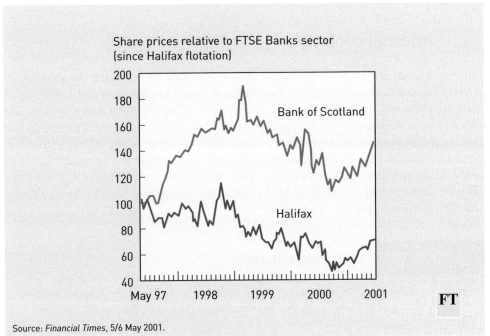

Source: *Financial Times*, 5/6 May 2001.

Figure 18.1

Pre-tax profits compared: Halifax/Bank of Scotland

Company directors have to watch share price movements. Unexpected movements might signal activity in the market that they ought to know about. For example, if another company is actively buying shares in the market and so raising the price, this might indicate they are planning a takeover bid. If a large shareholder is selling shares, thus pushing the price down, has performance in the company fallen short of expectations? In both circumstances the directors need to find out what they can about the market activities in order to take defensive action.

Case question 18.3

Look at the balance sheet for BASF Group. Calculate the proportion of the finance for the company that is attributable to the shareholders, and the proportion attributable to the liabilities.

Activity 18.7   **Comparing BASF and The Body Shop**

Look at the requirement for Case Question 18.3. Compute the same measure for The Body Shop. What strikes you about these measures? What do they tell you about these companies? Would it make a difference to your decision to buy shares in one and not the other? Can you explain why?

The directors and senior managers of a company cannot ignore what is going on in the markets outside their business. They operate in markets, some specific to their own activities, and some general – the capital and labour markets. Their performance is being evaluated all the time and they need to know what the buyers and sellers in the financial markets are thinking. Financial managers will be watching the share price. They have to convert external pressures from the market into pressure for internal action. This is what financial management is about.

18.6 Internal control

Most managers and employees can do little themselves to influence the share price directly. Nevertheless much of what they do has financial implications and eventually all their decisions will indirectly affect the share price. So management needs systems and procedures to ensure that the financial consequences of decisions are understood and that the action proposed is acceptable. An organisation cannot wait until the accountant prepares a financial report at the end of the year to see whether the operation has been profitable or not. It is too late to do anything. Profit does not just happen. It has to be planned (Horngren *et al.*, 2002). At least once a year management must prepare a financial plan, commonly known as a budget.

Activity 18.8 Preparing a budget

Prepare a simple cash budget for your own finances for next month. You will need to consider the cash you have available from savings in the past, how much cash you expect to receive during the month and what you plan to spend.

The budgeting process usually begins at the top level when the directors set a target or goal for the growth in shareholder value that will keep the business performing as well as, if not better than, its competitors. From this assessment they derive a profit target for the whole organisation. It may be expressed as a rate of return on invested capital (shareholders' funds) or as an absolute amount, but either way it will need to be translated into objectives that have meaning at lower operating levels within the business.

Controlling elements within an organisation

A large organisation will have a variety of products, markets and locations in which it operates. An international business may have highly independent operating divisions in a variety of locations, each expected to achieve a given rate of return.

In contrast, a smaller business may have just one location, but within it a range of functions such as purchasing, design, production, assembly, inspection, dispatch and accounts receivable. Each may be independently managed yet coordinated to ensure that they are all operating to achieve the required corporate objective. None of these divisions could be set a required rate of return or even a profit target because none of them has independent control over its activities. The volume of production will depend on sales, purchases will depend on production and accounts receivable on sales. However, each has control over certain aspects of the business. Purchasing must negotiate prices and specifications for supplies of material or components, but it has little control over volume. Based on the sales and production plan it will have a reasonable idea of volume, but it will be subject to change as the year progresses in light of actual sales and production. Similarly, the performance of the dispatch and shipping operation will depend on sales and customers' delivery requirements. They can base plans on the sales projections but, as with all plans in business, the actual activities will inevitably be different.

All parts of the organisation, then, have to be flexible and adaptable in response to market opportunities and customers' requirements. For this reason it is vital to establish and maintain good relationships with other organisations that the firm deals with. It is not unusual in smaller organisations to hear managers complain that the process of planning and budgeting is a waste of time because events always turn out differently. They certainly do, but this is no reason not to plan. As circumstances change plans should also change. Since desktop computers can easily perform the mechanics of budget preparation, budgets should always be up to date and reflect contemporary operating and market conditions.

Earnings per share at The Body Shop

management in practice

The earnings per share (profit after tax divided by the number of shares issued) for The Body Shop increased from 6.8 pence in 2003 to earnings of 10.7 pence in 2004. It cannot be known what plans the directors have for the future. The annual report does not include forecasts or plans. However, it can be seen from the executive chairman's and chief executive's letter that the improvement in the rate of profit was probably attributable to expansion and consolidation.

Plans consistent with the future strategic direction outlined in the letter will have been incorporated into the 2004/5 budget, although we cannot know the details. The achievable earnings per share will have been planned.

Source: The Body Shop *Annual Report*, 2004.
Reproduced with kind permission of The Body Shop International PLC.

Without a plan there is no sense of direction or clarity of purpose at operating levels. The process of budget preparation in itself is a useful exercise: not only does it enable the various parts of an organisation to relate their activities to others, but it is also a valuable coordination device to help the various parts of the organisation to focus on the same objective. The starting point for planning at operational level is generally the sales plan in a profit-oriented organisation. In not-for-profit organisations it may be the desired level of service to its constituency, for example the number of units of blood to be collected by the transfusion service.

In all cases the capacity to achieve the desired volume will depend on the resources available – especially people, equipment and finance. If added resources are needed management can anticipate both what is required and when. For example, if more people are required they have to be recruited and trained so that they will be ready to contribute to productive activity at the appropriate time. If more cash is needed to pay for added supplies of raw materials, it is important to have a financial plan to present to the bank manager well in advance of the time that a cash crisis begins to occur. Crises often arise because there has been insufficient care and attention with planning – and failure to update plans as circumstances change. Plans need to be changed as activity grows for the simple reason that growth requires added finance. Labour, supplies of materials and services will have to be paid for before cash begins to flow back from customers.

Case question 18.4

You have read aspects of the annual report of BASF. Now use your imagination to think through the process that might have been adopted in the construction of the budget for the year ended 31 December 2004. To help you, think about the following:

● Where did the process begin? How were the various elements or product groups brought together into a coherent plan?

● What steps might have been involved in arriving at an agreed budget?

Planning growth and improved performance

The length of the planning cycle depends on the kind of product or service. It may be no more than a couple of months or it could be much longer. Companies can fail as they grow simply because the rate of growth outpaces the ability to generate cash or because they have not anticipated the need for cash and made the necessary plans. Coordination of the various aspects has to be supervised centrally in the organisation to ensure that the overall objectives are achievable in the plan.

Much of the detail has to come from the operating units, especially performance targets related to work activity. It is here that there is likely to be a process of negotiation with central coordinators. Their activity is to improve productivity, whereas the objectives at the lower level may be to ensure that the performance targets do not put excessive pressures on employees. A process of genuine negotiation and cooperation may well lead to a budget that is acceptable both to operating divisions and to the central organisation. However, a budget cast in conditions of fear and apprehension can lead to attempts to create budget slack. This is exemplified by the readiness or otherwise of employees to introduce improved working methods. It is conceivable that more efficient working methods can be discovered through experience. Staff and management may choose not to disclose or introduce them at the earliest opportunity. Instead they may keep them in reserve to cushion the effects of a tight budget at some future time. Such behaviour is not in the best interests of the business as a whole, but it shows how budget preparation can lead to conflicts. The subject of participation in the process of budget preparation has been a topic for extensive research in recent years (Drury, 2004).

Typically a corporate budget will include:

● *Sales budget* – showing expected revenue for each product in each market
● *Materials budget* – showing purchases for each component, from each supplier
● *Labour budget* – showing deployment of employees and staff to each activity
● *Overhead budget* – showing the consumption of resources that cannot be identified with particular products, e.g. advertising, directors' fees, energy
● *Capital budget* – showing planned spending on new equipment, buildings and acquisitions of other companies
● *Research and development budget* – showing planned spending on particular projects
● *Cash budget* – showing the cash receipts and payments
● *Budget balance sheet*.

Once the budget is negotiated and agreed, it becomes an operating plan that reflects expectations about the conditions in which the organisation is operating. Each budget will be identified with a responsibility centre, i.e. with managers responsible for achieving the budget expectations. Sometimes alternative budgets are prepared for different purposes. For example, the performance targets incorporated for operating divisions may have been negotiated at a tighter level than past achievements with the objective of improving productivity. Although these targets may be achieved during the period of the budget, the process may take some months. If the cash or profit forecast given to the bank is based on these targets, it is likely that the cash or profit projections will not be achieved. So the cash budget may be based on looser performance. Similarly, a sales budget might reflect a higher sales level than that incorporated in the profit plan. The risk of having different budgets is the possibility that they will lose credibility within the organisation.

Performance measurement

Another favourite research topic has been the way in which budgets are used to judge performance. The behaviour of managers can be seriously influenced by the budget style in an organisation. If this is authoritarian and unthinking in manner, in which achieving the budget is the primary objective of management, it may lead to suboptimal performance. The pressure may be translated into action that is against long-term interests. For example, a salesperson might threaten customers with a price increase in the coming month to boost current sales and achieve a sales target.

In some organisations the immediate reaction to employees who fail to achieve budget is to presume that they are to blame. Any idea that the budget itself may be inappropriate or unachievable is not entertained. If this style is carried forward to performance evaluation it can be very destructive. In contrast, a budget can be prepared after discussion with those who know the area. It can then be used as a guide for judging performance after allowing for changing circumstances. This approach is more likely to achieve employee support.

Consistent failure to achieve budget should first lead to a review of the budget to ensure that the targets are fair and achievable. Only then should there be an attempt to take remedial action to improve an activity. The successful use of budgets depends on those affected, managers and staff alike, developing a sense of ownership towards them. As conditions change, the budget should be revised so that it continues to be credible.

A budget is, in essence, short term – usually for no more than one year. Nevertheless it has to be set in a longer-term context and be consistent with the strategy for the future development of the organisation. Long-term investments in research and development, product and market development, new plant and equipment or even the acquisition of other businesses have to be included in the short-term budget, and cash requirements in the cash budget.

If, in the longer term, a product is going to be phased out, it would be senseless to mount a major promotion campaign to strengthen its market position. It may make sense to promote it at a discount in stores in order to clear inventories. This further illustrates coordination, but, in particular, it shows a link between short-term action and longer-term strategy.

This conventional approach to budgeting is being challenged as businesses operate in rapidly changing conditions. More authority has to be delegated, with faster response times. So the emphasis is shifting towards value creation and benchmarking with other organisations rather than mere cost control.

18.7 Decision making

The one certainty in any organisation is that conditions will change. The budget cannot be revised every time minor changes occur or fresh opportunities arise. An organisation has to be flexible and responsive. Frequently opportunities arise that require prompt action – for example, a special order for a normal product or service, but to be sold at a low promotional price into a new market. In these circumstances the normal measurement of the average cost of producing and delivering the service may be an inappropriate starting point for computing potential profit. Many of the costs will not change as a result of accepting this opportunity: there will be no further research and development, no requirement to increase productive capacity (assuming that capacity is available) and, possibly, no added labour cost. In these conditions consideration need only be given to the costs that will increase directly as a result of choosing to accept this order: delivery, materials or additional resources consumed. Depreciation can be ignored and, in the very short term, so too can the labour cost since the employees will already have been paid for their time.

Let us suppose that Osram has an opportunity to make and sell electric light bulbs to a retailer. The bulbs will be packaged especially for the retailer and not identified with Osram. How will the costs be estimated?

- Is there enough manufacturing capacity without having to reduce normal production? If so, there is no need to take account of any additional capital costs.
- Are additional employees required or will existing employees have to work longer? If so, the extra costs will be attributable to this order; otherwise there are no added labour costs.
- Materials will be required according to the retailer's specification.
- Are there packaging costs? In this case there may be design and printing costs as well as costs of packaging material. The set-up costs will have to be included.
- Will the retailer collect the bulbs, or do they need to be delivered? Will there be added costs, or will existing transport arrangements be adequate?

The important issue is to identify costs that are directly traceable and attributable to this opportunity. The normal average cost of producing light bulbs may be irrelevant, since that includes research and development, capital equipment costs and administrative overheads which will not necessarily increase with this order.

Undoubtedly the retailer is looking for a special price, lower than that which Osram might normally charge. If this price exceeds the identified cost it may be an attractive opportunity. The critical issue for Osram to decide is whether or not this might damage its own long-term market position. Against this is the threat that the retailer will probably also be negotiating with a competitor to supply the light bulbs.

Suppose that the normal selling price is 80 cents and that the usual cost is made up (per unit) as follows:

	cents
Labour	10
Materials	20
Packaging	5
Delivery	3
Overheads	25
	63
Contribution to profit	17
	80

The retailer wants to buy lamps at a price of 60 cents. If we establish that Osram's overheads will not increase, that labour costs will be 8 cents, materials 20 cents and packaging 10 cents, then the appropriate cost per unit will be 38 cents. If additional delivery is $100 per journey for up to 10,000 light bulbs, the design and set-up costs for printing the packaging are $10,000 and the order is for 100,000 bulbs, is it acceptable to sell at 60 cents?

	cents
Unit costs: labour	8
material	20
packaging	10
	38
	$
Cost for 100,000	38,000
Delivery cost	1,000
Design, set-up	10,000
Relevant cost	49,000
Revenue	60,000
Contribution to profit	$11,000

This appears to be an acceptable sales opportunity as long as it does not erode Osram's normal market and as long as the existing customers do not expect the normal price to be lowered.

It is the job of the cost or management accountant to process financial information quickly in order to assist managers to take decisions of the kind described above. It is not usual for the information to be directly available from the financial records. The accountant will have to find out the alternative courses of action, extract the appropriate financial data from the system, process it and report in a coherent and understandable way to those responsible for taking the decision. Accountants are more likely to be useful if they understand the processes of service or product delivery. They also need to appreciate that they are providing a service to other managers.

Routine information for managers

Another aspect of internal financial measurement is more routine. Unlike the system of financial reporting for the organisation as a whole, which is geared to the needs of the capital market, internal information has to be related to the needs of the managers. They will be interested in financial measurements related to their own area of responsibility. For example, a marketing manager will need information about groups of products, brands, customers, regions and marketing areas. In research and development, costs accumulating for each project might be compared with research progress to date. This approach runs right through the value chain, recognising that value can be added from research, development and design, through to distribution and customer service. It is not just the manufacturing process or service delivery process that adds value and requires measurement.

As organisations develop stronger alliances and cooperative arrangements, at both the strategic and operational levels, the role of the accountant is expanded beyond the limits of the organisation within which he or she works. Cooperation in the supply chain can result in improved performance for both organisations involved. To achieve benefits of cost reduction and/or improved profitability through quality improvement, there has to be an open relationship and trust between the organisations. Accountants play a role in this cooperation by advising on the financial consequences for both organisations (Atkinson *et al.*, 2003).

18.8 International aspects of financial reporting

Internal financial analysis and control processes are generally designed to meet the needs of management and are not constrained by legal requirements. The principles and methods are universally applicable, although in some locations cultural factors and custom may mean that accountants go about their tasks in a different manner.

External financial reporting is rather different. In the English-speaking world financial reports appear to be similar, terminology aside, but fundamentally there have been different measurement systems and disclosure requirements. Nonetheless, across the modern world the system of double-entry book-keeping is at the foundation of all financial record-keeping systems. Within the United Kingdom, the limits to acceptable methods of reporting are governed by the Companies Acts and the Accounting Standards Board.

Different legal systems, industry financing, taxation systems, structure of the accounting profession, language and traditions mean that financial reporting has varied from one country to another. France, Germany, Portugal, Spain and Japan have historically required compliance with a rigid framework for financial reporting (Alexander and Nobes, 2004). This is now changing as International Financial Reporting Standards (IFRS) are being introduced in more than 90 countries from 2005.

Case question 18.5

Look at the summary of significant accounting policies in the BASF annual report. Do these help you to understand the report? Can you explain why?

The Accounting Standards Board in the United States will not adopt the IFRS, and the EU will not apply them all. The US system has been much more prescriptive and conservative than the standards previously applied in the UK. For example, it generally requires all research and development costs to be subtracted from revenue as incurred and not carried forward in the balance sheet to be offset against future gains, whereas in other regimes, development cost could under certain circumstances be carried in the balance sheet. The prescriptive approach in the USA has encouraged adherence to the letter of the standards rather than the spirit, and this has enabled companies to construct dubious, and allegedly fraudulent, arrangements to enhance reported earnings, as in the cases of Enron and WorldCom.

IFRS should help to overcome the difficulties in comparing the financial performance of companies in different countries and promote their access to international capital markets. Reported results will not be directly comparable with results reported under the previous standards, and this difference will be a challenge for readers who will find that in most companies profits are likely to be lower under the new regime. Taking two examples, in future the cost of executive stock options and the impairment of intangibles will have to be charged against revenue in the profit statement.

IFRS2 to hit company profits

Some of the UK's top companies will see a reduction in profits when share-based payment accounting standard IFRS2 comes into effect next year, a new study has revealed. The charge is predicted to wipe an average 5.42% a year, or £68m, from the profits of the top 25 FTSE100 companies by 2007.

Drinks producer Diageo would be the worst-hit FTSE100 company if the standard was applied now, taking a 43% charge on its latest year profits of £76m, while BSkyB and Standard Chartered would also suffer huge dents to their profits.

The new standard will also prove troublesome for many Finance Directors, such as ICAP's Jim Pettigrew. The study found the broker company would take a charge of more than £7.5m, or nearly 9%. It would also adversely affect the profitability of FTSE250 companies such as Trinity Mirror, P&O and EMI.

'IFRS2 is not merely another change to accounting standards', said Halliwell principal consultant Jon Dymond. 'The charge will impact on profits, recruitment, retention, reward structures, performance management and relationships with shareholders.'

The report said the charge on profits could also lead to a dramatic effect on the shape of executive remuneration practice in the future, as companies would need to consider their aims and to whom options should be granted.

But Ken Wild, Deloitte technical partner, suggested that although IFRS2 would have an impact on businesses and the investment community, education about the implications would be key to allaying fears. 'I'll be surprised if the market changed its assessment of a company merely because it accounted for its share-based schemes in a particular way, when it is essentially presenting the same information in a different way', said Wild.

'We get all these new standards, and it's like, "the world is going to end", and it doesn't. I'm not underestimating their impact, but it's short-term and the markets see it through.'

Source: Kevin Reed, *Accountancy Age*, 11 August 2004.

Whatever happens to the development of standards, possibly the most pressing need for accountants is to value internally generated intangible assets which cannot be included as assets under IFRS. Modern successful service companies including dot.coms often have few or no significant tangible assets, but brands and a very sophisticated workforce, which is where the value of the business resides.

Activity 18.9 Anticipating changes

Look at the 2004 annual report for BASF. Can you identify some of the items that will change in 2005 when IFR standards are applied?

Summary

1 **Understand the role of the finance function in management:**
   - Management needs funds, along with other resources, to help achieve the objectives of the business.
   - It must choose between investment opportunities.
   - Shareholders expect management to invest in projects to add shareholder value.
   - Management requires adequate financial information.
   - The finance function offers a system for assessing the financial consequences of decisions in a relatively objective way.
   - Management is required to communicate financial information about the company to actual and prospective shareholders through the financial reports.

2 **Be able to interpret basic financial reports:**
   - Operating profit, EBIT, and net profit as a proportion of sales is a useful basis for comparing firms in the same industry and for each firm through time.
   - Net profit as a proportion of shareholder's funds appears to be a measure of overall performance.
   - All measures of performance based on accounting numbers are subject to the opinions of those who prepare them.

3 **Know the difference between profit and cash:**
   - Profit is based on accounting interpretation of financial data.
   - Cash flow measures actual cash transactions and is less subject to opinion than profit.

4 **Know what a simple financial plan contains and its purpose:**
   - A financial plan sets out the financial implications of anticipated actions for a future period.
   - In most businesses a plan will show expected sales, costs, resources needed to fulfil the plan, a cash forecast and an expected balance sheet.
   - The plan sets out a course of action for the future.

5 **Understand the importance of financial results to evaluate performance:**
   - Owners and shareholders, and the capital market generally, exercise significant influence over managers.
   - The capital markets' reaction to reports of financial performance affects the ability of the company to raise capital.
   - Top management will experience this external pressure and transmit it internally.
   - Financial information also helps to measure management performance internally – actual revenue and expenditure can be compared with the budget.
   - Financial information can help control the management of projects, to ensure that what is spent corresponds to what has been planned.

6 **Know the basic steps in calculating the financial consequences of a management decision:**
   - Understanding the objectives of an organisation is essential in order to discriminate between alternative opportunities.

- Increments to profit may not require the recovery of all costs so long as incremental revenue exceeds incremental costs.
- Costs and revenue for decision purposes are estimates which reflect expected future operating conditions.

7 Be able to explain how budgets aim to ensure internal activities are directed at meeting external financial requirements:

- Budgets give focus and direction to the plans that management makes to achieve objectives.
- Budgets help to coordinate the activities of different functions and activities.
- The levels at which budgets are set have effects on motivation – impossible or very slack budgets have little beneficial effect. Those that are challenging but achievable have a positive effect on commitment.
- Organisations normally have a regular cycle of budgeting activity, conducted between those at the centre and those in the operating units.
- In some companies line managers are heavily involved in decisions about budgets; in others the budgets are imposed from the centre in an authoritarian manner, which affects the degree to which employees and managers accept ownership of the budgets.

Review questions

1 Why do companies have to make a profit? Check the website for Marks & Spencer plc. What do the directors have to say about profit and recent performance?

2 How is profit measured?

3 Explain why profit is different from cash. Look up any company report on **http://www.carol.co.uk** and see if you can explain the main difference between profit and cash for the company.

4 What does a balance sheet tell us about an organisation? What can you discover about the activities of Solvay (**http://www.solvay.com/business/**) from the balance sheet?

5 Can you explain how the external pressures on a company to generate a profit are translated into internal planning systems? Explain how this occurs in BASF.

6 What is the purpose of a budget?

7 How does a budget operate as a control mechanism?

8 Explain why the financial information prepared for external purposes is not necessarily appropriate for managers.

9 Explain the notion of contribution to the profit of a business. What do the directors of BASF or Solvay have to say in the 2004 annual report about sources of profit?

10 What are international financial reporting standards of accounting? Explain how they differ from requirements which applied in your country prior to their introduction.

Concluding critical reflection

Think about the ways in which your company, or one with which you are familiar, deals with financial reporting and management accounting matters. Then make notes on these questions:

- What examples of the issues discussed in this chapter struck you as being relevant to practice in your company?

- To what extent do you experience the external pressures from the financial markets for high performance and for frequent and positive financial statements? To what extent do you feel the financial community has a realistic understanding of your business? Has the need to meet short-term financial targets affected long-term performance (e.g. by affecting investment decisions)?

- Is the budget setting process conducted fairly, and in a reasonably participative way? What assumptions about the effects of budgets on motivation appear to guide those who set them? Are those who must meet the budgets adequately involved in setting them?

- What factors such as the history or current context of the company appear to influence the way the company handles these financial and budgeting processes? Does the current approach appear to be right for the company in its context – or would a different view of the context lead to a more effective approach?

- Have people put forward alternative approaches to budget systems, based on evidence about other companies? If you could find such evidence, how may it affect company practice?

Further reading

Coggan, P. (2002), *The Money Machine*, Penguin, Harmondsworth.

A useful introduction to the mechanisms that management can use to raise capital and the expectations they have to satisfy.

Alexander, D. and Nobes, C. (2004), *International Introduction to Financial Accounting*, Financial Times/Prentice Hall, Harlow.

Provides a European perspective on the topic.

Horngren, C.T., Foster, G. and Datar, S.M. (2002), *Cost Accounting* (10th edn), Financial Times/Prentice Hall, Harlow.

A standard text that covers all areas of the topic in great detail.

Drury, C. (2004), *Management and Cost Accounting*, Thomson Learning, London.

A useful concentration on behavioural aspects of management accounting.

Atkinson, A., Kaplan, R. and Young, S. (2003), *Management Accounting*, Financial Times/Prentice Hall, Harlow.

A pioneering text introducing modern concepts of cost accounting.

Ross, S., Westerfield, R. and Jordan, B. (2002), *Fundamentals of Corporate Finance*, McGraw-Hill/Irwin, New York.

A sound introduction to principles of corporate finance.

Henry, D. (2004), 'Fuzzy numbers', *Business Week*, 4 October, pp. 79–87.

A critical review of the ways in which financial reports can be manipulated.

The Economist (2003), 'True and fair is not hard and fast', *The Economist*, 16 April, pp. 59–61.

A review of the limitations of financial reporting and the quality of auditing.

You should also visit company websites to access financial reports. As well as illustrating the financial issues covered in this chapter, they usually provide a lot of information that relates to other chapters. In addition you can get useful information from these sites:

www.carolworld.com to access a variety of corporate reports

www.iasb.org the International Accounting Standards Board for IFRS.

Weblinks

These websites, among others, have appeared in the chapter:

www.thebodyshop.com

www.basf.com

www.solvay.com

www.siemens.com

Visit the websites in the list, or any other company that interests you, and navigate to the pages which include their annual report or investor relations (see also 'recent trading statements'). Sometimes they may include 'presentations to analysts' (who advise fund managers on investment decisions).

- What kind of information do they include in these pages, and what messages are they trying to present to the financial markets? If performance has been poor, what reasons do they give, and what do they promise to do about it? What implications might that have for people working in the company?

- You could keep the most recent trading statement, and then compare it with the next one, which will be issued in a few months.

- Gather information from the media websites (such as www.FT.com) which relate to the companies you have chosen. What stories can you find that indicate something about the financial performance of the companies you have chosen?

Annotated weblinks, multiple choice questions and other
useful resources can be found on
www.pearsoned.co.uk/boddy

Chapter 19
Managing operations and quality

Aim

To set the operations function in its historical context and show how it supports business performance.

Objectives

By the end of your work on this chapter you should be able to outline the concepts below in your own terms and:

1 Understand how the operations function can support performance in manufacturing and service organisations

2 Describe five types of transformation and their physical layout

3 Analyse the five main activities that make up an operations function

4 Compare the process approach to operations with the functional approach

5 Recognise the need to manage operations across an extended supply chain

6 Explain how the idea of 'order winners' and 'order qualifiers' links operations to the strategic process of meeting customer needs profitably.

Key terms

This chapter introduces the following ideas:

craft producers
factory production
inventory
system
line layout
cell layout
functional layout
concentric layout
quality
delivery
demand lead time
supply lead time
cost
partnering
order winner
order qualifier

Each is a term defined within the text, as well as in the glossary at the end of the book.

There are many aspects to the success of Benetton. One of these is undoubtedly its unusual operations management system.

With a radical approach to knitted goods, the Benettons in effect created a knitted pullover as a seasonal fashion good rather than a garment for comfort intended for years of service. Their bold colours brought a youthful image and created a need for dedicated retail outlets working to a closely defined and controlled specification. As a two-person business there was little need for systems. Giuliano designed and produced while Luciano sold. Their early success encouraged them to buy new machines and recruit local staff to produce a small range of goods in greater volume.

Where production was in Benetton factories, employees' suggestions for improvement were encouraged and acted upon while, early on, the company used subcontractors as producers. Initially these were outworkers to whom part-made garments would be delivered in their homes for completion and later collected. Larger groups of such workers formed a subcontractor network around the main Benetton factories. These grew up at a time when Benetton could not raise its own capital to build capacity internally. Instead, Luciano devised a partnership agreement with them such that, in return for providing a steady stream of work, the suppliers would invest in fixed assets.

The nature of the relationship with the retailers also impacts on Benetton's operations systems. The retail outlets are separate businesses (that do not pay royalties to their parent company).

The product line has increased each year with new garments and materials being used, but the essence of the Benetton system remains in operation terms dependent on a large number of independent entrepreneur suppliers working very closely in partnership with Benetton, growing and developing with them.

Benetton Autumn/Winter 2004–5 campaign, shot by photographer David Sims

Benetton thus demonstrates many of the characteristics of the Japanese auto companies in their supply system relationships: tiers of subcontractors collaborate to make their supply chains effective against Benetton's competitors. All of this is done without compromising the core of the Benetton belief system that customers deserve choice, variety, value for money and a guaranteed level of quality and service.

Source: Based on *Building the Benetton System*, European Case Clearing House, No. 390-042-1.

Case questions

- What business practices did Benetton introduce that seem unusual to you?
- What particular issues do you think would arise in managing an organisation with so many independent suppliers and shop owners?
- What contrasts and similarities are there between Benetton and The Body Shop from a management point of view?

19.1 Introduction

This chapter sets the operations function in its historical context and shows how this function supports other manufacturing or service activities. It then considers the current state of development of the management approaches inside the function and the increasingly cross-boundary aspects being demonstrated in the best organisations. The boundaries being crossed include those between departments of the same organisation. The role of the operations function often incorporates the management of the whole integrated supply chain. This begins with the supplier of raw material and ends with the delivery of the product or service to the customer. Thus the function has a major strategic dimension where it can hinder or help the achievement of corporate goals.

The first section outlines the main historical events, people and techniques. These have shaped our understanding of what we mean by operations and quality and how they support business activities. The chapter then describes five types of operations system, and the advantages of each. It outlines how operations contributes to quality in both manufacturing and services, and how the discipline extends beyond one organisation into other stages of the supply chain. It concludes by showing the link to marketing, and thus to the strategic position of operations in management.

19.2 Historical development

Craft production

The operations activity has existed for as long as there have been intelligent beings working with tools to transform base material into something different and desirable. In this regard, management created the specialism earlier than marketing, information systems and human resources. These latter depend more on size and complexity to justify separate status. Nevertheless, in some European cultures, management saw the purpose of operations as being to provide whatever the rest of the business wanted. They often did (in some fashion), but often this was due mainly to the abilities of the people in the function, not to a coherent approach.

This chapter looks at how the evolutionary process has changed the nature of the need that the operations function has to fill. It also examines how some organisations are paying more attention to designing and operating this transformation function. Their intention is to benefit customers and providers alike.

Activity 19.1 Visiting a craft worker

Visit a craft fair and talk to one or two of the craft workers about the way they work, how they sell, if they design to order or according only to their ideas, and how they organise the production of goods and the supply of materials.

Craft production refers to a system in which the craft producers do everything. With or without customer involvement they design, source materials, make, display, sell, perhaps service and do the accounts.

From the beginnings of trade, **craft producers** have embodied their ideas and skills in a product or service, and usually some elements of both. Craft producers do everything themselves. With or without customer involvement they design, source materials, make, display, sell, perhaps service and do the accounts. Once they generate income they reinvest and often train apprentices to continue the skills.

Craft producers conduct each stage of the complete product life cycle. Their output is unique and very variable. Sometimes batch production is possible – for example, a limited edition of 500 prints from an original piece of artwork, each signed by its creator.

The range of skills employed by a craft worker is a microcosm of the operations function. The flexibility that craft producers can achieve, and their ability to modify ideas to suit customer requirements, are now sought by large producers. Craft workers also gain a personal satisfaction from completing the whole set of tasks that is often absent in factories.

Factory production

Factory production made it possible to increase the supply of goods to rapidly growing populations. It broke down the integrated nature of the craft worker's approach. Management realised that dividing work into smaller units allowed workers to concentrate on developing a narrow range of specialised skills. The division of labour was between different tasks and between the thinking and doing tasks of manager and worker. This division began the evolution towards narrow, functionally defined boundaries with jealously guarded 'patches of turf'. These would become the focus of territorial wars across the organisation.

> Factory production broke down the integrated nature of the craftworker's approach and made it possible to increase the supply of goods by dividing tasks into simple and repetitive sequences.

Activity 19.2 Visit a factory

Many large manufacturers offer visiting facilities. Try to visit several to see if you can understand the way that they work. Alternatively you can visit the Cameron Balloons virtual factory at **www.bized.ac.uk/virtual/cb/welcome.htm**. This site is structured to give a broad view of many of the issues covered in this chapter.

Dividing tasks into simple and repetitive sequences allowed managers to employ a wider range of people in the factory and so enabled them to increase production.

Managers found that they needed two other techniques to enable high-volume production – standardisation and interchangeability. If several people are producing sets of parts that must fit together at some stage, they must work to a standard specification. Moreover, each part must be completely interchangeable with its equivalent produced by someone else. This was not an issue for the craft worker as he or she could work on only one product at a time, and had the skill to shape the parts to ensure a good fit.

Management in the developing factory system wanted to avoid this 'fitting' effort, so they designed both processes and machines to be regular and repeatable. This also influenced the nature of capital investment. At first, factory owners used this mainly to provide motive power for essentially human-based machines – they invested largely to supplement human muscle power. By removing variable human effort and increasing machine power, the machines themselves worked more precisely, so it became easier to make interchangeable parts.

Case questions 19.1

- Is Benetton a craft or a factory system?
- Review the information about the system Benetton uses and list its advantages and disadvantages.

Twentieth-century developments

The aim of Frederick Taylor (1917) and the Gilbreths (1911, 1914) in creating a 'scientific' approach to management was to move away from methods that were very variable and dependent on individual abilities and motivation (see Chapter 2). Some Western commentators have devalued Taylor's approaches to work measurement. Yet people who are performing a sequence of related activities need to know how long to allow for each stage and what resources they need. The method study approaches that the Gilbreths pioneered as they searched for the 'one best way of working' have a great deal to offer. What has changed is that management often expects operating staff themselves to look for improved ways of working. This is part of the continuous improvement effort.

A disadvantage of the scientific school was the concentration on finely subdivided tasks that a worker would repeat thousands of times in a working life. This process was deskilling and dehumanising – it permitted no variation or individuality.

This reached its peak with Henry Ford's automobile assembly plants. Ford brought high levels of interchangeability to moving production lines, highly 'scientific' management and vertical integration along the lines of supply (Ford, 1922). That is to say, Ford owned all the stages of production from raw materials through to final distribution to customers. In the 1920s his system could transform iron ore into a finished car in 81 hours, of which only about 5 hours were taken up by manufacturing and assembly. It was economically very efficient and reduced the real cost of producing a car over many years of continuous improvement. Over an 18-year period the retail price of the Model T Ford decreased from just over $3000 to less than $900. Ford's was a single model system, but General Motors later offered more varied products. They used different organisational principles, and created severe competition for Ford.

At the height of Ford's capability one of the many visitors was Taichi Ohno, who was the production engineer at the fledgling Toyota car company in Japan. While some of the Ford system impressed Ohno he learnt more from US supermarkets. He noted in particular how stores satisfied the needs of customers with minimal shelf space in the store. As customers took products away staff restocked the shelves. This is the logic behind what many observers regard as the world's best manufacturing company. It was also an early example of the two-way technology transfer (of managerial technologies) between west and east.

It was around this time that engineers developed a statistical approach to control quality. The method used control charts and sampling plans. Control charts tried to prevent people creating defects. Sampling plans ensured that any defects did not pass beyond the sampling stage. This statistical process control was instrumental in supporting production effort in the Second World War. It was also during that war that a different applied mathematical approach began its development. Operational research, or management science, attempted to create mathematical models of management situations. Staff could then manipulate these models to develop optimum results that management could use to inform their decisions. The assumptions needed to make some problems feasible for mathematical models were sometimes too great for managers to regard them as suitable surrogates for the real world. Nevertheless some of the approaches still offer utility to practising managers. A prime example is critical path analysis, which helps people to manage complex projects.

It was during the 1960s that availability of relatively cheap computing power encouraged people to develop techniques for managing production and **inventory**, known as material requirements planning (MRP) systems (Orlicky, 1975). These aimed to manage the production activity by controlling every part at every stage, and seemed to offer the complete computer integration of the manufacturing process. The reality was often less

Inventory consists of materials and part or finished goods that are held in anticipation of need by customers along a chain of supply from raw materials through to final consumption (and recycling?).

than ideal. Nevertheless it caused managers in the western world to look to computers to solve the problems of managing increasingly complex production systems.

Management in resource-starved Japan followed a different approach. Ford's model of mass production had not made sense to Toyota. Ohno began to build a system that used the supermarket model of simplicity and customer-driven operations. This approach did not need computers, but did need dedicated and capable people working together.

> ### Activity 19.3   Visit McDonald's
>
> - Visit a McDonald's or similar fast-food outlet and try to discover the material inventories that are used. What non-material inventories will there be? Given their attempt to meet the 'healthy living' agenda by introducing new salads and lower-fat meals, what impact will this have on their inventories?
> - Consider a hospital accident and emergency unit. What inventories are normally stored in such units? Remember that inventories are not just about products or things: other resources can be stored in some ways.

Systems thinking and models

Any operation can be represented as a **system** that takes inputs of various kinds and transforms them into some kind of desired output. Inputs may include materials, equipment, finance and people. Outputs include products, services, reputation and waste. The aim of systems thinking is to use an abstract view of the total system and then to operate each subsystem according to the defined 'best way' for the complete system. This can be drawn as a simple systems diagram. A control mechanism is included to ensure that the outputs expected are delivered and that they meet customers' needs. A feedback control loop measures, analyses and modifies the inputs, as shown in Figure 19.1.

A **system** is a set of interrelated parts designed to achieve a purpose.

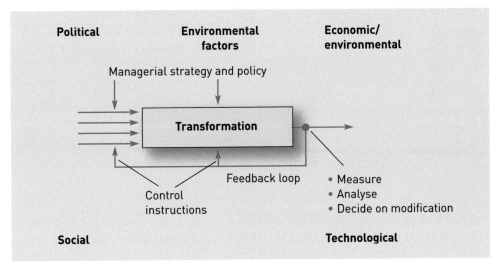

Figure 19.1

Basic systems diagram

The transformation stage can take many forms, only one of which is production. Service-oriented types are more numerous, although the history of the subject concentrates on production.

Case questions 19.2

● Draw a systems diagram that represents the Benetton production system.

● What are the main sources of feedback?

● How critical are they to input activities?

Table 19.1 lists the transformation types. Operations systems need to deal with two distinguishing features. The first is whether the system results in a tangible 'product' that can be stored. If not, either someone consumes the output immediately or the system has wasted the capability. If nobody occupies a hotel room or an airline seat it creates no output. The companies cannot store the capacity and have lost for ever the opportunity to sell it. A car, on the other hand, embodies its value in a less time-dependent form.

The second distinguishing feature is that in a pure service transformation (such as a visit to the hairdresser) the customer must be present throughout the transformation and largely defines the details of the transformation. In product production both design and transformation can be done without contact with the customer. In service businesses the people with whom the customer interacts *are* the service. In practice some service businesses are becoming more like factories, especially in back-office areas that have no contact with customers. An example is the cash dispenser system providing cash and sometimes other transactions with their customers without direct contact between bank staff and the customers. Conversely, many factories are trying to become closer to their customers to satisfy needs more precisely.

Table 19.1

Transformation types

Transformation	System	Variations
Physical	Production	Additive, e.g. automobile assembly
		Subtractive, e.g. oil refining
Locational	Transportation	Goods, people
Attitudinal	Education	Statutory or voluntary
	Entertainment	Escapist or informative
Physiological	Healthcare, fitness	Remedial/preventive
Presentational	Fashion	Clothes, hair, cosmetics

The objectives of operations managers are to select and manage the best mix of resources and transformation process to meet customer requirements. They must also do this in a way that permits the organisation to make an acceptable financial return on its investments. The customer requirements will cover aspects of product or service design, delivery, reliability, speed and quality. All must be at an acceptable cost.

Characteristics which differentiate operational systems

- **Output volume**
- **Nature of processing** (continuous or intermittent)
- **Outputs are continuous or discrete** (e.g. electricity or cars)
- **Specificity to actual customer requirements** (degree to which the output and the flexibility of the system's response are specific to or specified by the customer)
- **Physical layout** of transformation equipment

Volume ranges from unique items, such as a dam or fine art picture, through multiple copies or batches of similar items, to mass production. The latter can be continuous (e.g. cement) or discrete (e.g. video recorders). Figure 19.2 shows these systems with examples of each. It lists across the top the physical layouts that tend to match each type.

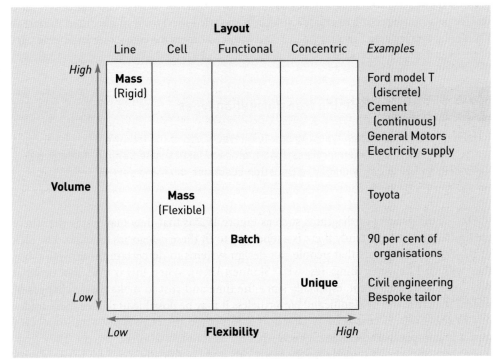

Figure 19.2

Forms of operations system

Line layout is specified by the sequence of activities needed to perform a given transformation. It is relatively fixed but may have similar processes scattered through the line as and when needed. It will tend to have specially designed process equipment and use people with a limited range of skills.

Cell layout permits more variety by creating multiple cells (which look like small line layouts) dedicated to producing families of output types. Within the cell people have several skills and move between jobs as required to keep the flow of transformation steady. The people are likely to have a wider range of skills and more decision-making authority.

Both of these types focus on the transformed materials or customer. The aim is to keep them flowing through the system without delay. If necessary, operators use parts of the transformation system at less than the theoretical capacity to keep the process moving.

Line layout is completely specified by the sequence of activities needed to perform a given transformation.

A cell layout creates multiple cells dedicated to producing families of output types.

A **functional layout** groups similar physical processes together and brings materials and/or customers to these areas.

Concentric layout occurs in, for example, shipbuilding where the product is so large that it remains static while labour and materials come to the centre to assemble the ship.

In **functional layout** the thinking is different. Here the system tries to keep the elements of the transformation process fully used and able to produce the required variety of output. Similar physical processes are located together, and the materials and/or customers visit these areas as required by the product or service design. This produces a very tangled flow round these locations, often involving extensive queuing time between the different processing stages. This system needs high levels of inventory while the operating staff perform highly specialised tasks. It is a common way of organising manufacturing and service operations.

In a **concentric layout** people focus activity on an area where something – such as a dam or a ship – is being assembled. The process is one of bringing the resources together in the required sequence and time to create a unique output. People have extensive skills. Integration is complex, so staff often use the critical path analysis technique to plan activities.

It is important to realise that these stereotypes are simply that. They are labels that bring certain assumptions with them so that using the label paints a mental picture as a form of shorthand in discussions. In practice organisations can often display a number of these stereotypes under one roof. For example, a restaurant might have a functionally organised kitchen producing batches of meals for parties of diners. The waiter is a pure service person interacting to create a uniquely specified meal for a single diner. If there is a buffet or carvery area this may be in a line with customers moving along and being part of the transformation process.

> ### Activity 19.4 Defining transformation types
>
> Define the transformation type and possible layout form of the following: (a) university matriculation or enrolment process, (b) a motorway fast-food servery, (c) a hospital accident and emergency unit, (d) a Benetton customer sales and service area.

One of the dangers of diagrams such as Figure 19.2 is that they may imply that there are limited choices. Certainly there is a tendency to fit these categories together. The idea of the trade-off suggests that people can design systems to do certain things well – but they will then do other things less well (Skinner, 1969). When this is true, that original decision is very important, especially since the time and cost to make major changes of system structure will be significant. Nevertheless it may be possible to reduce these trade-offs in some way. If customer satisfaction is improved then this will be an important aspect of competitive advantage. This is what the best organisations try to do. They challenge the assumptions underlying the trade-offs and continually strive to do more with less while ensuring continuing and expanding customer support.

19.3 A framework for analysing operations

Providing goods and services to a customer depends on five key operations activities, and these provide a useful way of describing and analysing an organisation's operations system (Sprague, 1990). Figure 19.3 shows these activities of

- Capacity
- Standards
- Scheduling

- Materials
- Control

and that each of these activities is connected to the others.

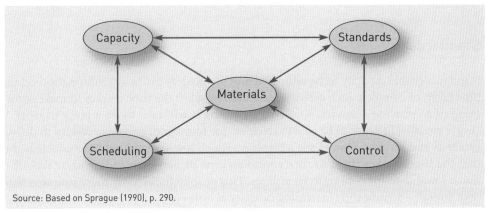

Source: Based on Sprague (1990), p. 290.

Figure 19.3

Framework for analysing operations management

Capacity

Capacity is the ability to yield an output – it is a statement of the ability of the numerous resources within an organisation to deliver to the customer: it indicates the limitations of a system. Defining capacity depends on identifying the main resources required to deliver a saleable output – staff, machinery, materials and finance. Capacity is limited by whichever of these is in shortest supply. Moreover, the matter is made more complicated by the fact that there will be a mix of resources within each category – a hospital's capacity to conduct a particular operation will be determined by some minimum number of specifically competent surgeons, nurses, technicians, and related professions, as well as more transferable staff such as catering and domestic staff. In service organisations all aspects of capacity may be visible to the customer – who can see not only the quality of the staff, but also the state of the physical equipment and material resources being used.

Technology may sound as if it relates only to the physical facilities available, but experience suggests otherwise. Technology depends on people who are able and willing to use it to best effect. If managers in a government service dealing with pensions or other benefits aim to increase capacity by installing a new computer system, but then do not ensure that staff are willing and able to use the system to improve performance, capacity will not increase as hoped. 'It is the mix of physical technology – machines, equipment, buildings, the physical assets – and labor-embodied technology that establishes the organization's capacity' (Sprague, 1990, p. 273). The previous section (19.2) outlined alternative ways of physically laying out the technology, by distinguishing the line, cell, functional or concentric approaches.

A vital aspect of the operations function is to ensure an adequate supply of the many material resources needed to deliver an output: in late 2004 Nissan announced that it was halting car production for five days because it was unable to obtain adequate supplies of steel in a world market suddenly experiencing shortages. One of the dilemmas is that holding stocks of materials is expensive – it ties up finance and incurs storage costs, and there is a risk, in rapidly changing markets, that stocks of components become out of date because of a change in model. Too much material can be as costly as too little. An organisation's capacity is also determined by the amount of money it has available. Small firms in particular can suffer from this – to grow they need to take on larger orders, but to be able to meet those orders they need to have invested previously in sufficient resources (staff, machinery, materials). They may be able to raise the finance needed from a bank – but this carries the risk of financial trouble, since if the order is delayed the company will not be able to repay the loan on the due date.

Standards

Standards enable capacity to be estimated and planned by providing information on the time taken to complete each activity. Standards establish the time it takes to make something or to provide a service. Knowing how long it will take to do a piece of work is clearly essential in order to be able to calculate the number of people necessary to deliver products and services. One of the advantages which low-cost airlines have established is that the time it takes them to turn round an aircraft between landing and take-off is much lower than for conventional airlines. This enables them to fly more journeys with each aircraft – significantly increasing capacity at little cost.

Scheduling

This is the function of coordinating the available resources by time or place – specifying which resources need to be available and when in order to meet demand. It begins with incoming information about demand and its likely impact on the available capacity. Service, productivity and ultimately profitability depend on matching supply with demand. Capacity management generates supply; scheduling links demand with that capacity. It can be carried out over several time periods. *Aggregate scheduling* is done for the medium term, and is closely associated with planned levels of capacity: as airlines plan their future fleets, which they need to do several years ahead, they make judgements about both their capacity and the likely demand (translated into frequency of flights on particular routes). *Master scheduling* deals with likely demand (firm or prospective orders) over the next few months, while *dispatching* is concerned with immediate decisions about which rooms to allocate to which guests.

Materials

Materials, otherwise known as inventory, is a major asset for organisations, representing, from a financial point of view, money tied up in stocks of raw materials. From a sales point of view, it represents the chance to make an immediate sale of goods that have been produced, so enabling them to be turned into cash. Those closest to the customers will argue forcefully for the benefits of large stocks.

A traditional view of inventory was that it can serve to solve manufacturing and distribution problems – to smooth demand and cover for unexpected production difficulties – and that it was generally something useful to have, 'just-in-case'. A modern view is fundamentally different, stressing the powerful cost implications of inventory and seeing it as something to be avoided. This approach also focuses on solving the underlying manufacturing problems that inventory could avoid, rather than relying on expensive inventory to cover them up.

Control

Control is intended to check whether the plans for capacity, scheduling and inventory actually worked. Without control, there is little point in planning, as there is no mechanism then to learn from the experience. There are three steps in the control process:

- Observe – see what actually happened
- Compare – relate what actually happened to what was expected to happen
- Decide – what action to take in view of that, and what longer-term changes to make for the future.

Only by engaging in this can immediate operations be kept moving towards objectives, and lessons learned for future improvements in the operations function.

19.4 The operations function and its contribution

The operations function has been set in its historical context and some models have been provided of the balance between market need and supply capability. The chapter now examines how the operations function can support the rest of the business.

In what follows it is assumed that management has made decisions on product or service design. Ideally it will have discussed the options with the operations function – but the marketing and design staff play the major role in that. The operations function can help ensure that people implement design decisions in a way that adds value to the business. The main contributions are in the areas of innovation, quality, delivery and cost.

Innovation

In products, the impetus for change comes from two sources. Market pull occurs when customers make new demands or when competitors try to change the strategic balance in some way. Such innovations are low risk. It is likely that there will be a demand for the new product. Since the product is based on what is known and understood it should be easy to estimate costs. The danger is that such innovations are too incremental – while safe, they do not advance quickly enough to gain a competitive advantage.

Benetton – the case continues – innovation in dyeing

CASE STUDY

One famous innovation took place in 1972, at a time when the colours were still simple, i.e. one colour per garment and no complicated patterns. Traditionally, wool is dyed its final colour when it is still a yarn, i.e. a long time before being used in a garment and a long time ahead of actual customer demand. By designing a process to dye the completed garment Benetton incurred some increased production costs but greatly reduced the cost of carrying the inventory of coloured garments formerly needed to react to customers' demands. Instead, the decision about colour was moved much closer to customers' buying decision, thus removing much risk and complexity. It also meant that stocks that were selling well could be replenished, while stocks of less popular goods could be minimised.

As the company grew it continued to rely on a network of subcontractors – often created by internal groups being encouraged to become independent contractors to Benetton. By 1987 only 5 per cent of final garment sewing assembly was done internally by Benetton.

Source: Based on *Building the Benetton System*, European Case Clearing House, No. 390-042-1.

CHAPTER 19 MANAGING OPERATIONS AND QUALITY

Technology push is the other main force for innovation. Here an expert with an idea proposes a new and often dramatic innovation. The danger is that no customer has yet requested this item, and many will not be able to express a need for it. Such innovations are high risk. There are no forecasts of market demand and no historical data for cost estimates. Many innovations of this type fail. Those that succeed, however, can change companies, industries and societies, as the Benetton case demonstrates. Only think of the photocopier, jet engine or scanning electron microscope to realise the importance of major breakthrough innovations. In reality management needs to consider both possibilities. It can seek incremental innovation continuously while the essentially intermittent nature of a breakthrough needs a different management approach.

Technology is more likely to stimulate process innovation. Even here multiple small changes can create wide competitive gaps if continued over a long period.

Organisations need innovation in both products and processes – and not just those in the production area. Many office systems and most service businesses repay a serious effort to redesign them in more effective ways. Telephone-based and Web-enabled insurance companies have dramatically increased their market share by innovations in the way they deliver the service. Banking is going in the same direction. Inditex shows the role of innovation in fashion retailing reaching new heights with Zara's attempts to remove 'seasons' from the business.

 **Inditex group** www.inditex.com

This fast-growing group of fashion-related companies has Zara, Pull and Bear, Massimo Dutti, Berschka and Stradivarious in its list. In 2004 it had 2181 stores in 55 countries. Over 200 designers help meet the aim to be close to their customers and do away with seasons in fashions. They now introduce 20,000 new items a year – and to do this they need to be even more responsive than Benetton.

In effect they have redefined the interaction with the customers who now know that, because of the high rate of new product introduction, if they do not buy a product when it appears in the shops then they might miss the opportunity altogether since that same item may never appear again. This also has the benefit of forcing the customers to keep visiting the stores to catch the new ideas before someone beats them to it.

In difficult trading conditions they increased sales by 16 per cent in 2003 and opened another 360 stores.

Source: Company website and other published information.

Quality

The **quality** of a product or service is the (often imprecise) perception of a customer that what has been provided is at least what was expected for the price he or she paid.

In craft production the **quality** of output is crucial, for without it customers may not pay and will certainly not return. Craftspeople also tend to have pride in their work and continuously strive to improve their mastery of the craft. During the evolution of the factory system this ideal suffered as management subdivided the work process. Management separated quality approval from production. Even quality control charts were tools for quality inspectors, not production workers.

Benetton – the case continues – response to new market trends

Without giving up the strongest aspects of its networked model, Benetton is integrating and centralising, instituting direct control over key processes throughout the supply chain. Vertical integration has meant establishing state-of-the-art production poles in Benetton's foreign locations. The Castrette pole, near its headquarters, decides what each of the foreign poles should produce (on the basis of the skills and experience of the local population), and the foreign poles contract out production tasks.

Benetton also has increased its upstream vertical integration to exercise greater control over its supply of textiles and thread. At the retail end, the company is supplementing its network of small, independently owned shops with large, directly controlled megastores. To stay ahead of fashion's ever-changing whims, Benetton is streamlining its brands and collections, supplementing two basic collections with smaller, flash collections.

Source: Camuffo *et al.* (2001).

During the 1950s the Americans sent a number of their statisticians to Japan to help rebuild their productive capability. The Japanese learned from Joseph Juran (Juran, 1974), W.E. Deming (Deming, 1988) and Armand Feigenbaum (Feigenbaum, 1993), and applied the lessons widely and conscientiously. They also recognised the fundamental truth of craft production – that the person who performs the transformation is the best person to ensure quality is correct at the moment of its performance. History has thus come full circle, with individuals taking pride in doing quality work and striving to make regular improvements.

Another realisation is that quality and customer satisfaction are responsibilities for all in the business and not simply the producer at the end of the chain. Each customer throughout the chain must receive top quality performance. This is a message top management must believe in and then act on accordingly.

Principles of total quality management (TQM)

key ideas

- **Philosophy**: waste reduction through continuous improvement
- **Leadership**: committed and visible from top to bottom of the organisation
- **Measurement**: costs involved in quality failures – the cost of quality
- **Scope**: everyone, everywhere across whole supply chain
- **Methods**: simple control and improvement techniques implemented by teams

The underpinning philosophy of TQM is that not having perfect quality wastes resources. Some of these wastes are obvious – scrapped material through equipment failure – but other wastes come through bad systems or poor communications and may be more difficult to find and measure. The philosophy advocates that a constant effort to remove waste pays dividends. Progressive, small improvements repay mightily from both customer satisfaction and revenue viewpoints. They reduce costs as the system uses resources more effectively. Leadership of a visible and tangible type is needed to keep the efforts going. It also avoids a tendency to consider delivery of any product as more important than the delivery of the correct product. Crosby introduced the idea that 'quality is free': it is getting it wrong that costs money (Crosby, 1979).

In contrast to the scientific management approach, modern writers propose that quality should not be separated from production. Everyone has to take responsibility for his or her proportion of the quality effort. This includes those people outside the organisation who nevertheless contribute towards the total quality of the supply chain. The whole supply chain must function as a total quality system. Methods used include simple descriptive statistics, brainstorming techniques and simple statistical process controls (Oakland, 1994). The people performing the transformation are the ones trained and encouraged to use these tools and they will often display the results in their work area to spur further improvement. In this they will work as a team, calling on different people to support them as required.

Company teams can take part in Quality Award schemes. The Deming prize in Japan set the tone, with the winners enjoying high prestige. In the United States, the Baldrige Quality Award has set a pattern of very wide-ranging definitions of quality, and this has influenced the equivalent European Quality Awards (see the EFQM website **www.efqm.org**). At a more local level various national standards for quality are often demanded of organisations to qualify as approved providers of goods or services (see **www.iso.ch**). The key is not the award but the thought processes of all the people in the organisation and their commitment to the total quality ideals.

---

key ideas **Sources of quality cost**

- **Prevention**: getting the systems right
- **Appraisal**: measuring how the systems are performing
- **Internal failure**: faults found during checks inside the operation
- **External failure**: faults found by users – the worst kind

Quality is never completely free because of the investment in prevention. It is clear, however, that switching proportionately more resources into prevention cuts other costs such that the total reduces.

 **management in practice** **Happy Computers** www.happycomputers.co.uk

In 2003 Happy Computers was announced the overall winner of the *Management Today* Service Quality Award. Happy Computers is a computer training company which believes that learning should be fun. It was established to combine technical expertise and excellent training skills with an enjoyable learning environment. All their training is based around the age-old principle:

- Tell me and I will forget
- Show me and I will remember
- Involve me and I will understand

There are no lectures at Happy Computers. All their courses are designed to involve delegates to the full, ensuring active learning and enabling people to reach their potential. Happy Computers is not the largest IT training company, although they are in the top 50 by size. Happy Computers is the only training company in the UK to be rated in the top three by the Institute of IT Training in each of the past three years.

Source: *Management Today*, October 2003, Service Excellence Awards Supplement.

Thinking about quality at the design stage brings important benefits. Choices here should incorporate ideas and information from as many insiders, customers and suppliers as is sensible. Such processes capture the prevention and 'right first time' ideals and create opportunities to save cost and time. Waste minimisation is the goal. Waste is any use of resources that does not add value for the customer. Note that customers are not the only stakeholders. Management may be able to justify an activity not directly related to the requirements of a direct customer. Environmental considerations fall into this category, as do those based on legislation.

Many western organisations have been trying to catch up with best Japanese experience and practice in understanding and applying the lessons of quality control. They will have active measurement and improvement programmes in place, but many will not yet be paying the same attention to delivery.

Dell Computing   www.dell.com

management in practice

By redesigning their whole supply chain Dell have made a virtue out of speed and response to customers in a way that repays Dell by efficient use of money. Customers buy online and pay for their product in advance. Dell also tries to manage the elective choices customers make by offering discounts for inventory that is moving too slowly. Their operational control system is such that a customer can call into Dell to check progress in the manufacture of their order. By then Dell has the use of their money and some time later will pay their suppliers' bills for the materials they have provided. This system is so responsive that Dell is able to change its pricing structure daily to take advantage of material price fluctuations and to price aggressively for certain markets in ways that their less flexible competitors find difficult to match.

Activity 19.5   Defining quality

Define what quality means in the following: (a) a fast-food hamburger restaurant, (b) a five-star hotel, (c) an executive automobile, (d) a travel agency, (e) the products sold by Zara, (f) the service provided by Zara sales staff.

Delivery

Each link in the chain of supply from raw material to final consumer is formed between an individual or group acting as a customer to a supplier. The customer is in turn the supplier to another. Thus the next customer along the chain immediately feels any failure in quality, unless large amounts of inventory hide the failure. This is a direct benefit of reducing inventory: it exposes quality problems so that people can deal with them permanently.

Benetton – the case continues – innovations in ordering

The fashion cycle for the important spring/summer season begins in February with selection of around 500 items. During May–July small samples are produced to allow retailers a chance to place orders for the season seven months ahead. As the first orders roll in, production plans are made and subcontractors informed. The shop owners are then obliged to buy the goods produced as Benetton does not accept any returned goods unsold at the end of the season. Most of the shop orders are delivered between November and the following May as the Basic collection in readiness for the new season.

The balance of the orders fall into two categories: 'Flash' consists of reactions to new trends or competitor offerings while 'Reassortment' allows for individual choice of product mix in a particular store, and possibly for those late-dyed popular colours.

Thus the operations system has to cope with fairly stable production runs of the 'standard order' for 80–90 per cent and 'specials' on a much faster response time for the late variations.

Source: Based on *Building the Benetton System*, European Case Clearing House, No. 390-042-1.

Delivery relates to the achievement of all promises made by any supplier to a customer.

As with quality, so with **delivery**. Any failure to supply the customer when expected causes the wastes of delay, remedial action and extra effort. The first step in delivery performance is total reliability. Every downstream customer is dependent on every upstream supplier fulfilling his or her delivery promise, otherwise there is more waste. Every chain needs reliability, but sometimes it also needs speedy delivery. Speed is crucial when a company is bringing a new product to the market. It wants to make sales to early adopters before competitors can produce alternatives that will drive the price down. In competitive situations speed of response may be the distinguishing factor that wins the order. Figure 19.4 captures the relative timescales on the supply and demand side.

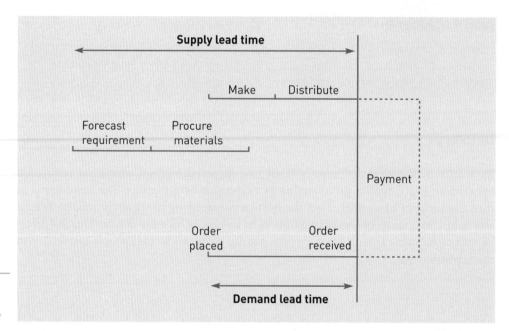

Figure 19.4

Manufacturing supply/demand lead time balance

Figure 19.4 illustrates a manufactured product for which the customer is prepared to wait some time between placing and receiving the order – the **demand lead time**. In some markets, such as retailing, this time is zero. That is, supply has to be instantaneous (off the shelf) or the buyer goes elsewhere or selects another product. In most manufacturing situations the addition of all the supply-side activities that constitute the **supply lead time** far exceeds the demand lead time. The critical fact is that all of the investment tied up in decisions to the left of the order placement point are at risk. In these areas there is no guarantee that a customer will place an order. So there is continual pressure to reduce the time needed on the supply side of the balance. Ideally the supply total would be less than the demand total. That would guarantee sales success, but only markets producing customised products to order are like this.

In service businesses the situation is different since the customer must be present during the service (see Figure 19.5). The service processing time will extend through the need to provide capacity (people and equipment) plus any consumable materials needed for the service. Generally there is likely to be a closer balance. Here, however, the customer perception of what is an acceptable service time can produce difficulties for the supply system if the system cannot match expectations effectively.

Demand lead time is the elapsed time that a customer is prepared to allow between placing an order for a product or service and actually receiving it; in certain situations this time is effectively zero.

Supply lead time is the total elapsed time between the decision to obtain the basic input resources to the final delivery of the product or service to the customer.

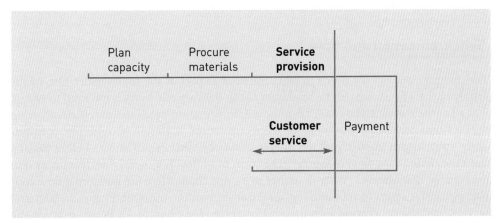

Figure 19.5

Service supply/demand lead time balance

One of the most effective ways to reduce the supply lead time in any linked supply chain is to consider the flow of materials through to the final customer as the real challenge. The task then is to synchronise all of the tributary flows into the main stream to maximise the main flow and minimise waste. Such synchronisation calls for coordinated effort in scheduling deliveries from internal and external suppliers according to an integrated master plan and reinforces the need for absolute control of quality and delivery performance.

| Activity 19.6 | Consider the lead time for a dress |

Consider the total supply lead time for a bridal dress made from Chinese silk. List and guess the timescales for the different stages of production and supply up to the final garment being made for the bride.

Cost

Cost expresses in money units the effect of activating or consuming resources. It is an internal control process of the producing organisation and is not visible to outside parties.

There is no disputing the need for the real **cost** of a transformation process to reduce with time. If organisations continually innovate to improve their systems and remove waste, and given that the learning effect of operating the systems also reduces waste and time taken, then cost should decrease. There is, however, a preferred sequence. An organisation must first build a solid base of quality performance and reinforce it with careful control over delivery. Doing these things correctly will lead to lower cost. If, on the other hand, the organisation tries to reduce costs and simply take resources away, this is likely to lower overall quality and delivery performance.

Cost is also an internal factor that customers do not always need to know. What they need to understand is what pricing possibilities the organisation can offer as a result of its performance on cost reduction. It is also important that an organisation does not concentrate solely on the direct money aspect of the business transaction, since many of the factors that go towards creating a satisfied customer will not necessarily be reflected in the unit price quoted for the good or service. The operations function has an important role to play as part of the supply chain team that delivers the goods and/or services in the most effective manner.

Synchronisation and flow

The operations area now needs to be considered as part of the much wider idea of the supply chain. The essence of the argument about delivery reliability is the need to ensure that all of the wastes in the chain are removed. Information needs to flow efficiently from the consumer to the producers at all points upstream. Materials should flow continuously downstream to satisfy all the intermediate customer requirements before passing from the chain to the final consumer. The concept of flow is a useful one. It is implied in the concept that Michael Porter describes as a value chain. Here the horizontal flow consists of the five stages of inbound logistics, transformation, outbound logistics, sales and service, and the generation of a financial margin (see Chapter 8). Porter extends the value system idea to include the output from one organisation's value chain being the input to another one. It is then similar to the supply chain model described above (Porter, 1980b).

The key part of this concept is that final consumers want to receive their chosen goods as they require them without hindrance or problem. So organisations need to make the flow as smooth, speedy and consistent as possible. Anything interfering with this smooth flow is a waste, causing customer dissatisfaction. Speed of flow also brings financial benefits: the quicker the flow becomes a sale, the quicker the company can recover the investment incurred in supply.

Case question 19.3

Consider the supply lead time for the Benetton Basic collection and for the Flash or Reassortment goods. What is the demand lead time for each of these categories?

This concept lies behind the just-in-time system of production where the total quality management and synchronised flow approaches are coupled with a cross-trained and committed workforce to produce very effectively (Schonberger, 1983). The synchronisation is not internal to just one organisation, so managements try to establish a complete supply chain working collaboratively on this basis.

Nissan Motor Manufacturing Company www.nissan.com

The suppliers of colour coordinated seats for Nissan cars are located close to the main factory and are connected electronically to the workflow on the Nissan line. When cars leave the paint oven and are accepted as ready for assembly, this is the signal for the particular colour of car seat to be produced and matched to the flow on the car line. The complete seat assembly with all electronic equipment, position adjusters, etc., must then be produced and delivered direct to the point of use on the Nissan line in less than 30 minutes. It must be in a condition such that the Nissan workers need only position it into the car and fix it to its mountings with complete confidence that everything about the seat is completely correct.

To make synchronisation possible management has to attack the problem that led to a functional focus. This is the traditional view that the best way to make a financial return on a piece of equipment is to keep it producing. The new thinking is that the equipment has to support the flow and no more. Thus, if the output is already sufficient then the process should stop and not build inventory for which there is no immediate demand. Management also needs to attack the thought that if it is expensive to change over from one production run to another it should do this less often; in other words it should produce large quantities before changing. This builds those costly inventories again. A better approach is to reduce the costs of changing, so that the pressure for large production runs is no longer there. Management can then approach the just-in-time ideal of making a little of everything every day. When this is achieved, the system can produce to customer order with no delays and no inventory.

Bottling and packaging www.scmg.co.uk

During work with a bottling company and a supplier of high-quality printed cartons, the extent of potential cost reductions became clearer the wider the investigation spread. Initially the buyer was trying to reduce its costs of buying the cartons by around 5 per cent per year over a three-year period. This was worth around £242,000 per year. However, the opportunities for real cost reduction in product design over the same period were £1 million, in ordering procedures they were £135,000, in production they were worth £153,000, and in planning they were worth £14,000. Many of these potential savings required action across many functions in both companies and were not as easy to obtain as a demand for a price reduction, but the impact on the business was clearly much bigger.

Source: www.scmg.co.uk.

The bottling and packaging example shows that the impact of a decision does not fall in only one organisation. There needs to be a mechanism by which all the interested parties come together to decide a course of action that will be an effective solution for all.

This form of system awareness is important when possible cost reductions in the supply system are considered. Each organisation or unit has an interest in supporting both the immediate and the final customer. Each also has to look good in terms of its own current performance. The difficulty is that sometimes the best supply chain solution means that one part operates less efficiently (from a local perspective) to improve overall chain performance.

---

key ideas — Conflicting performance targets

The classic description of the problem of each part trying to maximise its own performance relates to the ideal specifications for the production area and the sales area. The manufacturing stereotype is a preference for long runs of a standard product. The sales stereotype is a preference for providing unique products that meet particular customer requirements. There has to be a balance. It is possible for an organisation to become bankrupt satisfying customer requirements that it is not designed to satisfy, so the maxim cannot be 'customer satisfaction at all costs' since some costs are unacceptable.

Thus cost reduction is a continuing necessity but needs to be done with care. Suppliers can reduce some costs without any impact on the customer simply by doing things more smartly. One waste worth challenging is the amount of material held in the various categories of stock. By re-examining where to hold protection stocks and eliminating all others, a supplier can make large savings at no risk to customer service.

Case questions 19.4

Examine the points in the Benetton supply chain where inventory is stored and identify why it is likely to be held there.

The major leverage point for cost reduction is, however, at the initial design stage. Staff make decisions here that incur costs later. By thinking through both quality and operational logistics issues at this stage, people can avoid creating unnecessary costs at the source.

19.5 The business process view

The concept of flow as horizontal through the organisation is opposed to the vertical orientation of traditional organisational principles based around functions. This is in accord with a greater focus on customers and their satisfaction. The functional structure reflects the same thought patterns that lead to the functional layout discussed earlier. Both optimise internally regardless of the effect on the customer.

To escape from this mindset, organisations are trying to restructure their activities around basic business processes that all organisations will use to meet their customers' requirements. By defining these in generic terms they hope to create new insights. The essence of flow also means removing the waste from the interfaces between the traditional functions. Since organisations are unique there are no universal definitions of these core processes. They will vary between organisations, but it is possible to identify some relatively common ones.

Direct Line Insurance   www.directline.com

Re-engineering business processes has been critical for this company, which redefined the insurance business in the United Kingdom. Most other providers were then forced to copy this model just to remain in the same marketplace.

Each of Direct Line's products is designed with the same basic philosophy: to offer consumers *clear*, *straightforward*, *good value* alternatives to products that are sold through traditional distribution channels. This is especially so where those channels involve a 'middleman' that can be cut out to reduce costs.

As the company conducts the vast majority of its business using the telephone, customer service is at the core of the Direct Line proposition. It introduced new levels of service to the financial services sector, putting customer needs and considerations first in everything that it does.

To ensure that standards are maintained the company provides all staff with extensive customer care training and re-engineers sales processes to cut out complicated forms and jargon. In one of its first revolutionary moves Direct Line removed the need for 'cover notes' by arranging for all documents such as policy and insurance certificates to be laser printed immediately and forwarded by first-class post to customers – usually in time for the following day.

Innovative technology helps Direct Line keep down costs that, in turn, helps to reduce premiums. For example, most Direct Line products are paid for using credit cards or direct debits so that all payments are processed electronically. This keeps staffing levels and overheads to a minimum. Automated call handling systems also ensure that the company's 15 million customer calls each year are quickly and effortlessly rerouted between Direct Line's six call centres to ensure the minimum wait for an available operator.

Of course, the option to provide such call centre activity from outsourced and off-shored providers in, for example, India is one that many such companies are now considering.

Source: Company website and other published sources.

Create and capture customers' intent to buy the product or service

This process recognises the two sources of innovation – technology push and market pull – and uses either or both to define new product or service packages to bring to the customer market. Defined as a business process, this will cover activities often associated in the past with marketing, product design, prototype production, trial marketing, and product advertising and launch. The creative process is intended to bring together all of the interests associated with a forward look at customers. The aim is to fully define their requirements. In the case of truly innovative ideas the intention is to specify the product or service in a way that determines what the operations systems have to do to support these new market requirements.

Customer order fulfilment

Having created the intention to buy, this process does everything necessary to deliver the product or service to the customer. It aims to do this in such a way that the transaction satisfies both the customer and the supply system.

The process starts with capturing a customer order. From here it will cover all of the planning stages that allocate resources to produce and deliver the order. It also recognises the need to source resources from other suppliers in the chain. Thus the traditional functions of sales processing and forecasting, production planning and control, manufacture or service provision and resource procurement (buying) can all be included. So too can those concerned with the physical movement of materials and ensuring people are available to do the work. The flows in this process are clearly two-way: from customers to supply system about demand, and from supply system to customers with the order. The flow returns again with money to pay for the exchange. There are many interfaces between activities in this business process, often acting in very short timescales, and clearly this is one of the major (direct) value-adding sets of activities in the organisation.

management in practice   e-Government

In a different context of delivering services rather than products, the EU Commission is coordinating member states as they move towards e-government which is believed to be capable of delivering 'better, more efficient public services and improve the relationship between citizens and their governments. The resulting benefits to the quality of life, industrial competitiveness and society will only be realised, however, if administrations change the way they operate'. Expected benefits include: 'cost for both businesses and governments can be reduced, cutting the tax burden and boosting competitiveness; the public sector can be made more open and transparent, delivering governments which are more comprehensible and accountable to citizens, improving civic involvement in policy making and reinforcing democracy at every level across Europe; administrations can be made more user-centred and inclusive, providing 24/7 personalised services to everyone, no matter their circumstances or special needs'.

Source: http://europa.eu.int/information_society and other published sources.

Depending on the nature of the demand (a forecast or a firm customer order) the planning process can be aimed either at building inventory or at meeting the customer order. Speed is not always necessary, although delivery reliability is. In building for inventory, management strikes a balance between the costs of making a large and economical batch now and the costs of holding stocks of finished goods. If it produces too much for immediate requirements it has to store and care for the product until it is sold. The economic order quantity can be calculated by making assumptions about actual cost patterns. Management can then establish and manage stockholding policies.

Computerised planning approaches are appropriate when demand is known or can be calculated. Every order for a family car will generate an order for five wheels. Planners then add to this how long they believe it will take to produce or purchase the wheels. They can then decide when they need to place an order for the earlier parts of the supply system.

The just-in-time approach omits the computer calculations. It replaces them with a simple 'pull' signal sent when a customer removes some material from the end of the previous stage of the supply chain. This action sends a replenishment signal (a *kanban*) upstream telling the supplier to produce replacement parts. The signal can then ripple its way upstream and, ideally, the supply chain then operates quickly and with a much reduced level of inventory compared with both of the other ways described.

Pure service operations concentrate on scheduling service staff to ensure that they are available to deal with the customers as they arrive.

Cash handling and reporting

Transactions to transfer the ownership of goods or to pay for services must be properly accounted for. It is also necessary to create an audit trail to establish that the activities have been done legally. This process also provides the funds with which the organisation pays its own bills. More businesses fail through mismanaging their cash flow than fail for lack of customers. This is another reason to look for speed through the business processes in order to convert customer interest into cash.

Cash handling process in supermarkets

Supermarkets have a very profitable cash handling process. They receive cash or credit transfers almost instantaneously but pay their suppliers as long as 30 days from the date of the invoice. Meanwhile they can earn interest on both sets of money in the short-term financial marketplace. It is perhaps not surprising that the larger retail chains are providing their own banking opportunities for their customers. In some ways they have been behaving as banks for years. At the same time they have been highly efficient at converting shelf space to sales with minimum in-store inventory. Remember the Toyota story and their production system which was inspired by the supermarkets.

New ways of working eliminate many paper-based and costly transaction-processing activities. They use simplified techniques and place greater responsibility on the suppliers to do what they have contracted to do without the customer checking. In the car wheel example, all cars leaving the assembler's premises must have five wheels. Rather than arrange a transaction for each delivery of wheels, common practice now is to record the number of cars leaving the system (which is done anyway). The system multiplies that number by five and regularly pays the supplier for that number of wheels. As an alternative, for low-value items all purchasers can be issued with the equivalent of a plastic bank card so that orders can be sent in, deliveries made and a fully detailed statement sent to the purchasing organisation at the end of the month for one payment.

These are well-established examples of what has come to be called electronic or e-commerce. The speed of web-based electronic communications allows for more efficient markets to be established. Whole industries are trying to move in this direction and companies are creating business opportunities where previously none were possible – look, for example, at the success of eBay.com.

Maintaining service

In many product areas management has come to realise that it is much cheaper to retain a customer than to find a new one (a common estimate of the ratio is 1:10). This has caused them to re-examine the nature of the customer relationship and to support valued customers well beyond any contractual or warranty requirement. In service areas the degree of direct involvement with the client or customer changes the nature of the considerations again. The arguments about customer retention are even more important in this environment and often there will be a need to keep in regular contact (special newsletters, magazines, offers) to try to keep the relationship going.

In all cases current customers have great value in evaluating new product or service ideas at the trial market stage. They also help secure new customers through recommendations and contact names. This will be the case particularly where the price for a single transaction is not the most important factor in the buying decision.

19.6 Interfaces with other functions – partnering in the supply chain

In traditionally structured organisations the operations function has many interfaces as it contributes to nearly all crucial decisions relating to business performance. In some of these the operations function will be in a distinctly subordinate position, in others more to the fore. The aim should be to meet business requirements by satisfying the customer at the end of the chain. To do this all parts of the organisation need to understand each other's strengths and weaknesses. They then need to build a system that recognises the first and improves on the second. The new way of looking at the needs of the business in terms of the business processes recognises explicitly the need to manage across boundaries. Most commonly, change teams focus on processes that cross department functions. Some also review processes that cross the boundaries between organisations into (upstream) suppliers or (downstream) customers.

The argument here is that certain parts of the chain are experts at their portion of the total task. Those at other stages should allow them to perform those tasks without interference from customers telling them what to do. Those in the chain need to manage the relationships so that the chain as a whole meets the needs of the final customer. So the tasks are now about influence, information and coordination between independent but cooperating organisations. This is a different form of management from that which exercises command and control within an isolated business. It is also about encouraging, recognising and implementing innovation from all in the chain to the chain's competitive advantage and the ultimate customers' delight.

Partnering describes a business relationship based on taking a long-term view that the partners wish to work together to enhance customers' satisfaction.

When separate organisations use this approach they often refer to it as **partnering** (Macbeth and Ferguson, 1994). The logic applies to all management activities that cross boundaries, not only those with different ownership. The essence is to recognise complementary capabilities, look for ways to coordinate informational and logistical flows, and invest for the long term in a jointly planned way.

Principles of cooperative supply chain management

key ideas

- **Philosophy**: sharing information to reduce waste, increase value added and generate joint competitiveness
- **Leadership**: led by the experts wherever they are
- **Measurement**: reducing real costs demonstrated by measurement of both parties' behaviour
- **Scope**: cascaded from each buyer–supplier link to the extended network of interacting organisations
- **Methods**: joint benchmarking and joint improvement teams

---

Case questions 19.5

- What would a partnering approach imply for Benetton's management?
- What benefits might the company obtain from such a practice?
- What benefits might its suppliers and shop owners obtain?
- What could be the obstacles?

This recognises that internal competition is no longer the only way to demonstrate value for money. Rather it is about demonstrating that by removing the wastes from the chain the whole chain becomes more competitive than other chains. Working together increases the chances of success and of obtaining the rewards of success. It is not a comfortable or easy option since the pressures to stay expert in each area are intense. The need to innovate constantly to reduce waste further and to enhance the offer to the final consumers is unrelenting. In addition, the need to fully support the partner organisation creates its own dynamic pressure.

In order to make this a reality partners must be chosen carefully. The parties then need to create joint teams to address, in a planned manner, areas where improvements can be made that benefit both sides. They also need to measure and reward joint performance in new and creative ways (Supply Chain Management Group, 1995, and see www.scmg.co.uk). In all of this they aim to apply the essential operations management practices that have been described across all aspects of the joint organisations. Companies have to be best in class in three areas: inside each of the partner organisations and in the areas of explicitly joint responsibility.

The future orientation of the partnering process means that each has a responsibility to scan its field of expertise and interest. The customer organisation has to keep sight of developments in its own marketplace. It has to get close to its customers and watch its competitors' movements. It must also watch for new entrants with developments that threaten the whole chain. The supplier should scan its environment in a similar way. In particular, it should look for new technologies that might improve service to the immediate and ultimate customer. In this view organisations, departments and individual people are both customers of and suppliers to others. While the roles may take a different importance at different times, the responsibility to manage proactively in both directions is not diminished.

19.7 Strategic position of operations

Section 19.5 has demonstrated a new realisation of the importance of the operations function in an integrated approach to managing the supply system in support of the customer. The key questions relate to the capabilities that the system needs currently and which should be developed for future requirements. A related issue is the selection of those complementary suppliers who can provide the other aspects of the product or service, and finally the choice of market segments in which to compete. This latter decision might be still more influenced by factors associated with financial returns and market positioning. The broad nature of the operations activity means that making these decisions without reference to the ability of the system to respond and change will in turn make it difficult to achieve the objectives.

Customer demands in the markets usually change faster than production systems. These latter are made up of investments in hardware, software and people – not all of which can be changed rapidly. There needs to be an iterative process involving all interested parties deciding what the company must do well to succeed in the market. The concepts of order winners and order qualifiers can help to frame the discussion and bridge the language gap between the marketing and the operations staff (Hill, 2004).

An **order winner** is some feature or combination of features of the product and service that positively differentiates it from those of competitors and makes customers want to buy it in preference to those others. Ideally it is something that is unique which competitors cannot replicate. An **order qualifier** is the ticket to the game. It is a feature that is

> An **order winner** is some feature of the product that so positively differentiates it that customers want to buy it in preference to competing products.

> An **order qualifier** is a necessary but not sufficient requirement to be considered by a customer.

645

a necessary but not a sufficient requirement for purchase. Customers will not consider you without it. Qualifiers get the seller into the race but do not guarantee that it will win the prize. Some qualifiers are so critical that any deviation from the expected standard means instant disqualification. Customers will ignore otherwise attractive features if the seller does not meet this basic requirement.

These concepts are useful in opening up the debate between marketing and operations personnel since they can be defined in terms that both can understand. The operations staff can convert them into system specifications for process design once the parties agree them. It is also possible to rein in the wilder flights of fancy from marketers who see a new opportunity that the operations system has no prospect of satisfying in a sensible time. It is better to recognise this and to modify the target market than to risk everything to make a total change of operating system.

Of course, such order winners and qualifiers are dynamic. They change as customers become more demanding and as competitors become more proficient.

Japanese colour television production

management in practice

When the Japanese producers of colour televisions first entered the European market they created the order winner of quality and produced at such an improved level that they captured a large market share. The European producers took up this competitive challenge and attempted to match the quality standards. Quality then became a qualifier and the Japanese moved the order winner to price. In doing so they further improved their competitive position. The Europeans had failed to understand and implement cost-efficient ways of ensuring quality, so they were unable to compete as they were spending more than the Japanese merely to reach the qualifying levels of quality. They were certainly not able to reduce their production costs enough to compete on price as well.

Source: Various industry reports.

Thus the discussion of order winners and qualifiers needs to be a regular part of the chain process. Often it is a service-related feature that distinguishes qualified products. It is these aspects that are most likely to occur at the boundaries between traditional organisations. An integrated view of the whole supply chain helps management to improve them.

Activity 19.7 Defining order winners and qualifiers

- Define the order winners and qualifiers for the following: (a) a music, food and drink club catering for students; (b) a personal computer.
- Highlight those features most likely to change and comment on the implications for the operations system design needed to support them.
- How might new communication technologies (for example, the Internet) affect the supply chain for food shopping?

Summary

1 Understand how the operations function can support performance in manufacturing and service organisations:

- By improving the capabilities of the organisation to achieve high standards of innovation, quality, delivery, cost and flow.
- Operations developed in factories but now applies to service areas as well as products. It needs to be seen as part of an integrated approach to business connected with other functions internally and externally to customers and suppliers.

2 Describe five types of transformation and their physical layout:

- Transformation types are:
  - Physical (production)
  - Locational (transportation)
  - Attitudinal (education, entertainment)
  - Physiological (healthcare, fitness)
  - Presentational (fashion).
- Layout options are:
  - Line
  - Cell
  - Functional
  - Concentric.

3 Compare the process approach to operations with the functional approach:

- The functional approach organises activities 'vertically' within distinct functional specialisations, between which communication can be difficult. An alternative is to focus on horizontal flows of business processes which are directed at meeting customer needs. Such processes vary between businesses, but commonly important ones are those aimed at:
  - creating and capturing customers' interest and purchase decisions
  - fulfilling customer orders
  - handling and reporting cash
  - maintaining service.

4 Recognise the need to manage operations across an extended supply chain:

- Each stage in a supply chain has particular expertise, and the relations across the chain should be managed to maximise the scope for each player to do what they do best – recognising complementary capabilities. Further benefits come if the players in the chain coordinate their activities and invest for the long term in a jointly planned way.

5 Explain how the idea of 'order winners' and 'order qualifiers' links operations to the strategic process of meeting customer needs profitably:

- While order qualifiers are an essential ticket to offer a product or service, order winners are those combinations of features that positively discriminate a company from its competitors. This concept is familiar to both marketing and operations: operations' contribution is through being able to specify the implications for process design of particular order winners.

Review questions

1 Describe systems concepts as they apply to an operating system.

2 What are the major categories of operations system and their associated physical layout types?

3 Why is control over quality at source so important?

4 Why is delivery reliability more important than delivery speed?

5 Describe and discuss the importance of the demand/supply balance.

6 In what ways is the business processes approach different from traditional approaches?

7 List and discuss the main features of a partnering approach to business relationships. (See **www.scmg.co.uk** or **www.pslcbi.com** for ideas.)

8 Discuss the concepts of order winners and order qualifiers.

Concluding critical reflection

Think about the ways in which your company, or one with which you are familiar, deals with operational issues – such as innovation, quality or cost. Then make notes on these questions:

- What examples of the issues discussed in this chapter struck you as being relevant to practice in your company?

- To what extent do you experience external pressures from customers for rapid and sustained operating improvements? Which of the areas to which operations can make a contribution (innovation, flow, etc.) are most relevant to your situation? To what extent does your organisation seek to create long-term relations with adjacent players in the supply chain?

- How much attention is paid to identifying order qualifiers and order winners, and to ensuring that internal processes are redesigned to support order-winning features of your services or products? How good is the relationship between operations and marketing?

- What factors such as the history or current context of the company appear to influence the way the company handles operations issues, and the relation between operations and other functions? Does the current approach appear to be right for the company in its context – or would a different view of the context lead to a more effective approach?

- Have people suggested a greater or more prominent role for operations, based on evidence about other companies? If you could find such evidence, how may it affect company practice?

Further reading

Bicheno, J. (1998), *The Quality 60: A guide for service and manufacturing*, Picsie Books, Buckingham.

A simply presented collection of many of the quality approaches you are likely to need.

Brown, S. (1996), *Strategic Manufacturing for Competitive Advantage*, Prentice Hall International, Hemel Hempstead.

Provides much detail about operations management in a product environment and offers extra material about many of the concepts covered in this chapter.

Womack, J.P. and Jones, D. (1996), *Lean Thinking*, Simon and Schuster, New York.

Develops the theme established in *The Machine that Changed the World* by Womack *et al.* (1990), which first comprehensively described the Toyota production system as clearly superior to other car assemblers' systems by means of a benchmarking study. It sets JIT, TQM and supply chain thinking in an integrated framework. The latest book uses a number of case examples.

Heller, R. (2001), 'Inside Zara', *Forbes Global*, 28 May, pp. 24–25, 28–29.

Comments on the development of this fashion brand and the company founder behind it.

Kay, J. (1993), *Foundations of Corporate Success*, Oxford University Press, Oxford.

A highly rated text on strategy that, interestingly, also emphasises a number of key capabilities that are related to operations and the supply chain view as described here.

Krajewski, L.J. and Ritzman, L.P. (2004), *Operations Management: Strategy and analysis* (7th edn), Pearson Education, London.

This is a US textbook that provides a wealth of extra materials including useful website exercises.

Slack, N. and Lewis, M. (2002), *Operations Strategy*, Financial Times/Prentice Hall, Harlow.

This UK book has a wealth of good material about most of the issues covered in this chapter.

http://bized.ac.uk/virtual/cb/

This is an excellent interactive learning site based on the successful real company which built the round-the-world balloon Brietling Orbiter 3 which was the first to circumnavigate the globe.

Weblinks

These are some of the websites that have appeared in the chapter:

www.benetton.com

www.inditex.com

www.happycomputers.co.uk

www.dell.com

www.directline.co.uk

- Visit two of the websites in the list (or any other company that interests you) and navigate to the pages dealing with the products and services they offer. This is usually the first one you see, but in some it may be further back.

- What messages do they give about the nature of the goods and services they offer? What challenges are they likely to raise for operations in terms of their emphasis on, for example, innovation, quality, delivery or cost? What implications might that have for people working in the company?

- See if you can find any information on the site about the operating systems, or how they link with their suppliers.

- Gather information from the media websites (such as **www.FT.com**) which relate to the companies you have chosen. What stories can you find that indicate something about the performance of the companies you have chosen?

> Annotated weblinks, multiple choice questions and other useful resources can be found on **www.pearsoned.co.uk/boddy**

Chapter 20

Managing information systems

Aim

To examine why managers need information and how they can use technology to make the most of this resource.

Objectives

By the end of your work on this chapter you should be able to outline the concepts below in your own terms and:

1 Explain how information systems are critical to management performance

2 Explain the difference between data, information and knowledge

3 Explain the technical and social elements of computer-based information systems, and the management questions they raise

4 Distinguish information systems in terms of their type, scope and functions

5 Understand how information systems affect the tasks and roles of management

6 Explain how the Internet enables radical changes in organisations and their management.

Key terms

This chapter introduces the following ideas:

data
information
knowledge
information system
information systems management
databases
Internet
intranet
extranet
organisational systems
inter-organisational systems
knowledge system

Each is a term defined within the text, as well as in the glossary at the end of the book.

The Student Loan Company

The Student Loan Company (SLC) is a non-profit-making company which is owned by the UK government and responsible to the Department for Education and Skills (DfES) and the Scottish Executive. It was established in 1989 to administer loans which eligible undergraduate students in UK higher education receive to help meet their living costs during their period of study. In 2004 it delivered services to some 3.0 million customers, including providing 800,000 loans to current students with an average value of over £3000. It pays the loan to a student, maintains their accounts, and liaises with the Inland Revenue on the collection of repayments after the student has finished the course. The amount collected depends on the former student's income: 9 per cent of any income over £10,000 is collected directly by the employer and remitted to the Inland Revenue.

Borrowers repaying under an earlier loans scheme make repayments directly to SLC. Administering these accounts forms a large part of the company's business, and includes pursuing debts from those who have not met their obligations. The company provides several other services – such as paying the public contribution towards tuition fees to universities and colleges throughout the UK.

The company structure is based on four functional units, all of which report directly to the Chief Executive:

- *Finance and Administration*: dealing with financial services, corporate services, assurance services and human resource management.
- *Operations*: administering the various products, including the loan schemes, and recovering debts. This includes providing direct customer services through the call centre, and the documentation service departments such as correspondence, printing and mailing. It also handles relations with over 180 local Award Authorities throughout the United Kingdom and works closely with over 600 Higher Education institutions. Among other duties the HEIs supply details of all eligible undergraduate courses to a course database which is regularly updated and distributed to the Award Authorities.
- *Information and Communications Technology*: ensures that the information systems on which SLC depends function efficiently, and develops new systems for 'Front Office' and 'Back Office' applications.
- *Change Programmes*: created in 2003, and responsible for managing major change and development programmes.

Once SLC has paid a loan, the company maintains the student's account, including updating the customer's personal information such as address and bank details. A collection payments system manages customer contacts as payments become due, notifying the Inland Revenue when the borrower is due to start repayments and also giving daily management information on customers' repayment details. The system also includes an automated response facility which allows borrowers to access their account information directly through their telephone keypads.

Ariel Skelley/Corbis

Desktop applications include the Windows suite of office products, and Lotus Notes is used for email, running on a series of servers. The company has developed an intranet for internal use, and has deployed web technologies for the future development of the student financial support administration systems.

Source: Based on information provided by the company and the company website.

Case questions

- What are the inputs and the outputs of the SLC information systems?
- What are the objectives of the main loan administration system?
- How have developments in information systems affected the service SLC provides to customers?

20.1 Introduction

Managers at SLC run an organisation which depends on information – it relies on gathering, processing and disseminating information from and to a range of people and organisations. All have different requirements and work in different ways, yet SLC must develop information systems which integrate these different needs so that students receive their loans at the right time, and that eventually they repay the debt. The computer-based information systems (IS) have developed from standalone systems within SLC to ones that are linked to computer systems in other organisations such as the Award Authorities. Customers can now access their accounts directly from a telephone keypad, and web technologies will allow further enhancements to the SLC service.

This pattern of relatively simple systems evolving into more complex ones, with wide management implications, is common. Banks such as ABN AMRO and Barclays were early users of computer-based information systems, as they offered a more efficient way of handling huge volumes of routine transactions. They still perform that function – but have also enabled the banks to offer many new services through alternative distribution channels, such as online banking or through joint ventures with retailers such as Tesco. More radical applications of the available technology have come from completely new dot.com companies such as ebay.com or lastminute.com, whose managers have built completely new businesses around the technology of modern information systems.

People managing activities of all kinds depend on information. As you manage your work on an assignment you need information – such as what your teacher requires, the due date, advice from previous assignments and which theories and evidence you should use. People at all levels of an organisation need to add value to the resources they use, and to do that they need information – about inputs, the transformation process and the outputs. Information about inputs could include the cost and availability of materials, staff and equipment; information to help manage the transformation process could include delivery schedules, capacity utilisation, efficiency, quality and costs; output information could include prices, market share and customer satisfaction. The IS gathers data about inputs, transformation processes and outputs, and feeds the resulting information to those working at different levels of the organisation, to help them add value. Figure 20.1 shows how information systems support these fundamental management processes.

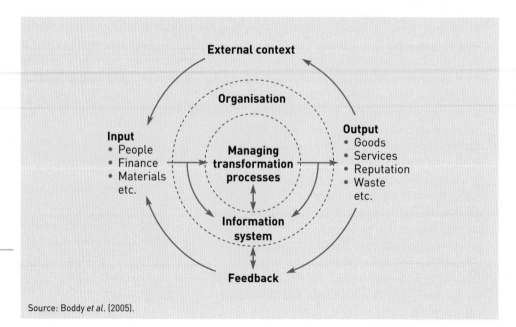

Figure 20.1

The role of information systems in organisations

Source: Boddy *et al.* (2005).

Computer-based information systems make internal processes more efficient and also create electronic links with suppliers, customers and business partners. Technological developments change the way people gain access to information, and to other people and services. Customers can compare prices more readily, professional staff can exchange ideas and proposals with others around the world almost instantaneously, and planners can collect and analyse sales data in infinite detail. These and countless other applications of IS can affect the strategy and competitiveness of an organisation. The challenge managers face is to ensure that their organisation uses, rather than squanders, the potential of such systems. This responsibility has become more widespread as IS has come to be used not just in background activities (like accounting and stock control) but also in foreground activities (like an online banking website) which directly affect the customers. So while the design of information systems depends on the skills of IS experts, managers are responsible for ensuring that IS staff develop systems that suit the business.

Jean-Pierre Corniou – Renault's CIO www.renault.com

Frankly my job (as Chief Information Officer) consists of being a bilingual guy: I speak both the language of business and the language of technology. Renault, like other companies, started investing in information technology (IT) in the middle 1960s. It was pioneering work – there were just a few people in IT, working on large systems of great complexity. People inside still have that pioneering attitude, of an era when IT was seen as secret, and complex . . . but we need to open up, to build transparency, to build the confidence and trust of all stakeholders in the company.

We have invested a lot of money in [advanced applications] and websites, and when we analysed the level of utilization of these products and tools, we were very surprised to see how much money had been spent on products that people were not using.

I spend a lot of time in plants, in discussions with foremen in the field, trying to understand how they use technology to increase their efficiency. I spend lots of time in commercial departments too, to understand the key business processes. Bringing IT to the business community means the CIO has to be embedded in the day to day life of the organization, and of course to have a seat on the board. I consider myself more a business guy than an IT guy.

FT

Source: *Financial Times*, 17 September 2003.

The chapter begins by outlining how managers depend on information and knowledge, and the different types of information systems they use. It then describes the technical elements of computer-based systems, showing in particular the management issues which arise in relation to each element. The evolution of such systems from background to foreground applications is illustrated, leading to the critically important organisational aspects of computer systems. Final sections trace their effects on the tasks and processes of managing.

Activity 20.1 Applying the open systems model

Apply the open systems model in Figure 20.1 to an organisation that you know.
● What are the inputs and outputs?
● Describe the transformation process.
● List examples of information systems that provide information about inputs, outputs and transformations.

20.2 Managing depends on information and knowledge

Data, information and knowledge

The terms 'data', 'information' and 'knowledge' are sometimes confused with each other, so it is worth being clear about their meaning.

Data are raw, unanalysed facts, figures and events.

- **Data** refers to recorded descriptions of things, events, activities and transactions – their size, colour, cost, weight, date and so on. It may be a number, a piece of text, a drawing or photograph, or a sound. In itself it may or may not convey information to a person.

Information comes from data that has been processed so that it has meaning for the person receiving it.

- **Information** is a subset of data that means something to the person receiving it, which they judge to be useful, significant, urgent and so on. It comes from data that has been processed (by people or with the aid of technology) so that it has meaning and value for the recipient – by linking it to other pieces of data to show a comparison, a sequence of events, or a trend. The information so provided is still subjective since what one person sees as valuable, another may see as insignificant data. They may interpret it in different ways, depending on their background and interests.

Knowledge builds on information and embodies a person's prior understanding, experience and learning.

- 'Knowledge builds on information that is extracted from data' (Boisot, 1998, p. 12). While data is a property of things (size, price, etc.) knowledge is a property of people, which predisposes them to act in a particular way. Knowledge embodies prior understanding, experience and learning, and is either confirmed or modified as people receive new information.

The significance of the distinction is that people use knowledge to economise on the use of resources. Accurate knowledge enables them to react more intelligently to information and data than those without relevant experience and learning. Someone with good knowledge of a market will use it to interpret information about current sales. They will be able to identify significant patterns or trends, and so attach a different meaning to the information than someone without that knowledge. They can act in ways that add more value to the resources they use.

key ideas   Quality of information

The quality of information depends on four criteria:

1 **Reliability** (accuracy) People expect information to reflect accurately the situation it describes – that a sales report is an accurate account of sales made, that the reported costs of an activity represent the reality.

2 **Timeliness** Information is only useful if it is available in time. A manager who needs to keep expenditure within a budget requires cost information frequently enough to be able to act on any unfavourable trends. If the information arrives in three months it will be too late to act on it.

3 **Quantity** Most managers suffer information overload, in the sense that they are not able to use and digest all the information they receive – there is simply too much. This suggests that those designing a system need a close understanding of how much information, and in what detail, the user requires to perform well.

4 **Relevance** This depends on a person's tasks and responsibilities. A manager with daily responsibility for production wants a daily report about output, cost, scrap, etc. of each machine. A senior manager wants more aggregated data such as overall production costs, and the balance between capacity and likely future demand.

The data that is the basis of this system is of many kinds and from many sources. It could be the manager's informal system (such as a conversation with a colleague) or a formal company system that collects data regularly. In itself, data is of little value – it needs to be converted into information or knowledge before people can use it to add value. Information systems perform this function – Figure 20.2 shows the relation between data, information, knowledge and information systems.

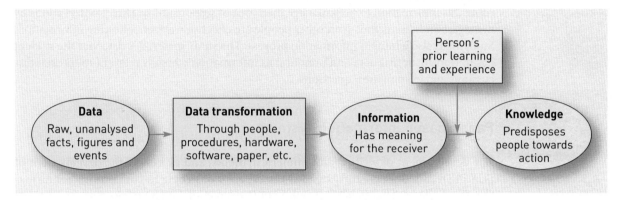

Figure 20.2 The links between data, information and knowledge
Source: Boddy *et al.* (2005).

Activity 20.2   Gathering information

Arrange a short discussion with someone who works in an organisation (or use your experience of being in an organisation).

- Ask them to give examples of some information that is used regularly by
  (a) a senior manager
  (b) a departmental manager
  (c) a professional specialist.
- Ask them how they receive that information, and how it helps them in their work.
- What information do you need regularly from your bank or from your university?
- What information does it provide that is relevant to you?

20.3   Types of information systems

Information systems

An **information system** is a set of people, procedures and technology that collects data which it transforms and disseminates. Human societies have developed successively more powerful ways of communicating with one another over space and time. This has *not* meant that all communication has become electronic. For all the power of computer systems to handle internal and external data, organisations have infinite networks of informal communication. People use these to pass gossip, rumour and useful information between colleagues with often astonishing speed. These informal systems exist in parallel with formal, computer-based information systems.

An **information system** is a set of people, procedures and resources that collects and transforms data into information and disseminates this information.

Human information systems

The earliest humans communicated through sign language, painting and drawing, and speech. These are informal information systems. Everyone uses sense organs to receive impulses from the environment; the brain interprets these impulses that lead to decisions on how to respond. From this perspective, everyone is an information system. For managers, this means observing events in the organisation and in the environment and using this information to help manage their area of responsibility. Direct observations by managers and discussions with other people are effective ways of collecting information. Studying is also a human information process. The study material is data, but the student has to transform that data and present it as information which is relevant to tutorial discussions and examination questions.

Paper-based information systems

The development of writing and numeric symbols, and especially the development of printing technology, greatly extended the capacity of people to communicate information to people in distant places. People could now record data on paper, transform it into information and present it on paper. People still use many paper-based systems as they are cheap to implement and easy to understand. Paper systems have some virtues and the genuinely paperless office is rare. Companies often define their procedures on paper, and staff are confident with information on paper. They can file a hard (paper) copy and use it easily for audit purposes. Staff often use paper systems when traceability is important and responsibility is high. Consider an insurance company in which senior directors must still write and sign cheques of high value. The format of paper information systems is often a piece of A4 paper with printed instructions or boxes to complete. It may be a label attached to a part being routed through a shop floor with instructions on what work to do. A manual, paper-based attendance list kept by a lecturer is another example, as is an address book or diary.

> ### Activity 20.3 Evaluating information systems
>
> Identify two formal but paper-based information systems that you use, or that affect you. What are the advantages and disadvantages of a paper-based system?

Computer-based information systems

Computer-based systems, which transform other symbols into digital form, dramatically extend this process of lowering the cost of processing and disseminating information. Most information systems beyond the smallest now use electronic means to collect and record data and to transform it into information. Electronic devices often collect the initial data, such as the barcodes and scanners that capture product details in shops. Thereafter electronic systems process, manipulate, distribute and record the data. The systems can provide paper output if required at various stages – such as a till receipt for the customer or a sales report for managers. Table 20.1 in Section 20.6 below lists some examples of electronic systems.

Evaluating computer-based systems

List three computer-based information systems you use or that affect you.

- What are the objectives of these systems?
- Could you process that information without using computers?
- What advantages and disadvantages have you experienced with these systems? Are computer-based systems always better?

Figure 20.3 shows the elements of a computer-based information system. It shows that an information system does not consist only of hardware and software, but also includes people and procedures. This system is part of a wider system – the organisational context, which significantly affects the performance of an information system.

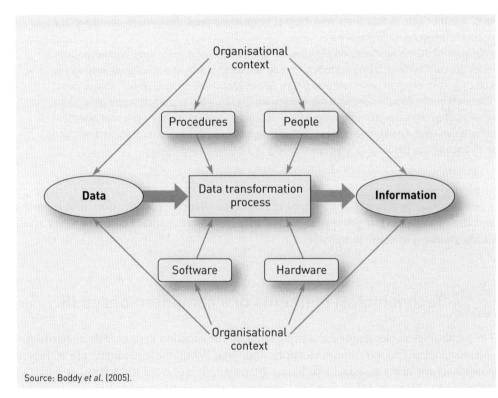

Source: Boddy *et al.* (2005).

Figure 20.3

The elements and context of a computer-based IS

Information systems are about organisations as well as technology   key ideas

An IS project is not a matter of managing a technical project, but an organisational one. Promoters need to be able to change both the technology and the organisation . . They design an IS to meet what they understand to be the requirements of senior managers. They must also take account of the elements in the context. How other people (users, managers, etc.) react to the resulting system will be influenced by *their* view of the system entering the context. Will it increase or decrease their power? Is it consistent with the prevailing culture? Will they be better off in some way? These are ▶

the areas to which promoters and project managers need to give attention. As well as investing in the technology, they need to reconstruct other aspects of the organisational context in which people are working. The outcomes of the project (success, embarrassing failure or something in between) will depend on how they manage these contextual elements.

Source: Boddy *et al.* (2005), pp. 17–18.

A computer-based student record system

This description of part of the information system in a university illustrates each of the elements in Figure 20.3. The system requires people (e.g. administrative staff) to enter data (name and other information about students and their results) following certain procedures. For example, there is a rule that only employees may enter data on student results into the system. The rules do not permit students to do this. Another rule is that a student cannot graduate unless the system confirms that the student has paid their fees and library fines.

   The hardware consists of the computers and peripherals such as printers, monitors and keyboards. This runs the student record system, using software to manipulate the data in a particular way and to print out the results for each student. Another procedure sends results to each student – for whom it is information. The staff in the department and the faculty want to be able to compare the pass rates of all the courses – so the results system then becomes an element of the university's management information. Staff will use their knowledge (based on learning and experience) to interpret trends and evaluate the significance of any patterns.

Information systems management is the planning, acquisition, development and use of these systems.

Information systems management includes the planning, acquisition, development and use of information systems to ensure that information meets certain quality standards, affecting its value to managers.

20.4 Technological elements of a computer-based IS

The technological elements of a computer-based information system include hardware, software, networks, telecommunications and data. While these elements are technical products, each raises management issues. Managers do not need to be familiar with the technical questions, but they do need to be aware of the management ones.

Hardware

Hardware refers to the physical components within a computer system. These consist of:

- *Input devices* (such as keyboard, mouse, joystick, scanner, touch screen, camera, microphone, sensor)
- *Central processing unit* (manipulates data and controls the computer system)
- *Storage devices* (the primary (internal) storage, and secondary storage such as disks)
- *Output devices* (such as screens, printers or mobile phones)
- *Communication devices* (to link the computer with other computers or the Internet).

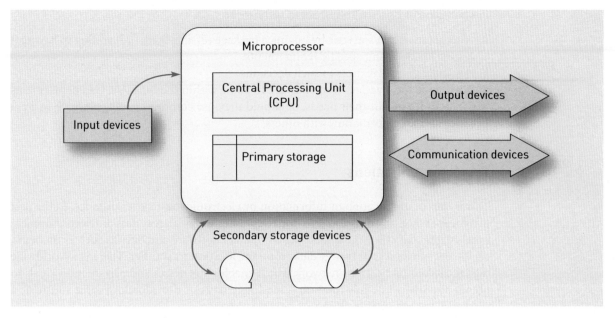

Figure 20.4 Physical elements of a computer system

Figure 20.4 shows the relationship between these hardware elements.

Mainframes are very large computers with massive memory and very rapid processing power, used in large businesses and government. Users work with passive terminals or workstations to enter data and receive information from the mainframe. A mini-computer is a mid-range computer often used in factories and middle-sized companies. Personal computers (PCs) sit on a desktop or are carried around by the user (portable laptops, notebooks and many mobile phones). A network to link PCs enables users to share files, software, printers and other network resources. A network requires specifically designed server computers with large memory and disk storage capacity. Laudon and Laudon (2004) and Turban *et al.* (2001) examine these points in more detail.

Management issues with respect to hardware are:

- Whether to use the latest hardware. It is easy to be attracted by the promotional literature about a new technical development, but much harder to show that the benefits will justify the investment.
- Which applications will best support the current strategy – such as whether to develop a new service such as a customer loyalty programme.
- Whether to provide all mobile staff with personal computers which enable them to remain connected to office and colleagues at all times.
- Whether to invest directly in computer systems, or to buy these services from other companies.

Software

Software is a set of instructions written in a specialised language which controls the operation of the computer. *System software* is a set of programs that manage the resources of the computer, such as the central processor, communication links and peripheral devices. Windows, Unix and Linux are examples of system software. *Application software* enables users to apply the computer to specific tasks, such as email, word-processing or stock control.

Management issues with respect to software are:

- Whether to obtain software by buying a package off-the-shelf, or investing in having it custom-made to suit specific requirements.
- How fully to involve users in such decisions.
- How much local variation of software to allow within the business. Can departments use software to suit their needs, or should they use common packages which make it easier to share information with others?

Telecommunications

This is the communication of information by electronic means over distance. In the past this meant voice transmission over the telephone. Today a great deal of telecommunication is digital data transmission, using computers, software and devices such as modems, cables and satellites to transmit data from one location to another. There is a worldwide digital telecommunications network which enables businesses and private individuals to obtain and distribute information – sending emails or downloading some music or a video clip to their mobile phone.

---

key ideas **The death of distance**

In time . . . it will be no more expensive to telephone someone on the other side of the world than to talk to someone in the house across the street . . . The death of distance as a determinant of the cost of communicating will probably be the single most important factor shaping society in the first half of the next century. Technological change has the power to revolutionize the way people live, and this one will be no exception. It will alter, in ways that are only dimly imaginable, decisions about where people work and what kind of work they do, concepts of national borders and sovereignty, and patterns of international trade. Its effects may well be as pervasive as those of electricity, which led in time to the creation of the skyscraper cities of Manhattan and Hong Kong, and transformed labor productivity in the home.

Source: Cairncross (2001), p. 1.

A telecommunication system is a set of compatible hardware and software (computers, input/output devices, communication channels and communications software) which makes it possible to send and receive information. Communication networks are a linked group of computers. They can be local area networks (LANs), usually limited to a single building, or wide area networks (WANs) which cover greater distances.

Management issues with respect to telecommunications are:

- How they can use the falling costs and increasing speed of telecommunications to expand the business, or to support the existing business more effectively.
- While it is technically possible to link many business units together, is it managerially wise to do so?
- Whether the company will face competition from unexpected quarters, as distance provides less protection.

Data

Technology makes it possible for people in organisations to use data much more effectively than when they could only analyse it with manual, paper-based systems. Many now put great effort into capturing data that is generated with each transaction, and making portions of that data available to people who can use it in their work. They do so by creating **databases** – collections of data organised to service many applications at the same time, using the same integrated set of data. Distributed databases are stored and updated in more than one location, yet the data remains consistent. When a database is designed around major business subjects such as customers, vendors or activities, it may be called a 'data warehouse'. Using such data to discover trends, patterns or behaviours is called 'data mining'.

A **database** consists of items of data stored in a way that enables them to be organised and retrieved in many ways.

Customer relationship management systems

management in practice

CRM systems collect and integrate information about customers – such as their buying patterns, personal characteristics, income bracket, demographics and lifestyle (Peppard, 2000). Companies use such data to strengthen the ties with their more profitable customers and to attract other customers by special offers or promotions carefully targeted to suit their individual circumstances. For example, when a customer calls their insurer to ask about their car insurance, the agent gets an immediate overview on the computer of all the policies that customer has. The system also suggests some questions. So when the agent has answered the car insurance question they can then say, 'You also have a fire insurance policy – do you think it still provides sufficient cover for you?'

Management issues with respect to database technologies are:

- Whether to develop a fully integrated customer database to enable more effective marketing.
- How to balance the advantages of this with possible ethical issues of privacy and data protection.

20.5 The evolution of information systems

From background to foreground

Between 1965 and 1975 organisations concentrated on automating those administrative functions where they could make large efficiency gains – often referred to as back-office or background functions. Typical targets were those that processed many routine transactions, such as payrolls, inventory and financial transactions. Department managers often delegated responsibility for information management to their IS department. These became very skilled at running large, routine and usually centralised systems. The IS function also became influential, and line managers were rarely involved in discussions on IS strategy and development. The technologies had little effect on smaller organisations. The objective of most applications was to process routine transactions more efficiently.

In the following decade automated systems spread widely. Technical developments made smaller systems possible and more attractive to managers in other parts of the organisation such as planning, manufacturing and distribution. More departments discovered the possibilities of computer-based information systems and their managers became familiar with issues of budgeting for hardware, requesting support, defining requirements and setting priorities – alongside established IS departments. Suppliers developed systems that were suitable for smaller organisations.

Since the mid-1980s the information systems environment has changed significantly. Systems that support the background functions of finance, manufacture and distribution continue to develop and employ more modern technology. In addition, technical developments have brought IS to the foreground of the organisations, changing the way the company deals with customers, by offering new channels of communication or even of delivering services. Information systems often support managers and professional staff directly through decision-support systems or video-conferencing. People throughout an organisation, and often those beyond it, depend on the quality of the computer-based information systems.

Examples of such new developments are:

- The emergence of fast, relatively cheap and portable computer power
- The ability to link these into networks (local and in a wider environment)
- The use of the Internet to link computer systems with those in other organisations
- Using information technologies for communication – such as email and video-conferencing
- Creating integrated databases that staff can use in different applications throughout the organisation, for example in customer relationship management (CRM).

Convergence of voice, vision and data

The most dramatic changes in the management of data, information and knowledge are coming from the rapid convergence of three technologies that developed independently of each other, which are transforming the cost of transporting information and knowledge. Three core technologies in the current revolution have long histories – 'the telephone was invented in 1876, the first television transmission occurred in 1926, and the electronic computer goes back to 1946, if not earlier. For much of that time the pace of change was slow, but began to gather pace in the late 1980s' (Cairncross, 2001, p. 27). Major developments include the following:

- *The telephone.* The ability to send signals along glass fibre-optic cables has increased capacity, and reduced cost, dramatically. The cost of carrying additional calls is virtually zero, irrespective of distance. This reduction of cost has encouraged people to use the telephone not only for speech, but for passing data and pictures not only between fixed computers, but between them and the growing range of mobile devices. The cost of long-distance communication will continue to fall, with major implications for managing businesses around the world.
- *The television.* Although consumers rapidly adopted television after the launch of the first commercial station in 1947, the technology changed little for many years. A breakthrough came with the development of communications satellites, which enabled viewers to see that they were in some respects part of a global community. The other big change was when broadcasters began to transmit programmes in digital form, which greatly increased the capacity of available channels, but also foreshadowed the convergence of televisions and computers.

- *The networked computer.* By fitting more power into the microchips which are at the heart of a computer, engineers are able to roughly double computing power every two years. As the power of each microchip multiplies, so the price of computing falls, leading to smaller computers and greater capacity. From being standalone calculators, computers are now embedded in many other gadgets – games, video cameras, etc.
- *The Internet.* The invention of the Transmission Control Protocol/Internet Protocol (TCP/IP) provides a common language and a set of rules that enable computers all over the world to talk to each other. TCP/IP does this by specifying the format in which all data sent over the Internet must be packaged – and thus enables telephone networks, cable-television networks and networks of computers to connect with each other as if they were a single network. Linking mobile phones to the Internet has led to the explosive growth of the 'Wireless Internet', which in effect liberates the computer from the desk top, enabling information to pass readily between people wherever they are.

> The **Internet** is a web of hundreds of thousands of computer networks linked together by telephone lines through which data can be carried.

Figure 20.5 shows the widening role of information systems. The early stages featured single, unconnected systems for separate business functions. In stages 3 and 4 managers are linking systems together and using them to make radical changes to previously separate processes. In stage 5 they are using common information systems based on the Internet to move information between organisations and often having direct electronic links with their customers.

Managing over the Internet

The significance of the Internet for everyone who works in organisations can scarcely be overstated. It affects all aspects of organisational activity and enables new forms of organisation and new ways of doing business (Phillips, 2003).

The Internet, a linkage of many small computer networks throughout the world, works because there are agreed rules about how computers exchange information. Specific drivers and search engines facilitate information exchange over the Internet. This now includes graphics, audio and video transmission and interactive communication. The Internet assists business processes, business transactions and communications. An important improvement in the attributes of the Internet has been the development of the World Wide Web, which allows users to connect documents and access locations with a web address.

The management importance lies in applying Internet technologies to support business processes, communications and transactions. This includes selling a product or service over the Internet and using the Internet to integrate an organisation's processes from its suppliers through to its customers. Another relevant term is an **intranet**. This refers to a private computer network, operating within an organisation. It uses Internet standards and protocols and is protected by various forms of security. Intranets operate as separate networks within the Internet. The opposite is an **extranet**, that is, a closed collaborative network that uses the Internet to link businesses with specified suppliers, customers or other trading partners. Extranets usually link to business intranets where information is accessible through a password system.

> An **intranet** is a version of the Internet that only specified people within an organisation can use.

> An **extranet** is a version of the Internet that is restricted to specified people in specified companies – such as major customers or suppliers.

The simplest Internet applications provide information, enabling customers to view product or other information on a company website; conversely suppliers use their website to show customers what they can offer. Internet marketplaces are developing in which groups of suppliers in the same industry operate a collective website, making it easier for potential customers to compare terms through a single portal. The next stage is to use the Internet for interaction. Customers enter information and questions about

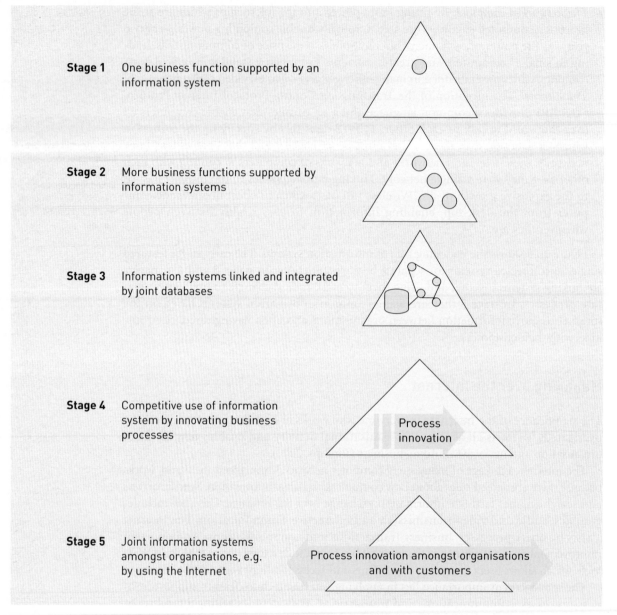

Stage 1 One business function supported by an information system

Stage 2 More business functions supported by information systems

Stage 3 Information systems linked and integrated by joint databases

Stage 4 Competitive use of information system by innovating business processes

Process innovation

Stage 5 Joint information systems amongst organisations, e.g. by using the Internet

Process innovation amongst organisations and with customers

Figure 20.5 The widening effects of information systems

(for example) offers and prices. The system then uses the customer information, such as preferred dates and times of travel, to show availability and costs.

A third use is for transactions, when customers buy goods and services through a supplier's website. Conversely a supplier who sees a purchasing requirement from a business (perhaps expressed as a purchase order on the website) can agree electronically to meet the order. The whole transaction, from accessing information through ordering, delivery (in some cases) and payment, can take place electronically.

Finally, a company achieves integration when it links its own information systems and (within limits) links them in turn to customers and suppliers and transforms into an e-business. Dell Computing is a familiar example amongst many others. As customers decide the configuration of their computer and place an order, this information moves to the systems that control Dell's internal processes and those of its suppliers. Figure 20.6 shows these stages. Established companies such as IBM use all of these stages.

Novotel www.novotel.com

The hotel group Novotel has the strategic objective of putting the customer first, and is determined to relate every action to satisfying their needs. It has for many years used information systems to support this strategy. As the Internet became available managers analysed how best to use it to support their strategy. They identified several possible applications. In setting priorities the main factor was the impact on satisfying existing customers and attracting new ones. Novotel decided to give priority to having a presence on the Internet, an easily accessible website, an online reservation system and useful information for customers.

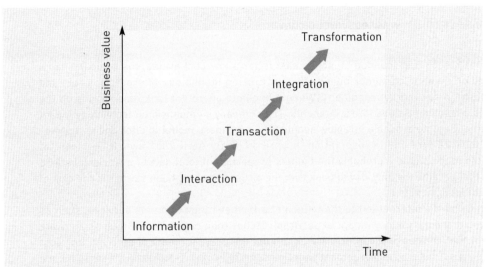

Figure 20.6

Stages in using the Internet

Internet applications at IBM www.ibm.com

IBM aims to become the premier e-business company in the information technology industry, and also to be recognised as a leading Internet business regardless of industry. As well as providing goods and services to other Internet firms, the company uses the Internet for its own activities, as shown below:

- **Information** The company website gives information about the company, including products, employment opportunities and financial performance.
- **Interaction** Prospective online purchasers can select options and configurations for their chosen machine and receive information on price and delivery. The company places current purchase orders for suppliers on a secure Internet website – to which suppliers respond.
- **Transaction** Customers can order their computer or other products online; suppliers can accept orders and send invoices online.
- **Integration** The production planning system takes customer orders and automatically translates those into the quantity of components required. This passes electronically to a buyer, who in turn releases it to the extranet site. Contracted suppliers access this and indicate their acceptance or otherwise. After delivering the physical goods, the supplier converts the original electronic purchase order into an electronic invoice, which passes to IBM for electronic payment.

Source: Interviews with company managers and public documents.

Other companies use the Internet to create and orchestrate active customer communities. Examples include Kraft (**www.kraftfoods.com**), Intel (**www.intel.com**), Apple (**www.apple.com**) and Harley Davidson (**www.harley-davidson.com**). These communities enable the companies to become close to their customers, and to learn how best to improve a product or service much more quickly than is possible through conventional market research techniques.

Wide Internet access has generated a huge increase in businesses offering new services. These include electronic auctions, search engines, electronic retailers and electronic hubs (Dutta and Segev, 1999; Timmers, 2000; Kaplan, 2000) – though as Weiss *et al.* (2004) point out, merely investing in Internet technology without considering the wider issues is a sure way to fail.

 **Easygroup** **www.easygroup.com**

From the day that Stelios Haji-Ioannou launched easyJet as a low-cost airline, the company had a strategy centred on meeting customer needs efficiently, using technology wherever possible and adapting processes to suit market conditions. When it began to operate it took reservations on the telephone, so paid no commissions to travel agents. The company's emphasis on technology meant that as the Internet became available it rapidly adapted their business model to offer online reservations. easyJet took its first online reservation in April 1998. By April 2001 over 85 per cent of reservations were made online – probably the highest proportion of total sales for any established business. Soon that became the only way to book with the airline – making huge savings in the cost of printing and distributing tickets.

Its success in using the Internet led to the launch of a further range of online services, such as easyCar (car rental) and easyMoney (financial services). Stelios then created easyGroup as a private holding company that creates new ventures based around the easyJet model of efficient, low-cost ventures. In late 2004 it reached an agreement with Deutsche Telekom's T-Mobile business to launch a low-cost mobile service – renting air-space from T-Mobile.

Source: *Financial Times*, 24 November 2004; published information and company websites.

The Internet is evidently challenging many established ways of doing business. People can communicate quickly and cheaply without regard to distance. Companies can do business with people and organisations that were previously beyond reach. Combined with political changes, this is creating a wider, often global, market for many goods and services. The challenge for managers is to make profitable use of these possibilities. This includes looking beyond technology – which receives most attention – to some wider organisational issues. A manager who played a major role in guiding Internet-based changes at his company commented: 'The Internet is not a technology challenge. It's a people challenge – all about getting structures, attitudes and skills aligned'.

20.6 Applications of computer-based IS

Computer-based information systems vary in the scope of their operation and this affects their influence on management and organisations. Table 20.1 illustrates some common applications, and the section then illustrates individual, departmental, organisational and inter-organisational examples.

The Student Loan Company – the case continues   CASE STUDY

SLC is in partnership with other organisations to provide its services, as they supply information and management that is essential for its work. These include over 180 Award Authorities (mainly Local Education Authorities), all of which receive the students' applications for a loan, and if they judged the student is eligible, pass this approval direct to SLC. The company pays the loan direct to the student once their attendance at an HEI has been confirmed, normally doing so automatically through the Bankers' Automated Clearing System (BACS).

A data warehouse is used to provide an effective information service internally to SLC and also to a wide range of external partners. It receives and processes information overnight, every night, ready to provide updated figures the following morning. The aim of the system is to provide a central point of contact for consistent management information; to analyse the management information requirements, and to identify the best delivery route for the information. Currently, the data warehouse provides mainly financial information for operational, middle and senior management but from the new Student Finance Direct system, information on Student Financial Support applications and assessments will also be provided.

Source: Based on information provided by the company and the company website.

Case questions 20.1

- What other organisations are now linked to the SLC computer systems?
- What will be the management implications of widening the scope of systems in this way?
- How will the development of such inter-organisational systems affect the service SLC provides?

Sector	Example	Description
Retailing	EPOS terminals	Provide faster customer checkout, identify customer preferences and improve inventory control. This control is linked with suppliers' computer systems
Financial services	ATMs, telephone banking	Support 24-hour-a-day banking services. Telephone banking enables customers to make transactions from their home. Online and Internet banking
Travel	Computer-based reservation systems	Provide up-to-date information to agents that makes it possible to advise travellers better and to alter prices depending on circumstances
Manufacturing	Computer-aided design and manufacturing	Linking design and manufacturing improves the time to market significantly. Better logistics by computer-based material requirements planning. Electronic data interchange with suppliers and customers

Table 20.1

Examples and descriptions of computer-based information systems

Individual systems

Many people use word-processing systems, spreadsheet programs and database systems to manage their work. It is also possible to download data from company-wide systems for use on individual tasks. The main advantage of such systems is that the user is deciding what to use the system for and is able to control the way they work. The disadvantage is that the quality of the software varies greatly. The data extracted from the corporate database quickly becomes out of date and the systems may not link easily with the systems of other users. Two examples are secretaries or professional staff using individual word-processing and office systems, and schedulers using standalone scheduling systems.

Local or departmental systems

If separate units or departments in companies have a distinct task to perform, it may be worthwhile having their own information systems. Management often creates these as separate systems, though many are now being integrated into the systems network of the whole company. For example, a department of a university uses a system that provides information about courses and assessments on the local departmental network which students can access.

Organisational systems

An **organisational system** is a computer system that enables data and information to pass between units of an organisation.

Organisational systems integrate departments, and people throughout the organisation use them. For example, in hospitals many units use centralised patient data to retrieve or update information about a patient. Such systems make it easier for staff from various departments to treat a patient in a consistent way. If the hospital is to implement such a system successfully it needs to discourage the continued use of standalone systems – such as a list of one doctor's patients held on a spreadsheet that he or she considers to be the definitive list, but which will not contain data on the lists of other doctors.

Inter-organisational systems

An **inter-organisational system** is a computer system that enables data and information to pass between organisations, such as electronic orders or invoices.

Many systems now link organisations electronically by using the Internet, which makes it easier to set up **inter-organisational systems** and introduce new ways of managing transactions between companies. For example, in 1998 IBM announced that, by the end of 1999, 95 per cent of its transactions with suppliers (of whom there are many thousands around the world) would be conducted over the Internet. This enables much faster and more efficient ordering, automatic invoicing, faster payments and substantial savings in clerical costs.

Whichever kind of application is being considered, the benefits (see Key Ideas) will depend on managing a range of human and organisational issues.

Five functions of information systems

Markus (1984) distinguished five functions that information systems can perform:

1 **Operational** These process routine transactions in an efficient, reliable and uniform way. Management uses them widely for activities such as payroll calculations, order entry and invoicing.
2 **Monitoring** These check the performance of a system at regular intervals. The factor being monitored can be financial, quality, departmental output or personal performance. Being attentive to changes or trends gives the business an advantage. It can act promptly to change a plan to suit new conditions.
3 **Decision support** These can help managers to calculate the consequences of different alternatives, and so make better decisions. This happens for instance by simulation and 'what-if' analysis. A decision support system incorporates both data and models to help a decision maker solve a problem.
4 **Knowledge (or expert)** These help people to make decisions by incorporating human knowledge into the system. A knowledge engineer tries to learn how the experts make decisions and incorporates that into the knowledge base of the system.
5 **Communication** People design communication systems to overcome barriers of time and distance. They make it easier to pass information around and between organisations.

Activity 20.5   Collecting examples of applications

The media regularly report new applications of computer software. Collect examples over the next week of new inter-organisational systems. Identify what they are likely to mean for the way people will work and manage in organisations adopting such systems. Compare notes with others and decide which of the systems you have found is likely to be of greatest organisational significance over the next two years.

20.7 The social elements of a computer-based IS

People

However sophisticated the technical elements of an IS, it will depend on people to make it work effectively. They include staff and managers who enter data into the system and those who receive information from it and use the results. The latter include staff in supplier or customer organisations who, as their systems become more closely linked, may be dealing directly with the organisation's IS system. It may also include members of the public visiting the website or entering data and receiving information from the system. We discussed in Chapter 15 how all have unique needs and interests and will see the system from a different point of view from those who designed it.

Management issues with respect to people include:

● Ensuring that systems are designed in a way that encourages the motivation and commitment of staff to enter data accurately and to use it appropriately.
● Acknowledging that people interpret the information they receive, and asking whether they understand it.
● Finding out what customers or members of the public expect of an information system (such as a website) and how well it meets their expectations.

Electronic Patient Record systems: convincing doctors

Healthcare experts have been preaching the benefits of electronic patient records (EPR) for at least two decades but adoption has been slow: most healthcare institutions still maintain the majority of patient records on paper. 'Technology is not the problem', says Eva Deutsch, a leader of IBM's healthcare business. The concerns about technical standards and immature technology that so worried buyers a decade ago have largely disappeared. But the problem of persuading people to use EPR remains complex. 'Before, an EPR system was looked at as just another IT project', says Ms Deutsch. But it is more of an organisational project, which means you have to analyse processes and convince doctors the system can bring value to them.

ERP systems are often seen as tools designed to help administrators rather than clinical staff. Doctors are more likely to support an EPR initiative if told of the clinical benefits: better use of scarce resources, reduced testing, better reporting and more complete documentation.　**FT**

Source: *Financial Times*, 21 May 2003.

Procedures

These are the rules or routines that people (staff or others) are expected to use when interacting with the IS. When staff enter data, they must follow certain procedures – which may be tightly specified in the system itself, or be left flexible. Implementing an IS can make procedures more rigid, with less opportunity for staff to use their initiative: this is not a force of nature, but a management choice. Another issue is whether the procedures require people to use the system, or whether it is voluntary – systems used by professional staff are sometimes of the latter kind.

Management issues with respect to procedures could include:

● Whether the procedures around an IS mirror earlier procedures or differ from them.
● Whether or not staff see them as supporting their established ways of working.
● Whether the procedures should be flexible or inflexible.

Organisation

Figure 20.3 showed that procedures and the people using the system are the immediate elements of an IS – and that these are set within a wider organisational context. There is abundant evidence (McLoughlin, 1999; Walsham, 2001; Boddy *et al.*, 2005) that organisational factors such as culture, structure and distribution of power affect the way people see and use information systems. Some organisational contexts are such that people generally welcome new systems, while in others (especially where there is a history of failed or inconvenient systems) people react with indifference or hostility.

Management issues with respect to organisational factors could include:

● Whether to use the capabilities of an IS to centralise or decentralise certain activities.
● Whether a proposed system will affect the relative power of different groups or functions, and how this may affect their reaction.
● Whether a system is consistent or inconsistent with the prevailing culture in some parts of the organisation.

Implementing systems

Implementing information systems is not just a technical activity of developing or buying a package that provides the information needed. Information systems have social, technical, organisational, economical and political dimensions. Many systems fail to realise their potential because managers have given insufficient attention to these aspects.

Reasons for failed systems

key ideas

An article in *Forbes Magazine* described a number of failed systems development projects. The main reasons for these failures were:

● User needs were not fully understood.
● User requirements were made secondary or even disregarded in favour of technical enthusiasm for the latest or most exciting, but inappropriate, method.
● Business changes during the development period were not reflected in the system by the implementation date.
● The time and money needed to develop and implement systems were underestimated. This caused overspending, partial implementation and dissatisfied users.
● During implementation politics and conflicts emerged as departments protected old systems.

Source: *Forbes Magazine*, 29 August 1994.

Many authors suggest that organisational culture, interest groups, the user community and the structure have a major influence on systems development (Keen, 1981; Markus, 1983; Markus and Robey, 1983; Noble and Newman, 1993; Boonstra *et al.*, 2004). This is consistent with the idea in Chapter 1 that managers work within a context, made up of the eight factors shown in Figure 1.3. Changing an information system involves a change in technology – but will also involve changes in several other of the elements shown – such as structure, power or culture (Markus and Keil, 1994). Boddy and Gunson (1996) found that managers who took account of these factors were likely to have successful projects, by establishing a coherence between the elements in Figure 1.3. The issues to be managed in implementing an information system are exactly the same as those to be handled in any of the change projects that Chapter 13 examined.

These extensive organisational consequences imply that the process of introducing information systems is especially important. Mumford and Weir (1979) argued that in many system development projects there is an overemphasis on the technical side, leading to neglect of the human side. To balance this, they developed the ETHICS method. ETHICS is an acronym for Effective Technical and Human Implementation of Computer-based Systems. The assumptions of this method are:

● Many kinds of computer technology are sufficiently flexible to allow for the design of systems that take into account the need of employees for satisfying work. Therefore designers should work on both the technical and the human parts of a system with this objective in view.

● Even in situations where designers have produced a technical system, it is still possible to redesign jobs in a way that will make them more satisfying.

The method follows two tracks: the technical track and the human track. Each side is worked on independently and brought together in a later stage. This method is intended to ensure that developers give enough time and attention to both dimensions. Figure 20.7 shows the Ethics approach.

The approach leads not only to working systems (from a technical perspective) but also to more attractive systems from a human point of view, enhancing motivation and job satisfaction. It develops the idea of an organisation as a sociotechnical system – discussed in Chapter 2.

These principles have been developed from research into many kinds of information system – and are likely to be just as true of attempts to implement information systems based on Internet technology.

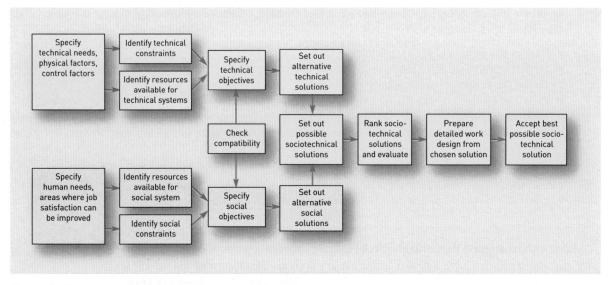

Figure 20.7 Ethics approach to system development

Activity 20.6 Critical reflection on IS applications

Consider a system which has been implemented in an organisation you know.

● How did it affect the social dimensions of the organisation?

● Did those managing the project pay sufficient attention to those issues and in what ways?

● How did that affect the outcomes of the project?

20.8 | IS and the tasks of managing

Chapter 1 presented the management job as being the pursuit of objectives through the tasks of planning, organising, leading and controlling the use of resources. Whatever their level, managers perform these tasks in a fluid, interactive way, and through their relations with other people. Modern computer-based information systems have considerable implications for how they do so.

Planning

This deals with the overall direction of the work to be done. It includes forecasting future trends, assessing actual and potential resources and developing objectives and targets for the business. Chapter 8 introduced Porter's five forces, widely used as a tool for identifying the competitive forces affecting a business. Figure 20.8 shows that modern information systems can alter each of these forces. Information systems are a source of competitive advantage if a company can use them to strengthen one or more of these forces. They can equally represent a competitive threat if other organisations use them more effectively.

Table 20.2 illustrates some of the many possibilities.

Managers also use information systems to support their chosen strategy – such as a differentiation or cost leadership. Information systems can support a cost leadership strategy when companies substitute robotics for labour, use stock control systems to reduce inventory costs, use online order entry to reduce order processing costs, and reduce downtime and scrap by systems that automatically identify a machine fault about to occur.

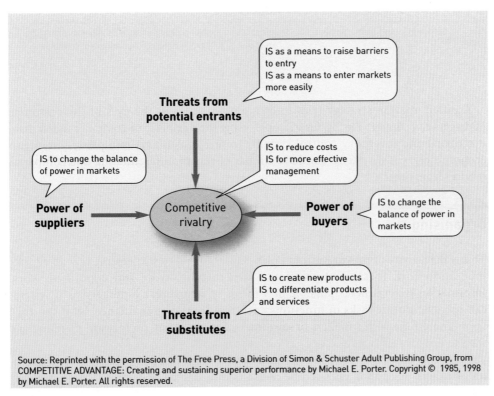

Figure 20.8

How information systems can change competitive forces: Porter's model

Table 20.2 Using information systems to affect the five forces

Porter's five forces		Examples of information systems support
Threat of potential entrants	Raise entry barriers	Electronic links with customers make it more costly for them to move to competitors. Supermarkets use electronic links to banks and suppliers, and so gain a cost advantage over small retailers
	Entering markets more easily	Bertelsmann, a German media group, entered book retailing by setting up an online store. Virgin offers financial services by using online systems
Threat of substitutes	Creating new products	Telephone banking (a threat to branch banking) has only been possible with modern information systems
	Differentiating their products	Using database technology and CRM systems to identify precise customer needs and then create unique offers and incentives
Bargaining power of suppliers	Increasing power of suppliers	Airlines use yield management systems to track actual reservations against capacity on each flight, and then adjust prices for the remaining seats to maximise revenue
	Decreasing power of suppliers	Auto companies have set up electronic marketplaces that suppliers must use, and which allow the customers (such as Ford or General Motors) to compare prices offered more easily, and identify new suppliers
Bargaining power of buyers		Buyers in many industries and sectors can use the Internet to access more suppliers, and to compare prices for standard commodities
Intensity of rivalry	Using IS to reduce costs	Enterprise Resource Planning systems make it possible to make radical changes in manufacturing systems, leading to greater consistency in planning and lower costs
	More effective management	Information systems provide more detailed information on trading patterns, enabling management to make

A differentiation strategy tries to create uniqueness in the eyes of the customer. Managers can support this by, for example, using the flexibility of computer-aided manufacturing and inventory control systems to meet customers' unique requirements economically. CRM systems can have similar effects in differentiating one company's services from others.

Organising

This is the activity of moving abstract plans closer to reality, by deciding how to allocate time and effort. It is about creating a structure to divide and coordinate work. Information systems make possible new forms of structure. Computer-based systems can remove routine tasks in functions such as purchasing or finance. Staff can then spend more time with suppliers or customers, concentrating on forward planning and ways to improve efficiency.

Computer-based systems allow organisations to centralise some functions and decentralise others. Telephone sales can be centralised to single call centres. This is currently

The Student Loan Company – the case continues   CASE STUDY

The UK government has established a Modernising Government agenda, through which it hopes to greatly increase the number of services which it can provide electronically. This is intended to

- simplify business processes so they are easier and quicker to use
- simplify regulations, forms and methods of application
- use new technologies, including the Internet, effectively
- Support government policy objectives.

SLC management was asked to establish the Student Finance Direct service which would support these wider objectives, and this enabled SLC to take a more central position within the student financial support system. Known as Student Finance Direct, this will be an online system which would allow borrowers to apply, be assessed, and be paid through a single electronic system. This will simplify the application process. The initial system has four main areas:

- *Online application*: information on available grants and loans will be online, and students will be able to apply, and have their eligibility assessed, online.
- *Centralised assessment*: once their eligibility has been assessed, their formal application can be assessed centrally.

- *One-stop customer support*: The customer contact centre will provide advice through web-based frequently asked questions (FAQs), telephone enquiry, postal correspondence, email and face to face via Award Authorities.
- *Shared knowledge*: all information – such as the course database and the student records – will be held centrally, so that all decision makers have shared access to the same information. Data will be entered once, and from a single source – with SLC responsible for developing and maintaining it.

Source: Based on information provided by the company, and the company website.

Case questions 20.2

- Use Porter's five forces model to analyse the possible effects of these changes on SLC's strategic position.
- Have they strengthened its position in relation to other players, and if so, how may they react?

---

proving massively successful with banks and other services. This centralisation reduces the cost of sales and allows the companies to compete with new entrants. Chapter 10 showed how Siemens had used the Internet to bring more centralised control to many functions. The Management in Practice feature summarises the main elements.

Centralisation at Siemens   www.siemens.com

A senior manager at Siemens outlined the steps the company has taken to use the Internet to bring more central control to the business. The plan included:

1 Knowledge management – using a company-wide system to capture and share knowledge about scientific and technical developments throughout the business.
2 Online purchasing (or e-procurement). Large savings are expected from pooling the demands of buying departments through a company-wide system called click2procure.
3 Online sales. Most of Siemens' customers are other companies who can click on 'buy from Siemens' on the website and place orders for most Siemens products.

4 Internal administrative processes – such as by handling 30,000 job applications a year online, or expecting employees to book their business travel arrangements over the Internet.

If you want to transform a company to an e-business company, the problem is not so much e-procurement and the face to the customer. All this can be done rather fast. What is truly difficult is to reorganise all the internal processes. That is what we see as our main task and where the main positive results will come from.

Source: Boddy *et al.* (2005) and company website.

A **knowledge system** is a system that incorporates the decision-making logic of a human expert.

Other companies have used the power of information systems to decentralise aspects of their operations. While Kwik-Fit initially used the EPOS system to centralise the business, it then moved on to decentralise more power to the newly created geographic divisions – supported by the same information system (Boddy and Gunson, 1996).

Others businesses use expert systems to help people make decisions by incorporating human knowledge into the system. A knowledge engineer works with one or more experts in the domain under study to build a **knowledge system**. He or she tries to learn how the experts make decisions, and incorporates this into that part of the software known as the knowledge base.

Examples of expert systems

ABN AMRO Bank uses a knowledge system to analyse proposed bank loans. The system incorporates the experience of experts in the field and enables loan decisions to be processed automatically at head office rather than by staff in the branches.

The Amsterdam Medical Centre, a large Dutch hospital, uses an expert system that enables people with relatively little experience to deal with emergency calls. The system proposes the questions they should ask, interprets the answers given, and recommends a plan of action.

Aegon, a Dutch insurer, uses a knowledge system to process applications, which enables agents to make insurance contracts with clients without involving the insurer.

Many systems of this sort do not replace the experts, but support them in making their decisions (Balachandra, 2000; Flores and Pearce, 2000). The system makes suggestions to the human experts, but does not take over their jobs. In this context Hirschheim and Klein (1989) distinguished between 'systems for experts' (these are supportive to the human experts) and 'expert systems' (which replace people who are expert in a certain field).

Leading

This is the activity of generating effort and commitment towards meeting objectives. It includes influencing and motivating other people to work in support of the plans. Most computer-based information systems have significant effects on the organisation. They can change the tasks and the skill levels required for them. In a hospital, the emergency room receives telephone calls that require some action. This room could be staffed by a two-person team consisting of a nurse and a doctor. Alternatively an operator with less medical knowledge can use an expert system that prompts the operator to ask questions. The operator enters the responses and the system suggests the most appropriate action. This allows medical staff to be employed in other areas.

Research into many computer-based information systems (Boddy and Gunson, 1996) shows that some managers use them in a way that reduces the intrinsic quality of work (see Chapter 15) while others use them to enhance it. This has little to do with the nature of the technology itself, but with how managers choose to design and implement it.

Computer systems in an ambulance service

The organisation transports patients to and from hospitals for routine treatment at a clinic. The Patient Transport Service work involves ambulance crews transporting patients between their homes and clinics within a hospital. The manual procedures that the service used to plan drivers' routes were flexible but labour intensive. To reduce costs the service had invested heavily in computer systems, including a route-planning system.

Planning officers received orders and keyed them into a computer that stored them until the day before the appointment. It then sorted them by area and allocated them to an available ambulance crew. The list was then printed, checked for feasibility and issued to the crew. Two years after implementing the system a control manager said:

> The basic system has not changed but we have made some changes in how we use it. We used to tell the crew how to do the run: what we do now is put all the patients in a geographic area on to a log sheet, with their appointment times. We have devolved responsibility to the crew members to decide how best they should schedule that journey to meet the appointments. Initially we told them in much more detail, manually intervening with the computer data. But it was very labour intensive, and we did not see the traffic jams. We hand out the work in the morning, and we only want to hear if the crews are having operational problems.
>
> The planning officer's role has developed into a liaison role with the hospitals, building up a relationship with them. The planner becomes a crucial personality, not just a worker. Someone coming into the job now could take two years to build up those working relationships. The machine does the routine bits. At first the planning officer did that: now we have pushed it down.

Source: Based on a case in Boddy and Gunson (1996).

Business becomes more dependent on skilled and committed people as technology increases. Since the business world is dynamic and uncertain there will be changes, errors and uncertainty to cope with. Staff need to be able and willing to use their initiative to deal with that, to exploit the hidden potential of the system, and generally to contribute imaginatively to the work. That can best be achieved by paying attention to how their jobs change with the introduction of the new system. Chapter 15 includes the theoretical basis for this, in terms of the work design model.

Controlling

Computer-based monitoring systems can check the performance of an operation at regular intervals. The factor being monitored can be financial, quality, departmental output or personal performance. Being attentive to changes or trends gives the business an advantage as it can act promptly to change a plan to suit new conditions.

Universities in The Netherlands use student trail systems that monitor the academic progress of students. These systems link to the national institution that provides scholarships. This information enables the institution to stop or reduce the scholarship when results are below the required standard.

Information systems allow management at head office to control subsidiaries or branch offices much more tightly. Head office can gather information much more frequently and measure branch performance almost as it happens rather than by weekly or monthly reports. It is a matter of management judgement whether that is a wise or unwise move.

Nestlé struggles with enterprise systems www.nestle.com

Nestlé is a food and pharmaceuticals company that operates all over the world. Traditionally it allowed local units to operate as they saw fit, taking into account local conditions and business cultures. The company had many purchasing systems and no information on how much business they did with each supplier: each factory made independent arrangements. Nestlé's management concluded that these local differences were inefficient and costly. They wanted to integrate the systems to act as a single entity, using the company's worldwide buying power to lower prices. Managers therefore started a programme to standardise and coordinate its processes and information systems, by installing common financial, purchasing, sales, and distribution systems throughout every Nestlé USA division.

A year after the project started, a stock market analyst in London doubted its success: . . . 'it touches the corporate culture, which is decentralised, and tries to centralise it. That's risky. It's always a risk when you touch the corporate culture'. Jeri Dunn from Nestlé later agreed: at an American plant most of the key stakeholders failed to realise how much the project would change their business processes. Dunn said: 'they still thought it was just software'. A rebellion had taken place when the plant moved to install the manufacturing modules. Staff did not understand how to use the new system and did not understand the changes. Management stopped the project and removed the project leader. This person had put too much pressure on the project and the technology. By doing so the team had lost sight of the bigger picture.

Source: Laudon and Laudon (2004).

20.9 IS and the process of managing

Chapter 1 introduced Henry Mintzberg's (1973) analysis of the roles of management as consisting of interpersonal, informational and decisional. How do computer-based information systems affect these roles?

Interpersonal roles

Interpersonal roles arise directly from a manager's formal authority and status, and involve relationships with other people both in and out of the organisation. Information systems can affect the leader role, which defines the manager's relationship with other staff, including motivating, communicating and development. The way they introduce and relate information systems to the work of employees has major influence on their commitment, as shown by the Chem-Tec example. If information systems take away their routine aspects of work they then allow managers to spend more time on interpersonal contacts. Conversely there is also anecdotal evidence that some managers can use the technology as a substitute for personal contact, thus becoming more distant from staff and colleagues.

Informational roles

Information systems by definition support the monitor role by providing access to much greater sources of information than were previously accessible. Intranets and extranets make it much easier to communicate consistent information quickly, so reducing the scope for error and misunderstanding. Modern information systems bring with them the danger of providing managers with too much information, beyond their capacity to absorb.

Decisional roles

In the entrepreneurial role the manager initiates change within the organisation. Managers see opportunities or problems and create projects to deal with them. Developments in information systems offer many opportunities for them to exercise this role, either within the business or as part of a new venture. The resource allocator role involves choosing amongst competing demands for money, equipment, personnel, and other demands on a manager's time. Decision support systems (DSS) can help managers to calculate the consequences of different alternatives, and so make better decisions. This happens for instance by simulation and 'what-if analysis.' A DSS incorporates both data and models to help a decision maker solve a problem. Some businesses use decision support systems to calculate the expected financial consequences of alternative investments.

Focused use of IS at Inditex www.inditex.com

management in practice

Inditex is a highly successful clothing manufacturer based in North-west Spain. In 2004 it had higher operating profits than Gap, H&M and Benetton and yet spends less than the industry average on information systems. Andrew McAfee (2004) believes this is because the company has developed some very clear principles to guide the way it uses IS. The first of these is that IS is an aid to judgement, not a substitute for it: the company relies heavily on the decision-making abilities of its staff. Information systems help managers deal with the huge amounts of data about trading patterns but do not decide, or even recommend, what styles or quantities they should order. Store managers make those key decisions. Information systems are as simple as they can be made, being designed to fit precisely the key processes in the store, and contain only the most essential features. And new IS projects always start from those managing the business, not the IS specialists.

Source: McAfee (2004).

Summary

1 Explain how information systems are critical to management performance:

- People at all levels depend on information about inputs, outputs and transformation processes to help them add value to the resources they use.

2 Explain the difference between data, information and knowledge:

- Data is the recorded descriptions of things, events or activities – such as their size or cost

- Information is processed data that has meaning for the person receiving it – they judge it to be useful
- Knowledge builds on information by using experience to evaluate its significance.

3 Explain the technical and social elements of computer-based information systems, and the management questions they raise:
- Technical elements consist of hardware, software, telecommunications and data
- Social elements include people, procedures and the wider organisational context, especially structural, cultural and political factors
- All raise management issues which will affect the value or otherwise of an information system far more than purely technical capabilities.

4 Distinguish information systems in terms of their type, scope and functions:
- Type – human, paper-based and computer-based
- Scope – individual, departmental, organisational and inter-organisational
- Functions – operational, monitoring, decision support, knowledge (or expert) and communication.

5 Understand how information systems affect the tasks and roles of management.
- Computer-based IS can potentially affect all tasks of managing:
  - *Planning* – e.g. modern IS can affect all of the forces in Porter's model
  - *Organising* – e.g. IS can enable the removal of routine tasks, break down barriers between departments and functions, and enable work to be more centralised or more decentralised
  - *Leading* – e.g. IS enable changes in the design of work, and can increase or decrease the motivational potential of jobs
  - *Controlling* – e.g. IS can greatly increase the frequency and detail with which activities can be monitored, irrespective of distance.
- They can also affect management roles (Mintzberg):
  - *Interpersonal* – e.g. IS can take over routine aspects of management work, enabling them to spend more time in contact with customers, colleagues or subordinates
  - *Informational* – e.g. IS can provide managers with access to much more information than is possible with manual systems, though with the danger of causing information overload
  - *Decisional* – e.g. some applications of IS, such as decision support systems, are specifically designed to enable managers to evaluate options more thoroughly and quickly than is possible with manual systems.

6 Explain how the Internet enables radical changes in organisations and their management:
- The effects will depend largely on the stage the company has reached in using the Internet – information, interaction, transaction, integration or transformational
- The benefits or otherwise obtained will depend largely on the skill with which managers deal with organisational as well as technical issues.

Review questions

1 Give some examples of data and of information that you have at this moment. Use these to explain the difference between the two.

2 What information do you lack that harms your work or study performance? How could this information be generated?

3 Give examples of the use of information systems in a business you know. How are they helping or hindering the managers in performing their tasks? Compare the needs of senior and lower-level managers if possible.

4 What are the advantages of human and paper-based information systems over computer-based ones, and vice versa?

5 What are the four criteria that define the value of information?

6 Give examples of how an information system can affect at least two of the forces in Porter's model, and so affect the competitiveness of a business.

7 Describe how an IS can support either a cost leadership or a differentiation strategy, with an example of each.

8 How do information systems affect the other functions of management – such as leading or controlling?

9 How do they affect the roles of management as set out by Mintzberg?

10 How are companies in an industry of your choice (e.g. finance, music, news, manufacturing) using the Internet, and how is this affecting the structure of the industry and the power of the different players?

Concluding critical reflection

Think about the main computer-based information systems that you use in your company, or that feature in one with which you are familiar. Review the material in the chapter, and perhaps visit some of the websites identified. Then make notes on these questions:

● What examples of the themes discussed in this chapter are currently relevant to your company? How have information systems helped or hindered managers' performance? How well have the social as well as the technological aspects of new systems been managed? How, if at all, have they altered the tasks and roles of managers, staff or professionals? What stage have you reached in using the Internet?

● If the business seems to pay too much attention to the technical aspects of IS projects, and not enough to the social and organisational aspects, why is that? What assumptions appear to have shaped managers' approach? Have recent applications served to increase or decrease the degree of centralisation – and is that in the best interests of the business?

● What assumptions about the nature of information systems seem to shape your approach to implementing them – are they typically seen as technical or sociotechnical systems? In view of the evidence about the influence of organisational factors on IS investment, are those assumptions appropriate?

● Have managers considered whether IS projects should be managed differently to improve their return on the funds invested? Do they regularly and systematically review IS projects after implementation to see whether they have achieved their intended objectives, and to learn for future projects? Do they typically compare their approach with that in other companies?

Further reading

Applegate, L.M., McFarlan, F.W. and McKenney, J.L. (2000), *Corporate Information Systems Management: Text and cases* (5th edn), Irwin, Chicago, IL.

Provides a broad perspective on the management implications of the rise of information systems. The book is organised around a management audit of the information services activity.

Laudon, K.C. and Laudon, J.P. (2004), *Management Information Systems: Organization and technology in the networked enterprise*, Prentice Hall, Harlow.

This text, written from a management perspective, focuses on the opportunities and pitfalls of computer and communications technologies.

Earl, M.J. (1998), *Information Management: The organizational dimension*, Oxford University Press, Oxford.

A useful non-technical book that looks at ways of exploiting information systems strategically. It emphasises the relation between corporate strategy and IS strategy.

Kalakota, R. and Robinson, M. (1999), *E-business: Roadmap for success*, Addison-Wesley, Harlow.

Shows how companies can build strategies that are strongly based on the opportunities which the Internet offers.

Phillips, P. (2003), *E-Business Strategy: Text and cases*, McGraw-Hill, Maidenhead.

A comprehensive European perspective on Internet developments relevant to business and strategy.

Weblinks

These websites are among those that have appeared in the chapter:

www.renault.com
www.novotel.com
www.ibm.com
www.easyGroup.com
www.siemens.com
www.nestle.com
www.inditex.com

Visit two of the business sites in the list, and answer these questions:

● If you were a potential employee, how well does it present information about the company and the career opportunities available? Could you apply for a job online?

- Evaluate the sites on these criteria, which are based on those used in an annual survey or corporate websites:
  - Does it give the current share price on the front page?
  - How many languages is it available in?
  - Is it possible to email key people or functions from the site?
  - Does it give a diagram of the main structural units in the business?
  - Does it set out the main mission or business idea of the company?
  - Are there any other positive or negative features?

Annotated weblinks, multiple choice questions and other
useful resources can be found on
www.pearsoned.co.uk/boddy

Part 6 Case   Airbus Industries and the A380

www.airbus.com

During the 1970s European manufacturers produced only 10 per cent of all commercial aircraft, trailing well behind the sales of companies like Lockheed, McDonnell Douglas and especially the market leader, Boeing. They realised that no single European company could hope to prevent Boeing's growing domination of the civil aviation market and, with strong political support, four major European aerospace companies decided to join forces. Aérospatiale (France), Deutsche Airbus (Germany), British Aerospace (UK) and Constructions Aeronauticas (Spain) came together to form a new company, Airbus Industries (Airbus). If successful, it would be a powerful symbol of cross-border industrial collaboration in Europe.

The partners in the company continued to operate as independent companies, supplying aircraft parts for final assembly at Toulouse (France) or Hamburg (Germany). This arrangement was costly and unresponsive, with regular disputes over the distribution of work and production facilities between the national partners. Airbus continued to depend heavily on state subsidies and internally generated funds, which limited its ability to invest in new models and production facilities. Boeing continued to dominate the civil aircraft market. The company wanted to invest in at least one major new model, but doing so would be beyond its financial resources. Private investors could provide this capital, but would only do so if Airbus operated as a market-oriented business. Therefore in July 2001 three of the Airbus partners combined to form the European Aeronautic, Defence and Space Company (EADS). The exception was British Aerospace (now known as BAE) which remains outside the group while retaining a financial stake: EADS owns 80 per cent of Airbus, and BAE 20

per cent. The partners relinquished all control over design, manufacturing and operations to Airbus itself, which was now able to operate as an independent commercial business. Headquartered in Toulouse, the company manages, designs, makes, sells and supports a family of aircraft:

- A319/A320/A321 (124–185 seat single-aisle)
- A300/A310 (220–266 seat wide-body)
- A330/A340 (263–340 seat wide-body)
- A380 (555 seat double-deck, wide body).

In addition to 150 design and manufacturing sites, the company manages an international network of some 1500 suppliers in more than 30 countries, including 800 suppliers in the United States. In 2004 it announced it was increasing the amount it would buy from China, where five companies already make many parts for Airbus aircraft – such as emergency and rear doors for the A320. China is also an important market for the company, with more than 250 Airbus planes delivered.

The company requires suppliers to be flexible and highly competitive. It used the concept of 'total cost of ownership' to evaluate suppliers, taking into account not just the purchase price but also factors such as quality, delivery and reliability of the parts supplied throughout the life of the aircraft. It developed long-term agreements with suppliers to decrease costs and increase efficiency, and to allow them to make investments in their business which also benefit Airbus. For example, it has worked closely with Alcoa, a leading US-based aluminium supplier, to develop new materials for use throughout the A380, including wings, fuselage and landing gear. These advances are the result of close collaboration between Alcoa staff and Airbus design teams, in which the supplier does not just offer specified components but works with the customer to develop innovative solutions to the underlying problem. Suppliers typically deal directly with the company, but for the A380 work is organised into packages which are the responsibility of about 50 major contractors. They alone deal directly with the company and manage a larger group of smaller suppliers. In return for long-term deals, suppliers have to bear more of the risks of the A380 project.

In 2003 Airbus secured more orders than Boeing for the fourth time in five years, and delivered more planes than its American rival for the first time (300 against 285). It also reported that it now had 129 orders for the A380 (from Emirates, Virgin Atlantic, Lufthansa, Air France and FedEx) – half-way to break-even point. Boeing had sought to counter the success of Airbus, including several challenges to the subsidies which it alleges Airbus still receives from European governments. In 2004 it demanded an end to the repayable 'launch aid' that European governments have long contributed towards the cost of launching new Airbus models. Airbus counters by pointing out that Boeing has received large subsidies from Washington State (where the company manufactures its planes at Seattle), and that the Japanese government also subsidises Boeing in return for the company ordering components from Japanese companies. Airbus also claims that Boeing receives indirect aid from the US government through defence-related contracts which allow cross-subsidies between models. The US government paid most of the development costs of the best-selling 747, which was originally designed as a military aircraft.

In 2000 Airbus faced a major strategic issue – whether to approve production of a new plane. The company believed that a sufficient market existed for a very large plane, while Boeing believed a greater demand existed for a smaller craft of 200–250 seats. The smaller aircraft would meet a perceived need amongst airlines to provide more direct services between cities, rather than through hubs served by large aircraft.

In December 2000 Airbus decided to introduce what will be the world's largest commercial airliner – the Airbus A380 – at an estimated investment cost of 13 billion euros. The plane will have a standard seating capacity of 555 passengers, though this will vary depending on how the cabins are laid out. Production began in 2002, and the first deliveries are planned for August 2006. Airbus has predicted a lifetime demand for this type at over 1100, though Boeing predicts the total market will be only 320. It has instead chosen to develop the 7E7 Dreamliner, a much smaller aircraft with 200–250 seats to replace the ageing 757 and 767 ranges.

The A380 uses very advanced technology which Airbus claims will ensure seat-per mile costs 20 per cent lower than those of other aircraft. It would offer more space and wider seats than the Boeing 747, generate less noise at take-off, emit less exhaust gases and carry 35 per cent more passengers. Weight is a critical aspect of aircraft performance, and Airbus uses carbon composite materials throughout the aircraft to minimise this – some 45 per cent of the parts will be made of these.

To be competitive, Airbus needs not only to deliver aircraft, but to ensure that airlines can use and maintain them economically. In the case of the A380, the height of the aircraft raises unusual challenges – at 24.1 metres, this is almost twice the height of a Boeing 747. It will therefore fit few existing hangars. Moreover most operators will have relatively small fleets, and will need to consider whether to invest in dedicated buildings, engineering, maintenance and test facilities. Many are expected to rely on specialised maintenance contractors, and Airbus will help them in this by creating a support plan for each of the airports around the world where the A380 will land. For example, it is planning to augment the support it provides at Los Angeles and New York JFK airports, where both Emirates and Singapore Airlines are expected to offer flights in 2006. Emirates, the largest customer for the A380, is building its own facilities for the plane at Dubai – which it may also use to offer maintenance services to other airlines.

Spares will also be a problem, with Emirates estimating that airlines will need to invest tens of millions of dollars in spares. An aircraft with many new and advanced systems, and with so many passengers, risks inconveniencing many customers if things go wrong.

The airlines are therefore considering optimising their investment by establishing a common pool of spares – upon which all the (competing) A380 users could draw. Major suppliers to the A380 are also involved in discussions about maintenance planning, and are expected to offer inventory access and repair packages to the airlines. Some are forming joint ventures to offer worldwide support and maintenance services to the airlines. Some spare parts are so large that they will require special transport – Airbus has been consulting with users about where to position these around the world should customers require them.

Assembling the A380 is a vast logistical exercise. Major parts come from 15 manufacturing plants across Europe and are moved to Toulouse for final assembly. Major sites include Broughton (UK), Hamburg (Germany), Puerto Real (Spain) and St Nazaire (France). A380 wings are made in the UK, the main fuselage parts in France and Germany and the tail in Spain. This cross-border network has enabled many suppliers to contribute to the A380 project. Transporting these for final assembly in Toulouse will be a major task, with parts being shipped by barge up the River Garonne to Langon, south of Bordeaux. There they are transferred to specially designed trucks for the 240 km journey to Toulouse – travelling only at night when the roads will be closed to other traffic.

The way the A380 is being managed establishes a new way of working that overrides the earlier national, work-sharing traditions. Transnational groups have been set up to focus on various aspects of the new aircraft's production. The group working on wings has not only British experts (reflecting BAE's wing expertise) but also French and Spanish engineers, whose role is to challenge accepted ways of doing things. Similar teams work on other critical aspects of the aircraft's design. For the first time at Airbus a single individual, the A380 project manager, is responsible for keeping the project on time and within budget.

Information systems clearly play a major role throughout Airbus. To support the close relationships with suppliers on which it depends, it has introduced a web-based portal, which aims to integrate more closely the company's activities across 150 sites and 1500 suppliers. Eventually 80,000 people (Airbus and suppliers' staffs) will be able to use the site – for example, enabling the company's buying staff and its suppliers to exchange information online about their requirements and proposals. Airbus can place requirements on the web page, and suppliers can inform Airbus about their capabilities to meet those needs. For routine ordering by staff in any one of the company sites (from potentially 1500 suppliers in 30 countries), there is an electronic catalogue of items available from approved suppliers. Using this to identify, select, order and pay for components and other supplies dramatically reduces the administrative burden of such transactions, and ensures a standard process across the company.

Other systems enable engineers to specify and record the specific requirements of all planes ordered by a customer, including specific cabin layouts required. This is then used to coordinate and integrate the manufacturing process, including all the requirements from suppliers to meet the customer's requirements. Other systems plan and control the widely dispersed manufacturing process, and carefully monitor the costs of meeting each order.

Source: Published information and the Airbus website.

Part case questions

- What are the main problems of control in a company of this sort?
- How do you expect that Airbus's investment in (a) the Airbus A380, and (b) information systems to support its manufacturing operations, will have affected specific items in (a) the profit and loss statement, and (b) the balance sheet of the parent company (EADS – www.eads.com)?
- How will the information systems have helped the internal control of decision making? With what financial consequences, explicitly?
- What can you discover from the financial press about the movement in the EADS price over the past year and the reasons for this? Is there any evidence of it affecting internal management policy and practice?

- What were the main operational problems that Airbus management will have had to deal with as the consortium has grown?
- What are the main business processes in Airbus that are crucial to satisfying customer requirements?
- What operations concepts will be especially important in supporting the strategic position of Airbus? How will implementing them have affected the roles of managers?
- What information does management at different levels need in order to do its job well?
- How will information systems help management to exercise control over current operations, and to support its competitive strategy?

Part 6 Skills development

To help you develop your skills, as well as knowledge, this section includes tasks which relate the key themes covered in the Part to your daily life. Working through these will help you to deepen your understanding of the topic, and develop skills and insights which you can use in many situations.

Task 6.1 Budgeting

Managers typically have fewer resources than they would like, so need to work with budgets – a tool to help them allocate resources between the various tasks they need to carry out. As a planning tool, budgets help identify what activities are important to the wider task, and how much resource to devote to each. Then as a control tool they help people to compare how the resources they have actually used compare with what they planned to use. Managers can then take corrective action if needed.

You can develop your skills of budgeting by working on this task.

1 Identify a project that you need to work on over the next few weeks. It could be a major study assignment or dissertation, a piece of research, a charity or student union activity you are taking part in, or an activity at work. The main criterion is that the job is one that matters to you, and will involve using scarce resources, probably of time and money. It could even be a simple personal budget for the next month.

2 List the resources you will need – your time, other people's time, materials, money, information. Think widely, as the more requirements you can anticipate now, the easier it can be to arrange for them to be available in good time. Also think how much of each you will need, being as realistic as possible: it is probably safer to overestimate what you need than to underestimate.

3 Map out when you will need these resources to be available. Do this by listing the tasks down the left-hand side of a sheet, and time (in weeks) across the top. Then work out when you will start and finish each part of the task, to show when you will need a resource. Along the bottom of the sheet you could include a row for money, indicating the total cost, if any, you will be incurring in each week. Alternatively, use that space to summarise the non-financial resources you will be needing that week (such as time).

4 As you work through the task, note regularly what activities you have completed. This is using the budget as a control tool. Compare the resources you planned to use for that with the resources you have actually used.

5 You may also have to act to ensure the budget is in line with what you planned, or take some other action such as trying to secure more resources or changing the objective.

6 Use any deviations as a basis for learning from the experience. If there is a gap, consider why that is, and whether there are any lessons to draw from it (such as being too optimistic or pessimistic, the power of unexpected events, or the influence of other people having different priorities). Use the results and lessons from this task as a starting point for future budgeting activities.

Task 6.2 Analysing a factory operation

Go to the website for the Cameron Balloons virtual factory, at **http://www.bized.ac.uk/virtual/cb/**. Do not confuse it with Cameron Balloons' own commercial website (**http://www.cameronballoons.co.uk**).

The Cameron Balloons virtual factory site contains background theory and concepts, as well as information about the company's operations.

Write a two-page report analysing the company by using the ideas in Chapter 19, such as:

- What is the business, and what are the main factors upon which the company competes?
- Which represent order winners and which represent order qualifiers?
- What affects the demand for Cameron Balloons' products and services? How variable is the demand likely to be? How can it be forecast?
- What is the main transformation performed in Cameron Balloons?
- Draw a system diagram for the company.
- What workflow systems do you think will be appropriate for the company – line, cell, functional, or concentric?
- How do you think Cameron Balloons should manage resources (human, equipment, and materials) to deal with variation in demand?
- What quality management philosophies and techniques are appropriate to use in Cameron Balloons?

You could then use the same framework to analyse another company with which you are familiar, or about which you would like to find out more.

Task 6.3 Analysing information systems

Choose an organisation of which you have some direct knowledge – one you work in, or in which you are studying. Write a short report analysing the organisation's main information systems using themes from Chapter 20, and from other relevant chapters in the book, such as:

- What types of information systems do different people in the organisation use to coordinate and control organisational activities?
- What types of computer-based systems do people use (including examples of both background and foreground systems)?
- Do the information systems provide users with information which meets the usual criteria of high quality information? If not, is the problem mainly technical or mainly organisational?
- How do the information systems affect the ability of the organisation to compete in terms of innovation, quality, delivery or cost?
- What emerging information systems may help the organisation to sustain, or radically change, its competitive position?
- What specific effects would a major investment in those technologies have on the annual financial statements of the organisation?

Administrative management is the use of institutions and order rather than relying on personal qualities to get things done.

The **administrative model of decision making** describes how people make decisions in uncertain, ambiguous situations.

Ambiguity is when people are uncertain about their goals and how best to achieve them.

Applied ethics is the application of moral philosophy to actual problems, including those in management.

Assessment centres are multi-exercise programmes designed to identify the recruitment and promotion potential of personnel.

Assets are the property, plant and equipment, vehicles, stocks of goods for trading, money owed by customers and cash: in other words, the physical resources of the business.

Authority refers to the rights inherent in a position to give instructions and to expect others to follow those instructions.

The **Balanced Scorecard** is a performance measure that looks at four areas: financial, customer, internal processes and people/innovation/growth that contribute to organisational performance.

Balance sheet shows the assets of the business and the sources from which finance has been raised.

Behaviour is something a person does that can be directly observed.

Behaviour models of leadership attempt to identify the behaviours that effective managers use to influence subordinates.

Behaviour modification is a general label for attempts to change behaviour by using appropriate and timely reinforcement.

Benchmarking is a process of comparing organisational performance and practices with others (preferably leaders).

Bounded rationality is behaviour that is rational within a decision process, which is limited (bounded) by an individual's ability to process information.

Bureaucracy is a system in which people are expected to follow precisely defined rules and procedures rather than to use personal judgement.

A **business plan** is a document which sets out the markets the business intends to serve, how it will do so and what finance they require.

The **business process** view puts satisfying customer's requirements at the heart of a design process to develop a supply system that will operate without waste. The orientation is towards speed of response and two-way flow of information and other resources.

The **capital market** comprises all the individuals and institutions that have money to invest, including banks, life assurance companies and pension funds and, as users of capital, business organisations, individuals and governments.

Cash flow statement shows the sources from which cash has been generated and how it has been spent during a period of time.

A **cell layout** creates multiple cells dedicated to producing families of output types.

Centralisation is when a relatively large number of decisions are taken by management at the top of the organisation.

Certainty describes the situation when all the information the decision maker needs is available.

A **channel** is the medium of communication between a sender and a receiver.

Coding is translating information into symbols for communication.

Coercive power is the ability to obtain compliance through fear of punishment.

Collectivism 'describes societies in which people, from birth onwards, are integrated into strong, cohesive in-groups which ... protect them in exchange for unquestioning loyalty.' (Hofstede, 1991, p. 51).

Communication is the exchange of information through written or spoken words, symbols and actions to reach a common understanding.

Competence (1) Competence concerns the actions and behaviours identified by change agents as contributing in their experience to the perceived effectiveness of change implementation. (2) Competences are those behaviours required for satisfactory ('threshold competence') or excellent ('superior competence') performance in a job.

Competitive advantage 'arises from discovering and implementing ways of competing that are unique and distinctive from those of rivals, and that can be sustained over time' (Porter, 1994).

A **competitive environment** is the industry-specific environment comprising the organisation's customers, suppliers and competitors.

Competitive or business strategy 'is concerned with the firm's position relative to its competitors in the markets which it has chosen' (Kay, 1996).

Complementarities Practices are said to be complementary when doing more of one increases the returns from doing more of another.

Concentric layout occurs in, for example, shipbuilding where the product is so large that it remains static while labour and materials come to the centre to assemble the ship.

Consideration is a pattern of leadership behaviour that demonstrates sensitivity to relationships and to the social needs of employees.

Consumer-centred organisation is focused upon and structured around the identification and satisfaction of the demands of its consumers.

Consumers are individuals, households, organisations, institutions, resellers and governments that purchase the products offered by other organisations.

Content is the specific substantive task that the group is undertaking.

Contingencies are factors such as uncertainty, interdependence and size that reflect the situation of the organisation.

Contingency approaches to organisational structure are based on the idea that performance depends on having a structure that is appropriate to the environment.

Core competencies are an organisation's major value-creating skills, capabilities and resources that shape its choice of strategy.

Corporate responsibility is the awareness, acceptance and management of the implications and effects of all corporate decision making.

Corporate strategy 'is concerned with the firm's choice of business, markets and activities' (Kay, 1996), and thus it defines the overall scope and direction of the business.

Cost expresses in money units the effect of activating or consuming resources. It is an internal control

process of the producing organisation and is not visible to outside parties.

A **cost leadership strategy** is one in which a firm uses low price as the main competitive weapon.

Counterimplementation refers to attempts to block change without displaying overt opposition.

Craft production refers to a system in which the craft producers do everything. With or without customer involvement they design, source materials, make, display, sell, perhaps service and do the accounts.

A **critical perspective** is one which evaluates an institution or practice in terms of its contribution to human autonomy, responsibility, democracy and ecologically sustainable activity.

Critical success factors are those aspects of a strategy that must be achieved to secure competitive advantage.

Current assets can be expected to be cash or to be converted to cash within a year.

Data are raw, unanalysed facts, figures and events.

A **database** consists of items of data stored in a way that enables them to be organised and retrieved in many ways.

Decentralisation is when a relatively large number of decisions are taken lower down the organisation in particular operating units.

A **decision** is a specific commitment to action (usually a commitment of resources).

Decision criteria define the factors that are relevant in making a decision.

Decision making is the process of identifying problems and opportunities and then resolving them.

A **decision support system** is a computer-based system, almost interactive, designed to assist managers in making decisions.

Decoding is the interpretation of a message into a form with meaning.

Delegating occurs when one person gives another the authority to undertake specific activities or decisions.

Delivery relates to the achievement of all promises made by any supplier to a customer.

Demand lead time is the elapsed time that a customer is prepared to allow between placing an order for a product or service and actually receiving it; in certain situations this time is effectively zero.

Determinism is the view that an organisation's structure is determined by its environment.

Differentiation (1) consists of offering a product or service that is perceived as unique or distinctive on a basis other than price. (2) The state of segmentation of the organisation into subsystems, which develop attributes relevant to their external environment.

A **divisional structure** is when tasks are grouped in relation to their outputs, such as products or the needs of different types of customer.

Emergent models of change emphasise that in uncertain conditions a project will be affected by unknown factors, and that planning has little effect on the outcome.

Enlightened self-interest is the practice of acting in a way that is costly or inconvenient at present, but which is believed to be in one's best interest in the long term.

Equity theory argues that perception of unfairness leads to tension, which then motivates the individual to resolve that unfairness.

Escalation of commitment is an increased commitment to a previous decision despite evidence that it may have been wrong.

Ethical audits are the practice of systematically reviewing the extent to which an organisation's actions are consistent with its stated ethical intentions.

Ethical consumers are those who take ethical issues into account in deciding what to purchase.

Ethical decision-making models examine the influence of individual characteristics and organisational policies on ethical decisions.

Ethical investors are people who only invest in businesses that meet specified criteria of ethical behaviour.

Ethical relativism is the principle that ethical judgements cannot be made independently of the culture in which they are made.

Existence needs reflect a person's requirement for material and energy.

Expectancy theory argues that motivation depends on a person's belief in the probability that effort will lead to good performance, and that good performance will lead to them receiving an outcome they value (valence).

Expertise power is evident when a person's knowledge of the topic enables them to influence decisions.

The **external context** consists of elements beyond the organisation such as competitors, or the wider PESTEL factors.

External fit is when there is a close and consistent relationship between an organisation's competitive strategy and its HRM strategy.

An **extranet** is a version of the Internet that is restricted to specified people in specified companies – such as major customers or suppliers.

Extrinsic rewards are valued outcomes or benefits provided by others, such as promotion, a pay increase or a bigger car.

Factory production broke down the integrated nature of the craftworker's approach and made it possible to increase the supply of goods by dividing tasks into simple and repetitive sequences.

Feedback (in communication) occurs as the receiver expresses his or her reaction to the sender's message.

Feedback (in a system) refers to the extent to which people receive information about performance.

Femininity pertains to societies in which social gender roles overlap.

Five forces analysis is a technique for identifying and listing those aspects of the five forces most relevant to the profitability of an organisation at that time.

Fixed assets are the physical properties that the company possesses – such as land, buildings, production equipment and vehicles – and which are likely to have a useful life or more than one year. There may also be intangible assets such as patent rights or copyrights.

Flexible manufacturing is a manufacturing technology using computers to automate and integrate manufacturing components such as robots, machines, design and engineering.

A **focus strategy** is when a company competes by targeting very specific segments of the market.

Formal authority is the right that a person in a specified role has to make decisions, allocate resources or give instructions.

Formal structure is the official guidelines, documents or procedures setting out how the organisation's activities are divided and coordinated.

A **formal team** is one that management has deliberately created to perform specific tasks to help meet organisational goals.

Formalisation is the practice of using written or electronic documents to direct and control employees.

Functional managers are responsible for the performance of a common area of technical or professional work.

A **functional layout** groups similar physical processes together and brings materials and/or customers to these areas.

A **functional structure** is when tasks are grouped into departments based on similar skills and expertise.

The **general environment** (sometimes known as the macro-environment) includes economic, political, social and technological factors that generally affect all organisations.

General managers are responsible for the performance of a distinct unit of the organisation.

Global companies work in many countries, securing resources and finding markets in whichever country is most suitable.

Globalisation refers to the increasing integration of internationally dispersed economic activities.

A **goal** is a desired future state for an activity or organisational unit.

Goal-setting theory argues that motivation is influenced by goal difficulty, goal specificity and knowledge of results.

Groupthink is 'a mode of thinking that people engage in when they are deeply involved in a cohesive in-group, when the members' striving for unanimity overrides their motivation to realistically appraise alternative courses of action' (Janis, 1972).

Groupware systems provide electronic communication between members of geographically dispersed teams.

Growth needs are those which impel people to be creative or to produce an effect on themselves or their environment.

High-context cultures are those in which information is implicit and can only be fully understood by those with shared experiences in the culture.

A **high-performance team** is one that meets all the requirements of a real team, but in addition shows commitment to the personal growth of members and performs beyond expectations.

Horizontal specialisation is the degree to which tasks are divided among separate people or departments.

Human relations approach is a school of management which emphasises the importance of social processes at work.

Human resource management is the effective use of human resources in order to enhance organisational performance.

Hygiene factors (or maintenance factors) are those aspects surrounding the task which can prevent discontent and dissatisfaction but will not in themselves contribute to psychological growth and hence motivation.

People use an **incremental model** of decision making when they are uncertain about the consequences.

They search for a limited range of options, and policy unfolds from a series of cumulative small decisions.

Individualism pertains to societies in which the ties between individuals are loose.

Influence is the process by which one party attempts to modify the behaviour of others by mobilising power resources.

An **informal group** is one that emerges when people come together and interact regularly.

Informal structure is the undocumented relationships between members of the organisation that inevitably emerge as people adapt systems to new conditions and satisfy personal and group needs.

Information comes from data that has been processed so that it has meaning for the person receiving it.

Information overload arises when the amount of information a person has to deal with exceeds their capacity to process it.

Information richness refers to the amount of information that a communication channel can carry, and the extent to which it enables sender and receiver to achieve common understanding.

An **information system** is a set of people, procedures and resources that collects and transforms data into information and disseminates this information.

Information systems management is the planning, acquisition, development and use of these systems.

Initiating structure is a pattern of leadership behaviour that emphasises the performance of the work in hand and the achievement of production or service goals.

Innovation covers incremental and/or step (breakthrough) changes in products and/or processes which change function, form, performance or resource use in an advantageous way.

Institutional advantage 'is when a not-for-profit body performs its tasks more effectively than other comparable organisations' (Goold, 1997).

Instrumentality is the perceived probability that good performance will lead to valued rewards, measured on a scale from 0 (no chance) to 1 (certainty).

Integration is the process of achieving unity of effort amongst the various subsystems in accomplishing the organisation's task.

The **interaction model** is a theory of change which stresses the continuing interaction between the internal and external contexts of an organisation, making the outcomes of change hard to predict.

Interdependence is the extent to which departments depend on each other for resources or materials to accomplish their tasks.

The **internal context** consists of elements within the organisation such as its technology, structure or business processes.

Internal fit is when the various components of the HRM strategy support each other and consistently encourage certain attitudes and behaviour.

International management is the practice of managing business operations in more than one country.

Internationalisation is the increasing geographical dispersion of economic activities across national borders.

The **Internet** is a web of hundreds of thousands of computer networks linked together by telephone lines through which data can be carried.

An **inter-organisational system** is a computer system that enables data and information to pass between organisations, such as electronic orders or invoices.

An **intranet** is a version of the Internet that only specified people within an organisation can use.

Intrinsic rewards are valued outcomes or benefits that come from the individual, such as feelings of satisfaction, achievement and competence.

Inventory consists of materials and part or finished goods that are held in anticipation of need by customers along a chain of supply from raw materials through to final consumption (and recycling?).

Job analysis is the process of determining the characteristics of an area of work according to a prescribed set of dimensions.

A **job enrichment model** represents the idea that managers can change specific job characteristics to promote job satisfaction and so motivate employees.

Knowledge builds on information and embodies a person's prior understanding, experience and learning.

A **knowledge system** is a system that incorporates the decision-making logic of a human expert.

Leadership refers to the process of influencing the activities of others towards high levels of goal setting and achievement.

Legitimate power flows from the person's formal position, which gives them authority over defined matters.

Liabilities of a business as reported in the balance sheet are the debts and financial obligations of the business to all those people and institutions that are not shareholders, e.g. a bank, suppliers.

Life cycle models of change are those that view change as an activity which follows a logical, orderly sequence of activities that can be planned in advance.

A **limited liability** company has an identity and existence in its own right as distinct from its owners (shareholders in Europe, stockholders in North America). A shareholder has an ownership right in the company in which the shares are held.

Line layout is completely specified by the sequence of activities needed to perform a given transformation.

Line managers are responsible for the performance of activities that directly meet customers' needs.

Low-context cultures are those where people are more psychologically distant so that information needs to be explicit if members are to understand it.

Management is the activity of getting things done with the aid of people and other resources.

Management as a general human activity occurs whenever people take responsibility for an activity and consciously try to shape its progress and outcome.

Management as a specialist occupation develops when activities previously embedded in the work itself become the responsibility not of the employee but of owners or their agents.

Management role is the sum of the expectations which others have of a manager.

Management tasks are those of planning, organising, leading and controlling the use of resources to add value to them.

A **manager** is someone who gets things done with the aid of people and other resources.

Market segmentation is the process of dividing markets comprising the heterogeneous needs of many consumers into segments comprising the homogeneous needs of smaller groups.

Marketing is a management process that identifies, anticipates and supplies consumer requirements efficiently and effectively.

The **marketing environment** consists of the actors and forces outside marketing that affect the marketing manager's ability to develop and maintain successful relationships with its target consumers.

A **marketing information system** is the systematic process for the collection, analysis and distribution of marketing information.

The **marketing mix** is the mix of decisions about product features, prices, communications and distribution of products used by the marketing manager to position products competitively within the minds of consumers.

Marketing orientation is an organisational orientation that believes success is most effectively achieved by satisfying consumer demands.

Masculinity pertains to societies in which social gender roles are clearly distinct.

A **matrix structure** is when those doing a task report both to a functional and a project or divisional boss.

A **mechanistic structure** means there is a high degree of task specialisation, people's responsibility and authority are closely defined and decision making is centralised.

The **message** is what the sender communicates.

A **metaphor** is an image used to signify the essential characteristics of a phenomenon.

A **mission statement** is a broad definition of an organisation's operations and scope, aiming to distinguish it from similar organisations.

A **model** represents a complex phenomenon by identifying the major elements and relationships.

A **monitoring system** is a computer-based system that processes data to provide information about the performance of a business process.

Motivator factors are those aspects of the work itself that Herzberg found influenced people to superior performance and effort.

Motivation refers to the forces within or beyond a person that arouse and sustain their commitment to a course of action.

Multinational companies are based in one country, but have significant production and marketing operations in many others.

A **network structure** is when tasks required by one company are performed by other companies with expertise in those areas.

Networking refers to 'individuals' attempts to develop and maintain relationships with others (who) have the potential to assist them in their work or career' (Huczynski, 2004, p. 305).

Noise is anything that confuses, diminishes or interferes with communication.

Non-linear systems are those in which small changes are amplified through many interactions with other variables so that the eventual effect is unpredictable.

A **non-programmed decision** is a unique decision that requires a custom-made solution when information is lacking or unclear.

Non-receptive contexts are those where the combined effects of features of the organisation (such as culture or technology) tend to hinder change.

Non-verbal communication is the process of coding meaning through behaviours such as facial expression, gestures and body postures.

Observation is the activity of concentrating on how a team works rather than taking part in the activity itself.

An **open system** is one that interacts with its environment.

Operational plans detail how the overall objectives are to be achieved, by specifying what senior management expects from specific departments or functions.

Operational research attempts to solve complex problems by developing mathematical models to analyse the many variables.

Operational strategies are those deployed by the different functions of the organisation, such as manufacturing, marketing, finance and human resource management, and which contribute to the achievement of corporate strategy.

An **operational system** is a computer application that processes transactions in an orderly and efficient way to provide a desired output.

An **opportunity** is the chance to do something not previously expected.

An **order qualifier** is a necessary but not sufficient requirement to be considered by a customer.

An **order winner** is some feature of the product that so positively differentiates it that customers want to buy it in preference to competing products.

An **organic structure** is one where people are expected to work together and to use their initiative to solve problems; job descriptions and rules are few and imprecise.

An **organisation** is a social arrangement for achieving controlled performance towards goals that create value.

An **organisation chart** shows the main departments and senior positions in an organisation and the reporting relations between them.

Organisation culture is the collection of relatively uniform and enduring values, beliefs, customs and practices that are uniquely shared by an organisation's members and which are transmitted from one generation of employees to the next.

Organisation Development (OD) is a systematic process in which applied behavioural science principles and practices are introduced with the goal of increasing individual and organisational performance.

Organisation structure 'The structure of an organisation [is] the sum total of the ways in which it divides its labour into distinct tasks and then achieves co-ordination among them' (Mintzberg, 1989).

An **organisational capability** is an activity that an organisation can perform better than its competitors.

Organisational change is a deliberate attempt to improve performance by changing one or more aspects of the organisation, such as its technology, structure or business processes.

An **organisational system** is a computer system that enables data and information to pass between units of an organisation.

Outer context of change relates to environmental factors, such as competitor behaviour, customer demands or other factors in the external environment.

The **participative perspective** is the belief that if people are able to take part in planning a change, they will be more willing to accept and implement the change.

Partnering describes a business relationship based on taking a long-term view that the partners wish to work together to enhance customers' satisfaction.

A **perceived performance gap** arises when people believe that the actual performance of a unit or business is out of line with the level they desire.

Perception is the active psychological process in which stimuli are selected and organised into meaningful patterns.

Performance appraisal is a systematic review of a person's work and achievements over a recent period, usually leading to plans for the future.

Performance imperatives are those aspects of performance which are especially important for an organisation to do well, such as flexibility and innovation.

Performance-related pay refers to payment systems in which a percentage of pay depends on the assessed performance of individuals, groups or the organisation as a whole.

A **person culture** is one in which activity is strongly influenced by the wishes of the individuals who are part of the organisation.

PESTEL analysis is a technique for identifying and listing the political, economic, social, technological environmental and legal factors in the general environment most relevant to an organisation.

Philanthropy is the practice of contributing personal wealth to charitable or similar causes.

Planning is the task of setting objectives, specifying how to achieve them, implementing the plan and evaluating the results.

A **policy** is a guideline that establishes some general principles for making a decision.

Political behaviour is 'the practical domain of power in action, worked out through the use of techniques of influence and other (more or less extreme) tactics' (Buchanan and Badham, 1999).

The **political model** is a model of decision making that reflects the view that an organisation consists of groups with different interests, goals and values.

Political models of change emphasise that change is likely to affect the interests of stakeholders unevenly and that those who see themselves losing will resist the change despite the rationality of the arguments or invitations to participate.

The **political perspective** reflects the view that organisations are made up of groups with separate interests, goals and values, and that these affect how they respond to change.

Power concerns 'the capacity of individuals to exert their will over others' (Buchanan and Badham, 1999).

A **power culture** is one in which people's activities are strongly influenced by a dominant central figure.

Power distance is the extent to which the less powerful members of organisations within a country expect and accept that power is distributed unevenly.

Preferred team roles are the types of behaviour that people display relatively frequently when they are part of a team.

A **problem** is a gap between an existing and a desired state of affairs.

A **procedure** is a series of related steps to deal with a structured problem.

A **process** is the way people interact with each other in performing a task, such as how they make decisions.

Process consultation is an OD intervention in which an external consultant facilitates improvements in an organisation's diagnostic, conceptual and action planning skills.

Product is a generic term used to identify both tangible goods and intangible services.

The **product life cycle** suggests that products pass through the stages of introduction, growth, maturity and decline.

Product position is the position in which consumers place a product relative to that of an alternative supplier.

Profit and loss statement reflects the benefits derived from the trading activities of the business during a period of time.

A **programmed decision** is a repetitive decision that can be handled by a routine approach.

A **project manager** is someone who is responsible for managing a project, usually intended to change some aspects of an organisation.

A **pseudo-team** is a collection of individuals who could perform more effectively but have shown no interest in developing the necessary skills and methods.

A **psychological contract** is the set of understandings people have regarding the commitments made between themselves and their organisation.

The **quality** of a product or service is the (often imprecise) perception of a customer that what has been provided is at least what was expected for the price he or she paid.

The **rational model of decision making** assumes that people make consistent choices to maximise economic value within specified constraints.

Real goals are those to which people give most attention.

Receptive contexts are those where features of the organisation (such as culture or technology) tend to help change.

Referent power (or charismatic power) arises when subordinates want to identify with the leader, on account of some personal characteristics of the leader.

Relatedness needs involve a desire for relationships with significant other people.

Relationship marketing is an approach that focuses on developing a series of transactions with consumers.

Responsibility refers to a person attempting to meet the expectations others have of them.

Reward power is the ability of someone to reward another through possessing resources the other values.

Risk refers to situations in which the decision maker is able to estimate the likelihood of the alternative outcomes.

A **role** is the sum of the expectations that other people have of a person occupying a position.

A **role culture** is one in which people's activities are strongly influenced by clear and detailed job descriptions and other formal signals as to what is expected of them.

A **rule** sets out what someone can or cannot do in a given situation.

Satisficing is the acceptance by decision makers of the first solution that is 'good enough'.

Scenario planning is an attempt to build plausible views of a small number of different possible futures for an organisation.

Scientific management The school of management called 'scientific' attempted to create a science of factory production.

Selection tests are formal, often psychologically based methods of assessing candidates' likely suitability for a job.

Selective attention is the ability, often unconscious, to choose from the stream of signals in the environment, concentrating on some and ignoring others.

Self-efficacy is an individual's belief that he or she is capable of performing a task.

A **sensitivity analysis** tests the effect on a plan of several alternative values of the key variables.

Sensitivity training is a technique for enhancing self-awareness and changing behaviour through unstructured group discussion.

Shareholders are the principal risk takers in a company. They contribute the long-term capital for which they expect to be rewarded in the form of dividends – a distribution from the profit of the business.

Shareholders' funds are the capital contributed by the shareholders plus profits that have not been distributed to the shareholders.

Situational models of leadership attempt to identify the contextual factors that affect when one style will be more effective than another.

Skill refers to a person's ability to perform various types of cognitive or behavioural activity effectively.

The **social contract** consists of the mutual obligations that society and business recognise they have to each other.

A **sociotechnical approach** is a systems development strategy that attempts to improve simultaneously the performance of the organisation and the quality of the working life of the workers.

A **sociotechnical system** is one in which outcomes depend on the interaction of both the technical and social subsystems.

A **span of control** is the number of subordinates reporting directly to the person above them in the hierarchy.

Staff managers are responsible for the performance of functions that provide support to line managers.

Stakeholder mapping is a means of identifying the expectations and power of different stakeholders.

Stakeholders are individuals, groups or other organisations with an interest in, or who are affected by, what the organisation does.

Stated goals are those which are prominent in company publications and websites.

Stereotyping is the practice of consigning a person to a category or personality type on the basis of their membership of some known group.

A **strategic alliance** is when firms agree to cooperate to achieve commercial objectives.

A **strategic business unit** consists of a number of closely related products for which it is meaningful to formulate a separate strategy.

Strategic management is an organisation-wide task involving both the development and implementation of strategy.

A **strategic plan** sets out the overall direction for the business, is broad in scope and covers all the major activities.

Strategy is concerned with deciding what business an organisation should be in, where it wants to be, and how it is going to get there.

Structural choice approaches emphasise the scope management has for deciding the form of structure, irrespective of external conditions.

Structure is the regularity in the way a unit or group is organised, such as the roles that are specified.

Subjective probability (in expectancy theory) is a person's estimate of the likelihood that a certain level of effort (E) will produce a level of performance (P) which will then lead to an expected outcome (O).

Subsystems are the separate but related parts that make up the total system.

Succession planning is the use of a deliberate process to ensure that staff are developed who are able to replace senior management as required.

Supply lead time is the total elapsed time between the decision to obtain the basic input resources to the final delivery of the product or service to the customer.

Survey feedback is an OD intervention in which the results of an opinion survey are fed back to respondents to trigger problem-solving on the issues which the survey identifies.

A **SWOT analysis** is a way of summarising the organisation's main strengths and weaknesses relative to external opportunities and threats.

A **system** is a set of interrelated parts designed to achieve a purpose.

A **system boundary** separates the system from its environment.

A **system of supportive relationships** refers to the inter-actions and experiences that build a person's sense of personal worth.

The **systems approach** looks at the different parts of an interacting set of activities as a whole and considers the best way for the whole to function.

A **target market** is the segment of the market selected by the organisation as the focus of its activities.

A **task culture** is one in which the focus of activity is towards completing a task or project using whatever means are appropriate.

A **team** is 'a small number of people with complementary skills who are committed to a common purpose, performance goals, and approach for which they hold themselves mutually accountable' (Katzenbach and Smith, 1993b).

Team-based rewards are 'payments or non-financial incentives provided to members of a formally established team and linked to the performance of the group' (IPD, 1996).

Technology is the knowledge, equipment and activities used to transform inputs into outputs.

Teleology is the practice of evaluating a decision against the criterion of whether the outcome achieves the original goal.

Traits are a variety of individual attributes, including aspects of personality, temperament, needs, motives and values.

A **transactional leader** is one who treats leadership as an exchange, giving followers what they want if they do what the leader desires.

Transactional marketing is an approach that focuses upon one-off exchanges with consumers.

A **transformational leader** is one who treats leadership as a matter of motivation and commitment, inspiring followers by appealing to higher ideals and moral values.

Transnational companies operate in many countries and delegate many decisions to local managers.

Uncertainty is when people are clear about their goals, but have little information about which course of action is most likely to succeed.

Uncertainty avoidance is the extent to which members of a culture feel threatened by uncertain or unknown situations.

Utilitarianism is the practice of evaluating a decision against the criterion of its consequences for the majority of people.

Valence is the perceived value or preference that an individual has for a particular outcome.

Validity occurs when there is a statistically significant relationship between a predictor (such as a selection test score) and subsequent measures of on-the-job performance.

Value is added to resources when they are transformed into goods or services that are worth more than their original cost plus the cost of transformation.

GLOSSARY

A **value chain** 'divides a firm into the discrete activities it performs in designing, producing, marketing and distributing its product. It is the basic tool for diagnosing competitive advantage and finding ways to enhance it' (Porter, 1985).

A **value for money service** is one that is provided economically, efficiently and effectively.

Vertical specialisation refers to the extent to which responsibilities at different levels are defined.

Virtual organisations are those that deliver goods and services but have few, if any, of the physical features of conventional businesses.

A **working group** is a collection of individuals who work mainly on their own but interact socially and share information and best practices.

Academy of Management (1996), Human Resources Division, *News*, Summer.

Ackroyd, S. and Thompson, P. (1999), *Organizational Misbehaviour*, Sage, London.

Adair, J. (1997), *Leadership Skills*, Chartered Institute of Personnnel and Development, London.

Adams, K. (1996), 'Respecting the difference: international competences for managers', *Competency*, vol. 4, no. 1, pp. 24–30.

Adams, J. S. (1963), 'Towards an understanding of inequity', *Journal of Abnormal and Social Psychology*, vol. 67, no. 4, pp. 422–436.

Adams, S. (1998), *The Dilbert Principle*, Boxtree, London.

Alderfer, C. (1972), *Existence, Relatedness and Growth: Human needs in organizational settings*, Free Press, New York.

Alexander, D. and Nobes, C. (2004), *International Introduction to Financial Accounting*, Financial Times/Prentice Hall, Harlow.

Alvesson, M. and Billing, Y.D. (2000), 'Questioning the notion of feminine leadership: a critical perspective on the gender-labelling of leadership', *Gender, Work and Organization*, vol. 7, no. 3, pp. 144–157.

Alvesson, M. and Wilmott, H. (1996), *Making Sense of Management*, Sage, London.

Anderson, T. and Metcalf, H. (2003), *Diversity: Stacking up the evidence. Executive briefing*, Chartered Institute of Personnel and Development, London.

Andersen, T.J. (2000), 'Strategic planning, autonomous actions and corporate performance', *Long Range Planning*, vol. 33, no. 2, pp.184–200.

Ansoff, H.I. (1965), *Corporate Strategy*, Penguin, London.

Ansoff, H.I. (1991), 'Critique of Mintzberg's "Design School"', *Strategic Management Journal*, vol. 12, no. 6, pp. 449–461.

Applegate, L.M., McFarlan, F.W. and McKenney, J.L. (2000), *Corporate Information Systems Management: Text and case studies* (5th edn), Irwin, Chicago, IL.

Argenti, J. (1997), 'Stakeholders: the case against', *Long Range Planning*, vol. 30, no. 3, pp. 442–445.

Argyle, M. (1988), *Bodily Communication*, Methuen, London.

Armstrong, G. and Kotler, P. (2000), *Marketing: An introduction* (5th edn), Financial Times/Prentice Hall, Harlow.

Armstrong, J. (1982), 'Value of formal planning for strategic decisions', *Strategic Management Journal*, vol. 3, no. 3, pp. 197–211.

Arnold, J., Hope, T., Southworth, A. and Kirkham, L. (1995), *Financial Accounting* (2nd edn), Financial Times/Prentice Hall, Hemel Hempstead.

Ashkenas, R. (1995), *The Boundaryless Organisation: Breaking the chains of organisation structure*, Jossey-Bass, San Francisco, CA.

Aslani, A. and Luthans, F. (2003), 'What knowledge managers really do: an empirical and comparative analysis', *Journal of Knowledge Management*, vol. 7, no. 3, pp. 53–66.

Atkinson, A., Kaplan, R. and Young, S. (2003), *Management Accounting* (4th edn), Financial Times/Prentice Hall, Harlow.

Babbage, C. (1835), *On the Economy of Machinery and Manufactures*, Charles Knight, London. Reprinted in 1986 by Augustus Kelly, Fairfield, NJ.

Balachandra, R. (2000), 'An expert system for new product development', *Industrial Management and Data Systems*, vol. 100, no. 7, pp. 317–328.

Bandura, A. (1997), *Self-efficacy: The exercise of control*, Freeman, New York.

Barnard, C. (1938), *The Functions of the Executive*, Harvard University Press, Cambridge, MA.

Baron and Greenberg (1997) *Behaviour in Organizations*, Pearson Education, Upper Saddle River, NJ.

Bartlett, D. (2003), 'Management and business ethics: a critique and integration of ethical decision-making models', *British Journal of Management*, vol. 14, no. 3, pp. 223–235.

Bass, B.M. (1990), *Handbook of Leadership: A survey of theory and research*, Free Press, New York.

Bate, P. (2000), 'Changing the culture of a hospital: from hierarchy to networked community', *Public Administration*, vol. 78, no. 3, pp. 485–512.

Batt, R. (2002), 'Managing customer services: human resource practices, quit rates and sales growth', *Academy of Management Journal*, vol. 45, no. 3, pp. 587–597.

Baum, J.R. and Locke, E.A. (2004), 'The relationship of entrepreneurial traits, skill and motivation to subsequent venture growth', *Journal of Applied Psychology*, vol. 89, no. 4, pp. 587–598.

Beall, A.E. (2004), 'Body language speaks: reading and responding more effectively to hidden communication', *Communication World*, vol. 21, no. 2, pp. 18–20.

REFERENCES

Beaumont, P.B. (1996), 'Trade unions and HRM' in B. Towers (ed.), *A Handbook of Human Resource Management* (2nd edn), Blackwell, Oxford.

Becker, B., Huselid, M.A. and Urich, D. (2001), *The HR Scorecard*, Harvard Business School Press, Boston, MA.

Beer, M. (1985), 'Note on performance appraisal', in M. Beer and B. Spector (eds), *Readings in Human Resource Management*, Free Press, New York.

Beer, M. and Cannon, M.D. (2002), 'Promise and peril in implementing pay-for-performance', *Human Resource Management*, vol. 43, no. 1, pp. 23–48.

Beer, M. and Spector, B. (eds) (1985), *Readings in Human Resource Management*, Free Press, New York.

Belbin, R.M. (1981), *Management Teams: Why they succeed or fail*, Butterworth/Heinemann, Oxford.

Belbin, R.M. (1993), *Team Roles at Work*, Butterworth/Heinemann, Oxford.

Bennis, W.G. (1969), *Organization Development: Its nature, origins and prospects*, Addison-Wesley, Reading, MA.

Bessant, J. (1991), *Managing Advanced Manufacturing Technology: The challenge of the New Wave*, Blackwell, Oxford.

Biggs, L. (1996), *The Rational Factory*, The Johns Hopkins University Press, Baltimore, MD.

Birsh, D. and Fielder, J.H. (eds) (1994), *The Ford Pinto Case: A Study in applied ethics, business and technology*, Albany State University of New York Press, NY.

Bjorn-Andersen, N. and Turner, J. (1994), 'Creating the twenty-first century organization: the metamorphosis of Oticon', in R. Baskerville *et al.*, *Transforming Organizations with Information Technology*, Elsevier Science/North-Holland, Amsterdam.

Blackwell, E. (2004), *How to Prepare a Business Plan* (4th edn), Kogan Page, London.

Blake, R.R. and Mouton, J.S. (1979), *The New Managerial Grid*, Gulf Publishing, Houston, TX.

Blake, R.R. and Mouton, J.S. (1964), *The Managerial Grid*, Gulf Publishing, Houston, TX.

Blakstad, M. and Cooper, A. (1995), *The Communicating Organization*, Institute of Personnel and Development, London.

Blau, P.M. (1970), 'A formal theory of differentiation in organizations', *American Sociological Review*, vol. 35, no. 2, pp. 201–218.

Bloemhof, M., Haspeslagh, P. and Slagmulder, R. (2004), *Strategy and Performance at DSM*, INSEAD, Fontainebleau (Case 304-067-1, distributed by The European Case Clearing House).

Boddy, D. (2002), *Managing Projects: Building and leading the team*, Financial Times Prentice Hall, Harlow.

Boddy, D., Boonstra, A. and Kennedy, G. (2005), *Managing Information Systems: An organisational perspective* (2nd edn), Financial Times/Prentice Hall, Harlow.

Boddy, D. and Gunson, N. (1996), *Organizations in the Network Age*, Routledge, London.

Boddy, D., Macbeth, D.K. and Wagner, B. (2000), 'Implementing collaboration between organisations: an empirical study of supply chain partnering', *Journal of Management Studies*, vol. 37, no. 7, pp. 1003–1017.

Boisot, M.H. (1998) *Knowledge Assets: Securing competitive advantage in the information economy*, Oxford University Press, Oxford.

Boonstra, A., Boddy, D. and Fischbacher, M. (2004), 'The limited acceptance by general practitioners of an electronic prescription system: reasons and practical implications', *New Technology, Work and Employment*, vol. 19, no. 2, pp. 128–144.

Boselie, P. and Dietz, G. (2003), *Commonalities and contradictions in research on human resource management and performance*, paper presented at the Academy of Management Meeting in Seattle, WA, August 2003.

Bowen, D.E. and Lawler, E.E. (1992), 'The empowerment of service workers: what, why, how and when?' *MIT Sloan Management Review*, vol. 33, no. 3, pp. 31–39.

Bowen, D.E., Ledford, G.E. and Nathan, B.R. (1996), 'Hiring for the organization, not the job', in J. Billsberry (ed.), *The Effective Manager: Perspectives and illustrations*, Sage, London.

Bowman, C. and Asch, D. (1996), *Managing Strategy*, Macmillan Business, Basingstoke.

Brech, E.F.L. (1957), *Organization: The framework of management*, Longmans Green, London.

Brews, P.J. and Hunt, M.R. (1999), 'Learning to plan and planning to learn: resolving the planning school/learning school debate', *Strategic Management Journal*, vol. 20, no. 10, pp. 889–913.

Brewster, C. (1994), 'European HRM: reflection of, or challenge to, the American concept?' in P. Kirkbride (ed.), *Human Resource Management in Europe*, Routledge, London.

Buchanan, D. (2001), *The Lived Experience of Strategic Change: A hospital case study*, Leicester Business School Occasional Paper 64.

Buchanan, D. and Huczynski, A.A. (2004), *Organizational Behaviour: An introductory text* (5th edn), Financial Times/Prentice Hall, Harlow.

Buchanan, D. and Boddy, D. (1992), *The Expertise of the Change Agent*, Prentice Hall International, Hemel Hempstead.

Buchanan, D. and Badham, R. (1999), *Power, Politics and Organizational Change: Winning the turf game*, Sage, London.

Burnes, B. (1996), *Managing Change*, Pitman, London.

Burns, J.M. (1978), *Leadership*, Harper & Row, New York.

Burns, T. (1961), 'Micropolitics: mechanisms of organizational change', *Administrative Science Quarterly*, vol. 6, no. 3, pp. 257–281.

Burns, T. and Stalker, G.M. (1961), *The Management of Innovation*, Tavistock, London.

Butt, J. (ed.) (1971), *Robert Owen: Prince of cotton spinners*, David & Charles, Newton Abbott.

Cairncross, F. (2001), *The Death of Distance 2.0: How the communications revolution will change our lives*, Orion, London.

Campbell, A. (1997), 'Stakeholders: the case in favour', *Long Range Planning*, vol. 30, no. 3, pp. 446–449.

Camuffo, A., Romano, P. and Vinelli, A. (2001), 'Back to the future: Benetton transforms its global network', *MIT Sloan Management Review*, vol. 43, no. 1, pp. 46–52.

Cannon, T. (1996), *Basic Marketing: Principles and practice* (4th edn), Cassell, London.

Cappelli, P. (2000), 'Managing without commitment', *Organizational Dynamics*, vol. 28, no. 4, pp. 11–25.

Carlson, S. (1951), *Executive Behaviour*, Stromberg Aktiebolag, Stockholm.

Carr, N.G. (2004), 'In praise of walls', *MIT Sloan Management Review*, vol. 45, no. 3, pp. 10–12.

Carroll, A.B. (1999), 'Corporate social responsibility', *Business and Society*, vol. 38, no. 3, pp. 268–295.

Catterick, P. (1995), *Business Planning for Housing*, Chartered Institute of Housing, Coventry.

Chaffey, D. (ed.) (2003), *Business Information Systems* (2nd edn), Financial Times/Prentice Hall, Harlow.

Champy, J. and Nohria, N. (1996), *Fast Forward*, Harvard Business School Press, Cambridge, MA.

Chandler, A.D. (1962), *Strategy and Structure*, MIT Press, Cambridge, MA.

Chapman, D. and Cowdell, T. (1998), *New Public Sector Marketing*, Financial Times Management, London.

Chen, M. (2004), *Asian Management Systems*, Thomson, London.

Cherns, A. (1987), 'The principles of sociotechnical design revisited', *Human Relations*, vol. 40, no. 3, pp. 153–162.

Child, J. (1972), 'Organizational structure, environment and performance: the role of strategic choice', *Sociology*, vol. 6, pp.1–22.

Child, J. (1984), *Organisation: A guide to problems and practice* (2nd edn), Harper & Row, London.

Chow, I. (1994), 'An opinion survey of performance appraisal practices in Hong Kong and the People's Republic of China', *Asia Pacific Journal of Human Resources*, vol. 32, pp. 62–79.

Christensen, C.M. and Raynor, M.E. (2003), *The Innovator's Solution*, Harvard Business School Press, Boston, MA.

Chrysalides, G.A.D. and Kale, J.H. (1993), *An Introduction to Business Ethics*, Chapman & Hall, London.

CIPD (2002), Pensions and HR's Role, Chartered Institute of Personnel and Development, London.

Clarke, F.L. (2003), *Corporate Collapse: Accounting, regulatory and ethical failure*, Cambridge University Press, Cambridge.

Clutterbuck, D. (1994), *The Power of Empowerment*, Kogan Page, London.

Clutterbuck, D. and Dearlove, D. (1996), *The Charity as a Business*, Directory of Social Change, London.

Coggan, P. (2002), *The Money Machine*, Penguin, Harmondsworth.

Cooke, B. (2003), 'The denial of slavery in management studies', *Journal of Management Studies*, vol. 40, no. 8, pp. 1895–1918.

Cooke, S. and Slack, N. (1991), *Making Management Decisions* (2nd edn) Prentice Hall, Hemel Hempstead.

Coombs, R. and Hull, R. (1994), 'The best or the worst of both worlds: BPR, cost reduction, and the strategic management of IT', paper presented to the OASIG Seminar on Organizational Change, London, September.

Corfield, R. (1999), *Successful Interview Skills*, Kogan Page, London.

Cravens, D.W. (1991), *Strategic Marketing* (3rd edn), Irwin, Chicago, IL.

Critchley, W. and Casey, D. (1984), 'Second thoughts on team building', *Management Education and Development*, vol. 15, no. 2, pp. 163–175.

Crosby, P. (1979), *Quality is Free*, McGraw-Hill, New York.

Cusumano, M. (1997), 'How Microsoft makes large teams work like small teams', *MIT Sloan Management Review*, vol. 39, no. 1, pp. 9–20.

Cusumano, M.A. and Nobeoka, K. (1998), *Thinking Beyond Lean*, The Free Press, New York.

Cyert, R. and March, J.G. (1963), *A Behavioral Theory of the Firm*, Prentice Hall, Englewood Cliffs, NJ.

Daft, R.L. (2000), *Management* (5th edn), The Dryden Press, Fort Worth, TX.

Damasio, A.R. (2000), *The Feeling of What Happened*, Heinemann, London.

Daniels, J.D. and Radebaugh, L.H. (1998), *International Business* (8th edn), Addison-Wesley, Reading, MA.

Davenport, T.H. (1998), 'Putting the enterprise into enterprise systems', *Harvard Business Review*, vol. 76, no. 4, pp. 121–132.

Davis, K. (1960), 'Can business afford to ignore social responsibilities?' *California Management Review*, vol. 2, no. 3, pp. 70–76.

REFERENCES

Davis, K. (1971), *Business, Society and Environment: Social power and social response*, McGraw-Hill, New York.

Deal, T.E. and Kennedy, A.A. (1982), *Corporate Culture: The rites and rituals of corporate life*, Addison-Wesley, Reading, MA.

Deming, W.E. (1988), *Out of the Crisis*, Cambridge University Press, Cambridge.

Delaney, J.T. and Huselid, M.A. (1996), 'The impact of human resource management practices on perceptions of organizational performance', *Academy of Management Journal*, vol. 39, no. 4, pp. 949–969.

Delmar, F. and Shane, S. (2003), 'Does business planning facilitate the development of new ventures?', *Strategic Management Journal*, vol. 24, no. 12, pp. 1165–1185.

Dent, C.M. (1997), *The European Economy: The global context*, Routledge, London.

Department of Trade and Industry (1996), *The Rewards of Success: Flexible pay systems in Britain*, DTI, London.

de Wit, B. and Meyer, R. (2004), *Strategy: Process, Content and Context, an International Perspective*, International Thomson Business, London.

Dibb, S., Simkin, L., Pride, W.M. and Ferrell, O.C. (1997), *Marketing: Concepts and strategies* (4th edn), Houghton-Mifflin, New York.

Dicken, P. (1992), *Global Shift: The internationalisation of economic activity*, PCP, London.

Dimbleby, R. and Burton, G. (1992), *More Than Words: An introduction to communication* (2nd edn), Routledge, London.

Dobson, P., Starkey, K. and Richards, J. (2004), *Strategic Management: Issues and cases*, Blackwell, Oxford.

Donaldson, L. (1995), *Contingency Theory*, Dartmouth, Aldershot.

Donaldson, L. (1996), *For Positive Organization Theory*, Sage, London.

Donaldson, L. (2001), *The Contingency Theory of Organizations*, Sage, London.

Drucker, P.F. (1954), *The Practice of Management*, Harper, New York.

Drucker, P.F. (1985), *Innovation and Entrepreneurship*, Heinemann, London.

Drucker, P.F. (1999), *Innovation and Entrepreneurship* (2nd edn), Butterworth-Heinemann, Oxford.

Drummond, H. (1996), *Escalation in Decision-Making*, Oxford University Press, Oxford.

Drury, C. (2004), *Management and Cost Accounting*, Thomson Learning, London.

Druskat, V.U. and Wheeler, J.V. (2004), 'How to lead a self-managing team', *MIT Sloan Management Review*, vol. 45, no. 4, pp. 65–71.

Dutta, S. and Segev, A. (1999), 'Business transformation on the Internet', *European Management Journal*, vol. 17, no. 5, pp. 466–476.

Dutton, J.E., Dukerich, J.M. and Harquail, C.V. (1994), 'Organizational images and member identification', *Administrative Science Quarterly*, vol. 39, no. 2, pp. 239–263.

Economist Intelligence Unit (1992), *Making Quality Work: Lessons from Europe's leading companies*, Economist Intelligence Unit, London.

Egan, J. and Wilson, D. (2002), *Private Business – Public Battleground*, Palgrave, Basingstoke.

Elliott, B. and Elliott, J. (2003), *Financial Accounting and Reporting* (6th edn), Financial Times/Prentice Hall, Harlow.

Engel, J., Kollatt, D. and Blackwell, R. (1978), *Consumer Behavior*, Dryden Press, Boston, MA.

Equal Opportunities Commission (1999), *Facts About Women and Men in Great Britain*, EOC, Manchester.

Ezzamel, M., Lilley, S. and Wilmott, H. (1994), 'The "new organization" and the "new managerial work"', *European Management Journal*, vol. 12, no. 4, pp. 454–461.

Fayol, H. (1949), *General and Industrial Management*, Pitman, London.

Feigenbaum, A.V. (1993), *Total Quality Control*, McGraw-Hill, New York.

Fenton, E.M. and Pettigrew, A.M. (2000), 'Theoretical perspectives on new forms of organizing', in A.M. Pettigrew and E. Fenton (eds.), *The Innovating Organization*, Sage, London.

Fiedler, F.E. and House, R.J. (1994), 'Leadership theory and research: a report of progress', in C.L. Cooper and I.T. Robertson (eds.), *Key Reviews of Managerial Psychology*, Wiley, Chichester.

Finkelstein, S. (2003), *Why Smart Executives Fail: and what you can learn from their mistakes*, Penguin, New York.

Fleishman, E.A. (1953), 'The description of supervisory behavior', *Journal of Applied Psychology*, vol. 37, no.1, pp. 1–6.

Flores, S.L. and Pearce, S.L. (2000), 'The use of an expert system in the M3-competition', *International Journal of Forecasting*, vol. 16, no. 4, pp. 485–493.

Flynn, N. (2002), *Public Sector Management* (4th edn), Financial Times/Prentice Hall, Harlow.

Fogel, R.W. (1989), *Without Consent or Contract: The rise and fall of American slavery*, Norton, New York.

Follett, M.P. (1920), *The New State: Group organization, the solution of popular government*, Longmans Green, London.

Fombrun, C., Tichy, N.M. and Devanna, M.A. (1984), *Strategic Human Resource Management*, Wiley, New York.

Ford, H. (1922), *My Life and Work*, Heinemann, London.

French, J. and Raven, B. (1959), 'The bases of social power', in D. Cartwright (ed.), *Studies in Social Power*, Institute for Social Research, Ann Arbor, MI.

Friedman, M. (1962), *Capitalism and Freedom*, University of Chicago Press, Chicago.

Gabrial, Y. (1988), *Working Lives in Catering*, Routledge, London.

Gerwin, D. (1979), 'Relationships between structure and technology at the organizational and job levels', *Journal of Management Studies*, vol. 16, no. 1, pp. 70–79.

Ghoshal, S. and Bartlett, C.A. (1998), *The Individualized Corporation*, Heinemann, London.

Gilbreth, L.M. (1914), *The Psychology of Management*, Sturgis & Walton, New York.

Gillespie, R. (1991), *Manufacturing Knowledge: A history of the Hawthorne experiments*, Cambridge University Press, Cambridge.

Glaister, K.W. (1991), 'Virgin Atlantic Airways', in C. Clark-Hill and K. Glaister, *Cases in Strategic Management*, Pitman, London.

Glaister, K.W. and Falshaw, J.R. (1999), 'Strategic planning: still going strong?' *Long Range Planning*, vol. 32, no. 1, pp.107–116.

Glass, N. (1996), 'Chaos, non-linear systems and day-to-day management', *European Management Journal*, vol. 14, no. 1, pp. 98–106.

Goldratt, E. and Cox, J. (1989), *The Goal*, Gower, Aldershot.

Goold, M. (1997) 'Institutional advantage: a way into strategic management in not-for-profit organizations', *Long Range Planning*, vol. 30, no. 2, pp. 291–293.

Govindarajan, V. and Gupta, A.K. (2001), 'Building an effective global business team', *MIT Sloan Management Review*, vol. 42, no. 4, pp. 63–72.

Graham, P. (1995), *Mary Parker Follett: Prophet of management*, Harvard Business School Press, Boston, MA.

Grant, R. (2002), *Contemporary Strategy Analysis* (4th edn), Blackwell, Oxford.

Grant, R.M. (1991), 'The resource-based theory of competitive advantage: implications for strategy formulation', *California Management Review*, vol. 33, no. 3, pp. 114–135.

Greenberg, J. (1990), 'Employee theft as a reaction to underpayment inequity: the hidden costs of pay cuts', *Journal of Applied Psychology*, vol. 75, no. 5, pp. 561–568.

Greenwood, R.G., Bolton, A.A. and Greenwood, R.A. (1983), 'Hawthorne a half century Later: relay assembly participants remember', *Journal of Management*, vol. 9, Fall/Winter, pp. 217–231.

Greer, C.R. (2001), *Strategic Human Resource Management*, Prentice Hall, New Jersey.

Gronroos, C. (2000), *Service Management and Marketing: A customer relationship management approach* (2nd edn), Wiley, Chichester.

Guest, D.E. (1987), 'Human resource management and industrial relations', *Journal of Management Studies*, vol. 24, no. 5, pp. 502–521.

Guest, D. (1988), 'Human resource management: a new opportunity for psychologists or another passing fad?' *The Occupational Psychologist*, February.

Guest, D.E. and Conway, N. (2001), *Organisational Change and the Psychological Contract: An analysis of the 1999 CIPD Survey*, Chartered Institute of Personnel and Development, London.

Guirdham, M. (1995), *Interpersonal Skills at Work*, Prentice Hall International, Hemel Hempstead.

Habermas, J. (1972), *Knowledge and Human Interests*, Heinemann, London.

Hackman et al. (1975), 'Development of the job diagnostic survey', *Journal of Applied Psychology*, vol. 60, no. 2, p. 161.

Hackman, J.R. (1990), *Groups that Work (and Those that Don't)*, Jossey-Bass, San Francisco, CA.

Hackman, J.R. and Oldham, G.R. (1980), *Work Redesign*, Addison-Wesley, Reading, MA.

Hage, J. and Aiken, M. (1967), 'Program change and organizational properties: a comparative analysis', *American Journal of Sociology*, vol. 72, pp. 503–519.

Hagman, E. (2000), Keynote address to Arthur Anderson European Business and Environment Network Annual Conference, 15 September.

Hales, C. (2001), *Managing through Organization*, Routledge, London.

Hamel, G. and Prahalad, C.K. (1996), *Competing for the Future*, Harvard Business School Press, Boston, MA.

Hall, W. (1995), *Managing Cultures*, Wiley, Chichester.

Handy, C. (1988), *Understanding Voluntary Organizations*, Penguin, Harmondsworth.

Handy, C. (1993), *Understanding Organizations* (4th edn), Penguin, Harmondsworth.

Hardaker, M. and Ward, B. (1987), 'Getting things done', *Harvard Business Review*, vol. 65, no. 6, pp. 112–120.

Hargie, O.D.W. (1997), *Handbook of Communication Skills*, Routledge, London.

Harris, P.R. and Moran, R. (1991), *Managing Cultural Differences*, Gulf Publishing, Houston, TX.

Harrison, E.F. (1999), *The Managerial Decision-Making Process* (5th edn), Houghton Mifflin, Boston, MA.

Hartley, J., Bennington, J. and Binns, P. (1997), 'Researching the roles of internal change agents in the management of organizational change', *British Journal of Management*, vol. 8, no. 1, pp. 61–74.

Heffcutt, A.I. and Arthur, W. (1994), 'Hunter and Hunter (1984) revisited: interview validity for entry-level jobs', *Journal of Applied Psychology*, vol. 79, no. 2, pp. 184–190.

Heil, G., Bennis, W. and Stephens, D.C. (2000), *Douglas McGregor, Revisited*, Wiley, New York.

Heller, R. (2001), 'Inside Zara', *Forbes Global*, 28 May, pp. 24–25, 28–29.

Helgesen, S. (1995), *The Female Advantage: Women's ways of leadership*, Currency/Doubleday, New York.

Hellriegel, D. and Slocum, J.W. (1988), *Management* (5th edn), Addison-Wesley, Reading, MA.

Hellriegel, D., Jackson, S.E. and Slocum, J.W. (2002), *Management: A competency-based approach*, South Western College Publishing, Cincinatti, OH.

Henderson, D. (2001), *Misguided Virtue: False notions of corporate social responsibility*, Institute of Economic Affairs, London.

Herzberg, F. (1959), *The Motivation to Work*, Wiley, New York.

Herzberg, F. (1987), 'One more time: how do you motivate employees?' *Harvard Business Review*, vol. 65, no. 5, pp. 109–120.

Heydebrand, W.V. (1989), 'New organizational forms', *Work and Occupations*, vol. 16, no. 3, pp. 323–357.

Hill, C.W.L. and Pickering, J.F. (1986), 'Divisionalization, decentralization and performance of large United Kingdom companies', *Journal of Management Studies*, vol. 23, no. 1, pp. 26–50.

Hill, T. (2004), *Operations Management* (2nd edn), Palgrave Macmillan, London.

Hiltrop, J.M. (1995), 'The changing psychological contract: the human resources challenge of the 1990s', *European Management Journal*, vol. 13, no. 3, pp. 288–294.

Hofstede, G. (1980), *Culture's Consequences: International differences in work-related values*, Sage, Beverley Hills, CA.

Hofstede, G. (1989), 'Organizing for cultural diversity', *European Management Journal*, vol. 7, no. 4, pp. 390–397.

Hofstede, G. (1991), *Cultures and Organizations: Software of the mind*, McGraw-Hill, London.

Honderich, T. (ed.) (1995), *Ethical Reasoning: The Oxford Companion to Philosophy*, Oxford University Press, Oxford.

Hoppe, M.H. (1993), 'The effects of national culture on the theory and practice of managing R&D professionals abroad', *R&D Management*, vol. 23, no. 4, pp. 313–325.

Horngren, C.T., Foster, G. and Datar, S.M. (2002), *Cost Accounting* (10th edn), Financial Times/Prentice Hall, Harlow.

House, R.J. (1996), 'Path–goal theory of leadership: lessons, legacy and a reformulation', *Leadership Quarterly*, vol. 7, no. 3, pp. 323–352.

House, R.J. and Mitchell, T.R. (1974), 'Path–goal theory of leadership', *Contemporary Business*, vol. 3, no. 2, pp. 81–98.

Howard, P. (1999), 'Fair play is better business', *Business Review Weekly*, March.

Howard, J.A. and Sheth, J.N. (1969), *The Theory of Buyer Behavior*, Wiley, New York.

Huczynski, A.A. (2004), *Influencing Within Organizations* (2nd edn), Routledge, London.

Huselid, M.A. (1995), 'The impact of human resource management practices on turnover, productivity and corporate financial performance', *Academy of Management Journal*, vol. 38, no. 3, pp. 635–672.

Ibbott, C. and O'Keefe, R. (2004), 'Transforming the Vodafone/Ericsson relationship', *Long Range Planning*, vol. 37, no. 3, pp. 219–237.

Ichniowski C., Kochan, T.A., Levine, D., Olson, C. and Strauss, G. (1996), 'What works at work: overview and assessment', *Industrial Relations*, vol. 35, no. 3, pp. 299–333.

IPD (1999), *Organisational development: whose responsibility?* Institute for Personnel and Development, London.

IRS (1997), 'The state of selection: an IRS survey', *Employee Development Bulletin*, 51, pp. 5–8, Industrial Relations Services, London.

Jackson, T. (1993), *Organizational Behaviour in International Management*, Butterworth/Heinemann, Oxford.

Janis, I.L. (1972), *Victim of Groupthink*, Houghton-Mifflin, Boston, MA.

Janis, I.L. (1977), *Decision Making: A psychological analysis of conflict, choice and commitment*, The Free Press, New York.

Jennings, D. (2000), 'PowerGen: the development of corporate planning in a privatized utility', *Long Range Planning*, vol. 33, no. 2, pp. 201–219.

Jobber, D. (2004), *Principles and Practices of Marketing* (4th edn), McGraw-Hill, London.

John, K.A., Northcraft, G.B. and Neale, M.A. (1999), 'Why differences make a difference: a field study of diversity, conflict and performance in work groups', *Administrative Science Quarterly*, vol. 44, no. 4, pp. 741–763.

Johnson, G. and Scholes, K. (eds.) (2000), *Exploring Public Sector Strategy*, Prentice Hall, Harlow.

Johnson, G. and Scholes, K. (2002), *Exploring Corporate Strategy* (6th edn), Financial Times/Prentice Hall, Harlow.

Johnston, R.A., Kast, F.E. and Rosenzweig, J.E. (eds) (1967), 'People and systems', in *The Theory and Management of Systems*, McGraw-Hill, New York.

Judd, V.C. (2003), 'Achieving customer orientation using people power – the 5th P', *European Journal of Marketing*, vol. 37, no. 10, pp. 1301–1313.

Judge, T.A., Piccolo, R.F. and Ilies, R. (2004), 'The forgotten ones? The validity of consideration and initiating structure in leadership research', *Journal of Applied Psychology*, vol. 89, no. 1, pp. 36–51.

Juran, J. (1974), *Quality Control Handbook*, McGraw-Hill, New York.

Kakabadse, A. (1993), 'The success levers for Europe: the Cranfield executive competences survey', *Journal of Management Development*, vol. 12, no. 8, pp. 12–17.

Kanter, R.M. (1979), 'Power failure in management circuits', *Harvard Business Review*, vol. 57, no. 4, pp. 65–75.

Kanter, R.M. (1983), *The Change Masters*, Unwin, London.

Kaplan, S. (2000), 'E-hubs: The new B2B marketplaces', *Harvard Business Review*, vol. 78, no. 3, pp. 97–113.

Kaplan, R.S. and Norton, D.P. (1996), *The Balanced Scorecard: Translating strategy into action*, Harvard Business School Press, Cambridge, MA.

Katzenbach, J.R. and Smith, D.K. (1993a), 'The discipline of teams', *Harvard Business Review*, vol. 71, no. 2, pp. 111–120.

Katzenbach, J.R. and Smith, D.K. (1993b), *The Wisdom of Teams*, Harvard Business School Press, Boston, MA.

Kay, J. (1993), *Foundations for Corporate Success: How business strategies add value*, Oxford University Press, Oxford.

Kay, J. (1996), *The Business of Economics*, Oxford University Press, Oxford.

Keaveney, P. and Kaufmann, M. (2001), *Marketing for the Voluntary Sector*, Kogan Page, London.

Keef, S.P. (1998), 'The causal association between employee share ownership and attitudes', *British Journal of Industrial Relations*, vol. 36, no. 1, pp. 73–82.

Keen, P. (1981), 'Information systems and organization change', in E. Rhodes and D. Weild (eds), *Implementing New Technologies*, Blackwell/Open University Press, Oxford.

Kipnis, D., Schmidt, S.M. and Wilkinson, I. (1980), 'Intra-organizational influence tactics: explorations in getting one's way', *Journal of Applied Psychology*, vol. 65, no. 4, pp. 440–452.

Klein, G. (1997), *Sources of Power: How people make decisions*, MIT Press, Cambridge, MA.

Klein, N. (2000), *No Logo: Taking aim at the brand bullies*, Flamingo, London.

Kleiner, A. (2003), *Who Really Matters: The core group theory of power, privilege and success*, Doubleday, New York.

Knapp, M.L. and Hall, J.A. (2002), *Non-verbal Communication in Human Interaction*, Thomson Learning, London.

Knights, D. and Murray, F. (1994), *Managers Divided: Organizational politics and information technology management*, Wiley, Chichester.

Kochan, T.A. (1992), *Principles for a Post-New Deal Employment Policy*, Sloan School of Management, MIT, Working Paper 5.

Kochan, T.A. *et al.* (2003), 'The effects of diversity on business performance: Report of the diversity research network', *Human Resource Management*, vol. 42, no. 1, pp. 3–21.

Kolb, D., Rubin, E. and Osland, J. (1991), *Organizational Psychology*, Prentice Hall, Englewood Cliffs, NJ.

Komaki, J. (2003), 'Reinforcement theory at work: enhancing and explaining what workers do', in L.W. Porter, G.A. Bigley and R.M. Steers (eds), *Motivation and Work Behavior* (7th edn), Irwin/McGraw-Hill, Burr Ridge, IL.

Komaki, J.L., Coombs, T., Redding, T.P. and Schepman, S. (2000), 'A rich and rigorous examination of applied behavior analysis research in the world of work', in C.L. Cooper and I.T. Robertson (eds), *International Review of Industrial and Organizational Psychology*, Wiley, Chichester, pp. 265–367.

Kotler, P. (2003), *Marketing Management* (11th edn), Pearson Education, Upper Saddle River, NJ.

Kotler, P. and Andreasen, A. (1991), *Strategic Marketing for Nonprofit Organizations*, Prentice Hall, Upper Saddle River, NJ.

Kotler, P., Armstrong, G., Saunders, J. and Wong, V. (2002), *Principles of Marketing* (3rd European edn), Financial Times/Prentice Hall, Harlow.

Kotler, P. and Armstrong, G. (1997), *Marketing: An introduction* (4th edn), Prentice Hall International, Hemel Hempstead.

Kottasz, R. (2004), 'How should charitable organizations motivate young professionals to give philanthropically?', *International Journal of Non-Profit and Voluntary Sector Marketing*, vol. 9, no. 1, pp. 9–27.

Kotter, J.P. (1982), *The General Managers*, Free Press, New York.

Kotter, J.P. (1991), *A Force for Change: How leadership differs from management*, The Free Press, New York.

Kotter, J. and Cohen, D. (2002), *The Heart of Change: Real-life stories of how people change their organizations*, Harvard Business School Press, Boston, MA.

Kotter, J.P. and Heskett, J. (1992), *Corporate Culture and Performance*, Free Press, New York.

Kotter, J.P. and Schlesinger, L.A. (1979), 'Choosing strategies for change', *Harvard Business Review*, vol. 57, no. 3, pp. 106–114.

Krackhardt, D. and Hanson, J.R. (1993), 'Informal networks: the company behind the chart', *Harvard Business Review*, vol. 71, no. 4, pp. 104–111.

Lancaster, G. and Messingham, L. (1993), *Essentials of Marketing* (2nd edn), McGraw-Hill, New York.

Laudon, K.C. and Laudon, J.P. (2004), *Management Information Systems: Managing the digital firm* (8th edn), Prentice Hall, Upper Saddle River, NJ.

REFERENCES

Laurent, A. (1983), 'The cultural diversity of western conceptions of management', *International Studies of Management and Organization*, vol. 13, nos 1/2, pp. 75–96.

Lawler, E.E. (1986), *High Involvement Management: Participative strategies for improving organizational performance*, Jossey-Bass, San Francisco.

Lawrence, P. and Lorsch, J.W. (1967), *Organization and Environment*, Harvard Business School Press, Boston, MA.

Lawson, P. (2000), 'Performance-related pay', in R. Thorpe and G. Homan (eds.), *Strategic Reward Systems*, Prentice Hall, Harlow.

Leach, S. (1996), *Mission Statements and Strategic Visions: Symbol or substance*, Local Government Management Board, London.

Legge, K. (1978), *Power, Innovation and Problem Solving in Personnel Management*, McGraw-Hill, London.

Legge, K. (1995), *Human Resource Management: Rhetorics and realities*, Macmillan, London.

Lengel, R.H. and Daft, R.L. (1988), 'The selection of communication media as an executive skill', *Academy of Management Executive*, vol. 11, no. 3, pp. 225–232.

Levitt, T. (1960), 'Marketing myopia', *Harvard Business Review*, vol. 38, no. 4, pp. 45–56.

Levitt, T. (1983), 'The globalization of markets', *Harvard Business Review*, vol. 61, no. 3, pp. 92–102.

Lewin, K. (1947), 'Frontiers in group dynamics', *Human Relations*, vol. 1, pp. 5–41.

Likert, R. (1961), *New Patterns of Management*, McGraw-Hill, New York.

Likert, R. (1967), *The Human Organization: Its management and value*, McGraw-Hill, New York.

Lindblom, C.E. (1959), 'The science of muddling through', *Public Administration Review*, vol. 19, no. 2, pp. 79–88.

Linstead, S., Fulop, L. and Lilley, S. (2004), *Management and Organization: A critical text*, Palgrave Macmillan, Basingstoke.

Lock, D. (2003), *Project Management* (8th edn), Gower, Aldershot.

Locke, E.A. (1968), 'Towards a theory of task motivation and incentives', *Organizational Behavior and Human Performance*, vol. 3, pp. 157–189.

Locke, E.A. (1996), 'Motivation through conscious goal setting', *Applied and Preventive Psychology*, vol. 5, pp. 117–124.

Locke, E.A. and Latham, G.P. (1990), *A Theory of Goal Setting and Task Performance*, Prentice-Hall, Englewood Cliffs, NJ.

Lodge, D. (1989), *Nice Work*, Penguin, London.

Lorsch, J.W. (1986), 'Managing culture: the invisible barrier to strategic change', *California Management Review*, vol. 28, no. 2, pp. 95–109.

Lucas, H.C. (1996), *The T-form Organization: Using technology to design organizations for the 21st century*, Jossey-Bass, San Francisco, CA.

Luthans, F. (1988), 'Successful vs effective real managers', *Academy of Management Executive*, vol. 11, no. 2, pp. 127–32.

Lynch, R. (2003), *Corporate Strategy* (3rd edn), Financial Times/Prentice Hall, Harlow.

Macbeth, D.K. and Ferguson, N. (1994), *Partnership Sourcing: An integrated supply chain approach*, Financial Times Pitman, London.

Magd, H. and Curry, A. (2003), 'Achieving best value in public-sector organisations', *Benchmarking International Journal*, vol. 10, no. 3, pp. 261–286.

Magretta, J. (2002), *What Management Is (and why it is everyone's business)*, Profile Books, London.

Maltz, E. (2000), 'Is all communication created equal?: An investigation into the effects of communication mode on perceived information quality', *Journal of Product Innovation Management*, vol. 17, no. 2, pp. 110–127.

Manz, C.C. and Sims, H.P. (1993), *Business Without Bosses: How self-managing teams are building high-performing companies*, Wiley, New York.

March, J.G. (1988), *Decisions and Organizations*, Blackwell, London.

Markus, M.L. (1984) *Systems in Organizations*, Pitman, London.

Markus, M.L., Manville, B. and Agres, C.E. (2000), 'What makes a virtual organization work?', *MIT Sloan Management Review*, vol. 42, no. 1, pp. 13–26.

Markus, M.L. (1983), 'Power, politics and MIS implementation', *Communications of the ACM*, vol. 26, no. 6, pp. 430–444.

Markus, M.L. and Robey, D. (1983), 'The organizational validity of management information systems', *Human Relations*, vol. 36, no. 3, pp. 203–226.

Markus, M.L. and Keil, M. (1994), 'If we build it, they will come: designing information systems that people want to use', *MIT Sloan Management Review*, vol. 35, no. 4, pp. 11–25.

Martin, J. (2002), *Organizational Culture: Mapping the terrain*, Sage, London.

Martinko, M.J. and Gardner, W.L. (1990), 'Structured observation of managerial work: a replication and synthesis', *Journal of Management Studies*, vol. 27, no. 3, pp. 329–357.

Maruca, R.F. (1998), 'How do you manage an off-site team?' *Harvard Business Review*, vol. 76, no. 4, pp. 22–35.

Maslow, A. (1970), *Motivation and Personality* (2nd edn), Harper & Row, New York.

Mayer, M. and Whittington, R. (1996), 'The survival of the European holding company: institutional choice and contingency', in R. Whitley and P.H. Kristensen (eds.), *The Changing European Firm*, Routledge, London.

Mayo, E. (1949), *The Social Problems of an Industrial Civilization,* Routledge and Kegan Paul, London.

McAfee, A. (2004), 'Do you have too much IT?', *MIT Sloan Management Review*, vol. 45, no. 3, pp. 18–21.

McClelland, D. (1961), *The Achieving Society*, Van Nostrand Reinhold, Princeton, NJ.

McGregor, D. (1960), *The Human Side of Enterprise*, McGraw-Hill, New York.

McLoughlin, I. (1999), *Creative Technological Change*, Routledge, London.

McSweeney, B. (2002), 'Hofstede's model of national cultural differences and consequences: a triumph of faith – failure of analysis', *Human Relations*, vol. 55, no. 1, pp. 89–118.

Mercado, S., Welford, R. and Prescott, K. (2001), *European Business*, Financial Times/Prentice Hall, Harlow.

Michaels, E.G. (1982), 'Marketing muscle', *Business Horizons*, May/June, pp. 63–74.

Micklethwait, J. and Wooldridge, A. (2003), *The Company: A short history of a revolutionary idea*, Weidenfeld and Nicolson, London.

Miles, R.E. and Snow, C.C. (1994), *Fit, Failure and the Hall of Fame*, The Free Press, New York.

Milgrom, P.R. and Roberts, J. (1990), 'The economics of modern manufacturing: technology, strategy and organization', *American Economic Review*, vol. 80, pp. 511–528.

Mill, J. (1994), 'No pain, no gain', *Computing*, 3 February, pp. 26–27.

Miller, S., Wilson, D. and Hickson, D. (2004), 'Beyond planning: strategies for successfully implementing strategic decisions', *Long Range Planning*, vol. 37, no. 3, pp. 201–218.

Mintzberg, H. (1973), *The Nature of Managerial Work*, Harper & Row, New York.

Mintzberg, H. (1979), *The Structuring of Organizations*, Prentice Hall, Englewood Cliffs, NJ.

Mintzberg, H. (1994a), *The Rise and Fall of Strategic Planning*, Prentice Hall International, Hemel Hempstead.

Mintzberg, H. (1994b), 'Rethinking strategic planning. Part I: Pitfalls and fallacies', *Long Range Planning*, vol. 27, no. 3, pp.12–21.

Mintzberg, H., Raisinghani, D. and Theoret, A. (1976), 'The structure of unstructured decision processes', *Administrative Science Quarterly*, vol. 21, no. 2, pp. 246–275.

Moncrieff, J. and Smallwood, J. (1996), 'Strategic management: ideas for the new millennium', *Financial Times*, 19 July.

Moore, J.I. (2001), *Writers on Strategy and Strategic Management* (2nd edn), Penguin, London.

Morgan, G. (1997), *Images of Organization*, Sage, London.

Morse, J. and Lorsch, J. (1970), 'Beyond Theory Y', *Harvard Business Review*, vol. 48, no. 3, pp. 61–68.

Moutinho, L. (1995), *Cases in Marketing Management*, Addison-Wesley, Wokingham.

Mowday, R.T. and Colwell, K.A. (2003), 'Employee reactions to unfair outcomes in the workplace: the contribution of Adams' equity theory to understanding work motivation', in L.W. Porter, G.A. Bigley and R.M. Steers (eds), *Motivation and Work Behavior* (7th edn), Irwin/McGraw-Hill, Burr Ridge, IL.

Mumford, E. and Weir, M. (1979), *Computer Systems in Work Design: The Ethics method*, Associated Business Press, London.

Newell, S. and Tansley, C. (2001), 'International uses of selection methods', in C.L. Cooper and I.T. Robertson (eds), *International Review of Industrial and Organizational Psychology*, Wiley, Chichester.

Newell, S. (1999), 'Ebank: a failed knowledge management initiative', in H. Scarbrough and J. Swan (eds), *Case Studies in Knowledge Management*, Institute for Personnel and Development, London.

Newman, A.J. and Patel, D. (2004), 'The marketing directions of two fashion retailers', *European Journal of Marketing*, vol. 38, no. 7, pp. 770–789.

Noble, F. and Newman, M. (1993), 'Integrated system, autonomous departments: organizational invalidity and stem change in a university', *Journal of Management Studies*, vol. 30, no. 2, pp. 195–219.

Nugent, N. and O'Donnell, R. (1994), *The European Business Environment*, Macmillan, Basingstoke.

Oakland, J. (1994), *Total Quality Management*, Butterworth/Heinemann, Oxford.

Obeng, E. (2001), 'Harnessing technology, thinking and action', in *Financial Times Handbook of Management*, Financial Times/Prentice Hall, Harlow.

Ogbonna, E. and Harris, L.C. (1998), 'Organizational culture: it's not what you think', *Journal of General Management*, vol. 23, no. 3, pp. 35–48.

Ogbonna, E. and Harris, L.C. (2002), 'Organizational culture: a ten-year, two-phase study of change in the UK food retailing sector', *Journal of Management Studies*, vol. 39, no. 5, pp. 673–706.

Orlicky, J. (1975), *Material Requirements Planning*, McGraw-Hill, New York.

Ouchi, W.J. (1981), *Theory Z*, Addison-Wesley, Reading, MA.

Parker, D. and Stacey, R. (1994), *Chaos, Management and Economics: The implications of non-linear thinking*, Hobart Paper 125, Institute of Economic Affairs, London.

Parker, M. (2000), *Organizational Culture and Identity: Unity and division at work*, Sage, London.

Pascale, R.T. (1984), 'Perspectives on strategy: the real story behind Honda's success', *California Management Review*, vol. 26, no. 3, pp. 47–72.

Pascale, R. (1990), *Managing on the Edge*, Penguin, London.

Pendleton, A., Wilson, N. and Wright, M. (1998), 'The perception and effects of share ownership: empirical evidence from employee buy-outs', *British Journal of Industrial Relations*, vol. 36, no. 1, pp. 99–124.

Peppard, J. (2000), 'Customer relationship management in financial services', *European Management Journal*, vol. 18, no. 3, pp. 312–327.

Peters, T.J. (1987), *Thriving on Chaos: Handbook for a management revolution*, Alfred A. Knopf, New York.

Peters, T.J. and Waterman, D.H. (1982), *In Search of Excellence*, Harper & Row, London.

Peters, T. (1996), *Liberation Management*, Ballantine Books, New York.

Pettigrew, A. (1985), *The Awakening Giant: Continuity and change in Imperial Chemical Industries*, Blackwell, Oxford.

Pettigrew, A. (1987), 'Context and action in the transformation of the firm', *Journal of Management Studies*, vol. 24, no. 6, pp. 649–670.

Pettigrew, A.M. and Whipp, R. (1991), *Managing Change for Competitive Success*, Blackwell, Oxford.

Pettigrew, A., Ferlie, E. and McKee, L. (1992), *Shaping Strategic Change*, Sage, London.

Pettigrew, A.M., Whittington, R., Melin, L., Sanchez-Runde, C., Van Den Bosch, F., Ruigrok, W. and Numagami, T. (2003), *Innovative Forms of Organizing*, Sage, London.

Pfeffer, J. (1992a), *Managing with Power*, Harvard Business School Press, Boston, MA.

Pfeffer, J. (1992b), 'Understanding power in organizations', *California Management Review*, vol. 34, no. 2, pp. 29–50.

Pfeffer, J. (1994), *Competitive Advantage Through People*, Harvard Business School Press, Cambridge, MA.

Phillips, P. (2003), *E-Business Strategy: Text and cases*, McGraw-Hill, Maidenhead.

Pinto, J. (1998), 'Understanding the role of politics in successful project management', *International Journal of Project Management*, vol. 18, no. 2, pp. 85–91.

Porter, M.E. (1980a), *Competitive Strategy*, Free Press, New York.

Porter, M. (1980b), *Competitive Advantage*, Free Press, New York.

Porter, M.E. (1985), *Competitive Advantage: Creating and sustaining superior performance*, Free Press, New York.

Porter, M.E. (1990), *The Competitive Advantage of Nations*, Free Press, New York.

Porter, M.E. (1994), 'Competitive strategy revisited: a view from the 1990s', in P. Barker Duffy (ed.), *The Relevance of a Decade*, Harvard Business School Press, Boston, MA.

Prastacos, G., Soderquist, K., Spanos, Y. and Van Wassenhove, L. (2002), 'An integrated framework for managing change in the new competitive landscape', *European Management Journal*, vol. 20, no. 1, pp. 55–71.

Pugh, D.S. and Hickson, D.J. (1976), *Organization Structure in its Context: The Aston Programme I*, Gower, Aldershot.

Quinn, J.B. (1980), *Strategies for Change: Logical incrementalism*, Irwin, Homewood, IL.

Quinn, R.E., Faerman, S.R., Thompson, M.P. and McGrath, M.R. (2003), *Becoming a Master Manager* (3rd edn), Wiley, New York.

Recardo, R. (1991), 'The what, why and how of change management', *Manufacturing Systems*, May, pp. 52–58.

Reed, D. (2000), *Is e-cruitment Working? A new report on maximising the effectiveness of Internet recruitment*, Reed Executive, London.

Ritzer, G. (1993), *The McDonaldization of Society*, Pine Forge Press, London.

Robbins, S.P. (2000), *Managing Today!* Prentice Hall, Englewood Cliffs, NJ.

Rivard, S., Bennoit, A.A., Patry, M., Pare, G. and Smith, H.A. (2004), *Information Technology and Organizational Transformation*, Elsevier/Butterworth-Heinemann, Oxford.

Robbins, S.P. and Coulter, M. (2003), *Management* (7th edn), Prentice Hall, Upper Saddle River, NJ.

Robbins, S.P. (2001), *Organization Behaviour: Concepts, Controversies and Applications* (9th edn), Prentice-Hall International, Upper Saddle River, NJ.

Robertson, I. (1996), 'Personnel selection and assessment', in P. Warr (ed.), *Psychology at Work* (4th edn), Penguin, Harmondsworth.

Robey, D., Schwaig, K.S. and Jin, L. (2003), 'Intertwining material and virtual work', *Information and Organization*, vol. 13, no. 3, pp. 111–129.

Roddick, A. (1991), *Body and Soul*, Ebury Press, London.

Roddick, A. (2000), *Business as Unusual*, Thorsons, London.

Roethlisberger, F.J. and Dickson, W.J. (1939), *Management and the Worker*, Harvard University Press, Cambridge, MA.

Rosen, S. (1998), 'A lump of clay', *Communication World*, vol. 15, no. 7, p. 58.

Rosener, J.B. (1997), *America's Competitive Secret: Women managers*, Oxford University Press, Oxford.

Ross, S., Westerfield, R. and Jordan, B. (2002), *Fundamentals of Corporate Finance*, McGraw-Hill/Irwin, New York.

Rousseau, D.M. (1995), *Psychological Contracts in Organizations: Understanding the written and unwritten agreements*, Sage, London.

Rousseau, D.M. and Schalk, R. (2000), *Psychological Contracts in Employment: Cross-national perspectives*, Sage, London.

Rugman, A. (2000), *The End of Globalisation*, Random Books, New York.

Schein, E.H. (1985), *Organizational Culture and Leadership*, Jossey-Bass, San Francisco, CA.

Schonberger, R.J. (1983), *Japanese Manufacturing Techniques*, Free Press, New York.

Schwartz, B. (2004), *The Paradox of Choice*, Ecco, New York.

Schwartz, P. (2003), *Inevitable Surprises: Thinking ahead in a time of turbulence*, Gotham Books, New York.

Semler, R. (2003), *The Seven Day Weekend: Finding the work/life balance*, Century, London.

Shaw, W.H. (1991), *Business Ethics*, Wadsworth, Belmomt, CA.

Shaw, C.T., Shaw, V. and Enkit, M. (2004), 'Relations between engineers and marketers in UK and Germany', *European Journal of Marketing*, vol. 38, no. 5/6, pp. 694–719.

Simon, H. (1960), *Administrative Behavior*, Macmillan, New York.

Simons, R. (1995), 'Control in an age of empowerment', *Harvard Business Review*, vol. 73, no. 2, pp. 80–88.

Sinha, D.K. (1990), 'The contribution of formal planning to decisions', *Strategic Management Journal*, vol. 6, pp. 479–492.

Sinickas, A.D. (2004), 'Intranets anyone? Take the guesswork out of using electronic channels', *Communication World*, vol. 21, no.1, pp. 30–34.

Skinner, B.F. (1971), *Contingencies of Reinforcement*, Appleton-Century-Crofts, East Norwalk, CT.

Skinner, W. (1969), 'Manufacturing: the missing link in corporate strategy', *Harvard Business Review*, vol. 47, no. 3, pp. 136–145.

Smith, A. (1776), *The Wealth of Nations*, ed. with an introduction by Andrew Skinner (1974), Penguin, Harmondsworth.

Smith, N.C. (1990), *Morality and the Market*, Routledge, London.

Smith, R.J. (1995), *Strategic Management and Planning in the Public Sector* (2nd edn), Longman/Civil Service College, Harlow.

Soothill, K., Mackay, L. and Webb, C. (eds.) (1995), *Interprofessional Relations in Health Care*, Edward Arnold, London.

Sparrow, P. and Hiltrop, J. (1994), *European Human Resource Management in Transition*, Prentice Hall International, Hemel Hempstead.

Sparrow, P.R. and Cooper, C.L. (2003), *The Employment Relationship, Key Challenges of HR*, Butterworth-Heinemann, Oxford.

Sprague, L. (1990), 'Operations management: productivity and quality performance', in E.G.C. Collins and M.A.Devanna, *The Portable MBA*, Wiley, New York.

Spriegel, W.R. and Myers, C.E. (eds.) (1953), *The Writings of the Gilbreths*, Irwin, Homewood, IL.

Stacey, R. (1994), *Managing the Unknowable*, Jossey Bass, San Francisco, CA.

Stark, A. (1993), 'What's the matter with business ethics?' *Harvard Business Review*, vol. 71, no. 3, pp. 38–48.

Steinbock, D. (2001), *The Nokia Revolution*, American Management Association, New York, NY.

Stewart, R. (1967), *Managers and their Jobs*, Macmillan, London.

Stajkovic, A.D. and Luthans, F. (2003), 'Social cognitive theory and self-efficacy: implications for motivation theory and practice', in L.W. Porter, G.A. Bigley and R.M. Steers (eds), *Motivation and Work Behavior* (7th edn), Irwin/McGraw-Hill, Burr Ridge, IL.

Steers, R.M., Mowday, R.T. and Shapiro, D.L. (2004), 'The future of work motivation theory', *Academy of Management Review*, vol. 29, no. 3, pp. 379–387.

Sternberg, E. (2004), *Corporate Governance: Accountability in the Market Place* (2nd edn), Institute of Economic Affairs, London.

Stogdill, R.M. (1974), *Handbook of Leadership: A survey of the literature*, Free Press, New York.

Storey, J. (1992), *Developments in the Management of Human Resources*, Blackwell, Oxford.

Storey, J. (ed.) (1995), *Human Resource Management: A critical text*, Routledge, London.

Supply Chain Management Group (1995), *The Supply Chain Improvement Process and the Relationship Positioning Tool*, SCMG Ltd, University of Glasgow, Glasgow.

Sutton, T. (2003), *Corporate Financial Accounting and Reporting*, Financial Times/Prentice Hall, Harlow.

Suutari, V. (1996), 'Leadership ideologies among European managers: a comparative study in a multinational company', *Scandinavian Journal of Management*, vol. 12, no. 4, pp. 389–409.

Swartz, M. and Watkins, S. (2002), *Power Failure: The rise and fall of Enron*, Aurum, London.

Symon, G. and Clegg, C.W. (1991) 'A study of the implementation of CADCAM', *Journal of Occupational Psychology*, vol. 64, no. 4, pp. 273–290.

Tannenbaum, R. and Schmidt, W.H. (1973), 'How to choose a leadership pattern: should a manager be democratic or autocratic – or something in between?', *Harvard Business Review*, vol. 37, no. 2, pp. 95–102.

Tayeb, M.H. (2000), *The Management of International Enterprises: A socio-political view*, Macmillan, Basingstoke.

REFERENCES

Tayeb, M.H. (1996), *The Management of a Multicultural Workforce*, Wiley, Chichester.

Taylor, B. (1997), 'The return of strategic planning: once more with feeling', *Long Range Planning*, vol. 30, no. 3, pp. 334–344.

Taylor, F.W. (1917), *The Principles of Scientific Management*, Harper, New York.

Thomas, A.B. (2003), *Controversies in Management: Issues, debates and answers* (2nd edn), Routledge, London.

Thompson, J.D. (1967), *Organizations in Action*, McGraw-Hill, New York.

Thompson, P. and McHugh, D. (2002), *Work Organizations: A Critical Introduction*, Palgrave, Basingstoke.

Thurley, K. and Wirdenius, H. (1989), *Towards European Management*, Pitman, London.

Timmers, P. (2000), *Electronic Commerce: Strategies and models for business to business trading*, Wiley, Chichester.

Toffler, B.L. and Reingold, J. (2003), *Final Accounting: Ambition, greed and the fall of Arthur Andersen*, Broadway Books, New York.

Towers Perrin (1999), *Euro Rewards 2000: Rewards, challenges and changes*, Towers Perrin, London.

Trevino, L.K. and Nelson, K.A. (1999), *Managing Business Ethics*, Wiley, Chichester.

Trevino, L.K. (1986), 'Ethical decision-making in organisations: a person–situation interactionist model', *Academy of Management Review*, vol. 11, no. 3, pp. 601–617.

Trist, E.L. and Bamforth, K.W. (1951), 'Some social and psychological consequences of the Longwall Method of coal getting', *Human Relations*, vol. 4, no. 1, pp. 3–38.

Trompennaars, F. (1993), *Riding the Waves of Culture: Understanding cultural diversity in business*, The Economist Books, London.

Tuckman, B. and Jensen, N. (1977), 'Stages of small group development revisited', *Group and Organizational Studies*, vol. 2, pp. 419–427.

Turban, E., Rainer, R.K. and Potter, R.E. (2001), *Introduction to Information Technology*, Wiley, Chichester.

Tyson, S. and Fell, A. (1985), *Evaluating the Personnel Function*, Hutchinson, London.

Uhl-Bien, M. and Graen, G.B. (1998), 'Individual self-management: analysis of professionals' self-managing activities in functional and cross-functional teams', *Academy of Management Journal*, vol. 41, no. 3, pp. 340–350.

Vallance, E. (1996), *Business Ethics at Work*, Cambridge University Press, Cambridge.

Van der Heijden, K. (1996), *Scenarios: The art of strategic conversation*, Wiley, Chichester.

van Houten, G. (1989), 'The implications of globalization: new management realities at Philips', in P. Evans, Y. Doz and A. Laurent (eds), *Human Resource Management in International Firms*, Macmillan, Basingstoke.

Van Knippenberg, D. and van Schie, E.C. (2000), 'Foci and correlates of organizational identification', *Journal of Occupational and Organizational Psychology*, vol. 73, pp. 137–147.

Venkatraman, N. and Henderson, J.C. (1998), 'Real strategies for virtual organizing', *MIT Sloan Management Review*, vol. 40, no. 1, pp. 33–47.

Volberda, H. (1997), 'Building flexible organizations for fast-moving markets', *Long Range Planning*, vol. 30, no. 2, pp. 169–183.

Volberda, H.W. (1998), *Building the Flexible Firm: How to remain competitive*, Oxford University Press, Oxford.

Vroom, V.H. (1964), *Work and Motivation*, Wiley, New York.

Vroom, V.H. and Yetton, P.W. (1973), *Leadership and Decision-making*, University of Pittsburgh Press, Pittsburgh, PA.

Walsham, G. (1993), *Interpreting Information Systems in Organisations*, Wiley, Chichester.

Walsham, G. (2001), *Making a World of Difference: IT in a Global Context*, Wiley, Chichester.

Wastell, D.G., White, P. and Kawalek, P. (1994), 'A methodology for business process redesign: experience and issues', *Journal of Strategic Information Systems*, vol. 3, no. 1, pp. 23–40.

Watson, T.J. (1994), *In Search of Management*, Routledge, London.

Weber, M. (1947), *The Theory of Social and Economic Organization*, Free Press, Glencoe, IL.

Weiss, L.M., Capozzi, M.M. and Prusak, L. (2004), 'Learning from the Internet giants', *MIT Sloan Management Review*, vol. 45, no. 4, pp. 79–85.

West, M. and Allen, N. (1997), 'Selecting for teamwork', in Anderson, N. and P. Herviot (eds.), *International Handbook of Selection and Assessment*, Wiley, Chichester.

Whetten, D.A. and Cameron, K.S. (2002), *Developing Management Skills*, Prentice Hall International, Upper Saddle River, NJ.

Whipp, R., Rosenfeld, R. and Pettigrew, A. (1988), 'Understanding strategic change processes: some preliminary British findings', in A. Pettigrew (ed.), *The Management of Strategic Change*, Blackwell, Oxford.

Whitley, R. (1996), 'The social construction of economic actors', in R. Whitley and P.H. Kristensen (eds.), *The Changing European Firm*, Routledge, London.

Whittington, R., Pettigrew, A., Peck, S., Fenton, E. and Conyon, M. (1999), 'Change and complementarities in the new competitive landscape: a European panel study,

1992–1996', *Organization Science*, vol. 10, no. 5, pp. 583–600.

Wickens, P.D. (1995), *The Ascendant Organisation*, Macmillan, Basingstoke.

Williams, K., Haslam, C. and Williams, J. (1992), 'Ford vs Fordism: the beginnings of mass production?' *Work, Employment and Society*, vol. 6, no. 4, pp. 517–555.

Wilson, F. (1996), 'Research note. Organizational theory: blind and deaf to gender?' *Organization Studies*, vol. 17, no. 5, pp. 825–842.

Womack, J.P., Jones, D.P. and Roos, J. (1990), *The Machine that Changed the World*, Macmillan, Basingstoke.

Wood, S. (1999), 'Human resource management and performance', *International Journal of Management Review*, vol. 1, no. 4, pp. 367–413.

Wood, S. and Wall, T. (2002), 'Human resource management and business performance', in P. Warr (ed.), *Psychology at Work* (5th edn), Penguin, London.

Woodward, J. (1958), *Management and Technology*, HMSO, London.

Woodward, J. (1965), *Industrial Organization: Theory and practice*, Oxford University Press, Oxford (2nd edn 1980).

Woodward, J. (1980), *Industrial Organization: Theory and practice* (2nd edn), Oxford University Press, Oxford.

Woodward, J. (1997), *Construction Project Management*, Thomas Telford Publications, London.

Wright, P.M., Gardner, T.M. and Moynihan, L.M. (2003), 'The impact of HR practices on the performance of business units', *Human Resource Management Journal*, vol. 13, no. 3, pp. 21–36.

Yukl, G. and Falbe, C.M. (1990), 'Influence tactics in upward, downward and lateral influence attempts', *Journal of Applied Psychology*, vol. 75, no. 2, pp. 132–140.

Yukl, G. and Tracey, J.B. (1992), 'Consequences of influence tactics used with subordinates, peers and the boss', *Journal of Applied Psychology*, vol. 77, no. 4, pp. 525–535.

Yukl, G.A. (2001), *Leadership in Organizations* (5th edn), Prentice Hall, Upper Saddle River, NJ.

Zolkiewski, J. (2004), 'Relationships are not ubiquitous in marketing', *European Journal of Marketing*, vol. 38, no. 1/2, pp. 24–29.

Index